Nomads on Pilgrimage

# Brill's Inner Asian Library

*Edited by*

Michael R. Drompp
Devin DeWeese
Mark C. Elliott

VOLUME 33

The titles published in this series are listed at *brill.com/bial*

# Nomads on Pilgrimage

*Mongols on Wutaishan (China), 1800–1940*

*By*

Isabelle Charleux

BRILL

LEIDEN | BOSTON

Library of Congress Cataloging-in-Publication Data

Charleux, Isabelle.
  Nomads on pilgrimage : Mongols on Wutaishan (China), 1800-1940 / by Isabelle Charleux.
    pages cm. -- (Brill's Inner Asian library, 1566-7162 ; volume 33)
  Includes bibliographical references and index.
  ISBN 978-90-04-29601-5 (hardback : acid-free paper) -- ISBN 978-90-04-29778-4 (e-book) 1. Mongols--
China--Wutai Mountains--History. 2. Mongols--China--Wutai Mountains--Social life and customs. 3.
Pilgrims and pilgrimages--China--Wutai Mountains--History. 4. Wutai Mountains (China)--History. 5.
Wutai Mountains (China)--Religious life and customs. 6. Wutai Mountains (China)--Ethnic relations. 7.
Mongols--Antiquities. 8. Inscriptions, Mongolian--China--Wutai Mountains. 9. Nationalism--China--
History. 10. Anti-clericalism--China--History. I. Title.

  DS793.W8222C47 2015
  305.894'2305117--dc23

                    2015012315

This publication has been typeset in the multilingual "Brill" typeface. With over 5,100 characters covering
Latin, IPA, Greek, and Cyrillic, this typeface is especially suitable for use in the humanities.
For more information, please see brill.com/brill-typeface.

ISSN 1566-7162
ISBN 978-90-04-29601-5 (hardback)
ISBN 978-90-04-29778-4 (e-book)

Printed by Printforce, United Kingdom

*I dedicate this book to my family, who helped me at every stage of its realization, from its incubation to its incarnation.*

∵

# Contents

# Acknowledgements

The original idea for this project stems from the convergence of various research trails. My interest in pilgrimages arouse in the mid-1990s when I joined pilgrims on several sites of Inner Mongolia during fieldwork research on Buddhist monasteries. My studies on Sino-Mongol interactions in the field of material culture thus naturally led me to Wutaishan. I first visited Wutaishan in 1994, and, among the very few pilgrims I met, a couple of Mongols from Ulaanbaatar aroused my curiosity. During the same period, I was awakened to the importance of epigraphy for the social history of religion thanks to Kristopher Schipper and his research group "Peking as a Holy City" in Paris.

In May 12-13, 2007, I participated in the Columbia University conference "Wutaishan and Qing Culture," organized by Gray Tuttle and Johan Elverskog at the Rubin Museum of Art in New York, on the occasion of the exhibition "Wutaishan: Pilgrimage to Five Peak Mountain," held from May 10 to October 16, 2007. The majority of the contributions focused on Qing imperial patronage and on biographies and writings of Tibetan high clerics, while ordinary pilgrimages received scant attention. I started to work on this book project following the very stimulating remarks of the participants of the symposium, and I particularly thank Gray Tuttle and Susan Naquin, who encouraged me to work in this direction. My fieldwork visits in July 2007, October 2009, September 2010 and October 2012 had three main objectives: copying and taking pictures of the stone inscriptions; collecting written and oral material on the monasteries; and interviewing pilgrims and resident monks. My key informants were Inner Mongol and Eastern Tibetan lamas from Luohousi and Shifangtang (two main Gélukpa monasteries), lama-pilgrims from Amdo and lay pilgrims from Mongolia and Inner Mongolia. I followed several groups of devotees on their pilgrimages and recorded the acts and rituals they performed and the places they favored.

Previous avatars of this work were presented at the Mongolia & Inner Asia Studies Unit (MIASU, Cambridge, UK, March 7, 2008), at the Institut National des Langues et Civilisations Orientales (INALCO, Paris, March 21, 2008), at the European Mongolists' Conference (organized by the Embassy of Mongolia in Hungary and the Academy of Sciences, Budapest, November 24-25, 2008), and at two conferences held at the Centro Incontri Umani (Ascona, Switzerland) on "Pilgrimage and Sanctuaries: Ambiguity in Context" (November 12-14, 2010) and "Visual Art, Material Culture and Pilgrimage" (November 12-13, 2011).

I am grateful to several organizations whose generous funding and institutional support at various stages during my research and writing have made this work possible. My research institute, Group Societies, Religions, Secularisms (GSRL, Centre National de la Recherche Scientifique—École Pratique des Hautes Études, Paris) supported my initial fieldwork in July 2007, as well as part of my 2010 and 2012 fieldwork. The ANR (National Research Agency) project on the study of the use of texts in imperial architecture of the Qianlong period (headed by Françoise Wang-Toutain, UMR [Joint Research Unit] 8155: Centre de recherche sur les civilisations de l'Asie orientale) supported my 2009 and 2011 fieldwork and part of my 2010 fieldwork.

I would especially like to thank the wonderful staff of the Institute for Chinese Studies at the Chinese University of Hong Kong, who provided me with the best possible working conditions in which to start this research in 2007. I have become indebted to a number of libraries and their staff members, in Paris (INALCO, École Française d'Extrême-Orient, Institut des Hautes Études Chinoises, Musée du Quai Branly); in London (School of Oriental and African Studies), in Hong Kong (Chinese University of Hong Kong), in Inner Mongolia (Library of the Inner Mongolia Normal University, Archives of Inner Mongolia) and in Beijing (Beijing Library, Library of the Institute of Minorities).

My work has benefited from the inspiration, collaboration and assistance generously offered to me by many people, ranging from friends and colleagues to anonymous pilgrims. Raoul Birnbaum shared with me ideas and souvenirs from 1986 to 1994, when Wutaishan was a very quiet and poor place and "monks were a mixture of saints and rascals, including a few criminals." This book owes much to Chou Wen-shing, Vincent Goossaert and Françoise Wang-Toutain, who gave so much of their time and energy to help me. I am extremely grateful to Françoise Aubin, Katia Buffetrille, Ü. Hürelbaatar, Zsuzsa Majer, Krisztina Teleki and Uranchimeg Ujeed, who provided many insightful comments and suggestions as this book developed. I owe a special debt of gratitude to Erkhes Bayasgalan and Sayinzaya in Paris, and the monk Agwangsangjie of Luohou Monastery on Wutaishan, who helped me decipher the stone inscriptions and averted errors of interpretation; to Cao Xinyu, Elisabetta Chiodo, Olivér Kápolnás, Marie-Dominique Even, Gray Tuttle and Vladimir Uspensky, who brought new sources to my attention. I have also greatly benefited from the help of and interesting discussions with Elena Astafieva, Luboš Bělka, Anne-Marie Blondeau, Don Croner, Grégory Delaplace, Elvira Eevr Djaltchinova-Malets, Vincent Durand-Dastès, Caroline Gyss, Roberte Hamayon, Corneille Jest, Luo Wenhua, Pierre Palussière, Rodica Pop, Françoise Robin, Tadeusz Skorupski, Heather Stoddard, Simon Wickham-Smith and my colleagues of the GSRL. Thanks to their advice and assistance, many errors and inaccuracies have been avoided, but, needless to say, those that no doubt remain are my responsibility alone.

At Brill, I was fortunate to work with Patricia Radder and her excellent staff. I also wish to thank my copy-editor, Heddi Goodrich, and the anonymous readers of my manuscript for their careful and thoughtful comments, which greatly improved the quality and arguments of the book.

I wish to sincerely thank all the monks and pilgrims who helped and accompanied me on the Wutaishan paths, especially Badraltsetseg, Borjigid, Tserendorji, Dalai, Geden, Gedünshirab, Gesang Dorji (Baatar), Gesangsangji Jamyangsambuu, Lubsangjamso, Lubsangsambuu, Ngawang Gedan, Shirabdorji and Tinley.

It is my family who deserves the greatest thanks of all for their unwavering support, and especially my husband, who read and helped me improve the many drafts of the manuscript, participated in endless discussions and who is always in my heart.

# List of Tables, Maps and Figures

## Tables

## Maps

## Figures

# Note on Transcriptions and Other Conventions

I used Christopher Atwood's system (2002: xv-xviii) for phonetically rendering Mongolian terms and names in the text. When citing authors, book titles and quotations of texts in footnotes, appendices and bibliography, I used Antoine Mostaert's system to transcribe the traditional Uyghur-Mongolian script, but I replaced 'č' and 'ǰ' with plain 'c' and 'j' and transliterated the vowels that can be pronounced as 'o' and 'ö' within non-initial syllables as 'u' and 'ü' (following Ferdinand Lessing's dictionary, 1960).

I added the Cyrillic (Cyr. Mo.) transcription for place names and personal names of the Republic of Mongolia, as well as for some Mongol names which may be familiar to the reader (such as Zanabazar): 'j' for ж, 'z' for з, 'ts' for ц, 'ch' for ч," 'sh' for ш, 'ye' for e, 'yo' for ё, 'i' for й and ъ, 'y' for ы, 'yu' for ю, 'ya' for я.

Tibetan words (Tib.) are phonetically transcribed according to the THL Simplified Phonetic Transcription of Standard Tibetan System; the reader will find pp. 462-466 the correct spelling according to Wylie's system.

Romanization of Chinese words (Ch.) follows the *pinyin* system, and characters are included the first time a Chinese term appears in the text. Mongol or Tibetan names appearing in Chinese transcription are transcribed with hyphens between syllables.

Sanskrit terms follow the standard International Alphabet of Sanskrit Transliteration.

For some foreign words that have entered the English-language academic literature, I have departed from the transcription systems noted above and kept now familiar spellings, e.g., Panchen Lama, Dalai Lama, Tukwan (Thu'u-bkwan) and Kumbum. Likewise, I have spelled certain place names according to modern renderings; for example, Beijing (even when the capital city was renamed Beiping, from 1928 to 1949), Lhasa, Höhhot (for Khökhe Khota) and Urga—which is more familiar to Western readers than Yekhe Khüriye (modern Ulaanbaatar). When speaking of the pre-communist period, I use the term Chinese as denoting the Han 'ethnicity.'

The term 'Mongol' here refers to the Mongolic peoples of Inner Mongolia (now in the People's Republic of China), Mongolia proper before 1911, and Russia, and the term 'Mongolia' refers to the Mongol-inhabited historical and cultural areas. 'Mongolian' is here restricted to qualify the citizens of Mongolia proper after it gained its autonomy in 1911 and to the language; otherwise 'Mongol' is used. 'Eastern Inner Mongolia' designates the Jirim, Josotu and Juu Uda Leagues of Inner Mongolia, following the usage of the peoples there.

# Correct Tibetan Spellings

Alaksha Tutop Nyima · A lag sha mThu stobs nyi ma
Amdo · A mdo
Amnye Machen · A myes rma chen

*badang* · *ba dang*
*bardo* · *bar do*
Butön Rinchen Drup · Bu ston rin chen grub

*cham* · *'cham*
Chang Gyeltsen · lCang [?] rgyal mtshan
Changkya · lCang skya
*chisa* · *spyi sa*
*chöjé* · *chos rje*
*chöjel* · *mchod mjal*
*chöné* · *mchod gnas*
Choné Trashi Chökhor Ling · Co ne bkra shis chos 'khor gling
*chöyön* · *mchod yon*

*da* · *brda*
*dakzhing* · *dag zhing*
Damchen Chökyi Gyelpo · Dam can chos kyi rgyal po
Damchen Dorjé Lekpa · Dam can rdo rje legs pa
Dampa Künga Drak · Dam pa kun dga' grags
Déchok · bDe mchog
Dergé · sDe dge
Détri Jamyang Tupten Nyima · sDe khri 'Jam dbyangs thub bstan nyi ma
Deushen · rDe'u shan
Dewachen · bDe ba can
Dézhin Shekpa · De bzhin gshegs pa
Dhétsang · Dhe tsang
Dilgo Khyentsé · Dil mgo mkhyen brtse
Döndrup Pelden · Don grub dpal ldan
*dorampa lama* Lozang Zangpo · *rdo rams pa* lama bLo bzang bzang po
Dorjé gyel[tsen] · rDo rje rgyal [mtshan]
Drakkar Treldzong · Brag dkar sprel rdzong
Drakpa Özer · Grags pa 'od zer
Drépung Monastery · 'Bras spungs

| | |
|---|---|
| Drigungtil | 'Bri gung mthil |
| *drönnyer* | *mgron gnyer* |
| Drung Rinchen Tsön[drü] | Drung rin chen brtson ['grus] |
| *duk* | *gdugs* |
| *düzang* | *dus bzang* |
| Durtrö Chenpo Siljin | Dur khrod chen po bsil sbyin |
| | |
| Ganden (Namgyal Ling) | dGa' ldan (rmam rgyal gling) |
| Ganden Datsang Lhündrup Ling | dGa' ldan da tshang lhun grub gling |
| Ganden Podrang | dGa' ldan pho brang |
| Ganden Shireetü Khutugtu Lozang | dGa' ldan siregetü qutuɣtu bLo bzang bstan |
|   Tenpé Nyima |   pa'i nyi ma |
| *gau* | *ga'u* |
| Gélek Damchö | dGe legs dam chos |
| *gélong* | *dge slong* |
| Gélukpa | dGe lugs pa |
| Gen(Gam)po Karpo | rGan(sGam) po skar po |
| Gendun Chopel | dGe 'dun chos 'phel |
| *géshé* | *dge bshes* |
| Golong Champa ling | dGon lung byams pa gling |
| Gomang | sGo mang |
| Gönpo Kyap | mGon po skyabs |
| *gowé lha nga* | *'go ba'i lha lnga* |
| *gyanakpa* | *rgya nag pa* |
| *gyelkham dönmé nyülba* | *rgyal khams don med nyul ba* |
| *gyeltsen* | *rgyal mtshan* |
| *gyépok* | *'gyed phogs* |
| | |
| Jamchen Chöjé Śākya Yéshé | Byams chen chos rje Śākya ye shes |
| Jampel Nakpo | 'Jam dpal nag po |
| Jamyang | 'Jam dbyangs |
| Jamyang Zhépa | 'Jam dbyangs bzhad pa |
| Jangchup Tsültrim Pelzangpo | Byang chub tshul khrims dpal bzang po |
| Jarung Khashor | Bya rung kha shor |
| Jéba | Byes ba |
| Jikmé Püntsok | 'Jigs med phun tshogs |
| *jinchen* | *byin can* |
| *jinlap* | *byin rlabs* |
| Jokhang | Jo khang |
| Jowo Rinpoché | Jo bo rin po che |

| | |
|---|---|
| *Kanjur* | *bKa' 'gyur* |
| *karchak* | *dkar chag* |
| Karmapa | Karma pa |
| Katok | *Kaḥ thog* |
| Kawa Karpo | Kha ba dkar po |
| Kelzang Tupten Wangchuk | sKal bzang thub bstan dbang phyug |
| Kham | Khams |
| Khangsar Rinpoché | Khang gsar rin po che |
| *khatak* | *kha btags* |
| Khédrup Gélek Pelzang | mKhas grub dge legs dpal bzang |
| Khédrup Jé | mKhas grub rje |
| Könchok Jikmé Wangpo | dKon mchog 'jigs med dbang po |
| Kongtsé Trülgyi Gyelpo | Kong tse 'Phrul gyi rgyal po |
| *kor* | *bskor* |
| *kubum* | *sku 'bum* |
| Kumbum Jampa Ling | sKu 'bum byams pa gling |
| Künga Özer Mergen | Kun dga' 'od zer mergen |
| Künga Trashi | Kun dga' bkra shis |
| Künrik Nampar Nangdzé | Kun rig(s) rnam par snang mdzad |
| Küntu Dewé Sel | Kun tu bde ba'i gsal |
| | |
| Labrang Tashi Khyil | bLa brang bkra shis 'khyil |
| Labrang | bLa brang |
| Lama Chenpo Sanggyé Pel | bLa ma chen po sangs rgyas dpal |
| *Lamrim chenmo* | *Lam rim chen mo* |
| *lendza* | *lan dza* |
| *lentsa* | *lan tsha* |
| Lhalé bappé düchen | Lha las babs pa'i dus chen |
| Lhamo | Lha mo |
| *lharampa* | *lha rams pa* |
| *lhari* | *lha ri* |
| Lhatsün Dargyé Nomönhen | Lha btsun dar rgyas no mon han |
| Lhündrup | Lhun grub |
| Longdöl Ngakwang Lozang | kLong rdol ngag dbang blo bzang |
| Loppön Chenpo | sLob dpon chen po |
| Lozang Chökyi Nyima | bLo bzang chos kyi nyi ma |
| Lozang Chökyi Nyima Gélek Namgyel | bLo bzang chos kyi nyi ma dge legs rnam rgyal |
| Lozang Menlam | bLo bzang sman lam |
| Lozang Pelsang | bLo bzang dpal sangs |

| | |
|---|---|
| Lozang Penden Tenpé Drönmé | bLo bzang dpal ldan bstan pa'i sgron me |
| Lozang Tendzin | bLo bzang bstan 'dzin |
| Lozang Tendzin Gyatso | bLo bzang bstan 'dzin rgya mtsho |
| Lozang Tenpé Gyeltsen | bLo bzang bstan pa'i rgyal mtshan |
| Lozang Trashi | bLo bzang bkra shis |
| *lüjin* | *lus sbyin* |
| *lungta* | *rlung rta* |
| *lungten* | *lung bstan* |
| | |
| Mahākāla Gur Gönpo | Mahākāla Gur mgon po |
| *mangja* | *mang ja* |
| *margyur semchen* | *mar gyur sems can* |
| Migön Karpo | Mi mgon dkar po |
| Milarépa | Mi la ras pa |
| Mitséring | Mi tshe ring |
| Mönlam | sMon lam |
| | |
| *namtar* | *rnam thar* |
| *néchen nga* | *gnas chen lnga* |
| *néjel* | *gnas mjal* |
| *nékor* | *gnas bskor* |
| *nékorwa* | *gnas skor ba* |
| *néri* | *gnas ri* |
| *néshé* | *gnas bshad* |
| *néyik* | *gnas yig* |
| Ngakwang Lhündrup Dargyé | Ngag dbang lhun grub dar rgyas |
| Ngakwang Lozang Chöden Pelzangpo | Ngag dbang blo bzang chos ldan dpal bzang po |
| Ngakwang Lozang Tenpé Gyeltsen | Ngag dbang blo bzang bstan pa'i rgyal mtshan |
| Ngakwang Tendar | Ngag dbang bstan 'dar |
| Ngakwang Tuptsen Wangchukden Trinlé Gyatso | Ngag dbang thub btsan dbang phyug ldan 'phrin las rgya mtsho |
| Norzang | Nor bzang |
| *nyellam* | *dmyal lam* |
| *nyenné* | *bsnyen gnas* |
| Nyima Dorjé | Nyi ma rdo rje |
| Nyingmapa | rNying ma pa |
| | |
| Orgyen Lingpa | O rgyan gling pa |

| | |
|---|---|
| Pabongkha Rinpoché | Pha bong kha rin po che |
| Padampa Sanggyé | Pha dam pa sangs rgyas |
| Pakpa Lama | 'Phags pa bla ma |
| Pakpa Lodrö Gyeltsen | 'Phags pa blo gros rgyal mtshan |
| Peltang | sPel thang |
| *pen* | *'phen* |
| | |
| Ramoche | Ra mo che |
| Rangjung Dorjé | Rang byung rdo rje |
| *rapné* | *rab gnas* |
| Ribo Tsénga | Ri bo rtse lnga |
| *riksum gönpo* | *rigs gsum mgon po* |
| Rölpé Dorjé | Rol pa'i rdo rje |
| | |
| Sakya pandita | Sa skya pandita |
| Śākya Yéshé | Śākya ye shes |
| Sakyapa | Sa skya pa |
| Samyé | bSam yas |
| *sang* | *srang* |
| Sanggyé Gyatso | Sangs rgyas rgya mtsho |
| Séra | Sera |
| Serthar | gSer thar |
| *sipaho* | *srid pa ho* |
| Situ Panchen Chökyi Jungné | Si tu pan chen chos kyi 'byung gnas |
| Sönam Dorjé | bSod nams rdo rje |
| Sönam Gyatso | bSod nams rgya mtsho |
| Songtsen Gampo | Srong btsan sgam po |
| *söpön* | *bso'i dpon* |
| Sumpa Khenpo Yéshé Penjor | Sum pa mkhan po ye shes dpal 'byor |
| *sungbum* | *gsung 'bum* |
| *sungdü* | *srung mdud* |
| | |
| Tangtong Gyelpo | Thang stong rgyal po |
| *Tanjur* | *bsTan 'gyur* |
| Tashilhunpo | bKra shis lhun po |
| Tendzin Gyatso | bsTan 'dzin rgya mtsho |
| Tenpa | bsTan pa |
| Terdrom | gTer sgrom |
| *terma* | *gter ma* |
| *terné* | *gter gnas* |

| | |
|---|---|
| *thangka* | *thang ka* |
| *tongchö* | *stong mchod* |
| Tongkhor Khutugtu Yönten Gyatso | sTong 'khor qutuɣtu Yon tan rgya mtsho |
| *torma* | *gtor ma* |
| *tranglam* | *phrang lam* |
| Tsampa Lozang Könchok | mTshams pa blo bzang dkon mchog |
| Tsangyang Gyatso | Tshangs dbyangs rgya mtsho |
| *tsatsa* | *tsha tsha* |
| Tsawa Lama Tamdrin Lozang Tayang | rTsa ba bla ma rta mgrin blo bzang rta dbyangs |
| *tsennyi* | *mtshan nyid* |
| Tsongkhapa | Tsong kha pa |
| Tukwan Lozang Chökyi Nyima | Thu'u bkwan bLo bzang chos kyi nyi ma |
| | |
| Yéshé Döndrup | Ye shes don grub |
| Yéshé Penden | Ye shes dpal ldan |
| Yéshé Rinchen | Ye shes rin chen |
| Yéshé Tenpé Gyeltsen śrībhadra | Ye shes bstan pa'i rgyal mtshan śrībhadra |
| *yidam* | *yi dam* |
| *yönchö* | *yon mchod* |
| *yöndak* | *yon bdag* |
| *yöndak chöné* | *yon bdag mchod gnas* |
| Yönten | Yon tan |
| *yüllha* | *yul lha* |
| | |
| *zhappé* | *zhabs spad* |
| *zhaser* | *zhwa ser* |
| *zhiba* | *bzhi ba* |

# Introduction

•••

Un lieu saint ne peut exister sans l'action centrifuge des saints et des religieux, et l'action centripète des pèlerins. Les religieux proposent et les
pèlerins disposent.[1]

∴

The Chinese and Western travellers among the Mongols in the nineteenth and
early twentieth centuries repeatedly noticed the spectacular devotion of these
Buddhist pilgrims on the way to and at pilgrimage sites. They were so numerous
on the roads to Tibetan sacred sites that Westerners and Japanese alike found it
easy to disguise themselves as Mongols and mingle in their midst.[2] But the most
popular Mongol pilgrimage was that of Wutaishan 五臺山 ('Five-Peaked
Mountain,' Mo. Utai Uula[3]), the famous Buddhist mountain in Shanxi Province
and a main place of Sino-Tibeto-Mongol encounter in China. The Scottish missionary James Gilmour (1843-1891), who visited Wutaishan in 1872, even compared the Wutaishan pilgrimage for Mongol Buddhists to Jerusalem and Mecca:

> As Jerusalem to the Jews, as the Mecca to the Mahometans, so is Wu Ta'i
> Shan to the Mongols. All over Mongolia, and wherever Mongols are met
> with in North China, one is constantly reminded of this place. It is true
> that the mania which possesses the Mongols for making pilgrimages car-
> ries them to many other shrines, some of which are both celebrated and
> much frequented, but none of them can be compared to Wu T'ai. At all

---

1 "A sacred place cannot exist without the centrifugal action of saints and clerics and the cen-
   tripetal action of pilgrims. The clerics put something forward and the pilgrims make use of
   it." (Buffetrille 1996a: 390). Unless otherwise stated, all translations from non-English-language
   sources are my own.
2 Such as Hisao Kimura (1922-1989), a young Japanese recruited by the Japanese intelligence
   service, who traveled to Tibet assuming the disguise of a Mongol monk from 1943 to 1945.
3 Or Udai, Utai Shan, Udaishan Uula. One of the earliest occurrences of the term Udai is in the
   fourteenth-century Mongolian inscription of Juyongguan Pass, northwest of Beijing (see
   Chapter 4). Wutaishan is also translated as Tabun Üjüürtü Uula or Tabun Uula, 'Five-Summit
   Mountain,' 'Five Mountains.' To Tibetans, it is known as Ribo Tsénga.

seasons of the year, in the dead of winter, in the heat of summer, pilgrims, priests, and laymen, male and female, old and young, rich and poor, solitary and in bands, on foot and mounted, from places far and near, may be seen going to and returning from this, the most sacred spot on earth to the Mongol Buddhist, the object of his devout aspirations during life, the place where he desires his bones to be thrown at death. The Mongols speak of it as one of the blessed spots on the earth, holy, purified, everlasting, indestructible ...[4]

In the nineteenth and early twentieth centuries, the Mongols went to Wutaishan in droves, and their donations greatly contributed to the development of Wutaishan's monasteries and to their maintenance after the decline of Manchu imperial patronage. Dmitri Pokotilov, then attaché of the Russian diplomatic mission in Beijing, described in 1889 the uninterrupted flow of Mongol pilgrims—Chinese and Tibetans being apparently much less numerous.[5] R.W. Swallow, a Western traveler, wrote in 1903:

The Mongols were the chief supporters of the various temples in the financial sense, and it was considered the right thing for every rich Mongol to make one journey at least to this place, bringing with him gifts from his tribe and friends.[6]

The pilgrimages stopped in the late 1930s, when Wutaishan became a conflict zone between Japanese and communist forces. Nowadays, after seventy years of Soviet atheism in the Republic of Mongolia and a century of anti-religious policy in China, many young urban Mongols have never heard about Wutaishan. However, the prominence of the Wutaishan pilgrimage in their religious landscape is still recorded in the memories of Mongol elders. In the mid-1990s, pilgrimages and festivals were revived in remote places of Inner Mongolia and Mongolia, and Mongols once more started to journey to Wutaishan, though they found themselves diluted among the crowds of Chinese pilgrims and tourists. Wutaishan is now one of the wealthiest Buddhist centers in China, along with Shaolin Monastery in Henan Province. In June 2009, it was named a World Heritage Site by UNESCO and received more than three million visitors that same year.[7] On this occasion, the provincial authorities decided to carry out

---

4   Gilmour 1970 [1883]: 141, 143.
5   Pokotilov 1935 [1893]: 66, 70, 79.
6   Swallow 1903: 182.
7   Unesco 2009.

major investments to improve infrastructure and attract tourists from China and abroad. Already in 2008, the 2.8 million paying visitors had brought 1.4 billion *yuan* (US\$ 206 million) in tourist revenues, according to government figures.[8]

## Focus of the Book

Although it was present-day observations that first aroused my interest in Wutaishan and later helped me understand some of the mechanisms of the pilgrimage, I am interested here in the genesis and the development of Mongols' journeys to this Chinese mountain from a historical perspective. Mongol pilgrimages to Wutaishan started in the seventeenth century and reached an apex in the late Qing period (from the nineteenth century to 1911)—a time of economic stagnation and political weakness, generally seen as a period of decline in China and Mongolia yet one of relative peace—and in the early Republican period, when Mongols struggled for autonomy while their land became the focus of conflicts between various foreign powers.[9] The aim of the book is to understand why Mongols went to Wutaishan, especially at a time of rising nationalisms, anticlericalism, spiritual revivals and Buddhist reforms.

The imperial patronage of the Wutaishan monasteries has attracted the attention of past and present scholars, and many Chinese articles and books deal with the imperially founded temples and the steles and poems calligraphed by emperors. The participants of the 2007 conference "Wutaishan and Qing Culture," as well as earlier scholars who have worked on the subject (such as David Farquhar 1978), have generally focused on Qing imperially centered historiography (Gray Tuttle, Natalie Köhle, Vladimir Uspensky, Patricia Berger) or on treatises, poetry and arcane scriptures produced by small groups of learned clerics (Kurtis Schaeffer).[10] Following recent trends in Qing studies that tend to shift the focus from China-centered historiography towards local, non-Chinese historiography, Johan Elverskog was one of the few scholars who took into account the Mongol perspective by looking for mentions of Wutaishan in Mongolian literature. He showed that it is necessary to reintroduce the Mongols' agency in the making of Wutaishan as a pilgrimage site.[11]

---

8    Saiget 2009.
9    Bawden 1989 [1968]; Atwood 2002.
10   Their articles were published in a special issue of the *Journal of the International Association of Tibetan Studies* 6 (2011): http://www.thlib.org/collections/texts/jiats/.
11   Elverskog 2011.

For this book, I have followed Elverskog's suggestion but have gone much further in exploring Mongol ideas and practices—I have mostly used sources other than Mongolian literary works and official histories. The specific purpose of my study is to document and analyze the reasons and motivations for such pilgrimages, the actual journeys made not only by nobles and lamas but also by ordinary Mongols, as well as their representations and ritual practices on the sacred mountain. Worship of Wutaishan in fact extended far beyond the world of learned clerics and was deeply rooted in popular traditions. Considerable hardship was endured by many monks and lay men and women who devoutly journeyed to Wutaishan, sometimes performing great prostrations all the way. This book is therefore not an intellectual, doctrinal or imperial history of Wutaishan but focuses on the pilgrims themselves. I was much inspired by the work of the Indianist Gregory Schopen, who stressed the importance of archaeological sources and especially stone inscriptions that express donors' intentions and tell us what a fairly large number of Buddhists actually did, as opposed to what—according to literary sources—they might or should have done. Schopen was not preoccupied with what

> small, literate, almost exclusively male and certainly atypical profession-alized subgroups wrote, but rather with what religious people of all segments of a given community actually did and how they lived.[12]

The aim of Chapter 1 is to understand the Mongols' engagement with Wutaishan compared to other pilgrimage sites in Mongolia (including 'pragmatic' pilgrimages to mountains, springs and rocks) and abroad—in Tibet, Nepal and India, the historical core of the Buddhist religion—but also in China. I investigate the respective spiritual and practical advantages of the different pilgrimage sites (including trade opportunities) in order to propose a hierarchy according to a scale of 'spiritual magnetism,' to use James Preston's terminology,[13] and to the types of pilgrims.

A general geographical, spiritual and historical presentation of the site (Chapter 2) will help us understand how Wutaishan was chosen as a mountain of spiritual significance, first by Chinese, by Buddhists of all East and Central Asia, and then by Mongols. The notion of liminality developed by Victor Turner,

---

12    In several of his articles, Schopen stressed that both the monastic elites and the less learned participated actively in a wide range of ritual practices and institutions that have heretofore been labeled as 'popular' (1997, esp. "Archaeology and protestant presuppositions in the study of Indo-Tibetan Buddhism," 1-22).

13    Preston 1992: 38-40.

can apply not only to the state of mind of the pilgrims but also to the place itself: Wutaishan appeared as an almost otherworldly place, where one had the possibility of establishing contact with supernatural powers, and at the same time, for the Mongols, as a familiar place. A presentation of its layered, sedimented history shows how Wutaishan has gradually developed into a formalized pilgrimage structure, to become a central place for the ritual protection of the empire. It helps understand why Yuan-dynasty Mongols became interested in this powerful site.

In the Qing period, the Manchu emperors developed Tibetan Buddhism on Wutaishan to such a point that Wutaishan became a 'Tibet in China.' Chapter 3 questions David Farquhar's 1978 thesis on the role of Qing imperial patronage in the promotion of the pilgrimage among the Mongols through two means of propaganda—imperial tours and the publication of gazetteers. I then investigate the strategies of the resident clergies to attract pilgrims and their donations when the imperial subsidies were reduced, before drying up in 1911. Lastly, the Tibetan, Mongol and Monguor high clerics also played a role in promoting the pilgrimage and transformed the spiritual landscape of Wutaishan by diffusing new narratives and discovering new sites.[14]

Chapter 4 moves the focus to Mongol narratives and restores the Mongols' agency in the development of the pilgrimage. It first introduces the Mongols' veneration of Mañjuśrī and Wutaishan before the Qing dynasty, and then presents their literary, oral and visual productions about Wutaishan. I will contrast Tibeto-Mongol clerical conceptualizations and Mongol popular views of the sacred mountain, in order to highlight the specificities of the Mongol *imaginaire*, or social imaginary, of Wutaishan compared to Chinese and Tibetan representations. Finally, I question whether the proliferation of Mongolian guidebooks and maps of the mountain was a cause or a consequence of the success of the pilgrimage, in order to understand when the popularity in Mongol pilgrimages to Wutaishan actually arose.

Chapter 5 addresses the social and economic side of the pilgrimage, taking as a main source the stone inscriptions erected within Wutaishan monasteries: Who were the Mongol pilgrims? What were their geographical origins and social backgrounds? And to what extent was Wutaishan a pan-Mongol pilgrimage? Was the Wutaishan pilgrimage a refuge in times of troubles, to escape poverty and debts and ask for divine help, or rather linked to the Mongols' feeling of being 'Qing Buddhists'?[15] To explain the extraordinary amounts of

---

14  Monguors (Ch. *tuzu* 土族) are an ethnic group living in Amdo (Qinghai Province), related to the Mongols, and followers of Tibetan Buddhism.

15  Elverskog 2006.

donations, I will look at the importance of trade and ask whether the pilgrims were only noblemen, wealthy commoners and lamas. A typology of pilgrims according to their identity, origins, material and spiritual motivations, modes of travel and material details of their journey will highlight the variety of pilgrims and pilgrimages. A particular motivation to undertake the pilgrimage was to bury a relative on the mountain. I will focus on how Wutaishan could have become a main burial place for Mongol pastoralists accustomed to burying their dead in their homeland so that their ancestors might protect the pastures, while at the same time allowing herders to claim the pastures surrounding the burial spot.

Chapter 6 focuses on what Mongol pilgrims actually did on Wutaishan. I will introduce the sacred sites they tended to visit, as well as the specific merit/chance-producing activities and rituals they engaged in, to understand whether or not they made the same pilgrimages as the Tibetans and the Chinese and whether they adopted Chinese practices in addition to their own. This chapter also deals with interactions and encounters between Mongols and other ethnic and religious communities and questions Elverskog's theory on the role of Wutaishan in the creation of a 'Mongol identity,' a 'Qing identity,' a 'Qing culture,' and Qing 'cosmopolitanism' uniting Mongols, Chinese and Tibetans.[16] Were there forms of *communitas* between 'ethnicities' and between the Mongols themselves on Wutaishan?

Chapter 7 focuses on the Mongol pilgrims' appropriation of Wutaishan through their practices, rituals and interpretations of its natural numinous sites; in fact, they disrupted the clerical Buddhist project by introducing some of their own pilgrimage practices. I take the example of the Mongols' ritual practice at the Mother's Womb-Cave to highlight the fact that Wutaishan was not only a Buddhist pilgrimage center in China but also a Mongol popular pilgrimage. This process of appropriation went as far as to claim that sites of the Mongol countryside were equivalent or identical to Shanxi's Wutaishan. But could these fully replace the pilgrimage to Wutaishan?

### The Sources to Study Mongols' Pilgrimages

Because of the multifaceted nature of sacred places and the diversity of pilgrims' quests, scholars of pilgrimages generally agree on the necessity of an interdisciplinary approach. I have therefore favored an ethno-historical approach

---

16     Elverskog 2011.

that includes the study of both the sacred place and the pilgrims, by combining a great diversity of written and visual sources.

### Mongolian Stone Inscriptions on Wutaishan

My main sources to document the pilgrims themselves are the stone inscriptions commissioned by groups of Mongol devotees (Fig. 1). Wutaishan today mostly appears as a Chinese site, making these ostentatious marks of religious patronage the only visible historical traces left by Mongol pilgrims. The practice of erecting steles recording donations was an old Buddhist tradition; they are found on the railings surrounding Indian *stūpa*s and in cave temples since the second century BCE.[17] The multiplication of steles on Wutaishan, and also near Datong 大同, on the way to Wutaishan, marks the Mongols' appropriation of this sacred site and of parts of the roads that leads to it.[18] The Mongol donors had more than 340 inscriptions carved on stone steles to commemorate their offerings and vows. They are dated between 1658 and 1940, but the great majority are dated to the late Qing (1875-1911) and Republican periods (1912-1940). They tell us about the identity of pilgrims, the date, amount and purpose of their donation, as well as the pilgrims' wishes and aspirations.

Between 2007 and 2012, I took pictures of all the inscriptions I could find in situ and copied those which were not legible in photos. I have built a database to study this corpus and try to quantify its different variables (see Appendix 2 and Online Appendix A1). The list of steles is presented by monastery in chronological order in Online Appendix A2, with the name and origin of the main donor, the date and the amount of the donation, as well as the steles' location in the monastery, and a summary of the text for the most important ones.[19] Except for some which are broken or have fallen down and have been moved to a corner, these steles still stand on Wutaishan, and eighty-five percent of them are located within the precinct of three monasteries: Shifangtang 十方堂, Tayuansi 塔院寺 and Luohousi 羅睺寺 (Table 5). Modern Mongols occasionally read the stone inscriptions and show respect towards this heritage by pasting gold leaf or Chinese coins on them. Unfortunately, a few steles covered by coins pasted with the wax of lamps have become illegible (Fig. 56).

---

17    Ray 1994: 38-39; Schopen 1997.

18    In many cultures, vertical steles are like seals that mark the possession of the soil. See for instance the Tibetan pillars and steles erected to signify possession of the ground (Stein 1987 [1962]: 138). On the functions of Chinese steles in pre-Buddhist and early Buddhist China: Wong 2004.

19    I here refer to the steles by their number in Online Appendix A2 and by their date. For instance, 'SF144, 1927' is the 144th stele of Shifangtang in chronological order and is dated 1927.

TABLE 1      *Number and dates of imperial, Chinese non-imperial and Mongolian steles in*
             *thirteen monasteries (in bold: Tibetan Buddhist monasteries of the Qing and*
             *Republican periods)*

| Monasteries | Number (and date) of imperial steles | Number (and date) of non-imperial steles in Chinese | Number (and date) of non-imperial steles in Mongolian as the main language | Number of steles in Tibetan |
|---|---|---|---|---|
| Tayuansi | 8 (1408?-1601) | 13 (1323-1934) | 61 (1853-1934) | - |
| Xiantongsi | 6 (1458-1677) | 5 (1636-1925) | 5 (1918-1935) | 1 |
| **Pusading** | 8 (1671-1811) | - | 1 (1936) | - |
| **Yuanzhaosi** | 5 (1458-1569) | 4 (1569-1917) | 7 (?) | - |
| Luohousi | 4 (1417-1710) | 1 (1624) | 47 (1658-1935) | - |
| **Shifangtang** | - | - | 182 (1835-1933) | 3 |
| **Cifusi** | - | - | 7 (1920-1940) | - |
| Shuxiangsi | 3 (1591-1749) | 4 (1328-1665) | 1 (1665) | - |
| Dailuoding | 3 (1582?-1786) | - | 2 (1691 and 1874) | - |
| Bishansi | 4 (1487-1525) | 6 (1504-1929) | 1 (Guangxu period?) | - |
| **Zhenhaisi** | 1 (1711) | - | 5 (1829-1866) | - |
| Nanshansi | 1 (1339) | 20 (1885-1935) | 2 (1894 and 1895) | - |
| **Shouningsi** | 1 (1711) | 2 (Yuan and 1691) | 2 (Kangxi and 1774) | |
| Total for 13 monasteries | 44 | 53 | 321 | |

Chinese steles, especially imperial ones, have attracted more attention than Mongolian steles; thus, most of the pre-Qing inscriptions and Qing imperial inscriptions have been published, while Qing and Republican non-imperial inscriptions have not.[20] Yet the Mongolian steles largely outnumber pre-1949 Chinese inscriptions: few inscriptions commemorating donations from other ethnicities before the twenty-first century are found on Wutaishan (Table 1).[21] The small number of Chinese inscriptions comes as a surprise considering the

---

20    A collection of steles published by Zhou Zhenhua et al. (1998) lists only 112 Chinese stone inscriptions (including funerary steles—not included in my corpus—and the Chinese version of a few polyglot steles erected by Mongols); see also Cui Zhengsen and Wang Zhichao 1995 and articles published in the journal *Wutaishan yanjiu* recording Chinese inscriptions. Only the Chinese texts of the few polyglot imperial steles have been published.

21    Hundreds of steles in Chinese were carved since the 1990s, commemorating Han Chinese and Inner Mongol donations. Modern Chinese visitors often have a look at stone

popularity of the Wutaishan pilgrimage among Chinese devotees.[22] Indeed, the geographer and Buddhist layman Zhang Dungu,[23] who visited Wutaishan in 1911, noticed than one or two steles out of ten were in Chinese, the rest being in Mongolian or Tibetan.[24]

This corpus of Mongolian inscriptions forms a unique heritage that has not attracted much attention before I started studying it and raising awareness among my Inner Mongol colleagues. Except for Rev. Joseph Edkins (1823-1905) and Zhang Dungu (1866-1933),[25] early twentieth-century pilgrims and visitors who wrote diaries, records and guidebooks did not notice them. The Japanese guidebooks and surveys published in the first half of the twentieth century and modern studies on Wutaishan occasionally mention multilingual steles but say nothing of Mongolian inscriptions.[26] To my knowledge, none of these texts (or stone rubbing of them) have been published yet. In 1999 the *Catalogue of Ancient Mongolian Books and Documents of China* listed 249 inscriptions.[27] I found 94 more inscriptions, and 21 inscriptions listed in the *Catalogue* have disappeared between 1999 and 2012.[28] Several steles that I copied or photographed in 2007 had disappeared by 2012, or were hidden or moved to a remote corner of a monastery.[29]

These steles are not 'eternal' testimonies as their title usually suggests,[30] and many of them have become completely illegible because of natural degradation or vandalism. Some inscriptions mentioned by written sources, such as a

---

     inscriptions when visiting a temple and express their surprise when discovering steles written in Mongolian.

22     I also recorded the Chinese non-imperial and imperial steles within the monasteries, first because I used them as historical sources and, second, to highlight their location in comparison to Mongolian steles.

23     Zhang Dungu 1911: 1a.

24     I found a dozen steles written in Tibetan only: three in Shifangtang, located among the Mongolian steles east of the Buddha hall, two in Baohuasi, one in Qifosi, one in Sanquansi, one in Xiantongsi and two in Mimoyan.

25     Edkins 1893 [1878]: 228; Zhang Dungu 1911: 1a.

26     Except for Altanzayaa 2010.

27     *Catalogue of Ancient Mongolian Books and Documents of China* 1999: 2141-2147 n° 12610-12647 and p. 2178-2211, n° 12786-12996. It gives the title, date, location on Wutaishan, name and origin of the main donor, size and language(s) but not the full text.

28     Altanzayaa (2010: 145-146) mentions thirty-five 'important' inscriptions, but includes in this total the Qing polyglot imperial steles.

29     In 2012, I could not find again steles I previously saw in Fomudong and Pujisi on the Southern Terrace and fragments of steles in Yuanzhaosi and Sanquansi.

30     The steles' 'head' (upper part, Mo. *tologai*) often expresses in Mongolian or in Chinese the wish of lasting forever, or at least 'a thousand *kalpas*.'

Tibetan stele written by the Fourth Jebtsündamba Khutugtu[31] at Fomudong 佛母洞, have disappeared during the twentieth century.[32] Many inscriptions were carved on a poor-quality stone that did not withstand time—probably sandstone, whereas granite was used for the imperial steles. Others have been broken, mutilated, covered with Chinese graffiti or with a black pigment, stored in a corner, abandoned or used as tables or as construction materials. Some have even been scratched and re-carved. Evidently, Mongolian steles erected in Chinese Buddhist monasteries do not present any interest for present-day communities. However, my work has inspired my colleague Hürelbaatar Üjeed from the Normal University of Höhhot (Mo. Khökhe Khota, capital of the Inner Mongolian Autonomous Region), who has since made several fieldtrips to Wutaishan with his students to record the texts of these steles.[33]

Among the Mongolian steles, seventeen imposing inscriptions record exceptional donations and especially important donors. Some of them stand symmetrically opposite Chinese inscriptions in front of the Buddha hall, showing the public acknowledgement of some major Mongol donations. But the great majority of Mongolian steles are embedded in a low wall, a balustrade or in a special place inside three monasteries: Shifangtang, Luohousi and Tayuansi.

I counted twenty-three multilingual steles—in Mongolian and/or Tibetan, and/or Chinese, sometimes with a prayer in Lantsa script[34]—written by Mongol donors (Table 9). In bilingual Mongolian-Chinese inscriptions, the Chinese text is not a translation of the Mongolian one, and is shorter, probably because Chinese texts were often written and signed by the abbot of the monastery, who wanted to record the material aspect of the donation, while the Mongolian texts follow Mongol patterns.

Pilgrims whose donations were too small to be recorded on stone received paper certificates. These were issued in considerable numbers by the Wutaishan monasteries, and some are now found in the archives of Höhhot and Ulaanbaatar (Fig. 2; Online Appendix A3).[35] They often adopt a vertical format

---

31    *Khutugtu* is the title given to reincarnated lamas of the highest rank.

32    According to the Dilowa Khutugtu, interviewed by Lessing 1957b: 97. Stein (1988: 3), who visited the place, did not find it either.

33    Kürelbayatur (forthcoming) found a total of 353 steles, of which 23 are incomplete or illegible.

34    Lantsa (*lañja*, Tib. *lentsa* or *lendza*) is a sacred script elaborated in Nepal to write Sanskrit, especially *dhāraṇīs*, particularly in architecture (for consecration formulas) and books.

35    Hundreds of such receipts are preserved in the Archives of Inner Mongolia; one is preserved in the Royal Library of Copenhagen (Heissig and Sagaster 1961: 252, Mong. 214). Others are sold on ebay.com and in antique shops of Ulaanbaatar. I thank Olivér Kápolnás, who purchased four certificates for me in Ulaanbaatar.

FIGURE 1    *The 'stele wall' on the northern side of the Great White Stūpa, Tayuansi.*
© ISABELLE CHARLEUX, 2010.

modeled on the shape and frame of the stone inscriptions. They are printed or pre-handwritten sheets of paper with the same formulas as the steles; blanks were left to be filled in by hand (in darker ink) at the time of the donation to record the name and origin of the donor(s), the amount and nature of the donation as well as the date. Red seals of the monastery are added, such as that reading "Seal of Three-Stūpa Monastery" (*gurban suburgan-yin temdeg*). Certificates of donations thus imitate steles in their form and content and can be viewed as cheap paper versions of the stone inscriptions or, in some cases, as a double of the stele to be carried back home by pilgrims (one certificate also mentions the carving of a stele).

### Other Emic Sources
The literary style of the steles and certificates is often too formal and codified to give us much information about what made the pilgrimage to Wutaishan unique for those Mongols. A more personal kind of record that gives an insider's viewpoint is pilgrims' diaries. Diaries of pilgrims to Urga, Lhasa, India and

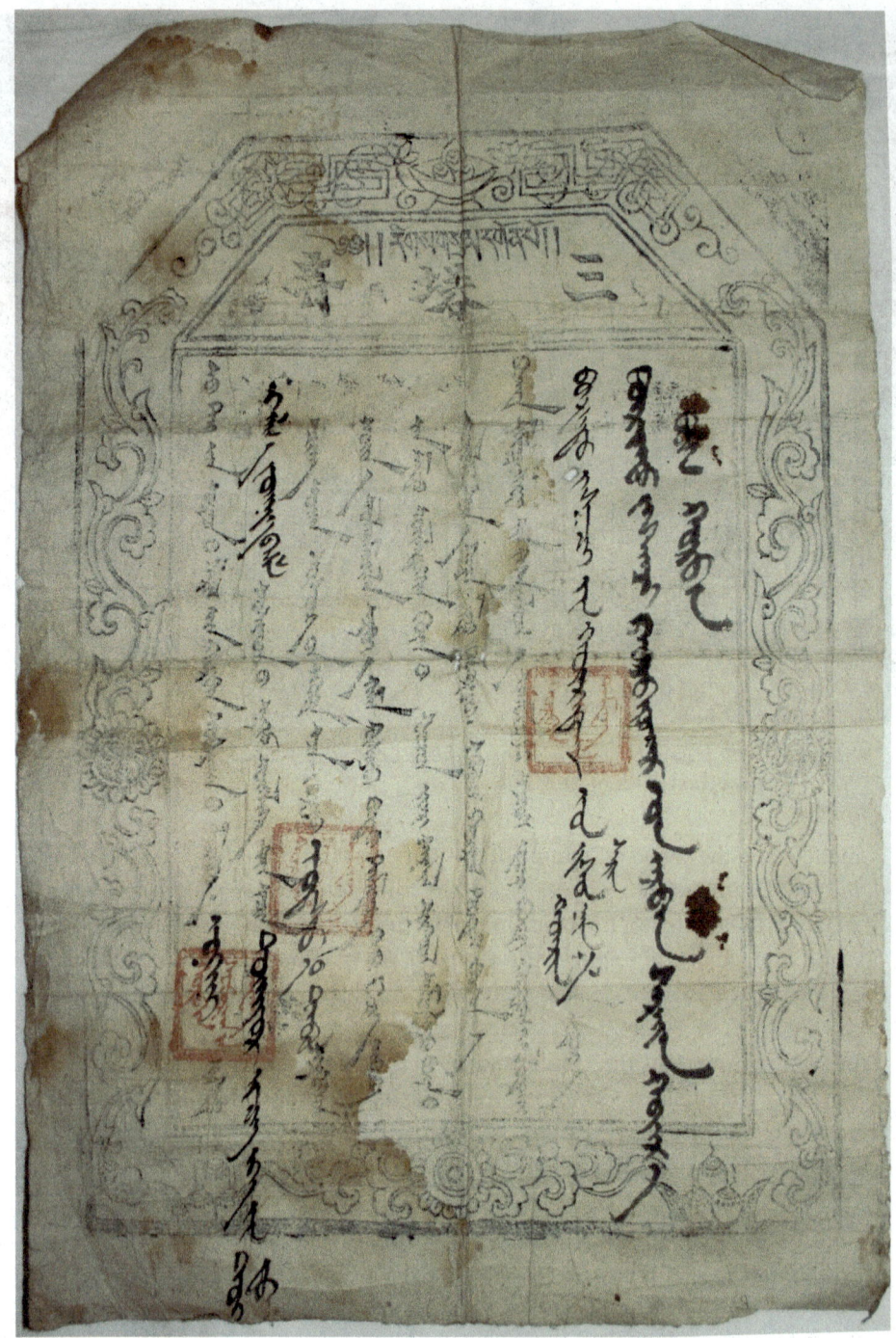

FIGURE 2     *Paper certificate of donation from Santasi, 1863.* © ISABELLE CHARLEUX, 2011.

Nepal include Gombojab Tsybikov's (1873-1930) famous detailed diary to Lhasa,[36] and diaries of Kalmyk and Buryat lay and monk pilgrims between 1882 and 1905. [37] As for Wutaishan, the travel account of Duke Migwachir (1893-1958), a writer, traveler, artist, poet and pious Buddhist from Inner Mongolia, describes his visit to the sacred Chinese mountain in 1938 with his younger brother after a long journey to Tibet, India and Beijing.[38] Other Mongolian diaries to Wutaishan did certainly exist. According to a stone inscription standing in Pusading 菩薩頂,[39] Prince Ardsedi of the Abaga Banner and deputy chief of the Shili-yin Goul League (Inner Mongolia) wrote an account (*oron-u dangsa*) of the pilgrimage he made to Wutaishan in 1848.[40] In the early 1930s, two Westerners visiting Wutaishan met "a group of Mongol pilgrims, the leader of whom was busily engaged writing down in Mongol script in a very modern notebook descriptions of the places of interest visited for the edification of those at home."[41]

In addition, short descriptions of Wutaishan are found in the autobiographies and memoirs of high clerics.[42] For instance, the Kanjurwa Khutugtu (1914-1978), a renowned reincarnation from Inner Mongolia,[43] and the famous Buryat diplomat monk Dorjiev (1854-1938)[44] wrote down factual details of their

---

36    This famous Russian Buryat explorer, Buddhologist and anthropologist left a travel account that is a unique source for the history of Tibet and Tibetan politics (Tsybikov 1992 [1919]). He also served as an interpreter for the Dalai Lama who had taken refuge in Urga in 1904.

37    Five Kalmyk manuscript diaries are listed by Tsybikov 1904; Bormanshinov 1998: 10, n. 43 and 44, 13, 16-17 and n. 71, 19. Some are preserved in the Archive of the Russian Geographical Society. See also Andreyev 2001c: 349, n. 1. Several travel records by Buryat lamas are preserved in the Russian Academy of Sciences, Saint Petersburg (Sazykin 1988: I, 295-296, n° 1635, 1636, 1638, 1639, 1640; Tsyrempilov, comp. 2004: 263-165, n° 549, 551, and 553; Tsyrempilov, comp. 2006: 287-289, n° 825, 826 and 827).

38    *Alaša qosiyun-u barayun güng-ün iledkel šastir* ("Report of the Western Duke of Alashan Banner"], Miγvacir 2008 [1942]: 403-407. See an abstract of his journey to Wutaishan in Online Appendix C.

39    Pusading, Bodhisattva Peak or Bodhisattva's Uṣṇīṣa [Monastery], was built during the Yongle reign on the ruins of old Da Wenshusi 大文殊寺, or Zhenrongyuan 真容院, that sheltered the 'true image' of Mañjuśrī. It was the Gélukpas' principal monastery, sponsored by the Manchu emperors.

40    Online Appendix A2, stele PSD1, 1936.

41    Alley and Lapwood 1935: 118.

42    Yang Jizeng, ed. 1997.

43    Jagchid and Hyer 1983: 106-107.

44    Martin and Norbu (1991) translated an autobiography written in 1923, of which several manuscripts and lithograph copies in Tibetan and Mongolian exist (I thank Gray Tuttle for having sent me a copy of this article).

journeys to Wutaishan. Over the past decade, a few Inner Mongols' memories of their pilgrimages from years back have been recorded.[45] But since the pilgrimages stopped in the late 1930s (the last stone inscription was written in 1940), there is little hope of finding any more elderly pilgrims who still have a clear recollection of the pilgrimages they performed more than seventy years ago.

A few guidebooks were written in or translated into Mongolian. They are of two different types: firstly, guidebooks translating parts of Chinese gazetteers (Ch. *shanzhi* 山志, 'mountain gazetteers') on Wutaishan, which offer a comprehensive clerical and/or imperial presentation of its religious geography; and secondly, guidebooks modeled on Tibetan guides to holy places, which fit with Katia Buffetrille's definition of Tibetan guidebooks as "literary stereotyped projections of an internal vision of spiritual reality destined to convey the pilgrim towards a supernatural level."[46] Since some of them reached a wide audience,[47] advertising the sanctity of Wutaishan in Mongolia, they helped shape the Mongol representations of Wutaishan. Other writings by Mongol lamas that evoked their visits to Wutaishan generally dealt with their initiations and visions; like the Tibetan-style guidebooks, they give a symbolic, 'mandalic' topography of Wutaishan, viewed as the otherworldly abode of *bodhisattva* Mañjuśrī.[48]

There was a gap between popular piety and the Buddhist spirituality of the literate;[49] hence, unfortunately, we still know little about what ordinary Mongols (and, especially, the illiterate or poorly literate masses) actually thought about Wutaishan during the Qing and Republican periods. Mongol historiography dealing with the history of Buddhism over the course of its transmission from India to Mongolia, the genealogies of nobles and reincarnated lamas and records of how they spread the faith and founded monasteries are of no help in documenting pilgrimages. However, oral and written literature such as tales, folk songs, wise sayings, prayers and prophecies can provide some insight, as they occasionally refer to Wutaishan as a holy and even mythical place.[50] For instance, a sixty-seven-verse popular song recorded among the Khorchins in

---

45    Nan Yang 1998; Ha-si-wu-la 哈斯烏拉 and Feng Qiuzi 馮秋子 in Tian Chang'an and
        Liang Heng, eds. 2003: p. 41-48 and p. 62-71.

46    Buffetrille 1998: 19; also Buffetrille 1997: 89.

47    Especially the *Uta-yin tabun ayulan-u orusil süsüg-ten-ü cikin cimeg orusiba*, hereafter
        *UTAOSC* (see Chapter 4).

48    Schaeffer 2011.

49    About the gap between popular piety and Buddhist spirituality in pilgrimage practices in
        Tibet: Macdonald 1998: x.

50    For an example of such prayers, see the manuscript prayer from Ordos: "U-tai-yin
        maγtaγal orusiba" (Yang 2000: 231-238): Online Appendix E.

eastern Inner Mongolia describes the route of pilgrims to and on Wutaishan (see Appendix 3).

The National Archives of Mongolia and the Provincial Archives of Inner Mongolia preserve interesting materials documenting pilgrimages such as passports for groups of pilgrims giving them authorization to cross their banners' frontiers,[51] in addition to "petitions of grievances," which provide us with some insight as to how nobles' pilgrimages may have impacted local populations. Russian archives have preserved an incomplete manuscript manual written for Buryat pilgrims with notes on the distance between various monasteries and sacred places in Mongolia, Eastern, Central and Southern Tibet, and Nepal.[52]

The most complete Mongol representations of the sacred mountain are maps. The oldest is a mural on a wall of the assembly hall of Badgar Choiling Süme in Inner Mongolia,[53] painted at some point between 1757 and 1835, which represents Wutaishan together with seven monasteries of Central and Eastern Tibet (Fig. 16). The second oldest map is a woodblock xylograph map carved by a Khalkha monk in 1846 at Cifusi 慈福寺, a Gélukpa monastery of Wutaishan, of which sixteen prints are known (Fig. 3). It had a wide circulation in Inner and Northern Mongolia in colored and uncolored prints; owing to its success, in 1874 new blocks were carved in China.[54] The Cifusi map locates the main monasteries and evokes the lore of the mountain, including apparitions of deities, historical narratives and symbolic interpretations of the landscape;[55] it certainly played a significant role in the development of the Wutaishan cult in Mongolia.

### Etic Sources

Although the Chinese language gazetteers do not discuss pilgrims, the Republican-period Chinese and Japanese guidebooks have different values and concerns: they are at the same time practical guidebooks investigating history and

---

51    I thank Cao Xinyu for having given me access to the digitalized archives of Alashan League, which keep fifty-seven passports of pilgrims from Alashan (n° 101-05-0098-011-0016-01).

52    Tsyrempilov and Vanchikova, comp. 2004: 164, n° 551.

53    Known in Chinese as Wudangzhao 五當召, this monastery, founded around 1749 northeast of Baotou, was the main academic monastery of Inner Mongolia.

54    Chou 2007; Chou 2011a. The prints that circulated and were colored in China and Tibet, however, cannot be considered as emic representations.

55    The Rubin Museum of Art in New York proposes a digitalized interactive version of its print of the Cifusi map: http://wutaishan.rma2.org/rma_viewer.php?image_id=1&mode=info (accessed on November 1, 2011).

FIGURE 3    *"Panoramic Picture of the Sacred Realm of the Mountain of Five Terraces," carved by*
*the monk Lhunrub, 1846, woodblock print on linen, hand colored, 118 × 165 cm. Rubin*
*Museum of Art, New York; Gift of Deborah Ashencaen, acc. no. C2004.29.1.*
© KARL DEBRECZENY.

architecture, and sometimes travel accounts.[56] More useful for us is the genre
of travel accounts, which often offers glimpses of the Mongol pilgrims' practices.
Western (including Russian), Chinese and Japanese travelers, as well as Chinese
pilgrims, wrote a number of records of their peregrinations mostly during the
period 1870-1940: they were tourists, officials, scholars, Buddhist clerics, lay pilgrims, Christian missionaries, geographers, explorers, diplomats and engi-
neers.[57] They offer different perspectives on the pilgrimage. The travel records
of Chinese literati and officials, though often written by lay Buddhists (such as
Zhang Dungu 張沌谷 in 1911 and Jiang Weiqiao 蔣維橋 in 1918),[58] do not give
much information on the pilgrimage and pilgrims but simply note the Mongols'

56    Li Xiangzhi 1932; Ono Katsutoshi and Hibino Takao 1940.

57    See the list of travelers and short presentations of the main accounts in Online Appendix
      C.

58    On the genre of literati travel accounts to pilgrimage sites in China: Naquin and Yü 1992:
      18.

presence. By contrast, Chinese pilgrim accounts—such as renowned Chan master Xuyun 虛雲 (b. 1840 or 1864, d. 1959), who traveled in 1882-1883, and lay pilgrim Gao Henian 高鶴年 (n.d), who made pilgrimages in 1903 and 1912—put emphasis on dialogues with monks and encounters with Mañjuśrī. As for Westerners' descriptions, Christian missionary accounts by J. Gilmour and J. Edkins, who travelled to Wutaishan in 1872 and who were especially interested in converting Mongols, give a very different viewpoint from that of scholars like D. Pokotilov (in Wutaishan in 1889),[59] H. Hackman (1900) and W.W. Rockhill (1887 and 1908), that of travelers like E. Fischer (1917) and that of Buddhist scholars like J. Blofeld (1935-1936).

Travelers' accounts offer us some vivid descriptions of the Mongol pilgrims' journeys and of practices that are absent from other sources. Indeed, some sacred spots on the mountain were known through stories that had a wide circulation and were often recorded in imperial gazetteers, while others became known through local monks or ethnic groups of pilgrims and thus circulated in narrower circles. For instance, some relics (such as the long tooth of Mañjuśrī in Jingangku 金剛窟, the Vajra Cave) or the Mother's Womb-Cave ritual were described only by a few witnesses who actually went to these places. Western and Chinese travel literature is of an uneven quality, but it remains a major primary source to reconstruct the pilgrimage, in particular when it concerns lesser known practices and places.

### Secondary Literature

The secondary literature on Mongols' pilgrimages to Wutaishan is extremely lean. Three short articles have been published in Mongolian and Chinese: Altanzayaa published a 2000 article documenting the pilgrimage of nobles and lamas and Mongolian guidebooks mostly from archival documents; in the same year, Song Wenhui 宋文輝 wrote an article about a document written by a Kharachin lama, preserved in the Archives of the Kharachin Right Banner, and Yan Tianling 閻天靈 (2004) listed some Chinese and Western sources on the pilgrimage. Although the libraries of Inner Mongolia and of the Republic of Mongolia possess a few guidebooks and religious writings on Wutaishan, as well as archival documents such as passports and paper certificates, Mongol and Chinese researchers have generally not been interested in pilgrimages. Chinese specialists of Wutaishan, such as Wang Zhiyong 王志勇 and Cui

---

59    Two out of the four chapters were translated from Russian into German in 1935. At the
       time of its translation, the Russian original was already rare; the translator W.A. Unkrig
       obtained it from A.M. Pozdneev in 1918 (introduction to the translation, Pokotilov 1935
       [1893]: 38). I only had access to the German translation.

Zhengsen 崔正森, who in 2000 published a two-volume general historical survey on Wutaishan, and scholars who write for the periodical *Wutaishan yanjiu* 五臺山研究 (Wutaishan studies), such as Gao Minghe 高明和, Wang Lu 王璐, Wei Guozuo 魏国祚, and Xiao Yu 肖雨, all focus on Chinese history and architecture, Chinese Buddhism, Chinese steles, calligraphies and poems.[60] Neither have researchers been interested in the Wutaishan pilgrimage from an anthropological perspective.

Modern Mongol pilgrims do not have much material written in their language to learn about Wutaishan. I only know of two modern Mongolian guidebooks. The first is the *Utai-bar juyacaysad-tu*, published in Chifeng 赤峰 in 1988, the translation of Wei Guozuo's *Wutaishan daoyou* 五臺山导游 (Guide to Wutaishan); in 2007 and 2012, a few copies could be purchased in the bookshop of Taihuai 臺懷, the central village of Wutaishan. The second one is a small guidebook in Cyrillic script by lama Ishtavkhai, published in 1998 in his booklet *Mörgölchidöd zoriulsan tailbar* (Explanations to pilgrims). The Qing period Mongolian guidebooks have not been reprinted since the early twentieth century and are found only in archives, except for the eighteenth-century imperial gazetteer *Cing liyang šan ayulan-u sine ji bicig* (hereafter *CLŠASB*), which was published in 2000 in a modern version. The Mongols from Inner Mongolia now use Chinese guidebooks, such as Wei Guozuo's, and lamas who read Tibetan mostly use one of the recently published Tibetan guidebooks.[61]

### Present-Day Observations

Observation of the Mongols' journeys through the lens of historical and visual sources gives us only part of the story. No Qing or Republican source tells us about pilgrims rubbing their hands on miraculous footprints, or about icons and springs that had to be worshipped in order to complete the pilgrimage. We will never know what past pilgrims thought, felt and experienced. Nonetheless, field observation and interviews with today's pilgrims on the site and with Buddhist devotees in Mongolia can help apprehend mental representations of the sacred geography, hierarchy of places to visit, motivations, beliefs, personal histories and ritual practices, along with their emic interpretations that are absent from historical sources. However, we must be extremely careful in our attempts to compare the pilgrimage in the twenty-first century with that of the

---

60    The articles by Yan Tianling and Song Wenhui are the only two articles about Mongols' pilgrimages to Wutaishan in *Wutaishan yanjiu*, a periodical published four times a year since 1985.

61    For instance, Ngag dbang bstan dar 2007. On recent Tibetan guidebooks: Chou 2011b: 134, 161-162.

nineteenth century. The revival of the Wutaishan pilgrimage, including the behavior of present-day pilgrims, the respective roles of pilgrims in a group ('the
leader/guide,' 'the translator,' 'the lama,' 'the pilgrim who has already performed
the pilgrimage and knows what to do,' 'the negotiator' [with Chinese merchants,
taxis] and so on) and, above all, the many individual stories would deserve to
be the subject of a separate book-length study. I have focused here on the Qing
and Republican period pilgrimages, only occasionally using observations on
contemporary pilgrimages as comparison.

### Questions of Vocabulary

#### Nineteenth- and Early Twentieth-Century Mongols: Geography and Diversity

Before entering into the world of pilgrims, it is necessary to specify what I mean
by 'Mongols,' 'Mongol Buddhism' and 'pilgrimage.' The main category of pilgrims we will encounter in this book is that of Mongols from Inner Mongolia,[62]
and Khalkha/Northern/Outer Mongolia (present-day [Republic of] Mongolia),[63]
both included in the Qing empire. They formed the vast majority of the Mongols: according to early twentieth-century censuses, there were 828,000
Mongols in Inner Mongolia (for 1911) and 611,000 Mongols in Khalkha Mongolia
(for 1918). A small minority of Mongols lived in other parts of the Qing empire,
such as the Khoshuud of Kukunor (present-day Qinghai Province), the Torguts
resettled in Turkestan (Xinjiang) and bannermen from Beijing. In addition,
Mongols living outside the Qing empire (Buryats of Siberia and Kalmyks of the
Volga) and Tuvans (of Turkik origin) are also mentioned among pilgrims to
Wutaishan.

The geographical origin of Mongols is defined by their 'banner' (*khoshuu*)—
the basic territorial, administrative and military unit of Qing Mongolia—and
by their league (*chuulgan* or *aimag*). The Mongol banners were administrated

---

62 'Inner Mongolia' (Dotood Monggol, Ch. Nei Menggu 内蒙古), renamed in Mongolian
'Southern Mongolia' (Öbör Monggol, but the Chinese denomination kept the appellation
Nei Menggu) in 1947, originated in the alliance between Mongol princes with Manchu
power in 1636.

63 I consider the terms 'Khalkha Mongolia,' 'Northern Mongolia' (Aru Monggol) and 'Outer
Mongolia' (Gadaadu Monggol, Ch. Wai Menggu 外蒙古) as more or less synonymous
('Outer Mongolia' lost its raison d'être when the Qing dynasty was abolished in 1912; it was
renamed the Mongolian People's Republic in 1924).

by local ruling princes called *jasag*,[64] and they enjoyed some autonomy, particularly during the first half of the Qing;[65] besides, some were managed by monasteries and reincarnations, thus functioning as monastic estates. The outer frontiers of the Qing empire (represented in Map 6) are mere indications since real frontiers moved according to the movements of frontier guards and herders.

### Tibeto-Mongol Buddhism and Chinese Buddhism

In the Qing period, Tibetan/Tibeto-Mongol Buddhism was practiced by Tibetans, Mongols, Monguors, Tuvans, as well as some converted Manchus and Chinese. I here prefer the non-ethnic term Gélukpa Buddhism, since from the Qianlong period (1736-1796) to the end of the dynasty, the Qing support of Tibetan Buddhism was restricted to the Gélukpa School, and non-Gélukpa traditions of Tibetan Buddhism were not represented in Wutaishan's clerical institutions. To a certain extent, the non-ethnic and encompassing terms 'lamaist' and 'Lamaism,' which are no longer in use in the academic world,[66] would also be appropriate.

The Wutaishan monasteries belong to two different clergies, the Chinese Buddhist and the Tibeto-Mongol Buddhist. It is difficult to avoid the term 'Chinese Buddhism' since, during the period studied here, there were no longer Chan, Avataṃsaka, Pure Land, Vinaya or Esoteric Schools but only monasteries

---

64    Except for the Tümed, the Chakhar of Inner Mongolia and the Khölön Buir banners, which were under direct Qing governmental control. The Inner Mongols and the Northern Khalkhas, whose aristocracy was linked to Chinggis Khan's family, were generally called 'Eastern Mongols,' while the Mongols of Alashan, Ejene Torgut, Qinghai, Xinjiang and Khobdo were Oirads (Western Mongols) who had survived the violent conquest and destruction of the Jungar (Zunghar) empire by Emperor Qianlong, or who had previously allied or taken refuge with the Qing. The populations of the Chakhar and Bargu banners were mixed, composed of Mongols resettled there by the Qing.

65    Khalkha Mongolia was divided into four *aimags* (divided into 86 banners from 1759 to 1912, plus eight monastic territories) located north of the Gobi, plus Darigangga (a special banner for imperial herds), the 'Khobdo frontier' and the 'Tannu Uriyangkhai.' Inner Mongolia included six leagues (divided into 49 banners), plus the Chakhar, Alashan and Ejene Torgut banners. The Bargu banners (in Khölön Buir) were part of Heilongjiang Province. On the administrative hierarchy and military organization of the banner: Vreeland 1962 [1957]: 13; Di Cosmo 1998: 301; Atwood 2004: 30-32.

66    The term 'Lamaism,' which has no Tibetan or Mongol equivalent, comes from Qing imperialism and was vulgarized by Western orientalism. It is repudiated by Tibetan Buddhists for its pejorative connotations, setting Tibetan Buddhism apart, as if different from Buddhism: Lopez 1998: Chapter 1, esp. p. 17-20.

combining these different traditions, with a general Chan or Pure Land orientation.

The Chinese and Tibeto-Mongol traditions both stem from Mahāyāna but differ in the texts and the organization of the canons they rely on (the Chinese *Tripiṭaka* 大藏經 on the one hand, the Tibetan *Kanjur* and *Tanjur* on the other),[67] the liturgical language, rituals, the monastic way of life, the pantheon and its iconography, and paraphernalia. Moreover, Tibetan Buddhism emphasizes esotericism and the presence of reincarnated lamas, whereas Chinese Buddhism does not. The popular understanding of the distinctions between these two forms of Buddhism have been studied by Gray Tuttle, who argues that before the 1930s, when Buddhism was constructed as a world religion, Tibetans and Chinese even perceived the two traditions as different religions. He nevertheless acknowledged that "the seventeenth- and eighteenth-century Mongol and Monguor lamas who served at the court ... tended to have a better understanding [than Tibetans] and more sympathy for Chinese Buddhists and their practices."[68] The present study will show that Mongols did not view these traditions as distinct religions and even built bridges between them, especially on Wutaishan.

On Wutaishan, the Gélukpa and Chinese Buddhist traditions are distinguished by colors: Chinese Buddhism is identified as *qing* 青, or 'green-blue/ grey,' due to the color of the monks' robes (in Mongolian, *khökhe*, 'blue'). Its monks are called 'monks in blue robes' (*qinggyi seng* 青衣僧) and Chinese Buddhist monasteries are thus 'blue monasteries' (*qingsi* 青寺).[69] The Gélukpa tradition is called *huang* 黃, or 'yellow': the lamas are 'monks in yellow robes' (*huangyi seng* 黃衣僧) and Gélukpa monasteries are 'yellow monasteries' (*huangsi* 黃寺)—the Gélukpas being known as the 'Yellow Hats' (Tib. *zhaser*).[70] During the period under study the Mongol word for Buddhism was *shira shashin* ('yellow religion/tradition/doctrine/teaching'), the Gélukpas being in the majority in Mongolia.[71]

---

67    The *Kanjur* and *Tanjur* also exist in Mongolian (and Manchu) translation, but since the eighteenth century, save a few exceptions, the Mongol monasteries have relied on the Tibetan canons.

68    Tuttle 2005: 26, 70-71, 262, n. 7.

69    Monks and nuns of North China are dressed in grey (blue-grey), or combine brown and grey, but ceremonial and abbots' robes are yellow and red.

70    As opposed to the 'Red Hats' i.e., the other schools of Tibetan Buddhism, and more specifically the Nyingmapas. Although this colored terminology is rejected by Tibetans and Tibetologists for being a Sino-Manchu invention, it is commonly used by Mongols.

71    The yellow of the Mongol church contrasts with the black of the laymen (*khara khümün*) and of popular religion (*khara shashin*), a pejorative term. Modern Mongols now call

I refer to Gélukpa monks as 'lamas,' as in the current Mongolian usage, i.e., fully ordained monks,[72] to distinguish them from Chinese Buddhist monks (*heshang* 和尚). Qing and Republican period Chinese sources on Wutaishan call them lamas 喇嘛 or *fanseng* 番僧 ('foreign monk').

### Definition of Pilgrimage in a Mongol Context

In China, the liberalization of state policy toward religion in the 1980s allowed for the revival of national and local pilgrimages and at the same time provided an opportunity for research on this phenomenon. A number of studies on the subject have appeared over the last twenty years, and the reference book on the subject, *Pilgrims and Sacred Sites in China*, was published in 1992.[73] Simultaneously, scholarly interest in Tibetan pilgrimage sites has grown rapidly among Tibetologists.[74] Though these studies are not numerous in the larger field of Chinese and Tibetan religious studies, they do nevertheless exist; in comparison, no book has yet been written on Mongol pilgrimages. One explanation is that Mongol pilgrimage guides are rare and difficult to obtain compared to Tibetan guidebooks. Besides, most anthropologists working on Mongolia have up to now chosen not to focus on Buddhism, and the revival of pilgrimages in the 1990s went unnoticed in the scholarly world.

In this book, I use the conventional, restricted definition of pilgrimage: "a journey to a sanctified place, undertaken with the expectation of future spiritual and/or worldly benefit," distinct from regular worship in time (long journeys) and space (separation from home).[75] Pilgrimage is a transaction, 'an investment in the future,'[76] from which the pilgrims, through their prayers, offerings and physical involvement (walking, circumambulation, prostrations), expect to obtain benefits as a reward. Yet a pilgrimage also involves much more than a physical journey and worship of a sacred place: it is 'a complete cultural phenomenon'[77] involving a wide range of actors—ranging from the political authorities to the residing monks, traders, beggars—and of motivations,

---

Buddhism *burkhan-u shashin* or *budda-yin shashin* ("religion/tradition/doctrine/teaching of the Buddha").

72   The term 'lama' should be restricted to designate the master, the guru; but Mongol monks, whatever their position and knowledge, are commonly called and addressed as lamas.

73   Naquin and Yü, eds. 1992.

74   Among others, Anne-Marie Blondeau; Katia Buffetrille (1996a, 1998, 2000, 2003); Alexander W. Macdonald (1998); Alex McKay (ed. 1998); Toni Huber (1999; ed. 1999). For a critical review of Tibetan pilgrimage research: Huber 1994; Huber 1999: 231, n. 2.

75   McKay 1998: 1.

76   McKay 1998: 2.

77   Buffetrille 2003.

including tourism and trade. It has a political, sociological, economic, as well as an ecological, impact and participates in the construction of cultural identities. Mongolian language distinguishes 'pilgrimage' from ordinary worship, called *mörgöl*, by referring to its 'size,' plus adding a verb denoting departure or travel.[78] The most common expression is (*yekhe*) *mörgöl-dür yabu-* (or *khi-* or *üiled-*), literally 'to go on/to make a (big) prayer.'[79] *Yekhe*, meaning 'big' or 'large,' evokes the adventure and emotional intensity inherent in long-distance pilgrimages. The term *mörgöl* refers all at once to bowing ('kowtow, knocking one's forehead against the ground'), public prayer, religious worship, religious ceremony, as well as pilgrimage. It comes from the verb *mörgö-*, which originally meant 'to butt, to hit, knock's one's forehead against something, to gore' for a horned animal,[80] and also designates the shaman's gestures imitating the goring attitude of the stag in order to please the spirit who gives game.[81] *Mörgö-* is also used in expressions meaning 'a collision, a car accident.' In the Buddhist context, it means 'to touch with one's head, to bow, to pray, to make a prostration, to pay religious homage'; Mongols commonly say: "I pray until my forehead is pierced." Interestingly, the Mongolian terminology of pilgrimage and worship does not use specific Buddhist terms but rather terms for concrete body language: the worshipper touching the ground with his forehead is comparable with the goring deer and the gesticulating shaman wearing antlers and imitating a cervid's butt.

Prostrations, more than circumambulation, therefore seem to characterize Mongol worship and pilgrimage; by contrast, the Tibetan vocabulary emphasizes circumambulation of the sacred site, generally in a clockwise direction, as prescribed in ancient Buddhist Sanskrit sources.[82] The generic Tibetan term for 'pilgrimage' is *nékor*, lit. 'circuiting, going around (*kor*) a place (*né*),' or (more honorific) *néjel*, lit. 'to meet a *né* (a holy place), to encounter, to pay respect to a holy place.'[83] A pilgrim is a *nékorwa*, 'the one who goes around the sacred place.'

---

78    The verb *ayala-* means 'to travel, set out on a journey, go on a military or hunting expedition, or a pilgrimage'; *ayalaltsa-*, 'travel, go on pilgrimage or on an expedition in a group.'

79    A worshipper and a pilgrim are both called *mörgölchin* (or *mörgöltön, jochin mörgölchin*; *jochin* meaning 'guest, visitor'); to make a full prostration is *mörgöjü dokhi* or *tologai mörgökhü*; a place of worship (temple, sacred place, pilgrimage site) is called *mörgöl-ün oron* or *mörgögdekhü-yin oron*.

80    Tsevel 1966: 345.

81    'Shamanizing' is *böge mörgö-* (Hamayon 1990: 142, 361, 497-499).

82    Buffetrille 1996a: 347-355; Huber 1999: 13.

83    *Jel*: 'paying respect to, the paying of respects.' Tibetans generally make a distinction between long-distance pilgrimages to a major holy place and regular, short-term

However, there are lesser-used Mongolian expressions that also refer to circum-ambulations: Antoine Mostaert gives for the Ordos dialect *mörgöl ergil* or *ergil mörgöl*, 'pilgrimage' (lit. 'circumambulation while praying/bowing') and *mörgöl ergil khi-*, or *mörgöl ergilte yabu-*, 'to make a pilgrimage.'[84] *Ergil*, 'turning, rota-tion, circumambulation of a temple or a *stūpa*,' translates the Sanskrit *pra-dakṣiṇa* and the Tibetan *kor*. In Mongolia, monks also say (Cyr. Mo.) *goroo-* or *gorool-* (< Tib. *kor*): 'to go round, circumambulate,' such as in *Bogd uulin go-roond yava-*, 'make the circumambulation of Bogda Mountain.'[85]

The notion of *né*, the translation of the Sanskrit *pratiṣṭhitā*, is central to un-derstanding Tibetan and Mongol pilgrimages. *Né* can be translated as 'abode,' 'power place,' 'holy place,' 'potential source of sacred energy,' as well as 'the (temporary or permanent) abode of a deity or a saint.'[86] A *né* place can be a mountain, a cave, a temple, a relic, an icon, or a human incarnation of a deity such as the Dalai Lama. *Né* sites are 'empowered' as a result of the contact with enlightened beings, such as Padmasambhava,[87] and by the religious practices performed there. As Huber puts it, "*gnas* [*né*] in the term *gnas-skor* [*nékor*] al-ways carries the double meaning of the actual physical place, and of the resi-dence or existence of deities, entities or beings believed to be powerful or significant in some way by the pilgrims who go there."[88] Meditating lamas can 'read' a *né*, i.e., interpret it by making a link between the 'actual plane' and a more subtle level of reality.[89] *Né* have the primary quality of being potential sources of 'sacred energy' or 'empowerment, blessing' (*jinlap*, Skt. *adhishthāna*) and wield transformative power over pilgrims. *Né* places both attract and emit: they attract pilgrims and emit a sort of magnetic field.[90]

*Né* is also a key notion of Mongol pilgrimages. According to the context, Mongols translate *né* as *oroshigsan*, lit. 'contained in, which dwelled in

---

individual worship at a local shrine, for a festival, for instance, which is called *chöjel* ('to pay respect with an offering'). But "the boundaries between these words (*mchod-mjal*, *gnas-bskor, gnas-mjal*) are subject to change and are blurred" (Ekvall and Downs 1987: 26). For other definitions of a Tibetan pilgrimage: Large-Blondeau 1960; Ekvall 1964: 244; Ekvall and Downs 1987: 26; Huber 1994: 23-39; Buffetrille 1996a: 478; for a comparative perspective in East Asia: Naquin and Yü 1992: 1-38.

84    *Mörgül ergül / ergül kī / ergült'u jawu-* (Mostaert 1941-1944: 470).
85    Lubsangdorji 2002.
86    Huber 1994: 23, 30-31; Huber 1999: 13.
87    Renowned eighth-century yogin reputed to have introduced Tantric Buddhism in Tibet and revered by the Nyingmapas as a second buddha.
88    Huber 1994: 31.
89    Huber 1999: 13.
90    Ramble 1997: 133.

something,' or *adistid-un oron, adistidlagsan oron* ('blessed site'). *Adistid*, or *adis*, from Sanskrit *adhishthāna*, means 'blessing, benediction, consecration, bestowal of miraculous power by a deity.' *Adis* is obtained (or transferred) by touching a lama's hand, an icon, or a *stūpa* with one's forehead (*adis ab-*, 'to receive [lit., take] the blessing'; *adislagsan gajar*, a 'blessed ground, blissful place'; *adisla-*, 'to bless, pronounce a benediction, consecrate'). Deities and saints such as Padmasambhava "blessed the Five[-Terraced] Mountain [i.e., Wutaishan] with their feet [i.e., footprints]."[91] These Buddhist notions coincide with properties of Mongol mountain gods who are said to possess *ide shidi* (supernatural power, magic) and *sür* (majesty, might, splendor).

While accumulating merit for oneself or a living or dead relative (hence the possibility of making substitution pilgrimages) is the official, 'orthodox' goal— and often the only expressed goal—of all Buddhist pilgrimages, the pilgrims generally also have more mundane objectives.[92] This is reflected in the Mongolian term *buyan* (< Skt. *punya*), which conflates the Buddhist notion of 'merit' and the more mundane notions of 'good luck, fortune, prosperity.' The meanings of *buyan* show that 'pragmatic' practices cannot be separated from more orthodox Buddhist beliefs and rites.[93]

Pragmatic cults, beliefs and rituals aim at bringing good fortune and blessings and warding off bad influences. They are believed to increase flocks and herds; provide heirs; keep evil spirits from sucking the fortune out of the household; prevent illnesses, epidemics and attacks by wolves; ward off thieves, pollution and dangers encountered during travels in this world or in the hereafter; and 'repair' misfortune. They encompass a wide range of collective and individual practices, some of which are commonly labelled as 'popular Buddhist practices'—including "the cults of saints (the cults of holy persons), the cult of

---

91   *Qoyar köl-iyer-iyen tabun ayula-yi adistidlayad*, in UTAOSC 11r, also 44v-45r.

92   For similar observations in Tibetan pilgrimages about orthodox benefits (notions of karma and accumulation of merit) and more mundane ones (such as good luck, purification of sins, transgressions and pollution, life energy, longevity), see Huber 1999: 10, 16-19.

93   Mongolists, like Tibetologists, often use the terms 'popular religion,' 'living religion,' 'real religion,' 'everyday religion, or 'elders' religion': see Heissig (1973 [1970]: Chapter 5: "The folk religion of the Mongols and its pantheon"); Bawden 1990; Bawden 1994; Kelényi 2003; Humphrey 1995; Atwood 2004: 466; Ujeed 2009. I will avoid using the term 'popular religion' for the reasons expressed by Teiser 1996, Dawson 2001 and others. Besides, it is not an organized, institutionalized and theoricized system with a doctrine, belief in gods and discernible church that excludes others.

relics (the cult of holy things) and pilgrimage (the cult of holy places)"[94]—and some of which are cults of non-Buddhist origin, though more or less influenced by Buddhism.[95] Because all of these pragmatic practices aim at bringing good fortune and removing bad influences, their Buddhist or non-Buddhist origin cannot be a criteria of classification: it is more pertinent to categorize them according to the officiant (lay member of a community, lay or Buddhist religious ritualist),[96] to distinguish group from individual practices and to differentiate rituals using a textual support from purely oral ones.[97] These practices are not restricted to laypersons: monks also individually go on pilgrimages, worship saints and use apotropaic amulets. Individual practices include milk aspersions, offerings to the fire, acts of purification and cult worship of saints, while

---

94    Martin 1994: 279. On 'popular Buddhism' being part and parcel of Buddhism in the Tibeto-Mongol world: Martin 1994; Atwood 1996 (who quotes Melford E. Spiro's work); Lindahl 2010. Geoffrey Samuel (1993: 5-6) terms it 'Shamanic Buddhism' in the Tibetan context, because the lamas act as shamans in rites of daily life.

95    By non-Buddhist rituals and practices, I do not mean 'shamanism.' Shamans were persecuted by Buddhist missionaries and, except in peripheral areas and pockets of resistance, have disappeared from the Mongol religious landscape. It is more fitting to speak of 'elements of shamanism' in areas which no longer have shamans. Besides, shamanism and lay practices are different though ideologically connected. See Caroline Humphrey's distinction (1995) between 'chiefly landscapes' (where the lay elders of a lineage are the main social agents) and 'shamanic landscapes.'

96    Some rituals necessitate the intervention of a religious specialist (for beckoning fortune, recovering one's life force, curing or protecting flocks, for the fire cult and so on), who might be a tantric practitioner (*lüjin*, belonging to the 'red' tradition), a lama astrologist, an oracle lama (*gürtüm* or *choijing* attached to a monastery, *laiching*), a lay diviner, a seer, a bonesetter, or a shaman.

97    Although many of these practices have much in common with the shamanist and old Turkic vision of the world, it is inadequate to call them pre-Buddhist or clearly distinct from Buddhism, first and foremost because Buddhism is present in the Asian steppes as early as the first centuries CE. Secondly, even if we assume that a ritual is of non-Buddhist origin, it can be indigenous, or of Tibetan or Central Asian origin and assimilated by Buddhism before its introduction to Mongolia. For instance, it is generally assumed that cairns (*oboo*) erected to worship local deities are of non-Buddhist origin and are also found in Tibet because Mongols and Tibetans share many similarities in their representation of the world. However, while the cult of mountain deities is attested in ancient Mongolia, we have no trace of *oboo* worship before the eighteenth century (see Lindahl 2010: 245, n. 23). Lastly, some Buddhist practices were already present in Inner Asia (sometimes with a different meaning) and merged with Indian practices when the Mongols converted to Buddhism: this is the case with the clockwise motion of the circumambulation and the fire cult.

predominant group rituals are communal lay offerings at *oboos*,[98] performed to propitiate the master-spirits of the land.[99] In contrast to Buddhist monastic rituals in which laypersons are most of the time spectators only, pragmatic cults and rites are open to laypersons as actors.

Some of these cults and practices, especially those performed at natural numinous sites such as sacred rocks, mineral springs and womb-caves, may have inherited from non-Buddhist practices or have partly developed in tandem with, or in reaction to, Buddhism. Buddhist authorities have striven hard to adapt Buddhism to the needs of ordinary social life, for instance by composing prayers to local deities, in order to appropriate and reorient local sacred sites within Buddhist space and time.[100] Conversely, indigenous beliefs and practices have perpetuated themselves by absorbing Buddhist influences (arriving in different waves), thus gaining in efficacy.[101]

At a pilgrimage site, there is no syncretism between an orthodox system and a pragmatic system but rather superposition, negotiation, symbiosis and a cultural 'do-it-yourself.'[102] A pilgrim can express different and sometimes contradictory discourses according to the context.[103] The same has been observed in pilgrimages to Tibetan mountains, reflecting different modes of religious expression. Wutaishan is a multi-confessional and multi-ethnic pilgrimage site, and we thus have to ask ourselves: How did rites and practices of different religious traditions, different clergies and different ethnicities cohabitate, prevail or influence each other? This study will contribute to a new understanding of the complexity of this shared pilgrimage site.

---

98   Ritual cairns that serve as a dwelling-place for local deities (*gajar-un ejen*). They are erected on summits, close to encampments yet still within the wild territory of these local deities.

99   In Mongolia, misfortune and prosperity are generally seen as intimately connected with the spirit-masters of the land.

100  Heissig 1973 [1970]: Chapter 5; Lindahl 2010.

101  Ujeed 2009.

102  Buffetrille 1996a; Henrion-Dourcy 2007 (referring to Stewart and Shaw 1994: 17).

103  For popular interpretations of the Buddhist doctrine: Humphrey and Hürelbaatar 2013.

CHAPTER 1

# The Pilgrimage Sites of the Mongols: An Overview

The aim of this chapter is to clarify the specific Mongol engagement with Wutaishan in the late Qing and Republican periods, compared to other pilgrimage sites in Mongolia and abroad. I will first introduce the mountains of the Tibeto-Mongol and Chinese Buddhist cosmologies and then present the different pilgrimage sites in Mongolia and abroad in order to propose a stratification of sacred sites and the relations between them according to a scale of 'spiritual magnetism,' to borrow from James Preston's terminology (1992). I will introduce the respective spiritual and practical advantages of the different pilgrimage sites, from local centers to international shrines, try to evaluate their respective power of attraction and question whether they form networks linking one site to another. Among pilgrimages abroad, did not Mongols prefer to journey to Tibet, the core of their religious tradition, rather than China? Mongolia itself also had a large number of places sanctified by the presence of living and dead Buddhist saints and reincarnations, of various relics and miraculous icons, and of sacred mountains, caves, springs and rocks. As we will see, in Mongolia pragmatic cults to mountain deities and Buddhist circumambulation and worship of 'mandalized' mountains often coexisted at the same pilgrimage sites. Since the journey to Wutaishan is a pilgrimage involving both monasteries and a sacred mountain with numinous sites, can it be compared to pilgrimages to sacred mountains in Mongolia?

### Sacred Mountains—The Tibetan Buddhist and Chinese Buddhist Cosmologies

Wutaishan is believed to be the 'field of activity' or 'place of practice' (*daochang* 道場, Tib. *maṇḍala*) of Mañjuśrī, the embodiment of all the buddhas' wisdom, the *bodhisattva* who preaches there and guides the devotees towards enlightenment. Tibetans and Mongols make a distinction between 'heavens' (called 'pure lands' by the Chinese), such as Sukhāvatī, and 'pure (or purified) lands' (*arilug-san orun*), which belong to this human world:[1] Wutaishan clearly belongs to the

---

1  Though we will see in Chapter 4 that this distinction is not always obvious in the Mongol *imaginaire*.

latter because it is located on earth and is reachable by foot. In Mongolian[2] and Tibetan literature,[3] there are five pure lands, also called 'Especially Excellent Sites of Empowerment' (néchen nga) of Jambudvīpa (the continent of the ter-restrial, human world): Vajrāsana in the center, Wutaishan in the east, Potala Moutain in the south, Udyāna in the west and the Shambhala kingdom in the north. The guidebook to Wutaishan written by the Second Changkya Khutugtu, Rölpé Dorjé (1717-1786), completed by his disciples and translated into Mongolian, starts with the enumeration of these five sites.[4] Vajrāsana is Bodhgayā, the place in India where Śākyamuni reached enlightenment, now in the state of Bihar. For Tibetans, Potala, the abode of Avalokiteśvara, was identified with the place where the Fifth Dalai Lama, Ngakwang Lozang Gyatso (1617-1682), built the Potala Palace in Lhasa, while for the Chinese it was identified with Pu-tuoshan 普陀山 (Potala 'Mountain') Island in Zhejiang, China. The physical location of medieval Indian Udyāna/Uddayana/Oḍḍiyāna is disputed and open to conjecture,[5] and Shambhala, the Northern kingdom, can now only be visited by some extraordinarily empowered lamas.

Although Tibetan Buddhists had their own network of sacred sites, they also heard about the 'Four Grand and Famous Mountains of China' (si da ming shan 四大名山) where bodhisattvas dwell.[6] These four mountains, which have formed the main pilgrimage circuit for devout Chinese Buddhists since the Ming dynasty, are Wutaishan, abode of Mañjuśrī; Putuoshan, abode of Avalokiteśvara; Jiuhuashan 九華山 (in Anhui Province), abode of Kṣitigarbha; and Emeishan 峨嵋山 (in Sichuan Province), abode of Samantabhadra. Some Tibetan Buddhists went on pilgrimage to these Chinese sites. In the late

---

2  Damdinsüren 1977.

3  Chandra Das 1991 [1902]: 751; Damdinsüren 1977. This list appears in eighteenth-century works, but Pakpa Lama's "Explanation of the Knowable," written in 1278, already mentions Udai/Utai, Udyāna and Potala in its description of Jambudvīpa (see Chapter 4).

4  *Zhing mchog ri bo dwangs bsil gyi gnas bshad dad pa'i padmo rgyas byed ngo mtshar myi ma'i snang ba*, hereafter ZMRBDB, Chinese translation "Sheng di Qingliangshan zhi" 1990: 8. This does not appear in the Mongolian version (OMSA)—I thank Vladimir Uspensky for having sent me photographs of the first thirteen pages plus the colophon of the Mongolian xylograph preserved in Saint Petersburg; for the rest of the guidebook I had only access to the Chinese translation of the Tibetan text. I also thank Chou Wen-shing, who worked on the two Tibetan versions published in Xining (1993) and Chengdu (1998) for sharing with me her insights into this guidebook.

5  This ancient kingdom is usually thought to be located in the present-day Swāt Valley in north-eastern Pakistan.

6  The gazetteer compiled by Rölpé Dorjé et al. also lists the Four Grand and Famous Mountains of China (ZMRBDB, Chinese translation 1990: 8).

eighteenth century, 'lamas' (whose ethnicity is unknown) undertook pilgrimages from Wutaishan to Putuoshan.[7] The publication in 1920 of a Mongolian guidebook to Putuoshan, translated from Chinese, attests to the Mongols' interest in Putuo Island in the early twentieth century.[8] At that time, some Mongols may have subscribed to the identification of Putuoshan with the Potala Pure Land. Tibetans also undertook pilgrimages to Putuoshan and Emeishan.[9]

The Buddhist world, whose cosmologic axis was the mythical Mount Sumeru, has no center comparable to Jerusalem for Christians or Mecca for Muslims, but for Mongols, Wutaishan, Lhasa (the seat of the Dalai Lamas and location of the Potala) and Bodhgayā were, according to Buddhist literature, the three most powerful sites to visit.

### Buddhist Pilgrimages Abroad

In practice, Mongol pilgrimages favor four main destinations abroad: Wutaishan, Kumbum, Lhasa and Beijing. In the words of the Kanjurwa Khutugtu:

> A very important activity of our religion was making visits or pilgrimages to sacred places and historic sites. The most important destination ... was a pilgrimage to Lhasa in Tibet and tens of thousands of our people have made this trip. The next important place was the famous Kumbum monastery, but both of these are very distant and the great majority of our people could never travel so far; thus, a very popular place, that was more accessible, was the sacred site of Wu-t'ai-shan ("five-peaked mountain") in Shansi province. The esteem in which this place was held would remind one of the veneration in which the Chinese hold P'u-t'ou shan.[10]

As the crow flies, Höhhot is 3,000 kilometers from Lhasa, about 1,000 kilometers from Kumbum and 400 kilometers from Beijing, but it is just over 300 kilometers from Wutaishan (Map 1). The pilgrims followed the trade routes that crossed

---

7    Reference in Naquin 2000: 472, n. 62. On the emergence of Putuoshan as a national and
     international pilgrimage center: Yü 1992.

8    *Emünetü dalai-yin bodulang orun-u namtar* ("History of the Potala of the Southern Sea"),
     transl. by 'Vang Küve Jiyug' from the Kharachin Right banner, 1920, in *Catalogue of Ancient
     Mongolian Books and Documents of China* 1999: no. 4822.

9    I did not find references of Mongols' pilgrimages to Emeishan, probably because it is
     located far from the Sino-Mongol border and also because Samantabhadra was not
     especially popular in Mongolia.

10   Jagchid and Hyer 1983: 106-107.

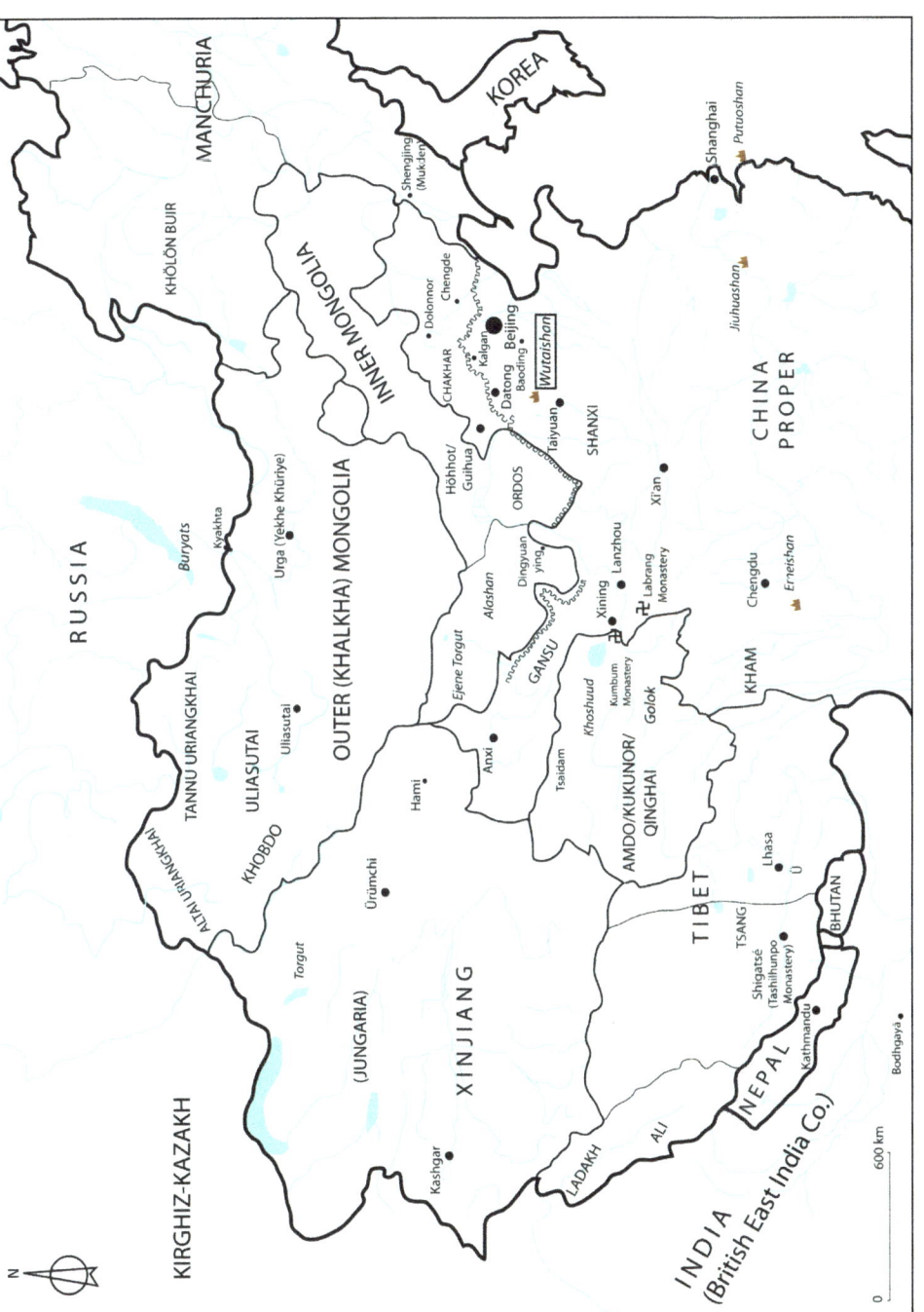

MAP 1          *Map of the Qing empire focusing on its northern and western 'dependencies,' ca. 1820.*

Mongolia from north to south (Buryatia-Urga-Höhhot) or from east to west, and often joined trade caravans. Those who journeyed to Lhasa generally visited Kumbum on the way. Biographies of Mongol lamas mention monks spending years on the road, visiting Wutaishan, Kumbum, Labrang Tashi Khyil and Lhasa, sometimes going as far as Nepal and India in the same journey. However, lay pilgrims who journeyed to Wutaishan usually did not go to Kumbum on the same trip.[11]

### Kumbum: The Birthplace of Tsongkhapa

Kumbum Jampa Ling (Mo. Gumbum or Gümbüm, in present-day Qinghai Province), founded on Tsongkhapa's (1357-1419) birthplace, was known to Mongols as the 'Second Garden of Lumbinī.'[12] It is conveniently located on the caravan route that connected Urga to Lhasa.[13] According to Gombojab Tsybikov, who undertook the pilgrimage to Lhasa in the guise of a monk in a group of Buryat and Kalmyk pilgrims from 1899 to 1902, the Mongol pilgrims to Lhasa stayed about two months in Kumbum before leaving for Central Tibet. Some visited their relatives there: two thousand monks from Inner Mongolia studied in Kumbum. Labrang, an equally major monastery in Amdo, sponsored by local Mongols, appears to have been a less important place to visit for Mongols from Inner and Khalkha Mongolia.

The main relic of Kumbum was the 'Tree of Great Merit,' a white sandalwood tree which allegedly sprung up miraculously from the placenta blood shed at Tsongkhapa's birth. Its supposed one hundred thousand leaves were said to bear impressions of the Buddha's face and *mantras*, hence the etymology of Kumbum (*kubum* means 'one hundred thousand images'). The leaves were sold to pilgrims who used them in infusions to facilitate difficult births. The tree eventually died in the twentieth century and was preserved inside a large *stūpa* covered with 1,500 kilograms of silver in the Golden Tiled Temple. Other relics included the skull of Tsongkhapa's mother with a golden circling that contained grains of rice distributed to pilgrims—these were said to multiply spontaneously and cure illnesses—as well as contact relics left by the Third, Fourth, Fifth and Seventh Dalai Lamas and by the Third Panchen Lama.[14] The most devout pilgrims performed one hundred thousand full-length prostrations on the circumambulation path surrounding the monastery. Tsybikov stressed the

---

11   Nowadays Mongolians from Mongolia who travel abroad for pilgrimage often go to 'Utai-Gümbüm' in the same trip, but Inner Mongols prefer to journey to Wutaishan only.

12   Serruys 1977: 602-603. Lumbinī is the birthplace of Śākyamuni.

13   Tsybikov 1992 [1919]: Chapter 2.

14   Tsybikov 1992 [1919]: 33, 39; see also Prjevalsky 1876, II: 155-156.

importance of trade during the festival season. But for Mongols who had no relatives in Kumbum, or did not plan to continue on to Central Tibet, Kumbum was a less attractive destination than Wutaishan.

### Lhasa, Nepal and India: A Risky Expedition

Mentions of Mongol pilgrims going to Lhasa are found in sources from the seventeenth to the twentieth century and especially in biographies of great lamas and in travel records of Buryat and Kalmyk pilgrims.[15] As early as 1631, thousands of Khalkhas, Oirads and Tümeds visited the holy city.[16] The pilgrimage was highly dependent on the political situation. For instance, it was not possible for Mongols to reach Lhasa during the Dungan Insurrection (1862-1877) in western China.[17]

The Buryats, Kalmyks from the Volga and Torguts from Xinjiang (Eastern Turkestan) accounted for a much higher proportion of pilgrims to Lhasa than of pilgrims to Wutaishan.[18] Kalmyks and Torguts traveled directly to Tibet by crossing Jungaria (northern Xinjiang Province) and western Gansu. From the second half of the eighteenth century on, the Buryats and Kalmyks, being subjects of the Russian empire, were forbidden to enter Tibet.[19] Incurring exclusion as foreigners and severe punishment, they nevertheless made secret pilgrimages as late as the 1910s (when they were not sent back at the border), concealing their identity by saying they were Khalkha.[20]

The great majority of Mongols going to Lhasa consisted of male pilgrims.[21] Although Antoine Mostaert asserted that only the wealthy, or else the begging

---

15    See Introduction, notes 37 and 38.

16    Ahmad 1970: 109-110, quoting the biography of the Fifth Dalai Lama.

17    Prjevalsky 1876: 78.

18    As early as 1698, the Kalmyk Arabjur journeyed to Tibet together with two to five hundred of his people (DeFrancis 1993: 172-173). On Kalmyk pilgrimages and failed attempts to reach Tibet: Bormanshinov 1998.

19    On the refusal of the Russian government to issue passports and the obstacles placed in their way by Chinese authorities: Bormanshinov 1998: 2, 20; Andreyev 2001c.

20    Tsybikov 1992 [1919]. Their number sharply decreased after the flight of the Dalai Lama from Tibet in 1904. Both Agwan Dorjiev in 1878 and Tsybikov in 1900 called themselves Khalkha to enter the forbidden country (Martin and Norbu 1991: 11, 16).

21    Prjevalsky 1876: 72. In addition to trade and pilgrimage, Mongols had other motivations to journey to Lhasa. For instance, Khalkhas organized caravans to search for the reincarnation of the Jebtsündamba Khutugtu. The embassy that departed to Lhasa in 1873 to search for the Eighth Reincarnation (1869-1924) was composed of five princes, high-ranking lamas, with a thousand tents and a thousand camels (Prjevalsky 1876, II: 257-258; Andreyev 2001b: 173).

itinerant monks, could undertake such long-distance journeys,[22] according to Tsybikov, those who had bought mules and female hinnies in Amdo for a good price could recoup all their travel expenses and even make a profit.[23] But the Khalkhas and Buryats were poor among the Mongols; they had to rent horses or mules to reach Lhasa and were recruited as servants in caravans for the journey back. There was no resident Mongol community in Lhasa itself, and some poor Khalkha pilgrims survived there by begging.

The Khalkha and Buryat pilgrims usually joined the two large yearly caravans which brought monastic trade missions from Urga to Lhasa and which departed in autumn or in spring. The dangers of the road, the difficulty of obtaining travel permits, the physical hardship and the financial cost were limiting factors for Mongols. Noblemen and wealthy reincarnations, loaded with alms, were frequently attacked by brigands on the way, and frightening tales from their returning compatriots circulated among the Mongols, about the rarefied air, or the attacks of the Goloks and the Black Tanguts.[24] In the nineteenth century, a reincarnated lama from Badgar Choiling Süme, who had gathered three thousand taels of silver to go on pilgrimage to Lhasa, was robbed and attacked by bandits and left for dead. When he managed to make his way back to his monastery, he found his own new 'reincarnation' having already taken his throne.[25] Russian geographer and explorer Nicholas Prjevalsky (1839-1888) wrote that

> [c]asualities to men and beasts are frequent. So many of the latter perish that a large reserve of camels or yaks is always taken; but notwithstanding this precaution, the men have sometimes to abandon all they possess, and to think only of their own safety. In February 1870, a caravan which left Lhassa 300 strong, with 1,000 beasts of burden, in a violent snow-storm, followed by severe cold, lost all the animals and fifty men besides. One of the survivors related to us how, when they found that their beasts were dying by the score every day ... only three men were kept alive ...[26]

Tsybikov's descriptions of the journey from Urga to Lhasa provide practical details about these expeditions. One month after his departure (on November 25, 1899), he reached Dingyuanying 定遠營 (modern Bayankhota) in Alashan, an important stop for merchants and pilgrims. From there, he joined six Khalkha

---

22    Mostaert 1956: 289.

23    Tsybikov 1992 [1919]: 75. See also Dorjiev's biography: Martin and Norbu 1991: 12-13.

24    Tsybikov 1992 [1919]: 40.

25    David 1867-1868: 9.

26    Prjevalsky 1876, vol. II: 185-186.

lamas on their way to Kumbum, two Buryat lamas going to Labrang and a Tibetan trader. In the 'celestial sands' (Tngri elesü) of Alashan, some pilgrims dismounted their camels because they believed that crossing that part of the Gobi on foot gave merit equal to the recitation of the eight thousand verses of the *Prajñāpāramitā sūtra*. Tsybikov spent some time visiting Kumbum and Labrang and then joined a caravan of Amdo Tibetans and Mongol pilgrims on their way to Lhasa. He bought four horses (at 18 to 50 taels apiece) and ten mules (25 to 40 taels apiece) to sell in Lhasa. The date of departure was fixed by the Labrang oracle for April 24, 1900. While crossing the Tsaidam, the caravan was ransomed by a local brigand, who levied a tax of two sapeques per Mongol pilgrim to 'protect them.'[27] During the trip, the pilgrims made offerings, especially to the master-spirits of the land—to ask for a safe passage and avoid high-altitude sickness—and avoided pronouncing the true names of mountains. Those who carried a weapon went hunting, including lamas who temporarily broke their vows to face the difficulties of the journey, but some pilgrims tried to save the animals' lives.[28] The caravan stopped for fifteen days among the Mongols of Tsaidam so the animals could regain their strength.[29] The Mongols stayed in the yurts of acquaintances of those who had made the pilgrimage before, or found one following the recommendations of their predecessors. Those who planned to return from Lhasa following the same route left behind some of their animals and provisions in Tsaidam.[30] The pilgrims visited monasteries along the way and rushed to arrive first in Lhasa in order to sell their hinnies and mules to Tibetan merchants at a good price. A Mongol lama sent by the Khalkha monks of Drépung (one of the main Gélukpa monasteries, near Lhasa) came to greet them before arriving in Lhasa and organized their lodgings. The caravan had covered the 1,850 kilometers from Kumbum to Lhasa in about a hundred days (including fifteen full days' rest and seventeen stops of one day each).[31]

The rush of Mongol pilgrims to the holy city entailed a well-organized trade. When in Lhasa, the two priorities were obtaining an audience with the Dalai

---

27    Tsybikov 1992 [1919]: 29, 48-51.
28    Tsybikov writes that Amdo Tibetans usually carried weapons, while Mongol pilgrims did not. Prjevalsky (1876, I: 72) informs us that every man in his caravan, including pilgrims, carried weapons.
29    Tsybikov 1992 [1919]: 64.
30    Tsybikov 1992 [1919]: 71.
31    Tsybikov 1992 [1919]. Agwan Dorjiev made the journey from Urga to Lhasa in record time, arriving after ninety days (Martin and Norbu 1991: 70 n. 180). The account of Prjevalsky, who traveled in autumn with camels (for the first part of the road) and yaks, provides additional details.

Lama and visiting the Jokhang and its famous Jowo ('Lord') statue of twelve-year-old Śākyamuni Buddha. They queued to enter the Jokhang, which was open to devotees three times a day. Tsybikov gives an abundance of details on devotional practices, along with the corresponding prices charged to the pilgrims: pouring butter into lamps; application of gold on the statues' faces, and so on. The pilgrims offered their own jewels and reliquary boxes to the temples. They bought statues and *thangka*s and paid for a coin per twenty-four hours to place them in front of the Jowo or hang them on the wall so that such objects could be consecrated by the Jowo [32] The monks even sold the dead mice that had eaten the barley offered on the altars: their meat was believed to cure difficult births.[33] The pilgrims also apposed their forehead on the right knee of the statues while whispering wishes and embraced the 'wish-granting pillar.' Some invited Buryat lamas to recite prayers and offered 'one hundred lamps' to the Jowo of the Jokhang and the Akṣobhya Vajra Jowo of the Ramoché temples.[34]

To be received by the Dalai Lama, pilgrims first had to send him 8 taels each through a translator (one yak was worth 6.5 to 7.5 Chinese taels). Three days later they were received in small groups for a ten-minute audience; they prostrated and offered scarves to the pontiff, who blessed them and tied around their neck a *janggiya* (thread blessed with his breath and used as a talisman).[35] Then they made the three concentric circumambulations around the Jowo Śākyamuni (inside and outside the Jokhang, and around the whole city), gave offerings to monks of the monasteries in and around Lhasa (such as the 'thousand offerings'[36]), and consulted oracles. They visited the Mongol monks residing in the great monasteries of Central Tibet, especially the Gomang College of Drépung and the Jéba College of Séra.[37] The Mongols stayed two or three months in Lhasa, usually making the vow to come back in this lifetime or a future one.[38]

Some Mongol pilgrims went further, to Tashilhunpo (to have an audience with the Panchen Lama),[39] to Ganden, Samyé and monasteries of Central Tibet,

---

32    Tsybikov 1992 [1919]: 89.
33    Tsybikov 1992 [1919]: 90.
34    Tsybikov 1992 [1919]: 126.
35    Tsybikov 1992 [1919]: 129-131; similar account in Prjevalsky (1876, I: 250), who adds that the Dalai Lama provided lodging and food to the poorest pilgrims and that princes brought very valuable presents.
36    Tsybikov 1992 [1919]: 95-96. On the 'thousand offerings' on Wutaishan, see Chapter 6.
37    Tsybikov 1992 [1919]: 191.
38    Prjevalsky 1876, II: 184-185.
39    An eighteenth-century Mongol painting depicts Mongol nobles in audience with the Panchen Lama (Narantuya 2005: 67).

and to Bodnāth Stūpa in Nepal. Bodnāth was especially holy for Mongols, who had replicas of the *stūpa* (Tib. and Mo. Jarung Khashor) erected in the steppe.[40] The Bodnāth Stūpa was said to have the "power of granting all prayers for worldly wealth, children, and everything asked for."[41] Only a few pilgrims, mostly lamas, went as far as India, especially to visit Bodhgayā, where Buddha had attained enlightenment.[42] The pilgrimage to India was more common in the early twentieth century thanks to improved means of transportation and to the publication of Tibetan guidebooks such as the one by the Amdo intellectual Gendun Chopel (1903-1951) in 1939.[43] In 1937-1938, Mongol duke Migwachir and his brother worshipped at many monasteries of Lhasa, enquired about their construction, icons and rituals and bought a copy of the *Kanjur*; then they crossed the Himalayas in a group of ten Mongol pilgrims and visited the main Buddhist pilgrimage sites of India.[44] In the mid-1920s, Chinese scholar politician Ma Hetian met two Mongolian lamas in Ejin Gol returning from a pilgrimage to India, part of a group of seventeen men and a number of camels and horses. Carrying heavy loads, they had crossed Kukunor and Tibet; three of them had died of malaria. It took them a total of seven years, chiefly on foot, except for a short train ride.[45] The Mongol pilgrims to Lhasa and beyond therefore represented a small minority of devout male laymen and lamas who could undertake such a long and perilous trip.

### The Pilgrimage to Beijing

From the seventeenth century on, Beijing was a major center of Tibetan Buddhism, especially for its numerous Mongol followers. The sanctity of the capital of the Qing empire mostly resided in one pan-Buddhist sacred icon (the Sandalwood Jowo) and in its reincarnated lamas. Most of the Mongols in Beijing were first and foremost noblemen and reincarnated lamas on official visit,[46] and traders from Inner and Outer Mongolia. They came in winter, in large

---

40   In Gandan (Gandantegchilen) Monastery (Ulaanbaatar); Damba Dorji Kheid (northeast of Ulaanbaatar); Khan Öndör Monastery (Arkhangai Province). The Bodnāth Stūpa is a common theme of Mongol *thangka*s and block prints.

41   Waddell 1985 [1895]: 315.

42   For biographies of reincarnations and high-ranking lamas who visited India and Nepal: Yang Jizeng, ed. 1997; Lokesh Chandra 1961: 14

43   "Guidebook for travel to the sacred places of India" (Huber 2000; Huber 2008: 117-136).

44   Miγvacir 2008 [1942]: 126-289. Agwan Dorjiev and Sanjiev went to Bodnāth and Bodhgayā (Martin and Norbu 1991: 18).

45   Ma Ho-t'ien 1949: 14-15.

46   The Qing imposed noblemen and reincarnated lamas from Mongolia to bring tribute and wish longevity to the Manchu emperor for New Year celebrations according to a six-year

delegations that camped in the 'Khalkha District' in the northern suburb, around the Yellow Monastery (Huangsi 黃寺), or stayed in hotels.[47] When the Fifth Jebtsündamba Lubsang Tsültem Jigmed (1815-1842) stayed two months in Beijing in 1840-1841, 175 yurts were laid for four hundred members of the pontiff's retinue near the Yellow Monastery.[48] These delegations stayed two or three months, selling cattle and dairy products and purchasing tea, silk, Tibetan and Mongol books, and Buddhist images. Qing-dynasty Beijing thus had a winter Mongol population of about a hundred fifty thousand.[49] Besides, the majority of the Tibetan Buddhist lamas in Beijing were Mongols.[50]

The propaganda orchestrated by the first Manchu emperors contributed to turning Beijing into a holy city for Mongols: Emperor Shunzhi (r. 1644-1661) invited the Fifth Dalai Lama in 1652; Kangxi (r. 1662-1723) rebuilt Hongrensi 弘仁寺 (or Zhantansi 旃檀寺) in 1665 to enshrine the Sandalwood Buddha (Mo. Tsandan Juu), and Qianlong founded Yonghegong 雍和宮 in 1743-1744 as a training center for Mongol lamas.[51] The fourteen eminent reincarnations from Amdo who resided part of the year in Beijing (zhujing khutugtu 住京呼圖克圖), especially Changkya Rölpé Dorjé and his master, Ganden Shireetü Khutugtu Lozang Tenpé Nyima (1689-1762), played a decisive role in the creation of Beijing as a holy city. The 1780 visit to Beijing by the Sixth Panchen Lama, Lozang Penden Yéshé (1738-1780), drew crowds of pilgrims from near and far, and his sudden death caused by smallpox helped create a new sacred site, the marble stūpa of the Yellow Monastery. In the summer of 1908, after his stay on Wutaishan, the Thirteenth Dalai Lama Tupten Gyatso (1876-1933) arrived by train in Beijing, where he was greeted by Qing dignitaries and lamas from twenty-eight monasteries and had several audiences with the emperor and the

---

rotation (Mo. jishiyan-du suu-): this 'audience to the court,' chaojin 朝覲, has been translated as 'pilgrimage to the emperor' (Chia 1993).

47   Naquin 2000: 470. In 1694, the Lifanyuan 理藩院 (the Court of Colonial Dependencies that regulated the relations between the Qing and the Inner Asians) had to provide accommodation for more than ten thousand Mongols who came to Beijing to bring the tribute. In 1762, the size of these delegations was reduced by an edict (Chia 1993: 74-75).

48   Pozdneev (1978 [1887]: 352), quoting the account of a lama in the retinue of the Jebtsündamba.

49   This also includes resident Mongols of the Eight Banners and noblemen from Eastern Inner Mongolia who had a residence in the Inner City.

50   Uspensky 2011: Chapter 3.

51   Yonghegong was headed by a Tibetan representative of the Dalai Lama but was mostly staffed by Mongol lamas; during the late eighteenth century, about one thousand Mongols studied in its colleges.

empress. So many people traveled from Mongolia to see him in Beijing that they looked like an army ready to invade the capital.[52]

Some Mongols especially journeyed to Beijing to worship the Sandalwood Jowo, which had become for the Mongols one of the three holiest 'Lords' (Mo. Juu, < Tib. Jowo), equal to the Jowos of Jokhang and Ramoché temples in Lhasa.[53] On November 14, 1892 in Mongolia near the Khangai Mountains, Russian Orientalist Aleksei Pozdneev met two Mongol foot travelers who told him they were on their way to Beijing to worship the Sandalwood Jowo.[54] When visiting Beijing, Mongol and Tibetan reincarnations asked the emperor for permission to worship the Sandalwood Buddha. In 1695, the First Jebtsündamba, Zanabazar (1635-1723), was received in audience by Kangxi in front of the icon, which became witness to their lama-patron relationship. In fact, the Sandalwood Jowo statue was considered so sacred that commoners seldom had an opportunity to view it (the monastery's doors probably opened for the New Year festival only) and had to content themselves with circumambulating the monastery's walls. Nevertheless, the story of the statue circulated in Mongolia through popular tales and official narratives.[55] Its fame reached an apex with the wide diffusion of Rölpé Dorjé's short treatise on the "History of the Sandalwood Jowo" (written in Tibetan in 1770 and translated into Mongolian the following year).[56] The sacred icon disappeared in 1900 during the Boxer Rebellion; some believe it was hidden on Wutaishan and later sent to Buryatia. The Buryats now claim that the statue enshrined in Egita Monastery (Egetü Dacang), located east of Ulan-Ude, is the original Sandalwood Jowo from Beijing.[57]

Another holy place for Mongols in Qing-dynasty Beijing was the White Stūpa Monastery (Baitasi 白塔寺, known as Miaoyingsi 妙應寺 in the Qing period), built by the Yuan emperor Khubilai Khan (r. 1260-1294) between 1289 and 1315. Sometime after 1753, Rölpé Dorjé composed a pilgrimage guide to the White Stūpa Monastery for Mongol pilgrims.[58] Earth from Bodhgayā and from

---

52    Liddle 1909: 155.

53    The Sandalwood Buddha, or Udayana Buddha, and the Jowos of Lhasa were believed to be the only true portraits of Śākyamuni, sculpted in India and dating from the Buddha's very lifetime; they embody Śākyamuni's presence in Tibet and in China (Charleux, forthcoming).

54    Pozdneev 1971 [1896]: 399, also Gilmour 1893: 31.

55    Charleux 2011a.

56    *Candan jovo-yin domuy ergikü kemjiye aci tusa-luya qamtu tobcilan quriyaysan erdeni erike neretü orusiba*, xylograph in the Royal Library of Copenhagen.

57    Terentyev 2009.

58    It was composed in Tibetan and translated into Mongolian: *Qayan-u yeke balyasun-u örüne-yin qayalya-daki cayan suburyan-u garcay süsüg-i nemegülügci kemekü orusiba* (Heissig 1954: 116-117, n° 129).

Wutaishan was found among the deposits of consecration within the *stūpa* when it was partly destroyed by the 1976 earthquake.[59] Interestingly, the two main pilgrimage sites of Beijing have their counterparts on Wutaishan: the Great White Stūpa of Tayuansi and the replicas of the Sandalwood Buddha (Fig. 38).

To sum up, a common feature of Mongol pilgrimages abroad was trade, which was a significant component of journeys to Beijing, to Lhasa and, as we will see, to Wutaishan. All pilgrimages abroad created the transfer of goods and wealth from the Mongol areas to China and Tibet, and appeared to have brought a substantial contribution to the economic wealth of Central Tibet in particular. Beijing first attracted (male) merchants, Buddhist dignitaries and nobles from eastern Inner Mongolia, for whom worshipping was generally a secondary motivation. The capital city was probably more attractive for Mongols during the eighteenth century—the heyday of Tibetan (or Gélukpa) Buddhism, when numerous holy reincarnated lamas resided in and visited the capital—but lost its appeal as a pilgrimage center when the Sandalwood Buddha disappeared in 1900. Lay pilgrims to Lhasa were mostly men who were able to leave their families for at least a year to risk their lives undertaking a perilous adventure. Lhasa probably attracted a much greater number of lamas than Wutaishan, ranging from the monks who toured the great Tibetan centers to the lamas who enrolled in the great colleges of Drépung and Séra for several years, passed the highest academic degrees and sometimes never went back to their homeland. For some traveling monks, Wutaishan was only one stop in their pilgrimage circuits, which included Amdo, Central Tibet and sometimes Nepal and India. Yet the following chapters will show that Wutaishan seems to have had a larger Mongol audience than Tibet or Beijing and attracted more ordinary pilgrims on a more frequent basis, women included.

### Pilgrimages to Reincarnations and Saints in Mongolia

Pilgrimages were often motivated by the possibility to see, to be blessed and to receive teachings and initiations from living reincarnations. These included pilgrimages to fixed places where reincarnated lamas resided, such as Lhasa, Urga and Beijing, and to their temporary residences. The largest temporary gatherings on the Mongol territory were due to the presence of the highest Buddhist reincarnations. At a more local level, other reincarnations, as well as hermits, wandering monks, and thaumaturgists also attracted pilgrims from afar. After death, these saints left relics that performed miracles.

---

59      Franke 1994: 181.

### Reincarnated Lamas Touring Inner Mongolia

The first pontiff who toured Inner Mongolia, between 1585 and 1588, was the Third Dalai Lama, Sönam Gyatso (1543-1588), who consolidated the enterprise of conversion initiated by Altan Khan (r. 1542-1582). His tour, his death in Inner Mongolia and his reincarnation among the Tümed royal family were decisive for the (re)conversion of the Mongols. But the two traveling reincarnations who caused the most massive movements of pilgrims in Inner Mongolia were the Fifth Dalai Lama, en route to Beijing in 1652 at the invitation of Emperor Shun-zhi, and the Ninth Panchen Lama, Lozang Chökyi Nyima Gélek Namgyel (1883-1937), who traveled in Inner Mongolia between 1927 and 1935. According to his biography, in 1652 the Fifth Dalai Lama taught to 5,000 Chinese, Tibetans, Mongols and Monguors at Kumbum; in Ordos, some 20,000 Mongols gave him offerings; in the Tümed banners, 4,100 Tümeds came to see him; in Beijing he met with and taught to some 12,000 people, mostly Mongols.[60] Gray Tuttle has counted a total of some 40,000 Mongols who attended the Dalai Lama's tour in Inner Asia and in the Qing capital and offered precious gifts that "led to a tremendous transfer of wealth from the Mongols to the Dalai Lama."[61]

Almost three hundred years later, the Ninth Panchen Lama traveled through Inner Mongolia, where he performed Kālacakra initiations (the Wheel of Time, an advanced *tantra*). His popularity was enhanced by the belief that the future reincarnation of the Panchen will reign as the King of Shambhala and lead the Buddhist army in the final war between Buddhists and heretics. Anyone who took the Kālacakra initiation from the current Panchen Lama was ensured a later rebirth in the kingdom of Shambhala; he/she would participate in the final victory and would be liberated.[62]

The Panchen traveled from one banner to the next with seven to fifteen motor cars and an escort of more than two hundred people. All the travel expenses of the pontiff and his retinue were paid by the Inner Mongol banners (i.e., the commoners). The Mongol princes competed with each other to invite him, offering him gold, silver, camels, horses, cows and sheep, and they built temples and residences in his honor. From 1928 to 1934, the Panchen gave Kālacakra initiations in four sites in Inner Mongolia and in Beijing, each time gathering

---

60   Tuttle 2006b: 75, 77, 81.

61   For instance, Ordos Mongols offered him 1,750 horses, 100 camels, 10,000 sheep and a total of 3,000 ounces of silver (Tuttle 2006b: 75-75).

62   The Panchen lineage has been influential in Inner Mongolia until the present day. In the 1980s, thousands of Inner Mongols went to Beijing to attend an audience with the Tenth Panchen Lama (Borjigin 2006: 30). Mongols also attended Kālacakra initiations given by high reincarnated lamas who were believed to preside in Shambhala, such as the Duingkhor Khutugtu of Badgar Choiling Süme (Jagchid and Hyer 1983: 162).

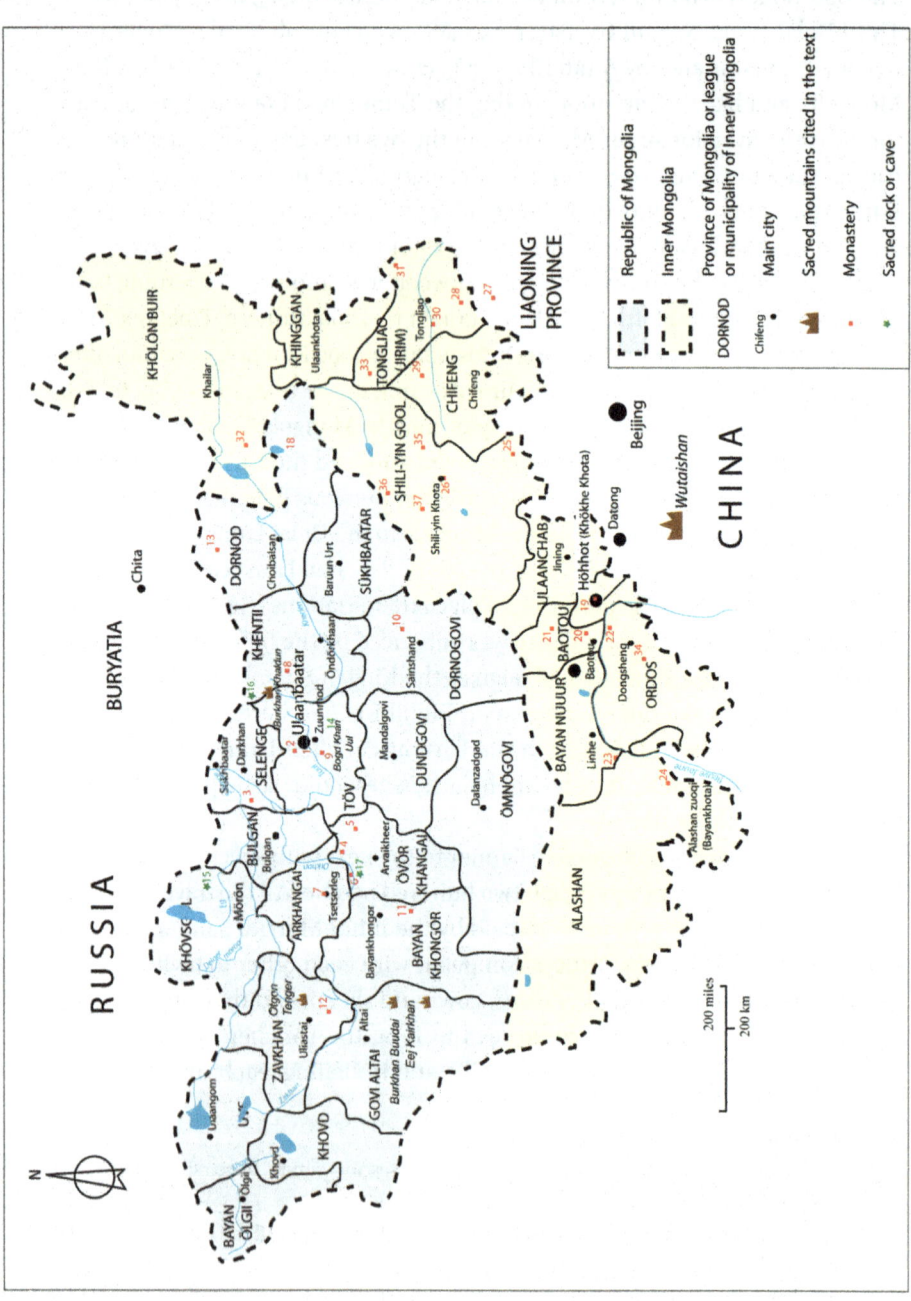

MAP 2      *Map of the main sites of pilgrimages cited in the text, with the equivalents in Cyrillic transcription and Chinese, and present-day*

Republic of Mongolia

1. Urga, Mo. Yekhe Khüriye/Ikh Khüree
2. Damba Dorji Kheid/ Dambadarjaa Khiid
3. Amurbayaskhulangtu Kheid/Amarbayasgalant Khiid
4. Erdeni Juu/Erdene Zuu
5. Baruun Khüriye/Khüree or Shankh Kheid/Khiid
6. Tövkhen Kheid/Tövkhön Khiid
7. Jaya-yin Khüriye/Zayayn Khüree
8. Baldan Bairawun Kheid/Breeven Khiid
9. Manjushiri Kheid/Manchir or Mandshiriin Khiid
10. Khamar-un Kheid/Khamryn Khiid
11. Lama-yin Gegeen-ü Kheid/Lamyn Gegeenii Khiid
12. Narobanchin Gegeen-ü Khüriye/Narvanchin
    Gegeenii Khüree
13. Ugtum Monastery
14. Mother Rock
15. Dayan Deerekhi/Dayan Deerkh Cave
16. White Rock
17. Mogoit, 18. Utai Uula-yin Kheid/Utai Uulyn Khiid

Inner Mongolia (Inner Mongolia Autonomous region, China)

19. Höhhot
20. Badgar Choiling Süme (Ch. Wudangzhao 五當召)
21. Batu Khaalga Süme or Beile-yin Süme (Ch. Bailing miao 百靈廟)
22. Yekhe Juu (Wang-un Gool-un Juu, Ch. Wang'ai zhao 王愛召)
23. Lobonchinbu Süme, or Agui-yin Süme (Ch. Aguimiao 阿貴廟)
24. Baruun Kheid (Ch. Helanshan nansi 賀蘭山南寺)
25. Dolonnor, Mo. Doloon Nuur
26. Bandida Gegeen Süme (Beizimiao 貝子廟)
27. Chagan Diyanchi-yin Kheid (Ch. Ruiyingsi 瑞應寺)
28. Khüriye (Ch. Kulunsi 庫倫寺, Xingyuansi 興源寺)
29. Gilubar Juu, Gilubar-un Agui (Ch. Houzhaomiao 後召廟) [White Utai]
30. Moroi-yin Süme (Molimiao 莫力廟)
31. Malchin Süme (Ch. Huifengsi 慧豐寺)
32. Ganjuur Süme
33. Altan Shirguul
34. Chinggis Khan's Eight White Tents
35. Red Utai.
36. Abural Nüüleskhüitü Süme (Green Utai)
37. Old Khorgo Mountain (Blue Utai).

Buryatia

38. Alkanay

between thirty thousand to more than three hundred thousand devotees from near and far. Processions of princes carrying incense led the way, followed by hundreds of devotees in prostration.[63] Thousands of yurts surrounded the monasteries where he presided over the ritual. These very high figures may not be reliable; but even if they must revised downwards, compared to a population of less than two million inhabitants, they are still very impressive. Pilgrims "offered money, gold, silver, jewels and ornaments, whatever they had. Poor commoners donated more generously than did the rich and powerful. Their first priority was to seek religious blessings for this life and the next."[64] These huge meetings were not equipped with microphones: although the majority could not hear the rituals but only the live music being played, all the participants were happy. "They firmly believed that the Buddha would bless their souls and future lives simply because they had been present at the ceremony."[65]

### Urga (Yekhe Khüriye), Residence of the Jebtsündamba Khutugtu

The seat of the Jebtsündamba Khutugtu was the main pan-Mongol pilgrimage within Mongolia, attracting Khalkhas and Inner Mongols, as well as Buryats and Kalmyks of Astrakhan (Fig. 4).[66] Urga (Mo. Yekhe Khüriye, Da Khüriye)[67] was the main Khalkha religious center in the nineteenth and early twentieth

---

63    In 1928 at Malchin Süme (Khorchin Darkhan Wang Banner) to 170,000 nobles, monks and lay people from all over eastern Inner Mongolia; in 1928 in Jasagtu Banner to 84,000 Mongols; in 1929 at Bandida Gegeen Süme to 30,000 (or up to 100,000 pilgrims, including Khalkhas); at Batu Khaalga Süme (several times between 1932 and 1934) to more than 370,000 Mongols (in 1932); in 1935 at Shine Juu (Otog Banner, Ordos) to 100,000 devotees from Mongolia, Höhhot and nearby Chinese provinces, many of them in great prostrations all the way; at Beijing in 1932 to tens of thousands of Mongols from Outer and Inner Mongolia (Wuyungaowa 1997: 202; Lattimore 1942: Chapter 12; Hedin 1943, Part II: 74; Jagchid and Hyer 1983: 134; Jagou 2004, Part II; Bulag 2007: 29). On Bandida Gegeen Süme (Beizimiao 貝子廟) of Shili-yin Khota (Shilinhot) and Batu Khaalga Süme (Bailingmiao 百靈廟), see Charleux 2006: CD-ROM [88] [74].

64    Jagchid 1999: 27.

65    Jagchid 1999: 27, 42.

66    Pozdneev 1971 [1896]: 33, 35; Bawden 1989 [1968]: 162; Bormanshinov 1998: 9-10; Andreyev 2001c: 354. The first Kalmyk pilgrims to Urga are documented for 1880. Tsybikov mentions Alashan Mongols who came to Urga to pay homage to the Jebtsündamba (1992 [1919]: 21). Although the Ninth Jebtsündamba (b. ca. 1932-2012) has lost a great part of his prestige for modern Khalkha Mongols, more than seventy thousand pilgrims rushed from Russia and Mongolia when he gave a Kālacakra initiation in Tuva in 2003.

67    Urga (< Örgöö, 'residence' [of the pontiff]) was an itinerant monastery that moved more than twenty times; it definitively settled at its present location (i.e., modern Ulaanbaatar) in the nineteenth century.

FIGURE 4

1) *"Mongolian pilgrims on their toilsome way to Bogdo Kure (the Cloister of God)"*; 2) *"Pilgrims on the way to Bogdo Kure"*; 3) *"Having reached their goals, the pilgrims collapse exhausted outside the outer enclosure surrounding Bogdo Hutuktu Gegen's Palace. Here they remain in prayer for days and weeks."* © HASLUND-CHRISTENSEN 1954 [1932]: BETWEEN P. 73-74.

century, with more than a hundred temples, residences and colleges, and thirteen thousand to twenty thousand inhabitants—half of whom were monks.[68] It was also a major trade center between Russia, China and Tibet. To receive blessings from the Jebtsündamba was the first aim of a pilgrimage to Urga.[69] Pilgrims also went to Urga for medical treatment and prophecies.[70]

The pilgrims were part of city life. During the daytime, people were allowed to freely enter the central area, the Eastern Monastery,[71] but after six in the

---

68 Pürevjav 1961: 19-30; Pozdneev 1971 [1896]: Chapter 2; Jambal, ed. Bawden 1997.

69 Seven other reincarnated lamas had a residence in Urga.

70 Geleta, ed. Forbath 1936: 258-259.

71 The monastic city had split into two parts when the temples of Gandan were built on a western hill in 1838, hence its name 'Western Monastery.' The old and main part of the monastery was then called the 'Eastern Monastery.'

evening women had to leave. The pilgrims visited the temples in the morning, and were received and blessed by the Jebtsündamba, who absolved them of their sins.[72] They offered him horses, camels, sheep, brick tea, meat, dairy products and so on, and later, in return of the blessing, a consecrated scarf or a gift of money. The sick among them were given medicine.[73] At eleven in the morning, the ceremony was finished for the day, and the gate of the Jebtsündamba's palace was closed. After that time, the pilgrims either sat in the yurts of their lama friends or spent the whole day at the market place.[74] From the 1910s to the 1930s the crowds of pilgrims were so large that most of them could not enter anymore, so

> a long rope was let out from one of the buildings. Kneeling, the Mongols reverently touched the rope, which was gently waggled from the other hand, supposedly by the Hutuktu ... then the Mongols rode away, silent with awe at having been blessed by the living god.[75]

It was presumed that the rope carried their prayers to the holy man and the blessings back to them.[76]

From morning to evening, hundreds of pilgrims circumambulated the Eastern Monastery, following the circular road delimitated with prayer wheels and small shrines.[77] They also circled Gandan Monastery along the path delimitated on the north and west side by twenty-eight *stūpas* erected by devotees. Gandan was accessible to the lay population only on the 15th day of the first summer month; this rule was loosened after the Eighth Jebtsündamba passed away, in 1924. Then, laypersons certainly had access to Megjid Janraisig Temple of Gandan to worship the twenty-five-meter-high statue of Avalokiteśvara built in 1911.[78] The pilgrims also worshipped the funerary and contact relics of the past Jebtsündambas,[79] and climbed the surrounding mountains to worship 'natural'

---

72   Pozdneev 1971 [1896]: 64; Ramstedt 1978: 55.

73   Geleta, ed. Forbath 1936: 260-261.

74   Pozdneev 1971 [1896]: 64.

75   Andrews 1921: 69 (who traveled in 1916-1919).

76   Geleta, ed. Forbath 1936: 259-261.

77   Ramstedt 1978: 44-45; Geleta, ed. Forbath 1936: 258-259; Majer and Teleki 2006: 32.

78   Andrews 1921: 72; Majer and Teleki 2006: 86.

79   The funerary *stūpas* of the Fifth, Seventh and Eighth Jebtsündambas were enshrined in temples of Gandan; that of the Second Jebtsündamba was at Damba Dorji Kheid, northwest of Urga. The hat and clothes of the First Jebtsündamba were enshrined in the White Temple (Jambal, ed. Bawden 1997: 6-9); his throne, cap and staff, as well as the

TABLE 2    *Number of worshippers who visited the Thirteenth Dalai Lama in Urga, Kumbum and Wutaishan*

|  | Urga ('Takulan'), 1904-1906 | Kumbum ('Ta Ehr sui,' i.e. Taersi, Amdo) | Wutaishan ('Yutai shan'), 1908 |
|---|---|---|---|
| In winter | 1,500 Mongols and Buryats | 3,000 Tibetans<br>70-80 Mongols | 2,000-2,500 Mongols<br>70-80 Tibetans |
| In summer | 10-20 Tibetans<br>4,-5,000 altogether | 1,000-2,000 Tibetans<br>20-30 Mongols | 1,000-1,500 Mongols<br>10-20 Tibetans |

SOURCE: MANNERHEIM 1969 [1940]: 695.

relics such as footprints of famous lamas in the rock, as well as springs, caves and rocks having supernatural properties.[80]

Pilgrims especially converged in Urga for special events such as the enthronement of a Jebtsündamba, bringing with them herds of horses to offer him. Egor Fedorovitch Timkowski, attached to the Russian Orthodox Mission of Beijing, described in 1820 crowds of Mongols gathering in Urga to worship the six-year-old fifth reincarnation of the Jebtsündamba, just arrived from Tibet.[81] The Thirteenth Dalai Lama's two-year sojourn in Urga (1904-1906) increased the city's popularity as a center of pilgrimage and attracted an especially large number of Buryats.[82] Every day hundreds of Mongols, laypersons and monks asked the Dalai Lama to bless them. It is said that the Jebtsündamba was jealous of the pontiff's popularity, and the tensions between the two may have forced the Dalai Lama to leave the city earlier than planned.[83] The Finnish baron Carl G.E. Mannerheim compared the number of worshippers who visited the Thirteenth Dalai Lama during his stays at Urga, Kumbum and Wutaishan (Table 2). Although his stay on Wutaishan was much shorter than in Urga, greater numbers of Mongols—mostly from the easternmost part of Mongolia—visited him on Wutaishan, in winter, than in Urga and Kumbum.

In several major pilgrimage sites in Mongolia and abroad, most pilgrims had no opportunity to enter the main shrine and approach the holy objects or the

---

statues he made with his own hands, were kept in the great Batutsagan assembly hall of the Eastern Monastery (Pozdneev 1971 [1896]: 56).

80    Majer and Teleki 2006: 86, 110.
81    Timkowski 1993 [1827]: 57.
82    Jambal, ed. Bawden 1997: 35-46; Tsybikov 1904: 96.
83    Jambal, ed. Bawden 1997: 38-39; also Geleta, ed. Forbath 1936: 101; Lomakina 2006.

reincarnation because of huge crowds, or because monasteries were open on certain festival days only. They had to content themselves with circumambulating and worshipping in front of the temple doors. Similarly, pilgrims traveling to see the Panchen Lama in Inner Mongolia generally could not see him; they could not even hear his teachings. This must have been frustrating, even if apparently, according to Sechin Jagchid, "all were happy." Conversely, on Wutaishan, monasteries and shrines were open to all visitors.

## Pilgrimages to Buddhist Monasteries

Urga was the only pan-Mongol pilgrimage site within Mongol territory that gathered in the same place Khalkhas, Buryats and Inner Mongols, but many monasteries that possessed reincarnations, relics and sacred icons became sites of local and supra-local pilgrimages. Of these more local attractions, the most visited in Inner Mongolia was certainly Badgar Choiling Süme. In his *Ordos Dictionary*, Antoine Mostaert has an entry for the expression *Badyartu mörgü-*, "make a pilgrimage to Badgar Choiling Süme."[84] Although this 'academic' monastery did very little to attract pilgrims—it organized only three festivals a year, without any *cham* dance, and was located in a remote place—at the end of the nineteenth century, about five thousand pilgrims came every year, sometimes from great distances away.[85]

### Pilgrimages to Relics and Ancient Icons

Erdeni Juu (Cyr. Mo. Erdene Zuu, 'Jowo Rinpoché,' Övörkhangai Province), built by Abadai Khan (1554-1588) in 1585-1586 above the ruins of the imperial capital Kharakhorum, was the holiest monastery of the Khalkhas due to its ancient and prestigious origin and to its number of relics and especially holy icons. These icons included one of Śākyamuni (probably made after Höhhot Yekhe Juu's Jowo), a copy of the Sandalwood Buddha, an especially revered Yuan-dynasty statue of Mahākāla Gur Gönpo, and a relic of Śākyamuni offered by the Third Dalai Lama to Abadai Khan.[86] Pilgrims circumambulated the fortified wall

---

84    Mostaert 1941-1944: 470.

85    Prjevalsky 1876, I: 155.

86    "The very mention of Erdeni Dzuu arouses love for his native land in the heart of every Mongol, and ultimately, moves him to fall on bended knee in trembling delight before this holy place" (Pozdneev 1971 [1896]: 282). Southeast of Erdeni Juu, Baruun Khüriye (Shankh Kheid) enshrined the black standard of Chinggis Khan and the statue of Vajrapāṇi given by the Dalai Lama to Abadai Khan.

topped with *stūpas* before entering to worship the Jowo in the central temple (Gool Juu). The renowned Mongol Buddhist scholar and hermit Jaba (Zava) Damdin Lubzang Tayang (1867-1937) wrote a poem entitled "Eulogy to Erdeni Juu," explaining that this monastery was the most sacred place of pilgrimage because it possessed 'life power for this life.'[87]

The funerary *stūpas* and mummies of great lamas and reincarnations were precious relics that could turn a monastery into a local pilgrimage center. Besides Urga, a dozen monasteries linked to Öndör Gegeen Zanabazar and enshrining some of his relics and relics of his reincarnations attracted pilgrims from all Khalkha Mongolia. Amurbayaskhulangtu Kheid/Amarbayasgalant Khiid (Selenge Province), built from 1727 to 1736 by Manchu emperors to enshrine the remains of Zanabazar, each year attracted thousands of pilgrims from every Khalkha league (*aimag*) and from Buryatia.[88] The pilgrims worshipped the funerary *stūpas* of the First and Fourth Jebtsündambas, in the third courtyard of the central complex, and a statue said to have been offered by the Third Dalai Lama to Abadai Khan, in the fourth courtyard.[89] In the 1890s, presentation of offerings before the funerary *stūpas* of these two reincarnations was held every day at five in the morning and again between eight and nine in the evening. The monks gave the pilgrims quarters in their homes, supplied them with water and fuel and sold votive scarves.[90] Like in Urga, excited crowds had to be contained by monk-policemen, who sometimes did not hesitate to beat people severely to prevent them from entering the holy of holies.[91]

Most of the large 'banner monasteries' that housed more than five hundred monks drew pilgrims from surrounding banners and leagues, especially at major festivals. As in medieval Europe, these monasteries boasted that they possessed the holiest relics and icons—which apparently could compare with those of Tibet. Worshiping the Jowo icons of Yekhe Juu of Höhhot and Yekhe Juu of Ordos (Wang-un Gool-un Juu) was considered equivalent to worshiping the Jowo of Lhasa.[92] Baruun Kheid Monastery, built in 1757 by a disciple of the Sixth Dalai Lama, Tsangyang Gyatso (1683-ca.1706), in the Helan Mountains

---

87   Lham 2011: 51-53.

88   Pozdneev 1971 [1896]: 25, 28.

89   The two *stūpas* were destroyed in 1937.

90   Pozdneev 1971 [1896]: 23.

91   "[T]o officiate at these services," writes Pozdneev, "five distinguished and most honored lamas are appointed in turn, whereas all the other more humble inhabitants of the monastery do not even have the right to approach these holy objects and must confine themselves to worshipping before the door of the temple in which they are" (Pozdneev 1971 [1896]: 24).

92   Charleux, forthcoming.

賀蘭山 (Alashan Banner, Inner Mongolia), enshrined the golden mummy identified as being that of the Sixth Dalai Lama. The lama believed to be his reincarnation in fact resided there,[93] as did the reincarnation of Tibetan regent, Sanggyé Gyatso (1653-1705). By creating a direct and tangible link between Mongolia and Tibet and even presenting themselves as surrogates of the pilgrimage to Lhasa, these monasteries played a crucial role in the acculturation of Buddhism in Mongolia, thus legitimating it as a sacred Buddhist place.

In the course of the nineteenth century, non-Buddhist ancestral shrines housing relics of Chinggis Khan and his family, whose worship was previously restricted to the nobility, also became a focus of pilgrimages for both nobles and commoners, illustrating the relative tolerance of the Buddhist authorities.[94] Although the ceremonies performed at the Eight White Tents, which enshrined Chinggis Khan's 'relics' in the Ordos region, included some Buddhist elements, they showed resistance to Buddhicization.[95] Other Chinggisid shrines of Ordos, such as that of Ishi Khatun (Khubilai Khan's mother) in Wang Banner, also became popular pilgrimage sites. Pilgrimages to Mount Burkhan Khaldun in Khentii Province (see below), designated as sacred by Chinggis Khan, may also have developed during that period as a major site of pilgrimage to the great Mongol emperor.

### Monasteries Renowned for Their Fairs and Trade Connections

Trade also contributed to moving pilgrims around Mongolia, since great fairs gathering Chinese and Mongol peddlers were held on the main festival days of the largest monasteries. In the nineteenth century, the greatest temporary monastic fair of Inner Mongolia, that of Ganjuur Süme (Kanjur Monastery, in the Left Banner of the New Bargu), gathered every year, from the 7th to the 15th day of the eighth lunar month, about twenty thousand pilgrims and traders from Mongolia, China and Transbaikalia. Mongol encampments formed a circle around the monastery, as large as three or four kilometers wide.[96]

Two cities located near the Sino-Mongol border with a large concentration not only of temples, monasteries and high reincarnations but also of markets and workshops were a powerful draw for visiting lamas, pilgrims and traders:

---

93    This lineage is therefore considered as a parallel line of reincarnation of the Dalai Lamas. The mummy was destroyed during the Cultural Revolution. On the 'second life' of the Sixth Dalai Lama, see Chapter 4.

94    Prjevalsky 1876, I: 205. In the nineteenth century, all Eastern Mongols came to recognize Chinggis Khan as their supreme ancestral deity.

95    Chiodo 1989-1991: 97; and 1992-1993; Hurcha 1999. On modern pan-Mongol pilgrimages to the Eight White Tents (now called 'Mausoleum of Chinggis Khan'): Khan 1997.

96    See articles on this fair in Xiao Guang et al., eds. 2003.

Höhhot (the Blue City, also known as the City of Temples) and Dolonnor (Doloon Nuur, Seven Lakes). By the nineteenth century, the fame of Höhhot as a religious center had declined, [97] and Dolonnor, being the administrative center for the Inner Mongol Buddhist administration, was too close to Manchu power to become a popular pilgrimage center. However, Mongol lamas going to Beijing generally stopped at Dolonnor to visit the residing reincarnated hierarchs,[98] and Tibetans traveling from Amdo to Beijing preferred to make a detour through Dolonnor (or Wutaishan) to avoid crossing Inner China.

### Monasteries Established on Natural Numinous Sites

As highlighted by Alphonse Dupront, all great pilgrimage sites superimpose modern worship to older cults, especially cults of natural elements.[99] As we will see, Wutaishan is not only a collection of famous temples, relics and icons; its natural numinous sites were also an important part of the pilgrimage. In Mongolia, Buddhist saints and reincarnations often established their monasteries on ancient sacred sites, to 'tame' and appropriate them, and discovered new numinous sites. Mongol herders therefore continued to practice old rituals within monasteries, sanctioned by Buddhist authorities.

These monasteries present a number of similarities to Tibetan pilgrimage sites: a dramatic configuration, on top of a vertical cliff or in a cirque sheltered by high mountains accessible by a narrow defile or steep path; sacred caves reachable by dangerous flights of steps carved into the cliff; 'traces' left by Buddhas and saints such as footprints in the rock; *mantras* and paintings that appeared spontaneously on a rock; and sacred springs, rocks and trees (Fig. 5). Four renowned examples are Tövkhen Kheid/Tövkhön Khiid, Baldan Bairawun Kheid, Gilubar Juu and Lobonchinbu Süme. Pilgrims visit Tövkhen Kheid, founded in 1653 by Zanabazar in Övörkhangai Province, Republic of Mongolia, for its womb-cave, its meditation cave and stone 'throne' of Zanabazar, a print of his boot, sacred wells and trees. At Baldan Bairawun Kheid (in the Khentii Mountains, Republic of Mongolia), pilgrims circumambulate the monastery, stopping at various holy places: a stone statue of White Tārā, a womb-tunnel cave and a throne-shaped seat in which everyone is advised to sit. The sides of the rock have numerous indentations shaped like various parts of the

---

97 Höhhot (Ch. Guihuacheng 歸化城) had eleven Gélukpa monasteries intra-muros plus twenty-eight extra-muros and twelve reincarnated lamas in the early Qing period.

98 Thirteen reincarnated lamas of Beijing had a summer residence in the two large imperial monasteries known as the 'Blue' and 'Yellow' monasteries. Both were destroyed by Russian troops in 1945.

99 Dupront 1987: 52.

body—back, elbow, head, etc. It is said that inserting parts of one's body into these indentations and massaging oneself against the stone has a beneficial effect on one's health.[100] In the 1930s, the Hungarian engineer Joseph Geleta followed inhabitants of Urga who visited Baldan Bairawun Kheid just before the White Month (first month of the lunar calendar) "to atone for their sins." He describes the

> endless procession of men, women and children [that] winds its way over the snow-covered mountain slope, mostly on foot, except for the very old, who ride on mountain ponies ... . The endless crowds climb the mountain in solemn silence, sunk in meditation, and only stop when they come to an *obo* [*oboo*]—a heap of stones—which they decorate with coloured *chadaks* [*khadag*], designed to propitiate the spirits of the mountain, so that they should not send a storm or a pack of wolves to endanger the lives of pilgrims. Some pilgrims leave on the *obo* an article of clothing, or a lump of dough mixed with the blood of a sacrificed animal, or a small clay Buddha brought from a Tibetan pilgrimage.[101]

During the Qing dynasty, Gilubar Juu, built in the 1770s around three Khitan (947-1125) Buddhist caves in the Left Baarin Banner (Inner Mongolia), attracted up to twenty thousand Mongols, who visited caves and sacred springs on its eighth lunar month festival (Fig. 5). [102] The biannual festival of Lobonchinbu Süme (< Loppön Chenpo, 'Great Teacher': Padmasambhava Monastery) [103] of Alashan, which commemorates the days Padmasambhava arrived and left the place (the 22nd day of the ninth month and the 10th day of the seventh month respectively), drew throngs of pilgrims, who worshipped the five caves (the most sacred one housed the golden statue allegedly made by Padmasambhava with his own hands), the sacred spring and the footprints of Padmasambhava and of a *ḍākinī*. As in Tibetan pilgrimage sites 'opened' by Padmasambhava, Lobonchinbu Süme's sanctity is supported by legends about the taming of a local deity and by tales of apparitions and miracles.

---

100   Croner 2008b.

101   Geleta, ed. Forbath 1936: 244-246.

102   Ch. Houzhaomiao 後召廟. See Galsang et al. 1994: 275-289; Yesibaljuur 2010.

103   Or Agui-yin Süme, Ch. Aguimiao 阿貴廟, in present-day Dengkou 磴□County. This Nyingmapa monastery is said to have been founded by Padmasambhava who, after having practiced Tantric exercises with five *ḍākinī*-sisters in each of the five grottoes, subdued a local demon and locked him in a cave (Charleux 2002b).

FIGURE 5    *Gilubar Juu, Baarin Left Banner, Chifeng Municipality, Inner Mongolia.*
© ISABELLE CHARLEUX, 1994.

## Pilgrimages to Mountains and Natural Numinous Sites of Mongolia

### Pilgrimages to Natural Numinous Sites

The term 'pilgrimage' must not be restricted to the great Buddhist sites (and Chinggisid shrines) but should be extended to the considerable number of isolated caves, trees, woods, strange rocks, springs, ponds, lakes, etc. of the Mongol countryside, which are often located in mountainous areas and not connected to a monastery. Mongol mountains are especially rich in healing springs and medicinal plants. Mongols used to (and still) bathe in mineral springs to cure diseases and afflictions, and worship specific sites reputed to grant fertility and healing. Many caves in fact are linked to fertility, and children's shoes are offered as ex-votos in front of their entrance. At Mogoit (Övörkhangai Province, Republic of Mongolia), after bathing in healing mineral springs, local pilgrims then climb the mountain to worship the Khanga-yin Oboo/Khangayn Ovoo, a hundred-meter-high vertical rock reputed to increase longevity.[104]

Modern Mongols and particularly (neo-)shamans explain that kinds of 'energies' circulate and connect several sacred sites in a way comparable to an

---

104    A modern example is detailed by Humphrey 1993. We will come back to pilgrimages to caves in Chapter 7.

electric grid; for instance, the Mother Rock (Eji-yin Khada/Eejiin Khad) in Khövsgöl Province and the one in Töv Province (about twenty kilometers south of Züün Mod, Sergelen District) in the Republic of Mongolia are believed to be connected to each other. However, the great majority of these natural sites are known only locally, and Mongols do not much like to discuss their location.[105]

### Pilgrimages to Mountains in Mongolia

All over Mongolia, specific mountains are worshipped on a local or supra-local level. Mountains are believed to be the property and abode of numinous forces—the master-spirits of the land and water (*gajar-un ejen*).[106] Traditional Mongol burial places were also located on mountain summits and upper slopes and thus associated with the spirits of ancestors. The territory of sacred mountains was consecrated as a sanctuary (*khoriul*), where it was forbidden to hunt, fell trees, plow fields; sometimes their access was restricted or forbidden (similar prohibitions protected lands surrounding monasteries).

The threefold typology elaborated by Allan Grapard for Japanese sacred mountains can be useful in understanding the Mongol cult of sacred mountains:

1.   the mountain as a sacred site, residence of an ancient divinity, where a contact with the divine world can be established;
2.   the mountain as a sacred area (a *maṇḍala*) where Buddhist pilgrims and monks come to accumulate merit, or practice meditation, asceticism, and search for Enlightenment;
3.   the mountain image of stability, that protects the sacred nation according to a syncretist Buddhist-local tradition.[107]

The first category was found all over Mongolia: every community was generally based around a local sacred mountain, [108] and propitiated the master-spirits of the land with seasonal sacrifices at *oboo*s located on the mountaintop. This category of mountain cult is close to what Tibetans call *lhari* (and their deity,

---

105   In addition, because they belong to what communists labeled as 'superstition' and were despised by the religious authorities, they have been poorly studied up to now.
106   They include the lords of mountains, hills, trees, lakes and rivers, who govern the weather and the environment. I here focus on mountains to compare mountain worship in Mongolia with the cult of Wutaishan.
107   Grapard 1982.
108   It is often said that clan-based communities worship a common forefather on the mountain. But Qing period Mongol communities were heterogeneous and did not share a common ancestor, except for aristocrats.

*yüllha*). The master-spirits of the land are ambivalent deities, responsible for bestowing prosperity, power, wealth, glory and progeny but also for sending calamities, such as droughts and snow storms, and punishing those who do not respect them. These mountain lords were feared and their personal name was taboo (at least locally): sacred mountains were generally called *khairakhan*, 'beloved, sacred' in place of their name. Every region had its own hierarchy of sacred mountains, whose deities were sometimes considered equal in rank to the Sky and Earth. Like in Tibet, some sacred mountains, or mountain lords, were anthropomorphized in tales and songs,[109] considered as being male or female, able to fall in love, marry each other and develop genealogical and hierarchical relations.[110] The pair mountain/lake, which is common in Tibet, is also found in Mongolia.[111]

*Oboo* sacrifices aiming at obtaining the mountain lord's favors—primarily, rain for pastures and fertility for flocks and herds—were traditionally restricted to the male members of the local community.[112] However, these men cannot be called 'pilgrims,' and the collective cult to local mountain-deities is clearly distinct from the above-mentioned individual pilgrimages to natural sanctuaries, though they generally are located on the same mountain.

These cults generally required the participation of lamas, who wrote prayers for mountain lords. The prayers show their attempt at Buddhicizing these territorial deities: as early as the sixteenth century, they were given a new Buddhist identity.[113] Eighteenth-century Mergen Gegeen Lubsangdambijalsan (1717-1766) of Urad wrote prayers for *oboo* worship, associating them with similar practices already established in Tibetan Buddhism, and protested against the slaughter of animals for offerings.[114] According to Buddhist narratives and

---

109    Pegg 2001: 98. On the personification of mountain lords: Humphrey and Onon 1996.

110    For instance, Mount Eji Khairakhan/Cyr. Mo. Eej Khairkhan, married to Aja Bogda/Aj Bogd, fell in love with Burkhan Buudai (Govi Altai Province, Republic of Mongolia) (Croner 2008a: 20).

111    The Dariganggas of Sükhbaatar Province (Republic of Mongolia) have a legend of origin about human lovers who became Dara/Dari Hill and Ganga Lake (the natural boundaries of their current homeland). They say that women go round the Ganga Lake in a clockwise direction, and men go to the top of the mountain and worship at the *oboo* erected there (Pegg 2001: 17). For the musical communication between mountains and lakes: Pegg 2001: 102-103.

112    These popular cults never disappeared in Mongolia and are now encouraged as an expression of Mongol national and cultural identity (Sneath 2000: 235-244).

113    Thousands of prayers to territorial deities have been preserved (Heller 1996).

114    Bawden 1994, "Two Mongol Texts Concerning Obo Worship." Up to now, sheep continue to be sacrificed to mountain deities in spite of the presence of lamas.

prayers but less frequently echoed by laypeople, Mongol sacred mountains, after being 'tamed' and bound by an oath into the service of Buddhism (generally by Padmasambhava), became associated with Buddhist mythical mountains such as Potala or Sumeru. This corresponds to the second category of Grapard's typology—the mountain as a sacred place in which to meditate and seek enlightenment. Mongol mountains/mountain lords were depicted as warrior deities riding horses and were sometimes also viewed as the abode of a transcendent buddha or *bodhisattva*, such as the deity of Bogda Khan Uula south of Ulaanbaatar being identified with the mythical bird Garuḍa. The Buddhist pantheon was 'fixed' into the landscape, thus turning the mountain into a *maṇḍala*;[115] for example, a Buddha was recognized in the shape of a peak, and deities and saints left their footprints on the rocks. Nonetheless, the mountain deity often kept his/her own identity; frequently, in fact, contradictory narratives about the deities coexisted. For instance, local Mongols worshipped the deity of Muna Mountain (west of Baotou in Inner Mongolia) as the main deity of their community, while at the same time they considered him a mere cook in a monastery of Tibet.[116]

Buddhicization was a gradual process that "involved the deployment of a great deal of local and imported ritual and narrative resources,"[117] and was never complete. In Mongolia, the process of Buddhicization of mountain/mountain lords seem to be much less advanced than in Tibet,[118] where in many cases the territorial god has disappeared,[119] and the mountain has become a *maṇḍala* presided by a transcendental buddha.[120] In Tibet, Buddhicized

---

115    On mandalization: Huber 1999: 26 and throughout.

116    Caroline Humphrey, personal communication, February 2009.

117    Huber 1999: 27.

118    Some scholars who have studied the incense-offering ritual texts for *oboo* worship stress the decidly Buddhist character of these prayers, which aim at reenacting a standardized ritual conversion of the local mountain deity to Buddhism and reduce the variety of indigenous practices (see Lindahl 2010). This is true when speaking of texts and rituals conducted by lamas at *oboos*; however, the beliefs, practices, gestures and (sacrificial) offerings of the laypeople who actually perform these rituals show how incomplete this attempt at Buddhicization is.

119    That said, different stages of Buddhicization are found in Tibet: some mountains, such as Amnye Machen (present-day Qinghai) and Kawa Karpo (present-day Yunnan), maintained the identities of both the territorial god and the transcendent Buddhist deity (Buffetrille 1996a: 193-208; Buffetrille 1997; Buffetrille 1998; Henrion-Dourcy 2007).

120    In Tibet, the Buddhicization of local mountains eroded the community-based cults and relegated them to the margins of the Tibetan territory (Huber 1999: 230). On the degree of Buddhicization of Tibetan sacred sites and the way Buddhist pilgrimages to mountains replaced or superimposed onto the cults of territorial gods in many areas: Blondeau

mountains are called *néri* ('mountains [that are] sacred places'). *Néri*, like Mount Kailash, are the abode of a transcendental buddha or a *bodhisattva*; male and female pilgrims practice circumambulations and perform prostrations and rites to obtain merit, a better future life and spiritual realization (according to the official Buddhist discourse).[121] Pilgrims do not climb up them anymore but instead circle around their base in the clockwise direction.[122]

Is there the equivalent of *néri* mountains in Mongolia?[123] Let us give two examples of mountains that are the focus of supra-local (Khalkha) pilgrimages: Burkhan Khaldun and Otkhon Tngri/Otgon Tenger. Burkhan Khaldun is a major site not only for pilgrims honoring Chinggis Khan but also for Buddhists (who recognize Chinggis Khan as an emanation of Vajrapāṇi).[124] The First Jebtsündamba Zanabazar went on a pilgrimage to Burkhan Khaldun and built a monastery at its foot for the benefit of Buddhist pilgrims.[125] C.W. Campbell recounts his own 1903 journey to a summit in the Khentii mountain range, which might well be Burkhan Khaldun:

> Every autumn the Manchu Amban [imperial resident] comes from Urga, with a retinue of magnitude, to make oblation to the great nature-spirits, and Mongols and Chinese alike make pilgrimages from great distances to enlist their favour ... Before a large tree *obo* [*oboo*], festooned with prayer flags, there are rough tables of larch, with a boarding in front, on which the Amban kneels ... The pilgrimages of centuries have marked recognizable paths, and Mongols ride the whole way up over tree-roots and fallen trunks.[126]

---

1996: ix-x; Karmay 2005 [1998]; Ramble 1995; Buffetrille 1996a: 193-210; Buffetrille 1998; Huber 1999: 23-32.

121  Pilgrims will never admit that they worship the mountain to obtain worldly benefits, but their practices and beliefs show that they constantly practice "religious bricolage" or to-and-fro movements between the official Buddhist discourse and pragmatic rites (Buffetrille 1998; Henrion-Dourcy 2007).

122  Even if at high-ranking pilgrimage sites like Kailash, shrines, curious rocks, *mani* stones, caves, springs and monasteries are so numerous that pilgrims, who stop to worship a dozen sites per day, are no longer aware that they are in fact making a circumambulation (Katia Buffetrille, personal communication, 2009).

123  Here I speak of actual beliefs and practices. We cannot assume, as does Jared Lindahl, that a mountain is a *néri* simply because there exists a Buddhist ritual text that presents it at the center of a *maṇḍala* (Lindahl 2010: 238, 242).

124  Mo. Wchirbani or Ochirbani, a martial *bodhisattva* deriving from Indra, the Indian god of thunder.

125  It was destroyed by the Jungar Mongols, who invaded Khalkha Mongolia in 1688.

126  Campbell 1903: 513-514.

Women were not allowed to ascend Burkhan Khaldun. Instead, they visited the temple at the base of the mountain and then went to the shores of the nearby Talkhit Lake, while men went to the summit to worship the *oboo*. Furthermore, the pilgrims did not make the circumambulation of the site. Burkhan Khaldun was thus not treated in the same way as a sacred *néri* mountain in Tibet: this 'pilgrimage' appears indeed to be a supra-local form of *oboo* worship.

The Buddhicization of Otkhon Tngri (also called Vajrapāṇi Mountain), the highest peak of the Khangai range,[127] seems to be more advanced than that of Burkhan Khaldun. At the end of the eighteenth century, Otkhon Tngri was said to be the residence of Vajrapāṇi.[128] Mongols commonly believe that Mongolia is the land of Vajrapāṇi,[129] Tibet is the land of Avalokiteśvara, and China is the the land of Mañjuśrī: the Buddhist landscape of North Asia is protected by these three major protector *bodhisattvas*.[130] Being the abode of a major *bodhisattva*, Otkhon Tngri is in some way the counterpart of Wutaishan, though the two are never mentioned together in cosmologies. Before 1921, Otkhon Tngri received sacrifices performed by the *amban*s, banner officials and local communities, and was visited by religious and lay pilgrims from the entire region.[131] Otkhon Tngri is also famous for its healing springs and the healing golden sand near the lake that surrounds it, as well as for its medicinal plants and the five varieties of juniper blessed by Vajrapāṇi that grow there.[132]

These different examples show that Grapard's categories of sacred mountains often overlap each other, that is, the same mountain can combine the three characteristics in different proportions. The third type—the mountain as protector of the sacred nation—is best represented by the cult to the Four Holy Mountains that enclose Urga—Bogda Khan, Songgina, Chenggeltü and Bayan Jirükhe,[133] which form a *maṇḍala* of Cakrasaṃvara. From the eighteenth

---

127   It is located three hundred kilometers west of Uliastai in Zavkhan Province.

128   Wallace 2008: 49.

129   In the 1990s Vajrapāṇi was reinstated by the Mongol government as the protector of the Mongol state, and its cult aims at bringing merit and security to the state and prosperity to the nation.

130   Tib. *riksum gönpo* (Barsbold 2004: 46; Wallace 2008).

131   The Fifth Dilowa Khutugtu mentions his pilgrimage to Otkhon Tngri in his autobiography: Lattimore and Isono 1982: 91.

132   Wallace 2008: 49.

133   Cyr. Mo. Bogd Khan, Songino Khairkhan, Chingelt Khairkhan and Bayanzürkh. See Dulam 2004. For a description of the *ambans'* worship of Bogda Khan Mountain: Jambal, ed. Bawden 1997: 16; Pozdneev 1971 [1896]: 50-51. It is not clear when the Qing state cult began; the earliest reference is the ceremony of 1778. According to legend, Bogd Khan was a

century on, the Qing state organized ceremonies to the Four Holy Mountains.[134] The two *amban*s of Urga had the political duty to make offerings of incense, candles and silk stuffs to Bogda Khan Mountain.[135] During the autumn celebration of Bogda Khan in the late nineteenth century, lamas presented offerings on the summit of the mountain, while the Jebtsündamba Khutugtu held a similar service in a small temple of Urga in honor of Padmasambhava, "who taught the Buddhists (how) to appease the spirits of the earth."[136] Like the terraces of Wutaishan (Fig. 5), the summit of Bogda Khan is a flat area that gives the impression of a large altar, with a temple named Bogda-yin Kheid (on Tsetsen Güng Peak), only open for ceremonies. The temple was dedicated to the mountain god, as well as to national heroes and ancestors of Mongols.[137] In some way, the configuration of Wutaishan resembles that of the great Urga monastic city surrounded by four sacred mountains.

In conclusion, there is no exact equivalent of a *néri* (Grapard's second category) in Mongolia. Otkhon Tngri and Bogda Khan were partially Buddhicized mountains, but pilgrims continued to ride on horses up to the summit and to make sacrifices to the mountain deity at the main *oboo*, and they did not practice circumambulation of the whole mountain. In some cases, however, in addition to the circumambulation of the *oboo*, pilgrims circumambulated the

---

sanctuary since the thirteenth century because Chinggis Khan was said to have been born at its foot.

134 During the third month, the traders of Maimaicheng (the Chinese traders' district) went to the summit of Bayan Jirükhe, because its master-spirit was seen as protecting fortune; monks and scholars went to Chenggeltü during the second month, because its master-spirit represented the literate world; residents of the western suburbs and soldiers went to Songgina, because its master-spirit was considered to be a warrior. But all venerated Bogda Khan, including statesmen, because its master-spirit was believed to be a protector of the state and of religion (Dulam 2004).

135 Pozdneev (1971 [1896]: 51) only mentions these offerings, but perhaps horses were also sacrificed, since the mountains were allocated their own horse herds to supply provisions for the rituals. The state sacrifice (*törö-yin takhilga-tai uula*) to Bogda Khan, Burkhan Khaldun and Otkhon Tngri, which were interrupted in the 1930s, were reinstituted in 1995 by a decree issued by P. Ochirbat (president of the Republic of Mongolia from 1990 to 1997). Once every four years, the president, followed by a large retinue, climbs the Burkhan Khaldun and makes offerings at the summit. A giant appliqué *thangka* representing Vajrapāṇi topped by Avalokiteśvara on his right side and Mañjuśrī on his left and, below, the three great Mongol emperors—Ögedei, Chinggis and Khubilai—was displayed on a slope of Otkhon Tngri during the 2010 sacrifice (Wallace 2008: 50).

136 Pozdneev 1971 [1896]: 42.

137 It housed a statue of Garuḍa, a set of armor, a helmet, saddles, bridles, bows and arrows belonging to two descendants of Chinggis Khan and a two-ton bronze kettle.

summit (at Otkhon Tngri, for instance), which may be related to Buddhist influ-ence.[138] In the twenty-first century, the Buddhicization process of Bogda Khan[139] and Otkhon Tngri[140] is continuing; circumambulation of Mongol mountains seems to be a new phenomenon.

By contrast, Wutaishan presents all the three characteristics in Grapard's ty-pology, and we will see in Chapter 4 how Tibetan and Mongol clerics strove hard to make Wutaishan enter the category of *néri*.

## Conclusion

The historical and anthropological evidence presented here suggests that Bud-dhist and non-Buddhist pilgrimages within Mongolia have played a larger role in Mongol religious life than usually assumed. They contributed to partially Buddhicizing Mongol territory through the assimilation of local cults, practices and deities. Gilubar Juu, Tövkhen Kheid and Lobonchinbu Süme—with their fantastic legends about the presence of buddhas, their caves, footprints of dei-ties and saints, and sacred springs—represent the transposition of typical Ti-betan pilgrimage themes to the Mongol landscape that we will find in Wutaishan too. Many sites possess several or most of the variables that characterize those 'spiritual magnetic sites,' as described by Preston:[141] miraculous cures (such as springs associated with healing), an awe-inspiring location (Gilubar Juu, Lobonchinbu Süme), the presence of living saints (high reincarnations), a sa-cralized geography and miraculous icons and relics (Urga, Lhasa), difficulty of access, trade opportunities and so on. Each site has its own 'power.'

---

138    Tatár 1976: 10, n. 41. The circumambulation of an *oboo* is slightly different from that of a Buddhist *stūpa*, temple or statue: devotees turn their body outwards around an *oboo*, while they turn inwards (sometimes touching the object of worship with their head) around a *stūpa* or a temple. Pilgrims also circumambulate specific holy places on the mountain, such as sacred stones or trees.

139    In July 2001, an ecologist movement, together with the monks of Ulaanbaatar's Dashichoiling Monastery, organized a circumambulation of Bogda Khan with the whole *Kanjur* and *Tanjur*, plus recitation of *sūtras* and tea aspersions. Participants were forbidden to get drunk, carry a weapon, dump garbage in nature or damage the trees and soil (*Email Daily News* 21/09/01). See also Croner 2008a: 12-14.

140    For a project of publication of a Mongolian and English pilgrimage guidebook "for the circumambulation route around Mount Otgontenger, including the shamanistic and pre-Buddhist folklore": Website Nekorpa: "Pilgrimage Guide to Otgontenger."

141    Preston 1992: 33-38.

Pilgrimage sites within Mongolia and abroad are varied and do not consti-tute a coherent and institutionalized network linking one shrine to another, comparable, for instance, to Hindu holy sites of India,[142] to the Four Grand and Famous Mountains of China or to Tibetan pilgrimage sites.[143] Rather, the many pilgrimage sites address different audiences. Lamas, deeply religious laypersons and trader-cum-pilgrims who were not afraid of a lengthy, far-flung adventure journeyed to Lhasa, while more 'ordinary' Mongol men and women simply looking for merit, blessings or cures found supra-local Mongol mountains and Wutaishan more accessible. It took only a few weeks for Inner Mongols to reach Wutaishan (even though for Kalmyks and Buryats, Wutaishan and Beijing were almost as difficult to reach as Lhasa and Kumbum). As we will see, women es-pecially favored Wutaishan, while few, if any, women traveled among groups of traders, lamas and diplomatic delegations journeying to Lhasa and Beijing. And while Mongols could content themselves with local or supra-local pilgrimages to holy monasteries and mountains, visiting Wutaishan once in their lifetime was almost an obligation for a good Buddhist from the nineteenth century on. The following chapter focuses on the spiritual and material reasons that make Wutaishan one of the most spiritually 'magnetic sites for Mongols.

The spiritual magnetism of pilgrimage sites also varied over time, according to the difficulties of travel, the political situation and the presence or absence of famous reincarnations, icons and relics. As early as the seventeenth century, Mongol devotees followed the Dalai Lama's travels in Mongolia and undertook pilgrimages to Lhasa and Kumbum, but they were only drawn in great numbers to Wutaishan later, as will be evidenced in the following chapters, with journeys there reaching an apogee in the late nineteenth and early twentieth centuries. On the other hand, pilgrimages to Chinggisid relics began to exert a powerful draw in the nineteenth century, when Chinggis Khan started to be viewed as the supreme ancestral deity of all Mongols. Pilgrimages to Beijing developed during the Qing period but stopped after 1900. Early twentieth-century Mon-gols were also interested in Chinese Buddhism and culture (see Chapter 6) and visited other pilgrimages centers of mainland China. The development of mod-ern transportation in the beginning of the twentieth century benefited Mon-gols' international pilgrimages not only to Wutaishan but also to Putuoshan, Lhasa, Bodnāth and India. Under the Manchukuo, some lamas had the oppor-tunity to study in the Buddhist schools of Japan and to visit Japanese holy sites. Yet in the 1990s and 2000s, revived and new pilgrimage sites emerged in the Republic of Mongolia, making local sites once more appealing, while pilgrim-ages abroad were almost abandoned.

---

142    Bhardwaj 1973.
143    Huber 1990; Kapstein 1998: 112.

CHAPTER 2

# The Invention of Wutaishan

...

In the southeast of Tai-chou 岱州, there is the Five Terrace Mountain. Anciently, it was said to be the dwelling of divine transcendants. This mountain encompasses three hundred *li* square, and its terrain is exceedingly precipitous and lofty.

There are five tall terraces. Grasses and trees do not grow on its summits. A dense forest of conifers is overgrown on the valley floor. This mountain is extremely cold. Those to the south call it Mount Clear-and-Cool (Yanyi, *Guang Qingliang zhuan,* 1060, transl. Birnbaum 1986: 120).

··
·

As pointed out by Robert Gimello, Turner's notion of liminality in pilgrimages can apply not only to the state of mind of the pilgrims but also to the place itself. Wutaishan appears as a liminal yet relatively accessible site: it is at the same time a pure land, a 'buddha land' (*buddhakṣetra*, Mo. *burkhan-u oron* ['abode of buddhas/deities'], Ch. *fotu* 佛土)—and 'part of the ordinary world.'[1] In this kind of 'middle realm,'[2] ordinary men and women have the possibility to come in contact with the *bodhisattva*. Tang-dynasty Chan monk-pilgrim Daoyi 道義 had a vision of himself visiting a 'transformation monastery' along with an old man, who was none other than Mañjuśrī:

When I arrived to travel at the mountain I only saw hillocks, grass, and trees. Now I see here (in the temple) gold and jade towers. For this reason, I am uncertain as to whether Wutai is a pure 淨 (land) or a part of the ordinary 穢 (defiled world). I cannot resolve whether the holy and ordinary are distinguished (here).[3]

---

1 Gimello 1994: 503, 554-555 n. 2; Köhle 2008: 94 n. 99.

2 Birnbaum 2004: 215.

3 *Qingding Qingliangshan zhi*, translated by Andrews 2011: 148. This would be the origin of Jingesi that was eventually constructed according to Daoyi's vision (Gimello 1992).

This second chapter sketches an overview of the mountain's natural, human and divine geography, followed by its history before the Qing dynasty, in order to highlight the intrinsic characteristics of Wutaishan that explain why it was chosen as a mountain of 'spiritual significance,' first by the Chinese, then by Buddhists from all over Asia and eventually by Mongols. It will help measure Wutaishan's 'spiritual magnetism' according to three of Preston's four components: apparitions of supernatural beings; geography sacralized by history and by the presence of deities and spirits; and difficulty of access.[4]

## Earthly Wutaishan

Wutaishan literally means 'Five-Terraced Mountain(s),' referring to its five summits with flat tops, one at each cardinal point and the fifth in the middle. Its more canonical name in ancient Chinese sources is 'Clear and Cool Mountains' (Qingliangshan 清涼山).[5] Wutaishan is the most ancient and most prominent pan-Asiatic Buddhist sacred site in China. It is home to many of China's most important monasteries and temples and has preserved the oldest extant wooden buildings in China.[6]

Wutaishan is located relatively far from urban centers and was considered a Buddhist retreat, "a kind of spiritual rampart of the empire"[7] isolated from urban social life. From the Shunzhi period of the Qing dynasty until well into the Republican period, the holy mountain was a Tibeto-Mongol enclave on the edge of Chinese territory with a status of extraterritoriality, ruled by the representative of the Dalai Lama. However, its remote location has not hindered its institutional and economic development. Being at the crossroads between Tibet, Inner Asia and China, Wutaishan has served as a religious, economic and political meeting point for the populations from those three areas and was

---

4  Preston 1992: 33-38.
5  Translated in Mongolian as Serüün Tunggalag Uula ('Cool and Clear Mountains') and transcribed as Tsing Liyang Shan Uula.
6  The Buddha halls of Nanchansi 南禪寺 and Foguangsi 佛光寺 have survived since the Tang dynasty (618-907) (Rhie 1977). Not far from Wutaishan are found a great number of ancient historical sites, such as the Yungang Grottoes, Huayan 華嚴寺 and Shanhua Monasteries 善化寺 of Datong, Mount Hengshan 恒山 (one of the 'Five Great Peaks' of China) and nearby Hanging Monastery (Xuankongsi 懸空寺). On Wutaishan architecture: Wang Jinping 2005; Lin 2014.
7  Gimello 1992: 99.

connected with a Buddhist institutional pan-Asian network.[8] It has become the most important place in Inner China where Chinese and Tibetan traditions of Buddhism cohabit and mingle, allowing Wutaishan to become a place of encounter between monks and pilgrims from all of East and Central Asia.

### Geography, Climate and Ecology of Wutaishan

Wutaishan is located in Wutai County 五臺縣 (Xin Prefecture 忻州),[9] north of Shanxi Province, and belongs to the Taihang 太行山 mountain range, which stretches almost all the way to Beijing.[10] It lies about 530 kilometers southwest of Beijing, between Taiyuan (about 120 kilometers to its south) and Datong (about 230 kilometers to its north) (Map 7). Towering over the arid loess plain, this frontier region at the very edge of the Chinese empire, not far from the (Inner) Mongol border materialized by the Great Wall, was at certain periods the epicenter of non-Chinese powers, such as the Northern Wei dynasty (386-534), which sculpted the Yungang 雲崗 Grottoes.[11] Shanxi Province was from the Song to the Qing the center of trade and banking societies, as well as of coal and iron mining. In the Qing period, the Shanxi merchants (*jinshang* 晋商) conducted trade between China and Mongolia.

Despite their names, the five terraces are not exactly arranged according to the points of the compass; the Western, Central, Northern and Eastern Terraces lie fairly close to each other and belong to the same chain of mountains, while the Southern Terrace stands apart. 'Wutaishan' first designates the sacred area inside the boundary of the five terraces and is also the name of a larger mountain range belonging to the Taihang Mountains. The sacred area, with a perimeter of about 500 *li*, i.e., 250 kilometers, was in ancient days slowly approached from the four directions by four narrow mountain roads often blocked by snowfalls or landslides. The four 'gates,' where each road entered the sacred area, were marked by the presence of steles and temples. The southern road (nowadays taken by visitors coming from Taiyuan) crossed Wutai County; the eastern road was taken by the emperors coming from Beijing; the northern road was taken by Mongol pilgrims but was dangerous because of the high altitude and risks of snow and wind preventing visitors from going further; the western road

---

8    In some recent studies, Wutaishan is presented as a perfect example of the "union of minorities/nationalities" (*minzu tuanjie* 民族團結) (Zhao Gaiping and Hou Huiming 2006).

9    In the Ming and Qing dynasties, Wutaishan was under the jurisdiction of Dai Prefecture 代州. In the Republican period it came under the jurisdiction of Wutai Prefecture.

10   It extends approximately from 113°15' to 113°45' east longitude and from 38°45' to 39°45' north latitude.

11   The Han now represent more than 99 percent of the population of Shanxi.

was often preferred by Mongols coming from the north.[12] The spread-out configuration of Wutaishan, with five terraces and more than a hundred monasteries, is very different from that of the other Chinese holy mountains, such as Taishan 泰山 (Shandong Province) or Huashan 華山 (Shaanxi), most of which are vertical peaks in the middle of a plain that visitors climb in one day from bottom to top, following steep staircases.

The area's high altitude—all the terraces are about 2,500 to 3,000 meters high, the Northern Terrace, at 3,058 meters above sea level, being called 'the roof of North China'—renders the growing season short, and the mountainous, rocky terrain limits the amount of land suitable for farming. The valleys are moderately arable and the slopes are now thickly forested. Wutaishan has a residing Chinese population living in a dozen villages established in the valleys.[13]

Wutaishan possesses many unique features that predisposed it to being chosen as a holy mountain.[14] They include its natural configuration of the five terraces (five is a highly symbolic number in Buddhism and in Chinese beliefs, and is especially linked to Mañjuśrī),[15] its high altitude and pure air, its unusual flora (including rare medicinal herbs and mushrooms) and fauna, and its numerous strange caves and subterranean springs. The bare, flat-topped terraces almost devoid of vegetation and rising above the tree line are compared to reversed alms bowls, to thrones for deities or to altars,[16] contributing to the mountain's otherworldly appearance (Fig. 6). Wutaishan's cold weather and clear streams earned it the appellation 'Clear and Cool Mountains' in ancient Chinese sources. The weather is volatile, characterized by frequent rain, sudden snowstorms, thunderstorms and hailstorms that can strike even in mid-summer on the terraces, thick mist and the occurrence of rainbows and beams of light due to the interplay of sunlight with varying levels of humidity. Ice is found even during the summer months. Wutaishan can be difficult to access

---

12    For a description of the roads: Ono Katsutoshi and Hibino Takao 1942: 129-133.

13    On the customs, life and "bad habits" of Wutaishan farmers in the early twentieth century: Li Xiangzhi 1932: 156-160; Ono Katsutoshi and Hibino Takao 1942: 142-143. Many new villages were built in the late 2000s for the growing population of migrants.

14    On unusual features of climate and environment as evidence of the profound spiritual meaning of a mountain in Tibet: Kapstein 1998: 96.

15    Mañjuśrī's *mantra* has five syllables; one of Mañjuśrī's epithets, Pancacīraka, 'Possessing Five [Hair-] braids,' refers to his five tufts of hair (or topknots tied in the manner of a youth) or a tiara with five points. He presents affinities with a celestial musician named Pañcaśikha, 'Five-crested' or 'Five-peaked,' which provides additional justification for the association of the *bodhisattva* with a five-peaked or five-terraced mountain range in China (Lalou 1930: 66-70; Tribe 1994a).

16    Birnbaum 1986: 121.

FIGURE 6     *View of the Northern Terrace from the Central Terrace, and the Southern Terrace.*
© ISABELLE CHARLEUX, 2010.

from October to April: the long winters are extremely rigorous with low temperatures and heavy snow, keeping pilgrims and tourists off the mountain. The temperatures, ranging between minus thirty to thirty degrees Celcius, are comparable to those of the Mongol plateau. Nowadays on Wutaishan, winter is a time for study, seclusion and meditation, whereas summer, the pilgrimage season, is bustling with activity, but we will see that the cold season did not deter Qing-period Mongols from undertaking the pilgrimage.

The ecology of Wutaishan is close to that of the Tibetan plateau, and Tibetans who had great difficulties adjusting to the Beijing climate felt at home there. Furthermore, it is still today described by some older Tibetans as belonging to Tibetan territory.[17] In the Qing and Republican periods, Wutaishan was also seen as an extension of the nearby Mongol plateau, and Mongol herders used to pasture their flocks and herds on its slopes. Yet the ecology then was quite different from how it had been in ancient times and how it is now. Before the Ming period, Wutaishan occupied a strategic position: the extensive pine, larch, and birch forest covering its slopes functioned as an inner barrier defending China from 'barbarians.' Massive deforestation occurred around the year 1580, when timber merchants from neighboring counties and farmers cut down the forests, and the hermits retiring there from society were driven out.[18] The Chinese gazetteers all deplored that the beautiful landscape now looked like pastures, "like a steppe such as the barbarian Mongols inhabited."[19] Fearing intrusions of 'northern barbarians,' the Ming state then issued a strict prohibition against the sale of wood.[20] However, with the rise of Manchu power, considerable areas of land were opened to cultivation in the years following 1644. During the eighteenth century, due to massive population growth in Shanxi, even more land was opened for cultivation.

Deforestation continued to progress, both for agriculture and timber (which was then in huge demand) but also to open coal mines, quarries and lime kilns.[21] The tigers and other wild beasts, which were still encountered in the late

---

17    Kheru Khangyal, a fifty-seven-year-old Tibetan, describes Tibet as "stretching from the Great Mountains in the Upper Region (Stod) to Wu-t'ai-shan in the Lower region (Smed)" (Rinchen Sangpo 2009).

18    On monks and officials fighting to protect the forests: Wang Zhiyong and Cui Zhengsen 2000: 606, 678-679.

19    *Qingliangshan zhi* 1887 [1596]: *juan* 5, 25v, *Qingliangshan xinzhi* 1985 [1694]: *juan* 5, 20r; *Qinding Qingliangshan zhi* 1785: *juan* 21, 16r, quoted by Lowdermilk and Wickes 1938: 5.

20    Lowdermilk and Wickes 1938: 7.

21    They are located near Wutaixian and Daixian (Bai Meichu 2010 [1925]: *juan* 2, 92; Zhang Dungu 1911: 23).

seventeenth century, disappeared from the mountain.[22] Although Wutaishan was famous in all of China for its production of mushrooms, timber and medicinal plants,[23] by the early twentieth century, Chinese farmers were cultivating oats, millet, potatoes, soya beans, buckwheat, cabbages, rhubarb and even poppies. The forests had been completely cut down except for some preserved groves around a few monasteries. Horse dung was burned rather than wood to heat *kangs* 炕 (heated sleeping platforms) throughout the region. Fields of potatoes and hemp nearly reached the summits, and non-arable land suffered extensive grazing by herders.[24] The People's Republic of China made a massive effort of reforestation under Mao Zedong, and, although cultivation of the soil (in the valleys) and grazing (near the terraces) are still practiced, many of the slopes are now covered with forests, and Wutaishan has recovered its alpine atmosphere.

### The Human-built Buddhist Environment

In pilgrimage sites, the Buddhicization of a landscape is first realized by creating a Buddhist built environment, including monasteries and their statues, isolated shrines and *stūpa*s, texts written in Chinese and Tibetan,[25] images and footprints of deities carved in the rock, [26] and cemeteries—as explained by Raoul Birnbaum,[27] the mountain becomes an icon comparable to a painting with image and text. Secondly, the distinctive features of the landscape are perceived or reinterpreted as numinous sites,[28] that is, natural features endowed with numinous power. Although the Ming and Qing gazetteers make a clear distinction between built monasteries and numinous sites, there is much

---

22  But not completely, since Gao Henian (2000 [1949]: 117) saw tiger or leopard footprints in 1912 and wrote that monks used conches to frighten them.

23  Bai Meichu 2010 [1925]: *juan* 2, 73; Li Xiangzhi 1932: 154-156; Rockhill 1895: 765; Ono Katsutoshi and Hibino Takao 1942: 143. The staple food on Wutaishan was steamed oatmeal or oat porridge with butter from Mongolia (Pokotilov 1935 [1893]: 67).

24  See the comprehensive study of the ecology and soil use of Wutaishan by Lowdermilk and Wickes 1938.

25  Like in other sacred Chinese and Tibetan mountains, texts are carved on the rock faces and cliffs. They can be found on the cliff near Tailusi (Tailu ziyai 台麓字崖), on the way to and at Shouningsi, at Mimoyan and at Guanyindong (also Fischer 1923: 85, 87; Ono Katsutoshi and Hibino Takao 1942: 191: pl. 39).

26  Tibetan Buddhist deities carved in the rock are seen near Guanyindong, Sanquansi, Cifusi, Zhenhaisi and Mimoyan.

27  Birnbaum 1989-1990: 117.

28  Ch. *lingji* 靈蹟, 'numinous traces,' Mo. *adistidtu jokhiyal*, 'blessed creations/works' (*CLŠASB* 1701: 143)

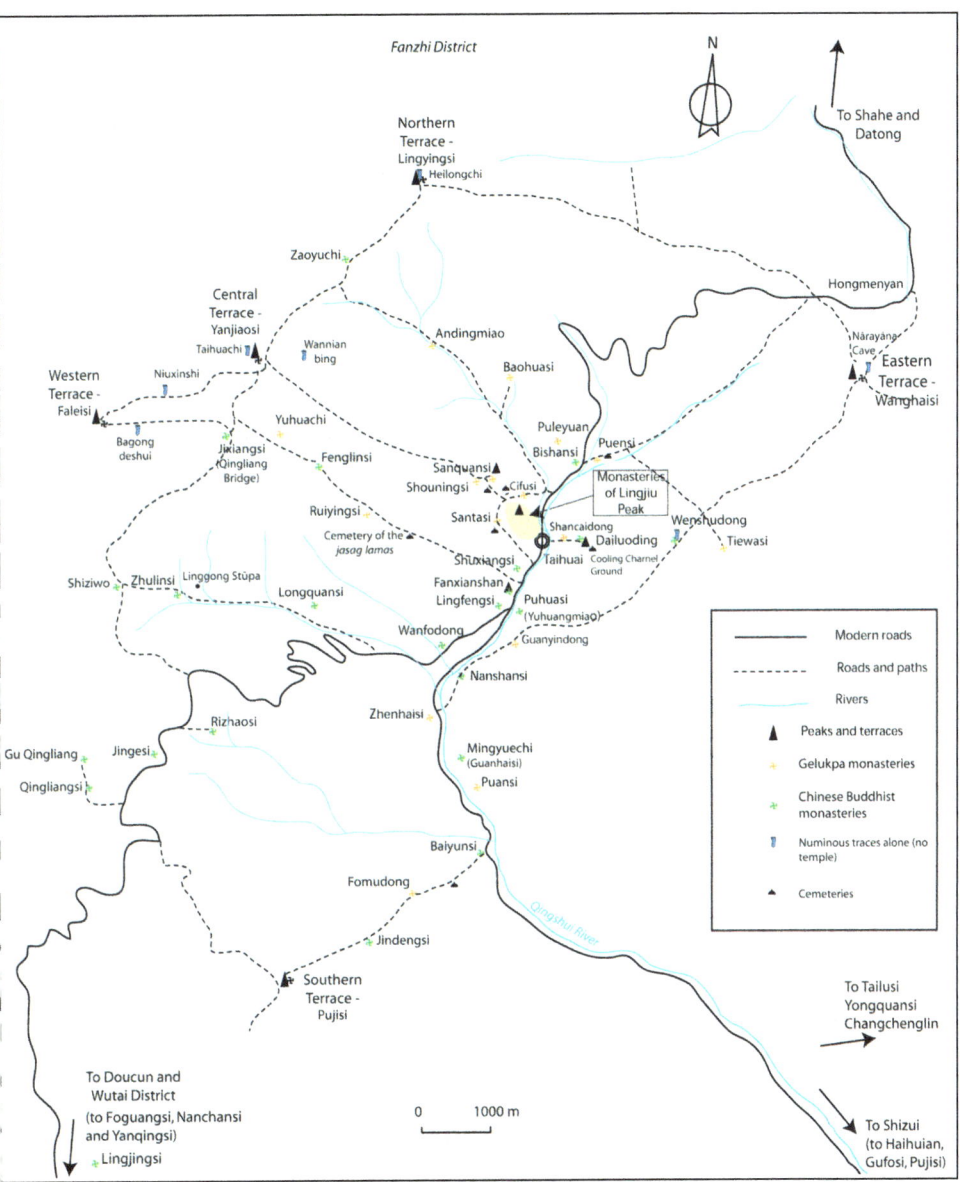

MAP 3    *General map of Wutaishan, distinguishing between the 'Yellow' and 'Blue' monasteries of the late Qing period.* © ISABELLE CHARLEUX.

*Note on the maps*: few modern maps of Wutaishan are accurate; I therefore used material such as Google-Earth satellite maps to complete and correct them.

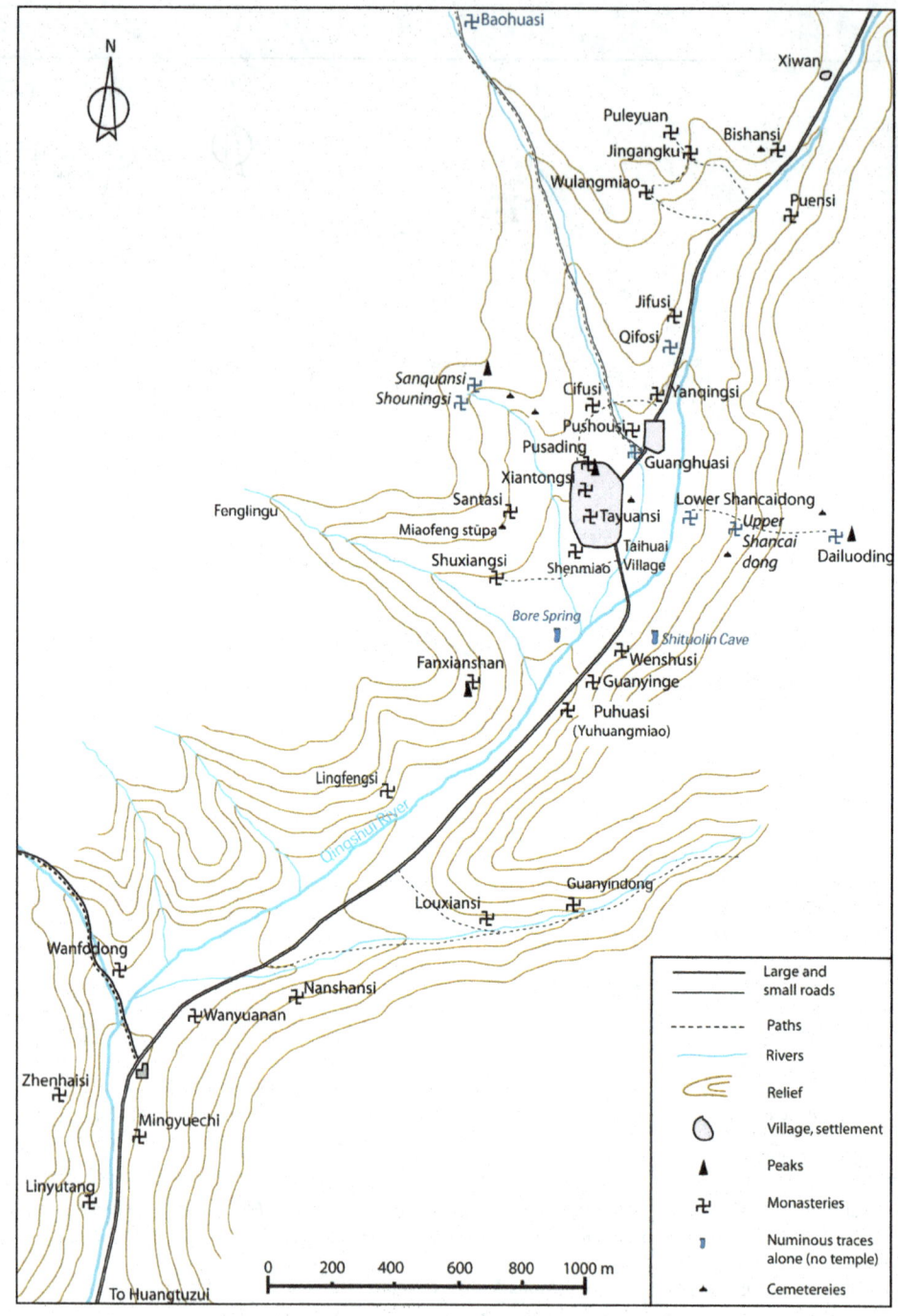

卍Baohuasi

Xiwan

Puleyuan
卍
Jingangku 卍 卍 Bishansi
▲
Wulangmiao 卍
Puensi
卍

Jifusi
卍
Qifosi
卍

*Sanquansi* 卍 Cifusi 卍 卍 Yanqingsi
*Shouningsi* 卍 ▲ Pushousi 卍
Pusading 卍
▲ Guanghuasi
Xiantongsi 卍 卍
Fenglingu Santasi 卍 Lower Shancaidong ▲
*Miaofeng stūpa* ▲ 卍 Tayuansi 卍 *Upper*
Shuxiangsi Taihuai 卍 *Shancai*
卍 Shenmiao Village *dong*
Dailuoding ▲

*Bore Spring* 𝕀
𝕀 *Shituolin Cave*
Fanxianshan 卍 Wenshusi
▲ 卍 Guanyinge
卍 Puhuasi
(Yuhuangmiao)

Lingfengsi 卍

Guanyindong
Louxiansi 卍 卍

Wanfodong 卍

Nanshansi 卍
卍 Wanyuanan

Zhenhaisi 卍

Mingyuechi 卍

Linyutang 卍

To Huangtuzui

0 200 400 600 800 1000 m

| | Large and small roads |
|---|---|
| --- | Paths |
| ～ | Rivers |
| ⊂ | Relief |
| ◯ | Village, settlement |
| ▲ | Peaks |
| 卍 | Monasteries |
| 𝕀 | Numinous traces alone (no temple) |
| ▲ | Cemetereies |

MAP 4      *Map of the central part of Wutaishan, from Ono Katsutoshi and Hibino Takao 1942, with some additions in italics.* © ISABELLE CHARLEUX.

overlap in this classification since several monasteries were built on or include numinous sites within their precincts. Besides, relics and the man-made *stūpas* that enshrine them are listed in the gazetteers as 'numinous traces.'

In the late Qing and Republican periods, there were up to twenty-seven Tibetan Buddhist monasteries and seventy-eight Chinese Buddhist monasteries on Wutaishan.[29] The gazetteers make a distinction between the monasteries located within the area delimited by the five terraces ('inside the terraces,' *tainei* 臺內) and those located outside the terraces (*taiwai* 臺外): the first ones form the core of the pilgrimage (Map 3). The Chinese further differentiate between monasteries 'of the Ten Directions' (*shifang* 十方)—'public' monasteries that were the property of the Buddhist order at large, and accommodate pilgrim monks and nuns (and for some of them, lay pilgrims too)—, and hereditary monasteries (*zisunmiao* 子孫廟), which function as a closed and local system, whereby an ordained monk teaches to a few disciples who do not travel to other monasteries; this distinction can also apply to Gélukpa monasteries such as Zhenhaisi 鎮海寺 and Pusading.[30]

A short physical description of the main places to visit may help the reader understand the configuration of the religious landscape (Map 3, Map 4). The most symbolic sight is the gigantic White Stūpa (Daci yanshou baota 大慈延壽 宝塔, shortened as Dabaota 大宝塔).[31] This bottle-shaped monument, which rises to just over fifty-four meters in height, is believed to enshrine one of the eighty-four thousand relics of Śākyamuni disseminated by the Indian Emperor Aśoka (r. ca. 274-ca. 236 BC). Visible from afar, it plays the role of a lighthouse that orients the pilgrims (Fig. 7, Fig. 8). The *stūpa* stands within the Tayuansi

---

29    According to official figures, 47 monasteries (and 24,108 statues) survived the Cultural Revolution and more than 20 were rebuilt or newly built in the 1990s-2000s thanks to donations from all over China, Taiwan, Japan, Korea and Nepal, etc. Among the 44 monasteries located in the core area in 2010, 7 are Tibetan Buddhist, 7 are Han Gélukpa, 25 are Chinese monk monasteries, and 5 are Chinese nunneries. Some of them changed affiliation during the twentieth century.

30    Szczepanski 2008: 123. Pilgrims are informed of a monastery's status because in the *lokapāla*s hall the statue of Weituo raises his *vajra* up in a *shifang* monastery and down in a *zisunmiao*. For a list of *shifangtang* and *zisunmiao* monasteries on Wutaishan in the 1980s: *Wutaixian zhi* 1988: 583.

31    The list of "Monasteries and numinous sites visited by Mongol pilgrims on Wutaishan" (Online Appendix B) presents the main numinous sites and the temples and monasteries, focusing on Qing and Republican history and connections with Mongols. It lists for each of them their different names in Chinese, Tibetan and Mongolian, and gives details on their history, architecture, iconography and special features, and their Chinese imperial and non-imperial steles. It is synthesized in Appendix 1.

FIGURE 7     *General ancient view of the Great White Stūpa and its surroundings.*
             © BOERSCHMANN 1923 (*photograph taken between 1906-1909*).

FIGURE 8     *General view of the Great White Stūpa and its surroundings.*
             © ISABELLE CHARLEUX 2009.

temple area and is the central place of worship for all pilgrims. Right outside its entrance is the Chinese temple of the Five Dragon Kings of Wutaishan (Wuye-miao 五爺廟, official name: Wanfoge 萬佛閣), where a well-attended opera is performed during festivals.

Tayuansi stands at the foot of a small peak (1,789 meters high), which has historically been viewed as the Chinese counterpart of the Vulture Peak (Gṛdhrakūta),[32] where Śākyamuni Buddha preached the scriptures, hence its ancient name, Numinous Vulture Peak (Lingjiu Fengding 靈鷲峰頂) (Map 5). The main, most ancient and prestigious monasteries cluster on this peak; they are accessible by Yanglin Street 楊林街 leading to the top. The oldest and largest Chinese Buddhist monastery on Wutaishan is Xiantongsi 顯通寺, which still preserves important Ming-dynasty architecture such as the Beamless Hall and the Gilded Bronze Pavilion. Facing Xiantongsi's entrance, Rāhula Monastery (Luohousi), an ancient Tibetan Buddhist site, is famous for its revolving lotus, an elaborate articulated sculpture that opens to 'reveal the buddhas.' Below it, Shifangtang (or Guangrensi 廣仁寺), anciently a dependence of Luohousi, was the main lodging center for Tibetan and Mongol lamas during the Qing and Republican periods. Up on Yanglin Street are Yuanzhaosi 圓照寺, which enshrines the funerary *stūpa* of Śāriputra Paṇḍita, a fifteenth-century Indian monk, and Guangzongsi 廣宗寺 Monastery. Reached by a 108-step stairway, the Great Bodhisattva (Mañjuśrī) Peak (or Bodhisattva's Uṣṇīṣa), Pusading, with its shining golden roofs, towers over the surrounding buildings (Fig. 12). This ancient imperial monastery run by Tibetan and Mongol lamas preserves stone inscriptions recording imperial favors. During the Qing and the Republican period up to 1937, it was the residence monastery of the *jasag lama* ('head lama'), who presided over the whole clergy of Wutaishan. Early twentieth-century travelers compared its splendor with that of the Beijing Imperial Palace.[33]

At the foot of the Numinous Vulture Peak, Taihuaizhen, the main village of Wutaishan (1,703 meters above sea level), offers hotels, guesthouses, restaurants and shops for pilgrims. South of the great *stūpa*, the Qing-dynasty palace called Imperial City (Huangcheng 皇城), built in 1760, is no longer extant; it served as

---

32   The name of this monastery comes from the place in Bihar (India) where Buddha set forth the second turning of the wheel of Dharma to an assembly of five thousand monks, nuns and laypeople, as well as innumerable *bodhisattva*s. Wutaishan was also compared to the first royal Buddhist city of Rājagṛha (modern Rajgir), circled by five hills, just west of Gṛdhrakūta.

33   Gao Henian 2000 [1949]: 112; Blofeld 1959: 122.

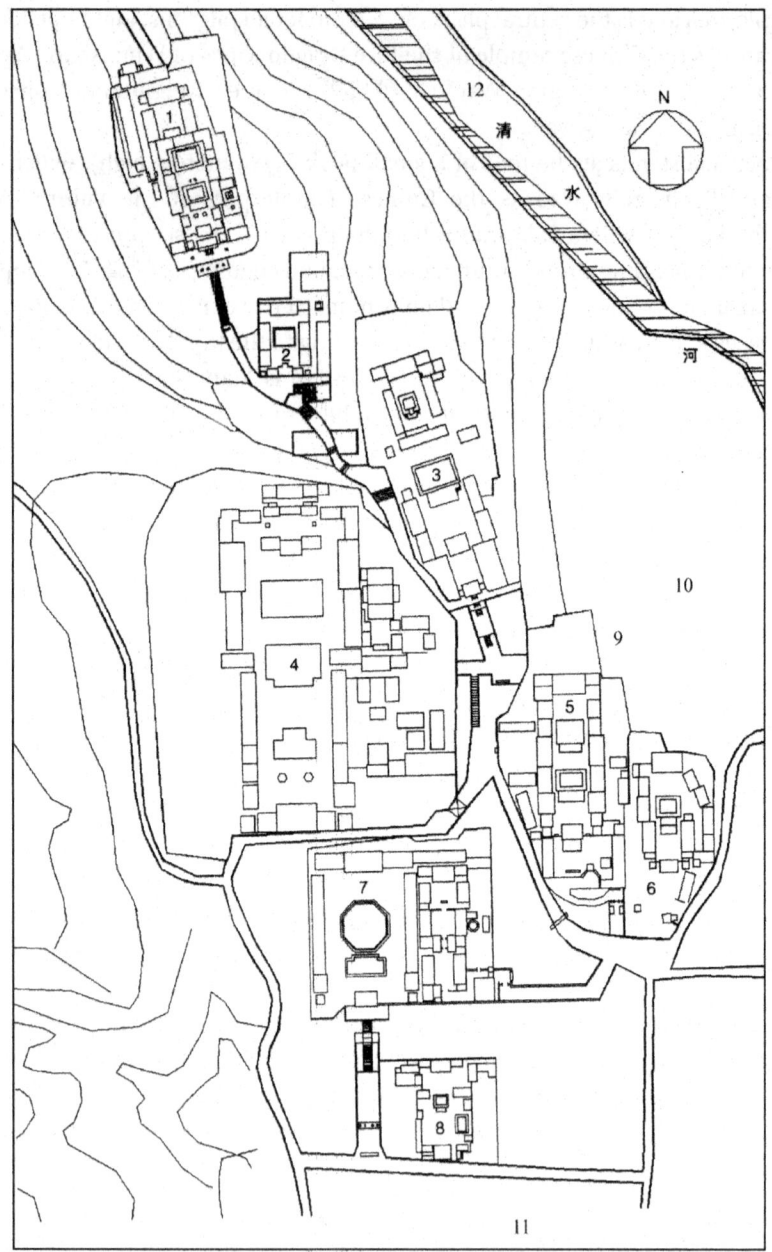

清水河

MAP 5        *Map of the Taihuai monasteries ( from Wang Jinping 2005: Fig. 1-31; Ono*
             *Katsutoshi and Hibino Takao 1942, with some additions).*

1. Pusading; 2. Guangzongsi; 3. Yuanzhaosi; 4. Xiantongsi; 5. Luohousi; 6. Shifangtang;
7. Tayuansi; 8. Wanfoge (Wuyuemiao); 9. Taiping Street; 10. Cemetery; 11. Ruins of the imperial
traveling lodge; 12. Qingshui River.

the touring palace and audience hall for Qing emperors,[34] and was already in ruins by the end of the nineteenth century. In the early twentieth century the remaining hall was used as stables for the soldiers' horses.[35]

North of Pusading, Cifusi was another lodging center for Mongol lamas. This monastery is where the woodblocks for the 'Cifusi map' were carved in 1846. West of Pusading, Santasi 三塔寺, with its three Tibetan *stūpas* in a row, was a branch monastery of Pusading. A mountain path climbing towards Shouningsi 壽寧寺 and Sanquansi 三泉寺 on top of a peak, overhangs a large cemetery for monks and laypersons. East of Taihuai, a bridge crossing the Clear Water River (Qingshuihe 清水河) gives access to Dailuoding Peak 黛螺頂, with the Lower and Upper Sudhana Cave Monastery (Shancaidong 善財洞) and, on its summit, Dailuoding Monastery, where the five Mañjuśrīs of the five terraces have been worshipped since the mid-Qing period. Dailuoding was a substitute pilgrimage for those who could not visit the five terraces due to bad weather (or to lack of time).

Other monasteries are located in the valley along or near the main road that follows the Qingshui River: Guanghuasi 廣化寺, Pushousi 普壽寺, Qifosi 七佛寺, Jifusi 集福寺 and Bishansi 碧山寺 towards the northeast (the road to Datong); and Shuxiangsi 殊像寺 (with its famous statue of Mañjuśrī), Puhuasi 普化寺, Nanshansi 南山寺, Zhenhaisi (enshrining the funerary *stūpa* of Rölpé Dorjé), Mingyuechi 明月池 and Puansi 普安寺 towards the south. Smaller monasteries are scattered in nearby valleys and ravines: Baohuasi 寶華寺 and its Nepalese-style *stūpa* believed to enshrine Tsongkhapa's lock of hair; Guanyindong 觀音洞, where the Sixth Dalai Lama is said to have meditated; Jingangku with its mysterious cave; Puleyuan 普樂院, a hermitage founded by Rölpé Dorjé; and, on the mountain slopes and passes on the way to the five terraces, Fomudong and its 'Mother's Womb-Cave,' Jingesi 金閣寺, Fenglinsi 楓林寺, Shiziwo 獅子窟, Jixiangsi 吉祥寺 and so forth. These off-track monasteries, temples and shrines were often built around natural numinous sites, like Zaoyuchi 澡浴池, erected around a sacred basin and Mañjuśrī's footprints.

Each terrace had a temple made of stone and vaulted in cave-dwelling style, dedicated to one of the five forms of Mañjuśrī, an attending *stūpa* and other

---

34    Li Xiangzhi 1932: 161-162; see its depiction on the 1846 Cifusi map. Besides the Taihuai Imperial City, the Qing emperors had two other travel palaces, in Baiyunsi (built under Kangxi's reign) and in Tailusi (built in 1685), but often liked to reside within Pusading (*Qinding Qingliangshan zhi* 1785: *juan* 10, 2v-5r).

35    Fischer 1923: 99.

small *stūpa*s of piled-up stones said to date from the Northern Wei dynasty.[36]
The Northern Terrace also has the Palace of the Black Dragon King (Heilong-
gong 黑龍宮).

The Qing-dynasty 'yellow' monasteries were concentrated in the main valley
of the Qingshui River, north and south of the village of Taihuai, and on the
mountain paths leading to the terraces (Map 3). The 'blue' monasteries were
scattered across a much wider area. In addition, every village had one or several
Chinese popular temples dedicated to Guanyin 觀音, the God of Wealth
(Caishen 財神), the Jade Emperor (Yuhuang 玉皇), the Three Emperors (Sanhuang 三皇: Huangdi 黃帝, Yao 堯 and Shun 舜) and so on.[37] Lingyingsi 靈應
寺, the Chinese temple of an ancient fox spirit who had become a Nainai 奶
奶-type of deity on Fanxianshan 梵仙山 Peak,[38] became one of the Buddhist
monasteries to visit in the pilgrims' circuits. The 1846 Cifusi map shows many
other human-built structures such as small fortified Chinese villages and settlements, bridges and isolated *stūpa*s (Fig. 3).

### *Homogeneity of Monastic Architecture*

The monasteries of Wutaishan all externally adopt Chinese architecture, with
compact layouts, narrow buildings, long staircases and high terraces that follow
the configuration of the landscape and, consequently, seldom respect the traditional southern orientation. Except for some vaulted stone temples (temples of
the five terraces and Lingyingsi), the buildings are Chinese-style wood and
brick halls composed of a framework supporting a large sloping roof covered
with tiles. They were continuously repaired, restored and enlarged, and the majority date to the Qing period. Some monasteries preserved *dhāraṇī* pillars
(*jingchuang* 經幢), multiple-storied pagodas and small *stūpa*s dating from the
Tang to the Ming dynasties.

Most of the monasteries have two small courtyards, sometimes three, with
an entrance hall also serving as a *lokapāla*s hall (hall of the guardian deities of

---

36   References in Birnbaum 1986: 120. Except for vaulted halls of the Southern, Eastern and
     Western Terraces, these temples were destroyed in the early twentieth century and rebuilt
     in the 2000s.

37   There was no Earth God Temple (Tudimiao 土地廟) on Wutaishan. Li Xiangzhi (1932:
     72-75) details his search of the Great Earth (God) of Shanxi and discovers it in a miniature
     shrine on a *stūpa* of Xiantongsi. Other Chinese shrines were located in caves (Shipendong
     石盆洞, Daxiandong 大仙洞 of Dong Xuanzhensi 東玄真寺) (Zhou Rubi and Li Guangyi
     2007: 377).

38   Generic name for female deities under the leadership of Bixia Yuanjun 碧霞元君, the
     Lady of Mount Taishan.

the four orients), drum and bell towers, a Buddha hall[39] with three colossal Buddha statues,[40] a Mañjuśrī hall,[41] and sometimes a two-storied scripture hall.[42] Venerable trees provide shade in the courtyards. The main monasteries display imperial signs in their central courtyards, such as name plaques that hang above doorways, written with the calligraphy of an emperor,[43] and large stone inscriptions, topped with dragons and standing on a tortoise, recording donations and poems by emperors.

Many Gélukpa communities had settled within ancient Chinese Buddhist monasteries and preserved their Chinese architectural heritage. Those that were built anew also adopted Chinese architecture with Chinese-style arch-ways, *lokapāla*s halls, refectories,[44] dormitories,[45] and so on, but the Chinese names of their pavilions sometimes do not correspond to the deities who are actually worshipped inside. For instance, instead of displaying a statue of Bodhidharma and paintings of deceased abbots, Pusading's ancestral hall enshrines statues of Padmasambhava and past masters. To the Chinese Bud-

---

39    The central building of the Chinese(-style) monastery is called Buddha hall (*fodian* 佛殿), big hall (*dadian* 大殿), or hall of the Great Hero (*daxiong baodian* 大雄寶殿), an epithet of Śākyamuni.

40    The Buddhas of the Three Times (Dīpankara, Śākyamuni and Maitreya) in Gélukpa monasteries and the Triad of Śākyamuni, Amitābha and Bhaiṣajyaguru in Chinese Buddhist monasteries.

41    When it enshrines statues of the three main *bodhisattvas* (Avalokiteśvara, Mañjuśrī and Samantabhadra), it is called 'Hall of the Three Holy Ones' (Sanshengdian 三聖殿) or 'Hall of the Three Great Masters' (Sandashidian 三大師殿).

42    A good introduction to Wutaishan Buddhist architecture is Wang Jinping 2005: Part I (see also Chai Zejun 1999). The oldest and most detailed description of Wutaishan monasteries, including their iconography, is Pokotilov 1935 [1893]: 58-89. On Chinese Buddhist architecture in general: Prip-Møller 1967 [1937]; on the different 'departments' of a Chi-nese monastery: Welch 1973 [1967].

43    In 2010, only Luohousi, Cifusi and Shifangtang had a Qing dynasty imperial name plaque written in the three (Chinese, Tibetan, Mongolian) or four languages (plus Manchu) of Qing Gélukpa Buddhism. But according to Zhang Dungu, who travelled there in 1911, since Mongol pilgrims were increasingly numerous, all the monasteries had a tablet in Chinese and Mongolian (1911: 1r).

44    The refectory (Wuguantang 五觀堂) is a lateral hall of the main axis. In *shifang* mon-asteries, the same building is used for residing monks and pilgrims.

45    Lamas on Wutaishan had to adapt their daily life to a Chinese-style monastery. In Tibet and Mongolia, monks have a much more independent life than in China; they sleep and eat in their own house or yurt, and monasteries do not have refectories, dormitories or collective meditation halls. Even contemporary lamas from Tibet and Mongolia feel very uncomfortable living in Wutaishan's Chinese-style monasteries (Chou Wen-shing, email, May 2010).

dhist-style layout were added temples to Padmasambhava, Tsongkhapa and wrathful deities who protect the *dharma*, bottle-shaped *stūpa*s, prayer wheels,[46] Tibetan roof finials (the two deers on either side of the *dharma* wheel above the entrance hall and small *stūpa*s on the ridgepoles) and formulas of consecration in Lantsa script on the beams.

The inner space does not differ greatly from that of a monastery in Tibet or Mongolia, with its large multicolored canopies, silk banners and *thangka*s hanging from the ceiling, ritual paraphernalia, statues of Tibetan masters, etc. The main difference is that Chinese deities and Chinese forms of Buddhas and *bodhisattva*s are sometimes added to the usual Tibeto-Mongol pantheon: a royal Mañjuśrī on a lion in the Mañjuśrī hall, a corpulent Maitreya and Weituo 韋馱 (or 陀, Skanda as a celestial general) in the *lokapāla*s hall, a Chinese-style Kṣitigarbha (in the refectory), or the Chinese warrior-god Guandi 關帝 (Guan Yu 關羽).[47] Some of these icons were donated by pilgrims. On the other hand, some Chinese Buddhist monasteries have or had Tibetan-style *stūpa*s, prayer wheels and Tibetan forms of Mañjuśrī,[48] as well as scriptures in Tibetan and Mongolian.[49] In addition, Tayuansi and Xiantongsi, two Chinese Buddhist monasteries that also housed a few lamas in the Qing and Republican periods, had Tibetan chapels and icons (see Chapter 3).[50]

The most common image of Mañjuśrī found in the Mañjuśrī hall follows the Chinese iconography developed on Wutaishan: in the posture of *lalitāsana* (posture of royal ease, with one leg drawn up) riding on his lion, the *bodhisattva* makes the *mudrā* of teaching and holds a large *ruyi* 如意 scepter.[51] This royal form is said to be modeled on the famous image that stood in Zhenrongyuan/dian 真容院/殿 (Cloister/Hall of the True Countenance) during the Tang dynasty (Fig. 9).[52] Gélukpa monasteries adopted either this Chinese iconography

---

46    Prayer wheels were destroyed during the Cultural Revolution but, according to earlier travel accounts, they were found in many monasteries (Gao Henian 2000 [1949]: 111, 119).

47    Guandi became a tutelary deity of Rölpé Dorjé who declared he was the protector of the Qing empire.

48    However, Tibetan *dharmapāla*s and *yidam*s are never found in Chinese Buddhist monasteries.

49    Jiang Weiqiao 1961 [1918]: 20.

50    Gao Henian 2000 [1949]: 110.

51    Mallmann 1964: 35-36. Birnbaum (1983: 18-19; also plates 1-2) details the origin of this form in the Tang dynasty. A *ruyi* is a auspicious Chinese symbol, discussion wand and staff of authority.

52    The oldest version of the story of this miraculous image was told by Japanese monk Ennin 圓仁 (posthumous name Jikaku Daishi 慈覺大師, 794-864) in the ninth century. See the references in Online Appendix B: "Pusading" and "Shuxiangsi."

FIGURE 9    *Statue of Mañjuśrī, Shuxiangsi and 'White Mañjuśrī' of Luohousi.*
© ISABELLE CHARLEUX 2007.

as their central image or a combination of this form with Mañjuśrī's Tibetan attributes: the sword of wisdom with a flaming point in his right hand and the *Prajñāpāramitā sūtra* in his left hand (both attributes can be placed on lotuses).[53]

Lastly, rare Tantric forms of deities that developed in the Tang-dynasty Esoteric School of Chinese Buddhism are usually mistaken as being Tibetan Tantric gods: they are the *dharmapāla bodhisattva* (a fierce black form of Mañjuśrī with nine heads and eighteen arms) of Mingyuechi and the Thousand-bowl Mañjuśrī of Xiantongsi.[54]

---

53    The Luohousi statue was described by Pokotilov 1935 [1893]: 69. See also the white Mañjuśrī on his lion, with a snake coiling up around a trident as his attribute in Cifusi (Zhou Rubi and Li Guangyi 2007: 231).

54    The Thousand-bowl Mañjuśrī originates in the text *Dacheng yujia jingang xing hai Manshushili qianbi qianbo dajiao wang jing* 大乘瑜伽金剛性海曼殊室利千臂千鉢大教王經 and the *Fanwangjing* 梵網經 (Shu Ren 1997: 12).

The ancient Chinese and Mongol guidebooks and gazetteers do not list the Chinese Buddhist and the Tibeto-Mongol Buddhist monasteries separately, and their names in both Chinese and Mongolian give no clue as to their affiliation—even though on the 1846 Cifusi map, the distinction is visually highlighted for some monasteries and caves by the presence of lamas and Tantric deities in clouds. To the visitor, in fact, the similarities between Gélukpa and Chinese Buddhist monasteries are often more obvious than their differences. Their apparent homogeneity, whatever their affiliation, was noticed by German scholar and missionary Heinrich Hackmann (1864-1935), who visited the mountain in 1911.[55] The transformation of several Chinese monasteries into Tibetan ones during the Qing period and of Tibetan monasteries into Chinese Buddhist or Han Gélukpa monasteries in the early twentieth century was partly responsible for their similarities. It is also possible that some Tibetan-style buildings existed but have not survived, such as the Changkya Khutugtu's residence in Zhenhaisi, built in the Republican period, and perhaps Puleyuan Hermitage, founded by Rölpé Dorjé and built in stone (Fig. 14). Travelers described Tibetan-style monks' houses in the streets leading to Pusading, which do not exist anymore.[56] The 1846 map shows that Tibetan-style *stūpa*s, in a variety of shapes, were more numerous in and outside monasteries than they are nowadays— *stūpa*s were a main target of destruction during the Cultural Revolution.

Although we have no proof of local or imperial pressure to 'keep things Chinese,' the lamas may not have had entire liberty to build as they wished since many Gélukpa monasteries were rebuilt on imperial order, with the exception perhaps of Puleyuan Hermitage. Rölpé Dorjé, the architect of several Qing-empire Gélukpa monasteries with a strong Tibetan flavor (in Beijing and Chengde for instance), did not build such temples on Wutaishan. He does not seem to have been interested in building on Wutaishan, where he wanted more than anything to find seclusion.[57] The only monastery influenced by Tibetan architecture in its conception is Cifusi, built after 1814: although its Buddha hall looks Chinese, the second story is a gallery allowing views of the central part of the first floor, comparable to skylights of Inner Mongol 'mandalic' assembly halls. In the rear courtyard, the small Milarépa hall, built to protect a cave, has

---

55    "The structure of the temple is for the greater part, Chinese, but the form of the pagodas is mostly Indo-Tibetan. The interior, too, forms a mixture of Chinese and Tibetan. Chinese and Tibetan idols stand side by side, Tibeto-Mongolian inscriptions are next to Chinese ones, Tibetan butter lamps, praying cylinders, also boards on which the monks throw themselves for prayer, all such things are seen here in Chinese temples" (Hackmann 1914 [1912]: 118-119).

56    Gilmour 1970 [1883]: 146.

57    According to Chou Wen-shing, email, May 2010.

Tibetan-style pillars and framework on the porch and door, with concentric motifs and consecration formulas, resembling those of Höhhot monasteries.[58] Yet these characteristics are unique on Wutaishan.

For the visitor, the salient feature of a Wutaishan monastery is not its current affiliation to Gélukpa or Chinese Buddhism but its peculiarity that distinguishes it in this complex religious landscape: the giant wooden lotus (Luohousi), the five Mañjuśrīs of the five terraces/directions (Xiantongsi, Puhuasi, Dailuoding, Shuxiangsi),[59] the Sandalwood Buddha (Dailuoding), the statue of Sudhana (Shancaidong), the eighteen-meter high statue of thousand-armed Avalokiteśvara in Jingesi and the natural numinous sites on which any given monastery is built. The pilgrims were informed that they must see certain particular icons, such as the ten main statues of Mañjuśrī,[60] or particular sights (or vistas) and nodes of interest.[61] Local stories provide justifications for worshiping the *stūpa* of Mañjuśrī's lock of hair (Tayuansi), the stele of the begging Mañjuśrī (Yuanzhaosi), the pond where an emperor shot an arrow at a monk who was bathing with two ladies (Zaoyuchi), the statue of Mañjuśrī pierced by an arrow (Pusading) and so on.[62]

### The Natural Numinous Sites in the Landscape

For pilgrims, the natural numinous sites (or 'numinous traces') were as important to visit as the monasteries.[63] In fact, the sub-section on the numinous traces in the Ming and Qing Chinese gazetteers, repeated in the guidebook by Rölpé Dorjé et al. (*ZMRBDB*/*OMSA*), comes before the section on the monasteries; it counts about 125 numinous traces, classified according to their

---

58    See the photo of Cifusi in Appendix B.

59    See Fang Qingqi and Wang Xuebin 1994, 2: 18-19. These are systematically represented in newly built monasteries such as Lingfengsi 靈峰寺.

60    See Chapter 6.

61    A list of ten scenic spots of Wutaishan (*jing* 景) has been drawn up on the model of literatis' lists of 'vistas': the bronze ox of Dashe 大社 Monastery (also known as Qixiansi); the five hundred *arhat*s of Yuhuachi 玉花池; the bronze cauldrons of Pusading; the *Avataṃsaka sūtra*, written in the shape of a *stūpa*, of Bishansi; the cliff inscribed with text near Tailusi; the archway of Gufosi 古佛寺; the lotus revealing the buddhas in Luohousi; the Bronze Hall; the iron stick of Song General Wulang 五郎; and the Great Earth (God) of Shanxi in Xiantongsi (Li Xiangzhi 1932: 150-154, 72-75).

62    Several of these stories are illustrated on the Cifusi map. See also Fang Qingqi and Wang Xuebin 1994: 2.

63    Contemporary Chinese and Mongolian guidebooks have no chapter on numinous traces, perhaps because practices associated with them, such as crawling into a cave or rubbing one's body against stones were disparaged as 'superstitious practices.' However, modern practices clearly evidence that these rites are central to pilgrims.

geographical location on one of the five terraces (Table 4). Such a profusion of numinous sites scattered over a wide area is characteristic of Chinese and Tibetan pilgrimage mountains; as explained by Susan Naquin and Yü Chun-fang, they are "the foundation on which much could be built, physically and imaginatively."[64] In the Gélukpa as in the Chinese Buddhist traditions, numinous sites are generally identified by high clerics who 'decipher' the landscape and perceive in some of its features the natural manifestation of the holiness and power of Mañjuśrī's abode.

The numinous sites listed in the Chinese-produced gazetteers were copied from earlier sources,[65] and many were not visited anymore, their actual location having been forgotten, while new ones had emerged. The last imperial gazetteer, the *Qinding Qingliangshan zhi* (1785), does not make any significant changes to the Ming-dynasty list of the *Qingliangshan zhi* (1596) and therefore ignores eighteenth- and nineteenth-century numinous sites, especially those worshipped by Tibetan and Mongol pilgrims. We will see in Chapter 4 how, in contrast, the Tibetan and Mongolian guidebooks reinterpret anew the five terraces and their numinous sites as a cosmic *maṇḍala*.

The most significant numinous trace of Wutaishan is the relic of Śākyamuni enshrined in the Great White Stūpa of Tayuansi—the same monastery is also known to preserve a stone carving of Śākyamuni's footprints and a lock of hair belonging to Mañjuśrī in a smaller *stūpa* (Fig. 42). However, most of the numinous sites are found on the slopes of the terraces, located more than ten kilometers from the village of Taihuai (the five terraces themselves are considered numinous traces). The main numinous traces to visit are *stūpa*s enshrining body or contact relics of great masters such as Tsongkhapa (at Baohuasi) or Mañjuśrī (at Tayuansi); footprints and handprints of *bodhisattva*s and great masters (at Zaoyuchi, Jingangku, Tayuansi, Luohousi); paw prints left by Mañjuśrī's lion (at the Central Terrace); springs with inexplicable variations in depth; ice that never melts (at the Central Terrace); and strange stones (at Qingliangsi 清凉寺, Niuxinshi 牛心石), peaks, cliffs, forests, ponds, springs, etc. About thirty of such sites are caves;[66] these generally greatly impressed

---

64    Naquin and Yü 1992: 22.

65    This was already the case for Song dynasty gazetteers: Birnbaum 1984: 18.

66    According to Chinese gazetteers' lists. For a classification of numinous caves, see Raoul Birnbaum's four categories: 'dwelling caves,' where ascetics live in solitary practices; 'paradise-caves' which can be entered through a hidden passageway (such as the Vajra Cave); 'manifestation caves' in which deities are believed to manifest themselves from time to time in response to devotees; and 'caves of initiatory rebirth' where one comes out endowed with a new spiritual body or a new karma. Birnbaum showed the interrelation

pilgrims.[67] Caves where saints disappeared, such as Vajra Cave (Jingangku) and Nārāyaṇa Cave, are part of both the Chinese Buddhist and the Daoist pilgrimage traditions,[68] but also belong to the Tibetan and Mongol tradition.[69] To every numinous site corresponds a miracle tale, an apparition, or a visit by ancient sages. Mañjuśrī was believed to have subjugated five hundred poisonous dragons on Wutaishan (one hundred on each terrace) and have become their master. Hence, several of the numinous sites make reference to them, such as the Dragon's Well (Longjing 龍井) and the Palace of the Black Dragon King.

The spiritual, natural and human-built environment partially explains the attractive power of Wutaishan. The numinous sites were visible and touchable traces of miraculous manifestations on Wutaishan, sought out by all pilgrims. As for the natural environment, the sacred mountain is located on the margins of China's territory and political power, at the juncture of Tibetan and Inner Asian cultures, and at a reachable distance from Beijing and Höhhot. For Mongols, who had to cross a part of Shanxi to get there, Wutaishan may have seemed more or less like a familiar place: like in Mongolia, the steppe-like ecology provided pasture for herds and flocks; the climate was similar; and the Tibeto-Mongol atmosphere (the yurts in the pastures, the *stūpa*, the interior of Gélukpa monasteries with the smell of butter lamps), as well as the cult of springs and caves, and the Mongolian-speaking monks made them feel they were not complete strangers in a foreign land. In the human-built environment, the ethnic and religious differences were smoothed over and merged into one coherent religious and aesthetic landscape.

### Otherworldly Wutaishan

Pilgrimage sites, according to Victor and Edith Turner, "are believed to be places where miracles once happened, still happen and may happen again."[70] Since ancient times, Wutaishan was associated with miraculous manifestations of lights and purple vapors, hence its name 'Purple Palace Mountain' (Zifushan 紫府山), given in a Daoist text from the first centuries CE.[71] The site was

---

of Buddhist and Daoist concepts and native Chinese traditions in the practices relating to the caves (1989-1990).

67    See He Zhang Lianjue 1934: 71; Li Xiangzhi 1932.

68    The Chinese Daoist *dongtian* 洞天 are celestial microcosms, places of initiation and refuge from civilization (Verellen 1995).

69    On a similar cave in Amdo: Epstein and Peng Wenbin 1994.

70    Turner and Turner 1978: 6.

71    Quoted by Huixiang 慧祥 in *Gu Qingliang zhuan* 古清涼傳 (Birnbaum 2004: 205).

particularly conducive to miracles, visions and mystical experiences that confirm the pilgrims' perception of Wutaishan as the abode of deities and spirits.[72]
These inexplicable phenomena experienced by monks in meditation, as well as
by laypersons in contemplation, were recorded in the earliest Chinese histories,
travel accounts and poetry.[73] Descriptions of these events became a literary
genre that was continued under many different forms in the following centuries: they were recorded in accounts of imperial visits,[74] popular tales, official
gazetteers and non-official pilgrimage guidebooks,[75] travel accounts of monk-
pilgrims, stone inscriptions,[76] poems of eighteenth- and nineteenth-century
Tibetan and Mongol clerics, pictorial representations of Wutaishan and travel-
ogues of foreign visitors. Such phenomena were observed on other Chinese
mountains, such as Emeishan, and their interpretations were inspired by Buddhist scriptures or explained by specific practices of meditation.[77]

The signs that testify to the presence of extraordinary beings are typically
intensified or incomplete sensory perception (perception by only one of the
five senses).[78] In ancient Chinese chronicles, the tolling of an invisible bell and
the smoke of invisible incense are interpreted as manifestations of Mañjuśrī.[79]
But although miracles perceived by these senses were occasionally recorded,
the main theme that dominates this literary genre is vision. Visions can be sub-
divided into apparitions of mirage monasteries; light phenomena and other
anomalies in the natural world (such as auspicious birds, five-colored clouds
appearing out of nowhere in a clear sky); visions of Mañjuśrī and other deities
in a human form; and interpretations of the landscape, that is, fauna and flora
as manifestations of the Buddhist doctrinal elements and deities. Apparitions
of mirage monasteries that seem to hover in the air ('transformation monasteries,' *huasi* 化寺), manifested by Mañjuśrī to monks or pious laymen such as

---

72    Gimello 1992: 133-134 n. 33; Birnbaum 1983: 19-24; Birnbaum 1986; Birnbaum 1989-1990:
      135-136; Birnbaum 2004: 195-226; Cartelli 2012.
73    See the Dunhuang manuscripts studied by Cartelli 2012.
74    See the description of an apparition at the Western Terrace on one of Kangxi's tours in
      *Qingliangshan xinzhi* (1694: *juan* 3, 19 a, translated by Köhle 2008: 91).
75    *Qingliangshan xinzhi* 1985 [1694]: *juan* 4; ZMRBDB; OMSA.
76    The stele "Zhenxiu Shi Zhengxiu zhuan bing shubei" 真休釋正秀撰並書碑, 1798 records
      miraculous lights that appeared above Mañjuśrī's Hair Stūpa (see Online Appendix B,
      "Tayuansi").
77    Visions that monk Shenying 神應 recorded in his eighth-century account would stem
      from his intense practice of the Lotus Samadhi, a seven-day meditation specific to the
      Tiantai tradition of Buddhism (Birnbaum 1986).
78    Merleau-Ponty 1945: 368.
79    Birnbaum 1983: 17.

Daoyi, are typically Tang-dynasty stories.[80] Although they are occasionally repeated in modern folklore, such as stories about the Kangxi emperor,[81] they are not found in the modern Chinese and Mongolian literature about Wutaishan.

### 'Buddha Lights'

Light phenomena, generally called 'Buddha lights' (foguang 佛光, Mo. burkhan-u gerel), were the most expected phenomenon on Wutaishan. They were described by all kinds of visitors and are still reported by modern travelers.[82] Yet they were not that frequent: a monk confessed to Japanese monk Ennin, who visited Wutaishan in 840, that he was happy to have seen one in his life.[83] They could take the form of altar lamps, rays of light, luminous multicolored clouds, flashes of lights like successive bolts, or great glowing spheres,[84] and were generally of short duration. These light formations are believed to have a transformative effect; they are commonly interpreted as a manifestation of Mañjuśrī's presence and power. Light, incandescence and radiance are generally connected to Mañjuśrī and to visions described in the Avataṃsaka sūtra.[85] They can also happen on the death of a Buddhist master who has attained spiritual achievement,[86] or emanate from his relics. Scientists have attempted to explain them as meteorological phenomena.

Buddha lights were generally spotted on two main places: the Great White Stūpa (or Lingjiu Peak) and the terraces. The supernatural halo emitted from Lingjiu Peak observed by Song statesman, literati, Daoist scholar and lay Buddhist Zhang Shangying 張商英 (1043-1122) and other pilgrims, that first appeared above a pine tree in Luohousi, then lightened the Great White Stūpa and the summit of Yuanzhaosi and disappeared at Pusading, was occasionally observed until the death of the pine tree in the Qing dynasty. The sacred tree

---

80    Birnbaum 1986: 119-120; Gimello 1992: 131 n. 30, 32; Andrews 2011.

81    Yang Zengwu 2005: 185-186.

82    For a classification of light phenomena into public/private, coming from within/from the outside, etc.: Birnbaum 2004.

83    Reischauer 1955: 251.

84    Great balls of fire were already recorded in Huixiang's gazetteer, the Gu Qingliang zhuan, published in 677, and are represented in painting on the west wall of Cave 159 at Dunhuang (Birnbaum 2004: 204). See also Gimello 1992, esp. p. 133-134 n. 33.

85    Birnbaum 1983: 11, 17; Gimello 1992: 133-134, n. 104; Wong 1993: 33-34; Birnbaum 2004.

86    As observed by Gray Tuttle in the 2000s on Wutaishan (personal communication, 2007); also Kapstein 2004. For description of Buddha lights on another Chinese sacred mountain: Hargett 2006: 17-19.

was then enshrined inside a *stūpa* in the first courtyard of Luohousi.[87] In 1885, from Dailuoding, Chan master Xuyun spotted fireballs that flew from the summit of the Northern Terrace to the Central Terrace, where it fell and then split into thirteen balls.[88] British Buddhist writer John Blofeld (1913-1987) gave a vivid description of these luminous phenomena he spotted from a terrace in 1935.[89] As summarized by Robert M. Gimello, "what we have here may be an example of sacred tradition conspiring with nature to transfigure unusual natural phenomena by investing them with spiritual significance."[90]

### Visions of and Encounters with Mañjuśrī

Mañjuśrī could manifest himself as a heavenly *bodhisattva* in a miraculous vision—in a cloud, astride a lion, surrounded by a nimbus of multicolored (or five)[91] rays of light emanating from all sides of his body—or as an ordinary human being, in a direct encounter. Such a vision was said to be able to deliver the spectator from sufferings. In his gazetteer, Ming-dynasty monk Zhencheng explains that "when pilgrims go to Wutaishan, what they desire to see is not the mountain but the countenance of the Great Sage [Mañjuśrī]."[92] Biographies of monks and accounts of pilgrims typically emphasize vision of, or a miraculous encounter with, Mañjuśrī as their central motif.[93] In popular tales and pilgrims' accounts, the *bodhisattva* appears in many guises: an old man, a hungry female beggar, a youth, a fox (in stories related to the Kangxi emperor), a cattle herder

---

87    This is recorded in his diary, the *Xu Qingliang zhuan* 續清涼傳 (Further Record of Clear and Cold), composed around the time of his visits to Wutaishan in 1088 and 1090 (*T.* 2100, vol. 51: 1127c-1135a, partially translated in Gimello 1992). References to texts in the *Taishō* canon are indicated by the text number (*T.*), followed by the volume, page and register (a. b. or c).

88    Birnbaum 2004: 206.

89    "Innumerable bolts of fire [that] floated majestically past. We could not judge their size, for nobody knew how far away they were, but they appeared like the fluffy woolen balls that babies play with seen close up. They seem to be moving at the stately pace of a large, well-fed fish aimlessly cleaving its way through the water; but, of course, their actual pace could not be determined without a knowledge of the intervening distance. Where they came from, and where they went after fading from sight in the West, nobody could tell. Fluffy balls of orange-coloured fire—truly a fitting manifestation of divinity!" (Blofeld 1959: 149-150).

90    Gimello 1992: 134, n. 104

91    The five colors are traditionally associated with the five Buddha families of the five directions.

92    *Qingliangshan zhi* 1887 [1596]: *juan* 8, quoted by Chou 2007: 115.

93    Birnbaum 1983: 22. For the period studied here: Gao Henian 2000 [1949]; He Zhang Lianjue 1934; Li Xiangzhi 1932.

riding on a cow (who is actually his lion) and accompanied by a child (his disciple Sudhana), a deer and so on. He sometimes guides pilgrims lost in the dark.[94] Anomalies of nature, such as butterflies and flowers blossoming in winter, or a fox waiting to be pursued, were interpreted as manifestations of the *bodhisattva*. It is still believed nowadays that the infinite potential manifestations of Mañjuśri on Wutaishan would make anyone behave gently towards any mendicant or poor creature on the mountain.

Chinese visitors, such as Zhang Shangying, had visions of theophanies described as pure lands populated by legions of *bodhisattvas* and divine figures in jeweled palaces.[95] Occasionally, a whole celestial imagery centered on Mañjuśrī could appear to large groups of people, such as a vision described at the occasion of the bestowal of an imperial gift to the Great Xiantongsi in 1420.[96] Theophanies, like light phenomena, rainbows and miraculous cloud formations, could be seen not only by monks in meditation but by all in attendance.

### Souvenirs and Materialization of Miracles and Visions

Because every rock, river, animal and tree on the mountain was viewed as a fragment of a holy place and therefore saturated with its power, all pilgrims used to carry back home some of Wutaishan's water, soil, herbs, stones, plants or mushrooms, believing them to have medicinal and spiritual virtues. The natural numinous sites have an even greater concentration of sanctity: they are the visible imprints of these mysterious phenomena on Wutaishan's landscape. The miraculous phenomena are not only temporary visions experienced by a

---

94   Gao Henian (2000 [1949]: 113-114) met an old man with his oxen; He Zhang Lianjue (1934: 72) met an old woman.

95   Gimello 1992: 106, 107, 137, n. 48.

96   "An auspicious light brilliantly issued forth, a five-colored radiance rising to illuminate the sky, covering the mountains and valleys, filling and spreading, with the brilliance of the sun and stars, lasting and not dissipating. Then Manjushri riding on a lion faintly emerged from the edge of the clouds, slightly revealing traces of his form. When the clouds and mist collected, you could see the lion displaying his whiskers and sticking out his tongue, raising his legs and moving his feet, prancing and dancing for joy, looking to the left and right, halting and standing on the mountain. The next day lohans came from Huayan Peak, some five hundred, some three hundred, some one or two hundred, one after the other, treading on each other's heels, soaring in close succession ... The group reached more than three thousand, manifesting and disappearing; the transformation was extraordinary. People who had travelled to Wutai from everywhere all bowed and sang in praise, regarding this as a rare event" (translation by Weidner 2001: 121 of the preface of the *Gequ ming jing* 歌曲名經, quoted in the *Qingliangshan zhi* 1887 [1596]: *juan* 4, 6v-7r).

few but can materialize in concrete 'traces' such as a rock, a spring, self-revealed statues, footprints of deities and relics, and even actual monasteries. Four large eighth-century monasteries, Jingesi, Zhulinsi, Fahuayuan 法華院 and Jingang-ku were erected as earthly replicas of extraordinary places manifested by Mañjuśrī.[97] Luohousi Monastery is said to have been founded near to a site where Mañjuśrī appeared and taught to a thousand devotees, and Qingliangsi was allegedly built around the large stone where Mañjuśrī preached the *dharma*. By erecting these earthly replicas or valorizing these traces, Mañjuśrī's Pure Land was made visible to all pilgrims.

Miracles were also recorded on two-dimensional mediums, such as paintings of Mañjuśrī on his lion on Wutaishan,[98] and the tenth-century panoramic map of Wutaishan in Cave 61 at Dunhuang, which represents the main monasteries with halos of light, multicolored clouds and supernatural manifestations.[99] Eighth-century pilgrims could buy paintings of Wutaishan focusing on extraordinary phenomena (called *Wutaishan huaxian tu* 五臺山化現圖); and make rubbings of stone inscriptions depicting marvelous manifestations (*linghua zhuanbei* 靈化傳碑).[100] These paintings could be inspired by theophanic visions but may also have influenced them.[101] Ancient block prints on paper cheaply reproduced the same images to be sold to pilgrims as objects of remembrance, protection and devotion.[102] In the period studied here, this role is played by prints of the Cifusi map recording miracles and by prints of the Buddha's footprints. More recently, paintings and prints were replaced by photographs evidencing miraculous apparitions, exhibited on the altars of Wutaishan's monasteries (Fig. 10).

To personally experience these phenomena and especially to encounter Mañjuśrī were the main goals of ordinary pilgrims as well as of meditating monks. They expected miraculous apparitions to infinitely repeat again and

---

97      Birnbaum 1986: 119-120; Gimello 1992: 131 n. 30, 32; Andrews 2011.

98      For instance, Pelliot EO 3588, reproduced in Schneider 1987: Fig. 1, showing the main Wutaishan monasteries.

99      It is located on the back wall of Cave 61, behind a votive pillar, dated 948 (Marchand 1976; Wong 1993). See also the painting of Cave 159, topped by glowing orbs of light and multihued light, and the twelfth-century paintings of Yanshansi 岩山寺, in the village of Tianyan 天岩村, north of Wutaishan. For representations of miracles on Wutaishan: Berger 2001.

100     Ennin, *Nittō guhō junrei kōki* 入唐求法巡礼行記, quoted by Demiéville 1952: 377; Zha Luo 1998: 97-101; see also Reischauer 1955: 269.

101     Gimello 1992: 137, n. 48.

102     Birnbaum 1983: 19 and Plates 1 and 2.

FIGURE 10
*Photograph of Mañjuśrī appearing among the clouds. This photograph was in 2009 'held' by the statue of Ganlu Mañjuśrī, Scripture Hall, Xiantongsi.*
© ISABELLE CHARLEUX 2009.

again. The depictions of apparitions of Mañjuśrī and other deities on the tenth-century Dunhuang map and those provided by the 1846 Cifusi map are comparable because they are timeless: they record past apparitions and seem to promise future ones.

Tales of miracles on Wutaishan show a striking continuity from the Tang period up to modern times, although they are variously interpreted by pilgrims depending on their religious and cultural system, and are often explained away as scientific phenomena by climatologists. Collective visions continue to be recorded in the twenty-first century. The perpetuation of ancient stories that are repeated and distorted, the apparition of new miracles, along with new interpretations and representations, add new layers to the ever-changing Wutaishan landscape. The gazetteers translated into Mongolian and Tibetan, the maps and paintings recording miracles, as well as the oral folklore propagated by traveling monks, informed pilgrims on what they were supposed to see and helped them interpret what they saw. The following chapters will highlight the degree to which the Mongol pilgrims of the late Qing and Republican period recognized, worshipped and reinterpreted ancient numinous sites and discovered new ones.

### Historical Wutaishan

The guidebooks and gazetteers inform us about the history of the Buddhicization of Wutaishan through the association with *bodhisattva* Mañjuśrī. Three main agents contributed towards the development and internationalization of the Wutaishan pilgrimage: the clergy(ies), the state and the pilgrims themselves. This development was progressive, made of different layers added one upon the next. The introduction of Tibetan Buddhism in the Yuan dynasty and the pilgrims coming from Tibetan and Mongol areas added new layers to this sedimented religious landscape, including new perceptions and interpretations. Then the Qing period Mongolian and Tibetan guidebooks and the Cifusi map merged these various histories and stories into one narrative. A short presentation of the early history of Wutaishan, including its link with imperial power, will give us the necessary background to understand the complexity of the site, the role of the state and the interactions between the different traditions.

### *Early History of Buddhism at Wutaishan and Its Association with Mañjuśrī*

In the first centuries CE, before the diffusion of Buddhism, the Daoists already regarded Wutaishan as a sacred place, an abode of immortals, and its forests were home to hermits.[103] From the fourth century CE, Wutaishan was appropriated by Chinese Buddhists, who began to consider it the earthly abode of the *bodhisattva* of transcendent wisdom. The construction of Wutaishan as a Buddhist holy land was a direct result of its association with Mañjuśrī. Etienne Lamotte has argued that the Chinese translation of the *Avataṃsaka sūtra* (Flower ornament scripture, Ch. *Huayanjing* 華嚴經)[104] between 418 and 421 has been falsified to assign Mañjuśrī a dwelling place on Wutaishan: the translator in

---

103   For the pre-Yuan history of Wutaishan, I am merely summarizing the secondary literature: Pokotilov 1935 [1893]: 50-53, who cites the *Shanxi tongzhi* 1990 [1892]; Ono Katsutoshi and Hibino Takao 1942: 2-87; Lamotte 1960; Wang Zhiyong and Cui Zhengsen 2000: 57-539; Wang-Toutain 2007.

104   For the history and different translations of this text: Cleary 1985-1986: "Introduction."

chief, an Indian monk named Buddhabhadra (359-429) made a slight addition to the chapter on the residences of the different *bodhisattvas* of the eight cardinal directions, locating Mañjuśrī in the northeast (versus the east, in the Indian original) and associating him with China's Qingliang Mountain.[105] This 'falsification,' supported by other monks who translated *sūtras* or wrote apocryphs, such as Bodhiruci 菩提流志 (672-727), Yijing 義淨 (635-713), Fuli 復禮 (fl. 681-703) and Fazang 法藏 (643-712), provided additional scriptural authority to the association of the mountain with Mañjuśrī.[106] The number five, associated with Mañjuśrī in ancient scriptures, and the configuration of five terraces covered with snow throughout the year fitted the description of the mythical abode of the *bodhisattva* and therefore further contributed to this identification.

Legends reported in Chinese gazetteers and repeated in Tibetan and Mongolian guidebooks tell that Buddhism came to Wutaishan sometime during the Eastern Han dynasty (25-220), not long after it appeared in China.[107] The first Buddhist foundation would date from the year 68. In 67, Emperor Ming (r. 58-65), inspired by a dream, sent envoys to India to seek Buddhist teachings; they returned to China with two Indian monks. When they visited Wutaishan in 68, the two monks discovered that it was the abode of Mañjuśrī and contained a *stūpa* erected by Emperor Aśoka. Since in their eyes one of the central peaks resembled Vulture Peak, where Śākyamuni Buddha had preached the *dharma*, they named it Numinous Vulture Peak and submitted a memorial to Emperor Ming to erect there a monastery named Dafu Lingjiusi 大孚靈鷲寺 (Great Faith Numinous Vulture [Peak]).[108] Dafu Lingjiusi (which was actually founded in the fifth century) is believed to be the most ancient Buddhist monastery in China, along with the White Horse Monastery (Baimasi 白馬寺), built the same year in Luoyang (Henan Province).[109]

With scriptures asserting that the mountain was the oldest Buddhist site in China, was the earthly abode of Mañjuśrī and sheltered relics of Śākyamuni, Wutaishan was completely legitimated as a sacred Buddhist place.[110] The

---

105 "Pusa zhuchu pin" 菩薩住處品 (The dwelling places of the *bodhisattvas*), in *Dafangguangfo huayanjing* 大方廣佛華嚴經, *T.* 278, vol. 9: *juan* 29.

106 Lamotte 1960: 84; see also Birnbaum 1983; Birnbaum 1984; Birnbaum 1986; Gimello 1992.

107 Guidebooks that repeat these legends are *OMSA* (3v-4r, 5v-7r); *TÜAG* (3v).

108 It is known by different names—Dafutusi 大孚圖寺, Dapusi 大鋪寺, Dabusi 大布寺 (Zheng Sen 1987: 28). The Aśoka Stūpa may have been initially located in Shouningsi (Wang Zhiyong and Cui Zhengsen 2000: 573-576).

109 Birnbaum 1986: 124-126.

110 By the seventh century, scriptures assert that a first temple dedicated to Mañjuśrī had been built by King Mu 穆王 of the Zhou dynasty (r. 1001-947 BCE). Mu would have been converted to Buddhism by Mañjuśrī himself and the sage Maudgalyāyana. Following his

presence of Buddhist sacred places such as Wutaishan on Chinese soil, along with the discovery of Śākyamuni's relics, contributed to creating a direct and tangible link between China and the holy land of Buddhism and to relocate peripheral China at the center of the Buddhist world.

Wutaishan's fame reached other Buddhist countries, and by the seventh century the abode of Mañjuśrī, then worshipped as a savior, had become a prominent pilgrimage destination for Buddhists from China and abroad—Central Asians,[111] Tibetans, Indians, Nepalese,[112] Kashmiris,[113] Singhalese, Koreans and Japanese.[114] The pilgrims themselves, through their writings about miracles and numinous features, oral narratives, travel accounts and reinterpretations of sacred texts, played a central role in the development of the cult of Wutaishan and the elaboration of its sacred geography.[115]

### Legitimization of the Temporal Power and Protection of the Chinese State

During the same period, Wutaishan was also a place linked to the legitimization of temporal power,[116] and the combination of religious and imperial interventions consecrated the mountain as a predominant Buddhist holy place. The cult of Mañjuśrī was expanded by the eighth-century arrival in China of esoteric forms of Buddhism in which the *bodhisattva* played a major and complex role. Empress Wu Zetian (r. 684-704), who presented herself as a *cakravartin* (universal emperor) ruler, strengthened the sacred character of Wutaishan with the help of Indian and Central Asian monks. The association between Wutaishan and Mañjuśrī was made even more explicit in the new translation of the *Avataṃsaka sūtra* into Chinese,[117] made on her request by the Khotanese monk

example, Emperor Aśoka would then have erected the *stūpa* containing Śākyamuni's relics on the mountain (Daoxuan 道宣, *Daoxuan lüshi gantong lu* 道宣律師感通錄, 644, T. 2107, vol. 52: 437a-b, translated in Birnbaum 1986: 120-121).

111   Lamotte 1960: 59, n. 138.

112   Schneider 1987.

113   Lamotte 1961: 84-91; Sen 2003: 79-86; Duan Jinjin 2008.

114   Gazetteers of Wutaishan authored by Chinese resident monks were brought by pilgrims back to Japan and Korea.

115   Wang-Toutain 2007.

116   Other non-Buddhist mountains such as Mount Taishan also served as legitimation of temporal power through communion with heaven that granted the emperor his mandate to rule on earth: Chavannes 1910.

117   "In the northeast there is a place called Cool, Clear Mountain, where enlightening beings have lived since ancient times; now there is an enlightening being there named Manjushri,

Śikṣānanda (657-710) in 695-699.[118] Empress Wu then restored Dafu Lingjiusi and renamed it Da Huayansi 大華嚴寺 (Big Avataṃsaka Monastery) by reference to this text.[119] In one of its cloisters a chapel was specifically erected for prayers for the well-being of the Tang imperial household and the prosperity of the empire.

Raoul Birnbaum has shown that by the mid- to late Tang, Mañjuśrī was perceived as a mountain deity, a national (and personal) protector of the emperor and guardian of the nation as well as a cosmic lord, at the core of the astrological tradition. This expansion occurred largely in connection with the spread of Esoteric Buddhism, in which deities assumed more abstract and symbolic identities than they had in the more traditional schools.[120] Wutaishan then developed into the center of a cult aiming at the ritual protection of the Chinese state. The main instigator of the promotion of Mañjuśrī as protector of the imperial throne was the Sri Lankan Tantric master and translator Amoghavajra (Ch. Bukong 不空, 705-774), who was all-powerful at the Tang court during the years 758-774.[121] Under the Tang dynasty, Wutaishan had thus become the most influential Buddhist site in China. The relation between the Tang court, Wutaishan and Mañjuśrī would serve as a model for the subsequent dynasties.

### The Construction of Temples and Monasteries

Several of the monasteries that came to be famous in the Ming and Qing dynasties were founded in the fifth and sixth centuries, when the Northern Wei, a non-Chinese dynasty of Tabghach origin that generously sponsored Buddhism, established a capital at Pingcheng 平城 (modern Datong) in northern Shanxi.[122]

---

with a following of ten thousand enlightening beings, always expounding the Teaching." (transl. Cleary 1985-1986, vol. 2: 218).

118   Sen 2003: 81. This version based on a more complete text imported from Khotan was translated into English by Cleary 1985-1986.

119   Wang-Toutain 2007; Ono Katsutoshi and Hibino Takao 1942: 38-45.

120   Birnbaum 1983: 9; also Birnbaum, 1986: 123-24; Gimello 1992: 99-101; Rhie 1977: 1-45; Yoshida Hiroki 1995: 26-28; Li Kecheng 1995: 21-27; Sen 2003: 76-86; Wang-Toutain 2007.

121   On his impetus, monasteries dedicated to Mañjuśrī were built throughout the empire, an image of Mañjuśrī was installed in the dining hall of every monastery, and five monasteries were rebuilt on Wutaishan. In these monasteries, esoteric rituals were regularly performed to protect the country (Birnbaum 1983: 25-38; Ono Katsutoshi and Hibino Takao 1942: 45-56). Nakata Nie (2009) showed how Amoghavajra combined the ideology of the *cakravartin* and the Mañjuśrī cult to create a new ideology of kingship.

122   Between 471 and 477, Emperor Xiaowen (r. 471-499) founded two large monasteries: Dafu Lingjiusi, composed of twelve courtyards and a flower garden; and Zhenrongyuan, on top of Numinous Vulture Peak. Zhenrongyuan was rebuilt and enlarged several times and popularly called Pusading in the Qing dynasty.

As early as the Northern Qi (550-570), the sources count two hundred temples and monasteries on Wutaishan, the largest being imperial foundations. The most flourishing period of foundations was the Tang, especially the Kaiyuan era (713-741), when there were as many as 360 temples and monasteries and thousands of monks and nuns.[123] The persecution of Buddhism in China in 846, although somewhat lessened by the remoteness of Wutaishan, entailed the destruction of many monasteries, and only 64 were left in the year 859. Soon after, the religious activities were resumed: the tenth-century map of Wutaishan painted in Cave 61 at Dunhuang shows 191 built and natural sites,[124] and the monasteries flourished under the Five Dynasties, the Song (960-1127), Liao (947-1125) and Jin (1115-1234) periods.[125]

### Early Tibetan and Mongol Interest in Wutaishan and Yuan-Dynasty Patronage

Tibetans undertook pilgrimages to Wutaishan as early as the ninth century,[126] and their interest in obtaining and painting maps of the mountain demonstrates their familiarity with its sacred geography.[127] In his history of Buddhism in Tibet, the Sakyapa master and historian Butön Rinchen Drup (1290-1364) asserts that King Songtsen Gampo (r. 617-650) went to Wutaishan and built 108 monasteries there:[128] Butön's assertion (which is repeated in later Tibetan and Mongolian chronicles)[129] shows how important the mountain had become for Tibetan Buddhists by the fourteenth century.

---

123    Monasteries of nuns were few on Wutaishan; two are known during the Tang period (Schneider 1987: 37).

124    Marchand 1976; Wong 1993; Heller 2008. The cave was excavated between 947 and 951.

125    Ono Katsutoshi and Hibino Takao 1942: 68-76; Wang Zhiyong and Cui Zhengsen 2000: Chapters 6 and 7.

126    Xiao Yu 1998: 33. On Tibetan pilgrimages to Wutaishan: Demiéville 1952: 188 n. 1, 376-377; Beckwith 1987: 7, 9, n. 30; Duan Jinjin 2008: 76; Wang Xiangyun 2004: 8; Tuttle 2006a: n. 2; Debreczeny 2011: 7-43.

127    In 824, the Tibetan king requested a map of Wutaishan from the Tang court (*Jiu Tangshu* 舊唐書: *juan* 17, "Jingzong benji 敬宗本紀;" transl. and text in Lee 1981: 162, 229; Demiéville 1952: 118; Zha Luo 1998). Around 980-995, Tibetans decorated Cave 117 of Dunhuang with a painted map of Wutaishan. A ninth- or tenth-century mural of Samyé Monastery in Central Tibet also depicts Wutaishan (reference in Chou 2007: 127, n. 44). It may have been drawn by Tibetan monks who had taken refuge to Deushen (Wutaishan?) during the ninth-century persecution of Buddhism in Tibet (Zha Luo 1998: 98). On other murals depicting Wutaishan in Tibet: Chou 2007: 127, n. 47.

128    Szerb 1990: 12.

129    For instance Galdan's *Erdeni-yin erike* (1859, ed. 1999: 100).

However, the permanent presence of Tibetan monks on Wutaishan is not attested before the thirteenth century, when the Mongol Yuan dynasty gave its preference to Tibetan over Chinese Buddhism and established Tibetan Buddhist communities.[130] On Wutaishan, Tibetan Buddhists were in charge of the ritual protection of the empire. During the brief reign of Tug Temür (r. 1329-1332), while expenditures on Buddhist rituals and palace expenses were curtailed, 'foreign monks'[131] were sent three times to the Shanxi mountain to perform rituals to protect the country and pray for peace.[132]

The monasteries of Wutaishan enjoyed generous imperial patronage and tax exemption. In 1265 Khubilai Khan ordered twelve monasteries on Wutaishan be restored and for a *Kanjur* to be sent to Shanzhuyuan 善住院 (later called Xiantongsi), which had to be read by monks to bless the population.[133] Emperors Temür (r. 1295-1307) in 1296 and 1301 and Shudibala (r. 1320-1323) in 1322, along with their empresses, personally journeyed to Wutaishan. With the coming of Pakpa Lama (Pakpa Lodrö Gyeltsen, 1235-1280), who administrated Wutaishan's clergy in 1257-1258 (before being appointed imperial preceptor in 1260), as well as other renowned masters, Wutaishan gained importance as a main center of Tibetan Buddhism in China and attracted more Tibetan monks. Pakpa Lama wrote eulogies on Wutaishan, which later became popular among Tibetan Buddhists.[134] Another renowned Tibetan dignitary who journeyed to Wutaishan was the Third Karmapa Rangjung Dorjé (1284-1339) on the occasion of his visit to the Yuan court in 1334.[135]

Pakpa asked one of his disciples at Khubilai's court, National Preceptor Dampa Künga Drak (Dan-ba Guoshi 膽巴國師, 1230-1303), known as a Tantric ritual

---

130   Ono Katsutoshi and Hibino Takao 1942: 77-85; Wang Lu 1995: 22; Gao Lintao 2000; Wang Xiangyun 2004; Zheng Lin 1997: 19. These lamas probably belonged to different schools of Tibetan Buddhism, since the Mongol princes did not restrict their patronage to the sole Sakyapa School.

131   *Fanseng*番僧 designates monks from Tibet but also from India and Nepal (Franke 1987: 297).

132   Wang Zhiyong and Cui Zhengsen 2000: 546. The Mongol Yuan also sponsored non-Buddhist Chinese mountains such as Wudangshan 武當山 (Lagerway 1992: 297).

133   *Qingliangshan zhi* 1887 [1596]: *juan* 4, 5v-6r.

134   "Garland of Jewels: Praise to Mañjuśrī at Wutaishan" (*'Jam dbyangs la ri bo rtse lngar bstod pa nor bu'i phreng ba*, 1257); also: *'Jam dpal la mtshan don gyi sgo nas bstod pa* and *'Jam dpal la nye bar bsngags pa me tog gi phreng ba*, in *Sa skya bka' 'bum*, vol. 15.

135   Toh 2004: 128-135. For other Tibetan monks who visited or were believed to have visited Wutaishan during that period, such as Sakya Paṇḍita: Li Jicheng 1988; Duan Jinjin 2008; Debreczeny 2011: 7-43.

specialist, to take residence on Wutaishan.[136] Dampa lived for almost ten years on the mountain; he was appointed abbot of Shouningsi before 1272,[137] restored twelve monasteries and built a temple devoted to performing rituals to the martial protector Mahākāla.[138] Shouningsi may have been the first Tibetan Buddhist establishment of Wutaishan (although it may have merged Chinese and Tibetan traditions).[139] Pakpa's disciple Yéshé Rinchen (1248-1294) also resided on Wutaishan and was the first high Tibetan cleric to die on the mountain.

Yuan imperial patronage was not restricted to the Tibetan Buddhist monasteries on Wutaishan but extended to Chinese Buddhist institutions. Following their predecessors, the Yuan emperors also sponsored the great Chinese Buddhist monasteries of Wutaishan and erected new ones.[140] They are known for having spent funds on monumental building projects. A chronology of construction will highlight the involvement of Yuan-period Mongols with the sacred mountain. In 1295, Temür asked the celebrated Newar artist Arniko (Ch. Anige 阿尼哥, 1245-1306) to build Wansheng Youguosi 萬聖佑國寺 to accumulate merit for the emperor's mother Hongjilie 弘吉烈. The construction, supervised by Dampa Künga Drak, was completed in 1297; the temple was later renamed Nanshansi.[141] This project proved to be very unpopular and raised sharp criticism from the officials at court: ten 'circuits' (*lu* 路) covering half of northern China, from Dadu to Shanxi, were mobilized to supply materials, and ten thousand artisans and laborers were levied. Although the project was at first in the hands of a high lama, the Tibetan imperial preceptor appointed Zhenjue Guoshi Wencai 真覺國師文才 (1241-1302), a famous Chinese cleric of the

---

136   Franke 1994 [1984] (translating his Chinese biographies); stone inscription "Danba bei" 胆巴碑, 1316, written by Zhao Mengfu 趙孟頫. His Tibetan biography has not yet been found. For other secondary sources: Debreczeny 2011: 19, n. 46.

137   Franke 1994 [1984]: 161, n. 18. Shouningsi was restored by Emperor Shudibala in 1322.

138   Pakpa Lama had a golden statue of Mahākāla under the form of Gur Gönpo, the special protector of the Sakyapa order, cast on Wutaishan. This statue is generally thought to be the same as the one sculpted around 1274, on the instruction of Pakpa Lama, by Arniko, then supervisor-in-chief of all artisans at the Mongol court. It was placed in a temple built by Arniko in Zhuozhou 涿州, south of Dadu (Beijing), and is credited with the Mongol victory over the Song armies.

139   Wang Zhiyong and Cui Zhengsen 2000: 569.

140   On the great Han Chinese masters of the Yuan period: Wang Zhiyong and Cui Zhengsen 2000: 566-573. On relic *stūpa*s of great Chinese masters: Ono Katsutoshi and Hibino Takao 1942: 222-226.

141   Construction of the temple was actually first ordered by Khubilai to Dampa in 1293, but the emperor died before work on it had started (*Qingliangshan zhi* 1887 [1596]: *juan* 4, 6r; Ono Katsutoshi and Hibino Takao 1942: 85-91; Jing 1994: 54-56; Xiong Wenbin 2003: 64-72).

Avataṃsaka School, as the first abbot.[142] The emperor's mother personally travelled to Wutaishan for the opening ceremony; she awarded Arniko ten thousand taels of silver and married him to a Mongol woman. The fourth abbot was the renowned Hongjiao Dashi 弘教大師 (1271-1337), a master of the Chinese Vinaya School, who in 1321 had received secret initiations from the (Tibetan Buddhist) imperial preceptor.[143] Later, as shown in his biography, Arniko built other monuments on Wutaishan for the imperial household as well as on his own initiative.[144]

Only four years later, another important project focused on the mountain's holiest relic. In 1301, on imperial orders, Arniko built a gigantic brick *stūpa*, the Daci Yanshou Baota 大慈延寿宝塔 (known as the Great White Stūpa, modern Tayuansi) upon the previous Tang-dynasty octagonal pagoda sheltering the relics of Śākyamuni allegedly brought there by Aśoka. Auspicious clouds and lights were said to have appeared in the sky at the beginning of the construction. In the same year, Temür personally visited Wutaishan with Fifth Imperial Preceptor Drakpa Özer (1246-1303).[145] The Great White Stūpa (restored and heightened in 1407, making it now 54.10 meters high) replicates the 52-meter-high White Stūpa of Beijing, erected thirty years before by Arniko to enshrine relics of Śākyamuni.[146] The latter stands in the main Tibetan monastery of Yuan Beijing (modern Baitasi), dedicated to Mañjuśrī and, as seen in Chapter 1, became a main locus of pilgrimage in Beijing for Mongols of the Qing period.

In 1309, Emperor Khaishan (r. 1307-1311) ordered the building of an imperial monastery, Puningsi 普寧寺, or Yuanzhaosi, which was staffed by Chinese Avataṃsaka monks.[147] During the years 1308-1310, imperial construction on Wutaishan required a total of 1,400 artisans and 11,500 mobilized soldiers.[148] In

---

142 He died less than two years after his appointment and was buried on the mountain. His disciple Huantang 幻堂 (1272-1322) was the second abbot.

143 Wang Zhiyong and Cui Zhengsen 2000: 566-567, 569; Li Kecheng 1995: 25.

144 Jing 1994; also Wang Zhiyong and Cui Zhengsen 2000: 541-543.

145 Jing 1994: 55.

146 This monastery was built in 1096; Khubilai had it reconstructed after supernatural radiance was observed from the relics it enshrined and renamed it Da Shengshou Wan'ansi 大聖壽萬安寺 (Franke 1994).

147 Other monasteries built or rebuilt by the Yuan court include Pumensi 普門寺, Tiewasi 鐵瓦寺, Xishouningsi 西壽寧寺, Huguosi 護國寺 (=Bishansi), Jindengsi 金燈寺, Wanghaisi 望海峰 (on the Eastern Terrace), Wenquansi 溫泉寺, Shitasi 石塔寺 and Qingyuansi 清源寺. Most of them were certainly staffed by Chinese Buddhist monks (Wang Zhiyong and Cui Zhengsen 2000: 546; list p. 878-880).

148 Wang Zhiyong and Cui Zhengsen 2000: 544, quoting the *Yuanshi* [1370] 1976, "Wuzong ji" 武宗紀 1: *juan* 22 and 23.

1326, Yesün Temür (r. 1323-1328) rebuilt Shuxiangsi and granted its community three hundred *qing* 頃 of land.[149] The great monasteries received large areas of arable land from the imperial throne, and the number of their monks was fixed to three hundred.[150] Besides enjoying imperial support, the large monasteries received incomes from their land and other activities such as iron mining, hotels and shops.

The Yuan-dynasty buildings on Wutaishan have been altered by later additions and repairs. Up to the early twentieth century, Mongol and Tibetan pilgrims visited the small Puensi 普恩寺, where Pakpa used to reside, and worshipped its Tibetan-style *stūpa*, said to enshrine Pakpa's monastic robe and hat.[151] Pakpa Lama was a key figure in the Tibetanization of Wutaishan, and remained in the memory of Qing-period Tibetan and Mongol high clerics, who made explicit mention of his poetry about Wutaishan.[152]

Individual lamas, including female lamas, also established new monasteries on Wutaishan. For instance, the Uyghur female lama She-lan-lan 舍藍藍 (1269-1332), from Gaochang 高昌 (near Turfan), founded Pumingsi 普明寺.[153] But we have no source mentioning the presence of Mongol lamas on Wutaishan during the Yuan and Ming periods.

With the construction of two prestigious monasteries, the appropriation of Aśoka's Buddha relics through the building of a big *stūpa*, the presence of some of the holiest Tibetan masters, and new literature in Tibetan praising the sanctity of the place, along with a new corpus of stories and legends, Tibetan Buddhism began to leave its mark on Wutaishan. From then on, the flow of Tibetan masters visiting Wutaishan never ceased.

### Ming-Dynasty Tibetan Buddhism on Wutaishan

The Ming dynasty continued the sponsoring of Wutaishan monasteries with the construction of a number of buildings and the performance of rituals to protect the state. The position of Wutaishan as central to imperial ideology was confirmed and even strengthened at least until the reign of Jiajing (1522-1567).[154] Like the Yuan, the Ming imperial family showed a continuous interest in

---

149    *Yuanshi* [1370] 1976, "Taiding di ji" 泰定帝紀: *juan* 30, 668.

150    Between 1267 and 1347 the Yuan granted a total of 32,861,000 *mu* 畝 to the Wutaishan monasteries (Wang Zhiyong and Cui Zhengsen 2000: 546). 1 *mu* = 614.4 sq.m.

151    Wang Lu 1995: 28. Nothing is left of this monastery except for Pakpa's *stūpa* and stone inscriptions (see Online Appendix B, "Puensi").

152    Schaeffer 2011: 219.

153    Yang Fuxue 2003: 42; Wang Zhiyong and Cui Zhengsen 2000: 565; quoting the *Fozu lidai tongzai* (before 1340).

154    Wang Zhiyong and Cui Zhengsen 2000: 594.

Tibetan Buddhism,[155] and, through its support of various Tibetan schools, appears largely non-sectarian in its sponsoring of Wutaishan's monasteries. Although bureaucrats denounced the conversion of Chinese people to Tibetan Buddhism and imperial edicts occasionally prohibited such conversions, more and more 'foreign monks' in China were in fact Han Chinese.[156] Like in Beijing, several monasteries on Wutaishan, such as Xiantongsi and Luohousi, housed both Chinese Buddhist and Tibetan Buddhist monks.[157] In Ming and early Qing sources, Tibetan Buddhism was simply called 'Buddhism of the Western Regions' (*Xiyu fojiao* 西域佛教), and its monks were 'foreign monks from the West' (*fanseng, xifanseng* 西番僧 or *xiseng* 西僧).[158] The distinction between the 'religion of the lamas' (*lama zhi jiao* 喇嘛之教)[159] and Chinese Buddhism would only be in use towards the end of the Qianlong reign of the Qing.

Although Tibetan Buddhist monasteries numbered few on Wutaishan, they acquired a prominent place in the fifteenth century thanks to Ming imperial patronage. Indeed, in his famous gazetteer printed in 1596, the monk Zhencheng 鎮澄 (1546-1617) publicly acknowledged the importance of Tibetan Buddhism on the mountain.[160] In the late fifteenth century, Tibetan monks were in charge of Wutaishan's clergies. From 1426 or 1448 until at least 1538,[161] the 'foreign' abbot of Yuanzhaosi was the overseer (*dugang* 都綱), in charge of administrating all of Wutaishan's 'Tibetan' (*fan*) and Chinese clergy as well as its lay

---

155    On Tibeto-Mongol Buddhism in the Ming period: Sperling 1983; Weidner 2001; Toh 2005; Köhle 2008; Köhle 2008: 79-84; Shen 2007; Robinson 2008: 371-382.

156    "In Ming times, the study of the Tibetan language and Tantric formulae became so much in vogue that there were more and more Chinese who desired to be honored as 'Tibetan masters'" (Toh 2004: 238-240). See also Charleux 2002a.

157    *Qingliangshan zhi* 1887 [1596]: *juan* 4, 9b; Sperling 1983: 117, n. 38; Weidner 2001: 130. The Great Huayansi, in ruins by the early Ming, was rebuilt and divided into two parts: Xiantongsi in the south and Da Wenshusi on top of the hill.

158    For instance, in Gao Shiqi 1989 [ca. 1700]: 8r.

159    The earliest known occurrence of this term is 1573 (Naquin 2000: 49, 208). See Charleux 2002a; Lopez 2003: Chapter 1.

160    Köhle 2008: 83. Zhencheng counted 100 monasteries, among which 64 were within the area delimited by the five terraces, and 36 were beyond (*Qingliangshan zhi* 1887 [1596]: *juan* 3, 1r and 9v).

161    Zheng Lin 1997: 21; Tuttle 2006a: 17. Köhle 2008: 81. During Zhengde's reign and at least up to 1538, the 'overseer,' with the title of *dharmarāja* (*fawang* 法王), was Zhang Jian-can 張堅參 (<Chang [?] Gyeltsen). In 1538 an "overseer of the prefectural Buddhist registration" (*senglusi dugang* 僧錄司都綱) with a Chinese name, Mingxu 明續, was concurrently residing at Xiantongsi: as pointed by Natalie Köhle, he may have been a second overseer, or else the seat of the office of overseer had been transferred to Xiantongsi (2008: 82-83).

Buddhists.[162] In 1481, on Emperor Chenghua's (r. 1465-1488) order, a monk with a Tibetan name, Duan-zhu-ban-dan (< Döndrup Pelden) Chanshi 短竹班丹禪師, was appointed abbot of the newly restored Da Wenshusi (later known as Pusading, on the site of the old Zhenrongyuan).[163] This monastery may have already been Tibetan Buddhist or mixed the two traditions.[164] These monks had to perform rituals for the protection of the state and "pray for the happiness of the country and the prosperity of the people."[165] On imperial order, the Tibetan monk Duo-er-zhi-jian 朵而只堅 (< Dorjé gyel[tsen]) erected Guang-zongsi in 1507 below Da Wenshusi/Pusading, and Yanjiaosi on the Central Terrace in 1512.[166]

However, it is unclear whether Tibetan or Chinese Buddhists were in charge of the mountain clergy after 1538, and there is no evidence of Ming patronage of Tibetan Buddhism on Wutaishan after the reign of Zhengde (1506-1522), when imperial largesse was re-directed towards Chinese Buddhist monasteries. Tibetan monasteries, such as Yuanzhaosi and Tayuansi, then became staffed by Chinese Buddhist monks. The second part of the Ming period witnessed an apogee for the Chinese Buddhist communities of Wutaishan.[167] Emperor Wanli (r. 1573-1620), a devout Buddhist, sponsored several Chinese monasteries and offered them copies of the Chinese Buddhist canon. His mother, Empress Dowager Li 李 (Cisheng 慈聖, 1546-1614), ordered new construction and renovations in Tayuansi and in Xiantongsi, in 1579 and 1606 respectively.[168] On that occasion, Wanli sent three thousand artisans from various parts of the empire to repair the Great White Stūpa. The talented Chan monk architect Miaofeng 妙峰 (Fudeng 福登, 1540-1613) was in charge of the restoration; in 1605 in Xiantongsi he also built the little Bronze Hall, with its ten thousand bronze buddha figures, and in 1606 the vaulted Beamless Hall (Wuliangdian 無樑殿) and cast

---

162    Köhle 2008: 80-82.

163    *Qingliangshan zhi* 1887 [1596]: *juan* 4, 8r; Silk 1996: 160, 163-166.

164    This monastery was offered the first copy of the Yongle (Tibetan) *Kanjur* (printed in 1410 in red ink) immediately after its completion.

165    *Qingliangshan zhi* 1887 [1596]: *juan* 4, 14r, Pokotilov 1935 [1893]: 74; Köhle 2008: 80; Xiao Yu 肖雨 1996: 10. As shown by Köhle, we have no evidence of the affiliation of Pusading to Tibetan Buddhism before that date.

166    Köhle 2008: 80.

167    See the biographies of great Chinese masters who lived in Wutaishan: Wang Zhiyong and Cui Zhengsen 2000: 609-619, 624-691.

168    Stele "Chijian Wutaishan Da Tayuansi beiji," dated to 1582 in Tayuansi (Beixin 1996: 34-35); *Qingliangshan zhi* 1887 [1596]: *juan* 4, 15v-18r; Weidner 2001: 129-130.

a bronze image of Mañjuśrī.[169] Xiantongsi thus appeared to be the most splendid imperial monastery on the mountain in late Ming times, as evidenced by the monumental stone inscriptions, great bronze bells and name plaques over doorways. On the empress dowager's order, in 1581 the famous Chinese monk Hanshan Deqing 憨山德清 (1546-1623)[170] and Miaofeng convened a great ritual to protect the country, with five hundred participants, lasting 120 days at Tayuansi. Chinese Buddhism was again entrusted with protecting the empire.

In the early Ming period, several 'foreign monks' visited the mountain. The Ming court invited Tibetan and 'Western' lamas, such as the Fifth Karmapa Dézhin Shekpa (1384-1415) in 1406; Jamchen Chöjé Śākya Yeshé (1354-1435),[171] several times between 1414 and 1419;[172] the Sakyapa lama Künga Trashi in 1413;[173] and Śāriputra Paṇḍita,[174] (Ch. Shilisha 室利沙, ca. 1335-1426), abbot of the Mahābodhi Temple of Bodhgayā in India and eminent Tantric master, in 1417.[175] On Wutaishan, these clerics gave initiations and teachings to crowds of devotees and performed rituals for the imperial family. The Fifth Karmapa performed anew the great ritual in honor of Yongle's (r. 1403-1425) deceased

---

169     Miaofeng was made abbot of the monastery with the title *huguo chanshi* 護國禪師 ("Chan master who protects the nation"). Prip-Moller 1967 [1937]: 275-281; Weidner 2001: 130. His funerary *stūpa* stands in the cemetery south of Santasi.

170     Hanshan Deqing, who was Miaofeng's close friend (and biographer), sometimes lived as a hermit at Wutaishan. He made a copy of the *Avataṃsaka sūtra* in his own blood mixed with gold, defended an abbot accused unfairly, contributed to protecting the forests against traders with the help of a prefect, pacified conflicts and obtained tax exemption for Wutaishan monasteries (Hsu 1979: 66-74).

171     Tsongkhapa's disciple and the founder of Séra Monastery in Central Tibet, sent to the Ming court to represent Tsongkhapa in 1414-1415.

172     *Qingliangshan zhi* 1887 [1596]: *juan* 8, 24r; *Qingliangshan xinzhi* 1985 [1694]: *juan* 2, 10rv; Sperling 1983: 184-185, n. 59, 152-154; Wang Zhiyong and Cui Zhengsen 2000: 585-586; Köhle 2008: 83.

173     Sperling 1983: 141.

174     *Paṇḍita*, 'learned, erudite' is a title given in India to erudite brahmans and in Tibet to lamas such as the Dalai and Panchen Lamas. For recent scholarship on Śāriputra: McKeown 2010.

175     Śāriputra had led a delegation to Emperor Yongle in Beijing in 1414, to whom he had offered five golden statues of the Jinas and a stone model of Mahābodhī Temple of Bodhgayā. Yongle conferred to him the title Great Preceptor of the Nation (*daguoshi* 大國師) (according to the imperial stone inscription of Zhenjuesi, 1475 (Miaozhou 1995 [1935]: *juan* 7, 71-72), of Yuanzhaosi, 1569 ("Chongxiu Yuanzhaosi beiji" 重修圓照寺碑記); 1996; Mighe [Ming period]: *juan* 25, "Dashan guoshi zhuan" 大善國師傳; Wang Zhiyong and Cui Zhengsen 2000: 691-696; Köhle 2008: 79-80; McKeown 2010.

imperial parents that he had performed in Nanjing,[176] and in 1424 Śāriputra
Paṇḍita performed the ritual of enthronement of the new emperor, Hongxi
(r. 1425-1426). They also encouraged imperial construction and restorations and
founded monasteries. [177] Śākya Yeshé 'founded' five Gélukpa monasteries for
Tibetan lamas, which means that he turned former Chinese Buddhist and Tibetan Karmapa and Sakyapa monasteries into Gélukpa ones.[178] Some of these
dignitaries remained on Wutaishan, like the Tibetan Tantric master Lama
Chenpo Sanggyé Pel, who had accompanied the Fifth Karmapa to Nanjing in
1407; appointed as abbot of Puensi, he stayed on Wutaishan for eleven years.[179]
The relics left by some of these 'foreign monks' after their deaths formed new
sacred sites that contributed to empower Wutaishan. Puningsi/Yuanzhaosi,[180]
a great Tibetan monastery of the Ming period, houses the *stūpa* containing one
third of Śāriputra's relics.[181]

Other 'foreign monks' visited Wutaishan in the Ming dynasty, such as Tibetan
lama Tangtong Gyelpo (ca. 1361-1485), famous for his construction of bridges: on
Wutaishan, "he gave a reading transmission of the *Litany of the Names of
Mañjuśrī (Mañjuśrīnāmasaṃgīti)* to an eager congregation of (Chinese?) mediators" and meditated for "eight months, during which time the five forms of
Mañjuśrī appeared to him in a series of visions and spoke a prophecy instruct-
ing him to build geomantic focal points (often taking the form of *stūpas*) to
suppress the four elements."[182] Other 'foreign monks' include Ashing Lama (d.
1636), a Gélukpa monk from Amdo whose influence was decisive in the conversion of Altan Khan in the early 1570s;[183] a Nepalese monk known as Ju-sheng
Jixiang 具生吉祥, or Che-ha-za shi-li 徹哈失里, who lived for five years in

176   *Qingliangshan zhi* 1887 [1596]: *juan* 8, 21r-23v; Sperling 1983: Chapter 3; Berger 2001.
177   At the request of the Fifth Karmapa, Yongle ordered the restoration of the Great White
       Stūpa in 1407 and the separation of its courtyard from Xiantongsi to create a new
       monastery, named Tayuansi (*Qingliangshan zhi* 1887 [1596]: *juan* 3, 2r; *juan* 4, 9b; Wang Lu
       1995).
178   These are Shouningsi, Pumingsi, Tayuansi, Puensi and Puningsi/Yuanzhaosi (Zheng Lin
       1997; Cai Hong 1999).
179   See the stone inscription "Xitian da lama Sangke bala xingshi bei" 西大喇嘛桑渴巴辣行
       實碑, 1459, in Huguosi (= Chong'ensi 崇恩寺) of Beijing, quoted by Huang Hao 1993: 11.
180   Puningsi was renamed Yuanzhaosi in 1434 (when Śāriputra's *stūpa* was erected), or in
       1458.
181   The two other parts were enshrined in Zhenjuesi 真覺寺 in Beijing (popularly known as
       Wutasi 五塔寺, Five-Stūpa Monastery, erected in 1466-1473 on Chenghua's orders, on the
       model of the Mahābodhī Temple in India), and in a monastery in Taiyuan, which was
       destroyed in 1547.
182   Debreczeny 2011: 26.
183   Elverskog 2003: 131 n. 204.

Shou'an Chanlin 壽安禪林, between 1369 and 1374, going on retreats and preaching Tantrism;[184] and a monk from Gaochang with a Tibetan name, Suo-nan-nang-jie 鎖喃曩結, who studied in Tibet, went to Wutaishan in 1598 and spent several years in Luohousi.[185] However, I found only one mention of a Mongol monk who visited Wutaishan during the Mongol Yuan period: the famous Tümed hermit Bogda Chagan Lama (d. 1627) visited Wutaishan and Tibet.[186]

## Conclusion

Geographical, supernatural and historical particularities of Wutaishan explain why this mountain became the site of a pan-Asian pilgrimage from the seventh century onwards and developed into an important site for the ritual protection of the Chinese state. While its ancient Chinese monasteries continued to receive generous imperial support from the Yuan, Ming and Qing courts, a significant and continuous Tibetan Buddhist presence was felt since its establishment in the thirteenth century, with the support of the Mongol Yuan and later the Ming imperial courts, who appointed lamas in charge of state rituals. But in spite of the Yuan court's involvement in Buddhism at Wutaishan, we have no trace of ethnic Mongol religious communities there.

During the Qing period, the Karmapa, Sakyapa (and perhaps Nyingmapa) monasteries all became Gélukpa. The history of Wutaishan monasteries is complex, and the following chapter will confirm that these institutions are not easily classified according to their affiliation to Chinese or Tibetan Buddhism since some of them changed affiliation or even housed both clergies. This chapter has shown that Wutaishan is ever-changing—from forests to pastures, from Daoist to Chinese and then Tibeto-Mongol Buddhist. The oldest layers are compressed and sedimented but not forgotten, since they are merged with more recent ones. While old stories are recycled, there is also room for innovation, new stories, new visions and new interpretations. When Mongols reconverted to Tibetan Buddhism in the late sixteenth century,[187] they certainly were not

---

184  Wang Zhiyong and Cui Zhengsen 2000: 699.

185  Wang Zhiyong and Cui Zhengsen 2000: 701-702.

186  Qiao Ji 2007: 135 sq., quoting his Tibetan biography.

187  The Mongol elite of the Yuan dynasty had converted to Buddhism and patronized monasteries and translations of texts. After the collapse of their empire, very few traces of Buddhism are found, and it is generally considered that Altan Khan is the initiator of the reconversion to Buddhism in the late sixteenth century.

unaware of the previous involvement of the Yuan court in Chinese and Tibetan Buddhism on Wutaishan; in addition, Ashing Lama, the main actor in the conversion of Altan Khan, came from Wutaishan (according to Altan Khan's biography). Wutaishan was a cultural and spiritual nexus that put Mongols into contact with Buddhists from Tibet, China and Central Asia; Mongols heard about Wutaishan from a variety of sources, which merged or superimposed to create a new Mongol *imaginaire*.

# CHAPTER 3

# Political and Clerical Promotion of Wutaishan in the Qing and Republican Periods

This chapter moves into the Qing and Republican periods and introduces the strategies implemented by the Qing empire and by the Wutaishan clergies to promote the pilgrimage among the Mongols. The first part focuses on how the Qing emperors developed Tibetan Buddhism on Wutaishan to such a point that Wutaishan became a 'Tibet in China' ruled by a representative of the Dalai Lama. In his seminal 1978 article "The Emperor as Bodhisattva in the Governance of the Ch'ing Empire," David Farquhar asserts that the Qing emperors expended an enormous amount of time and resources to promote the Wutaishan pilgrimage among the Mongols, which was part of their attempts at incorporating them within their empire:

> It may be, as has been asserted, that the emperors were interested in orienting the Mongols towards China and away from Tibet by this and other imperially supported Tibetan-style monastic establishments built on and near Chinese soil, but I suspect that the wish to spread the Mañjuśrī-emperor belief was the main reason for the new imperial concern with Mount Wu-t'ai.[1]

Yet it is quite possible that the role of the Qing imperial patronage of Wutaishan towards the Mongols has been overestimated. The second part of this chapter focuses on the local clergies' strategies to attract pilgrims. When the last Qing emperors had lost interest in the holy mountain and reduced their patronage, the resident clergies had to find new sources of income and adopted strategies to attract pilgrims and their donations. In the end, the high-ranking lamas who visited or resided on Wutaishan, authoring poems and pilgrimage guidebooks, played a significant role in attracting pilgrims to the Shanxi mountain.

### How the Manchu Emperors Reshaped Wutaishan

The Manchu dynasty's support of Buddhism on Wutaishan was in continuity with the previous dynasties' sponsorship: Wutaishan remained a major site for

---

1  Farquhar 1978: 29.

the protection of the state and the imperial family; in addition, the Qing emperors presented themselves as emanations of Mañjuśrī, with three emperors themselves journeying to the mountain. The emperors' promotion of Wutaishan also served as a means to strengthen their position in Inner Asia and to counterweight the power of the Dalai Lamas. Meanwhile, Gélukpa Buddhism acquired a prominent position on Wutaishan. The head lama presided over the whole clergy, including the Chinese monks (*heshang*), and Wutaishan became one of the headquarters of the Changkya Khutugtu's lineage. Discussing the continuities and innovations of the Manchu emperors' patronage will help us understand the position that Wutaishan acquired in the Tibeto-Mongol world, and their role in the development of the Mongols' pilgrimages.

### The Qing-Dynasty Administration of the Mountain

The Qing emperors reshaped Wutaishan into a predominantly Tibeto-Mongol Buddhist site, but the identity of the mountain also remained firmly rooted into its layered Chinese past. Their promotion and institutionalization of Wutaishan started in 1655, when forty Mongol lamas (*ge-long*, Tib. *gélong,* Mo. *gelöng,* Skt. *bhikṣu,* fully ordained monk) settled there on imperial order to conduct a forty-day ritual on behalf of the imperial family and the state. In 1657, fifty more lamas, including a doctor, were sent to Wutaishan, and in 1659 Emperor Shunzhi appointed a *jasag lama* (head lama, or chief administrative lama)[2] to preside over the mountain and take charge of Tibetan and Chinese affairs.[3] Since that time up to 1936, the Tibetan Buddhist clergy exercised spiritual and temporal authority over the monastic communities of Wutaishan.

This first *jasag lama*, A-wang-lao-zang 阿王老藏[4] (1601-1687), was a Gélukpa lama from the Western Hills (Xishan 西山), west of Beijing. He was certainly a sinicized Mongol,[5] since he bore the Chinese family name Jia 賈, a name that was used by Mongols living among the Chinese during the Ming.[6] In 1653, he

---

2   The full title is "Qinming guanli Wutaishan lama shiwu zhangyin zhasake da lama" 欽命管理五臺山喇嘛事務掌印扎薩克大喇嘛.

3   *Qingliangshan xinzhi* 1985 [1694]: *juan* 2, 10r, *juan* 3, 17r; Mongolian version *CLŠASB* 2: 169-170: "After the Great Qing had established its government at the city of Yan ging [Yanjing, i.e., Beijing], in the White Mouse year of the reign of Shunzhi (1660), Awanglobzang Lama was sent by imperial decree to administer Wutaishan, and he arrived by postal relay horses." On the Qing emperors' appointment of Tibetan and Mongolian monastic officials on Wutaishan: Tuttle 2011: 183-187.

4   Or A-wang-luo-bu-zang 阿旺羅布藏, Mo. Awanglobzang, < Tib. Ngakwang Lozang.

5   Besides, Mongolian sources identify him as a Mongol. The *UTAOSC* (71r) is the only source that says he came from Höhhot ("The famous wandering mendicant monk from Höhhot, Ng[a]gdwang blo bjang"). See Kara 2000: 15; Heissig 1953: 4; Heissig 1954: 12.

6   According to David Robinson, quoted by Tuttle 2011: 168, n. 18.

had taken vows from the Fifth Dalai Lama in visit to the capital, who predicted he would go to Wutaishan. A-wang-lao-zang was versed in esotericism and he translated texts from Sanskrit. In 1682 or 1683, Kangxi granted him the honorary title of *qingliang laoren* 清涼老人 ('elder of Qingliang').[7]

The chief administrative lama was an official of the first rank in the Qing hierarchy and wore a *longpao* 龍袍, the Qing official dress, which, for lamas, was yellow (Fig. 11). He was also the abbot of Pusading, which became the seat of the imperial administration of Wutaishan and thus the Gélukpas' principal monastery (Fig. 12). Long-life rituals to protect the country and the dynasty were performed in this monastery. A-wang-lao-zang performed such a ritual for Emperor Kangxi once in 1673 and twice in 1683.[8] Pusading was equipped with a lodging palace for the emperor and, since 1684, with a garrison under the command of a military official of the seventh rank, composed of ten horsemen and thirty infantrymen, who were in charge of keeping an eye on the monastery's precious objects. The *jasag lama* was assisted by a *da lama* in charge of administrative affairs,[9] who resided in Tailusi, as well as at least twelve other *da lamas*.[10] Pusading and Tailusi, supported by the Qing treasury, were thus 'imperial monasteries.'

A-wang-lao-zang remained in that position for more than twenty years. His successor in 1668 was the polyglot Mongol lama Lao-zang-dan-bei-(jian-can) 老藏丹貝(堅參)[11] (1632-1684), who came from Chongguosi 崇國寺[12] in

7    See *Qingliangshan xinzhi* 1985 [1694]: *juan* 7, 21v-24v, "Qingliang laoren A-wang-lao-zang taming" 清涼老人阿王老藏塔銘 (text in Zhang Yuxin 1988: 246-248); *Qinding Qingliangshan zhi* 1785: *juan* 16, 21r-v; Cui Zhengsen 1999; Wang Zhiyong and Cui Zhengsen 2000: 756-762; Tuttle 2011: 184.

8    See also the stone inscription "Yuzhi Pusading Dawenshuyuan bei" 御製菩薩頂大文殊院碑, 1671, text in Zhang Yuxin 1988: 241; partial English transl. in Köhle 2008: 87-88.

9    Title in the Qing imperial bureaucracy. The *da lama* supervises the internal organization of a monastery; the term is generally translated as 'abbot.'

10   The *jasag lama* proposed a candidate for the position of *da lama* to the Lifanyuan for approval. The Lifanyuan then sent the official document confirming the appointment and the rank (*Qinding Lifanyuan zeli* 1817: *juan* 56, 3r, 27r).

11   Or Luo-bu-zang-dan-bei 羅布藏丹貝, Mo. Lubzangdambi, < Tib. Lozang Tenpé (Gyeltsen).

12   In the first *jasag lama*'s funerary steles, Chongguosi is described as being located in the Western Hills; however, it can probably be identified with Huguosi 護國寺, called Dadu Chongguosi 大都崇國寺 in the Yuan dynasty, located north of Beijing's Imperial City. Huguosi was restored on the occasion of the visit of the Fifth Dalai Lama in 1652, then in 1722 and 1731. It was especially sponsored by Mongol monks (see the stele in Chinese and Tibetan "Yuzhi Chongguosi bei" 御制崇國寺碑文, 1722, in Huang Hao 1993: 92). It is no longer extant (*Rixia jiuwen kao*: 842-847; Huang Hao 1993: 10-14).

FIGURE 11
*Lama in Qing dynasty official dress.*
© BLOFELD 1938.

FIGURE 12
*Pusading imperial monastery.*
© OLIVÉR KÁPOLNÁS.

Beijing and bore the Chinese family name Zhao 趙.[13] He had first been appointed abbot (*da lama*) of Pusading, in 1659, and assistant to the *jasag lama.*

---

13   See his biography by Gao Shiqi 高士奇 in the 1685 stele of his funerary *stūpa*: "Da lama
     Lao-zang-dan-bei taming" 大喇嘛老藏丹貝塔銘 (in *Qingliangshan xinzhi* 1985 [1694]:
     *juan* 7, 24v–26v; *Qinding Qingliangshan zhi* 1785: *juan* 16, 21v-22r; Wang Zhiyong and Cui
     Zhengsen 2000: 756-764; Tuttle 2011: 193).

Sometime after Lao-zang-dan-bei's death, his disciple Lao-zang-dan-ba 老藏丹巴 became the third *jasag lama*. This ethnic Chinese lama, born in Shandong Province, in 1698 was granted the additional title *qingxiu chanshi* 清修禪師 ('meditation master') *jasag lama* in charge of Tibetan and Chinese affairs of Wutaishan, and was given a silver seal.[14] His successors also received the Chinese title *qingxiu chanshi*.

The first six *jasag lama*s were appointed by the Manchu emperors and all came from Chongguosi. However, from the seventh onward, they were appointed every six years by the Dalai Lama and became ambassadors for Tibetan religious affairs in China. Several *jasag lama*s served several terms— this is why there were only seventeen *jasag lama*s between the mid-eighteenth to the mid-twentieth century.[15] Whether Mongol or Tibetan, they were confirmed clerics who were trained in the main centers of the Tibetan Buddhist world and generally had earned a *géshé* degree.[16]

### The Foundation of Gélukpa Monasteries on Wutaishan

The Kangxi and Qianlong reigns were a period of large-scale construction and renovation of temples, monasteries and travel lodges. Since the Yuan and Ming, when the first Tibetan Buddhist monasteries were built on the mountain, and to a greater extent during the eighteenth and nineteenth centuries, when a significant number of lamas populated these monasteries, Wutaishan's sacred landscape included more and more Tibetan elements. The 1883 *New Gazetteer of Wutai* lists twenty-six Tibeto-Mongol monasteries for the Yonzheng period and more than a thousand 'monks in yellow robes.'[17] If we include temples managed by only one or two lamas, the total number of Gélukpa monasteries and temples reached thirty in the late nineteenth century.[18] In the heyday of Gélukpa Buddhism on Wutaishan, when Changkya Khutugtu Rölpé Dorjé, the

---

14    "Tidu Wutaishan fanhan da lama" 提督五臺山番漢大喇嘛 (in *Qingliangshan xinzhi* 1985 [1694]: *juan* 3, 23r, quoted by Tuttle 2011: 184, n. 91; Wang Zhiyong and Cui Zhengsen 2000: 762-764); stele "Chongxiu Wutaishan Zhenrongyuan ji" 重修五臺山真容院記 in Pusading. It is unclear whether he became *jasag lama* just after Lao-zang-dan-bei's death in 1684, or after A-wang-lao-zang's death in 1687 (A-wang-lao-zang would then have had a second term as *jasag lama* from 1684 to 1687). Tuttle (2011: 193) believes that A-wang-lao-zang was *jasag lama* from 1659 to 1687.

15    A list of the twenty-three *jasag lama*s is given in Online Appendix I.

16    Doctor in theology, first degree in academic studies.

17    Tian Pixu *et al.* 1883: *juan* 3, quoted by Zhao Gaiping and Hou Huiming 2006: 29.

18    Tian Pixu *et al.* 1883: *juan* 3, quoted by Zhao Gaiping and Hou Huiming 2006: 29. Of the 124 temples and monasteries inventoried in 1956, 99 were Chinese Buddhist and 25 were Tibeto-Mongol (according to the 1956 inventory made by the Wutaishan guji baohusuo 五

highest reincarnation of Inner Mongolia, spent summers on the mountain between 1750 and 1786, up to three thousand clerics lived on Wutaishan. The two
largest Gélukpa monasteries were Pusading, with five hundred to one thousand
lamas, and Luohousi, with about two hundred lamas in residence. Eleven Gélukpa monasteries were state-funded.[19]

Although the *jasag lama* presided over the entire clergy,[20] the Changkya
Khutugtu became more and more influential from the eighteenth century
on.[21] From the Yongzheng to the Republican period, twenty or twenty-one (according to the period) Gélukpa monasteries were under the jurisdiction of the
*jasag lama*, while five or six 'belonged' to the Changkya Khutugtu.[22] There were
more Mongol monks in the Changkya's monasteries than in the *jasag lama*'s.[23]

The *jasag lama* may have held an academic degree, but Gélukpa monasteries
themselves were not academic centers of learning proposing degrees. However,
in the late nineteenth century, there was one school of Buddhist doctrine (Tib.
*tsennyi*, Mo. *tsanid*), located behind Pusading, with twenty-six students.[24] In
addition, the residing and visiting great masters gave teachings and initiations.

Even with an increasing presence of Tibetan and Mongol lamas, the transformation of Wutaishan into a Tibeto-Mongol pilgrimage site was a gradual process. Fifteen Chinese Buddhist monasteries became Gélukpa over the course of
the Qing dynasty, and eight new Gélukpa monasteries and hermitages were
founded (Table 3).[25] By the eighteenth century, the Manchu emperors' support

---

臺山古蹟保護所, quoted in Wei Guozuo 1993 [1988]: 215-216). On other inventories and
names of monasteries: Wang Xiangyun 2004: 6.

19   According to the *Qinding Lifanyuan zeli* 1817: *juan* 56, 27r-v: Pusading, Tailusi, Luohousi,
Shouningsi, Yuhuachi, Jingangku, Yongquansi, Qifosi, Sanquansi, Shancaidong and
Puansi. Except for Tailusi and Luohousi, the others can be considered branch monasteries
of Pusading: the *jasag lama* chose their abbots, whose function was purely nominal.

20   The *jasag lama* was the supervisor of Wutaishan's clergies, including the Chinese Buddhist
monks. However, the Chinese Buddhist monasteries were administrated by the Wutaishan
Senggangsi 五台山僧綱司, based in Xiantongsi, which coordinated its decisions with
the *jasag lama*.

21   On the respective powers of the *jasag lama* and the Changkya Khutugtu on Wutaishan:
Song Yu 2010: 294.

22   Zhao Gaiping and Hou Huiming 2006: 31.

23   Song Yu 2010: 294.

24   Pokotilov 1935 [1893]: 76-77. It may be the monastery mentioned by Migwachir (Miɣvacir
2008 [1942]: 405) behind Pusading: Gebshi-yin Süme, Monastery of the *Géshé*.

25   The often-cited fact that ten Chinese monasteries were turned into Tibetan monasteries
by Emperor Kangxi in 1683, or in 1705, has no historical basis. Wang Xiangyun (2004: 8)
suggests that the number ten was simply drafted to parallel the ten main Chinese
monasteries (see also Köhle 2008: 77, n. 14).

TABLE 3     *Foundation date of twenty-seven Tibetan Buddhist monasteries in activity during the Qing period. In bold: the state-funded monasteries listed in the* Qinding Lifanyuan zeli *1817. The foundation date of three small Qing dynasty Gélukpa monasteries is not known:* Jinhuasi 金華寺, Nan'gemiao 南閣廟 *and Yu'naian* 魚耐庵. *The 'new Tibetan Buddhist monasteries' of the Qing period were completely new foundations or built on the ruins on former structures.*

| Former Chinese monasteries turned into Tibetan Buddhist monasteries under the | | | New Tibetan Buddhist monasteries |
|---|---|---|---|
| Yuan dynasty | Ming dynasty | Qing dynasty (date of conversion) | Qing dynasty |
| Shouningsi | Pusading[b] | Luohousi (early 17th century)[d] | Yongquansi (1683) |
| Puensi[a] | Yuanzhaosi[c] | Zhenhaisi (1710) | Tailusi (1671 or 1685) |
| | | Baohuasi (1711) | Guanyindong (18th |
| | | Wulangmiao (early 18th century) | century) |
| | | **Jingangku** (18th century) | Puleyuan (1765-1769) |
| | | Shancaidong (18th century) | Wenshusi (Qianlong |
| | | **Sanquansi** (18th century) | period) |
| | | **Qifosi** (18th century) | Cifusi (1814) |
| | | Tiewasi (18th century?) | Jifusi (19th century?) |
| | | Guanghuasi (19th century) | Shifangtang (1831) |
| | | Pushousi (end of the 19th century) | |
| | | Puhuasi (ca. 1872) | |
| | | Santasi | |
| | | **Yuhuachi** | |
| | | **Puansi** | |
| 2 monasteries | 2 monasteries | 15 monasteries | 8 monasteries |

[a]  It is unclear whether Shouningsi and Puensi remained Tibetan Buddhist institutions from the Yuan up to the Qing, or became Chinese Buddhist after the Yuan, and again Tibetan Buddhist in the Qing.
[b]  Pusading was staffed by lamas as early as 1481, but it may have become Chinese Buddhist from the late Ming up to 1656-1659, when a Gélukpa community settled in it.
[c]  Yuanzhaosi was turned into a Tibetan Buddhist monastery in the fifteenth century, but apparently became a Chinese Buddhist monastery in the last decades of the fifteenth century, and was again affiliated to Gélukpa Buddhism in the early Qing period.
[d]  Luohousi was staffed by both Chinese Buddhist monks and lamas during the Wanli period. It was affiliated to Gélukpa Buddhism in the Shunzhi period.

was restricted to monasteries of the Gélukpa tradition, while the other, 'red traditions (Karmapa, Sakyapa, Nyingmapa etc.) were viewed as heterodox and illicit. Hence, the 'red' communities that were active during the Ming dynasty and perhaps in the early Qing were turned into Gélukpa centers. However, some 'red' hermits and monks did reside on Wutaishan in Qing times, and small monasteries that do not appear in the official records may have belonged to

non-Gélukpa schools of Tibetan Buddhism. For instance, when the great eighteenth-century scholar and artist Situ Panchen Chökyi Jungné visited China, he
is said to have stayed on Wutaishan in a branch monastery of Katok Monastery
in Dergé (Kham/Western Sichuan), one of the main monasteries of the Nying-
ma School.[26]

### Wutaishan as a Tibeto-Mongol Enclave in Chinese Territory

The most splendid and lavishly decorated monasteries patronized by the Qing
court were staffed by Mongol and Tibetan monks and attracted so many Mongol pilgrims that, from the eighteenth to the early twentieth century, to Chinese
visitors Wutaishan had a strong exotic flavor.[27] The Gélukpa clergy not only had
more power, since the *jasag lama* presided over both the Gélukpa and Chinese
clergies, but the yellow monasteries were wealthier than the Chinese ones. Up
to twenty to thirty *li* (about ten or fifteen kilometers) to the north and south of
the village of Taihuai, the land belonged to Gélukpa monasteries, which did not
pay taxes to the Qing government. According to Edkins,

> the Pusading had landed estates supposed to bring into the treasury sev-
> eral tens of thousands of taels annually. The lands of the monasteries are
> in Shanse [Shanxi], but also in Pau-ting-foo [Baodingfu 保定府], Chen-
> ting-foo [Zhendingfu], etc., belonging to the metropolitan province. A
> large sum is conferred each winter by the Emperor on the Tibetan chiefs
> of the monastery during their visit to Peking, where they appear at the
> New Year festivities.[28]

The rent and produce from their lands were the first source of income for monasteries.[29] In 1935, the forty-one Chinese Buddhist and Gélukpa monasteries
'inside the terraces' still owned 83,817 *mu* 畝 of farmland scattered across Wutai,
Fanzhi 繁峙, Dai and Fuping 阜平 Counties, of which two to three percent was
farmed by the monks, the rest being rented to farmers; the annual income of
the rented lands was 1,082 tons of produce.[30] Li Xiangzhi wrote in 1932 that
all the farmlands and forests of Wutaishan's slopes belonged to Gélukpa

---

26  For the possible identification of this monastery: Debreczeny 2011: 46, n. 118.
27  Wang Chang 1999 [1792]: 22th day; Zhang Dungu 1911: 24; Jiang Weiqiao 1961 [1918]: 21; Li
    Xiangzhi 1932: 3.
28  Edkins 1893 [1878]: 239.
29  On the economy of the Wutaishan monasteries: *Wutaixian zhi* 1988: 586-788.
30  Pusading and Xiantongsi owned 22,550 *mu* and 6,013 *mu* of farmland respectively. See the
    land incomes plus the production of coal, wood and cattle in *Wutaixian zhi* 1988: 587-588;
    Xin Butang and Zheng Fulin 1995: 29-30.

monasteries. One monastery owned from 30 to 110 *qing* 頃 of land,[31] and rented them to ten to fifty families of Chinese tenant farmers. In the ninth or tenth month of every year, a lama from the monastery came to receive the payment and decide on the payment for the following year. The lama stayed nearly two months in every village, and sheep and pigs were killed to please him.[32]

The Buddhist monasteries also owned forty shops in Taihuai, which were rented out to Chinese merchants (in 1937). In 1946 a monastic business was set up to sell Tibeto-Mongol medicine and also cereals, flour, cloth, shoes, wool and antiques.[33]

Although the total amount of silver and gold offered to Gélukpa monasteries by the imperial throne was lower than that offered to the much more numerous Chinese Buddhist monasteries, the major Gélukpa monasteries individually received larger amounts than the Chinese ones,[34] along with copies of the *Kanjur* and *Tanjur*, Buddhist statues, ceremonial scarves (*khatak*), ceremonial robes and so on. The clergy of Pusading and Tailusi was entirely supported by the Qing treasury and by local taxes ('tribute') from all the counties of Shanxi.[35] Moreover, Pusading received a symbolical distinction, since in 1683 Kangxi authorized its Buddha hall to be covered with yellow glazed tiles—the imperial color reserved for use on imperial palaces. Pusading remained the wealthiest monastery during the Republican period; it had branch monasteries, such as Sanquansi, and one of its abbots went on to found Guanghuasi and Cifusi.

Through sponsoring these Tibeto-Mongol monasteries, the Qing reshaped the sacred landscape. The large Gélukpa monasteries were all located in the central part of Wutaishan, around the village of Taihuai (Map 3), whereas most

---

31    1 *qing* = 6.144 hectares.

32    Li Xiangzhi 1932: 157-158.

33    Xin Butang and Zheng Fulin 1995: 30.

34    Kangxi offered to Pusading 1,000 taels of silver and rebuilt Tailusi with 3,180 taels of gold; Qianlong spent 3,000 taels restoring Tailusi.

35    In the nineteenth century, according to Qing regulations, the sole Wutai County every year had to send 1,200 taels to the *jasag lama* and 1,200 to the *da lama* (Tian Pixu *et al.* 1883, quoted by the *Wutaixian zhi* 1988: 586: "The grass and beans which the lamas give to horses, the rice, wheat, tea and oil used by the lamas, come from [Wutai County] farmlands and in-kind contributions of an amount of 1,200 taels, and lamas can use them or sell them as they wish." See also Xin Butang and Zheng Fulin 1995: 29; Zhao Gaiping and Hou Huiming 2006: 32; Yan Tianling 2004: 41, quoting a petition of the *da lama* of Tailusi to the Meng Zang weiyuanhui (Mongol and Tibetan Affairs Commission): "Wutaishan Tailusi da lama Yi-she-peng-cuo yuancheng" 五臺山台麓寺達喇嘛依什捧磋原呈, *Mengzang yuebao* 蒙藏月報 1934: *juan* 2-2. For local stories on Shanxi peasants burdened by these taxes: Li Xiangzhi 1932: 15-17.

of the Chinese Buddhist monasteries were scattered across the slopes and in the valleys. And the Manchu emperors clearly indicated to all their subjects, through the imperial gazetteers written or prefaced by Gélukpa lamas and through their visible sponsorship of monasteries, that the Gélukpa communities were the central locus of patronage on Wutaishan.

Gélukpa monasteries were treated as a 'tributary territory' according to Qing regulations (*Qinding Lifanyuan zeli*). The *jasag lama* of Wutaishan and the *da lama* of Tailusi received a tribute from the counties of Shanxi and, in their turn, presented a tribute twice a year in Beijing, for the New Year and for the *duanwu* 端午 holiday (the 5th day of the fifth lunar month).[36] This tribute consisted of two boxes of mushrooms, which were sent by each of them to the Lifanyuan 理藩院 (Court of Colonial Affairs). The return gifts from the emperor consisted of silk, brocade and other fabrics.[37]

With Qing imperial support, Wutaishan became a Tibeto-Mongol enclave on the edge of Chinese territory, ruled by a representative of the Dalai Lama. Under the reign of Jiaqing (r. 1795-1820), because of its number of Mongol and Tibetan pilgrims, Wutaishan was called 'the Tibet of China' (Zhonghua Weizang 中華衛藏).[38] Lamas from this outpost of Tibetan civilization acted as diplomats in conflicts with Tibetans and Mongols. The Thirteenth Dalai Lama, who spent five months on Wutaishan in 1908, felt more secure and free on Wutaishan than in Beijing. He felt "so comfortable in these surroundings that he treated his Chinese escort with contempt, basically ignoring their sovereignty over this territory."[39] His sojourn allowed an unprecedented opportunity to interact with Westerners and Japanese without the interference of the Qing court.[40]

---

36    When in Beijing, they resided in Wumenmiao五門廟 (Huguosi 護國寺 Street), which was a branch of a Wutaishan monastery (Pusading?) (stele of Wumenmiao written by abbot Jian-can peng-cuo-le-shi 堅參朋錯勒石, dated 1722, quoted by Huang Hao 1993: 248). This small monastery had only three residing monks.

37    Uspensky (2007) considers the mushroom tribute symbolical, yet the Wutaishan mushrooms were highly valued in Chinese pharmacopeia. In fact, the mushroom tribute existed before the Qing dynasty.

38    The imperial stele "Qingliangshan ji" 清凉山記, 1811 (in Zhou Zhenhua et al. 1998: 81) says: *huangjiao wei zhu fanbu qingxin xinyang, jinguan chaoshan dingli zhe, jie zhong bu jue, cheng Zhonghua Weizangye* 黃教為諸藩部傾心信仰,進関朝山頂禮者,接踵不絕,誠中華衛藏也—"the yellow teachings are the faith of all the *fan* [Mongol and Tibetan] tribes who believe with their whole heart, and for those who enter China to pay homage to the mountain making prostrations one after the other without interruption; it is unquestionably the Tibet of China" (Weizang is an ancient name for Tibet).

39    Tuttle 2005: 267, n. 79 quoting Bell 1987 [1946]: 81-82.

40    American diplomat and Tibetologist William W. Rockhill (1854-1914), Finnish baron and Russian officer Carl Gustaf Mannerheim (1867-1951), French explorer Commandant Henri

Because of their heavy imperial patronage, their organization, the omnipresence of visible imperial signs (stone inscriptions, yellow roof tiles, name plaques above doorways), the presence of the Changkya Khutugtu and their 'ritualistic' or practice-oriented focus (as opposed to the academic orientation of university monasteries),[41] the Gélukpa monasteries of Wutaishan were comparable to the imperial monasteries of Beijing and Dolonnor. They were of crucial political importance for the Manchu emperors and benefited from a particularly high status.[42] However, in contrast with the imperial temples and monasteries of Beijing and Chengde,[43] they were open to all visitors and to their donations and enjoyed more autonomy in their internal affairs.[44]

## The Manchu Emperors' Promotion of Wutaishan

By reshaping Wutaishan as the 'Tibet of China,' the aim of the Manchu emperors was, according to D. Farquhar, to "orienting [orient] the Mongols towards China and away from Tibet," to spread among them belief in the emperor-Mañjuśrī and to ensure their unfailing devotion and fidelity. I will question this assertion by examining two main means the Qing used to bring the Mongols to Wutaishan: imperial tours and the publication of a new gazetteer that was translated into Mongolian, Tibetan and Manchu. But were the Mongols the main target of the imperial tours and gazetteers?

---

d'Ollone (1868-1945), British Ambassador to China Sir John Jordan (1852-1925), Russian Minister of Foreign Affairs Count Alexandr Izvolsky (1856-1919), German Consul Dr. E. Heintges and Japanese military attaché Fufushima Masanoni. On his meeting with Rockhill: Rockhill 1910: 77; Wimmel 2003: 167-168; Meinheit 2011; Sperling 2011.

41　According to the classification made by Japanese historian of religion Nagao Gajin 長尾 雅人, summed up by Miller (1959: 20-22), 'ritualistic monasteries' emphasize the performance of services towards laypersons and do not offer academic degrees.

42　Pokotilov 1935 [1893]: 58; Miller 1959: 82-84.

43　The private monasteries of the Manchu imperial family, located within the imperial palaces and imperial parks, were not accessible to the public; other monasteries of Beijing, such as Yonghegong or Zhantansi, were only opened on major celebrations like the New Year festival.

44　For instance, the Lifanyuan did not fix a number of lamas per monastery on Wutaishan (Uspensky 2007, quoting the *Qinding Lifanyuan zeli*). The monasteries of Beijing and Chengde, as well as the 'imperial' monasteries of Mongolia, had a fixed number of lamas, who received an official certificate (*dudie* 度牒); nevertheless, these quotas were not respected, and the majority of monks who resided in these monasteries had no certificate.

### The Mañjuśrī Emperor

Through the identification of the persona of the emperor with Mañjuśrī, the Qing naturally reinforced their connection to Wutaishan. The Manchus had inherited the cult of Mañjuśrī from the Mongols even before the conquest of China. When the Fifth Dalai Lama and the Fourth Panchen Lama identified the Manchu emperor as an emanation of the *bodhisattva* in a joint letter recognizing the legitimacy of Manchu power in 1640, Mañjuśrī was elevated as the protector of their empire then in formation.[45] The phonetic proximity between 'Manchu' and 'Mañjuśrī' added further weight to this identification, which endured until the end of the dynasty. Emperor Qianlong even represented himself as an emanation of Mañjuśrī in a much-discussed series of *thangka*s,[46] and he had the *dhāraṇī* of Mañjuśrī carved in his mausoleum.[47]

It is well known that, through imperial edicts, multilingual stone inscriptions and portraits in guises, the Manchu emperor simultaneously addressed the various constituencies of his empire according to their respective traditions of governance: he presented himself as a Indo-Tibetan Buddhist *cakravartin* (universal emperor) and emanation of Mañjuśrī for Tibetan and Mongol audiences, as an Inner Asian *khaan* for a Mongol audience, as a Confucian sage-king for a Han audience, and as a Manchu warrior for a Manchu audience.[48] However, recent scholarship has proved that the compartmentalization of these constituencies based on language was not completely hermetic,[49] references to the emperor-Mañjuśrī being found in Chinese sources too, such as a gazetteer of Wutaishan,[50] as well as a Qianlong imperial stone

---

45    Farquhar 1978: 8-9; Chayet 1985: 47. The extensive literature on this subject is aptly summarized in the most recent publications: Atwood 2000; Berger 2003a: 55-57; Wang Zilin 2006; Elverskog 2006. The connection between the Manchus and Mañjuśrī was already found in the Mongolian letters of the Manchu ruler Hungtaiji.

46    Farquhar 1978: 11-20, 22-34; Henss 2001; Berger 2003a and 2003b.

47    Wang-Toutain, personal communication, 2009. On Qianlong's cult of Mañjuśrī and Yamāntaka in Fanzonglou 梵宗樓 Temple in the Imperial Palace: Wang Zilin 2006.

48    Farquhar 1978; Crossley 1999.

49    Atwood (2000: 129-130) studied the 'language of loyalty' and showed it was also shared by Mongols, Manchus and Chinese.

50    The denomination 'holy emperor Mañjuśrī' or 'supreme lord, incarnation of Mañjuśrī' found in the Mongolian gazetteers of Wutaishan (colophon of the *UTAOSC* 73r; Farquhar 1978: 30), does not appear in the Chinese language gazetteers (Tuttle 2011: 182). However, Köhle (2008: 87 and n. 63) found a veiled reference to the emperor-Mañjuśrī in Lao-zang-dan-ba's preface to the 1701 *Qingliangshan xinzhi* and concludes, "The image of the emperor as an emanation of Mañjuśrī was also known and (carefully) propagated in Chinese-language publications," and thus this image must have been recognized by

inscription.[51] While the above-mentioned *thangka*s were directed at a very small audience or at no audience at all,[52] two colossal statues of Mañjuśrī enshrined in imperial monasteries were viewed as portraits of Qianlong in local Chinese folklore.[53]

As in the case of previous dynasties, Wutaishan was at the core of political legitimization for this essentially foreign dynasty ruling China. By presenting themselves as emanations of the *bodhisattva* residing on Wutaishan, the Manchu emperors could symbolically legitimate their stranglehold on Chinese territory. In a recent article, Natalie Köhle convincingly showed that they continued a tradition begun in the Tang dynasty of promoting the cult of Wutaishan for the ritual protection of the Chinese state and used the *cakravartin* political ideology much as their predecessors did.[54]

Yet the Qing emperors' patronage of Wutaishan must also be placed within their larger multifaceted support of Tibetan Buddhism. They patronized Buddhist institutions and practices both publicly—by founding monasteries and engaging in translation projects and rituals—and privately—by attending inner court rituals, teachings and private initiation ceremonies. Tibetan Buddhism was a key component of Qing political ideology and strategies of rule, and such rituals enacted for the longevity of the imperial family and for the protection of the state were central to the court.[55] The emperors, according to Marina Illich, cultivated relations with lamas

> not simply as a steely measure of *realpolitik* to get control over Tibetan Buddhist territories, as most scholars assert, ... but to gain control over the potent technology of empire that Tantric Buddhism had to offer," a technology "that endowed them with a kind of totalizing agency over the cosmos."[56]

---

certain circles of Chinese Buddhists. See also the painting of Qianlong as Mañjuśrī engaged in a discussion with Vimalakīrti (Berger 2003a: 1-4, plate 1).

51    The Chinese text of the imperial stele dated 1792 in Pusading mentions the emperor as "Great Emperor Mañjuśrī" and recalls the phonetic proximity between Manchu and Mañju(śrī).

52    Some were painted for private use, others were sent to Tibetan hierarchs: one was offered to the Dalai Lama to be exhibited in the Potala Palace.

53    Zhengjuesi 正覺寺, near Yuanmingyuan 圓明園 Park, west of Beijing (Pander, *The Lamaist Pantheon*, in Pander 1994 [1889]: 40-41) and Shuxiangsi of Chengde (Hedin 1933: 89).

54    Köhle 2008: 88-89; Wang-Toutain 2007; Tuttle 2011: Table 1.

55    Köhle 2008; Tuttle 2011: 176.

56    Illich (2006: 157, 318-320). What she calls 'Tantric technologies of empire' refer to the ideology of the *cakravartin* kinship based on state patronage of the Buddhist institution,

Therefore, the promotion of Tibetan Buddhism on Wutaishan may be explained by the necessity to continue esoteric rituals to protect the empire in the face of the disappearance of the Chinese esoteric tradition. In this perspective, then, the Manchu emperors' endorsement may amount less to a sponsoring of *Tibetan* Buddhism on Wutaishan than to a more general support of *esoteric* Buddhism.[57]

Nonetheless, the promotion of Mañjuśrī and Wutaishan was also part of a strategy to counter the growing power of the Dalai Lama, whose influence over the Mongols in the seventeenth century came to be seen as a major threat to the Manchus' sovereignty in Inner Asia: the Tibetan pontiff not only had become the temporal ruler of Tibet but also regularly legitimated Mongol khanships by bestowing seals, received military assistance from the Khoshuud kings and acted as a diplomat in Inner Asian conflicts.[58] By bestowing titles, thus endowing the Mongol nobility with the authority to rule, and by officially recognizing Buddhist reincarnations, the Manchu emperors appropriated the ritual power of the Dalai Lamas.

The question of the conversion of Qianlong and other Qing emperors to Tibetan Buddhism, which has caused much ink to spill, is not relevant here: whether they sincerely believed in Tibetan Buddhism or used it to ritually protect the empire and as a political expediency to manipulate their Tibetan and Mongol subjects seems to be of less significance than the fact that, in the eyes of the Mongols, they comported themselves as genuine believers.[59] Elverskog has shown the great success of this strategy: the Chinggisid Mongols saw

---

which offers "a broad range of ritual and ideological technologies with which to master the elements, subdue malevolent forces, vanquish enemies, dispel disease and see through the prism of time to future and past events alike," and that represents "a full repertoire of discursive and institutional practices to secure and maintain socio-cosmic harmony" (2006: Part I, Chapter 2, more specifically p. 172-173, drawing on Ruegg (1995) and other sources).

57    Köhle 2008: 105.

58    Illich showed that the Manchu promotion of the holy universal emperor who emanated from Mañjuśrī (the protector of China) was modeled on, rivaled and even outbid that of the Dalai Lama, who was the holy reincarnation (and emanation of Avalokiteśvara, the protector of Tibet) and temporal ruler (Illich 2006: 313-322; also Elverskog 2006: 75-78).

59    For some divergent opinions on whether the Qing emperors genuinely believed in Tibetan Buddhism or just used it as a political means: Farquhar 1978; Grupper 1984: 47-75; Chayet 1985: 58-65; Wang Xiangyun 1995; Stoddard 1999; Zhao Linen 2001; Berger 2003a; Ishihama 2005; Illich 2006; Ishihama 2011; Uspensky 2011.

themselves as subjects of the great Qing empire and addressed the Manchu emperor as 'Holy Emperor Mañjuśrī' in their writings.[60]

In any case, the emperors of the early and mid-Qing seem to have taken their role as emanations of Mañjuśrī very seriously, and the *bodhisattva*'s abode consequently occupied a significant place in the imperial ideology. The emperors sponsored monasteries and redaction of gazetteers, personally visited famous sites and wrote stone inscriptions, name plaques and poems for monasteries. By contrast, the Ming emperors did not tour Wutaishan nor sponsor gazetteers, and they wrote far fewer inscriptions.[61] For the Mongols of the Qing empire, Wutaishan was connected to the emperor-Mañjuśrī, who sanctified and empowered the place by his presence. But did they especially visit Wutaishan to pay their respects to the emperor?

### The Emperors' and Mongol Nobles' Tours to Wutaishan

According to D. Farquhar, Qing imperial tours to Wutaishan were kinds of 'pilgrimages' to recall and reinforce their connection with Mañjuśrī in the eyes of their Mongol subjects.[62] Emperor Shunzhi did not, at least officially, visit the mountain—a legend says that he did not in fact die in 1661, aged twenty-three, but rather secretly lived as a monk in a monastery on Wutaishan. His son and successor Kangxi visited Wutaishan five times: once in 1683 with his beloved grandmother, Empress Dowager Xiaozhuang 孝莊 (1613-1688), a Khorchin Mongol, a second time in 1683,[63] and then in 1698, 1702 and 1710. Yongzheng accompanied his father Kangxi in 1702 but did not visit Wutaishan as an emperor. Qianlong visited Wutaishan six times (in 1746, 1750, 1761, 1781, 1786 and 1792), and his mother, Empress Xiaosheng 孝聖, (1693-1777) accompanied him on three of his visits.[64] During their tours, Kangxi and Qianlong were especially generous towards Wutaishan's monasteries: the total amount of the offerings

---

60   Elverskog 2006, also in Atwood 2000.

61   Köhle 2008: 90.

62   Farquhar 1978: 29.

63   See Gao Shiqi 1989 [ca. 1700].

64   In 1761, Qianlong traveled with the empress dowager for her seventieth birthday; she was so taken by the most famous image of Wutaishan, the Mañjuśrī of Shuxiangsi, that she expressed the desire to copy it. To enshrine the replica, Qianlong founded Baoxiangsi 寶相寺 in the hills west of Beijing, close to Baodisi 寶諦寺, which had itself been established in 1751 as a 'replica' of Pusading. In 1774, another copy of the statue was enshrined in a temple of Chengde, which was also named Shuxiangsi (Berger 2003a: 161; Berger 2011: 362-363).

for Qianlong's reign adds up to 720,000 taels of white silver.[65] Jiaqing was the last emperor to tour the mountain, in 1811. The previous imperial tours represented a huge financial burden on the population;[66] by contrast, Jiaqing's visit was marked by an atmosphere of austerity.[67]

The touring emperors were often accompanied by Mongols. The Khalkha reincarnation, Zanabazar, accompanied Kangxi on his third tour in 1698; he gave the monks many teachings and gifts of tea and money and composed a benediction prayer.[68] On the same tour were Ööled (Eleuthes) nobles from the Kukunor region: Bkrashis Baatur, Tüshiyetü Daiching, Namtsar Erdeni, Puntsug Taiji and others.[69] In 1710, the Guihua City (Höhhot) Commander-in-Chief Wu-ji—probably a Mongol according to his name—journeyed in Kangxi's retinue. In 1811, when Jiaqing took Mongol nobles to pray on Wutaishan, they visited temples "in the spirit of a unique family of interior [China] and exterior [outside China]."[70] Yet, all in all, Mongols represented only a small proportion of the whole imperial retinue.[71]

Natalie Köhle has pointed out that Kangxi's tours to Wutaishan were not in actual fact pilgrimages and had very diverse underlying motives and objectives: they "were only one part of a larger project of imperial touring of the empire, and the tours were modeled after (Han) Chinese as well as Inner Asian styles of rulership."[72] They were the occasion for the emperor to perform literary and political activities such as composing and reciting classical Chinese poetry, competing with his sons and soldiers in martial skills, appraising or chastising local officials, or inspecting waterways and dike works. Kangxi also killed a tiger that had been terrorizing the region—an event linked to the construction of Tailusi. Directed towards multiple audiences—Han, Tibetans, Manchus and Mongols, lay and religious elites, literati, bannermen, officials, monks and even

65    Zhao Gaiping and Hou Huiming 2006: 29. This includes the 80,000 taels of silver Qianlong
       spent in 1786 to restore the Taihuai Imperial City, the roads and the bridges (Wang Zhiyong
       and Cui Zhengsen 2000: 726).

66    Zhao Gaiping and Hou Huiming 2006: 30.

67    Berger 2011.

68    According to a Mongolian biography of the Jebtsündamba lineage dated 1859 (transl. by
       Bawden 1961: 58-59 n. 5); Dharmatāla 1889: 342 (see also Altanzayaa 2000: 141). Curiously,
       no trace of his presence is found in the Qing Veritable Records (*Qing shilu* 清實錄).

69    *Subud erike* (Biography of the First Changkya), transl. Sagaster 1967: 117.

70    Stele "Qingliangshan beiji" 清涼山碑記: "You cui Menggu fanwang tong lai cong qi suo
       yu, gong ye fansi, shi zhongwai yijia zhi xin" 又催蒙古藩王同來從其所欲,共謁梵寺,
       示中外一家之心, 1811, which stands in Pusading (Zhou Zhenhua et al. 1998: 81).

71    Tuttle 2011: 178.

72    Köhle 2008: 95.

commoners—the imperial tours were also a means of governance and of taking possession of a sacred site visited by previous dynasties.[73] The religious activities of the emperor seem to have been limited to burning incense in monasteries, giving donations and sponsoring recitations of *sūtra*s in Pusading.[74] However, the visits Kangxi made with his aging Mongol grandmother, a devout Buddhist, and those made by Qianlong with his mother were certainly closer to pilgrimages than to tours of inspection.[75] In 1683, when he accompanied his grandmother, Kangxi prohibited his retinue from taking life on the mountain, sponsored a ritual for three days, made costly gifts to the clergy and prayed on behalf of his grandmother in the main monasteries. An apparition of Mañjuśrī among five-colored lights above the Western Terrace was interpreted (in Rölpé Dorjé's guidebook to Wutaishan) as a direct result of the emperor's prayers.[76]

Therefore, imperial tours were not mere Buddhist pilgrimages, for even those that may have been made out of sincere devotion were loaded with political benefits—at the very least, that of helping reinforce the emperor-Mañjuśrī connection. Furthermore, through the tours, as well as through the Mulan hunts and receptions at Chengde, personal relations were created between the emperor and the Mongol ruling elites and religious dignitaries who accompanied him. Also, as we will see in the following chapter, the tours had an impact on Mongols' representations of Wutaishan, and some of the stories about Kangxi that circulated in Mongolia were located on the Shanxi mountain.

In addition to the Mongol nobles and high-ranking monks who accompanied the emperor on his pilgrimage, the Mongol ruling princes (*jasag*s) and the highest reincarnations of Inner and Outer Mongolia were required by the Qing state to make pilgrimages to Wutaishan in turns in order to pay respect to Mañjuśrī. These tours were modeled after the New Year's audience to the court in Beijing. During the Qing period, each of the ruling families and the great reincarnations of the forty-nine banners of Inner Mongolia and of the four Khalkha *aimag*s had to go on pilgrimage to Wutaishan every four years, which means that each year twelve of the Inner Mongol ruling princes and their

---

73    Köhle 2008: 95-96, quoting Chang 2001: 22, 33.

74    Tuttle (2011: Table 1) lists the regular and exceptional rituals sponsored by imperial family members on Wutaishan, on behalf of the emperor, the empress dowager, the empire and its people. The regulations about imperial tours to Wutaishan are found in the *Qinding Lifanyuan zeli* (1817: *juan* 20, 17r-19v), which fixes the protocol of the imperial visits to monasteries. On these regulations: Uspensky 2007.

75    In addition, the Confucian literati who recorded these tours may have distorted the imperial activities by emphasizing worldly activities (Köhle 2008: 93).

76    References in Köhle 2008: 91-92.

families officially journeyed to the mountain.[77] They usually made the pilgrimage in spring, after their tour to Beijing.

### The Production of Imperial Gazetteers

The involvement of the imperial throne and the emperor himself in the publication of three imperial gazetteers between 1661 and 1811 was far from unusual in the Qing dynasty.[78] More gazetteers were published on Wutaishan than on any other site in the empire. The Qing rulers' engagement with this literary production was aimed at promoting their status as great patrons of Buddhism.[79] The first, second and third *jasag lamas* played an active role in the compilation of these imperial editions. In 1661, the first *jasag lama* A-wang-lao-zang wrote the preface (in Chinese) of the reprint edition of the 1596 *Qingliangshan zhi*,[80] and later commissioned a Mongolian gazetteer of the mountain.[81] Lao-zang-dan-ba, the third *jasag lama*, apparently started to translate the *Qingliangshan zhi* into Mongolian;[82] at the same time, he was compiling in Chinese, on Kangxi's order, the most important Qing-dynasty gazetteer of the mountain, which was published by the Palace Publishing House in 1694, the *Qingliangshan xinzhi* (New gazetteer of Qingliangshan). Qianlong not only commissioned a third gazetteer, the *Qinding Qingliangshan zhi* (Imperially commissioned gazetteer of Qingliangshan, compiled in 1785) but also authored its preface. The choice of Mongol and Han Gélukpa Buddhists as prefacers or compilers of Chinese editions of the gazetteer must have surprised the Chinese literati and attests to the public acknowledgement of the leading role that Tibetan Buddhists had on Wutaishan.[83] Their funerary *stūpa* epitaphs were added to the biography section of the gazetteers.

---

77    Li Xiangzhi 1932: 180. Li Xiangzhi mistakenly wrote 'Outer Mongolia' for 'Inner Mongolia.' This regulation does not appear in the *Lifanyuan zeli* and it is unclear to me whether it was strictly respected.

78    The production of Chinese gazetteers on Wutaishan has been extensively discussed: Birnbaum 1984: 17-19; Farquhar 1978; Köhle 2007; Tuttle 2011: 179-183. For the different editions of the Qing gazetteers, see Brook 2002: 99-100; Tuttle 2011: Table 3.

79    Tuttle 2011.

80    The preface was preserved in the 1755 edition but not in the 1887 reprint of the 1661 edition (Tuttle 2011: 182, n. 78).

81    *UTAOSC*, see Chapter 4.

82    Two out of three manuscript volumes of this translation are preserved in Beijing, dated 1680: *Cing liyang šan ayulan-u sine hi bicig* (*Catalogue of Ancient Mongolian Books and Documents of China* 1999: no 4824). They may have served later for the translation of the *Qingliangshan xinzhi* into Mongolian.

83    Tuttle 2011: 182.

All the Qing imperial gazetteers refer back to the major Ming-dynasty gazetteer, the *Qingliangshan zhi* (1596, 10 *juan*), compiled by the monk Zhencheng, who quotes from the earlier records of Huixiang, Yanyi, Zhang Shangying and others.[84] They present collections of lore about the numinous traces and the monasteries, merging genuine history with recollected legends, monks' biographies, miracles and manifestations of Mañjuśrī, as well as emperors' patronage and visits to the mountain. However, every new edition added new colophons; (invented) details about the life of past monks and about legends; descriptions of temples' relative positions, dimensions and architecture; new stele inscriptions and poems by Qing emperors; imperial renovations; inspection tours; and rituals performed. A comparison between the map of Wutaishan in the *Qingliangshan zhi* and the map in the later *Qinding Qingliangshan xinzhi* clearly highlights the reshaping of the Wutaishan landscape by the Qing emperors, since the 1785 gazetteer lists fifty-eight names of monasteries and other holy sites, thirty-six of which (nearly three-quarters) were not in the 1596 gazetteer. The last Chinese imperial gazetteer, Jiaqing's *Xixun shengdian* 西巡盛典 (Magnificent record of the Western Inspection Tour) by Peng Lin 彭齡, printed in 1812, is a twelve-volume work with twenty-one illustrations.[85]

The 1694 *Qingliangshan xinzhi* was later emended,[86] translated and published in 1701 into the three other languages of Qing Gélukpa Buddhism (Mongolia, Manchu and Tibetan) and prefaced by Kangxi himself. Lao-zang-dan-bei edited the Manchu-language translation (*Cing liyang šan alin-i ice jy bithe*).[87] The Mongolian version is entitled *Cing liyang šan aγulan-u sine ji-bicig* (other editions bear the title *U-tai serigün tungγalaγ aγula-yin jokiyangγui*).[88] Divided into ten chapters, it is the largest Mongolian gazetteer of the mountain. A few manuscripts and xylograph versions, some of them from Mongolia, have been

---

84 The first known gazetteer of Wutaishan, the *Gu Qingliang zhuan* (Ancient record of Clear and Cold), was composed around 677-680 by the monk Huixiang (*T.* 2098, vol. 51: 1092c-1100c). It was followed around 1060 by a more complete work called *Guang Qingliang zhuan* 廣清涼傳 (Expanded record of Clear and Cold), by Yanyi 延一, a Northern Song dynasty monk (*T.* 2099, vol. 51: 1101a-1127a). For a survey of the ancient Chinese Wutaishan gazetteers: Birnbaum 1984: 17-19.

85 Berger 2011.

86 On the different emended editions and reprints: Farquhar 1978: 24; Xiao Yu 1999; Wang Zhiyong and Cui Zhengsen 2000: 763-764; Brook 2002: 99; Tuttle 2011: Table 3.

87 Köhle 2007: 78.

88 *CLŠASB*. Farquhar 1978: 30, n. 88; Heissig 1954: 19-20, no. 10. On the possibility that it was printed in 1705 instead of 1701: Heissig 1954: 19-20, n. 5. A five-fascicle manuscript version in Saint Petersburg (IVAN, Mong. F-287) served as a proofreading copy for the xylograph edition (Kara 2005: 219-220, ill. p. 220).

preserved.[89] It includes many transliterations of the Chinese text. In contrast to the Tibetan version of the *Qingliangshan xinzhi*, which, being a nearly word-for-word translation or transliteration of the Chinese text, is not truly comprehensible for Tibetans,[90] the Mongolian version is legible for a modern Mongol.

D. Farquhar viewed Mongolian guidebooks commissioned by the Manchu emperors as a major instrument of promotion of the sacred mountain directed at Mongols, yet he included in his list non-imperial gazetteers. The translation of the 1694 *Qingliangshan xinzhi* is, in actual fact, the only imperial Mongolian gazetteer; as we will see in the following chapter, the other Mongolian guidebooks were not commissioned by Qing emperors. This limited production is in sharp contrast to that of Chinese-language guidebooks; therefore, we cannot say that the Manchu court strove very hard to encourage the Wutaishan pilgrimage among Mongols through publication of Mongolian-language guidebooks. As Gray Tuttle has evidenced, the re-edited and augmented Chinese imperial gazetteers first addressed a Chinese audience: ethnic Chinese Buddhists, including Han lamas, as well as Chinese and Manchu officials.[91]

### The Qing Emperors' Support of Chinese Buddhist Monasteries

Although the great Gélukpa monasteries enjoyed visible imperial patronage, the Qing also sponsored the renovation of Chinese Buddhist monasteries and supported their clergies. Imperial patronage was often addressed to all the monasteries of the mountain without distinction; for instance, on his first visit in 1683, "Kangxi 'offered incense,' and 'worshipped the Buddha,' in '*all* the temples,' and 'presented *each* monastery of the mountain with 200 taels of silver'"—except for Pusading, which received 1,000 taels of silver. Besides, after each imperially sponsored prayer ceremony, "*all* the foreign *and* Chinese monks

---

89    Manuscript versions are preserved in the Völkerkunde-Museum of Münich (Heissig and Sagaster 1961: 268-269, no. 500), in the Institute of Oriental Studies, Academy of Sciences, Saint Petersburg (Sazykin 1988: 297, cat. 1644 and 1645); and four in China (one dated Guangxu 18, 1892, three from the Republican period: *Catalogue of Ancient Mongolian Books and Documents of China* 1999: no. 4825, 4829, 4827, 4828). A xylograph version is in the Institute of Oriental Studies, Academy of Sciences, Saint Petersburg (Sazykin 1988: 297, cat. 1643, 1701); another dated to the Republican period and a lithography with illustrations are preserved in China (*Catalogue* 1999: no. 4823, 10 vol.; no. 4826). A complete three-language (Mongolian, Chinese and Tibetan) set dated to 1707 is preserved at the library of the Palace Museum in Taipei (I thank Chou Wen-shing for this reference).

90    Chou 2014.

91    Tuttle 2011: 185; also Köhle 2008.

received imperial subsidies."[92] In 1683 and 1698, Kangxi also paid out over 3,000 *taels* of silver and 9,000 *taels* of gold to restore Chinese Buddhist monasteries (among them, Bishansi and Shuxiangsi), to which should be added expenses such as the regular allowance provided to court-sponsored monks, the construction of roads and so on.[93] During his first tour, Qianlong offered 595 taels to each monastery, plus 530 taels for their communities; during his second tour, he offered 190 taels to Xiantongsi for burning lamps; and during his third tour, he donated 190 taels to each monastery and 260 taels for their communities.[94]

The Qing emperors wrote stone inscriptions, Chinese poems and name plaques for both Chinese Buddhist and Gélukpa monasteries.[95] The Qing imperial inscriptions represent about forty percent of all the imperial inscriptions preserved on Wutaishan; written in Chinese, only four of them are multilingual.[96]

In fact, if we only look at the number of monasteries and their presentation in the officially sponsored gazetteers, Wutaishan still appears to be primarily a Chinese Buddhist center. Not only were the Chinese Buddhist monasteries of Wutaishan sponsored by Qing emperors but they also preserved Chinese artistic and architectural heritage. The gazetteers do not list Chinese Buddhist and Gélukpa monasteries separately or say anything about their recent history: instead, they classify them according to their importance and location and recall their ancient Chinese past (without even mentioning the conversion of some of them to Tibetan Buddhism). Similarly, the inscriptions the emperors wrote for Gélukpa monasteries emphasize the continuity of imperial patronage from the Tang to the Qing and the ancientness of the foundation, but they make no reference to Tibetan Buddhism or the legacy of the Yuan emperors.[97]

To conclude, the Qing emperors were more involved in Wutaishan than the preceding dynasties, yet the promotion of Tibetan Buddhism on the sacred mountain was also part of the general 'technology of empire.' The tours, the

---

92    *Qingliangshan xinzhi* 1985 [1694]: *juan* 3, 18r-19v, translated by Köhle 2008: 85, references
      n. 49 and n. 50.
93    Tuttle 2011: Table 2.
94    Wang Zhiyong and Cui Zhengsen 2000: 724-725; Yang Zengwu 2005: 130.
95    See Köhle 2008: 84-86. Kangxi wrote 15 poems, 55 name plaques and more than 20 stele
      inscriptions (13 are preserved); Qianlong wrote 270 poems, 20 plaques and 11 inscriptions
      (Zhao Linen 2001: 61-65; Zhou Zhenhua et al. 1998).
96    One stele of Xiantongsi is written in Chinese and Manchu; three steles of Pusading were
      carved in the four official languages of Qing Tibetan Buddhism (Chinese, Tibetan,
      Mongolian and Manchu). See Online Appendix B, "Pusading" and "Xiantongsi."
97    Köhle 2008: 85.

gazetteers and even the references to the emperor-Mañjuśrī were directed towards multiple audiences—first and foremost towards the Chinese audience.
The Mongol nobles and high reincarnations were required to visit Wutaishan
every six years but, in short, they were not the main target of the imperial promotion of Wutaishan.

### The Wutaishan Clergies and Their Role in the Promotion of the Pilgrimage

From the mid-nineteenth century on, imperial support to the Wutaishan monasteries generally declined because of economic and political difficulties and
general disinterest in the former Qing policy towards Tibetan Buddhism. A look
at the dates of the Chinese steles confirms the decline of imperial patronage
after the eighteenth century (Table 1). The monasteries had to find new sources
of funding and turned towards Mongol donors, elaborating strategies to attract
them. During Pokotilov's visit in 1889, the main Gélukpa monasteries and the
two main Chinese Buddhist monasteries (Xiantongsi and Shuxiangsi) were still
flourishing thanks to Mongol pilgrims' donations, whereas smaller monasteries
were already dilapidated or in ruins.[98] What was the role of the residing clergy
in the promotion, management and control of Mongol pilgrimages?

#### The Wutaishan Clergies

First, a presentation of Wutaishan clergies will highlight some specific features
of the place. On the face of it, the 'monks in blue robes' (*heshang*s, or Chinese
Buddhist monks) and the 'monks in yellow robes' (lamas) seemed to form clearly distinct communities (Fig. 13).[99] Following Robert Hayden, because members of these communities distinguished themselves from each other, their
differences appeared more obvious than their common ground.[100] *Heshang*s
and lamas not only belonged (and still belong) to traditions of Buddhism that
differ in their canons, pantheon, liturgy, etc. but they also had different garments, habits and ways of life. Lamas lived a much more private life than *heshang*s; in the morning they shared tea in the central assembly hall but then
had their meals in their own quarters; they ate meat and had dinner in the late

---

98    Pokotilov 1935 [1893].
99    Two categories of religious specialists were in a minority at Wutaishan and are omitted
      from this list: Chinese Buddhist nuns and (Chinese Buddhist or Daoist) clerics who
      managed the Chinese temples.
100   Hayden 2002: 207, n. 4.

FIGURE 13
*Lamas in the 1930s.* © BLOFELD
1959: BETWEEN P. 48-49.

afternoon.[101] Conversely, *heshangs* shared their meals in a refectory, slept in a dormitory and meditated together in a meditation hall; they ate vegetarian food and were not supposed to have a substantial meal in the afternoon. *Heshangs* took their vows at collective ordination ceremonies,[102] while Gélukpa lamas were ordained individually by their master in the main monasteries. However,

101 However, some Gélukpa monasteries of Wutaishan, such as Luohousi, built a refectory for lamas and pilgrims. Nowadays, the lamas of Luohousi and Shifangtang share five-bed dormitories, and only few of them have individual rooms.

102 The two ordination centers on Wutaishan during the Kangxi period were Bishansi and Xiantongsi. Bishansi is equipped with a hall called Hall of the Ordination Platform (Jietandian 戒壇殿). Ordinations are expensive rituals that are now organized only once every ten years. On ordinations in the 1980s: *Wutaixian zhi* 1988: 585-586.

both communities borrowed from one another, and visual frontiers between religious communities were not always so clear.

The Tibeto-Mongol Buddhist clergy of Wutaishan had some unique features compared to the clergies of monasteries in Tibet and Mongolia. For instance, on Wutaishan, there was no reincarnation lineage in residence throughout the year. But the most noticeable difference was the clergy's ethnic and social make-up. The 'official' monasteries were exclusively Gélukpa and were staffed by Mongol, Monguor and Tibetan lamas and, in some cases, also by ethnic Chinese and Manchu lamas.[103] From the late eighteenth century up to the mid-twentieth century, Mongol lamas became more and more numerous.[104] Pokotilov even speaks of the 'colonization' of Wutaishan by Mongol monks and estimated that more than a half of the lamas were Mongols, which was linked to the great number of Mongol pilgrims.[105] Mongol lamas usually came from monasteries of Inner Mongolia, but some of them were ordained in a Gélukpa monastery in Beijing or took their vows directly on Wutaishan. Some families took their child to Wutaishan to place him in a monastery as a novice, and sometimes they eventually decided to settle on Wutaishan themselves.[106] Lamas of Wutaishan also occasionally 'bought' seven- or eight-year-old boys to make into novices, as told by Rockhill, who traveled there in 1887, a few years after a terrible famine in North China.[107] Mongols young and old still go to Wutaishan to become lamas, and stories of sudden conversion are many.[108] In the 1950s, a Mongol named Han-ga-da 韓嘎達 from the Khorchin Left Middle Banner brought the bones of his mother to Wutaishan to bury them; he

---

103    In 1912, Pusading was staffed by four to five hundred Tibetan, Mongol, Han Chinese and Manchu lamas (Gao Henian 2000 [1949]: 112-113). G. Tuttle argues that the great majority of lamas in China seem to have been Mongols because Tibetans had difficulties becoming accustomed to the Chinese climate and diet. According to his sources, the only Chinese monasteries that regularly housed Tibetan lamas were Beijing's Yonghegong and Wutaishan's Pusading (2005: 21).

104    In 1872 Edkins only counted about a hundred Tibetan lamas in the monasteries (1893 [1878]: 228, 236). He estimates the total number of lamas at between seven hundred and two thousand, apparently including pilgrim-lamas, and the number of Chinese Buddhist monks at several hundred only.

105    Pokotilov 1935 [1893]: 56-57, 66. Pokotilov also documents the monks' education, the ordination ceremony and the hierarchy within Gélukpa and Chinese Buddhist communities.

106    Nan Yang 1998.

107    Rockhill 1895: 262.

108    For instance Tsorigtu, a young Mongol student from the Ordos Khanggin Banner, suddenly decided to give up his studies to become a lama at Shifangtang on Wutaishan, against his parents' will (Tian Chang'an and Liang Heng, eds. 2003: 43).

eventually stayed on and became a lama.[109] Mongol pilgrims thus contributed to increasing the Mongol monastic community on Wutaishan.

The Mongol lamas in residence were "almost exclusively from Eastern Inner Mongolia, reflecting the importance of that region in regard to wealth and population,"[110] but also reflecting its social proximity to the Qing court—the Mongols from Juu Uda and Jirim Leagues were the first to ally with Manchu power. Many of these lamas, as noted by British Protestant missionary Joseph Edkins in 1872, could read Mongolian, whereas most Mongol lamas in monasteries of Mongolia and Beijing could only read Tibetan.[111] While Tibetan was the main liturgical language in the Gélukpa monasteries of Wutaishan, several sources suggest that Mongolian was also used for specific rituals requested by pilgrims,[112] as well as for debates.[113]

A small minority of Wutaishan lamas had obtained an academic degree in Lhasa or Kumbum.[114] A few of them became famous historical figures. An example is the twenty-second *jasag lama* of Wutaishan, who was influential at court and in Chinese and Tibetan networks, and helped bridge the two traditions. He was a Torgut Mongol from Xinjiang named Erdeni (1882-1955). At the age of seven, he took his novice vows in a Torgut monastery and was given the religious name Lozang Pelsang (Ch. Luo-sang-ba-sang). He studied in Drépung Monastery from 1902 to 1908 and had obtained the *lharampa* degree; he then served as a government official in Lhasa. Lozang Pelsang was fluent in Chinese, Mongolian and Tibetan. In 1919, he went to Beijing as secretary of the Thirteenth Dalai Lama, was appointed abbot of Yonghegong, then as *da lama* of Heisi 黑寺 (Black Monastery, in a northern suburb of Beijing). The same year, he was appointed *jasag lama* of Wutaishan and went on to serve three terms (1919-1936).[115] Lozang Pelsang had Tibetan *géshé* lamas come to Wutaishan to raise the level of studies and had a great influence on the religious life of the mountain. In 1936, he was invited by the lama Nenghai 能海 (1886-1967)[116] in Bishansi to teach Tibetan *sūtras* and became one of his masters. Lozang Pelsang

---

109 Tian Chang'an and Liang Heng, eds. 2003: 42.

110 Edkins 1893 [1878]: 228. Seventy-two percent of the Mongols of Inner Mongolia lived in the Jirim, Juu Uda and Josotu Leagues (1911 census).

111 Edkins 1893 [1878]: 228.

112 Fischer 1923: 90-91.

113 Blofeld 1948: 97, speaking about the Great Sixth Month Festival.

114 See the biography of an Inner Mongol lama named Jamyang (1897-1984), from Shili-yin Gool League, who obtained his *géshé* degree in Lhasa and resided in Tayuansi from 1951 to 1984: Wang Xuebin et al. 1994: 167-168.

115 Xiao Yu 肖雨 1996: 15; Gao Lintao 2004; see also Andreyev 2001c: 353.

116 On Nenghai: see below.

organized the Wutaishan army of monks against Japanese occupation and eventually acted as a diplomat in the Sino-Japanese conflict, trying to protect the monasteries (without real success). He then 'retired' in a monastery of one of the Chakhar banners in Inner Mongolia. In 1947 or 1948, Lozang Pelsang was again invited by Nenghai, this time to teach at Zhengci Monastery 正慈寺 of Chengdu (Sichuan). After 1949, he participated in the government of Shanxi and in the Chinese Buddhist Association. After 1953, he contributed to the religious revival on Wutaishan. Lozang Pelsang died in Beijing at the age of seventy-two.[117]

Lastly, a particularity of the Wutaishan clergy was the number of Han lamas, who had three possible origins: first, ethnic Han lamas who came from the Tibetan Buddhist monasteries of Beijing (such as Chongguosi) at the beginning of the Qing period; second, Han Chinese who converted to Tibetan Buddhism during the Ming and Qing dynasties; and third, Chinese Buddhist *heshangs* who adopted the yellow robe when their monasteries became Gélukpa.[118] The number of Han disciples of Tibetan Buddhist masters in Qing China was certainly higher that usually assumed.[119] Although there was no widespread conversion of Han Chinese to Tibetan Buddhism, there was a particular receptivity towards Tibetan Buddhism among Han officials living in Beijing and Tianjin, as well as among the Han communities on Wutaishan, in the Upper Monastery of Bingling 炳靈 Grottoes in Gansu Province and in other localities at the Sino-Tibetan border.[120]

In the early eighteenth century, when the *jasag lamas* began to be appointed by the Dalai Lama, Han lamas were progressively replaced by Tibetan and

---

117     Wang Zhiyong and Cui Zhengsen 2000: 754; Wang Xuebin *et al.* 1994: 148-152. For a photograph of his successor: Ono Katsutoshi and Hibino Takao 1942: 20.

118     Zhao Gaiping and Hou Huiming (2006) and Gao Lintao (2004), without quoting their sources, assert that when Chinese Buddhist monasteries converted into Gélukpa monasteries, the *heshangs* changed their robes into yellow ones and replaced the statues with Tibetan images.

119     As stressed by Matthew Kapstein, "it seems more prudent to admit that the question of Chinese popular involvement in Tibetan Buddhism during the dynastic period has not yet been adequately examined, and remains a topic of interest for future research" (2009: 9).

120     Chinese received initiations, took monastic vows during public festivals, visited Gélukpa monasteries and hired lamas for funerals (Charleux 2002a). Reincarnations of local masters were even found in ethnic Han families in the seventeenth century (Tuttle 2006b: 79 n. 53; Nietupski 2009: 194). When Qianlong founded Yonghegong as the first academic monastery of Beijing in order to raise the level of education of Mongol and Chinese lamas, he had three hundred Tibetan lamas come from the four main monasteries of Tibet to train two hundred Chinese, Mongol and Manchu novices.

Mongol lamas. However, a few monasteries were exceptions. In the imperial Tailusi, Edkins counted more than a hundred lamas, of whom only twelve were Mongols and the rest Chinese.[121] Luohousi was almost exclusively staffed with Han lamas in the nineteenth century,[122] and as late as 1872-1873, Edkins noticed on Wutaishan that there were still "many Chinese Lamas. The fashion is, when the Chinese become Lamas, for them to chant Tibetan prayers, and to have in their temples the same images and costumes which are customary in Tibet."[123] According to Gray Tuttle, the Chinese language gazetteers of Wutaishan primarily addressed this declining but still visible community of Han lamas.[124] Some of them could also speak Mongolian because it was the main language spoken in their monastery and/or because they needed to communicate with Mongol pilgrims: see the biography of Luo-bu-sa lama 羅布薩 (b. 1886), a Han Chinese lama who took vows in Pusading in 1904 and learned to speak and write Mongolian.[125] The relations between Han lamas and Tibetan and Mongol lamas are still poorly documented. In the nineteenth century, antagonisms occurred between the Han lamas of Luohousi and the Tibetan and Mongol lamas of its monastic hostelry, Shifangtang, who prayed alongside the Han lamas.[126]

The Qing authorities expected those of the Chinese and the Gélukpa Buddhist traditions to cooperate harmoniously on Wutaishan more than in any other place of the empire, and they may have encouraged some integration of the two communities. The cohabitation of lamas and *heshang*s in a few 'ecumenical' monasteries of the Ming (such as Xiantongsi) and early Qing periods explains why it is often difficult to date the conversion of a Chinese monastery into a Gélukpa one.[127] Besides, lamas and *heshang*s had to perform imperially sponsored rituals together, under the leadership of the *jasag lama*. For instance, in the eighteenth century, the fourth *jasag lama*, Ding-zeng-jian-cuo, led

---

121    Edkins 1893 [1878]: 223.

122    Cai Hong 1999: 24. Wang Chang (1792: twenty-fourth day) noticed in 1792 that the lamas of Luohousi all came from Shanxi and Zhili. Nowadays Luohousi is the main Mongol monastery of Wutaishan: its monks come from eastern Inner Mongolia (Tongliao and Chifeng Municipalities, Jirim League) plus a few from Ordos, Höhhot and the Chakhar banners.

123    Edkins 1893 [1878]: 236. Song Yu asserts that the liturgy performed by Han lamas was in Chinese only (2010: 293).

124    Tuttle 2011: 184-185.

125    Wang Xuebin et al. 1994: 147-148.

126    Cai Hong 1999: 24.

127    In the Ming period, such cohabitation was also the case in several Beijing monasteries: Naquin 2000: 208 n. 133.

*ge-long*s 格隆 (Tib. *gélong*)[128] and *ban-di*s 班弟 (Mo. *bandi*, < Skt. *vandya*, novice), along with all the other foreign and Han monks, to climb all together to Jingangku (Vajra Cave).[129] The 1729 biography of the First Changkya Khutugtu, Ngakwang Lozang Chöden Pelzangpo (1642-1715), also describes pilgrimages and rituals on Wutaishan that brought together Mongols, Tibetans and Chinese in festive religious celebrations.[130] The Qing emperors continued certain rituals of protection of the state established by the Ming dynasty, "but were explicit about elevating the role of Tibetan Buddhists in leading these rituals."[131]

Chinese *heshang*s also listened to the sermons and attended initiations given by Tibetan Buddhist masters. On the 11th day of the second month of 1653, three hundred Han Chinese monk retreatants (*jingxiuzhe* 靜修者) from Wutaishan came to see the Fifth Dalai Lama in Beijing's Yellow Monastery and offered him a precious vase that was said to have been held by Mañjuśrī.[132] As we will see, Rölpé Dorjé had Chinese *heshang*s among his disciples on Wutaishan.

The distinction between Chinese Buddhist and Gélukpa communities may have been less marked on Wutaishan than in other part of the Qing empire such as in Beijing. As seen in Chapter 2, visitors were often confused by the similarities in architecture and organization of Wutaishan's monasteries, whatever their tradition. The missionary H. Hackmann even noticed an "amalgamation of Chinese Buddhism and Lamaism" in the Wutaishan monasteries: "Both doctrines borrow from one another in habits and arrangements ... . In their services, too, one style blends with the other."[133] But whether there was some sort of syncretism of Tibetan and Chinese liturgy in the Qing dynasty, probably because of the presence of Han *heshang*s who had converted to Gélukpa Buddhism, is not clear and certainly deserves further study.

Although we have no such testimony for the Qing period, a twentieth-century Mongol monk educated both in Mongolian and in Chinese could, and still can, relatively easily change his affiliation. A boy named Dashi (b. 1931) from the

---

128    Köhle (2008: 85, n. 50) questions whether the term *ge-long* (< Tib. *gélong*) found in Chinese sources exclusively referred to foreign Tibetan Buddhists or whether it can also refer to Han Chinese lamas.

129    Köhle 2008: 88 quoting the stele inscription dated 1714 at Jingangku. This echoes the co-celebration of court rituals by Buddhist, Daoist and Confucian clerics in imperial China (*sanjiao heyi* 三教合一). Nowadays *heshang*s and lamas co-celebrate Mañjuśrī's birthday in Tayuansi, on the 4th day of the fourth lunar month.

130    Sagaster 1967: 265-268, quoting the *Subud erike*.

131    Tuttle 2011: 168.

132    Danjiong Rannabanza and Li Decheng 1997: 21.

133    Hackmann 1914 [1912]: 118-119, also p. 138.

Chakhar Rear Right Banner of Inner Mongolia took his first novice vows in 1937 as a seven-year-old with a *heshang* master in the Chinese Buddhist monastery of Tayuansi, where he studied the *Analects of Confucius* (*Lunyu* 論語) and other Confucian classics—his parents may have preferred to send him to the holiest monastery on Wutaishan, regardless of affiliation, rather than to a less prestigious Tibeto-Mongol one. At eighteen, he was ordained as a *gélong* by a lama of the small Tibetan Buddhist monastery of Wulangmiao 五爺廟 and received his Buddhist name, Sonamdorji (< Tib. Sönam Dorjé). He defrocked in 1947 but in 1953 returned to Tayuansi (he was probably again ordained as a *heshang*), where he participated in the restoration of the *stūpa*; he then became a *heshang* in Xiantongsi in 1977 and worked for the Buddhist Association of Wutaishan. In 1983, he was appointed abbot of Luohousi. He revived Tibeto-Mongol Buddhist activities and restored this famous Gélukpa monastery, now staffed by Mongol lamas from Inner Mongolia.[134]

The apparent harmony and blurred visual frontier between *heshang*s and lamas and between Chinese and Tibetan Buddhist monasteries, as well as the 'multiethnic' rituals may have contributed towards convincing the Mongol pilgrims even more firmly that Chinese Buddhism and Tibetan Buddhism belonged to the same tradition. Sanctity and efficacy (of relics, of sacred icons, of great Buddhist masters) were more important than sectarian and ethnic differences. Also, the importance of the residing Mongol community helped attract pilgrims by convincing them that Wutaishan was also a Mongol place.

### Strategies of Chinese Buddhist Monasteries to Attract Mongol Pilgrims

The fact that the cohabitation of lamas and *heshang*s endured into the twentieth century has a very practical explanation. After the cut of imperial subsidies in the late Qing period, monasteries relied on donations from pilgrims, especially Mongol pilgrims. For example, from the 1910s to 1937, Tayuansi—the central place of worship and one of the ten great Chinese Buddhist monasteries of Wutaishan in the early twentieth century[135]—had both Chinese *heshang*s and Mongol lamas in residence.[136] They performed two sets of rituals, one in

---

134   Nan Yang 1998.

135   Bai Meichu 2010 [1925]: *juan* 2, 153; Zhang Yuanji and Zhuang Yu 1925: 1; Li Xiangzhi 1932: 64.

136   Zhang Dungu 1911: 26; Gao Henian 2000 [1949]: 110; He Zhang Lianjue 1934: 70; David-Neel 1940: 173; Ono Katsutoshi and Hibino Takao 1942: 216. He Zhang counted a hundred monks and twenty lamas in a large monastery named Xiatasi 下榻寺, which can be identified with Tayuansi.

Tibetan and one in Chinese, both attended by Mongol pilgrims. According to
Fischer:

> The great number of temples which in the course of ages came under
> Chinese-Buddhist administration, uphold and intermix the Mongol-
> Tibetan form of service; these temples have their daily "Meng Ku Nien
> Ching" [Menggu nianjing 蒙古念經, *sūtra* reading in Mongolian] or
> Mongol Lama service of prayers, as well as the Chinese Buddhist service.
> For the former, Mongols are engaged by the Ho Shangs [*heshang*s], who
> give them their meals and homes, and a very small sum of cash monthly.... .
> So far as visitors are concerned the temples depend mostly on Mongol
> support, as there are but few Chinese who make pilgrimage to Wu Tai.... .
> At set hours religious services are going on daily that is, early in the morn-
> ing at daybreak and in the evening.[137]

Fischer continues with a description of the Chinese service, in which Mongol
pilgrims also participated and gave offerings:

> And while this Chinese-Buddhist service takes place, called the "Ho-Shang
> nien-ching," a second service in a small sanctuary on the upper platform
> of the pagoda also takes place, the "Lama nien ching" or Tibetan-Mongol
> prayers which are participated in also by the visiting pilgrims.[138]

Similarly, Pokotilov noted in 1889 that the main donors of Xiantongsi—the largest Chinese Buddhist monastery—were in fact Mongol pilgrims and that the
*heshang*s had to invite Mongol lamas in residence to receive them. These lamas
took residence in the most prestigious part of the monastery; in fact, four or five
lamas ran the small Bronze Hall.[139] In the same monastery in 1917, Fischer
counted, in addition to its hundred *heshang*s, a large number of Mongol lamas
and confirmed that the Bronze Hall was managed by Mongol gatekeepers who
lived in nearby buildings.[140] In the 1930s Li Xiangzhi met a Mongol monk
in Xiantongsi who did not speak a word of Chinese,[141] and counted in this
monastery 220 *heshang*s, plus 60 Mongols (lamas?) and a dozen traveling

---

137    Fischer 1923: 90-91.
138    Fischer 1923: 90-91.
139    Pokotilov 1935 [1893]: 71-72.
140    Fischer 1923: 95.
141    Li Xiangzhi (1932: 72-73) uses the term *dazi* 韃子, 'barbarian.'

monks.[142] Shuxiangsi, which, according to Pokotilov, owed its prosperity almost exclusively to Mongol donors, adopted the same strategy, although its *heshang*s invited Mongol lamas in residence also because "they enjoy incomparable confidence and respect of their fellow countrymen."[143] In 1938, Migwachir mentions both *heshang*s and lamas numbering fifty that were performing a ritual and playing music in Shuxiangsi.[144] In 1912, the abbot of Huayangu 華 嚴谷 (i.e., probably Puensi) was a lama, but two *heshang*s also lived in his monastery.[145]

This strategy of cohabitation certainly encouraged Mongol pilgrims not to neglect these Chinese Buddhist monasteries. Indeed, Tayuansi was the Chinese monastery that received the greatest number of donations from Tibetan and Mongol pilgrims (see Chapter 5).

### The Development of Syncretic Schools in the Late Qing and Republican Periods

At the same time, some Chinese monasteries enjoyed a revival thanks to charismatic religious leaders. In the late nineteenth century, Li Xiangshan 李向善, known as Monk Puji 普濟和尚, a famous master close to the Qing court,[146] and abbot of Nanshansi in 1884, trained about two hundred disciples.[147] Puji was above all a Buddhist master, but he was ordained by a Jiugongdao 九宮道 ('Way of Nine Palaces') leader and also propagated these teachings.[148] This northern Chinese religious movement, which took the name of an older 'redemptive society,' emphasized a syncretism between Buddhism, Daoism and Confucianism. Thanks to Puji's almsrounds in North and East China and in Manchuria,

---

142  Li Xiangzhi 1932: 77. In 1940, Ono Katsutoshi and Hibino Takao (1942: 237-238, 246, 253) mention Chinese monks as well as lamas in Xiantongsi, Yuanzhaosi and Shuxiangsi.

143  Pokotilov 1935 [1893]: 79.

144  Miγvacir 2008 [1942]: 403-404.

145  Gao Henian 2000 [1949]: 116.

146  It is said that when he was accused of heterodoxy and imprisoned in 1892, he went seven days in his cell without eating or drinking. Empress Dowager Cixi was deeply impressed; she worshipped him as a 'living Buddha' and offered him a name plaque (Wang Chien-ch'uan 2008 [2004]: 134-135).

147  Ono Katsutoshi and Hibino Takao 1942: 125-128; Wang Chien-ch'uan 2008 [2004].

148  Wang Chien-ch'uan's seminal article (2008 [2004]), based on stone inscriptions and contemporary sources, questions the links between Puji and the Jiugongdao (was he a Buddhist master or a sect leader?) as well as his supposed role in the Boxer Rebellion. On the Jiugongdao, its doctrine and its pantheon, see also Lu Zhongwei 2002: 36-61.

large amounts of donations invigorated the Wutaishan monastic economy. Besides receiving donations to build temples and support the clergy, the Jiugong-dao leaders sold expensive charms and amulets to protect one's body and home against dangers (bullets, swords, demons, suffering in the other world and so on). Based in Nanshansi, Puji and his disciples developed the Jiugongdao on Wutaishan and took over more than twenty monasteries,[149] spending seven million silver dollars to restore or rebuild them.[150]

These monasteries belonged to a national network that included Shuangtasi 雙塔寺 of Beijing and Baiyisi 白衣寺 of Tianjin, all of them branches of Nan-shansi.[151] Monasteries appropriated by the Jiugongdao adopted Daoist and syncretic deities of the Chinese pantheon.[152] The monasteries of the five terraces were turned into Chinese temples dedicated to the 'Emperors of the Five Peaks' and to Chinese deities.[153] Li Xiangzhi, in his 1932 guidebook to Wutaishan, was surprised by the presence of so many 'Daoist' deities in Buddhist monasteries:[154] it may be due to the influence of the Jiugongdao that other Chinese Buddhist monasteries and even Tibetan Buddhist monasteries also displayed Chinese deities on their altars. In the Republican period, the Jiugongdao initiated an artistic renaissance, with stone archways and screen-walls decorated with exquisite sculptures including these popular deities (in Nanshansi, Longquansi 龍泉寺, Puhuasi, Gufosi).

Puji's funerary Tibetan-style *stūpa* (1920-1924) in Longquansi represents him as Maitreya Buddha, of whom he was believed to be the ninth incarnation. The reputation of the Jiugongdao thus reached Beijing, South and East China, and the important donations it received contributed to the flourishing of the

---

149    Puji restored Nanshansi from 1877 to 1883, rebuilt Longquansi in 1877, Gufosi in 1896, Pujisi in 1903 (previously a branch monastery of Yuanzhaosi), Jingesi, Shigousi, Rizhaosi and Haihui'an. His disciples restored Nanshansi (between 1914 and 1937), Zunshengsi, Puhuasi, Wanfodong, Lingfengsi, rebuilt Gufosi, Wanghaisi of the Eastern Terrace and Yanjiaosi of the Central Terrace, and enlarged Longquansi.

150    They purchased several monasteries, but a few abbots spontaneously rallied their monastery to Nanshansi.

151    The Jiugongdao was divided into 'associations' (see the organization chart in Lu Zhongwei 2002: 51). The northern association was based in Pujisi, the central association had Gufosi, Nanshansi, etc.

152    Such as Laozi, the Three Saints (Laozi, Śākyamuni, Confucius), the Jade Emperor (Yuhuang), the Three Emperors (Sanhuang), the Three Officials (Sanguan 三官廟, of Heaven, Earth and Water), Songzi Niangniang 送子娘娘 (The Maiden Who Brings Children), the Eight Daoist Immortals, the stellar deity of longevity (Laoshouxing 老壽星), the heroes of the Three Kingdoms (Liu Bei 劉備, Guandi and Zhang Fei 張飛).

153    Li Xiangzhi 1932: 127-149.

154    Li Xiangzhi 1932: 127-149.

Chinese monastic centers on Wutaishan. Since the Jiugongdao recruited many followers and disciples in the three Manchurian provinces, some Khorchin Mongols became disciples of this movement, and two Mongolian stone inscriptions in Nanshansi, dated 1894 and 1895, are evidence of donations by Mongols. However, Mongol interest in this movement alone does not explain the proportion of Mongol donations being given to Chinese Buddhist monasteries.

While the Jiugongdao declined on Wutaishan in the 1940s, a syncretic Tibeto-Chinese tradition of Buddhism flourished, when three ethnic Chinese lamas—Nenghai,[155] Fazun 法尊 (1886-1980) and Qinghai 清海 (1922-1990)—were active on the mountain.[156] Fazun entered the *sangha* (monastic community) on Wutaishan aged eighteen in 1920, was later trained in China and Tibet and returned to Wutaishan in 1935. He was a pioneer in the translation of many of the major Gélukpa doctrinal texts into Chinese and trained many Chinese monks and nuns in the Tibetan tradition. His memorial *stūpa* was erected in 1980 in a side courtyard of Guangzongsi. Nenghai went to Wutaishan from 1934 to 1936 and intermittently between 1956 and 1966. He was appointed abbot of Guangji Maopeng 廣濟茅蓬 (more commonly known as Bishansi) in 1936 and later lived in Shancaidong and Qingliangqiao 清涼橋 (the old Jixiangsi). His attempts at introducing Tibetan esoteric elements into the liturgy encountered some opposition from the Chinese Buddhist monks. During the 1930s, and again after the Cultural Revolution, these masters began to appropriate former Gélukpa monasteries such as Santasi, as well as ancient Chinese Buddhist monasteries such as Guangzongsi, Bishansi and Jixiangsi.[157] With the help of his master (the twenty-second *jasag lama*, Lozang Pelsang), Nenghai established his own Vajrayāna School in Shancaidong, though in 1937 the Sino-Japanese War forced him to flee with his disciples to Chengdu.[158]

A new category of 'Han lama' thus emerged during the Republican period. Although this new trend has no connection with the Qing period Chinese lamas, it shows the continued interest of ethnic Chinese in Tibetan Buddhism on Wutaishan. Nenghai's tradition radiated from Wutaishan towards the whole of China. From the 1980s on, their second- and third-generation disciples, following Nenghai's disciple Qinghai, contributed to revitalizing the Sino-Tibetan

---

155    Nenghai studied in Lhasa with Pabongkha Rinpoché (1878-1941) and Khangsar Rinpoché
       for nine years (Wang-Toutain 2000; Tuttle 2005; Tuttle 2006a; Bianchi 2009).
156    Tuttle 2006a; Bianchi 2009, Bianchi and Rinaldo 2010.
157    For a synthesis on the organization of these monasteries, their canons, details on the diet,
       the color of monks' robes, etc.: Bianchi 2009.
158    Tuttle 2005: 11.

tradition on Wutaishan.[159] Since the 2000s, an increasing number of Inner Mongols have joined their monasteries.

### The Promotion of Wutaishan out on the Field

Although the monastic communities strove hard to attract Mongol pilgrims within their precinct, the donations received on Wutaishan were not sufficient, especially when a community wanted to restore a temple. This is why the Gélukpa and Chinese Buddhist communities of Wutaishan used to send groups of monks every year to Mongolia, China and Tibet[160] to collect donations. The lamas of Pusading, for instance, organized alms-collecting rounds to Tibet and to Mongolia.[161] These monks were the *ombo lamas* (Ch. *wenbu* 溫布), managers of practical affairs, of the Wutaishan monasteries. The practice is already attested in 1598, when monks from Luohousi organized subscriptions in Tibet.[162] Pokotilov, who traveled to Wutaishan in 1889, locates the peak season of the pilgrimage in winter: in summer the sacred mountain was relatively empty because many *ombo lamas* were away in Mongolia organizing almsrounds. James Gilmour confirms that alms-collecting lamas left Wutaishan in the spring and returned before winter.[163] Their role was crucial for the Wutaishan monasteries: they maintained relationships between their own monasteries and Mongol donors and increased the number of patrons.[164]

This practice seems to have intensified in the early twentieth century. In the 1920s, due to the rise of conflicts in China, the flow of pilgrims slowed down and the 'praying agents' of Wutaishan's monasteries were "regularly sent to Mongolia, where rich and poor subscribe in specie, or in products of barter, their annual subscription to Wu-T'ai Shan."[165] Writing in 1932, Li Xiangzhi explained that during the first month of every year, the Chinese monasteries of Wutaishan used to send *ombo lamas* to Hebei, Shandong and Manchuria to collect funds, while the Gélukpa monasteries sent *ombo* to the encampments, small cities and monasteries of Inner and Khalkha Mongolia.[166] Chen Xingya, who traveled in 1934 to Wutaishan, recorded that Chinese monks from Zunshengsi 尊勝寺

---

159 On the development of Nenghai's school under the Chinese communist government and the "indigenization of Tibetan Buddhism among the Chinese": Tuttle 2005: Chapter 7 and Postscript. On the revival of Chinese Gélukpa Buddhism on Wutaishan: Tuttle 2006a.

160 Andreyev 2001b: 175.

161 Gao Henian 2000 [1949]: 113.

162 Wang Zhiyong and Cui Zhengsen 2000: 701.

163 Gilmour 1970 [1883]: 151.

164 Pokotilov 1935 [1893]: 67.

165 Fischer 1923: 90.

166 Li Xiangzhi 1932: 159.

had collected twenty thousand silver dollars in Manchuria.[167] Among the Chinese Buddhist monasteries, it was mostly those belonging to Puji's school that sent collector monks to China and especially Manchuria. However, some Chinese Buddhist monasteries too, such as Qixiansi 棲賢寺, every year sent *ombo lamas* to eastern Inner Mongolia, and even up to Buryatia, because Mongols were said to be particularly generous and wealthy. These monks visited every family, rich and poor, and received food, felt, cattle and gold.[168] As for the Gélukpa monasteries, Yuanzhaosi's finances were entirely dependent on the expeditions of the *ombo lamas* who traveled to Khalkha Mongolia.[169]

Some of these lamas were Mongolian-speaking Chinese. Luo-bu-sa (b. 1886), a Han Chinese lama of Pusading who had learned to speak and write Mongolian, was in charge of receiving Mongol donors and lay Buddhist practitioners in the 1910s. He spent five years from 1913 to 1918 collecting donations in Inner Mongolia. Every year he brought many Mongols' offerings to Wutaishan. In 1918, in reward for his services, he was appointed *demchi* (business manager) of Pusading.[170]

*Ombo* monks often travelled together, setting off with carts and tents; others traveled alone and were called *badarchi lama*.[171] As noted by the missionary James Gilmour:

> [t]hese expeditions are numerous and indefatigable, and perhaps there is no tent, rich or poor, throughout the whole length and breadth of the eastern half of Mongolia, which is not visited by such deputation every year. These collectors penetrate even beyond the bounds of the Chinese empire, and carry off rich offerings from the Buriats, who compared with Mongols are wealthy. Food, tea, skins, cattle, money, all are eagerly received ... [172]

---

167   Chen Xingya 1936: 32.
168   Gilmour 1970 [1883]: 151; Ono Katsutoshi and Hibino Takao 1942: 147-148.
169   Li Xiangzhi 1932: 79.
170   Wang Xuebin et al. 1994: 147-148.
171   A *badarchi* (lit. one with an alms bowl) more generally designates itinerant monks, a loose category that includes monk-pilgrims, monks traveling on great distances to further their religious training in Mongolia and Tibet, monks traveling to collect funds, wandering Nyingmapa practitioners and lamas running away from taxes and debts. *Badar*, < Skt. *pātra*, alms bowl, donation, alms, contribution; *badar barikhu-* ask for alms, donations; *badarchila-*, to collect contributions for a religious purpose. See Gochoo 1970 [1963]: 73-77.
172   Gilmour 1970 [1883]: 151.

The alms-collecting lamas from Wutaishan went anywhere in Mongolia to solicit and collect contributions from a wide range of donors—from common
people and slaves to rich lords and princes—and actually came in competition
with those from the Mongol monasteries of Labrang and Golong Champa Ling.
The expeditions of Wutaishan's *ombo lamas* in the Kharachin Right Banner in
Inner Mongolia between 1840 and 1845 are known to us thanks to a document
written by a Kharachin lama, preserved in the Archives of the Kharachin Right
Banner (Chifeng Municipality, Inner Mongolia).[173] According to this document,
when the *ombo lamas* arrived in Mongol territory, they first went to a banner's
administrative seat and offered silk and other gifts to obtain the authorization
to collect alms.[174] Then, going from yurt to yurt, they delivered a speech about
the monastery they came from, the temples and *stūpas* in need of repair, asking
for the great compassion of the donors and telling them of the infinite merit
they could obtain. They presented an official paper issued by the Qing court
proving their affiliation to a monastery of Wutaishan. If a family agreed, they
welcomed the monk to enter, offering milk tea and food. The monks brought
small gifts (silk they had bought in Beijing, clothes for the children, silk scarves,
statues from the mountain and *adis*)[175] as well as children's shoes for childless
families as a promise to bring them offspring. Like other wandering *badarchis*,
they also transmitted news and stories.[176] They may also have offered or sold
maps of Wutaishan, such as prints of the Cifusi map.[177] Everyone, from ordinary
herdsmen to nobles, had great consideration for these Wutaishan monks, who
were generally welcomed and offered food and lodgings.

---

173    Song Wenhui 2000.

174    Similarly, before organizing an expedition, the monks from Inner Mongol and Khalkha
       monasteries had to report to the banner prince, who would obtain the permission from
       the Lifanyuan to collect contributions. The emperor could also grant a high lama the right
       to collect alms in a particular territory. For instance, the Second Neichi Toin Khutugtu
       (1671-1703) obtained the authorization to collect alms in the ten Khorchin banners and
       obtained from the herders fifty thousand taels of silver, three thousand heads of cattle
       and sheep, furs, silver bowls, etc., which he redistributed to monasteries in Höhhot and
       Beijing.

175    *Adis* are square packets of white paper (three or four *cun* wide) with Tibetan writing,
       filled with sugar, rice etc. to eat as a medicine in order to bring happiness, wealth and luck.

176    Song Wenhui 2000: 33.

177    According to Swallow's account (1903: 179): on Wutaishan, "We made the acquaintance of
       a Russian Mongol, and as he could not speak Chinese we thought he was a pilgrim and
       treated him as a guest, but next day he came and wanted to sell us rough colored maps of
       the place, and he asked such outrageous prices that we soon sent him about his business."

Once they had gathered enough funds, these monks returned to Wutaishan, sometimes with large sums of money, gold and silver, driving before them up to two thousand sheep and hundreds of horses. They usually sold some of the animals in exchange for taels of silver in the towns they went through.[178] They kept part of the donations for their travel expenses. In 1930, a certain Babu, after having deducted his traveling expenses, brought back as much as 1,300 silver dollars to his Wutaishan monastery.[179] Those who had traveled to eastern Inner Mongolia went via Beijing, where they purchased various artifacts to take to Mongolia. On their way back, they exchanged part of the gifts they had received for silk in Beijing. "In this way the final sum realized on a begging expedition depends to a great extent on the ability and address of the agent. Frequently large sums are collected, but accidents sometimes happen."[180] Gilmour mentions the case of the failed expedition of a Wutaishan lama who had collected a fairly large number of horses and some oxen and was driving southwards to the Chinese market. Just before reaching the frontier, the animals were seized by a Mongol pretending to be their true owner. The unfortunate lama was thrown into prison; he was later acquitted but only part of his property was restituted to him. He tried to obtain the full restitution of his property, "as without the money he could not show his face in Wu T'ai."[181]

Comparable observations were made about collector lamas from Baruun Kheid (Western Monastery) of the Alashan Banner. They usually left their monastery in spring and autumn for a maximum of three months, alone or in small groups of two or three, carrying a notice written by the reincarnation or the abbot, explaining the reason for the solicitation and expressing the hope of receiving help from people.[182] The lama's name, his monastery and visiting date were also written on the notice. They went from door to door, going as far as Central Mongolia or the Solon and Bargu banners in the northeast. After entering a home, the lama would present his notice and explain the purpose of his visit. Almost every herdsman would give something, even of little value: animals, money, cloth, flour, rice, sugar or brick tea. Those who did not make offerings promised to give something next time. After receiving a donation, the *badarchi lama*s would offer some gifts in return according to the amount of donation: those who gave a camel or a horse might receive a large scarf, a bottle

---

178     Song Wenhui 2000: 33; Gilmour 1893: 16-17.
179     Song Wenhui 2000: 33.
180     Gilmour 1893: 16-17.
181     Gilmour 1893: 16-17.
182     State Nationalities Affairs Commission of China 1986: 124-126.

of alcohol and a pound of sugar.[183] The collector lamas kept some of the animals for themselves and could even become individually wealthy after one or two expeditions.[184] Walter Bosshard, a German who traveled to Wutaishan in 1954, witnessed in one of the Sünid banners a whole caravan of oxcarts, sheep, horses and cows driven by *badarchi lamas* going back to their monastery after an entire summer of fundraising.[185]

The Wutaishan monasteries also directly entrusted Mongol banners with the task of gathering donations to repair their temples. A booklet on a "great enterprise of restoration of Ganjuur Süme on Wutaishan" (possibly relating to Yuanzhaosi),[186] written by the abbot of this monastery, was 'issued' by the Old and New Bargu Banners of Khölön Buir (on behalf of the Ganjuur Süme) and sent to the nearby Achitu Beise Banner of the Khalkha Setsen Khan. Dated the 15th of the second lunar month of 1919, it requested that Mongols provide the huge sum of fifty thousand taels to repair the monastery (Online Appendix F).[187] This booklet starts with a moving description of the poor state of preservation of the "central assembly hall of Ganjuur Süme," which had suffered heavy rains and flooding: now "the sunlight and moonlight come through," and the splendour of the Buddha statues and objects of worship is fading. The abbot explains that at first, after deliberation with eminent persons, he informed the authorities of the necessity of repairing the temple, hoping that a government decree would order that restoration be done within a thousand days; however, he received no answer and prayed to Mañjuśrī. He complains that there is no longer central power, that Buddha's teachings are no longer worshipped and that the Chinese have endured many sufferings. This is why he has now turned towards the 'strength of many donors,' starting with great compassionate princes. The aim of the booklet is not only to inform and arouse Mongols' pity but also, after having obtained donations, to record their names and clans:

---

183   The alms-collecting lamas brought gifts such as ceremonial scarves, sugar, alcohol and carpets. Another source mentions *badarchi lamas* from Yamun Süme (Yanfusi 延福寺) in Dingyuanying (Alashan Banner) who carried 30 scarves, 10 bricks (25 pounds) of tea, 20 pounds of sugar and 30 bottles of alcohol to offer.

184   For example, a lama from Baruun Kheid collected 30 camels but reported only 10; the monastic storehouse paid him 2 camels for his food and lodging expenses, thus leaving 8 camels. With his 22 camels he could build 5 houses (State Nationalities Affairs Commission of China 1986: 125-126).

185   Bosshard 1954 [1950]: 205.

186   In stele YZ4 (1898), Yuanzhaosi is called Golden *Kanjur* Monastery. On Wutaishan, the Fourth Jamyang Zhepa of Labrang visited Kangyur Temple, a place later listed as one of Labrang Monastery's properties, which Nietupski apparently did not identify (2011: 339).

187   I thank Olivér Kápolnas for having copied this text for me.

"once the restoration of this hall is completed, a stone inscription will be carved to show the names [of the donors] and erected south of the central assembly hall so that it will last ten thousand years." Great merit will result from these deeds, and this is the path to enlightenment to become a Buddha.

Why did the petition originate from the Bargu banners? Perhaps there existed a particular connection between the Ganjuur Süme of Wutaishan and the famous Ganjuur Süme of the Bargus. In any case, the subscription was not filled and was never returned to Wutaishan (it is preserved in the National Central Library of Ulaanbaatar): the forty-nine pages following the introductory text, destined to receive the names of donors, were left blank. It must be the same kind of document that a fundraising monk from Wutaishan showed to John Blofeld in Beijing around 1936-1937: a trilingual (Mongolian, Tibetan, Chinese) booklet of beautifully printed receipt form. It had taken him three months to walk from Wutaishan to Beijing, collecting funds.[188]

Wutaishan lamas who traveled through Mongolia for other purposes, such as to take back home ill or tired pilgrims, also received many gifts from Mongol families along the way:

> Sometimes a party of pilgrims reach Wu-T'ai on foot, but are [sic] so worn out by the journey that they feel unable to return home. The temple they lodge at sends them home under the care of one or two of its lamas, who receive gifts for their temple not only from the families of the pilgrims they have thus assisted, but also from the devout inhabitants of the neighbouring country, to whom the assisted pilgrims introduce them as their benefactors.[189]

Particular relations were therefore established between Wutaishan monasteries, Mongol banners and individuals in the mid-nineteenth century. The Mongol donors whose names were entered in a subscription list were not only ensured good merit through the act of donation but also assured that they had created a connection, a particular relation with a specific monastery of Wutaishan, so that when they went to the mountain they would then be welcomed to that monastery "as old acquaintances by those who experienced their hospitality in the desert, and were the recipients of their pious gifts."[190] Some even transferred all their property to some monastery on Wutaishan, "on condition that the temple will feed, lodge, and clothe him for the term of his life. It relieves

---

188    Blofeld 1959: 96-97.
189    Gilmour 1970 [1883]: 149.
190    Gilmour 1970 [1883]: 151.

them from anxiety about their temporal affairs, and permits to devote the close of their life without distraction to the duties of religion."[191]

These fundraising expeditions not only allowed some Wutaishan monasteries to survive and prosper in difficult times but also played a crucial role in the diffusion of knowledge about the mountain and acted as a living advertisement for the pilgrimage. The numerous *ombo lamas* from Wutaishan's monasteries spread the mountain's fame throughout Mongolia, Tibet and as far as Buryatia with such persuasion that, after the lamas' visit, the Mongol donors often made a vow to make a pilgrimage there. Wutaishan monasteries thus maintained an extensive network of clients, who could be encouraged to return again and again over the years.

*Ombo lamas* served as intermediaries between their Wutaishan monastery and the Mongol pilgrims; they tried to build confidence and establish personalized relations so that the Mongols would come again in the future. The monasteries functioned as travel agencies and organized facilities for pilgrims to make their sojourn comfortable. We will see in Chapter 6 that monasteries sent *ombo lamas* to Zhangjiakou, Datong or Höhhot in order to welcome princes and officials and personally accompany them to Wutaishan.

### Literary and Visual Production of the Resident Wutaishan Lamas Designed for Pilgrims

Wutaishan resident monks did not produce many guidebooks: I could identify only one guidebook authored by two Wutaishan lamas in 1652, and its diffusion was extremely limited. The most diffused Mongolian guidebook was commissioned by the *jasag lama* of Wutaishan to a lama from Inner Mongolia (see Chapter 4). Yet guidebooks had a smaller audience compared to woodblock images of Wutaishan, which were more accessible printed vehicles of information about the pilgrimage.[192] Xylograph printing of Buddhist scriptures and images had been used in China since the seventh century to disseminate Buddhist teachings and to accumulate merit by reproduction of holy texts and images.

191 Gilmour 1970 [1883]: 151.

192 Already during the first millennium, paintings of Wutaishan and its extraordinary phenomena played a significant role in the development of the cult of this sacred mountain in Asia (Demiéville 1952: 188 n. 1, 376-377; Sen 2003: 79). Shanxi painters were commissioned to create maps showing the topography of the mountain and its holy temples as well as the legends attached to them and descriptions of miraculous phenomena. When Japanese monk Ennin visited Wutaishan in 840, his fellow traveler asked a painter of Taiyuan to paint a map of the divine manifestations of the *bodhisattva* on Wutaishan, and Ennin took it back to Japan (Ennin, *Nittō guhō junrei kōki*, quoted by Demiéville 1952: 377; Zha Luo 1998: 97-101; transl. by Reischauer 1955: 269).

The map of Wutaishan produced in 1846 by a Mongol lama at Cifusi was widely diffused in Mongolia. While it can be studied as one of the local lamas' strategies to promote the pilgrimage, it is also a Mongol production stemming from the success of the pilgrimage; this is why it will be studied in the following chapter.

## The High-Ranking Lamas Who Contributed to Empowering Wutaishan

The famous Tibetan, Mongol and Monguor monks who temporarily resided at or visited Wutaishan enhanced its attractive power. Like with the above-mentioned travels of the Dalai Lamas and Panchen Lamas in Mongolia, these renowned masters were followed by disciples looking for initiations and empowerments. They contributed to 'empowering' Wutaishan by their presence and, after their death, by their relics.

### The Changkya Khutugtus and Wutaishan

In 1705, on Kangxi's order, the First Changkya Khutugtu restored Pusading and was entrusted with turning Chinese monasteries into Gélukpa monasteries.[193] Among his following reincarnations, only the second, Rölpé Dorjé, regularly resided on the mountain. Born in a Monguor family of Amdo, Rölpé Dorjé became a well-known hierarch within the Gélukpa School, as well as the state preceptor of Qianlong.[194] He was first attracted to Wutaishan because Tsongkhapa, the founder of the Gélukpa School, is said to have reincarnated as an erudite monk in a monastery of Wutaishan.[195] Besides, Rölpé Dorjé was connected to Yuan-dynasty Pakpa Lama, who is listed as a previous incarnation of the Changkya Khutugtu lineage in the biographies of Rölpé Dorjé and of his successor.[196] Both Pakpa and Rölpé Dorjé had a decisive influence on the

---

193   Xiao Yu 蕭宇 1990: 12; Wang Zhiyong and Cui Zhengsen 2000: 745.

194   His biography as well as his political, spiritual, architectural and artistic influence at court have been extensively studied: Biography of Rölpé Dorjé, transl. Chen Qingying and Ma Lianlong 1988: 305; Wang Xiangyun 1995; Illich 2006; Chou 2011b: Chapter 1.

195   According to Tsongkhapa's biography. See Chapter 4.

196   Biography of Rölpé Dorjé quoted by Illich 2006: 342-343; biography of the Third Changkya Khutugtu: *Cindamani-yin erikes* (after 1851), transl. Everding 1988: 110, 144. Śākya Yéshé, who resided on Wutaishan several times between 1414 and 1419, was also included among the previous incarnations of the Changkya Khutugtu lineage (Biography of the Third Changkya Khutugtu: transl. Everding 1988). Since Qianlong was viewed as a reincarnation of Khubilai Khan (both being emanations of Mañjuśrī), Rölpé Dorjé and Qianlong were

development of Wutaishan as a sacred Tibetan place and their relics became sites for pilgrimage on Wutaishan.

The thirty-four summers (generally from the fourth to the eighth lunar month) that Rölpé Dorjé spent on the mountain between 1750 and 1786 (i.e., every year except for 1757-1758, when he traveled to Tibet) correspond to a great material and spiritual prosperity for the Tibetan tradition on Wutaishan. He repeatedly expressed the wish he could stay longer, and he often complained that the emperor wanted him to return to Beijing—although the Qing emperors wanted the Changkyas to periodically tour Wutaishan, they did not especially expect them to reside there. Rölpé Dorjé played the role of a magnet, attracting Mongol masters and pilgrims when he resided at Dolonnor, Tibetan Buddhists from China when he was in Beijing, and Tibetans and Mongols when he resided on Wutaishan. During those periods when Rölpé Dorjé was there, Wutaishan was the main place where Gélukpa masters from Central Tibet, Amdo, Mongolia and Beijing converged.

Rölpé Dorjé's activity on Wutaishan was considerable.[197] He joined Qianlong four times in his imperial tours (in 1750, 1761, 1781 and 1786), conducted rituals of longevity for Qianlong's mother, lectured on Buddhist doctrine, had informal talks with the emperor and spent a lot of time practicing meditation and retreats (sometimes six months long). He also performed rituals that were decisive for the Qing military strategy: in 1772, he threw bolts of fire against the Jinchuan 'rebels' over a distance of hundred kilometers.[198] Between 1767 and 1786 he composed a pilgrimage guide to introduce the monasteries and famous Buddhist monks of Wutaishan,[199] as well as poems,[200] and a book about rituals to be performed at various monasteries of Wutaishan.[201] He also gave numerous initiations, empowerments and teachings (including secret teachings) at the request of Mongol princes, Chinese monks and laypersons, especially in the years from 1782 to 1786. For instance, he gave a Guhyasamāja initiation to an Oirad Mongol noble, to lamas from Höhhot, to the *jasag lama* of Wutaishan and to about two hundred devotees; a Vajrabhairava initiation to the Second

connected through many lifetimes, repeating the priest-patron relationship between Pakpa Lama and Khubilai.

197   About Rölpé Dorjé on Wutaishan: Xiao Yu 肖雨 1990 and 2003; Xiao Yu 蕭宇 1990; Wang Xiangyun 1995: 103-108; Illich 2006: Part II, Chapter VI.

198   Martin 1990: 7-10.

199   *ZMRBDB*; Mongolian translation: *OMSA*. See Chapter 4.

200   Schaeffer 2011: 222-227; Biography of Rölpé Dorjé, transl. Chen Qingying and Ma Lianlong 1988: Chapter 18.

201   *Ri bo rtse lnga'i gzhi bdag rnams la gtor bul 'phin bcol mdor bsdus pa bzhugs*. See Wang Xiangyun 1995: 104.

FIGURE 14    *Amdo pilgrims worshipping the ruins of Puleyuan.* © ISABELLE CHARLEUX, 2007.

Bandida Gegeen (see below) and two hundred pilgrim-monks; and a Kālacakra initiation to a Chakhar Mongol and three hundred pilgrim-monks. In 1769 he consecrated a statue of Lhamo for the Toin Khutugtu of Alashan. He had a countless number of disciples and followers among monks and laypersons, including Manchu princes (such as the twelfth son of Kangxi and the fifth, sixth and eighth sons of Qianlong) and Chinese.[202]

At first, Rölpé Dorjé lived in Upper Shancaidong (which he had had restored), Jingangku or Pusading. In 1765 or 1766 he founded a hermitage, which was completed in 1769 and called Universal Joy Cloister (Ch. Puleyuan, Tib. Küntu Dewé Sel) (Fig. 14).[203] After 1767, he resided in Zhenhaisi and it was there that he died, in 1786, in spite of the attention of the best doctors available. Although Rölpé

---

202    Xiao Yu 肖雨 1990: 6.

203    Biography of Rölpé Dorjé, transl. Chen Qingying and Ma Lianlong 1988: 304-305. The same name was given to two different monasteries: the lateral courtyard of Zhenhaisi, where the Changkya had his residence, and a now destroyed monastery near Jingangku that

Dorjé had expressly asked the emperor not to build a *stūpa* in his honor, Qian-long commissioned a relic *stūpa* for seven thousand taels of gold and silver decorated with precious stones to enshrine his mummy, which was buried in a subterranean stone chamber at the spot indicated previously by the master.[204] In addition, a seven-meter-high stone *stūpa* was erected in the Puleyuan court-yard of Zhenhaisi and became one of the most important places of pilgrimage for Mongols (Fig. 15). This latter monument enshrines the blessed salts used to dry and preserve the remains of the lama.

Through his charisma, but also through his guidebook and poems and, after his death, through his funerary *stūpa*, Rölpé Dorjé 'empowered' Wutaishan and considerably strengthened its Tibetan and Mongol Buddhist identity. From then on, Zhenhaisi became the headquarters of the Changkya lineage. The Third Changkya Khutugtu, Yéshé Tenpé Gyeltsen śrībhadra (1787-1846), lived there when he visited Wutaishan between 1806 and 1819. His funerary *stūpa* was built in the upper courtyard (it was destroyed during the Cultural Revolution). The Fifth Changkya, Lozang Tendzin Gyatso (b. 1878-d. 1887 or 1888), was buried on Wutaishan, and Emperor Guangxu offered a thousand taels for his funerals. The Sixth Changkya, Lozang Penden Tenpé Drönmé (1891-1958) spent a part of his life on Wutaishan, where he met President Yuan Shikai 袁世凱 (1859-1916) in 1912. He settled a conflict in 1917,[205] and established his office in the Puleyuan courtyard of Zhenhaisi in 1937.[206] He encouraged Wutaishan monks to enroll in the army and fight the Japanese. He died in Taiwan, but till recently his disciples were planning to carry his remains back to Wutaishan.[207]

---

looked more like a hermitage. According to his biography, Puleyuan here refers to the second one, "at the foot of Vajra Cave" (Illich 2006: 517).

204   According to most authors, the place remained secret, perhaps deep underground inside or near Zhenhaisi; according to others, a small temple was built on the spot (See Miaozhou 1993 [1935]: *juan* 5, 100; Wang Xiangyun 1995: 302-306; Wang Lu 1995; Zhang Yu 1996; Wen Ming 2006).

205   The illegal exorbitant taxation imposed by the *jasag lama* of Pusading on the local population had raised discontent in Wutai, Fanzhi and Dai Counties. Chinese warlord Yan Xishan, the then governor of Shanxi, asked the Changkya to organize a meeting in Zhenhaisi and find an agreement (Xiao Yu 蕭宇 1990: 14).

206   Daguoshi Zhangjia hutuketu banshichu 大國師章嘉呼圖克圖辦事處.

207   Fabienne Jagou, personal communication, 2007.

FIGURE 15    Stūpa *of Rölpé Dorjé in Zhenhaisi.* © ISABELLE CHARLEUX, 2010.

### Famous Tibetan Buddhist Dignitaries Visiting Wutaishan

Three categories of Tibetan Buddhist clerical visitors were encountered on the mountain.[208] The first were the ordinary pilgrim-monks; the second were monks who came to Wutaishan to study with great masters. For instance, Tsampa Lozang Könchok (1742-ca. 1822), a student of the Second Jamyang Zhépa from Labrang, was sent by the latter to Wutaishan to study with the famous encyclopedist Longdöl Ngakwang Lozang (1729-1794) and Rölpé Dorjé. [209] The third category was made up of renowned masters and reincarnations who toured China and Inner Asia, visiting Wutaishan, then Beijing and the great monasteries of Amdo and Mongolia, where they gave blessings and initiations. These Buddhist dignitaries came to Wutaishan to make their personal pilgrimage to the mountain by paying homage to the renowned temples and sacred sites. At the same time, they were themselves a locus of pilgrimage, attracting devotees who came especially to worship them: the pilgrimage to the mountain was also a pilgrimage to the great masters who lived or temporarily resided there. They contributed to 'empower' or 're-empower' certain sites of Wutaishan for future generations through their consecrations, blessings, miracles and rediscovery of hidden religious treasures, while themselves receiving blessings and power from the holy site.

These masters—like the Fourth Jamyang Zhépa, Kelzang Tupten Wangchuk (1856-1916), in 1898—were received by the *jasag lama* of Wutaishan and were expected to give blessings, initiations, ordinations and teachings.[210] They could meet and discuss with the Manchu emperor during his visits and with Chinese Buddhist monks. They also acted as diplomats and mediators. Wutaishan had thus become a node in religious and economic networks linking Amdo Tibetans, Central Tibetans, Mongols, Manchus and Chinese.

In the early twentieth century, two pontiffs took refuge on Wutaishan. The Thirteenth Dalai Lama, after having fled the British invasions of Tibet in 1904 and spending almost three years in Mongolia and six months at Kumbum, stayed five months on Wutaishan in 1908 with his retinue, at the (considerable) expense of the Shanxi governor. There, he established his court and dealt with

---

208   Most of the ancient and modern Chinese sources, such as Wang Zhiyong and Cui Zhengsen (2000: 734-743 and 799-800, mostly based on Yu Meian 1977 [1923], document the life and deeds of the great Chinese Buddhist masters who resided and visited Wutaishan, but no such documentation exists for Tibetan and Mongol dignitaries. One has to read biographies (*namtar*) and collected works (*sungbum*) written in Tibetan, and occasionally in Mongolian, to discover brief mentions of or poems on Wutaishan.

209   See the account of the trip of the Second Jamyang Zhépa to Wutaishan and the unusually detailed record of the Fourth Jamyang Zhépa (Nietupski 2011: 332-333, 338-339).

210   Nietupski 2011.

foreign diplomats, gave teachings, conducted rituals, performed miracles, visited temples and holy sites and recited the *Sūtra of Great Compassion* in Guanyindong for twenty-one days. D'Ollone mentions Mongol princes accompanied
by their numerous retinues visiting the Dalai Lama.[211] Mongols and Buryats
made the trip to Wutaishan carrying offerings to meet him (Table 2). Also, in
1925 the Ninth Panchen Lama went twice (by car) to Wutaishan , where he
meditated for twenty-one days; he gave two initiations of Long Life of Tārā, a
teaching of the Shambhala prayer attended by a thousand monks and laity, gave
three thousand silver dollars for a ritual at Pusading and distributed gifts to the
assembled monks.[212]

The majority of these high Gélukpa masters and reincarnations who visited
Wutaishan were Tibetans, Mongols and Monguors from Amdo, and Mongols
from Inner Mongolia. As shown by Schaeffer and Nietupski, they formed a
"closely knit intellectual community."[213] Amdo scholar Sumpa Khenpo Yéshé
Penjor (Mo. Ishibaljur, 1704-1788)—a polymath, linguist, physician, mathemati-
cian and astronomer of Oirad or Monguor origin, disciple of Rölpé Dorjé and
active at Qianlong's court—spent three years on Wutaishan in the 1740s.[214] The
Third Tukwan, Lozang Chökyi Nyima (1737-1802), visited Wutaishan several
times, first in his thirties to visit his master, Rölpé Dorjé.[215]

Lamas from Labrang and other Amdo monasteries, some of whom were of
Mongol origin, built a 'power network' on Wutaishan.[216] Among them were the
'reverend Chinese' (*gyanakpa*),[217] as were known the Tibetan lamas sent by
Labrang and other Amdo monasteries to propagate Tibetan Buddhism and to
promote their monasteries' political interests in China and in Mongolia. These
religious and political emissaries were especially active on Wutaishan and at

---

211    Ollone 1911: 362.
212    Wuyungaowa 1997: 201; Jagou 2004: 118, n. 21.
213    Schaeffer (2011: 219) notes that most of the writers on Wutaishan were born in Amdo. See
       also a list of high dignitaries from Amdo who visited Wutaishan in a Tibetan guidebook
       by Dznyā na shrī man, *Ri bo rtse lnga'i dkar chag rab gsal me long* (1994 [after 1827]) (Gray
       Tuttle, email, September 2011).
214    See his biography composed in 1776, included in his eight-volume complete work
       (translated into Mongolian), quoted by Schaeffer 2011: 220. He is the author of the *dPag
       bsam ljon bzang*, a history of Buddhism in India and Tibet.
215    See his biography composed in 1803, quoted by Schaeffer 2011: 220. Other examples in
       Schaeffer 2011.
216    Nietupski (2011) showed that the Labrang lamas sought to establish a presence on
       Wutaishan and, through Wutaishan, with Beijing.
217    Nietupski 2009: 337.

the Beijing court, as well as in Chinese communities.[218] Since Labrang maintained relations with several Inner Mongol monasteries, Wutaishan was a convenient place where the Mongols could meet its reincarnations. The Second Jamyang Zhépa of Labrang, Könchok Jikmé Wangpo (1728-1791), visited Wutaishan in 1770 and three years later wrote a description of Buddhism in China starting with a long discussion on the central importance of Wutaishan as being the heart of China.[219] He is also credited with the foundation of Gilubar Juu in the Baarin Left Banner of eastern Inner Mongolia, a place that was known as 'White Wutaishan' (see Chapter 7).[220]

The Third Détri Jamyang, Tupten Nyima (1779-1862), thirtieth abbot of Labrang, sojourned on Wutaishan in 1842, 1847 and 1856, where he worshipped Rölpé Dorjé's *stūpa* and experienced mysterious phenomena. In 1856, after having performed a rain ritual in a period of severe drought, he was recognized as a *bodhisattva* by Tibetans, Mongols and Chinese. A Mongol community invited him to visit, teach, ordain monks and perform ritual services on Wutaishan.[221] Other Amdo monasteries entertained links with Wutaishan; for instance, Choné Trashi Chökhor Ling (in present-day Gansu Province) used to send lamas to teach at Shifangtang (founded in 1831 by a lama from Choné), and lamas from Wutaishan went to Choné for advanced studies.[222]

Renowned Mongol clerics from Inner and Khalkha Mongolia journeyed to Wutaishan on their way to Beijing or to Tibet. For example, the First Jebtsündamba, Zanabazar, visited Wutaishan together with Emperor Kangxi in 1698. The Fourth Jebtsündamba, Lubsang Tübden Wangchug (1775-1813), visited Wutaishan in 1802,[223] and again in 1812; he died of pneumonia upon his return to Mongolia in 1813. The Fifth Jebtsündamba paid a visit to Emperor Daoguang (r. 1821-1851) in 1839 and on the occasion traveled to Wutaishan.[224] During his travels in Inner Mongolia and China, the First Jaya Bandida, Lubsangpringlei (1642-1715), of the Khalkhas, made a pilgrimage to Wutaishan in 1707. One of his

---

218    For instance, the Upper Monastery of the Bingling Grottoes in Gansu Province. Nietupski (2009) mentions eight lineages of *gyanakpas* from Labrang starting in the seventeenth century.

219    Nietupski 2011: 332-333.

220    Galsang et al. 1994: 280.

221    Nietupski 2011: 335.

222    Wang Xiangyun 2004, n. 52.

223    Dznyā na shrī man's Tibetan guidebook *Ri bo rtse lnga'i dkar chag rab gsal me long* mentions his 1802 pilgrimage (1994 [after 1827], passage transl. by Gray Tuttle, email, September 2011).

224    Several sources mention and document these trips. See, for instance, *Tabuduyar boydayin namtar* [Hagiography of the Fifth Bogda], MS. National Library of Mongolia.

disciples wrote the main guidebook on Wutaishan (see Chapter 4), and the modern museum located in his monastery, Jaya-yin Khüriye (Zayayn Khüree, Tsetserleg, Arkhangai Province), preserves a colored print of the Cifusi map.

The lineage of the Chagan Diyanchi from eastern Inner Mongolia was especially connected to Wutaishan. Samdan Sangbu (1633-1720 or 1728), the Mongol eremitic monk who founded Chagan Diyanchi-yin Kheid and received from the Dalai Lama the title Chagan Diyanchi, [225] repeatedly went to Wutaishan at the request of Emperor Kangxi.[226] He and several of his reincarnations were buried on Wutaishan. Another eminent Inner Mongol reincarnation who visited Wutaishan is the Second Bandida Gegeen (Changlung Arya Paṇḍita), Agwang Lubsang Danbi Jalsang (1770-1845), a great erudite scholar, artist, physician and musician of the Bandida Gegeen Süme. In 1783 he visited Wutaishan, where he received the Vajrabhairava initiation from Rölpé Dorjé; he traveled there again around 1800.[227] The Second Dagbu Gegeen or Deedü-yin Gegeen of Baruun Kheid, Lubsang Tübden Jamso (1747-1807) and later the Seventh Dagbu and the last Dagbu (in the 1930s) often journeyed to Wutaishan and stayed in Shancaidong.[228] The great poet, dramaturge and eccentric Nyingmapa lama Danjinrabjai (b. 1803 or 1804-d. 1856, Cyr. Mo. Danzanravjaa), the Fifth Noyan Khutugtu who was nicknamed the 'Drunkard of the Gobi,' went on pilgrimage from Dolonnor to Wutaishan along with his master, the Third Changkya, around 1825. The sanctity of Wutaishan inspired Danjinrabjai to write his twelve-verse poem "Saruul tunggalag" (Beautiful and Clear), which was dedicated to the Changkya Khutugtu.[229] Jaba Damdin (Cyr. Mo. Zava Damdin) Lubzang Tayang journeyed to Wutaishan after 1906.[230] To write his *gSer gyi deb*

225   White Hermit Monastery, Ch. Ruiyingsi 瑞應寺, in eastern Inner Mongolia, present-day Fuxin 阜新 Autonomous County, Liaoning Province.

226   According to his manuscript biography (*Caγan diyanci lam-a-yin namtar*, Vol 1, 56, see *Catalogue of Ancient Mongolian Books and Documents of China* 1999: no. 4761), quoted by Elverskog 2011: 249-250, n. 30.

227   His biography mentions his encounters with Rölpé Dorjé (*gSung 'bum*, 7 printed volumes [http://www.tbrc.org/]. He paid for the carving of the printing blocks for Rölpé Dorjé's guidebook (Chapter 4).

228   Miγvacir 2008 [1942]: 405. Lubsang Tübden Jamso received the title Iluugsan Bandida Nom-un Khan from the Panchen Lama; he was renowned for his literary works and paintings of goddess Lhamo.

229   Other poems of Danjinrabjai mention Wutaishan, such as "The High Mountain" (transl. by Wickham-Smith 2006: 70). I thank Simon Wickham-Smith for having sent me the poem "Saruul Tunggalag" from Tsagaan 1992.

230   Lokesh Chandra 1961: 27.

*ther* (Golden Annals), written in Tibetan between 1919 and 1931, he consulted Wutaishan guidebooks.

Wutaishan therefore appears as a must-do pilgrimage-cum-study or pilgrimage-cum-teaching in the hagiographies of high clerics from Amdo and Mongolia, from the eighteenth to the early twentieth century, and the list could go on. It is also worth mentioning the travels of Buryat monks: Buryatia and Mongolia were linked to Tibet by a 'Buddhist road' going through Wutaishan and Kumbum. The famous Buryat diplomat monk Dorjiev, on his first trip to Tibet at about twenty years old, left Russia with a caravan in 1873 and reached Wutaishan, where he spent two years (before 1878). There, he met and obtained initiations, teachings and practical guidance from great Tibetan masters, including the *jasag lama*, and started a long Vajrabhairava retreat. Dorjiev's main tutor, Jangchup Tsültrim Pelzangpo,[231] asked him to go with him to Tibet on an almscollecting tour to obtain money so that the *jasag lama* of Wutaishan could afford to go to Tibet in his own turn. Dorjiev left for Lhasa in winter with Jangchup Tsültrim Pelzangpo, via Xining, Chengdu and Dartsedo (Tatsienlu); on the road thousands of people asked for precepts and gave them offerings. He then returned to Wutaishan and gave the *jasag lama* the money he had collected. Since he was very successful in his almsround, the latter asked him to be his attendant on the journey to Tibet, and they went together to Lhasa in 1880. There, Dorjiev completed his Buddhist education and obtained the *lharampa* degree in 1888.[232] In 1907 he again spent a few months on Wutaishan.

In their travel records, autobiographies, songs and poems, Mongol masters and reincarnations mentioned visions and experiences of mysterious phenomena on Wutaishan, meetings with high-ranking lamas and visits to monasteries and caves. Most of them wrote in classical Tibetan, such as Alaksha (Alashan) Tutop Nyima (his disciple, the renowned philosopher, linguist and poet Agwandandar [1759-1840] also visited Wutaishan). Kurtis Schaeffer, who has studied the works of twenty-two Tibetan and Mongol clerics who wrote in Tibetan from 1257 to 2007, noticed that poetry was the preeminent form of Tibetan literary expression regarding Wutaishan. Some poems on Wutaishan were even written by clerics who never went there. [233]

---

231 Also known as Jadrel Rinpoché, Namnang Bagshi or Namnanai Gegeen, he was a prominent Buryat figure. He had completed the twenty-two-year Great Retreat of Vajrabhairava in the holy Alkanay Mountains and was thus known as the Buryat Milarépa (Martin and Norbu 1991: 12-13; Andreyev 2001b: 175.)

232 Martin and Norbu 1991: 12-13, translating his 1923 autobiography; also Andreyev 2001a: 34 and Andreyev 2001b: 176, quoting and translating a Russian memoir discovered in the archives of the Russian Academy of Sciences in Saint Petersburg (Oldenburg Collection).

233 Schaeffer 2011: 217.

After the death of the great hierarchs who visited Wutaishan, pilgrims worshipped the material evidence of their sojourns, such as the *stūpas* enshrining their relics and the caves where they are said to have meditated—regardless of whether their presence on Wutaishan was historical fact or pure legend.

## Conclusion

Wutaishan appeared in the Qing dynasty as a quasi-autonomous enclave enclosed within Chinese territory, a place with a particular status where different ethnic and religious communities resided, ruled by a lama-official originally appointed by the Manchu emperors and later by the Dalai Lamas. A part of the Chinese Buddhist landscape was turned into a Tibetan Buddhist landscape, which entailed a transformation of the sacred site. On this fertile ground, the encounter between Tibeto-Mongol and Chinese Buddhists led to exchanges and borrowings, which culminated with the development of the Chinese Gélukpa School in the twentieth century. In these encounters, a few lamas from Amdo and Inner Mongolia who were fluent in Chinese, such as Rölpé Dorjé, Sumpa Khenpo, the Third Tukwan and the twenty-second *jasag lama*, acted as mediators between the two religious communities, and between the Tibetan, Mongol, Han and Manchu worlds. When discussing these eminent masters who toured Wutaishan, we can speak of Gélukpa cosmopolitanism, because in their life and writings, it is almost impossible to distinguish high reincarnations of Amdo, Central Tibet and Mongolia. These traveling lamas from Amdo and Mongolia contributed to forge links between their own monastery and monasteries of Wutaishan, such as Shifangtang and Choné; similarly, *ombo lama*s from a Wutaishan monastery may have developed such links, such as between the Ganjuur Süme of Wutaishan and that of Inner Mongolia. Such links certainly encouraged pilgrims from the catchment areas of these Mongol monasteries to visit and primarily give offerings to their twinned monastery on Wutaishan.

The imperial visits—connected to the cult of the emperor-Mañjuśrī—and the presence of the Changkya Khutugtu and other renowned lamas empowered the mountain and added to the sanctity of Wutaishan: pilgrims could expect to receive imperial grace from the emperor-Mañjuśrī, as well as Buddhist blessings and initiations. The ordinary pilgrims were certainly not conscious of the complexity of these ethnic and doctrinal relations. Yet they probably witnessed an apparent ecumenical cohabitation between monastic communities and were certainly impressed by the heavy imperial patronage of the Qing emperors. Wutaishan was the ideal face of the multiethnic Qing empire at its border.

While the previous chapter introduced the worldly and otherworldly 'pull' factors that contributed to Wutaishan's appeal, this chapter has investigated the role of the imperial state and of the local clergy. The Qing emperors' promotion of the Wutaishan pilgrimage was not specifically directed at Mongol commoners; it also targeted nobles and great reincarnations. And in fact, the peak period of Mongol pilgrimages does not correspond with Kangxi or Qianlong's imperial patronage or with the presence of Rölpé Dorjé but to the late Qing and Republican periods, when the state ceased to show interest (Chapter 5). Thus, the role of Qing imperial promotion in the success of the pilgrimage has been overestimated. In other words, the Qing emperors' initial encouragement certainly contributed to the early success of the pilgrimage, but they cannot be given credit for the end result, which completely exceeded their expectations. Rather, it was the strategies implemented by the local clergies and the repeated visits by Tibetan and Mongol reincarnations that were certainly much more successful in encouraging Mongol commoners to undertake the pilgrimage. It is now time to explore the Mongols' own agency in the development of the pilgrimage.

# CHAPTER 4

# The Mongol *Imaginaire* of Wutaishan

The previous chapter has shown that different agents promoted the pilgrimage from the top down or contributed to attract Mongol pilgrims by their sole presence: the Qing emperors; and lamas from Wutaishan, Mongolia, Tibet and from the Qing court. This chapter aims at restoring the Mongols' agency in the development of the pilgrimage, first by investigating the Mongol veneration of Mañjuśrī and Wutaishan before the Qing dynasty, then by presenting the literature and images of the mountain produced by the Mongols themselves. Through these Mongol literary, oral and visual productions, I will investigate the Mongol clerical and popular *imaginaire*, or social imaginary, of Wutaishan, in order to highlight its specificities compared to Chinese and Tibetan representations. This chapter eventually questions when pilgrimages to Wutaishan actually developed and whether the proliferation of Mongolian guidebooks and maps was a cause or a consequence of the success of the pilgrimage.

### Wutaishan and the Cult of Mañjuśrī in Mongolia before the Qing Period

Johan Elverskog has convincingly pointed out that, even though the Qing emperors certainly encouraged the Mongols to undertake pilgrimages to Wutaishan, the cult of Mañjuśrī and its connection to Wutaishan were already well known to the Mongols long before the appearance of the Manchus.[1] Using various sources, I will first highlight the importance of the cult of Mañjuśrī and its connection to Wutaishan in Buddhist Mongolia, and the *bodhisattva*'s status in religious canonical texts, as well as in texts and narratives used in Mongols' daily lives, to question whether the worship of Mañjuśrī was strong enough to incite the herders to undertake a pilgrimage to his abode on earth.

The cult of Mañjuśrī developed in Mongolia during the Yuan period.[2] The oldest known Mongolian reference to Wutaishan may be Pakpa Lama's

---

1  Elverskog 2011.

2  In Mongolian, Mañjuśrī is called Manzushiri/Manjushiri, Jöölen egeshig-tü ('Melodious,' translating Mañjughoṣa, 'The Soft Voiced'), or Jöölen tsog-tu ('Tender and Strong') (Sárközi 1982: 557). He is described as being 'youthful' (*ori bologsan*), 'wise' (*bilig-tü*) and 'skillful' (*uran*). On the development of his cult in India, Nepal, India and China, see Etienne Lamotte's exten-

*Medegdekün-i belgeteye geyigülügci nere-tü šastir* (*Explanation of the Know-able*), written in 1278, in which, describing Jambudvīpa, he mentions Udai (Utai) as the abode of Mañjuśrī in the east, along with Udyāna and Potala.[3] Most scholars believe that Khubilai Khan was identified as an emanation of Mañjuśrī during the Yuan dynasty. In the inscription of the Cloud Platform (Yuntai 雲臺) of Juyongguan 居庸關 Pass built northwest of Beijing between 1342 to 1345 by the last emperor Togon Temür (r. 1333-1367), the sentence about Setsen Khan (i.e., Khubilai) on the west wall is usually understood as follows: "There would be someone named 'the Wise One from the vicinity of Mount Wu-t'ai' who would become a great emperor." [4] Other references to Khubilai identified as an emanation of Mañjuśrī are found in thirteenth- and fourteenth-century Tibetan sources.[5] This identification was confirmed later, in the late sixteenth-century Mongolian manual of government attributed to Khubilai, the *White History*.[6] Starting with Khubilai, the Mongol court was involved in both Tibetan and Chinese Buddhism on Wutaishan, including the expenditure of enormous amounts of money, manpower and resources in the construction of monasteries and in rituals and gifts to monks (Chapter 2). This prefigures the later Mongol pilgrims' involvement and expenditures that we will observe in the following chapters.

The Mongol emperors had a major hymn in praise of the names, qualities and activities of Mañjuśrī, the *Litany of the Names of Mañjuśrī* (*Mañjuśrīnā-masaṃgīti*), translated between 1295 and 1312 into Mongolian.[7] The *Litany* is

---

sive cross-cultural monograph (1960); also Mallmann (1964) for his iconography, and Tribe (1994a) for a discussion of the different hypotheses as to his origin and his role in Mahāyāna literature.

3   The "Explanation of the Knowable" was initially written in Tibetan (*Shes bya rab gsal*), at the request of Khubilai's son Jinggim, and was translated into Mongolian in the Yuan dynasty. The Mongolian version was published in transcription by Vladimir Uspensky (2006: 6, fol. 6v).

4   *Ut'ayi-yin horč'in mergen neret'u yéke qa·an bolju*, translated by Farquhar, basing his translation on Lajos Ligeti and Nicholas Poppe's studies (1978: 11-14; cf. Junast 1991: 171; also Murata 1957: I, 262-263, 342; Murata and Fujieda 1955: pl. 92). The translation of the Tibetan, Pakpa, Mongolian and Uyghur inscriptions has caused much ink to flow. G. Tuttle believes that the 'vicinity of [Mount] Wutai' simply refers to Khubilai's birthplace (2011: 165). Yang Fuxue (2003: 41) translates the same passage of the Uyghur inscription as "the region of Wutai can be called 'the abode/sacred area (Uyghur: *ulus*) of 'the Wise One' [Mañjuśrī]," with no reference to Khubilai Khan.

5   Debreczeny 2011: 22-23.

6   The *Cayan teüke* would be an apocryphal dated 1560-1570 (Sagaster 1976: 31).

7   This text was discovered in Turfan. It was already very important for the Uyghurs: Yang Fuxue 2003: 41-42. See Weiers 1967: 350-352; Sárközi 1982; Cerensodnom and Taube 1993: 101-106 no. 25.

one of the favorite texts recited by Tibetan Buddhists.[8] Several versions attest to the large popularity it enjoyed during the sixteenth-century renaissance of Mongol Buddhism.[9] It was one of the earliest texts brought from the Ming court to Altan Khan's descendants, who had it translated anew into Mongolian. It was later edited by Altan Khan's nephew *toin* (monk) Choijamso (d. ca. 1656) in a tetraglot version (Sanskrit, Tibetan, Chinese and Mongolian) in 1591-1592 and block printed.[10] An abridged version in three folios was found among the early seventeenth-century manuscripts on birch bark which were discovered in a *stūpa* in Kharbukhyn Balgas, Mongolia.[11] The recitation of this text is said to allow one to obtain countless worldly and spiritual benefits.[12] According to Elisabetta Chiodo:

> We may conjecture that the brief Xarbuxyn [Kharbukhyn] Balgas text must have consisted of verses of homage to *Mañjuśrī* which summarize the essence of the entire *Mañjuśrīnāmasamgīti*, and that to the recitation of these verses the same merits and benefits were attributed as those deriving from the recitation of the whole text ... According to the Buddhists the essence of the doctrine can be condensed in shortened texts. It can be also concentrated in one mantra or in one syllable.[13]

Devout Mongols used to carry small Buddhist books (referred to as 'bosom books,' *öbör nom*) in the pocket formed by the right flap of their *deel* (Mongol dress);[14] they may have carried the *Mañjuśrīnāmasaṃgīti* in an abridged form in their *deel*'s pocket or in amulet boxes.

---

8    On this text, see Davidson 1981: history, full translation and transliteration with annotations of the Sanskrit text; Wayman 1999 [1985]; and Tribe 1994b. *Mañjuśrīnāmasamgīti* is the abridged form of the *Mañjuśrījñānasattvasya paramārthā nāmasaṃgīti* (Mo. *Ilaju tegüs nögcigsen jögelen coγtu injan-a sadu-yin ünemleküi ber ner-e-yi ünen-iyer ügüleküi*), that is, Rehearsal of the supreme names of Mañjuśrī the knowledge-being.

9    For a list of independent Mongolian versions of the *Mañjuśrīnāmasaṃgīti* preserved in Europe and China: Chiodo 2009: 142-143 n. 3.

10   *Qutuγ-tu manjusiri-yin nere-yi üner/üneker-iyer ügüleküi* (late seventeenth or early eighteenth century xylograph preserved in Saint Petersburg); Bulaγ 2003: 637; Kara 2005: 123-124; Elverskog 2011: 248.

11   Chiodo 2009: 143-144 (XMB 139).

12   Chiodo 2009: 144: n. 9.

13   Chiodo 2009: 144.

14   Wallace 2009: 79.

New translations and commentaries of the *Mañjuśrīnāmasaṃgīti* from the Tibetan were made in the Qing period. [15] The *Litany* circulated in Mongolia as a separate text and was also included as the opening text of the manuscript Mongolian *Kanjur* translated in 1628-1629 at Ligdan Khan's order,[16] as well as in other collections.[17] As stressed by Elverskog, this is the "most telling piece of evidence for the Mongol interest in the cult of Mañjuśrī."[18] In present-day monasteries of Ulaanbaatar, lay donors offer donations for the recitation of the *Mañjuśrīnāmasaṃgīti* in its Tibetan version (Tib. *'Jam-dpal mtshan-brjod*, Mo. *Tsanjod*) in order to remove obstacles and to awaken intelligence and wisdom, in addition to other prayers (actually, portions of prayers) to Mañjuśrī (such as *bLa-ma dang*, a short prayer to Mañjugosha, or *rJe-btsun 'jam-dpal dbyangs-kyi bstod-pa*, Eulogy of the Noble Mañjuśrī).[19] Other Qing-dynasty texts dedicated to Mañjuśrī had a receptive audience among Mongols, such as Rölpé Dorjé's "Ülemji Manjusiri-yin taγalal-un cimeg" (Ornament of the favor of Mañjuśrī), translated into Mongolian (and matched with an old Mongol chanting tune) by the eighteenth-century Mongol cleric Biligündalai and carved on printing blocks in Beijing.[20]

Because of their great wisdom and impressive erudition, several Mongol reincarnated lamas of the pre-Qing period were recognized as emanations of Mañjuśrī and founded monasteries that bear the name of the *bodhisattva* of wisdom: for instance, the Second Tongkhor Manjushiri Khutugtu, Yönten Gyatso (1557-1587), from Tongkhor Monastery in Amdo;[21] Ashing Lama Manjushiri Khutugtu (d. 1636), who was perhaps trained in a Wutaishan monastery;[22] Künga Özer Mergen 'Manjushiri Bandida';[23] Ayushi Ananda Manjushiri

---

15    Sárközi 1982: 451.

16    Karénina Kollmar-Paulenz, personal communication, email May 30, 2013. It is also the opening text of the Imperial Mongolian *Kanjur* printed in Beijing in 1717-1720.

17    See a collection of *dhāraṇīs* in the Library of Congress (Farquhar 1955: 175, 23(2)).

18    Elverskog 2011: 249 and n. 28.

19    These prayers are recited during daily assemblies (Majer 2008: 131-233, 141).

20    This text was based on the "Precious Box" by Tsongkhapa (Ujeed 2009: 183).

21    He was conferred this title from the Third Dalai Lama, Sönam Gyatso, in 1578, at the meeting between Altan Khan and Sönam Gyatso. This lama was then charged to represent the Dalai Lama at Altan Khan's court, where he became the highest dignitary of Höhhot, taught the *dharma* to the Tümed ruling house, saved Altan Khan's life and performed the ritual at the *khan*'s funerals.

22    This title was also conferred at the meeting between Altan Khan and the Dalai Lama.

23    This Sakyapa lama, active at the court of Ligdan Khan, directed the translation of the *Kanjur* into Mongolian in 1628-1629 and authored the *Cayan lingqu-a neretü nom-un kölgen sudur* (The Mahāyāna *sūtra* called White Lotus"). He was also known as Mergen Daiching Bandida or Mergen Chakhar Lama.

Güüshi;[24] Neichi Toin Dalai Mañjuśrī;[25] and the Ganden Shireetü Khutugtu's lineage. A later incarnation of the Tongkhor Manjushiri Khutugtu founded Manjushiri Kheid (Manchir Khiid, Töv Province, Khalkha Mongolia) in 1733. In 1632, Ashing Lama Manjushiri Khutugtu was granted by the Manchu ruler Hungtaiji (r. 1627-1643) an independent monastic estate known as Manjushiri Khüriye (Mañjuśrī Monastery)[26] and, after 1646, as Shireetü Lama Khüriye Banner (Kulunqi 庫倫旗, Tongliao Municipality). Ashing's successors were appointed by the Qing, and later by the Republican administration until 1931, and bore the title Agwang Jamyang Lama (Jamyang being the Tibetan name of Mañjuśrī). The monasteries of this banner maintained links with Wutaishan monasteries, and many Mongol lamas of Wutaishan came and still come from the Shireetü Lama Khüriye Banner.[27]

While Mañjuśrī's residence on Wutaishan is not mentioned in the *Mañjuśrīnāmasaṃgīti*, the late sixteenth- and early seventeenth-century Mongols were aware of the association between the wise *bodhisattva* and Wutaishan. A prayer for rebirth among the Kharbukhyn Balgas manuscripts specifically links Mañjuśrī to Wutaishan: "On China's Wutaishan mountain dwells the victorious youth Holy Mañjuśrī."[28] The Kharbukhyn Balgas manuscripts also include an invocation to Mañjuśrī expressing the aspiration to disperse the darkness of ignorance and attain wisdom.[29] Fragments of a text on incense offering that mentions Wutaishan were also found among the manuscripts of Olan Süme in Inner Mongolia (dating somewhere between the end of the fifteenth century to the beginning of the seventeenth).[30] Although I did not find any mention of Mongol monks traveling to Wutaishan during the late sixteenth-century Buddhist revival, the cult of Mañjuśrī linked to the reputation of his abode was certainly one of the main factors that encouraged Mongols to visit Wutaishan.

---

24  Title of Ayushi Güüshi in the biography of Altan Khan (Elverskog 2003: 162, n. 300).

25  Neichi Toin was called 'Mañjuśrī Holy Lama' because he was considered by his disciples as being the second Tsongkhapa, who was viewed as the earthly manifestation of Mañjuśrī (Ujeed 2009: 220).

26  In the 1580s, Ashing Lama traveled in eastern Inner Mongolia to preach the *dharma* and was invited to Hungtaiji's court in 1629.

27  Oral information given by a lama of Luohousi, Wutaishan, fall 2009.

28  "Kitad utaisang aγulan-tur ilaγuγsad-un köbegün qutuγ-tu Manjus[ir]i saγun bülüge" (Chiodo 2000a: 96, repeated p. 98; Elverskog 2011: 248-249) (XMB 43).

29  Chiodo 2009: 145-149 (XMB 140); See also a fragment mentioning Wutaishan: Chiodo 2000a: 99 (XMB 45, 3 lines).

30  Heissig 1976b: 386, 392, OS IV/52r.

## The Production of Mongolian Guidebooks and Maps

### Guidebooks of Wutaishan Authored or Translated by Mongols

As seen in the preceding chapter, the *Cing liyang šan ayulan-u sine ji-bicig*—the 1701 translation of the *Qingliangshan xinzhi* compiled in 1694 by Lao-zang-dan-ba—was the only one imperially commissioned production in Mongolian. Even if the Qing court sponsored other Mongolian guidebooks, their writing was not made on its order: the other guidebooks were composed or translated at the request of pious Mongols who asked high clerics to write them or paid for the printing, or at the initiative of local lamas to promote the sacred place and legitimate its sacred status.

These guidebooks are of two types. Some resemble Tibetan *karchak, néshé* and *néyik*,[31] that is, they introduce the different deities and saints who 'opened' (discovered) and empowered the site; explain the significance of the monasteries, statues, *stūpa*s, springs and caves to worship along with their specific deities; instruct how to venerate them (e.g., the prescribed number of circumambulations); and explain which benefits will result from visiting certain places. These present an immaterial, spiritual vision of the pilgrimage site that must be seen as a *maṇḍala* of deities or as a *stūpa*. Other guidebooks, on the other hand, are closer to the structure of Chinese gazetteers, from which they borrow a great deal of information, and offer a comprehensive presentation of the Wutaishan religious geography. A chronological presentation of the different Mongolian guidebooks will help understand why and by whom they were written.[32]

1) The earliest known Mongolian work is a manuscript entitled *Kitad-un tabun üjügür-tü ayula-yin jokiyal-i todurayulan üiledegsen sümber-ün cimeg kemekü nere-tü sudur orusiba* (Ornament of the Sumeru composed to explain the composition of China's Five-Peaked Mountain), composed in 1652 by two monks, *toin* Janshonwa (Byang šon) and *gélong* Yondanrinchenjamso from Luohousi. Sazykin adds that it was translated by Sürüm on the request of Lobzang 'dgeslung' (*gélong*), which means that it was certainly originally written in

---

31    *Karchak* are catalogues that contain a list of the most important objects to worship and
       generally focus on the history and contents of just one temple in immense detail; *néyik*
       and *néshé* contain more historical material and touch upon the history and contents of
       many temples in one area. Yet these genres of religious geographic literature are
       overlapping (Wylie 1965).

32    The following presentation is mostly based on the colophons of guidebooks reproduced
       in the *Catalogue of Ancient Mongolian Books and Documents of China* (1999), on Altan-
       zayaa (2000) and on the four guidebooks I had access to: CLŠASB, UTAOSC, TÜAG, and
       OMSA.

Tibetan. According to the colophon, "all the monks, to begin with Jiyentseren Nanso of Pusading, learned it by heart."[33]

2) In 1680, a translation into Mongolian of Zhencheng's gazetteer *Qingliang-shan zhi* in three volumes by Lao-zang-dan-ba was in preparation (see Chapter 3). The editors may have given up this publication when Lao-zang-dan-ba had to compile the *Qingliangshan xinzhi*, which was published in Mongolian translation in 1701 (*CLŠASB*).

3) Then, chronologically, comes the *Uta-yin tabun ayulan-u orusil süsüg-ten-ü cikin cimeg orusiba* (A guide to the five mountains of Wutai. Ornament for the ears of the devotees, hereafter *UTAOSC*),[34] which is the guidebook that had the widest diffusion both as Peking xylographs (in seventy-four folios)[35] and manuscripts.[36] This work was written by *güüshi* Lubzangdanjin (Tib. Lozang Tendzin) at A-wang-lao-zang's behest. Lubzangdanjin, also called Su Madhi Shashina Dhara (or Sumadishasanadhara) according to the colophon, was a disciple of the First Jaya Bandida, Lubsangpringlei.[37] Apparently, he "gathered and

---

33    Other titles: *Ayulas-un qayan tabun üjügür-tü ayula-yin garcay geyigülügci jibqulang-tu cimeg neretü orusiba* (Guide to the Five-Peak Mountain, King of mountains, the One that Enlightens, Magnificent Ornament); *Kitad tabun üjeger-tü ayula-yin jokiyal geyigülügci jibqulang-tu cimeg neretü orusiba*. It is preserved in the National Central Library of Ulaanbaatar (Altanzayaa 2000: 144-145) and in the Institute of Oriental Studies, Academy of Sciences, Saint Petersburg (Sazykin 1988: 297-298, no. 1647, 25 fol., no.1649, no. 1647, 19 fol.).

34    It actually means "the most excellent thing to be heard." It is known under different titles; Altanzayaa (2000: 142-144) believes that the original edition was named *Degedü orun-u tabun üjügür-tü ayula-yin zadig kemegdekü orusiba*, and that the editions bearing other titles are later copies. Here I used the title of the edition I had access to, i.e., Mong. 254 preserved in the Library of the Hungarian Academy of Sciences, Budapest (Kara 2000: Mong. 4, Mong. 223, Mong. 254).

35    It is preserved in Budapest, Berlin (Heissig and Sagaster 1961: 267-269, no. 497-499); London; Washington (Farquhar 1955: 206, no. 73); Berkeley; Tokyo (Poppe, Hurvitz, and Okada 1964: 149-150, no. 152 and 153); China (*Catalogue of Ancient Mongolian Books and Documents of China* 1999: no. 4830, 4831, 4832); Saint Petersburg (Uspensky, comp., 1999: 281; Sazykin 1988: I, 298, no. 1650); Ulan-Ude (Tsyrempilov, comp. 2006: 287, no. 824), etc. See Heissig 1954: 12, no. 7; 53, no 58; Heissig 1959: 52 sq.

36    Manuscript copies are preserved in Ulan-Ude (Tsyrempilov, comp. 2006: 289-290, no. 831, 36 fol.); Saint Petersburg (Sazykin 1988: 298, no. 1651, 25 fol.; 1652, 29 fol.; 1653, 21 fol.).

37    Fol. 72r. At that time, the title *güshiri* or *güüshi* (< Ch. *guoshi* 國師) was given to translators. A Lubzangdanjin, also called Sumadishasanadhara, was a *güüshi* of the Tsebden Beile Banner of the Üjümüchin and participated in the translation of volume 95 of the *Tanjur*. But another Lubzangdanjin who translated volume 114 of the *Tanjur* was from the Shabi estate of the Khalkha Jaya Bandida and was granted the title *nomchi tsorji* (I thank Marie-Dominique Even for this information).

summarized works compiled by earlier wise men."[38] But except for a few passages, such as quotations from the *Avataṃsaka sūtra* and the *Mañjuśrī dharma ratnagarbha dhāraṇī sūtra*, its main source of inspiration is obviously Tibetan literature, such as the *Pad ma bka' thang*, the *Blue Annals*, and Tibetan astrological treatises such as the *White Beryl* (for the description of the terraces, see below). It also includes oral traditions.[39] This guidebook closely follows the genre of the Tibetan pilgrimage guides.[40]

In the colophon, the author explains that the book was engraved to "strengthen the longevity of the Supreme Emperor who makes the world prosper, incarnation of Manzushiri."[41] The woodblocks were prepared in Pusading in 1721 and then probably brought to Beijing to be printed. It was one of the first block prints printed in China for the Mongols, certainly with the support of the imperial court; Kangxi's grandmother, a pious Buddhist and Khorchin Mongol, may have been implied in this project.[42] Because of an incoherence in the date mentioned in the colophon, there is debate about the dating of this work. I personally subscribe to the date 1721.[43]

---

38    *UTAOSC* 71v.

39    *UTAOSC* 3v.

40    See a summary in Online Appendix D. Due to the absence of precise localization and of corresponding Chinese names (except for some monasteries and springs), many springs, 'thrones,' ponds, trees, stones and caves are difficult to identify.

41    *UTAOSC* 73r.

42    Heissig 1953: 4-5; Heissig 1954: 12-13, n. 4, 13; Kara 2000: Mong. 4, Mong. 223, Mong. 254; Farquhar 1978: 30.

43    The colophon reads: "... carved on the sixth year of Engkhe Amugulang [i.e., 1667], year of the White Iron Cow [i.e., 1721]." Heissig (1954), Aerdingdu (1997) and Elverskog (2007) retain the date of 1667, while Kara (2000: 287), the authors of the *Catalogue of Ancient Mongolian Books and Documents of China* (1999) and Altanzayaa (2000: 143-144) retain the date of 1721. Aerdingdu believes that the "blessings to the Holy emperor" refer to Shunzhi and not to Kangxi: Shunzhi was in poor health and the guide may have been written in his honor, but the author was not able to finish the book before the emperor's death. Farquhar (1978: 30) believes a second edition was published under a different title (*Tabun üjügür-tü ayula-yin zadig kemegdekü orusiba*) in 1721; while Kara thinks the date of the compilation, 1667, could have been telescoped with that of the printing, 1721 (2000: 287). In my opinion, the book was published in 1721. The colophon (fol. 73r-v) mentions that the "*ching-shiu-tsa-shi* [*qingxiu chanshi*, title of Lao-zang-dan-ba?] *tidu* [< Ch. *tidu* 提督, governor, administrator] Bsdan-ba [Tib. Tenpa] Khubilgan, the *tidu jasag lama* Tendzin Gélong of Pusading, and the monks of Pusading" asked Lubzangdanjin to compose this guidebook. Lao-zang-dan-ba was granted this title in 1698 and ceased his functions in 1704; Tendzin Gélong could be Ding-zeng-jian-cuo/Tendzin Gyatso, the fourth *jasag lama*, from 1705 to 1714, which would point to the date of 1721 for this edition.

4) The *Utayišan ayula-yin adistid-tu sitüged-ece tabun jayun bandida-yin cedig orusiba* (Biographies of the five hundred Pandits [*paṇḍitas*] from the blessed places of worship of Wutaishan Mountain), is a thirteen-folio Peking xylograph. According to its colophon,[44] the original work was written in Tibetan between 1725 and 1736 by Gombojab (< Tib. Gönpo Kyap, fl. 1692-1750), the famous scholar from Üjümüchin, translator, and teacher at the Tibetan School in Beijing. Gombojab based himself on a work by *diyanchi gelöng* Lubsang Bkrashis (hermit monk Lubsang Dashi). It was translated into Mongolian by *ubadini jasag blama güüshi* Shashin Dhara (or Danjinchoidar, from one of the Sünid banners) from Longfusi 隆福寺 in Beijing in the Qianlong period.[45] A manuscript copy was made in the Republican period.[46]

5) A fifth guidebook, entitled *Üjesküleng secig-ün erike kemegdekü orušiba* (The beautiful flower chaplet)[47] was written around 1813 and printed in Beijing. It was commissioned by Ganden Shireetü Khutugtu, Ngakwang Tuptsen Wangchukden Trinlé Gyatso (1773-ca. 1820), the second-ranking Buddhist reincarnation residing in Beijing, and written by *gelöng* Yéshé Döndrup (1782-1855) of the Tümed, a monk from Dafosi (Puningsi 普寧寺, Monastery of Universal Peace) of Chengde, according to the primary colophon, with the help of Alashan Buddhist grammarian Agwandandar (Ngakwang Tendar, b. 1759-d. 1831 or 1840). This twenty-nine-folio book of praise, which also exists in a contemporary Tibetan version,[48] focuses on Shuxiangsi, the Chinese Buddhist monastery that enshrines the holiest image of Wutaishan, and on its surroundings, including

---

44   *Catalogue of Ancient Mongolian Books and Documents of China* 1999: 902, no 4833; Altanzayaa 2000: 144. It seems that the Tibetan original has not been preserved. On the five hundred *arhat*s on Wutaishan, see Online Appendix B, "Yuhuachi."

45   Longfusi Monastery was well known for its trade fair; it was also a printing center.

46   *Catalogue of Ancient Mongolian Books and Documents of China* 1999: no. 4834.

47   Full title: *Serigün tungyalay ayulan-tu manjusiri lakšan-tu süm-e-yin* [/*süsüg-ün*] *yayiqamsiy: jibqulangtu gegen düri-yin cedig ergil-ün kemjiy-e-lüge selte süsügten arad-un durašil-i egüskegci üjesküleng secig-ün erike kemegdekü orusiba* [The marvels of the Mañjuśrī Body Monastery of the Cool, Clear Mountain. Together with the story of the miraculous bright image and the measure of its circumambulation, that engenders the desire of the believing people, which is called the beautiful flower chaplet] (Farquhar 1978: 30, n. 88; Heissig 1954: 163-164, no.208). It is preserved in the University of Chicago (Collection Laufer, Krueger 1966: 162, L-250); Toyo Bunko (Poppe, Hurvitz and Okada 1964: 148-149, no.151); in China (*Catalogue of Ancient Mongolian Books and Documents of China* 1999: no. 4836); in Ulan-Ude (Tsyrempilov, comp. 2006: 284, no. 820).

48   *Ri bo dwangs bsil gyi 'jam dpal mtshan ldan gling gi mtshar sdug sku brnyan gyi lo rgyus bskor tshad dang bcas pa dad ldan skye bo'i spro bskyod me tog 'phreng mdzes* [A beautiful garland to rouse the faithful: A history and circumambulation survey of the fine statue in the Sandalwood Mañjuśrī Temple of Mount Clear and Cool].

the nearby Prajña Spring (Borequan 般若泉). It was the last guidebook that received imperial sponsorship.[49]

6) The *Tabun üjügür-tü ayula-yin yarcay* (Guidebook of the Five-Peak Mountain, hereafter *TÜAG*) is a short manuscript text (sixteen folios) composed by the monk Badmin Tatra Zaya in the mid-Qing period (the first third of the eighteenth century). The front page bears a seal of Prince Yunli 允禮 (1697-1738), the seventeenth son of Kangxi, well known for his religious activities, his works and his collection of books and manuscripts. The original text was written in Tibetan, and the author acknowledged that he compiled Chinese sources and "many *sūtras* and *tantras*, including the *Avataṃsaka sūtra* and the Root *Tantra* of Mañjuśrī." It starts with a Tibetan-style prayer, followed by the Chinese history of the introduction of Buddhism in China, and more specifically in Wutaishan, and a description of fourteen monasteries and seven numinous traces which are clearly identifiable thanks to Chinese transcriptions and descriptions copied from Chinese sources. The name of the translator into Mongolian is unknown.[50] As with the *UTAOSC*, some sentences seem to be translated following Tibetan grammar, rendering them difficult for a Mongol to understand.

7) In 1831, the Mongolian translation of the main Tibetan language guidebook on Wutaishan, *Zhing mchog ri bo dwangs bsil gyi gnas bshad dad pa'i padmo rgyas byed ngo mtshar myi ma'i snang ba*, authored by Rölpé Dorjé and completed by his disciples, was printed and published in Beijing under the title *Orud-un manglai serigün ayula-yin orun-u nomlal süsüg-ün lingqu-a-yi delgeregülügci yayiqamsiy-tu naran-u tuy-a kemekü orusiba* (hereafter *OMSA*). The Tibetan original was written on Wutaishan between 1767 and 1786 and later revised and completed by Rölpé Dorjé's disciples. In 1831, the Second Changlung Arya Bandida, Agwang Lubsang Danbi Jalsang from the Left Sünid Banner, another of Rölpé Dorjé's disciples (see Chapter 3), wrote a colophon and paid for the blocks to be carved at Songzhusi in Beijing on the advice of the Eighth Dalai Lama.[51] The Mongolian edition was printed in the same year: according to the

---

49    Elverskog (2011: 250) labels this text as "the earliest 'indigenous' Mongol description of
        Wutai Shan;" however, it received sponsorship from the court and was printed in Beijing
        (Service 2007; Tuttle 2011: 181, 190). Therefore, an earlier Mongol description of Wutaishan
        is clearly the *UTAOSC*. On the Mongolian version and its author: Service 2007; on the
        Tibetan version: Tuttle 2011: 181, 190.

50    Archives of Inner Mongolia (*Catalogue of Ancient Mongolian Books and Documents of
        China* (1999: no. 4835); also Altanzayaa (2000: 142, and n. 19). Olivér Kápolnas and I will
        translate this text in a forthcoming publication.

51    A first version of the text was carved on Wutaishan: Chou 2014.

colophon,[52] the monk Damcho (*biligtü güüsri* Dgeleng Damchowas), of Jinong Beise Banner of the Khorchin, translated it on Achitu Vchir Dara (Vajradhara) Bandida Gegeen's order.[53] The Mongolian xylograph (156 folios) is longer than the Tibetan text (91 folios). This guidebook could rather be called a gazetteer in that it introduces Tibetans and Mongols to Chinese sites, history and lore: more than half of the text translates extracts from the *Qingliangshan zhi* and *Qingliangshan xinzhi*; however, Rölpé Dorjé sometimes switched the order around, at times mislabeling descriptions.[54] The only true Tibetan Buddhist touch added to the guidebook is Rölpé Dorjé's lengthy praise poem of Wutaishan "Cloud of offerings to please Mañjuśrī: A song coupled to a place-praise for Wutaishan," known to Mongols as "Orun-u maᵞtaᵞal" (Eulogy of the place), and composed as a concluding prayer. Except for this prayer, only a few Tibetan perspectives are included, such as a quotation from the *Arya Mañjuśrī mūlatantra* that prophecizes the apparition of a young Mañjuśrī in China (in the introduction), mentions of two monasteries built by Rölpé Dorjé himself (Shancaidong, Puleyuan) and of renovation projects by Mongol and Tibetan lamas (Tiewasi, Shouningsi, Baohuasi).[55] A few mistakes were corrected,[56] but overall there is faithful adherence to the original Chinese sources. Following the *Qingliangshan zhi*, the third chapter on eminent monks gives the biographies of forty-seven pre-Qing-dynasty clerics, of whom forty-four are Chinese Buddhists.[57] Rölpé Dorjé's guidebook and its concluding poem influenced later Tibetan and Mongol Buddhist masters in their own visions and in their accounts.

---

52  *OMSA* 155-156.

53  Peking xylograph, preserved in China (*Catalogue of Ancient Mongolian Books and Documents of China*: no. 4837), Saint Petersburg State University Library (Uspensky 1999: 282, no. 256); Institute of Oriental Studies, Academy of Sciences, Saint Petersburg (Sazykin 1988: 297, no. 1646).

54  In actual fact, Rölpé Dorjé wrote or orally transmitted only the first two chapters of this work (1. "Prophecy and recognition of the place;" and 2. "Distinctive features of this sacred land"), which were included in his *gSung 'bum* (Collected writings). The three other chapters are 3. "Great masters who visited the sacred place," 4. "Mañjuśrī's visionary manifestations to devotees," 5. "Imperial patronage." See Tuttle 2011: Table 3; Xiao Yu 肖雨 2003; Illich 2006: 519; Chou 2014.

55  This text "is probably the most frequently cited textual authority in various Tibetan works on China" (Chou 2014). Chou tries to understand why the authors strove hard to render such a faithful and legible translation from Chinese gazetteers, including some abstruse Chan dialogues.

56  Chou 2014.

57  The only non-Chinese monks included in both the *Qingliangshan zhi* and Rölpé Dorjé's guidebook are the Fifth Karmapa Dézhin Shekpa, Śākya Yéshé and a Ming dynasty Indian ascetic, Bei-sheng Jixiang 貝生吉祥 (whose funerary *stūpa* was built on Wutaishan).

8) The archives of Inner Mongolia possess a Mongolian manuscript about Wutaishan dated to the Republican period.[58]

9) Another manuscript of the Chinese archives dated to the Republican period introduces the statue of Shuxiangsi.[59]

Mongol and Monguor monks also authored a few guidebooks in Tibetan, such as the *Ri bo rtse lnga'i dkar chag rab gsal me long* (The clear mirror: A guide to Five-peaked Mountain), written sometime after 1827 by a cleric known as Dznyā na shrī man (Yé[shé] Pen[den], probably a Mongol).[60] Yet, even though Mongolian was the primary language of teaching and learning in monasteries of Mongolia,[61] only a small minority of monks could read and write Mongolian.[62] Thus, the educated pilgrim-monks certainly preferred reading Tibetan guidebooks. Some probably also had access to Chinese gazetteers on Wutaishan. Although they were theoretically forbidden to learn Chinese, during the nineteenth and twentieth centuries a growing number of literate Mongols could read and write Chinese.

Among the above-mentioned Mongolian-language guidebooks and gazetteers, we must clearly distinguish imperial productions—only one gazetteer was published by the Palace Publishing House with an imperial preface (*CLŠASB*)—from those books authored and commissioned by lamas (though sometimes printed with imperial support). The fact that a guidebook was printed in Beijing does not mean that it enjoyed official support: Beijing was the largest printing center of the Mongol world, and the printing of Mongolian books in Beijing was mostly supported by Mongol nobles.[63] All in all, two guidebooks were commissioned by high lamas at the service of the court and printed with imperial support, while four guidebooks did not receive any support from the court. Five (or six, if we include the *Üjesküleng secig-ün erike*

---

58    *Tabun ayula-yin quriyangyui*, 1936 (*Catalogue of Ancient Mongolian Books and Documents of China* 1999: no. 4840).

59    *Ülemji yeke aburaltu laqsin tegülder sitügen-ü namtar*, 1 vol. (*Catalogue of Ancient Mongolian Books and Documents of China* 1999: no. 4838).

60    For Chou (2014), Dznyā na shrī man's guidebook draws heavily from the guidebook by Rölpé Dorjé et al. but "also includes many more contemporaneous Tibetan and Mongolian materials." A list of the Tibetan-language guidebooks of Wutaishan, some of them authored by Mongols and Monguors, is given by Tuttle 2011: Appendix 1.

61    Ujeed 2009: 49-50.

62    Wallace 2009: 76-77.

63    Bawden (1989 [1968]: 84) stressed the fact that the great enterprise of printing 'lamaist books' in Beijing was patronized by wealthy and noble Mongols and was in no way encouraged by the Manchu emperors.

*kemegdekü orušiba*) are translations from Chinese or Tibetan, and only two (or one) would have been originally written in Mongolian.

### The Aims and Diffusion of the Mongolian Guidebooks

Whether Mongols of the Qing and Republican periods had access to and read the imperial ten-volume gazetteer (*CLŠASB*) is unclear, but we do know that the Mongol guidebook *UTAOSC* had at least three editions and a large circulation: I counted more than twenty xylograph prints and four manuscript versions kept in libraries and archives. Woodblocks of this text were found in twenty-three monasteries of Inner and Khalkha Mongolia, Buryatia and Beijing (Songzhusi).[64] I do not know whether the second and third edition also received the support of the imperial court, but the book was still being reprinted in the early twentieth century;[65] it was probably also printed in Pusading.[66] The circulation of the other guidebooks was more limited. The existence of manuscript versions attests to the popularity of the 1721 guidebook: it was common to copy precious Buddhist books by hand, in order not only to have one's own version but also to earn merit. The colophon specifies that A-wang-lao-zang commissioned a guidebook that was 'easy to understand,' adding:

> This is how this work about the place of Mañjuśrī and his remarkable creations [came to be]. The famous monk who wanders in the region of Höh-hot, Ng[a]gdwang Blö Bzang, 'adorning' with faith and donation, said, "Sort out from the many treatises composed by the wise men of the past and produce one collection, [so that] we will know everything about it and that it will be accessible," besides, one can worship it in invocation.[67]

Thus, the book itself claims to be an object of worship.

All in all, the guidebooks, the Tibetan erudite works, the biographies, and the poems about Wutaishan were read by a minority of learned Mongols and were certainly not the main means of promoting the pilgrimage.[68] They were first of

---

64    List of the monasteries in Shüreg 1976: 40-41, quoted by Altanzayaa 2000: 142.
65    Some printing blocks were dispersed around 1923; a curio dealer or bookshop manager in Beijing sold the odd-numbered folios to foreigners (Farquhar 1978: 30, n. 85).
66    Altanzayaa 2000: 142-143, 148.
67    *UTAOSC* 71r-v.
68    It is generally estimated that as late as 1935, less than five percent of the population of school age and above was literate. However, Bawden argues that the numerous cheap copies of stories and poems seem to point to a degree of literacy probably higher than generally believed (1989 [1968]: 87).

all used as cult objects—*sudur* books,[69] believed to be holy and have magical power. Stored in the most precious place in Mongols' tents, on the altar located opposite the entrance, they were read only on special occasions, and women were forbidden to read them: according to a saying, for a woman to look at a book is like a wolf looking at a settlement.[70] (As we will see in the following chapter, laywomen whose names are identifiable in the stone inscriptions represent about a third of the lay pilgrims to Wutaishan.) Although some of the guidebooks probably encouraged the pilgrimage, they were first of all objects of devotion, of pious merit, reflecting the importance of the pilgrimage. Those that translate Chinese gazetteers, such as the guidebook compiled by Rölpé Dorjé et al. and the *TÜAG*, did inform pilgrims about the main places to visit, but the 1721 guidebook was of little practical use for making an actual pilgrimage.

There was also a rich Mongolian oral tradition of poetry, eulogies and songs about Wutaishan that attests of the popularity of the pilgrimage. Some of these were recorded by folklorists in Khorchin (like the song "Utai-yin jam"), Ordos (the praise prayer "U-tai-yin maɣtaɣal orusiba") and Shili-yin Gool (the praise prayer "Utai sang-un mani") (see Online Appendix E).[71]

### The Mongols' Production of Maps of Wutaishan

While the Chinese gazetteers of Wutaishan include several maps and drawings, the Mongolian guidebooks only have a few illustrations of buddhas and *bodhisattva*s but no map of the mountain. Nevertheless, Mongols, who particularly excelled in pictorial representation of monasteries and holy sites,[72] produced portable and mural paintings of the mountain to help the pilgrims visualize the different holy places of Wutaishan.[73] Although photographs replaced painting

---

69    *Sudur* < *sūtra*, book of the *sūtra* section of the scriptures, now designates in Mongolian any palm-leaf format book. On the culture and cult of the book, and the various rituals related to books in Mongolia: Chiodo 2009: 144-145, n. 11; Wallace 2009: 90; Bazarov 2010. The scriptures generally believed to possess 'power' are the *Lotus Sūtra*, the *Diamond Sūtra*, the *Flower Ornament Sūtra* and the *Sūtra of the Master of Healing*.

70    Humphrey 1974: 275.

71    See also a praise prayer called "Utai šan-u maɣtaɣal" (late Qing dynasty): *Catalogue of Ancient Mongolian Books and Documents of China* 1999: 4839.

72    A great number of such paintings are preserved in the museums and archives of Mongolia such as the Zanabazar Museum of Fine Arts in Ulaanbaatar.

73    Since these maps present a bird's eye view showing the relief and frontal elevation of buildings with multi-focal perspective, historians of cartography generally prefer using the terms 'topographical art,' 'pictorial representation of space,' or simply 'picture map' or 'pictorial drawing' rather than 'map.'

in the course of the twentieth century, representations of monasteries are still worshipped as icons in Mongol monasteries.

A mural painting of Wutaishan in Badgar Choiling Süme represents Wutaishan together with eight monasteries of Central and Eastern Tibet.[74] It can be roughly dated between 1757 and 1822 (Fig. 16).[75] The monasteries, depicted according to a panoramic, multifocal view, are separated by mountains and scenes of nature. While the painting of the Tibetan monasteries follows the same Tibetan style as the other wall paintings of the assembly hall,[76] the representation of Wutaishan adopts the blue and green landscape style of Chinese painting and is obviously from a different hand. Beside each of the fifty-two Wutaishan monasteries is a trilingual cartouche with its name in Mongolian, Tibetan and Chinese. The Mongol names inform us about what the Mongols knew of these sacred sites. Apart from the representation of monasteries, the painting shows many curiosities such as palm trees and disproportionate peonies.

The Badgar Choiling Süme's map may have taken as models previous Chinese maps, or a hypothetical precedent of the 1846 Cifusi map, or portable paintings that circulated in Mongolia.[77] A.M. Pozdneev asserted that paintings of Wutaishan were common in Mongol monasteries and compared them to "our crude wood carvings of Mount Athos or of the Holy city of Jerusalem."[78] Except for the colored print of the Cifusi map, which was certainly hung in a temple of

---

74  Most probably a nunnery near Lhasa, the Potala Palace, Jokhang Temple, the monasteries of Ganden, Séra, Drépung, Samyé and Badgar Choiling Süme itself. The mural, located on the outer wall on the second floor of the central assembly hall is twenty-three meters long and two meters high (Charleux 2006: CD-rom [63]; Wang Leiyi et al. 2009: vol. II, 222-227).

75  1757 is the date of construction of the central assembly hall. Cifusi and Shifangtang, built respectively in 1822 and 1835, are not depicted on the painting of Wutaishan. Chou believes that the estimated date of the painting is around the turn of the nineteenth century (2011b: 49). The paintings of the Tibetan monasteries are in a much better condition and may be of a later date. I thank Chou Wen-shing for having sent me her photos of this painting and shared her observations with me.

76  The whole mural is said to be modeled on *thangka*s brought from Tibet by the first reincarnation of the Duingkhor Bandida, Lubsang Danbi Jialsan (b. 1614 or 1617-d. 1763 or 1766), the renowned scholar who founded the monastery.

77  Chou (2011b: 50-56) showed that the painting can be compared to maps of imperial Chinese gazetteers, and he concluded that copies of imperial Chinese gazetteers printed by non-imperial printing houses may have circulated in Mongolia and diffused their vision of Wutaishan. In my opinion, it is more probable that folded maps or leaflets depicting Wutaishan brought back by pilgrims circulated in Mongolia.

78  Pozdneev 1978 [1887]: 134-135.

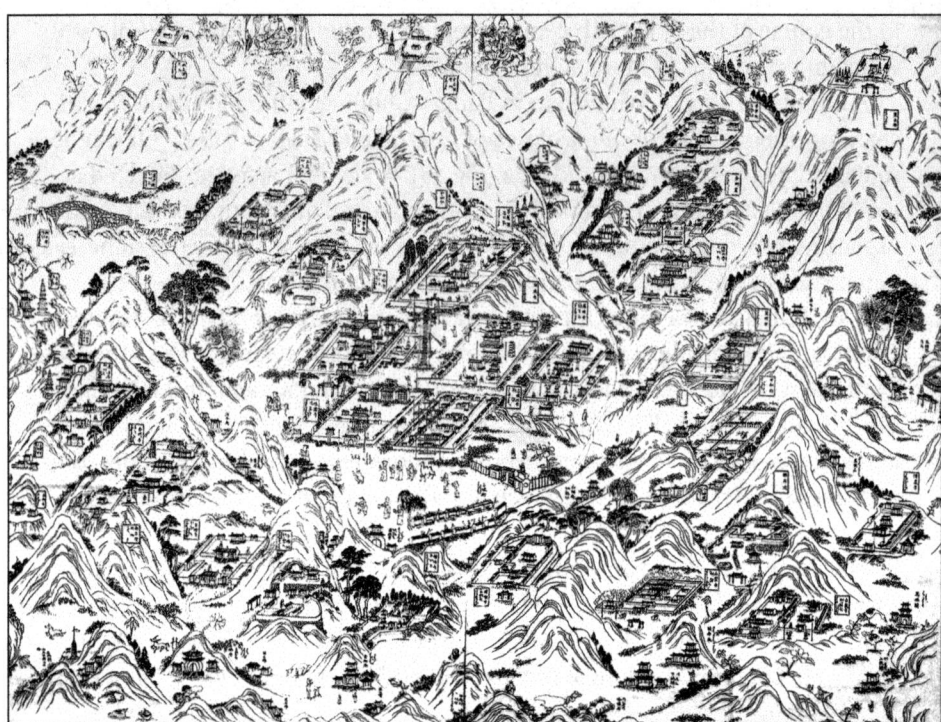

FIGURE 16      *Drawing of the map of Wutaishan painted on the second floor of the Assembly*
                *Hall (Tsogchin dugang) at Badgar Choiling Süme, between 1757 and 1835. The*
                *whole painting is 23 meters long for 2 meters high and depicts Wutaishan*
                *together with seven monasteries of Central and Eastern Tibet.* DRAWING BY
                WANG LEIYI, IN WANG LEIYI ET AL. 2009: VOL. II, 191, FIGURE 10-19.

Jaya-yin Khüriye in Tsetserleg (Fig. 17),[79] these paintings did not survive the
twentieth-century massive-scale destruction of the Mongol artistic heritage.

What is known as the 'Cifusi map'—a large xylograph map dated 1846, entitled "Panoramic Picture of the Sacred Realm of Wutaishan"[80]—was engraved
by a Khalkha lama named Lhunrub (Tib. Lhündrup) in residence at Cifusi (Fig.
3). According to the trilingual inscription (in Mongolian, Tibetan and Chinese)
at the bottom, Lhunrub came from the Sengge Department of the *shabi* (estate)
of the Holy Jebtsündamba of Yekhe Khüriye.[81] The map was printed at Cifusi—

---

79   It is now exhibited in the Museum of Arkhangai Province, installed in the residence of the
     Jaya Bandida reincarnations in Jaya-yin Khüriye.

80   *Ri bo dwangs bsil kyi gnas bkod* in Tibetan—*Wutaishan shengjing quantu* 五臺山聖境全
     圖 in Chinese—*Serigün tungyalay ayula-yin orun-u jokiyal* in Mongolian. The most
     detailed reproduction is Halén (1987).

81   See a Mongolian translation in Online Appendix G.

FIGURE 17     *Apparition of Tsongkhapa above the Eastern Terrace. Detail of the 1846 Cifusi map, print preserved in Güden Süme, Jaya-yin Khüriye, Tsetserleg, Republic of Mongolia.* © ISABELLE CHARLEUX, 2009.

this monastery is represented near to the center, much larger than its actual dimensions.[82] At least sixteen prints from the same woodblock set are preserved in Chinese, Mongolian and overseas museums and libraries.[83] They were sold or given away in Wutaishan and circulated in North and East Asia during the late nineteenth and early twentieth century. Dr. G. J. Ramstedt's Finnish

---

82    An antecedent of the Cifusi painting is the tenth-century map of Cave 61 at Dunhuang that shows a similar composition and iconography with depiction of temples, apparitions, miracles and pilgrims. For other possible sources of inspiration: Chou 2011b: 58-59.

83    Chou, who thoroughly studied this painting, counted fourteen prints (2011a: 374, n. 7). To this list must be added the Jaya-yin Khüriye's print and the one in the collection of the Hawaii State Art Museum.

FIGURE 18     *Pusading, detail of the 1846 Cifusi map, woodblock print on linen, hand-colored,*
              *118 × 165 cm. National Museum of Finland, Helsinki.* (PHOTOGRAPH PROVIDED
              BY THE NATIONAL BOARD OF ANTIQUITIES, FINLAND).

expedition purchased one in 1909 in a 'Beijing shop' (store selling goods imported from China) of Urga along with sixty-three *thangka*s (Fig. 18).[84] The
prints preserved in the Museum of the Mission of Fathers of Scheut (C.I.C.M.)
in Belgium and in the Etnografiska Museet in Stockholm from the collection of
explorer Sven A. Hedin (1865-1952) certainly come from Inner Mongolia.[85]

---

84    The *thangka*s and the map are now kept in the National Museum of Finland in Helsinki
      and were published by Halén in 1987.
85    Museum of China, Anderlecht, inv. Bouddhisme/n° 193, personal communication with
      Father Jean-Pierre Benit, 2007.

Another print was brought back from Wutaishan to Washington, D.C. by William Rockhill after his meeting with the Dalai Lama on the mountain.[86] Two were acquired in China in 1934 by Arthur W. Hummel (1884-1975).[87] In 1874, only thirty-two years after the first print, the Cifusi map was carved again on new woodblocks, probably somewhere in China, and, left uncolored, were widely distributed to donors on Wutaishan.[88] Other similar-style woodblocks also exist, and the 1846 map was copied on various supports such as silk scrolls and mural paintings.[89] The Cifusi map thus appears as a "prototype and model for depicting Wutaishan during the late Qing dynasty."[90]

The Cifusi image of Wutaishan provides an easily decipherable and comprehensible landscape and certainly helped spread knowledge of the mountain. It was more accessible than guidebooks and could be used by illiterate pilgrims. Besides, the image, measuring 118 × 165 centimeters, is precise enough to function as a map to find the must-see places (even though it presents some distortions of the actual geography). About seventy monasteries plus sixty shrines, caves, villages and hills have inscriptions written in Chinese with a Tibetan transcription (or vice versa): this way, a pilgrim could ask the way to any resident on the mountain. With its numerous scenes of apparitions of deities and saints in clouds (Fig. 17) or as earthly beings, the map can also serve as "a guide map for visionary encounters."[91] As shown by Chou Wen-shing, the pilgrim could visualize buddhas, deities and saints associated with each monastery, *stūpa* and cave: these apparitions are at the same time a record of past visions and a promise of future ones. The thousand-year history of Wutaishan and its myths, legends and apparitions were boiled down and reduced within the same representation, connecting present to past, the physical world to the spiritual world. The aim of the engraving is clearly exposed in the Chinese inscription:

> The benefactors from all four directions who make a pilgrimage to the sacred realm of Clear and Cool, see this map of the mountain, listen to and recount the spiritual efficacy and wondrous Dharma of the bodhisattva will in this life be free from all calamities and diseases, and enjoy boundless blessings, happiness, and longevity. After this life, they will be

---

86  He donated it to the United States Library of Congress, Washington, D.C., in 1905.
87  Now preserved in the Library of Congress.
88  Chou 2011b: 57.
89  Chou 2007: 116-117, 126, n. 2, n. 11 and 12; 127 n. 48, n. 49.
90  Chou 2007: 117.
91  Chou 2007: 116.

reborn in a blessed land. All these benefits can be acquired through the bodhisattva's merciful transformations.[92]

The inscription advises pilgrims to see and study the map so that one's troubles and misfortunes will disappear and one will be reincarnated in a blessed land. The act of looking at the Cifusi map is therefore a kind of pilgrimage per se: like a *thangka* and the guidebooks, the map is an object of meditation and devotion for the faithful. The inscription goes as far as to suggest that by worshipping the map the pilgrim could even make a pilgrimage equivalent to the physical pilgrimage.[93]

Once printed, some maps were perhaps hand-painted at Cifusi, but others were left uncolored and sold to pilgrims; they could later be painted in Mongolia, in Tibet or in China. This is why the same print gives very different results when colored: the process of coloring informs us about the different interpretations of the Cifusi image, as Chou has carefully studied.[94] The painters selected and accentuated some details while erasing others (because they did not see them or understand them, or by choice) and used colors to highlight the similarities or differences between details. Variations in colors applied to a same deity can even change his/her identity; for instance, a *bodhisattva* can be turned into a Daoist priest.[95] The coloring can highlight the coherent composition of the map, using techniques to render volume, or, on the contrary, give the impression of a flat composition. Some mistakes may be attributed to Mongol or Chinese painters who were not familiar with the Tibetan script, such as in the map of the National Museum of Finland.

Lastly, the uses of the maps were many. Some beautifully colored prints were mounted as *thangka*s (such as the print preserved in the Rubin Museum in New York), certainly to serve as an object of devotion and meditation to be placed in a temple or on a house altar. Others were left without paint, or unskillfully painted (like the Helsinki print);[96] they were sometimes folded up for prolonged

---

92   四方善士凡朝清涼聖境,及見此山圖, 聞講菩薩靈驗妙法者, 今生能消一切災難
     疾病, 享福享壽, 福錄綿長,命終之後,生於有福之地。 皆賴菩薩慈化而得也,
     transl. Chou 2007: 125, "Appendix." The Tibetan and Mongolian versions are very close to
     each other and omit this passage (Online Appendix G).

93   Chou 2007: 114, 124.

94   Chou 2011a.

95   Chou 2007; Chou 2011a.

96   Chou (2011a: 382) contrasts the Rubin Museum print with the Helsinki print: the former
     would be first a Buddhist icon, "timeless, ethereal, and devoid of earthly contexts in the
     imagination of its viewers," and the latter, painted in the genre of Chinese folk prints,
     would be more 'earthly.' Debreczeny (2011: 51) believes that the Rubin print was painted by

periods and could have been carried by pilgrims in a reliquary box, or kept in a reliquary on the altar of the yurt or house. The Cifusi map could thus be used at the same time as a guide-map, a model for painters, a souvenir, an object of worship and even as a substitute for the pilgrimage.

The Cifusi map was not the only map of the mountain available to pilgrims: in the late nineteenth century (and certainly before), simple Chinese maps of Wutaishan,[97] as well as travel guidebooks, were also sold to pilgrims.[98] Nowadays, pilgrims are unaware of the existence of the Cifusi map.[99]

### Mongol Buddhist *Imaginaire* of Wutaishan

Even though the first maps and guidebooks for Mongol pilgrims were produced on Wutaishan, pious Mongols reappropriated this production by commissioning copies, translations, new carving of blocks and new books, and by hand-copying guidebooks and giving new interpretations to images by coloring the black-and-white prints. These books and maps diffused a certain representation of Wutaishan that blended Chinese, Tibetan and Mongol elements, Buddhist concepts, imperial narrative and popular stories. New representations, images and narratives about Wutaishan developed and were superimposed above former layers.

---

a Mongol because of a misspelling of the Tibetan name of Wutaishan in the title and because of the coloring style.

97   See the "Chijian Wutaishan Wenshu pusa Qingliang shengjing tu 勅建五臺山文殊菩薩清涼勝境圖" (Map of the imperially established Wutaishan of the Clear and Cool realm of *bodhisattva* Mañjuśrī), late Qing period, Beijing National Library (Chou 2011b: 54 and fig. 2.29). For a reproduction of a Chinese map sold in the 1930s: Alley and Lapwood 1935: ill.

98   For instance, "Wutaishan jingdian tu 五臺山景點圖" (Map of scenic landmarks of Wutaishan); and "Wutaishan mingsheng tu 五臺山名勝圖 (Map of famous sites at Wutaishan).

99   Although the blocks were preserved on Wutaishan, the existence of the Cifusi map was forgotten during the second half of the twentieth century. Chou (2011b: 84) offered copies of the map to lamas of Wutaishan, thus inspiring the redaction of a Tibetan guidebook in 2007: the map was reproduced—but in a small, illegible format, in Ngag dbang bstan dar 2007.

### Tibeto-Mongol Buddhist Narratives: Mandalization of Wutaishan

Now this very Wutaishan is a particular supreme site that the Buddha pre-dicted to be a holy site of Mañjuśrī in the Avatamsaka Sūtra and the Mañjuśrī Root Tantra, and so forth, and that has been blessed by countless Buddhas, Bodhisattvas and holy beings from India and Tibet.[100]

Seen through the eyes of high lamas such as Pakpa Lama and Rölpé Dorjé, Wutaishan is, like Tibetan pilgrimage mountains, a *maṇḍala* that is embodied by the Five Buddha families. Both lamas identified the shape of the five terraces of Wutaishan as being the mounts of the Five Jina Buddhas (the central one being Mahāvairocana) (Table 4).[101]

The *White Beryl* (*Vaidūrya dkar-po*), a Tibetan manuscript on astrology and divination said to have been written in 1685 by Regent Sanggyé Gyatso, contains a description of the five terraces and its *stūpa*s as well as a three-folio illustra-tion of Wutaishan and the manifestations of Mañjuśrī (Fig. 19).[102] It presents the Mañjuśrī astrological system starting with Mañjuśrīnātha, a first emanation of Mañjuśrī from the gnarl of a *triṣa* tree, on the Central Terrace (or Peak); "im-mediately thereafter, he emanated as Mañjughoṣatikṣṇa on the eastern peak, as Jñānasattva on the southern peak, Vādisiṃha on the western peak, and Vimala on the northern peak."[103] The five terraces are arranged into a cosmic *maṇḍala* format, with each terrace made of gold or a precious stone placed in a cardinal direction plus the center, assigned a corresponding shape resembling the mount of a Jina and associated to one of the five Jina Pure Lands. The numinous sites on each terrace are difficult or impossible to match to actual places. This description of the terraces is repeated in the 1721 Mongolian guidebook and in a praise prayer from Ordos.[104]

Each terrace has some qualities linked to a particular deity: flowers of the five colors have the qualities of the Five *ḍākinī*s,[105] just as stones of the five

---

100 Biography of Changkya Khutugtu Rölpé Dorjé, composed by his student the Third Tukwan Lozang, Chökyi Nyima, between 1792 and 1794; passage translated by Illich 2006: 516.

101 ZMRBDB, Chinese transl. "Sheng di Qingliangshan zhi" 1990, p. 9-10. This idea originated in the eleventh-century *Guang Qingliang zhuan*: "Five Terraces is none other than the throne of the Tathāgathas of the five directions. It also resembles the five topknots on the *bodhisattva*'s head."

102 Dorje 2001: 22, pl. 1, 48-49.

103 Dorje 2001: 49.

104 The guidebook is UTAOSC (31v-32r, 43v-62v). For the praise prayer, see Online Appendix E.

105 Initiation goddesses of the five Buddha families: Vajra-*ḍākinī*, Padma-*ḍākinī*, Ratna-*ḍākinī*, Karma-*ḍākinī* and Buddha-*ḍākinī*.

TABLE 4      *The five terraces,* maṇḍala *of Mañjuśrī*

| Terrace | Northern | Eastern | Central | Western | Southern |
|---|---|---|---|---|---|
| Altitude | 3,058 m | 2,795 m | 2,894 m | 2,773 m | 2,485 m |
| Number of numinous races[a] | 27 | 14 | 28 | 17 | 21 |
| Form of Mañjuśrī | Stainless Mañjuśrī | Intelligent Mañjuśrī | Child Mañjuśrī | Mañjuśrī with the Lion's Roar | Mañjuśrī of Knowledge |
| - Sanskrit | Mañjuśrī Vimala | Mañjughoṣa-tikṣṇa | Mañjuśrī-nātha | Mañjuśrī Vādisiṁha | Mañjuśrī Jñānasattva |
| - Mongolian[b] | Khgir ügei Manjushiri | Btsana sadua (Jñānasattva?) | Jaluu Manjushiri | Arslan Manjushiri | Khurtsa Manjushiri |
| Manifestation of | Efficacy | Thought | Body | Speech | Wisdom |
| Corresponding realm | Amoghasiddhi | Akṣobhya | Vairocana | Amitābha | Ratnasambhava |
| Mount | Garuḍa | Elephant | Lion | Peacock | Horse |

According to ZMRBDB, Chinese translation 1990: 10-14.
From UTAOSC 31v, 44r, 47r, 54r, 58v.

colors have the qualities of the Five Herukas.[106] Each of the five kinds of stones and flowers is believed to remove five poisons, evils and obstacles.[107] In the Tibetan and Mongol contexts, a sacred mountain can be seen as both the abode of a deity and the embodiment of the divine itself.[108] Since it was and is still believed today that Mañjuśrī can manifest himself through any kind of being on Wutaishan, every part of the mountain—including its rocks, flora and fauna—is considered a manifestation of the *bodhisattva* and is therefore charged with power.[109] A long section of the eulogy "Cloud of offerings to please Mañjuśrī," composed by Rölpé Dorjé in 1767 and reproduced at the end of his guidebook and in his biography, is dedicated to the natural and supernatural wonders of Wutaishan that must be interpreted as 'signs' (Tib. *da*) indicating certain soteriological benefits for those who visit the site. K. Schaeffer translated the poem and sums it up as follows:

---

106    The wrathful forms of the five Buddha families: Vajra-Heruka, Padma-Heruka, Ratna-Heruka, Karma-Heruka and Buddha-Heruka.

107    *Khoura, todkhar, jedkher:* UTAOSC 25v-26v.

108    Huber 1999: 13.

109    See ZMRBDB.

FIGURE 19    *Painting of Wutaishan in the White Beryl (Dorje 2001: 48-49). Detail of the Eastern*
             *Peak: Asura Cave with a potent stream of nectar and its dragon-shaped source on*
             *the left; images of Samantabhadra and of Mañjuśrī dispelling ignorance,*
             *Mañjughoṣa's footprint in beryl, and Mañjuśrī's footprints.*

The mountain foot is liberation; its peak is wisdom. Flowers are virtue,
bees embody the doctrine of causation. Rivers flow with love, breezes call,
and birds teach. Fruit is contemplative, deer trot along the Buddhist path,
and the clouds are a celestial magic show.... As it moves the reader up and
down the mountains, it elicits each of the five senses: sight, hearing, smell,
touch, and taste. We hear the bees, the birds, the breeze and the rivers. We
smell the wild flowers and herbs. Cooling winds and forest breezes touch
us, as we reach out to rocky cliffs, high meadows, and waterfalls. We taste
sweet fruit, and savor aromatic restorative herbs.[110]

This eulogy was written for a wide audience of Tibetan and Mongol pilgrims,
not for his disciples only.

---

110    Schaeffer 2011: 225-226.

In the eyes of high clerics, Wutaishan thus had all the characteristics of the 'power-places' of Tibetan pilgrimages,[111] ones which capture the five senses of the devotees. The vision of celestial imagery in the natural features of the land-scape is a literary *topos* of Tibetan pilgrimage guides and mixes conventional images with actual places and phenomena experienced on Wutaishan.[112] 'Read-ing the landscape' to identify the presence of buddhas and deities is central to Tibetan pilgrimage guidebooks: drawing on Grapard (1982), Buffetrille (1998) speaks of 'mandalization' of the landscape. This religious landscape is continu-ally enriched or reshaped by new visions and reinterpretations.

### Divination, Hidden Books and Sacred Néri *Mountains*

In Chinese lore, Mañjuśrī is also connected to the stars and planets and is con-sidered a revealer of astrological knowledge.[113] Tibetans and Mongols believe that Mañjuśrī introduced divination and mathematics into China and even converted the Chinese to Buddhism while teaching astrology on Wutaishan. In Tibet, he began to be seen as the inventor of divination, at least since the four-teenth century: the *Padma bka' thang*, a biography of Padmasambhava discov-ered in Tibet by the treasure-revealer Orgyen Lingpa (1323-ca. 1360) in 1352, places the very origins of Tibetan elemental divination on Wutaishan.[114] This is later repeated in the *White Beryl* and in the *Grub mtha' shel gyi me long* (The clear mirror of philosophical tenets)[115] written in 1801 by the Third Tukwan Khutugtu, Lozang Chökyi Nyima (1737-1802). The 1721 Mongolian guidebook to Wutaishan, drawing from the *Pad ma bka' thang* without explicitly quoting it, explains how Mañjuśrī, having taken the decision to preach in China, was 'born' from a lotus on Wutaishan and gave teachings on divination:

> After having obtained Enlightenment, [Śākyamuni] turned three times the wheel of the Dharma, and from there he intended to make the Dharma enter in China .... He preached about favor and merit, and on crimes and sins, but people did not listen and despised his teachings. Then Śākyamuni, thinking about the method of converting [*nomugadkha-:*

---

111  Huber 1999: 13.

112  The study of Tibetan pilgrimage guides of Kailash or Amnye Machen reveals similar conventional descriptions of natural features that are often difficult to connect to actual sites (Buffetrille 1996a).

113  Birnbaum 1983: 92-99.

114  Transl. Douglas and Bays 1978: 224. It was translated into Mongolian and exists in a Beijing xylograph version (*Padma kadang sudur*).

115  Full title: *Grub mtha' thams cad kyi khungs dang 'dod tshul ston pa legs bshad shel gyi me long.*

'pacify, subjugate, conquer, tame'] people thanks to the Dharma, went to Mount Gederigüt [= Grhakūta [parvata]].... He then understood that converting the Chinese was the destiny of Mañjuśrī. At that time, on the Five Peak Mountain in China, in a land rising above the great plain of China, ... to the east of Jambudvīpa, there were five different *stūpa*s on five shining peaks of five different colors. At the feet of each *stūpa* grew a perfumed Jambu tree. A golden ray emitted by Buddha's *uṣṇīṣa* was absorbed by these trees, and from their seeds emerged lotus flowers from which Mañjuśrī was born in the world, without father or mother, without defilement and sin of the *saṃsāra*. He has a yellow body decorated of many kinds of jewels, and five golden [?] rainbows make circles on the top of his *uṣṇīṣa*.[116]

The newly born *bodhisattva* gave teachings on astrology:

He taught the seven root *tantra*s of astrology,[117] which include the number governing fate [associated with][118] obstacles in the lives of sentient beings, the number [associated with] searching for the dead's souls, the number [associated with] a wedding, the number [associated with] the sign of a place.[119] For each number [associated with] the sign of a place, he taught the 'gate of 21,000 numbers.' All the sentient beings of Jambudvīpa and especially of China and great China gathered around him and listened to his decrees.[120]

But the crowd of listeners did not stay to listen, and Mañjuśrī hid all the books of his advanced doctrine "in a place located north of Wutaishan." Sometime later, when disasters and troubles arose, Avalokiteśvara went to this place and blessed Wutaishan with the contact of his feet. Padmasambhava and Avalokiteśvara decided that it was time to 'rediscover' the hidden books. Avalokiteśvara ordered Mañjuśrī: "You, Mañjuśrī, I ask you (to go) where these books were hidden and to take them out." Having said that, Avalokiteśvara washed himself at

---

116    *UTAOSC* 6r-8v; see *Pad ma bka' thang*, transl. Douglas and Bays 1978: 224-227.

117    *Mengge-yin shiltagan*, lit. 'causation of birthmark': *mengge* is the distinctive mark that constitutes the astrological profile of a person; *shiltagan sudulul* translates as 'aetiology, the study of causations.'

118    *Too*, 'number, figure': the personal 'distinctive mark' of each person is composed of a color and a number, and is associated with a particular Buddhist deity and with a direction.

119    *Belge*, 'sign, symbol,' are astrological symbols indicating auspicious or inauspicious days (Mostaert 1969: 5).

120    *UTAOSC* 9v-10r.

one of the many springs of Wutaishan and left. Then Padmasambhava met with Mañjuśrī at the top of the Central Terrace, and they took the books out of their hiding place in order to divulgate their contents.[121] They started to teach the doctrine contained therein, this time with success. From then on, Mañjuśrī constantly resided on Wutaishan and appeared under many different guises to those who visit the mountain.[122]

The theme of hidden books refers both to the Chinese lore of Wutaishan— the Vajra Cave as a depository of extraordinary treasures (books, images and ritual objects)—and to the Tibetan *terma* tradition (texts which were hidden by great masters for future discovery at auspicious times by other masters). According to Samten Karmay, the first stage of the Buddhist conversion process of a Tibetan mountain is the discovery, usually by Padmasambhava, of sacred texts hidden in the mountain, which consequently becomes a *terné*, a place where a treasure (of texts) is concealed.[123] With these treatises on astrology hidden for a later revelation, plus the treasures hidden in Vajra Cave and, more recently, statues and treatises unearthed by Nyingmapa masters,[124] Wutaishan is undoubtedly a *terné* (Mo. *sang-un oron*), a place where Buddhist treasures are buried to be later revealed. These Buddhist treasures also contribute to 'consecrating' the holy mountain, like consecration texts and relics that are inserted inside icons, and thus to empowering it. Similarly, footprints and handprints of deities and *stūpas* empower and tame the mountain;[125] they are well-known devices used throughout the Buddhist world to seal the Buddhist appropriation of a site. The Pure Land of Mañjuśrī is therefore described by Tibetan and Mongol Buddhist authors as a sacred *néri* mountain. As discussed in Chapter 1, *néri* mountains are the abode of a transcendental buddha or a *bodhisattva* and are inhabited by deities forming a *maṇḍala*; typically they are worshipped through circumambulation.

---

121  The *Pad ma bka' thang* recounts that Padmasambhava revealed eight-four thousand volumes of astrological teachings that Mañjuśrī had concealed at Wutaishan (transl. Douglas and Bays 1978: 226-227).

122  *UTAOSC* 10v-12r.

123  Karmay 2005 [1998]: 47.

124  Such as Jikmé Püntsok in 1987, who not only uncovered but also buried Buddhist treasures (Chou 2011b: 135-136).

125  On *stūpas*, prints of hands and feet, *maṇḍala* and steles that bring a territory under subjugation: Buffetrille 1996b. See also the legend about the taming of local deities trapped underground at Zhenhaisi (Online Appendix B).

### Descriptions of Miraculous Manifestations in Tibetan and Mongolian Guidebooks

Stories and poems recording miraculous manifestations on Wutaishan and theophanies appear in both Mongolian and Tibetan poems, praise prayers and guidebooks of the mountain.[126] The 1721 Mongolian guidebook mentions manifestations of Mañjuśrī, lights, rainbows and *prajña* lamps (*belge bilig-ün jula*)[127] above the Northern Terrace: "merit and blessings ensuing from these visions are unimaginable."[128] By personally experiencing visions on Wutaishan and writing about it in guidebooks and poems, Mongol clerics thus subscribed and added to the long list of extraordinary perceptions on Wutaishan initiated by ancient Chinese narratives.

The main differences between Chinese and Tibeto-Mongol description of miraculous manifestations on Wutaishan are the nature of the visions and their interpretation: whereas Chinese accounts interpret all phenomena as manifestations of Mañjuśrī or theophanies surrounding him, the Tibetan and Mongolian writings also mention apparitions of crowds of *bodhisattvas*, buddhas, Indian and Tibetan masters of the past, and various transcendental beings. Some of these, such as Padmasambhava, Padampa Sanggyé (see below) and the Tibetan historian Tāranātha (1575-1634),[129] were believed to have dwelt, meditated and had visionary experiences on Wutaishan during their lifetime—or visited the mountain as reincarnation or emanation, or in a dream—thereby contributing to the taming and empowerment of the mountain. Many of them are represented in clouds above monasteries on the 1846 Cifusi map and on the eighteenth century manuscript painting of Wutaishan in the *White Beryl*. The master who is most often mentioned in relation to Wutaishan is Tsongkhapa, though he never visited Wutaishan in his lifetime.

### Tsongkhapa on Wutaishan

Tsongkhapa, who reformed Tibetan Buddhism following Mañjuśrī's instruction, came to be seen by his disciples as an incarnation of Mañjuśrī. His

---

126    Mongolian guidebooks: UTAOSC 18v-20r; TÜAG 14r-15v (text in Kápolnas 2008: 11); OMSA 5rv; Tibetan praise poems: Schaeffer 2011; Chou 2011b: 131. Dznyā na shrī man, an eighteenth-century Tibetan lama, made a complex classification of ten different 'Buddha lights' on Wutaishan (Schaeffer (2011: 227), translating a passage of the *Ri bo rtse lnga'i dkar chag rab gsal me long*, 1994 [after 1827]). See also Birnbaum 2004.

127    The same term, referring to Mañjuśrī's wisdom, is used in Chinese.

128    UTAOSC 6or-v.

129    Tibetan historian Tāranātha is said to have visited Wutaishan and written a *lungten* (revelatory account, prophecy) there. The 'Black Mañjuśrī' (Jampel Nakpo) would have summoned him to convert or annihilate the 'atheist' Chinese (Hummel 1971: 395, n. 9). On the Cifusi map, a *stūpa* is dedicated to Tāranātha.

biography recounts his many visions of Mañjuśrī, who gave him teachings and advice during his meditations.[130] One of these visions appeared before Tsong-khapa's own father in an auspicious dream, whereby a young monk, whom the father identified as an emanation of Mañjuśrī, came from Wutaishan asking for shelter. According to Tsongkhapa's biographies, Tsongkhapa is believed to have reincarnated as an erudite monk (*pandit*) on Wutaishan, teaching *sūtra*s in the morning and giving esoteric teachings in the afternoon.[131] Rölpé Dorjé, who himself belongs to the spiritual lineage of Tsongkhapa and is hence connected to Mañjuśrī,[132] recounts several details he heard or saw in a dream about Tsong-khapa's 'emanation body' and eventually told his biographer that Tsongkhapa's emanation resided in Qingliangqiao, a Chinese Buddhist monastery of Wutai-shan.[133] Tukwan Lozang Chökyi Nyima, the author of the biography, concluded that Rölpé Dorjé had personally met Tsongkhapa.[134] According to the 1721 Mon-golian guidebook, which targeted a much wider audience than Rölpé Dorjé's biography, Tsongkhapa said to Khédrup Jé (his disciple Khédrup Gélek Pelzang, 1385-1438) that he now and forever dwells on Wutaishan.[135] The five manifesta-tions of Tsongkhapa appear to the kneeling Khédrup Jé emanating above each of the temples of the five terraces on the 1846 Cifusi map (Fig. 17)[136] and on the panels above the architrave of the Buddha hall of Cifusi.[137] An apparition of Tsongkhapa would be at the origin of the carving of the map.[138]

---

130 Thurman, ed. 1982: 33.

131 Tukwan Lozang Chökyi Nyima's biography of Rölpé Dorjé, quoting a biography of Tsongkhapa, transl. Chen Qingying and Ma Lianlong 1988: 313-314. Actually, the reference is not found in any biography of Tsongkhapa but in a biography of his disciple Khédrup Jé (Chou 2011b: 20).

132 On Rölpé Dorjé's spiritual lineage and its connection to Wutaishan: Chou 2011b: Chapter 1.

133 Chen Qingying and Ma Lianlong restored the name of the monastery as Qingningsi 慶寧寺, but the original version has "Ching-lang-ch'ou" (Chou 2011b: 19).

134 Transl. Chen Qingying and Ma Lianlong 1988: 313-314.

135 *UTAOSC* 20r-v.

136 See Chou 2007: 115 and Fig. 8, 9.

137 Khédrup Jé is said to have had five visions of his master after his death: Tsongkhapa riding an elephant and making the *mudrā* of teaching, Tsongkhapa as the supreme Buddha Vajradhara, Tsongkhapa as Mañjuśrī on his white lion, Tsongkhapa *siddha* riding a tiger and holding a sword, and Tsongkhapa in his usual aspect. The five manifestations also appear in Tukwan Lozang Chökyi Nyima's biography of Rölpé Dorjé. They are carved in the rock of a mountain in eastern Inner Mongolia, known as Qianfoshan 千佛山 (or Agui-yin Süme, Khüriyetü Uula, Zhangwu County 彰武, Liaoning Province). For three small carved images and paintings in Mongol charm-boxes, representing the five forms of Tsongkhapa seen by Khédrup Jé: Meinert, ed. 2011: cat. 95, cat. 98, cat. 99.

138 Chou 2007: 115.

The Mongols especially revere Tsongkhapa, whom they view as a second buddha (*khoyadugar iluugsan bogda Zongkapa*, "the second victorious [one], holy Tsongkhapa") that Śākyamuni prophesized to rectify Buddhism when it fell into chaos. His birthday (or anniversary of his death), on the 25th of the tenth lunar month, is one of the main religious festivals in Mongolia. In addition, many modern Mongolians questioned about the main pilgrimage abroad cite 'Utai-Gümbüm': they believe that Kumbum (Tsongkhapa's birthplace) and Wutaishan are the same pilgrimage site, and I have even been told that Tsongkhapa was "born in Utai-Gümbüm." The two places are therefore connected, in the Mongol people's minds, through the person of Tsongkhapa.

### Vajrabhairava Yamāntaka on Wutaishan

Another figure of the Tibeto-Mongol pantheon who frequently appears in the Wutaishan spiritual landscape is Vajrabhairava Yamāntaka (Vajra Terror, Ender of Yama), a wrathful form of Mañjuśrī and the main protector in the Gélukpa School. In 1767, following a dream, Rölpé Dorjé proclaimed that the protector of Wutaishan was not a *nāga* (or a dragon king) as everyone believed but, according to a revelation he had in dream, Yamantāka (Tib. Damchen Chökyi Gyelpo), the fierce emanation of Mañjuśrī.[139] Yamāntaka thus appears as the overarching deity of the mandalized *néri* Wutaishan.

Vajrabhairava Yamāntaka and the *Vajrabhairava tantra* were very popular among the Mongols,[140] especially the eastern Inner Mongols, since the Mongol missionary Neichi Toin promoted the worship of this deity among the Khorchins, and treatises on various types of magic (such as hunting rites) came to be prefaced with invocations to Yamāntaka.[141] The worship of this *yidam* by Mongols dates back to the Yuan dynasty when Pakpa Lama composed prayers to Yamāntaka.[142] Vajrabhairava does not appear on the Cifusi map, perhaps because he was less important for pilgrims than he was for advanced practitioners; nevertheless, he is mentioned in the 1721 Mongolian guidebook as the main protector of Pusading.[143]

---

139    Biography of Rölpé Dorjé, transl. Chen Qingying and Ma Lianlong 1988: 310; Illich 2006: 531. Rölpé Dorjé's eulogy at the end of his guidebook also proclaims that Yamāntaka is the protector of Wutaishan (Illich 2006: 527).

140    See Ujeed 2009: 178 sq. The *Vajrabhairava tantra* belongs to the class of higher *tantras* (*anuttara yoga tantra*): see Siklós 1996.

141    Siklós 1996: 12.

142    Yamāntaka is also the designated Manchu imperial protector deity, as can be seen by his prevalence at the Beijing Imperial Palace (Bianchi 2008).

143    *UTAOSC* 34v.

### The Sixth Dalai Lama on Wutaishan

The Sixth Dalai Lama, Tsangyang Gyatso (1683-1706?), is believed to have come to Wutaishan and meditated for six years in a cave after his presumed death: many Mongols (and Tibetans) believed that he did not in fact die near Kukunor en route to Beijing after he was forcibly deposed by the Qing in November 1706, as described in official histories. Instead he is said to have escaped and started a new life, traveling as a beggar monk throughout East and South Asia and finally settling in 1716 in Alashan (western Inner Mongolia), where he built several monasteries and died in 1746.[144] His disciples founded Baruun Kheid in Alashan to enshrine his mummy. On Wutaishan, around the cave where he was said to have meditated, Avalokiteśvara Cave (Guanyindong) Monastery was founded. Tibetans share with Mongols the veneration for this cave, and the Thirteenth Dalai Lama specially visited the site in 1908. Three reincarnations of the Dagbu Gegeen of Baruun Kheid, recognized as a Mongol reincarnation of the dethroned Sixth Dalai Lama, visited Wutaishan (see Chapter 3).

### Mongols' Knowledge of the Ancient Chinese History of Wutaishan

What was the Mongols' knowledge of the official Chinese history of Wutaishan, and to what extent did their narratives differ from the Chinese narratives? Chinese additions to the *bodhisattva*'s biography were certainly acknowledged in Mongolian and Tibetan works on Wutaishan. Rölpé Dorjé's guidebook quotes ancient Chinese sources about a young Mañjuśrī with five hair braids dwelling on Wutaishan.[145] Eighteenth- and nineteenth-century Mongolian guidebooks and maps repeat information from the *Qingliangshan zhi* that quotes the Chinese translation of the *Avataṃsaka sūtra* locating Mañjuśrī in the northeast

---

144 His secret biography, *The Hidden Life of the Sixth Dalai Lama*, was written in 1757 by a Mongol monk named Ngawang Lhundrup Dargyé (religious name: Lhatsün Dargyé Nomönhen), himself being a reincarnation of the Tibetan regent Sanggyé Gyatso. Klafkowski (1979), Aris (1989), Miyvacir (2008 [1942]: Chapter 2), Jalsan (2002—Jalsan is the sixth reincarnation of Sanggyé Gyatso) and Wickham-Smith (Ngawang Lhundrup Dargyé 2011) have different hypotheses concerning the identity of the Mongol Sixth Dalai Lama.

145 *OMSA*, fol. 3v. Mañjuśrī was known by the Chinese since the Eastern Han dynasty and became one of the most important *bodhisattvas* in the Chinese Buddhist tradition. As early as the second and third centuries, over a dozen Buddhist *sūtras* in which Mañjuśrī plays an important role had been translated into Chinese (Lamotte 1960).

and associating him with Qingliang Mountain in China, [146] as well as the passage from a Chinese version of the *Mañjuśrī dharma ratnagarbha dhāraṇī sūtra* (Scripture on the *dhāraṇī* of Mañjuśrī's precious treasures of the *dharma*). According to this text, translated into Chinese by Bodhiruci in 710,[147] Śākyamuni declared after his death that Mañjuśrī would go to a country named Mahācīna, to a mountain called Pañcaśikha (Five Peaks, Ch. Wuding 五頂), to preach the Buddhist doctrine.[148] Mahācīna, translated and transcribed in Chinese as Da Zhenna 大振那, was understood as being China.[149]

Mongolian descriptions of the mountain, drawing on Chinese gazetteers, also acknowledge the presence of relics of the Buddha brought by Indian Emperor Aśoka, the story of Emperor Ming's dream and the legendary foundation of Dafu Lingjiusi in the Eastern Han dynasty. Two guidebooks explain how the Daoists of Wutaishan—called *terse* in Mongolian, 'heretics, heterodox, hostile'—threw themselves into the water or converted to Buddhism after they understood the superiority of the *dharma*: "One cannot compare the fox with the lion or the light of a lamp with the sun and the moon."[150]

In his praise poem entitled "Cloud of offerings to please Mañjuśrī," Rölpé Dorjé emphasized the possibility of encountering within the landscape of the mountain not only Chinese masters of the past, such as patriarchs of the Avataṃsaka School, but also Indian and Tibetan masters, from the Buddha to Tsongkhapa, who were believed to have preached on Wutaishan. Like Mañjuśrī, these masters may appear "to faithful disciples who keep the holy vow" in any guise (a sage, a boy, a man, a woman, a Chinese monk, a destitute beggar, a bird, a deer, flowers, plants and so on). Rölpé Dorjé "thereby collapses the historical narrative ... into an eternal present in which visitors may always encounter past masters in the landscape of Wutai Shan."[151]

---

146    *TÜAG* 2r-3r (text in Kápolnas 2008: 7); *OMSA* 3v-4r; text in the lower part of the 1846 Cifusi map (Online Appendix G).

147    Debreczeny 2011: 7. We do not have the Sanskrit version of this text. The Tibetan version does not mention the Clear and Cool Mountain.

148    Ch. *Wenshu shili fabaocang tuoluoni jing* 文殊師利法寶藏陀羅尼經, *T.* 1185A-B, vol. 20, transl. Birnbaum 1983: 11; Lamotte 1960: 84; Birnbaum 1986: 124; Wang-Toutain 2007.

149    *T.* 1185B, vol. 20: 798b. This identification is controversial (personal communication by Gérard Fussman, November 2011). The *Manjusrīmūlakalpa*, translated in Chinese, also located Mañjuśrī in Mahācīna.

150    *UTAOSC* 16v-17r; *TÜAG* 7r-8r, text in Kápolnas 2008: 8-9. In the modern period, a few Daoists are still mentioned in sources, but there was no residing community.

151    "With backward views clogged up with karmic stink,/ Sophist logicians possessing but fickle minds,/ Intoxicated with conceited hubris, Do not recognize them, but it's obvious." Transl. by Schaeffer (2011: 222-223), from Rölpé Dorjé's biography, verses 35-37. For

The ancient folklore of Wutaishan forms the background upon which later Chinese, Tibetan and Mongol stories were grafted, developed and distorted. Mongolian guidebooks and the Cifusi map represent several ancient Chinese stories, such as the Begging Mañjuśrī, the 'true portrait' made by a monk named Ansheng 安生, and the emperor shooting at a monk who was bathing with two women.[152] Later, Duke Migwachir in his travel account merges a story of Emperor Kangxi searching for his father with that of the buckwheat portrait of Mañjuśrī.[153] Other Mongol and Tibetan narratives distorted and reinterpreted stories, such as the encounter between the Kashmiri monk Buddhapāli (or Buddhapālita, Ch. Fotuoboli 佛陀波利) and Mañjuśrī. According to the legend transmitted since the Tang dynasty, Buddhapāli came on pilgrimage to Wutaishan in 676 and near the Southern Terrace encountered, or saw in vision, Mañjuśrī in the guise of an old bearded man in white, who instructed him to retrieve the "*Sūtra* of the *dhāraṇī* of the head protuberance that purifies all bad existences" (*Uṣṇīṣa vijayā dhāraṇī sūtra*). Buddhapāli returned to India, found a copy of the text and brought it back to the Tang capital, Chang'an 長安 (modern Xi'an), where he translated it along with a Chinese monk after 683 and offered it to the emperor.[154] Then he took the Sanskrit text with him to Wutaishan, and Mañjuśrī led him into Vajra Cave (Jingangku);[155] they both disappeared

---

descriptions of visions and dreams of Rölpé Dorjé on Wutaishan, see his biography, transl. Chen Qingying and Ma Lianlong 1988: Chapter 18, esp. p. 314-315.

152  On the stories of the Begging Mañjuśrī (about a monk who distributed porridge to the poor and did not recognize the *bodhisattva*, for his two attendants and his golden lion were disguised respectively as a beggar woman, her children and a dog), the 'true portrait' (Mañjuśrī appeared to a sculptor who could not make the head of a statue, after which the sculptor quickly made the head with buckwheat according to the apparition) and Kangxi shooting at Mañjuśrī disguised as a monk: Online Appendix B, "Tayuansi," "Pusading," "Shuxiangsi" and "Zaoyuchi." The tale of the Begging Mañjuśrī is depicted on a stele at Yuanzhaosi and on the 1846 Cifusi map.

153  Miγvacir 2008 [1942]: 405.

154  *Foding zunsheng tuoluoni jing* 佛頂尊聖陀羅尼經, *T.* 967, vol. 19: 349v. This text, which was believed to eliminate great calamities and diseases, had a wide diffusion at that period, particularly through banner-pillars (*jingchuang*) inscribed with it (see the banner-pillar in Zunshengsi of Wutaishan) (Liu Shufen 1996: 155-167).

155  Vajra Cave is typically a 'paradise-cave' where past masters, starting with Buddhapāli, are believed to have remained inside, withdrawn completely from human society and attained enlightenment or obtained various spiritual powers (Stein 1988: 6-9; Birnbaum 1989-1990: 120). Worshipped as early as the seventh century as the home of Mañjuśrī, it was believed to be the depository of extraordinary treasures such as sacred texts and musical instruments. Since the Tang or maybe the Song dynasty, the entrance has never been opened again, but pilgrims still today continue to visit the site. The location of the

within the cave, which closed by itself.[156] However, in Tibetan and Mongolian versions of this story and on the Cifusi map,[157] Buddhapāli is replaced by the South Indian *siddha* (Mo. *arshi*, hermit) Padampa Sanggyé (Paramapitri, d. 1117), who, in a late biography, is supposed to have visited Wutaishan between 1086 and 1097. On the road to Wutaishan, during a time when China was suffering epidemics, Padampa met an old sage, who told him to go to Vajrāsana (Bodhgayā) and obtain a *dhāraṇī* of Vijaya that could cure epidemics. According to the 1721 Mongolian guidebook, Padampa Sanggyé asked the hermit, "How can I get to a place so far and difficult to reach?" The hermit showed him a cavity in the rock cliff; Padampa entered the cavity, was transported to Vajrāsana (Bodhgayā) and obtained the *dhāraṇī* that he had 'invited' to Wutaishan.[158] A direct gate thus connects Wutaishan with the heart of the Buddhist world, the central Pure Land of Jambudvīpa. This legend was probably important for Mongol pilgrims, who especially worshipped Vajra Cave.[159]

Overall, Mongolian sources for pilgrims did borrow ancient Chinese stories and legends, but they molded and reinterpreted them over time. With the exception of Rölpé Dorjé's guidebook, which closely mirrors its Chinese sources, the Mongolian guidebooks I had access to make no mention of imperial visits and patronage, famous Chinese monks or ancient miracles from the Chinese history of Wutaishan.

---

encounter between Buddhapālita and Mañjuśrī was originally believed to have been Zunshengsi.

156   The encounter is recorded by Ennin, who visited Wutaishan in 840 (transl. Reischauer 1955: 246-247) and in the *Guang Qingliang zhuan*, ca. 1060, *T.* 2099, vol. 51: 1111. It is depicted twice in the tenth-century map of Wutaishan painted in Cave 61 at Dunhuang. See Lamotte 1960: 86-88; Stein 1988: 6; Birnbaum 1983: 10; Birnbaum 1989-1990: 120-132; Heller 2008: 43. This story may have been forged by the Buddhist clergy to promote Wutaishan as the abode of Mañjuśrī (Sen 2003: 80-81, 279 n. 111).

157   See Chou 2011b: Fig. 4.15.

158   This story occupies five folios of the *UTAOSC* 38v-40v. It is found in the fifteenth-century *Deb ther sngon po* (*The Blue Annals*, transl. Roerich and Gedun Choepel 1979 [1976]: 911-912); see also Chou 2011b: 136-237; Duan Jinjin 2008: 77; Debreczeny 2011: 13-16.

159   The Mongolian guidebook localizes the story at Vajra Cave, but the Cifusi map depicts Padampa sitting in Xitian Cave 西天洞, between Qingliangqiao and Fenglinsi (Chou 2011b: Fig. 4.15). I could not identify Xitian Cave; on the Cifusi map its localization does not correspond to that of Puensi/Xitiansi.

## Mongol Popular *Imaginaire* of Wutaishan

Let us now focus on specific Mongol developments that are sometimes shared with Tibetans but that do not come from clerical literature, paintings or local Chinese stories.

### *Mañjuśrī as the God of Wisdom and Astrology*

While lamas' visionary experiences and writings emphasize the apparition of many buddhas, deities and saints, Mongol popular devotion focused on Mañjuśrī. Although Mongols acknowledge that Mongolia is Vajrapāṇi's domain whereas Mañjuśrī's domain is China, Mañjuśrī is a key figure in the popular Mongol pantheon, as shown by the success of abrigded versions of the *Mañjuśrīnāmasaṃgīti* and the many objects of daily worship that represent him—such as miniature paintings or statues enshrined in amulet boxes,[160] icons for household altars, prayer flags, divination charts and amulets.[161] Being the embodiment of the transcendental wisdom (*prajñā*) of all the buddhas,[162] he symbolizes sacred esoteric knowledge, which has the highest value in Tantric Buddhism.[163] Mongols believe that by worshipping Mañjuśrī they will obtain intelligence, wisdom, eloquence and the ability to memorize the sacred texts.[164]

Like the Chinese, Mongol pilgrims personally hoped to meet Mañjuśrī in one of his guises or obtain a sign from him. Mañjuśrī is the main deity who is mentioned in the stone inscriptions of Wutaishan, which typically start with "Cool and Clear Mount Wutaishan, abode of the savior Mañjuśrī," and end with "May I/we/they be reborn under the lotuses of the golden feet of Holy Lama Mañjuśrī" (Appendix 1). Pilgrims especially visit his famous sculpted icons on Wutaishan.

---

160    Mañjuśrī is well represented in a corpus of 5,120 miniature paintings gathered by Davis (2010).

161    See the amulets in the Ferenc Hopp Museum of Eastern Asiatic Art in Budapest: Kelényi 2003: 97, Fig. 96; 93, Fig. 84; an amulet with the *sūtra* that disperses darkness to the ten corners of the universe: Le Calloc'h 1989: 278.

162    Tibetan Buddhists, and particularly the Gélukpas, also came to see Mañjuśrī as the source of inspiration of the Madhyamaka School of philosophy. Later Mahāyāna scriptures identified Mañjuśrī with Prajñāpāramitā (Perfection of Wisdom, or of Insight). He took on increasing importance in early Buddhist Tantric works, especially in the traditions of the *Kālacakra tantra* and the *Hevajra tantra*, which identified him with the Primordial Buddha (*ādibuddha*) (Wayman 1999 [1985]: 3).

163    His place is therefore primary in the Tibeto-Mongol pantheon. The study of the *Mañjuśrīnāmasaṃgīti* goes along with the study of Kālacakra (Wayman 1999 [1985]: 4-8).

164    Sárközi 1982.

On the map painted at Badgar Choiling Süme, several monasteries are simply called in Mongolian 'Old Mañjuśrī' (Ebügen Manzushiri, i.e. Shouningsi), 'Mañjuśrī with a Cart' (Tergetü Manzushiri, i.e., Qixiansi) or 'Mañjuśrī with a Buckwheat Head' (Gulir terigütü Manzushiri, i.e., Shuxiangsi), without even adding the term 'monastery' (Fig. 16).

Mongolian guidebooks relate that Mañjuśrī plays with different identities to test people's faith and sometimes to confuse and trick people.[165] The 1721 Mongolian guidebook explains how Mañjuśrī, disguised as a cunning mendicant monk (ayaga takhimlikh),[166] took possession of Wutaishan. The emperor of China saw him sitting on top of a tree and asked him how he had come to find himself in such a strange situation. The mendicant answered, "I sit here because I have not a patch of land that belongs to me; all this land belongs to the emperor." The emperor prostrated before the lama and said: "O wisest of all, ask me whatever you want." The mendicant answered, "In all this land I would only like to possess a patch of land that my carpet can cover." The emperor agreed to his request; the mendicant threw his carpet, which rose into the air, took the dimensions and shape of a cloud and covered with its shadow an area of five hundred li. The emperor and his courtiers were amazed by this marvel, while the mendicant, who was none other than Mañjuśrī Khubilgan (an apparition of Mañjuśrī), was standing before them all in great majesty, surrounded by ten thousand bodhisattvas. To commemorate this marvelous apparition, numerous temples and hermitages were founded on Wutaishan.[167] This tale, which recalls the well-known myth of the oxhide delimitating a territory,[168] does not appear in Chinese gazetteers; therefore, it may have an Indian or Central Asian origin.

Mañjuśrī is also the god of astrology, presiding over human destiny, and of science. Tibetan and Mongolian manuals of astrology and divination start with "I bow to Lama Mañjuśrī." The first day of the year is consecrated to Mañjuśrī.[169] A manual translated from Tibetan called "The Mirror of Mañjuśrī's Benevolence, the Refuge: The Method of Reckoning Calamities" locates Mañjuśrī on Wutaishan.[170] Divination charts represent Mañjuśrī wielding his flaming sword

---

165    *UTAOSC* 18v; *OMSA* 5v.

166    On the etymology of *ayaga takhimlikh*: Pokotilov 1935 [1893]: 47, n. 3. He is called *badir* (< Skt. *pātra*, alms –bowl) *ayaga* in the *TÜAG* (11v).

167    *UTAOSC* 22v-24r.

168    This tale had a wide diffusion from Scandinavia to South Asia and Kirghizia. It probably originates with the story of Carthage's foundation by Dido, who treacherously demanded "as much land as an oxhide can hold" (Svenbro and Scheid 1985).

169    See the manual introduced by Antoine Mostaert (1969: 2).

170    Late seventeenth or eighteenth century: Kara 2000: 229, Mong. 145, quoted by Elverskog 2011: 248.

FIGURE 20    *Divination chart (sipaho) topped by Mañjuśrī, painting on a wall at Zhenhaisi.*
© ISABELLE CHARLEUX, 2010.

in their upper part.[171] These charts, which are similar to the Tibetan astrological charts (*sipaho*), were printed on paper and carried as talismans, or on prayer flags to be hung outside one's tent (Fig. 20).

171    Kelényi ed., 2003: 50, fig. 27.

According to certain Tibetan sources, Mañjuśrī was reborn on Wutaishan as Confucius and under this avatar brought astrology to Tibet on a tortoise.[172] Large-size wind-horse flags carry depictions of the wind-horse (*khei mori*, the ever-living prospering spirit), the divination tortoise and a protective circle full of *mantra*s, Śākyamuni, Mañjuśrī and Kongtsé Trülgyi Gyelpo (i.e., Confucius) standing one above the other on a vertical axis.[173] On these same flags are represented the five personal deities born together with every human being (Tib. *gowé lha nga*), among whom is the White Mountain god (Migön Karpo, i.e., the White Old Man), who is said to reside on Wutaishan. Mongol families used to hang wind-horse flags on a pole just outside their yurts to protect the home.[174]

### Mañjuśrī in Popular Prayers and Rituals

Prayers, eulogies and evocations (*sādhana*, Mo. *büteel*) especially addressed to Mañjuśrī were composed in Mongolian by great lamas such as Mergen Gegeen Lubsangdambijalsan.[175] Mañjuśrī was mentioned in a great variety of prayers (such as prayers to Chinggis Khan) and rituals. In the popular ritual entitled "Offering of the Fox" (*Ünegen-ü sang*),"[176] from the sky Mañjuśrī speaks to the people, advising them to pray to the Seven Stars of the Plough, who in turn instruct them to apply for help to a *khan* named Guanchi. Guanchi tells them to kill the sinful fox.[177] Mañjuśrī also presided over gift-giving rituals of wedding ceremonies (probably due to the importance of divination in weddings)[178] and was worshipped in prayers for purification after funeral rites.[179] Several prophetic books are believed to have been sent by Mañjuśrī from heaven, and some appeared on earth after falling from the sky on Wutaishan, onto the top of the

---

172 Dorje 2001: 48; Lessing 1957a about a Qing dynasty Tibetan prayer to Confucius of Wutaishan found in Yonghegong.

173 Kelényi ed. 2003: 77 and 78, fig. 53; Lin 2007.

174 Wind-horse flags have been especially documented among the Ordos (Kler 1957) but were found in all of Mongolia (Bawden 1985b: 14; Bawden 1990).

175 "Cayan Manjusari [Manjušri]-yin bütügel"; "Manjuširi-yin maytayal," references in Chiodo 2009: 148, n. 23 and 149, n. 33; also Ujeed 2009: 168.

176 Bawden 1976: 440.

177 Bawden 1976: 452-453. The fox is an ill-omen in Mongolian literature.

178 Cf. a manual for marriage ceremonies from Ordos: Serruys 1974a: 253, translation p. 284, referring to the 'Clever Mañjuśrī' (*uran manchushiri*) at the beginning of the handbook (quoted by Elverskog 2011: 251); another manual from Ordos is mentioned in Chiodo 2009: 148, n. 23.

179 Pozdneev 1978 [1887]: 613.

Golden Bronze Monastery (Xiantongsi) or of the Golden Monastery of Tārā Mother.[180]

### Mañjuśrī the Dragon King

In Chinese lore, the relationship between Wutaishan and dragons was reinforced by Mañjuśrī's association with them in certain Buddhist scriptures, where he was called "the Supreme Tathāgatha King of the Dragon King."[181] On Wutaishan, Mañjuśrī was said to have subjugated five hundred poisonous dragons and to reside on the mountain with a retinue of ten thousand *bodhisattvas*, countless gods, *nāgas*/dragons and eight classes of spirits. In the early twentieth century, the cult of Wutaishan's main dragon king along with his family (the Wuye 五爺, 'Five Lords') rose in importance: he was worshipped both at the Northern Terrace and at Wanfoge and was identified as a fierce emanation of Mañjuśrī; hence the appellation 'Black Mañjuśrī' (Mo. Khara Manjushiri, see Chapter 6) (Fig. 21). As a master of the dragons and thus of weather, Mañjuśrī was also a god of agriculture, who brings rain to crops. This association of Mañjuśrī with dragon masters of the land was common in Mongolian literature: Mañjuśrī was praised during rituals to or at *oboos* to propitiate the master-spirits of the land (*gajar-un ejen*) solicited to send down blessings on a locality. A Mongolian prayer to the water spirits (*luus*) says:

> The rulers residing in the 3,000 kingdoms, rulers of localities, and dragons residing on Wutaishan, the supreme country of Mañjuśrī; in the Potala, the kingdom of Qongshim bodhisattva (Avalokiteśvara); in Shambhala, the country of secret dharanis ...[182]

---

180 The "Order of Holy Mañjuśrī" (*Qutuγtu manjusiri-yin jarliγ*); "Order of the Holy Panchen Erdeni, of His Brightness the Dalai Lama and of the Holy Chinggis Khan" (*Boyda Bancin erdeni Dalai blam-a-yin gegen boyda Cinggis qaγan-narun jarliγ-un bicig*) (Sárközi 1992: 70-73, 79-80).

181 *Gu Qingliangshan zhi*, 1093r, quoting the *Śūrangama samādhi sūtra*. The tenth-century map of Wutaishan in Dunhuang Cave 61 in its upper part depicts Mañjuśrī, along with the five hundred dragon kings.

182 Pozdneev 1978 [1887]: 524. See also Mergen Gegeen's prayer of *oboo* ritual "The Clear White Glass," 9v, wooden block print, translated into English by Uranchimeg Ujeed (personal communication).

FIGURE 21     *Dragon King identified as a fierce emanation of Mañjuśrī, Guanyindong (copy of the icon worshipped in Wanfoge/Wuyemiao).* © ISABELLE CHARLEUX, 2010.

### Old Mañjuśrī and the White Old Man

One of the characteristics of Mañjuśrī in Buddhist texts (repeated in Rölpé Dorjé and his disciples' guidebook of Wutaishan)[183] is his eternal youth. His official iconography depicts him as a sixteen-year-old *bodhisattva*. But in the Wutaishan lore he is more often depicted as a old man clad in white. Local iconography acknowledged this form, since statues depicting him as an old man riding on his lion and holding a *ruyi* stand in Shouningsi, Puhuasi, Jingangku, Baohuasi, Xiantongsi, Jindengsi and Jixiangsi. Shouningsi in particular was reputed for its (now destroyed) statue of Old Mañjuśrī. This iconography is supported by local narratives dating from at least the Tang period, starting with Buddhapāli disappearing with an old white-clad man in Vajra Cave; Mañjuśrī appearing as an old man in a vision to Master Fazhao 法照 in 769 to remind him that he had vowed to go to Wutaishan;[184] as an old man leading an ox to Chan master Wuzhu (or Wuzhao 無著); as an old man showing Tang-dynasty Chan

---

183   Rölpé Dorjé describes him as a young ascetic boy clad in white (*OMSA* 3v, 5v: *cagan deel-ün arshi*).

184   Stevenson 1996: 208, quoting the *Guang Qingliang zhuan*, 1060.

FIGURE 22
*Statue of Old Mañjuśrī in
Puhuasi.*
© CHRISTOPH BAUMER.

monk-pilgrim Daoyi a marvelous monastery floating in the sky (Jingesi); and
as an old monk holding a lantern to guide Emperor Kangxi to a monastery
(Jixiangsi) (Fig. 22). Padampa, who replaced Buddhapāli in Tibetan and Mongolian versions of the story, also met Mañjuśrī as an old man carrying a staff.
The 1721 Mongolian guidebook embraces this Wutaishan lore and describes
Mañjuśrī as an old man appearing on Wutaishan to teach arts and crafts to residents, as a beggar or as an old hermit.[185] The identification of Confucius as an
incarnation of Mañjuśrī on Wutaishan may have supported the *bodhisattva*'s
representation as an old sage.

185    *UTAOSC* 22v-25r, 64r.

According to Chinese gazetteers, in the Northern Wei dynasty, on the slope of the Jujube Tree Forest (Zaolinpo 棗林坡)—one of the numinous traces of the Eastern Terrace—Mañjuśrī appeared to a hunter as a white deer and then as an old man dressed in white holding a staff.[186] This tale is repeated in Rölpé Dorjé's guidebook, and may have contributed to the identification of Mañjuśrī with the White Old Man, who is generally represented with a deer and a staff (Chagan Ebügen, Tib. Gen/Gampo Karpo or Mitséring). This deity, who is particularly worshipped by Mongols, originates in pre-Buddhist times; he protects and multiplies herds and can help couples have children, but he can also cause diseases and epidemics if not correctly propitiated.[187] The White Old Man is also connected to the master-spirits of the land, or dragons, and to mountain deities. Given Mañjuśrī's apparitions as an old man clad in white and his association with dragons, it is easy to see how he may have been identified with the White Old Man in popular belief.[188] This may explain why several Mongol prayers and invocations assert that the White Old Man comes from Wutaishan: "I am the one, who arrived from the country of the five Mañjuśrīs/Of the Wut'ai-shan."[189]

### Wutaishan as the Place to Find Hidden Treasures

Some local stories were recycled and distorted to be incorporated within the Mongol ritual repertoire. The Inner Mongols, especially the Ordos and Khorchins, developed stories about Emperor Kangxi (Mo. Engkhe Amugulang), whom they acknowledged as a legitimate, exemplar and almost Mongol emperor, though he often makes blunders due to his ignorance of local customs.[190] Wutaishan certainly was a source of inspiration for Kangxi stories in Mongolia. His killing of a tiger, which is depicted on the Cifusi map, was interpreted by Qing propaganda—the Tailusi stele and the gazetteers—as the heroic feat of an emperor who subjugated a local demon, perpetuating the deeds of ancient rulers.[191] However, modern Mongols are shocked by this episode because they consider killing an animal on a sacred mountain a sacrilege: here, the imperial

---

186    ZMRBDB, Chinese translation 1990: 11.

187    He is also prayed to for protection against demons, slander, enemies, thieves and poisonous snakes (Heissig 1976a). His Tibetan and Mongol Buddhist iconography was borrowed from the Chinese stellar deity of Longevity (Shoulao 壽老 or Shouxing 壽星).

188    See also Hummel 1971: 395, 401.

189    Udui šang [Utai šan]-un tabun mangjusiri-yin orun-aca iregsen, Sárközi 1983: 361, transl. p. 365, quoted by Elverskog 2011: 250-251. See also Heissig 1976a: 55; Hummel 1971: 394, 402.

190    Charleux 2011b.

191    References in Köhle 2008: 92-93; Chou 2007: 123.

propaganda failed to shape the Mongol *imaginaire* accordingly.[192] This may be why the popular legend shifts the blame on his guards, who encouraged him to shoot the tiger.[193] Another Khorchin story about Kangxi amalgamates various legends:

> When Amgalang Ejen travelled incognito (*sifangla-*, < Ch. *sifang* 私访) on a donkey in search of his Jade Seal, he heard that his father Shunzhi was on Wutaishan. So he went to Wutaishan and, after many enquiries, he arrived at a cave where he thought his father was meditating. He knelt down and kowtowed as soon as he went into the cave and called the person inside 'father.' To this the person replied, "I am not your father. However, now that you have called me 'father' and kowtowed to me, I will give you the Jade Seal of the State." In fact, it turned out that the man in the cave was Li Zicheng,[194] who had rebelled against the Ming state and had seized the Jade Seal. When he was defeated, he took the seal and went to Wutaishan to become a monk.[195]

In this Mongol story, the true quest is not Kangxi's father, as in many Chinese stories, but the Seal Transmitting the Empire (*chuanguo xi* 傳國璽), the mythical and magical object that was so important in legitimizing new dynasties and that Manchu ruler Hungtaiji claimed to be in possession of in 1634.

Other legends about the most sacred objects of Buddhist China converging on Wutaishan recall the Tibetan *terma* tradition initiated by Mañjuśrī on the sacred mountain. Seventeenth-century Mongols are said to have found the Yuan-dynasty golden statue of Mahākāla on Wutaishan and brought it to the court of Ligdan Khan of the Chakhar (r. 1604-1634), the last of the Mongol emperors.[196] A more recent example is the statue of the Sandalwood Buddha,

---

192  Nietupski gives examples of two lamas of Labrang inspired by Emperor Kangxi (2011: 336, 338).

193  Charleux 2011b.

194  Li Zicheng 李自成 (1606-1645) was a Chinese rebel leader who overthrew the Ming dynasty and proclaimed a short-lived dynasty that lasted less than two months. He disappeared in unknown circumstances, but a legend says that Li survived after his defeats and became a monk for the rest of his life.

195  Story told by Bao Jinshan (from the Khorchin Left Flank North Banner) to her daughter Uranchimeg (Uranchimeg Ujeed, email, November 7, 2011).

196  The statue eventually ended up at the Manchu court, where it became a tool of legitimization for the Qing dynasty ("Shishengsi beiwen" 實勝寺碑文, stone inscription of Shishengsi of Mukden [Shenyang], 1638, Chinese version: Zhang Yuxin 1988: 209-211; transl. from the Manchu: Grupper 1984: 67, n. 19).

which was believed to have taken a temporary or permanent residence at Wutaishan (Chapter 1). Stories about extraordinary treasures locked inside Vajra Cave and about astrology books hidden by Mañjuśrī built the reputation of Wutaishan as the best hiding place for the most precious religious and political treasures.

### The Cult of Wutaishan Mountain in Mongolia

The Mongols also worshipped Wutaishan as a sacred mountain per se, with no allusion to Mañjuśrī or to other deities and saints. Ritual texts of offerings to master-spirits of the Mongol land at *oboo*s list the mountains of India, Mongolia and China, among which is Wutaishan.[197] But although the dragon king(s) can be considered its master-spirit, no prayers and songs are dedicated to Wutaishan itself as a mountain deity.

In Mongolian prayers, Wutaishan is often associated with other sacred Buddhist pure lands belonging to this human world (defined in Chapter 1). In rituals surrounding horse races, Wutaishan, Vajrāsana and Potala are offered nine aspersions of fermented milk.[198] In folk songs and prayers, Wutaishan sometimes appears as an otherworldly buddha land for the souls of the dead. A Khorchin folk song even locates Wutaishan in Sukhāvatī 'heaven' (Appendix 3). The mountain is praised in the following song, whose lyrics were recorded by the Russian emissary Timkowski (1790-1875) when he traveled around Mongolia in 1820-1821:

> Dzoungkhaba [Tsongkhapa], the prince of the law, is the powerful king of all what exists. O! happy people, born in the country of the gods ! we beg you to carry us beyond the great river, that our souls may freely soar towards the abode of Outai khan [sic]. And you, perverse men, who trouble the repose of your fellow creatures, know that there is a judge for good and evil; the equitable Eerlik Nomoun khan. The lamas teach us the dogmas of the faith; our parents good manners: let us endeavour to profit by their lessons; for, wandering at random in an obscure valley, we cannot walk securely, or penetrate the thoughts of the man who live with us; but

---

197   See the text called *Burqan-u bodisadu-a terigüten qamuy delekei-yin ejed-ün takiyu takily-a*, passage translated by Elverskog 2006: 138; and Mergen Gegeen's prayer for *oboo* ritual "The Clear White Glass" (this chapter, note 182).

198   "To the Vajra-throne of India; to Potala Mountain; to Wu-t'ai-shan (*uutai-san ayula-dur*); to each individually (I) offer a full nine aspersions" (Serruys 1974b: 50, quoted by Elverskog 2011: 251). "To Mount Sumeru, Kailash [...] to the Central Vajra Throne, to the Five-Peaked Eastern Mountain, to the Southern Potala Mountain" (Serruys 1974b: 84).

if the intercession of the Dalai Lama is favourable to us, we shall escape
the snares of our enemies, and our secret faults will be pardoned by the
three Bogda [The Panchen Lama, the Dalai Lama and the Jebtsündamba
Khutugtu].[199]

This song describes Wutaishan as a paradise to be reborn in; the study of Mongol pilgrimages in the following chapters will highlight the strong connection
between Wutaishan and rebirth and fertility rituals and the attempts of Mongols to be buried in the Pure Land of Mañjuśrī.

Mañjuśrī of Wutaishan was even invoked by shamans of eastern Inner Mongolia. Walther Heissig in 1942 recorded an exorcist invocation of a female shaman of the Khüriye Banner, which includes many Buddhist influences:

I pray to masterful Mañjuśrī Buddha (*uran manshir burkhan*)
Of the five peaks of Wutaishan!
I offer to the Five Peaks!
Juniper sprigs burning I purify
Prostrating towards ten directions
The tortures by the demons
I offer to the Aryabalu Monastery! ... Great Yellow Temple at Mukden;
    Monastery of the Golden Throne ... I offer to the monasteries ...[200]

Wutaishan is therefore viewed by the Mongols as a semi-mythical pure land of
their cosmology (like the kingdom of Shambhala, the cult of which also developed in the late nineteenth and early twentieth century) and as Mañjuśrī's
earthly abode, where the *bodhisattva* may be accessible.

### The Cult of Wutaishan: A Late Phenomenon?

The study of the production of maps, books, praise poems, songs and prayers
on Wutaishan and of the cult of Mañjuśrī allows us to restore the Mongols'
agency in the development and promotion of the pilgrimage. Images and texts,
stories and history, tales and orthodox Buddhist accounts influenced themselves mutually, and local lore was reappropriated, distorted, mixed or ignored.
The cult of Mañjuśrī and Wutaishan deeply permeated Mongol culture (already
reputed for its osmotic characteristics), including oral literature, songs and
shaman's invocations.

---

199    Timkowski 1827, vol. 2: 298-299, text p. 298.
200    Beginning of the invocation, Heissig 1950: 171-172.

This written, oral, and visual production that increased and spread the reputation and fame of Wutaishan in Mongolia propagated a collective *imaginaire* of the sacred mountain. A part of this social imaginary was shared by Mongols and Tibetans because it originated in the writings of famous lamas and was repeated in guidebooks. But Mongols also developed their own lore, such as the origin of the White Old Man on Wutaishan and the story of the imperial seal, thereby positioning Wutaishan as a central place in their cosmology.

Present-day observations allow me to assume that the promotion of the Wutaishan pilgrimage was mostly done on the field, through oral accounts of pilgrims and monks, through incitation by *ombo lama*s from Wutaishan and through the advice and prescriptions given by learned lamas and reincarnations encouraging Mongols to undertake the pilgrimage to cure an illness, accumulate merit and so on. Returning pilgrims must have recounted miracles, visions and encounters with Mañjuśrī or have come back miraculously cured from their illness: the Wutaishan sacred site stood as the primary advertisement for itself. Witnessing that their own relatives had accomplished the pilgrimage, meeting pilgrims as they stopped in yurts along the way and crossing paths with devotees making prostrations from their home to Wutaishan may have encouraged Mongols to make the pilgrimage themselves at least once in their lives. The Mongols also heard about Wutaishan in prayers, songs and stories that circulated in the steppe. Nowadays, advertisements on the radio and in the streets of Ulaanbaatar encourage Mongols to give their elderly parents a pilgrimage tour to Wutaishan.[201]

While Mañjuśrī is clearly linked to Wutaishan in pre- and early-Qing Mongols' minds—and we can safely assume that the Manchu adoption of Mañjuśrī as emanating in the persona of the Manchu emperor was successful precisely because the *bodhisattva* was already popular among the Mongols—this does not necessarily entail that Wutaishan was a favorite pilgrimage destination for them at that time. In his article "Wutai Shan, Qing cosmopolitanism and the Mongols," Elverskog argues that, although the Mongols knew about Mañjuśrī's presence on Wutaishan from long ago, they started to go there on pilgrimage only from the late eighteenth century on, and the pilgrimage only became a mass phenomenon in the nineteenth century.[202] A main argument in favor of this thesis is the date of the Mongolian stone inscriptions that stand on Wutaishan. As the following chapter will show, a close study indeed confirms that 3 percent of the 340 stone inscriptions are dated before 1800 and 7 percent are dated between 1800 and 1879, whereas 82 percent are dated to the period 1880-

201    "Tenger Travel internet website."
202    Elverskog 2011.

1940 (Table 6). In addition, the diffusion of the 1846 map and its re-carving in 1874 would confirm that the second half of the nineteenth century was the period that saw the greatest number of pilgrims. Another argument in favor of this thesis is that seventeenth-century travellers to Wutaishan, such as Gu Yanwu and Gao Shiqi, do not mention Mongol pilgrims, while later Chinese travelers do. Elverskog also bases his argument on the late mentions of Wutaishan in Mongol literature: "No early Mongol history ever mentions Wutai Shan; however, in nineteenth-century sources mentions of the mountain are commonplace."[203] The name Wutaishan does not appear in prophetic or ritual texts before the nineteenth century.[204] Mentions of Wutaishan are generally limited to a few lines. For instance, Dharmatāla's nineteenth-century "Rosary of White Lotuses" (written in Tibetan) briefly describes the imperial construction of monasteries and bestowal of gifts from the reign of Shunzhi up to the nineteenth century, as well as the administration of the Wutaishan monasteries by a *jasag lama*, and he counts only ten Gélukpa monasteries.[205] Nevertheless, the mere absence of sources is rarely conclusive proof; thus, Elverskog's hypothesis about the starting point of these pilgrimages and the means of propagation that caused the pilgrimage boom remains open to discussion. Firstly, we must consider the possibility that the steles may not be completely representative of the Mongol pilgrims' donations (see Chapter 5). Secondly, most of the Mongolian literature that has survived is that written *after* the 1760s (especially ritual texts and folk literature), so there are gaps in our understanding. Ordinary pilgrims left few traces of their pilgrimages. Thirdly, we have to be mindful when examining the causal relationship between the pilgrimage and its literary and visual production. To do so, let us highlight some developments of the seventeenth and eighteenth century:

a.   as we will see in the following chapter, the stele recording the most important donation to Wutaishan monasteries made by a Mongol is dated 1658;

b.   the first Mongolian guidebooks were published in the mid and late seventeenth century, and the main one, in 1721;

c.   the Badgar Choiling Süme's map was painted between 1757 and 1822;

d.   in 1728, an edict by the Yongzheng emperor prohibited burial within monasteries because Mongol demand was too important (Chapter 5);

---

203    Elverskog 2011: 250.
204    Elverskog 2011: 251.
205    *Padma dkar-po'i phreng-ba*, Dharmatāla 1987 [1889], transl. Klafkowski 1987: 226, 417-420.

e.    the second half of the eighteenth century saw a significant increase of
      the population of Tibetan and Mongol monks living on Wutaishan,
      which is linked to the presence of eminent masters such as Rölpé Dorjé;
f.    as demonstrated by K. Schaeffer, Tibetan poetry about Wutaishan,
      including poetry by Mongol authors, especially flourished between the
      1760s and 1830.

In his article, Elverskog attributes the late Mongol interest in the Wutaishan
pilgrimage to its late oral and written promotion by revered Buddhist hierarchs
who resided there and wrote about their visions. This would be confirmed by
the dates of steles and by the diffusion of maps of Wutaishan after 1846. Yet can
we actually say with certainty what the cause-effect relationship was between
the greater popularity of the Wutaishan pilgrimage and the increase in its related writings and maps? In other words, were the revered Buddhist hierarchs
responsible, through their oral and written promotion, for the pilgrimage's success or, on the contrary, did they praise Wutaishan because their lay devotees
and relatives already had the custom of visiting the place?

   My conclusion is that, even though the first Mongolian guidebooks were certainly media through which knowledge of the mountain was spread in the
steppe and played a role in the widespread adoption of the pilgrimage by Mongols, the later guidebooks were more a consequence of the success of the pilgrimage—in the same way that Tibetan pilgrimage guides were usually written
after a pilgrimage had already become institutionalized. It is indeed likely that
written histories and religious poetry appeared sometime after popular practices had already fully acknowledged Wutaishan as a prominent pilgrimage site.
This is why Wutaishan may have already been an important pilgrimage place
for Mongols in the early Qing period—much early than previously thought.
The second half of the nineteenth century certainly reflects a peak in its popularity, but, I believe, Mongols already journeyed to Wutaishan in the seventeenth century. But, regardless of the reason behind it, how can we explain that
the historical peak of the Mongols' pilgrimages to Wutaishan corresponds to a
period when Mongol nobles and commoners were becoming impoverished by
economic stagnation, Chinese exploitation and colonization? This is one of the
questions that I raise in the following chapter.

# CHAPTER 5

# The Mongol Pilgrims: Sociological and Economic Aspects

In the late Qing period, Mongol pilgrims became the main patrons of Wutai-shan's monasteries, and in the Guangxu era (1875-1909) their financial support almost completely replaced the declining imperial patronage. Foreign visitors, like Gilmour and Edkins in 1872 and Pokotilov in 1889, counted a large majority of Mongol pilgrims and hardly mentioned Chinese pilgrims.[1] The crowds of Mongol devotees were particularly noticeable among the other visitors because of the sumptuous female headdresses and ornaments (especially those of Khalkha women: Fig. 23), as well as their colorful garments, ostensible devotion and generous donations:

> The heads of many of the Mongolian women were weighed down with heavy silver ornaments in which precious stones were set.... . Generally speaking, the Mongols could be distinguished by their clothes of orange, red, purple and yellow, while the sober Chinese appear in simple silks and cottons of blue and white.[2]
> [Mongol women wore] massive headgear of silver ornaments threaded on to one or two ribbons, made of chased silver, like those worn by Mongolians and Tibetans, with medicines or images on their breasts.[3]
> The Mongol women are very kind to strangers, less selfish than the Chinese, part readily with milk and cheese ... [4] You meet them in the bazaar trafficking with the bazaar-keepers, going the round of the temples to worship, pushing the praying wheels, or mounted on camels on their way home.[5]
> [There were] pilgrim women with their hair braids hanging down, and with their silver and coral head and ear ornaments, all of a peculiar Mongol and Tibetan kind. The women visitors from Mongolia were in their

---

1  Edkins 1893 [1878]; Gilmour 1970 [1883]; Pokotilov 1935 [1893]: 66, 70, 79. Similarly, Hargett (2006: 182) noticed the continuous decline of the number of Chinese pilgrims to Emeishan after the Tongzhi reign (1862-1874).
2  Blofeld 1938: 30, 32.
3  Mannerheim 1969 [1940]: 688.
4  Edkins 1893 [1878]: 136.
5  Edkins 1893 [1878]: 236, 245.

FIGURE 23
*Mongolian pilgrims.*
© BLOFELD 1959: BETWEEN
P. 97-98.

better-looking leather coats and furs and in their neater-looking leather
boots; they were more attractive than the rustic looking Mongolian
nomad.[6]

Fascinated by the appearance of the humble and exhausted Mongol pilgrims,
R.W. Swallow writes in 1903:

> To me, however, the most interesting and fascinating thing about the
> place was the people. Not the greedy, apathetic, treacherous-looking
> priests who swarmed round the confiding pilgrims like wolves around a
> carcass, but the weird half-witted, half-ragged, mumbling, stumbling
> fanatic, who went round and round, and when not engaged thus, counting
> his beads and calling upon Buddha. Some of them had been weeks and
> even months, with no occupation save that of fulfilling a vow or earning
> merit for the next world. Madmen many of them were, but there
> was a terrible earnestness about them, and this contrasted with the

---

6   Fischer 1923: 92.

ill-concealed hypocrisy of the professional worshippers, whose faces filled one with distrust.[7]

These subjective descriptions, as well as photographs taken by Western and Japanese travelers, paint us a picture of an amorphous crowd, a colorful multitude and also, sometimes, a bunch of 'fanatics'—a term often used by Westerners to describe Mongol pilgrims.[8] Yet the Mongol devotees certainly did not form such a homogeneous group, and we can observe a great variety of pilgrims and pilgrimages. The close study of steles, complemented by travel records, allows us to establish a typology of pilgrims according to their identity (gender, social status, wealth and place of origin), their motivations (both spiritual and mundane) and their mode of travel. It also brings to the fore the astonishing amount of silver money and gifts offered to the Wutaishan monasteries, which helped the local economy flourish.

However, the nineteenth century was a period of economic stagnation, a fact that raises a few questions. How could impoverished herders go on pilgrimage, spending months on the road, despite their herds needing constant care, and offering money, horses and sheep and gifts to the monasteries on Wutaishan? Did nobles visit Wutaishan to leave their names and status on steles because they were living at a time when the nobility was in crisis? Did Wutaishan only attract, on the one hand, noblemen and wealthy commoners and lamas who had enough money and leisure time and, on the other hand, impoverished Mongols who had lost their means of subsistence and were thus fleeing troubles and conflicts, poverty and debts? After examining who the Mongol pilgrims were, this chapter will conclude by showing another dimension of Wutaishan: the mountain as a burial place for Mongol pastoralists. This appears to be in contradiction with their tradition of burying their dead in their homeland to protect it and claim the surrounding pastures.

### A Major Source on the Pilgrimage: The Stone Inscriptions

This chapter, which raises social and economic questions, takes as its main source the corpus of Mongolian stone inscriptions erected within the Wutaishan monasteries, records that inform us about the status of donors and the amounts donated (Table 5). The more than 340 inscriptions carved to commemorate Mongols' offerings and vows are invaluable documents on Mongol

---

7   Swallow 1903: 179.
8   For instance, Huc 1928 [1924]: 93-94.

society and on Wutaishan's economy (Appendix 2). They record practical information on the pilgrims themselves, on the amount, nature and purpose of their
donation, on the benefits expected from the donation and on the date of erection. As pointed out by Susan Naquin regarding the steles of a large Buddhist
monastery west of Beijing, "The texts emphasized the group's sincere devotion,
their offerings, and, through the lists of names, their numbers. Even for those
who could not read, the proliferation of such steles with their many names,
some large and impressive, others simple and plain, was ample testimony to the
drawing power of the temple."[9] Dorothy C. Wong adds about Chinese steles:

> In their most fundamental usage, stone steles are emblems of identity
> that embody the religious, social, cultural, and territorial identity of their
> users, who include those honored with steles, the patrons of steles, and
> the steles' audience or viewers. Through steles, these users articulated
> their aspirations, projected their ideals, and constructed notions of iden-
> tity in a public manner.[10]

For social historians, monasteries' steles are an inestimable source on monastic
history and on the history of religious communities.[11]

The Mongolian steles not only record donations from the wealthiest pilgrims
but also from groups of ordinary pilgrims. But are they representative of the
Mongol pilgrims? To answer that question we have to firstly take into consideration that many of them have disappeared or became illegible because of natural degradation, vandalism or re-use (re-carving). Secondly, the minimum total
donation required to carve a stele appears to have been fifty taels of silver[12]—or
its equivalent in cattle or sheep—for the late Qing period; groups of pilgrims
who offered less received paper certificates, and their names were not recorded
on steles (Fig. 2). Secondly, it is possible that before the mid-nineteenth century
donors were only given paper certificates for their offerings and that the practice of carving stone inscriptions in Mongolian only became fashionable after
1880, which would explain why eighty-two percent of the Mongolian steles
were erected between 1880 and 1935 (Table 6). Some institutions, such as Shifangtang, may have had a carver in residence (which would explain the high

---

9       Naquin 1998: 197.
10      Wong 2004: 9.
11      On the use of stone inscriptions in the study of Chinese pilgrimages: Naquin 1992 (corpus
        of 24 steles on Miaofengshan, dated 1689-1939, with seven thousand names); Lagerway
        1992 (corpus of 80 steles of Wudangshan).
12      For the value of the tael of silver in the late Qing period, see below.

TABLE 5    *Number and date of inscriptions, and origin of donors per monastery*

| Monastery | Number of inscriptions | Dates of the inscriptions | Origin of the donors |
|---|---|---|---|
| Shifangtang | 182 | 1862 to 1933 (mostly 1880-1933) | Majority from Shili-yin Gool League and the Chakhar banners |
| Tayuansi | 61 | 1853 to 1934 | Inner, Outer, Western Mongolia |
| Luohousi | 47 | 1658 to 1935 | Majority from Sünid Right and Chakhar banners |
| Cifusi | 9 | 1920 to 1940 | Gorlos, Khölön Buir, Üjümüchin |
| Yuanzhaosi | 7 | 1898 to 1890 | Khalkha Setsen Khan, Darigangga, Bogda-yin Shabi |
| Zhenhaisi | 5 | 1829 to 1866 | Khalkha Tüshiyetü Khan and Setsen Khan, Abaga, Ongniud |
| Xiantongsi | 5 | 1918 to 1939 | Jasagtu Khan, Abaga, Abaganar |
| Sanquansi | 4 | | *Illegible* |
| Dailuoding | 2 | 1691, 1874 | *Illegible* |
| Qifosi | 2 | 1934, ? | Khölön Buir, *illegible?* |
| Nanshansi | 2 | 1884, 1897 | |
| Fomudong | 2 | - | *Illegible* |
| Pusading | 1 | 1936 | Juu Uda |
| Lower Shancaidong | 1 | - | Khalkha, Ongniud |
| Upper Shancaidong | 1 | - | Üjümüchin |
| Guanyindong | 1 | - | Shili-yin Gool |
| Shouningsi | 2 | 1774 | various parts of Inner Mongolia, Beijing |
| Eastern Terrace | 1 | 1908 | *disappeared* |
| Southern Terrace | 1 | Guangxu | *disappeared* |
| Northern Terrace | 1 | Before 1912 | *disappeared* |
| Western Terrace | 1 | Before 1912 | *Illegible* |
| Central terrace | 1 | Before 1912 | *Illegible* |
| Shuxiangsi | 1 | 1665 | *Illegible* |
| Bishansi | 1 | Guangxu? | *Illegible* |
| Baohuasi | 1 | 1717 | *Illegible* |
| *Stūpa* near Zhenhaisi | 1 | - | |
| Total | 343 | Period: 1658-1940 | |

number of steles in this monastery), while other monasteries may have continued to give paper certificates for donations. Lastly, some steles may also have
been carved after a subscription organized by *ombo lamas* who had collected
donations in Mongolia, which means that the donors did not personally journey to Wutaishan (Online Appendix F). Whatever the case may be, these inscriptions remain our most complete and reliable source for the pilgrimage, at
least from the Guangxu era to the Republican period.

### Who were the Mongol Pilgrims?

#### *Mongol Society in the Nineteenth and Twentieth Centuries*
Firstly, a short presentation of nineteenth- and early twentieth-century Mongol
society will help us understand the degree of social stratification and gender
division of the pilgrims and situate Mongol patronage of Wutaishan in the
larger context of Mongol society, economics and politics. Specialists of the
Qing, such as Evelyn Rawski and Pamela Crossley, generally argue that the modern concepts of 'nation,' 'borders' and 'ethnicities' could not apply to the Qing
empire; they prefer to speak of 'constituencies' that changed over space and
time.[13] The common denominator between a Sinicized Mongol bannerman, a
Tümed farmer and a Khalkha lama may a priori not be obvious; besides, pre-
modern identity was mostly based on 'limited locality.' However, the Mongols
did form a well-defined cultural entity that shared a common language and
culture, a rich oral literature, a pastoral way of living with yurt-dwelling (for
most people), a common cosmology and religion—Tibetan Buddhism (for the
vast majority)—and a belief in a supra-natural world populated with deities of
mountains and rivers. In the course of the nineteenth century, a distinct Mongol identity, including not solely the hereditary aristocracy but also commoners, began to emerge. As a result of various forces weakening the boundaries
between aristocrats and commoners, the Mongols slowly came to perceive
themselves as one nation cemented by the heritage of Chinggis Khan.[14]

---

13    "The Qing political model was not the nation-state; the goal of the government was not to
      create one national identity, but to permit diverse cultures to coexist within the loose
      framework of a personalistic empire. Ethnicity in its modern sense did not exist, nor did
      the state seek to create it." However, the fact that the Qing did not conceive its diverse
      constituencies in modern day ethnic terms "does not mean that the Qing rulers did not
      have concepts concerning their own identities and the identities of other peoples"
      (Rawski 1998: 5). See also Atwood 2000; Elverskog 2006.
14    Munkh-Erdene 2006; Elverskog 2006: 155-162.

Yet, despite sharing a common culture and values, Qing Mongol society was highly stratified. A sharp divide existed between, on the one hand, the two aristocracies—the lay hereditary and ecclesiastical—who controlled political leadership (themselves being divided into a multiplicity of ranks and titles), and the commoners and slaves on the other.[15] As for the aristocracy, the Khalkha and Inner Mongol nobles (*taiji*) claimed to be descendants of Chinggis Khan or blood relatives of the Borjigid clan. Wealthy nobles owned thousands of head of cattle and sheep, as well as servants to care for them, and occupied the best pasturelands. They were distinguished by their dress and symbols of rank and were approached with special honorific terms of address. The aristocracy was itself not a homogeneous group. The highest nobility were bound to the Manchu royal house by a system of hierarchical ranks and titles, salaries, rewards and marriage alliances,[16] while minor noblemen (the *petite noblesse*, the younger sons of noble families who did not inherit titles) lived no differently from commoners. Nobles could become lamas by renouncing their status and upon approval from the emperor.

The commoners (*arad*)—otherwise known as 'black people' (*kharachuud*)—'belonged' to the estate of a banner ruler-prince (*jasag*), to a monastery or to a reincarnated lama, to which/whom they paid taxes and corvées. Those 'belonging' to the estate of a ruler-prince were called *albatus* ('one subject to requisitions'),[17] and those attached to a monastery or to a reincarnated lama were called *shabis* (ecclesiastical serfs). Although the *shabis* were exempt from taxation, they had to contribute towards the expenses of the monasteries (such as the funeral of a reincarnation). At the bottom of the social ladder were the domestic servants and the slaves (prisoners of war, etc.); devoid of their own herds, they were obliged to work for their masters as herders, servants or agricultural laborers and even to join them in battle.

In the nineteenth century, social differentiation was based more on wealth than on nobility. The special status of the minor nobility was eroded by their being made liable to pay taxes, like any commoner. Sometimes they were worse off than average commoners and were forced to work for their own subjects for a wage. After 1850, the banner administration was partly staffed with

---

15    Vreeland 1962 [1957]; Natsagdorj 1963; Sanjdorj, 1980 [1963]; Bawden 1989 [1968]: Chapters 3 and 4; Atwood 2004: 507-509; Elverskog 2006; Elverskog 2011.

16    One who married an imperial princess was called an 'imperial son-in-law' (*efü*).

17    Some of them were *khamjilgas* (nobles' personal retainers); the others were commoners belonging to a *sumu* (administrative unit below the banner level). The *khamjilgas* were associated with noble families in a special relationship characterized by a set of reciprocal rights and obligations; they had to help the noble meet his debts, and the noble had to pay for their funeral services, etc. (Vreeland 1962 [1957]).

commoners. Nobles could officially buy high ranks in exchange for large amounts of silver. In addition, the exogamic rule forced the Chinggisid nobles to take wives and to marry off their daughters among commoners (or among the Manchu aristocracy).

Counterbalancing the decline of the nobility, the Buddhist institutions occupied a position of wealth and power. The monasteries played a pivotal role in local society: they were not only spiritual centers but also centers of education, of arts and handicrafts, and of medicine.[18] They acted as trading companies and banks, lending out money, renting out farmland and coalmines, and running caravans. Thirty to fifty percent of the male Mongol population spent part of their time in monasteries:[19] the great majority were novices (they did not pass the full ordination of *gelöng*), lived as herders and came to their monastery for collective celebrations only.[20] These 'steppe lamas' performed rituals and cast horoscopes for lay Mongols. At the top of the hierarchy were learned clerics who had passed monastic degrees, clerical administrators and reincarnated lamas supported by their ecclesiastical serfs. Registered monks were exempt from taxes, military conscription and other duties. Of the 3,000 monasteries of Inner and Outer Mongolia, about 150 (on average one per banner) were large institutions gathering more than five hundred monks and novices, headed by high reincarnations and training their best clerics in their academic colleges; the others were small to medium-sized temples and monasteries. Large monasteries organized big annual festivals, which were opportunities for the entire population of a banner to meet and trade.

For an example of the increasing importance of wealth in Mongol society, let us take the example of the banner of Dalai Choinkhor Chin Wang Tserensodnom of Sain Noyan Khan Aimag, which during the late Qing dynasty counted 25,000 inhabitants, of whom 7,000 were lamas and 600 were noblemen. The wealthiest families owned more than 1,000 sheep, 300 to 500 horses, over 100 oxen and 50 to 60 camels and had servants working for them.[21] A family of average wealth generally owned 200 to 300 sheep, 20 cows and 3 or 4 horses (100 sheep was considered the minimum for a family to survive independently).[22] Various exchanges of goods and services (such as shearing sheep, making felt

---

18    For the organization and economy of the monasteries: Miller 1959; Vreeland 1962 [1957]:
      20 sq.
19    In 1921, the number of lamas was estimated at 113,000 in Khalkha Mongolia.
20    It is usually estimated that only a third of the Mongol lama population in general observed
      the vow of celibacy.
21    Shirendev 1997: 5-6.
22    Vreeland 1962 [1957]: 31. The relative importance of various animals varies from region to
      region.

and rope) existed between families or camps, and there was a variety of ways in which wealthy and poor families were dependent on each other. Management of herds, routes of nomadization and property rights on winter pastures were ruled by custom, and arguments were settled by the banner's authorities.[23] The gender division of labor was also codified. Women worked hard and had to run the family by themselves when the men were at war or requisitioned for cor-vées. [24] Only senior women appear to have been almost on an equal footing with their husbands. Agriculture was developed near the Chinese border in southern and eastern Inner Mongolia, and some herders practiced other activi-ties in addition to herding, such as metallurgy, carpentry, tannery and leather work, handicraft, trade and hunting. Chinese artisans, peddlers, carpenters, bricklayers and merchants crossed or settled in Mongolia in the nineteenth century, and the importation of cheap Chinese and Russian products caused a decline in the local craft industries. Money as a medium of exchange grew in importance in the nineteenth century, when Mongolia progressively entered into a market economy.

In the mid-nineteenth century, a serious economic depression ravaged Mon-golia. A great part of its wealth was drained off into China, and the remainder was spent wastefully inside the country. Mongol princes and dukes contracted huge debts with Shanxi merchants to buy luxury goods and build palaces in the steppe,[25] and the extravagance of the aristocracy led to the virtual enslave-ment of the population to Chinese usury. To redeem their debts, the nobles raised new taxes and sold arable lands to Chinese farmers, incurring the resent-ment of their Mongol subjects. The commoners, themselves indebted to Chi-nese merchants, were overburdened by taxation:[26] besides regular government taxes,[27] special levies collected at irregular intervals to meet extraordinary needs were raised to pay off princes' personal debts to Chinese merchants, to pay for the cost of their travels to Beijing and their pilgrimages to Urga (and to Wutaishan) and to sponsor public rituals, enthronement of reincarnations, weddings and funerals.

---

23    On pasture rights: Bawden 1989 [1968]: 90-91.
24    Mongols were recruited as soldiers to suppress Qing-dynasty popular uprisings such as those of the Taiping (1851-1864), the Nian (1853-1868), the Miao, the Chinese-speaking Muslims in Yunnan (1855) and the Dungans in northwest China (1862-1877).
25    Avery 2003; Maiskii 2001 [1921].
26    On taxation: Bawden 1989 [1968]: 148-152.
27    The mobilization of Mongol soldiers and animals during conflicts (including the Opium Wars), the cost of maintenance of watch posts and relay stations, the herding of imperial and army herds and so on were heavy burdens on the Mongol economy.

By the mid-nineteenth century, the majority of the Khalkha banners had completely given up hope of paying off their debts to the Chinese traders. Discontentment, protest and revolt grew among commoners. Petitions of grievances kept in the Ulaanbaatar archives inform us of such protests against greedy Chinese merchants and provide insight into the exploitation by Manchus and Chinese officials and by Mongols' own secular and ecclesiastical feudal lords.[28] Impoverished herders moved away from their lord to escape misery; crime developed, and paupers and beggars settled around monasteries and around the few towns. Some popular leaders took up arms, were executed or banished. Poor lamas had to work and sometimes had no other choice than to desert the monastery to avoid starvation. What's more, in the 1920s, venereal diseases affected a large part of the population.

From the late nineteenth century onwards, Inner Mongolia became ever more exposed to Chinese immigration: with the Chinese economic depression hitting Mongolia as well, homeless Chinese migrated to Mongolia and opened more land to cultivation, an influx that had a negative impact on the pastoral economy.[29] Nationalist, anti-Manchu and anti-Chinese movements arose, along with anti-clerical protests against the wealth and moral decay of the Buddhist institution, which at that stage possessed up to fifty percent of the banners' herds.[30] The growing anti-Manchu and anti-Chinese sentiment manifested itself in desertions, street riots and mobs against the Chinese communities. But even the more organized protests did not aim to usurp authority or change the system, and the nobility always manifested an unconditional loyalty towards the Manchu imperial house.[31]

The political events between 1911 and the 1930s are well documented: the collapse of the Qing dynasty, the autonomous movements, the fight for independence, the struggles between warlords, nationalists and communists, later strife with the Japanese and Russians, and the great religious repressions in the late 1930s in the People's Republic of Mongolia. Biographies of twentieth-century lamas, politicians and herders from Mongolia and Inner Mongolia reveal the bitterness and hardship of their lives. In spite of attempts at modernization encouraged by some enlightened princes, especially in the fields of education

---

28  See the petitions translated by Raṣidondug and Veit 1975.

29  It is estimated that the Chinese population in Inner Mongolia increased from 1 million in 1800 to 1.5 million in 1911, while the Mongol population decreased from 1.030 to 0.828 million during the same period. In 1918 Khalkha Mongolia, there were 611,000 Mongols, 100,000 Chinese and 5,000 Russians.

30  On the discontent within the Buddhist institution: Bawden 1989 [1968]: 170-176.

31  Elverskog 2006.

and health, the lives of ordinary people hardly changed from the nineteenth century to the 1920s.

### The Social Origin, Status and Gender of the Pilgrims

Thousands of names are recorded in the stone inscriptions; many are preceded by a rank, title, function, monastic degree or relationship within a family, or they combine several of these (such as 'son-monk,' or 'lama-uncle') (Online Appendix A1: Table A). I have made a distinction between the 'main donor' whose name is sometimes repeated in the text of the stele, and the other names. Some inscriptions bear only one name, whereas others have up to thirty (stele numbered SF69, dated 1897: see Online Appendix 2), but the average group size is seven or eight names. Another source, the many passports (*jam yabukhu temdeg*) to Wutaishan kept in the Inner Mongol archives, confirms that the majority of pilgrims came in groups mixing men and women, lamas and laypersons. For instance, a passport issued by the ruler prince of the Alashan Banner in 1836 gives eight people the authorization to cross the border, make a pilgrimage to Wutaishan and go back to their banner: five men (lamas and commoners) and three 'women and children'—along with eleven camels to carry people and belongings.[32]

About 78 percent of all donors (and 61 percent of the main donors) listed in the steles belong to the laity. The main patron is generally the head of a household, occasionally a woman (in seven cases only). He/she is followed by members of his/her family (of whom several are monks), usually of a lesser rank, and/or by groups of monks or laypersons. Most of the names indicate degrees of kinship with the main donor.[33] For instance, "the great supreme alms-master Sonombaljur, [his] wife Shirindaua, son Gombojab, daughter Chimedpil..." (LH12, 1908). Most of the inscriptions are multigenerational.

Forty-two percent of the main lay donors (and 11 percent of all the names of lay donors) were nobles with or without a civil or military rank. The status and/or rank of the main patron is specified before his/her personal name: 5 percent of the main lay donors have a rank in the Manchu imperial hierarchy;[34] 25

---

32    Digitalized archives of Alashan Banner, n° 101-05-0098-011-0016-01.

33    For instance: *echige* (father), *ekhe* (mother), *akha* (elder brother), *düü* (younger brother), *khüvüün* (son), *ekhener* (wife), *egechi* (elder sister), *kheükhen* (girl, young lady), *achi* (grandson), *emege ekhe* (grand-mother), *abaga* (paternal uncle), *beri* (daughter-in-law), *jee* (child of one's daughter or sister), *ergümel* (adopted child).

34    Such as *khoshoi chin wang* (*heshuo qinwang* 和碩親王, imperial prince of the first rank), *giyün wang* (*junwang* 郡王, imperial prince of the second rank), *beile* (prince of the third rank), *beise* (prince of the second rank), *güng* (duke or count).

percent have a civil or military function in the banner hierarchy;[35] 5 percent have a noble appellation;[36] the rest are called *arad* (commoners)[37] or *shabi* (ecclesiastical serfs).[38] The other names without the above ranks and titles, which form the great majority of recorded names, probably also designate commoners. The steles not only aim at informing visitors of the generosity and merit achieved by the donors but also record and expose to everybody their rank and distinction in the administration, allowing noblemen to reassert their status and legitimate their rule. The erection of steles by noblemen may in fact be primarily an issue of social status dynamics in the context of the waning power of the Chinggisid nobility. Sometimes the text specifies that the main donor was elevated to an upper rank thanks to his military achievements and rewarded by imperial order (SN1, ca. 1664). For instance, "the noble of second rank who received the *jingse* of fourth rank by decree,[39] named Tügji, of the camel herds of the Darigangga Right Wing" (LH11, 1906).[40] Some nobles left their names on several steles, indicating that they made the pilgrimage several times. Prince Magsurjab of the Sünid Left Banner appears as the main donor on nine inscriptions with his wives, brother, sons, etc.[41] Before 1908, he bears the title *jasag törö-yin giyün wang*; later he is named *jakhirkhu wang ye* and finally *khoshoi chin wang*.[42] The stele PSD1 (1936) gives a recapitulation of the names, ranks, number of pilgrimages and donations of eleven generations of princes of

---

35    *Jasag* (head of a banner: *jasag wang, jasag beise, jasag beile, jasag güng*), *tusalagchi* (deputy of the *jasag*), *jakhirugchi janggi* (superintendent, warrant officer of a *jasag*), *meiren-ü janggi* (deputy lieutenant of a banner), *jalan-u janggi* (commander of a regiment), *jangjun* (general), *sumun-u janggi* (commander of a *sumu*), *boshgo* (sergeant), *daruga* (chief), *khiya* (sergeant), *bichigechi* (clerc, scribe, secretary). Each banner office had two *tusalagchi*s (who were noblemen), one *jakhirugchi* (a commoner) and two *meiren*s (also commoners). Many of these titles have a Chinese or Manchu origin: see Brunnert and Hagelstrom 2007 [1912]; Miller 1959; Natsagdorj 1963; Jagchid and Bawden 1970.

36    *Noyan* (lord, prince, son of a prince), *taiji* (minor nobleman), *khatun* (princess, wife of a high dignitary), *abagai* (prince's wife, lady); *efü* (imperial son-in-law).

37    For example, Linchinjab [Rinchinjab], commoner of the Bargu District n° 7 of the Chakhar Plain Red Banner (LH12, 1894: *caqar siluyun ulayan qosiyun-u baryu doluduyar sumun-u arad lincinjab*).

38    I have assumed that *shabi* here designates the subject of a clerical estate, but it can also mean a 'religious disciple.'

39    Honorific button on imperial dignitaries' hats, made of a precious stone indicating rank.

40    See also SF13, 1881; LH11, 1906; LH13, 1906; SCD1, 1907; LH24, 1922.

41    In 1892 (SF47), 1898 (SF69), 1907 (SF94), 1908 (3 steles: SF97, SF98, SF99), 1910 (2 steles: SF104, SF105) and 1918 (SF115).

42    He is probably the same as the 'prince in leisure' Magsurjab, supporter of Prince De's Autonomy Movement, mentioned in Demchugdongrub's biography (Jagchid 1999: 62).

the Abaga Banner, who produced merit for 281 years without interruption. It highlights the title *khoshoi chin wang* granted to the fourth prince and explains that the actual donor and his son's pilgrimages re-enact the pilgrimages of their ancestors and entail an extraordinary accumulation of merit for their successors.

If we only take into account the lay donors whose gender is explicit, female donors represent more than one half of the total: 249 names are female lay donors, including 47 princesses (*khatun*), plus 43 female devotees (*chibagantsa*).[43] Of the 576 lay donors of whom we have only the name, it is often difficult to know if they are men or women. Some travelers noted that Mongol female pilgrims were generally more numerous than men, but they were also more visible because of their spectacular headdresses.[44]

The clergy, from novices to abbots and reincarnations, represents 22 percent of all the donors, but more than 39 percent of the main donors: in fact, lamas often led groups of lay donors.[45] Travelers' accounts confirm that many of the pilgrims were lamas.[46] R.W. Swallow writes in 1903:

> We saw many Mongols and some Thibetans, while others came from Turkestan and North Manchuria, and the one thing that seemed scarce was queues, for the numerous priests had all shaven heads.[47]

Edkins stressed in 1893 the difficulty of counting the monks on Wutaishan: he heard from a lama from Kalgan that there were one to two thousand (resident and pilgrim) lamas on Wutaishan, while others thought there were not more than seven hundred.[48]

---

43  *Chibagantsa*s or *shibagantsa*s are female devotees who shaved their hair and took certain vows; however, they continued to live a secular life and cannot be included among the clergy.

44  Ekvall and Downs (1987: 29) estimated that about two thirds of the pilgrims in Tibetan pilgrimages were women (traveling along with men).

45  Gregory Schopen showed from several thousand Theravada and Mahāyāna Indian donative inscriptions dated from the second to the first centuries BCE on the railings surrounding *stūpa*s, as well as in Buddhist cave temples, that between 40 to 70% of Buddhist donors were monks and nuns: these were here not pursuing 'higher' Buddhist goals, such as liberation from the cycle of reincarnations, but were involved in donative, merit-making activities connected with the *stūpa* cult, and especially the transfer of merits towards one's deceased relatives (Schopen 1997, esp. "Two problems in the history of Indian Buddhism," 23-55).

46  Edkins 1893 [1878]: 214, 225, 236.

47  Swallow 1903: 179.

48  Edkins 1893 [1878]: 236.

Statistics are difficult to procure on account of the floating character of the population. Lamas are fond of wandering, and, if of frugal habits, can easily obtain a hospitable reception in temples. They flock in crowds to Woo-tai, and prostrate themselves at the various shrines with great apparent fervour.[49]

The entire range of clergy members is represented among the pilgrims. The highest clerics are referred to by their appellations and titles;[50] others were ranked according to the vows they took,[51] their Buddhist degrees,[52] or their functions in a monastery.[53] The majority of monks mentioned as donors are referred to as *gelöng* or *khuwarag*.

Occasionally the home monastery of a community is mentioned, such as Mandultu Süme of the Chakhar Plain White Banner (SF35, 1888), Chagan Diyanchi-yin Kheid of the Monggoljin (TY28, 1907) and Gürüm-yin Süme of the Sünid Left Banner (TY49, 1923). However, the inscriptions do not reflect any organization comparable with Chinese pilgrimage associations (in pilgrimages such as that of Miaofengshan 妙峰山, near Beijing, these associations played a leading role in the general organization of the pilgrimage, either acting as travel agents and tour directors, helping maintain or repair specific halls of the temple).[54]

Since the great majority of so-called 'monks' were actually novices who made a living from their herds, the gap between a layperson and a monk in

---

49    Edkins 1893 [1878]: 236.

50    *Khutugtu* (highest title of a reincarnation granted by the Manchu court), *khubilgan* (general term for any reincarnated lama; title for minor reincarnations), *gegeen* (common designation for a reincarnation, corresponding to Tibetan *rinpoché*), *shaburung* (reincarnation of smaller monasteries, not recognized by the imperial court), *bagshi* (master, lama teacher), *tsorji* (curate), *lama* (lama, master), *toin* (monk), *güüsi* (high dignitary, translator), *diyanchi* (lama hermit), and *shabi* (disciple). *Toin* initially designated lamas of noble descent.

51    *Bandi* (novice), *getsül* or *gezül* (monk who received the preliminary ordination), *gelöng* (fully ordained monk), *khuwarag* (monk).

52    *Geshi* or *gebshi* (doctor), *rabjamba, doramba, laramba* (the three degrees in doctrinal studies), *juudba* (degree in esoteric studies).

53    *Khanbu* (abbot), *jasag lama* (abbot), *da lama* (chief lama), *demchi* (business manager), *shangjodba* (lama treasurer); *donir* (clerk, secretary), *gebkhüi* or *geskhüi* (master of discipline, proctor of a temple), *nirba* (cashier, storekeeper).

54    On these associations (temple associations or associations created specifically to organize a pilgrimage): Lagerway 1992: 304, 312; Naquin 1992: 345 sq.; Hargett 2006: 181. Chinese pilgrims visiting a mountain in such groups sometimes numbered as many as two hundred.

Mongolia is somehow reduced. The ordinary lama-pilgrims were included in the larger category of the *badarchi lamas* (traveling alms-collecting lamas): the majority of these were novices and were relatively free to travel and undertake journeys to other monasteries.[55] Going from tent to tent, the *badarchi lamas* played a fundamental role in propagating stories and became well-known figures of Mongol folklore. They were also the object of mockery, and many stories circulated about ignorant or tricky mendicant lamas who managed to obtain free meals and offerings.[56] *Badarchi lamas* used to go to Wutaishan, Kumbum, Lhasa and as far as India and Ladakh. Some brought back with them valuable scriptures and Buddhist relics. In the early twentieth century, many were Tantric practitioners who followed Nyingmapa teachings.

Sources on pilgrims are occasionally found in the national, provincial and local archives of Mongolia and Inner Mongolia. Mongol scholar Altanzayaa, who in the Ulaanbaatar archives found names of Mongols who journeyed to Wutaishan, such as reincarnated lama Lubsangdanjab from 'Skhakhajaal-un Kheid' of Setsen Chin Wang Banner in Sain Noyan Khan Aimag, the *jasag-un törö-yin giyün wang* Dorjijab of Tüshiyetü Khan Aimag (in 1801) or the Fourth Jebtsündamba Khutugtu (in 1814), concludes that the Khalkha pilgrims to Wutaishan were mostly nobles and high-ranking lamas.[57] However, the steles, the paper certificates and travelers' accounts show otherwise: commoners in fact formed the great majority of pilgrims.

### The Geographical Origin of the Donors Who Left Their Names on Stone Inscriptions

The stone inscriptions always mention the geographical origin—league (*chuulgan* and *aimag*), banner (*khoshuu*), *sumu* ('arrow,' subdivision of a banner)—of the donors, which allows us to identify the catchment area of Wutaishan. The majority came from Inner Mongolia; others came from central Outer Mongolia, inner China,[58] eastern Turkestan (Torguts of Xinjiang) and Amdo (Table 5, Online Appendix A1: Table E). Other groups, such as the Kalmyks of the Volga and the Buryats,[59] did not leave any inscriptions at all. Yet Rockhill in 1887 met la-

---

55   Pozdneev 1978 [1887]: 242.
56   See stories about *badarchi lamas* on pilgrimage to Lhasa or Wutaishan in Stuart, ed. 1995: 33-35; Gochoo 1970 [1963].
57   Altanzayaa 2000: 146.
58   The Mongols of Inner China include the Mongols of the Eight Manchu Banners as well as the Mongols living in China since the Ming dynasty.
59   Buryat pilgrimages to Wutaishan are mentioned by Mannerheim 1969 [1940]: 690. As for the Kalmyks, they generally preferred to go on pilgrimages to Lhasa or Urga (Bormanshinov 1998).

mas from Urga, Amdo and the Amur region coming to worship Mañjuśrī on Wutaishan.[60] These Mongols were perhaps less familiar with the practice of recording donations on stone or did not offer significant contributions. A certificate of donation to Guangzongsi and a prayer to Wutaishan kept in the National Library of Tuva attest that even Tuvans (a Turkic people that practiced Tibetan Buddhism) undertook the pilgrimage.[61]

The main Mongol group represented in the steles are the Sünids (144 inscriptions, i.e., 42 percent of all the inscriptions), the Chakhar banners (28 inscriptions), the Bargu banners (17 inscriptions) and the Darigangga (16 inscriptions). Pilgrims from the four *aimags* of Khalkha Mongolia commissioned 43 inscriptions (14 percent of the total) (Map 6 below and Online Appendix A1: Table E). Luohousi and Shifangtang in particular attracted pilgrims from central Inner Mongolia: the majority of Luohousi's donors come from the same geographical area—the Sünid Right (27 percent) and Chakhar banners (19 percent) and a minority from the Darigangga pastures, Bargu, other banners of Inner Mongolia, as well as Khalkhas and Dörbeds. Shifangtang's donors are even more homogeneous, with 86 percent of them coming from the Shili-yin Gool League and the Chakhar and Darigangga banners—56 percent belonging to the Left Sünid Banner alone—and a minority from the Bargu banners and the Khalkha *aimags*. On the contrary, the steles of Tayuansi show much more diverse origins: more than a third (39 percent) of the pilgrims comes from Khalkha Mongolia, 29 percent come from Shili-yin Gool, and almost a tenth are Western Mongols from Eastern Turkestan (Xinjiang), that is, Torguts from Khobog Sairi and Dörbeds. Western Mongols especially came in the years 1910-1911; but already in 1844 Father Huc mentioned Torgut Mongols performing journeys "occupying a whole year" and "with immense difficulty."[62] To sum up, in the inscriptions, 49 percent of all Mongol donors were from Shili-yin Gool, 14 percent were from Khalkha Mongolia, and 8 percent were from the Chakhar banners.

These figures raise some questions. Why were the Sünid, Chakhar, Üjümüchin and Darigangga people more numerous than other groups? It may be because they came to Wutaishan as pilgrims-cum-traders to sell their horses at the big fair—the Sünids and Üjümüchins were reputed for breeding excellent horses, especially ambling horses. The geographical catchment area of Wutaishan would therefore partly correspond to economic patterns: a great proportion of pilgrims brought flocks and sheep to trade and to offer to monasteries (see below).

---

60    Rockhill 1895: 766-768.
61    I thank Olivér Kápolnás for this information.
62    Huc 1928 [1924]: 94. Mannerheim (1969 [1940]: 693) also mentions Torguts.

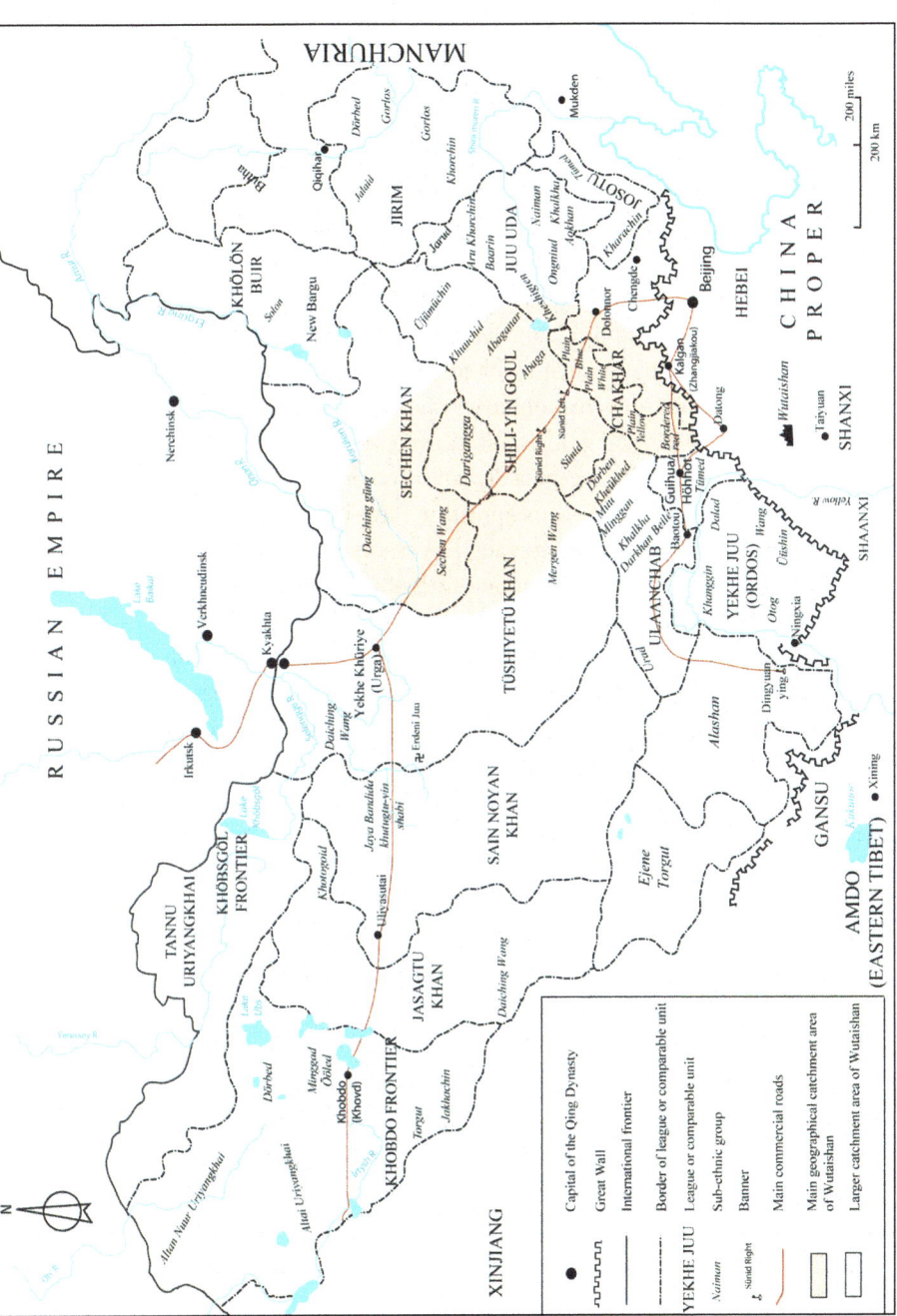

MAP 6   *Map showing the geographical origin of Mongol pilgrims in the late Qing dynasty: in pink, the main catchment area in Mongolia of Wutaishan pilgrims; in blue, larger catchment area.* © ISABELLE CHARLEUX, 2011.

Futhermore, why are the majority (53 percent) of steles located in Shifangtang, the main lodging center for pilgrims? The monks residing in this monastery may have encouraged the carving of steles, while other monasteries may
not have. But why were the Sünids especially generous towards (and perhaps
preferred to stay in) Shifangtang? A first hypothesis would be that the monastic
communities of Shifangtang may have hailed from the Shili-yin Gool League;
still today, Mongol pilgrims often have a relative or at least a contact from their
own banner residing in a Wutaishan monastery and go to that monastery to offer him gifts. However, we have no information on the geographical origins of
Shifangtang's lamas in the period under study.[63] A second hypothesis would be
the existence of specific links between Shifangtang and large monasteries of
the Shili-yin Gool League, such as Bandida Gegeen Süme—the Second Changlung Arya Bandida from this monastery had traveled twice to Wutaishan and
had printed Rölpé Dorjé's guidebook in 1831 (see Chapter 3). The *ombo lamas*
from Shifangtang may have especially collected offerings among the Sünids.

To conclude, the pilgrims thus appear to have been common people as well
as members of the Borjigid aristocracy, laypersons as well as lamas, men as well
as women. Lamas represent about one-fifth of the donors who left their names
on the inscriptions. Most Mongol pilgrims to Wutaishan came from central
Inner Mongolia, and half of lay pilgrims were women. Therefore, the profile
of a typical pilgrim who left his name on stone would be an Inner Mongol turning up with his family and relatives (including women), perhaps following a
lama, to pray for his deceased parents. Donations were recorded in stone inscriptions by the pilgrims' names alone (or by the qualitative 'commoner'), and
typically groups of a dozen persons collected fifty to a hundred taels as an
offering.

### The Pilgrimage to Wutaishan: A Refuge from Conflicts and Economic Stagnation?

#### When Did the Mongols Go to Wutaishan?

Did Mongols go to Wutaishan to escape from poverty and war, or did they make
the pilgrimage in times of peace? Eighty-two percent of the stone inscriptions
were carved between 1880 and the end of the Qing period (1880-1911: 43 percent) and during the Republican period (1912-1940: 39 percent), i.e., during a
period of economic depression (Table 6). A closer look at the periodicity of the

---

63    The present-day monks of Shifangtang are Tibetans from Amdo plus a few Mongols from
      eastern Inner Mongolia.

ABLE 6    *Number and date of the Mongolian stone inscriptions and their localization*

| Date | Tayuansi | Luohousi | Shifangtang | Other | Total | Percentage of the total |
|---|---|---|---|---|---|---|
| 7th century | - | 2 | - | 3 | 5 | 1.5% |
| 8th century | - | 1 | - | 4 | 5 | 1.5% |
| 800-1879 | 5 | 7 | 7 | 6 | 25 | 7.3% |
| 880-1911 | 34 | 7 | 98 | 8 | 147 | 42.8% |
| Republican period (1912-1940) | 18 | 28 | 77 | 12 | 135 | 39.3% |
| Date illegible | 4 | 2 | - | 20 | 26 | 7.6% |
| Total | 61 | 47 | 182 | 53 | 343 | 100 |

Mongolian inscriptions and at travel accounts shows that during the period 1880-1935, steles were erected almost every year, especially in Shifangtang, with peaks in 1888 (13 inscriptions), 1896 (12 inscriptions), 1898 (10 inscriptions), 1922 (10 inscriptions), 1923 (13 inscriptions), 1930 (11 inscriptions) and 1931 (17 inscriptions). Pilgrims were especially numerous during the visits of the Dalai Lama in 1908 and of the Panchen Lama in 1925 (leaving respectively 6 and 7 inscriptions, more than in the preceding and following years). Clearly, in spite of their economic difficulties, Mongols offered significant donations in times of peace.

The number of steles testifies to a revival of the Wutaishan pilgrimage among Inner Mongols in the 1920s and early 1930s, which was made easier by the improvement in transportation.[64] However, while the great Chinese Buddhist institutions enjoyed a revival, especially Puji's school, Wutaishan's fundraising lamas could no longer travel to Mongolia to collect alms; consequently, the Gélukpa monasteries suffered from the shortage of Mongol donors.[65]

According to written accounts, Mongol refugees also fled to Wutaishan to seek protection in times of trouble (such as during the 1870s' Dungan Insurrection, war, drought and starvation. But there were certain times of conflict that were just too harsh, making it too hard to Mongols to make the journey: no

---

64    The same phenomenon was observed by Susan Naquin for the pilgrimage to Miaofengshan (1992: 343).

65    Li Xiangzhi 1932: 159; Ono Katsutoshi and Hibino Takao 1942: 147.

inscription was carved (or preserved) in 1891 (during the Jindandao Uprising),[66] 1900-1902 (the Boxer Rebellion) or 1911-1915 (the first years of the Republic). Therefore, during some periods, the pilgrimage may have been almost impossible to make. As A.W.S. Wingate wrote in 1905:

> Scarcity of water along the routes had resulted in a large falling off in the number of Mongol pilgrims, consequently, as the Head Lama carefully explained to us, there was a heavy shortage in the amount of contributions.[67]

In 1917 Fischer was told that

> in former times, "Business was good" as the Mongol pilgrims frequently visited the Wu-Tai. But during recent years, (since the fall of the Manchus), political disturbances in China and Mongolia put a stop to the pilgrimages .... So far as visitors are concerned the temples depend mostly on Mongol support, as there are but few Chinese who make pilgrimage to Wu-Tai ... [68]

Natural disasters and epidemics, such as the smallpox epidemic that reached Urga in the 1920s and especially in 1928-1929, prevented the Mongols from going to Wutaishan. Political factors also curtailed Mongol pilgrimages. Khalkha donors were much less numerous after independence in 1911, when they consequently turned to Urga as their main place of worship. When the Mongolian People's Republic was proclaimed in 1921, they were forbidden to go to Wutaishan; those who managed to undertake the pilgrimage in spite of the interdiction incurred heavy fines and reprimand.[69] Still, the last Khalkha stone inscription is dated 1928 (TY53).

In the above-described context of economic depression and strife, the revived cult of Wutaishan in Mongolia may well be connected to the blossoming of eschatological and messianic movements such as the belief of reincarnation in the Pure Land Sukhāvatī or in Shambhala, and the cult of Maitreya. Whereas Maitreya will reign at a time in the far-distant future, the Shambhala war will occur in this present epoch of decline: we have seen in Chapter 1 that the Ninth

---

66    The Chinese members of this devotional movement slaughtered and expelled tens of thousands of Mongols from the Josotu League.

67    Wingate 1907: 276.

68    Fischer 1923: 90.

69    Li Xianzhi 1932: 180.

Panchen Lama, who traveled in Inner Mongolia giving Kālacakra initiations, caused massive movements of pilgrims who hoped to be reborn in Shambhala and participate in the final war. Therefore, Wutaishan appeared as an even more accessible refuge in a pure land in this lifetime, a place where pilgrims could pray for more immediate divine assistance.

### Wutaishan in the Conflicts of the Late 1930s

As we have seen, in time of troubles 'pilgrims' to Wutaishan may first have been refugees. This is particularly true of the late 1930s, a period of conflict, religious persecution, and warfare between nationalist, communist and warlord forces. Before 1937, Chinese warlord Yan Xishan 閻錫山 (1883-1960), himself born in the Wutaishan region, was able to protect the province, but from 1937 to 1946 Wutaishan became a conflict zone. The last *jasag lama* was dismissed in 1937. At the beginning of the Sino-Japanese conflict in 1937, groups of Mongols sought refuge on Wutaishan. French explorer and orientalist Alexandra David-Neel, who left Wutaishan during the Japanese attack, encountered along the road groups of terrified Mongols—fleeing Chakhars (including women and children) who were seeking refuge on Wutaishan.[70] In 1938 the Japanese occupation of northern Shanxi, including Wutaishan, almost put an end to the pilgrimage. That same year, "Japanese and Communist forces [the Eighth Route Army], along with the armies of a few warlords, took up residence in the mountains, taking over temple buildings for use as forts and causing many monks and nuns to leave to seek safety elsewhere."[71] Much of the forests were cut down, the monasteries were squatted and pillaged, and many inhabitants fled the area. Yet in 1940, the date of the last (Inner) Mongol stone inscription, Ono Katsutoshi and Hibino Takao still encountered pilgrims from Inner Mongolia.

During the period that lasted up to the first years of the People's Republic of China, Wutaishan thus appears as an isolated bastion, a refuge from the conflicts and economic disasters that ensued from them, attracting refugees, runaways and bandits. Many pilgrims died from hunger and exhaustion on the road before reaching their destination, and the survivors desperately flooded the monasteries in search of food and shelter. In addition, monks from monasteries all over China that were closed or turned into administrative offices and schools reached Wutaishan to continue their training or simply to survive.

The result was that, while the rest of the country experienced instability and economic ruin, the number of monks increased on Wutaishan, and monastic

---

70    David-Neel 1940: 155.

71    Szczepanski 2008: 58. On that period: Ono Katsutoshi and Hibino Takao 1942: 153-156. The residence of Mao Zedong in Tayuansi displays pictures of that period.

life and Buddhist practice were able to continue.[72] In 1936 a provincial census still counted on Wutaishan 130 monasteries and 2,200 registered monks and clerics, of which 800 were Tibeto-Mongol Buddhists, as well as 10,000 practicing lay Buddhists.[73] To accommodate the growing numbers of monks and nuns as well as lay pilgrims, the monasteries had to adapt, and most of them were turned into 'monasteries of the Ten Directions' (*shifangtang*) which were open to all members of the *sangha*.[74] It therefore seems that calamities and troubles entailed a rise in faith, an increase in the need for divine help and miracles, and pushed Mongol refugees to journey to Wutaishan.

### The Contribution of Mongol Herders to the Wutaishan Economy

This presentation of the economic and social difficulties of nineteenth- and early twentieth-century Mongols begs the question: How could herders over-burdened by heavy taxation make a pilgrimage and offer large quantities of money and cattle to the Wutaishan monasteries? How much did pilgrims spend on their journey in donations and travel costs? Here I will examine expenditures and donations made during the Mongols' pilgrimages.

#### *Expenditures on the Journey to Wutaishan*
Li Xiangzhi explains in 1932 that, as for pilgrims going to Wutaishan and making a vow so that their father or mother will recover from a disease,

> some will give over everything that they own; some will give a half or a third of their possessions to ensure the vow they made [will be fulfilled]... .

---

72    Ono Katsutoshi and Hibino Takao 1942: 152. Similarly, in this period of religious persecution, other great pilgrimage sites that relied mostly on individual donations and less on land property and were less linked to local power fared relatively well (Goossaert and Palmer 2011: 127).

73    Cui Zhengsen 2003: 13. In 1911, Zhang Dungu (1911: 26) counted 3,000 to 4,000 monks and novices. In their chapter on the Wutaishan clergy and monastic economy, Ono Katsutoshi and Hibino Takao (1942: 144-145) quote a survey listing 46 'blue' monasteries with 797 monks, and 20 'yellow monasteries' with 394 lamas in 1940. By 1958, however, there were only 582 monks on Wutaishan, according to the census (Bianchi and Rinaldo 2010: 362).

74    Speaking about Chinese Buddhist music, Beth Szczepanski points out that this transformation entailed a simplification of rituals to allow "participation by a large number of inexperienced novices from all over China" (2008: 55).

they sell all they possess, horses, oxen, sheep, pigs,[75] mules, donkeys, etc. in exchange for silver money, or they go themselves to Zhangjiakou 張家 □ [Kalgan, on the Sino-Mongol border], Suiyuan 綏遠 [Höhhot], Baotou 包頭 or another place to sell their mules and horses in exchange for silver money. [They take] whatever they get, 300 or 500 *yuan*.

As for princes or officials travelling in caravans, he added, "They directly sell their own herds and flocks and receive up to 12,800 silver [dollars, i.e., *yuan*]."[76] In other words, Mongol commoners either offered a part or all of what they possessed or went to Wutaishan as mendicants after they had lost everything. However, princes did not fund their pilgrimages from their own treasury but instead levied special taxes among their subjects to cover the costs.

Prince 'To' (Togtokhtör Wang, 1797-1868) of Setsen Khan Aimag (Khalkha Mongolia), famous not only for his attempts at modernization but also for his shocking spending, is the best-known example. His subjects wrote a petition of grievance to the league-chief of Setsen Khan Aimag in 1840 to accuse him of having levied too many taxes: "Wang Togtokhtör is squeezing us again and again with various oppressions and making it impossible for us to continue our living."[77] Among the forty counts of indictment (starting in 1821) were the taxes for the expenditures and supply animals for To Wang's wife's pilgrimage to Urga in 1827 (17 camels, 25 horses, 40 rams, 392.90 taels of silver);[78] for To Wang's journey to Beijing in 1829 (800 taels of silver plus 20 geldings); for his journey to Lhasa and back with the Fifth Jebtsündamba in 1835-1836; and for his journey to Beijing in 1837 and again in 1839. For the 1839 trip, his subjects were asked to pay extra taxes for a delegation that would meet the prince at Dolonnor for his journey back: 430 taels of silver for the rent of 40 camels, 50 horses, and 1,115.40 taels of silver for provisions, plus 38 camels, 47 horses, 366 taels of silver for tents and 28 taels for provisions. But while his people were sending him animals and money, the prince decided to go on pilgrimage from Beijing to Wutaishan in 1840. He left Wutaishan in the first month of 1840 and arrived home in the third month.[79] These petitions shed light on the financial burden these pilgrimages

---

75   It is, of course, highly improbable that Mongols possessed and sold pigs—unsuited as they are to nomadic life—except perhaps for some sinicized Mongols living at the Sino-Mongol border.

76   Li Xiangzhi 1932: 181.

77   Rasidondug and Veit 1975: 72 (Doc 23).

78   For the value of the tael of silver, see below.

79   Rasidondug and Veit 1975: 73-78 (Doc 23).

put on nobles' subjects and inform us about the equipment needed for nobles' caravans.

Mongol reincarnated lamas in pilgrimage brought important offerings from their personal treasury, but high clerics may also have gathered contributions from lay people living around their monastery. In 1911, Zhang Dungu noticed that "among the Mongols, princes, dukes, *taiji*, monks, and common people, the wealthiest of all were the monks."[80]

### Donations to Monasteries

The Mongolian steles record donations for amounts superior to 30 taels of white silver,[81] or 10 silver dollars when that currency was adopted.[82] The biggest recorded individual donation is 30,000 taels (Online Appendix A1, Table B). Peaks in donations are observed for the years 1869, 1907, 1915, 1926 and 1936, and smaller peaks can be seen in 1894, 1896, 1918 and 1922. In the late Qing period, groups of pilgrims commonly made an offering of 50 to 100 taels in silver ingots (or their equivalent in head of cattle),[83] plus cows and sheep.[84] Comparable amounts of donations are found on other Mongol pilgrimage sites. In 1827, a Mongol aristocratic lady who went to Urga to worship the Jebtsündamba Khutugtu offered him 17 camels, 25 horses, 40 sheep and 262.50 taels of silver.[85]

As seen above, the Mongols had to sell their cattle for cash before they could travel into Chinese territory. Nineteenth-century Mongol economy was partially monetized and integrated with the Chinese silver-based economy, but Mongols continued to use bricks of tea leaves as well as sheep and ceremonial scarves (*khadag*) as units of value, and barter was the main form of exchange (the value of the bartered item was measured by its equivalent in tea, sheep or

---

80   Zhang Dungu 1911: 25

81   Nineteenth-century Mongols did not use the Chinese copper currency but taels of 'white' silver, i.e., silver ingots (Ch. *bailiang* 白兩, Mo. *chagan mönggö lang*). A (*bai*)*liang* is a Chinese unit of weight equivalent to 36-37 grams of silver (see Atwood 2002: 1059-1060). I henceforth use 'tael' for 'tael of white silver.' The Mongols did not use taels of gold.

82   *Dayang* 大洋, Mo. *da yang*, also called *yuan* 元 (Atwood 2002: 1060-1061). The nineteenth-century silver dollar that circulated in Mongolia contained little more than 24 grams of pure silver. Some inscriptions (SF58, 1896) mention 'new and ancient taels': 'the 'new tael' could be an appellation for the silver dollar coin.

83   For example *tabin lang-un mal ergübe*: "[they] offered cattle for [a value of] 50 taels" (SF51, 1894).

84   Ten head of cattle (LH41, 1934); a good horse and 15 sheep (SF137, 1923); 2,500 silver dollars, 5 oxen and sheep (CF6, 1935).

85   Rasidondug and Veit (transl.) 1975: 73; other examples p. 74, 179.

silver).[86] Up to the Republican period, a combination of silver taels, 'tea units' and foreign notes and coins circulated in Mongol areas.[87] In the Republican period, Mongols continued to use taels of silver, whereas Chinese switched to the silver dollar (PSD1, 1936).[88] Only nine Wutaishan stone inscriptions record Inner Mongols' donations in silver dollars (*yuan*) after 1931. The inscriptions do not mention paper currency, and only one stele (SF149, 1928) mentions a donation in *tögrög*, which had become the sole legal currency in the People's Republic of Mongolia in 1928: a few Khalkha Mongols who visited Wutaishan in 1926 and 1928 continued to offer taels of silver (TY53, 1928; TY52, 1926).[89]

Nineteenth- and twentieth-century travelers also inform us regarding non-monetary donations to the Wutaishan monasteries. The Mongols donated livestock (sheep, oxen, horses) and urns of butter,[90] as well as gold and silver, women's jewelry and silver ornaments.[91] Temples' altars were not only covered with money but also votive lamps, brick tea, dairy products, sacrificial cakes, *maṇḍala*s, "dishes of fruits and of candies, and a row of bowls of pure water,"[92] as well as enormous amounts of other paraphernalia and gifts,[93] "many packages of Mongol robes"[94] and women's jewelry. Mongol pilgrims apparently also brought various gifts for bribes.[95]

---

86   Mongols used both coarse brick tea itself as well as paper currency based on tea bricks (*üne tsai*: lit. price-tea). There was a fixed relationship between tea and sheep: in 1786, 2 bricks of tea=1 three-year-old sheep=a package of tobacco=2 black lambskins=1/10 of a good horse, etc. A family of 4-5 people used a brick of tea a month (Sanjdorj 1980 [1963]: 88-90; Maiskii 2001 [1921]). On currencies and prices for the period 1911-1931 in Mongolia: Atwood 2002: Appendix D.

87   Bawden 1989 [1968]: 148-152.

88   The Republic of China officially issued the silver dollar as the national currency in 1914; it was valued at 0.72 taels. But, before 1935, multiple currencies (Guomindang currency, Japanese yen, local currencies issued by commercial, provincial and foreign banks) were circulating in China, Mongolia and Manchuria, all at different values.

89   Around 1860-1870, rudimentary banknotes appeared as the first paper money in Khalkha Mongolia, issued by the treasury of the Yekhe Shabi (Sanjdorj 1980 [1963]: 101). The Khalkhas used taels and silver dollars together with other circulating currencies until 1925, when they switched to the *tögrög* (*tögürig*) at a value equal to one Soviet ruble (one ruble or *tögrög* was equal to 18 grams of silver (Maiskii 2001 [1921]; Atwood 2002: 1061-1062).

90   Fischer 1923: 96.

91   Blofeld 1959: 128-129; Fischer 1923: 90.

92   Rockhill 1895: 767.

93   Swallow 1903: 179; Fischer 1923: 9.

94   Fischer 1923: 93.

95   Rockhill (1890: 6) does not specify who the Mongols had to bribe.

### Amounts of Donations Received by Wutaishan Monasteries

The total amount of donations that Wutaishan monasteries received every year from pilgrims is much higher than the sum of donations recorded in the surviving inscriptions, most donors being probably given paper certificates. According to a Chinese survey made in 1947, before 1935 forty-one monasteries received every year an average of 229,030 silver dollars in total donations from all pilgrims (including Chinese).[96] If we assume that this total was more or less the same for 1936, according to another survey, twelve monasteries concentrated almost eighty percent of this amount (Table 7). Five out of twelve were Gélukpa monasteries (which represented at that time thirteen percent of the all Wutaishan monasteries); they each received between 5,000 and 15,000 silver dollars in donations. The high amount of donations to Longquansi and Nanshansi is due to the exceptional fame of Master Puji, who collected considerable donations in North China (Longquansi's sumptuous archway built from 1926 to 1931 cost 47,000 silver dollars). In 1941, during the Japanese occupation, the main monasteries still received an average of 20,275 silver dollars each; in 1947 this figure fell to 553 silver dollars.

Out of 246 stone inscriptions, eleven percent (i.e., 27 inscriptions, of which 11 are in Tayuansi) record offerings superior to 500 taels or 500 silver dollars. Most of the donations come from princes, dukes and high reincarnations from Central Khalkha Mongolia and the Shili-yin Gool League. The largest ones are 30,000 taels (LH1, 1658), from the First Chakhar Diyanchi (d. 1671), the famous eremitic lama from Höhhot;[97] 12,200 taels from a Sünid prince, to Tayuansi (TY3, 1869-1887); 10,000 taels from the prince of Khalkha Tüshiyetü Khan in 1907, to Shancaidong (SCD1); and 8,800 taels from an Abaga prince, to Pusading in 1936 (Online Appendix A1: Table C). According to Li Xiangzhi, in the 1930s, princes used to offer 5,000 or 6,000 silver dollars to their 'main' monastery, plus 3,000 or 4,000 silver dollars to the other monasteries.[98]

Tayuansi donors were much more generous than those who donated to Shifangtang or Luohousi. The 182 steles of Shifangtang mostly record donations of between 50 and 100 taels (average: 92 taels), while Tayuansi and its Great White Stūpa received much higher amounts per inscription than the other

---

96    Xin Butang and Zheng Fulin 1995: 28, quoting the *1947 nian tugai gongzuotuan de diaocha baogao* 1947年土改工作团的調查報告.

97    Although the Chakhar Diyanchi's project of restoring monasteries on Wutaishan was approved by an imperial decree, the stele and his biography do not say that money was granted by the emperor; thus, we can assume that he gathered contributions from many different donors.

98    Li Xiangzhi 1932: 182-183.

TABLE 7    *Twelve Chinese Buddhist and Gélukpa monasteries that received more than five thousand silver dollars in donations (from all pilgrims) in 1936*

| Monastery | Tradition | Amount of donation |
|---|---|---|
| Longquansi | Chinese Buddhist (Puji's school) | 80,000 silver dollars |
| Tayuansi | Chinese Buddhist (+ resident lamas) | 17,000 silver dollars |
| Pusading | Gélukpa | 15,000 silver dollars (cf. PSD1) |
| Cifusi | Gélukpa | 11,000 silver dollars |
| Zhenhaisi | Gélukpa | 10,000 silver dollars |
| Puhuasi | Chinese Buddhist (Puji's school) | 10,000 silver dollars |
| Xiantongsi | Chinese Buddhist (+ resident lamas) | 8,500 silver dollars |
| Pushousi | Gélukpa | 7,000 silver dollars |
| Bishansi | Chinese Buddhist | 7,000 silver dollars[a] |
| Shuxiangsi | Chinese Buddhist (+ resident lamas) | 5,300 silver dollars |
| Jifusi | Gélukpa | 5,000 silver dollars |
| Nanshansi | Chinese Buddhist (Puji's school) | 5,000 silver dollars |
| **Total** | 7 Chinese Buddhist, 5 Gélukpa | 180,800 silver dollars |

[a]    Xin Butang and Zheng Fulin (1995: 28) wrote 70,000 silver dollars, which is a mistake for 7,000.
SOURCE: XIN BUTANG AND ZHENG FULIN 1995: 28.

monasteries (average: 650 taels). Still today, this temple with its brick pagoda is Wutaishan's greatest attraction.

The two most generous groups of donors are from Khalkha (mostly Tüshiyetü Khan and Setsen Khan, the two central provinces) and central Inner Mongolia (Shili-yin Gool, Chakhar and Darigangga). The first mostly came before 1911; they represent 14 percent of the stone inscriptions but offered 40 percent of the total recorded amount of donations. Conversely, even though the Mongols from Shili-yin Gool, Chakhar and Darigangga represent 62 percent of the donors (they were even more numerous during the Republican period), their donations account for only 50 percent of the total. The explanation could be that the Mongols from central Inner Mongolia, being closer to the Sino-Mongol border, were mostly commoners who were frequent pilgrims to Wutaishan and pilgrims-cum-traders who came every year to sell their herds, while pilgrims coming from afar, perhaps once in their lifetime, tended to make larger donations.

### Donations to Restore and Build Temples and Stūpas

The Wutaishan monastery that received the most Mongol donations for restoration was Tayuansi and its Great White Stūpa. Among the sixteen major restorations recorded during the Qing and Republican periods, eleven were carried out by Mongols:

- In 1703, a Mongol *da lama* (abbot) of the Kharachin called Cha-han de-li-ji 察漢得力吉 (Chagan Dorji?) financed some restoration.[99]
- In 1853, the Imperial Prince Ildeng of Khalkha Setsen Khan Aimag offered 300 taels of silver to the monastery (stele TY1).
- In 1869, Prince Namjilwangchug, ruler of the Sünid Left Banner, while visiting Wutaishan, made the vow to restore the *stūpa* and first offered 2,000 taels of silver to start the work. Then he asked all the nobles, officials and commoners of his banner to contribute towards the restoration and was able to collect a total of 10,000 taels. "The monks praised the merit and celebrated the virtues of the Mongol princes, who are the true protectors of the mountain" (stele TY3, abstract in Online Appendix A2). We obviously here have a case of 'forced contribution.'[100]
- In 1887, the *tsorji da lama* Galsangdondub of the ecclesiastical estate (*shabi*) of the Khalkha Jaya Bandida came on pilgrimage, stayed at Tayuansi and saw miraculous five-colored lights circling around the *stūpa* (stele TY7, Fig. 24). He offered 500 taels of white silver, four camels, and one yurt to restore the paintings and statues of the 'great central assembly hall,' to provide robes for the monks and to restore the prayer wheels.
- In 1894, a reincarnated lama named Longdanjamso, from Khalkha Sain Noyan Khan Aimag, offered 1,800 taels of silver to restore the Great White Stūpa (stele TY9).
- In 1915, a monk from Khalkha Setsen Khan Aimag offered 2,200 taels of white silver to restore the porch roof that protected pilgrims who circumambulated the Great White Stūpa, to make icons and prayer wheels and to fund the performance of rituals (stele TY40).
- In 1926, a high reincarnation from Khalkha Mergen Wang Banner offered 5,000 taels of white silver (stele TY52).
- In 1928, a certain Gombo from Urga offered 500 taels of white silver (stele TY53).
- In 1932, Prince Minjuurdorji from the Üjümüchin Left Banner offered 1,256 *yuan* (stele TY55).

---

99    Gao Minghe 1996: 14. I did not find any inscription recording this donation.

100   See the 'petitions of grievance' (Rasidondug and Veit 1975).

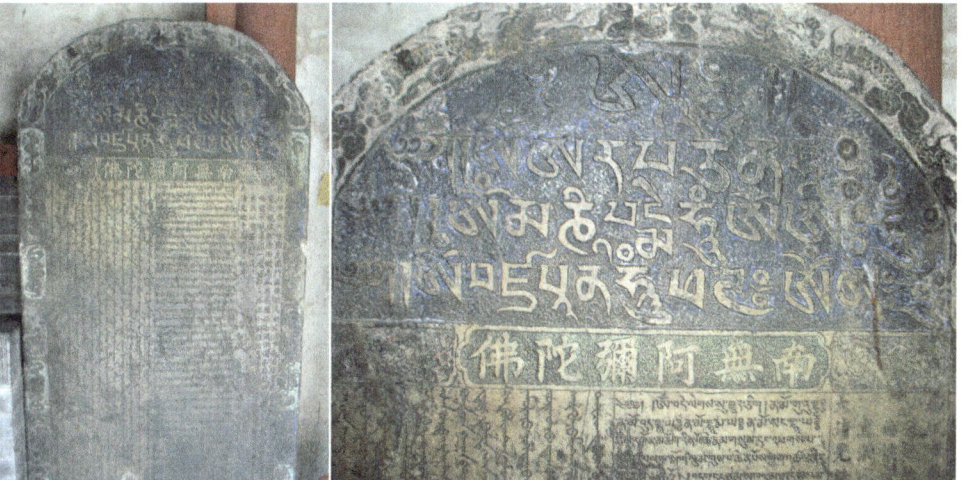

FIGURE 24      *Trilingual stele TY7 (1887) in Tayuansi.* © ISABELLE CHARLEUX, 2010.

- In 1934, Prince Rinchinwangdun from the Sünid Left Banner offered 1,046 *yuan* (stele TY56).
- At an unknown date, a noble from Abaga Banner offered 1,000 taels to restore the Mañjuśrī's Hair Stūpa.

The amounts of donations per stone inscription given to repair the Great White Stūpa range from 300 to 12,000 taels. In Qianlong's time, the construction of a monastery on Wutaishan cost about 10,000 or 20,000 taels of silver, and restorations cost between 1,000 and 2,000 taels. During the same period, the large monasteries of Inner Mongolia were built for 10,000 to 50,000 taels of silver. A two-meter-high bronze statue cost from 2,000 to 6,000 taels and a whole set of the *Kanjur* cost 1,200 taels in 1738.[101] In 1820-1822, the construction of the Maidari Temple of Yekhe Khüree cost 7,000 taels of silver. In 1906, with rising inflation (see below), the restoration of Narobanchin Gegeen-ü Khüriye, south of Uliastai, which took four years, eventually cost 60,000 taels of silver. In 1911, a Khalkha prince collected the enormous sum of 230,000 taels to build the Megjid Janraiseg temple of Gandan plus 100,000 taels of silver for its gigantic statue.[102] Donations by individual pilgrims to Wutaishan monasteries were thus significant amounts at that time.

---

101    Charleux 2006: 163.
102    Bawden 1989 [1968]: 147. The other destinations of Mongol pilgrims' donations will be detailed in the following chapter.

## Mongol Trade on Wutaishan

An important component of the Wutaishan pilgrimage (as in many pilgrimages the world over) is trade. Victor Turner and other scholars have already stressed the importance of trade fairs as "secular interludes between religious activities" in the study of pilgrimages of medieval Islam and Christianity, Japan and so on.[103] Some Mongols engaged in trade to pay for their pilgrimage, while others were just doing business.[104] Wutaishan became an important Sino-Mongol trade center in the late Qing and Republican periods. The pilgrims brought with them animals to give as offerings to the monasteries and also to sell. In the early twentieth century, according to Fischer, they brought

> their products, hides, furs, horses, sheep and cattle from the grazing grounds to Kwei Hwa Ting [Guihuacheng, or Höhhot] on the market, and either pay in specie or cash to Mount Wu-T'ai. The more profitable their dealings are, the more they will carry on their pilgrim-journey to Mount Wu-T'ai.[105]

Bai Meichu adds that:

> The wealthiest came with dozens of animals, the poorest with only a few head of cattle. They carry gold, silver, hides, camel hair, cheese and Mongol local products; when they arrive on Wutaishan, they either sell or offer to the monasteries all the things they have brought, and then they return home.[106]

Lamas too brought their herds to sell on Wutaishan. Gilmour encountered a large drove of horses:

> In the midst of this a lama, richly dressed and mounted on a fine steed ... saying he came from Wu T'ai, that he had been to Russia ... and that he was on a business journey.[107]

---

103    Turner and Turner 1978: 37.
104    On pilgrimages and concomitant forms of commercial activity in the Tibetan world: van Spengen 2000: 122-129.
105    Fischer 1923: 100.
106    Bai Meichu 2010 [1925]: *juan* 2, 154.
107    Gilmour 1893: 15-16.

During the sixth month of the lunar year, an important event called the Great Mule and Horse Fair (*luoma dahui* 騾馬大會) was organized on Wutaishan. The common opinion is that, from the eighteenth century on, the Mongols were no longer allowed to drive their surplus herds of horses, camels and oxen down into China, but rather traded with Chinese merchants who came to Mongolia.[108] That such a fair was allowed on Wutaishan counters this belief, for the Qing authorities apparently tolerated a Sino-Mongol market in their territory. In the Qianlong period,[109] this great fair was organized at the foot of Dailuoding and on the banks of the Qingshui River south of Taihuai.[110]

The Great Mule and Horse Fair attracted traders and herders from Inner and Outer Mongolia, northern and western China, Manchuria, Eastern and Central Tibet and Eastern Turkestan. The horses and mules mostly came from Baotou, Höhhot, the two Sünid banners, Dolonnor, Batu Khaalga Süme, Bandida Gegeen Süme and (Shireetü Lama) Khüriye Banner in Inner Mongolia, as well as from Tibet, Gansu and Xinjiang.[111] At the Great Mule and Horse Fair, Mongols exchanged sheep, mules, horses and donkeys for tea, food and everyday items. According to a late 1930s' survey, in one year 10,000 oxen came from Mongolia and Tibet; 700,000 horses, 20,000 donkeys, 10,000 mares and she-mules from Mongolia, Tibet, China and Xinjiang; 200,000 sheep from Mengjiang 蒙疆 (central Inner Mongolia, then under Japanese control); 1,000 camels from Mengjiang and Shaanxi; and 70,000 pigs and 90,000 chickens from Shanxi.[112] Annual taxes on cattle and horse trade reached more than 20,000 *yuan* in 1925 and 40,000 to 50,000 *yuan* in the 1930s.[113] Most of the horses, mares, oxens, camels and sheep at the fair came from the Mongol pastures (some could have been brought from Mongolia to Wutaishan by Chinese traders). Soldiers were sent

---

108 References on trade in Qing Mongolia generally focus on long-distance caravans, on itinerant Chinese merchants who eventually settled in trade cities and near monasteries, and on the implantation of the great Shanxi firms in Mongolia (Maiskii 2001 [1921]; Sanjdorj 1989 [1963]; Bawden 1989 [1968]: 95-96; Lu Minghui and Liu Yankun 1995; Avery 2003). Long-distance caravans run by monasteries were conducted by Mongols, but the great majority of the trade was in the hands of Hui Chinese (Lattimore 1928). Trade was also practiced at frontier towns such as Kalgan, Yulin, Shuiquanbao 水泉堡 and Shizuizi 石咀子.

109 Bai Meichu 2010 [1925]: *juan* 2, 92; Li Xiangzhi 1932: 176-177; Chai Zejun 1999: 68; Huang Yongsong and Dai Qing 1991: 1-23. For Chai Zejun, the history of this great fair dates from the Sui and Tang dynasties.

110 It has since been organized again, after 1990, on the pastures facing Zhenhaisi.

111 Li Xiangzhi 1932: 177.

112 Ono Katsutoshi and Hibino Takao 1942: 151-152.

113 Bai Meichu 2010 [1925]: *juan* 2, 92; Li Xiangzhi 1932: 177.

from Datong to prevent trouble, and officials collected taxes on the occasion.[114] The fair also attracted Chinese from the nearby counties as well as prostitutes,[115] and some pilgrims expressed their disapproval of secularized activities of the 'temple merchants.' For instance, the Kanjurwa Khutugtu writes in his biography that the pilgrims "criticized the questionable activities which took place there among the visitors and the less desirable local people."[116]

The Mongols usually put their herds out to pasture at least fifteen days and up to three months before selling them. They may have faced the following dilemma: Should they sell their animals at the Great Mule and Horse Fair on the sixth month or, following Mongol custom, wait till they are fat and sell them just before winter? The cool climate of Wutaishan and its pastures, which replaced the forests during the Qing dynasty, were said to be excellent for horses and cattle: the grass and water quickly fattened, strengthened and cured the animals (Fig. 54).[117] Travelers described large herds of sheep, horses, goats and cattle, "at times of over 500 head [head] strong,"[118] grazing on the pastures at the foot of Dailuoding, where a small temple to the horse deity stood,[119] and on the slopes of the Southern and Western Terraces.[120] According to Gilmour, the Mongols "say that any beast which eats the grass and drinks the water of the place is ensured to be born hereafter into a higher state."[121]

The trade fair and other economic activities were opportunities for economic, as well as social exchange between Mongols and Chinese and appeared to be much more than a mere by-product of the Wutaishan pilgrimage.

### Exchange Value

To give an idea of the exchange value of donations and trade, in 1808 Khalkha Mongolia one sheep or goat cost about 1.50 taels of silver, and one head of cattle cost 7.50 taels of silver.[122] In 1820 Khalkha Mongolia, a fat sheep cost 2 or 3 taels, a horse, 6 to 15 taels, and a good camel, 20 to 30 taels.[123] During the same period, the annual pay of the banner officers in Chakhar varied from 24 taels a year for

114    Zhang Dungu 1911: 24.

115    Li Xiangzhi 1932: 154.

116    Jagchid and Hyer 1983: 106-107.

117    Han Heping and Wang Miao 1999: 98-99.

118    Fischer 1923: 101, 85.

119    Pokotilov 1935 [1893]: 83.

120    Fischer 1923: 85, 101.

121    Gilmour 1970 [1883]: 143.

122    Rasidondug and Veit (transl.) 1975. The best study on the Khalkha Mongol economy for that period is Maiskii 2001 [1921], who cites the Mongol census of 1918.

123    Timkowski 1827, vol. 2: 318.

a sergeant up to 120 taels a year for a commander.[124] Monks who possessed a certificate received 1 to 2 taels of silver a month; this had risen to up to 6 or 8 taels by the end of the Qing dynasty. In 1892, Rockhill bought camels in Inner Mongolia at 16 to 40 taels per head. A donation of 50 taels therefore represented a significant amount for a Mongol family. Inflation progressed at a slow pace but accelerated in the 1900s, along with the rise in taxes.[125]

Prices of cattle, horses and sheep rose when one approached the Chinese border, in Höhhot and Kalgan, for instance, and were even higher in China. According to Sanjdorj, in 1786 Chinese merchants bought several three year-old sheep in Khalkha Mongolia for two bricks of tea each and took the animals to China, where one sheep could be sold for 3 taels of silver (or 30 bricks of tea), a horse for 18 taels (or 180 bricks) and a camel for 20 taels (or 200 bricks). So Chinese merchants buying livestock in Mongolia made a 29.5-brick profit on a sheep and 185 bricks on a camel. Even taking into account the expense of bringing back the flocks to China (5 bricks per sheep), by making a round trip Chinese traders could turn one sheep into fifty.[126] Such profits were therefore extremely appealing to Mongol herders, who were glad for the opportunity to cross the Chinese border themselves with their herds and sell them on Wutaishan at a much higher price than in Mongolia.

The study of the geographical origin of pilgrims has highlighted the high proportion of those who came from the vicinity of the Sino-Mongol border. If the majority of them were also traders, the profits they gained by trading large numbers of horses, oxen and sheep may be one of the factors that explain the large sums donated to Wutaishan's monasteries.

## The Expectations of Mongol Pilgrims

What prompted Mongols to step out of their daily activities to undertake a sacred journey? Were their motivations to go on pilgrimage different from that of Tibetans and Chinese? As seen before, the Mongols' reasons to visit Wutaishan

---

124  Timkowski 1827, vol. 1: p. 260-261. The monthly salary of the border guards of the Otog Banner was between 8 and 15 taels in 1921 (Atwood 2002: 1064).

125  Rockhill 1894: 15. For estimations of the rise in taxes in early twentieth-century inflation: Bawden 1989 [1968]: 151. According to Holmes Welch (1968: 5), a silver dollar was generally worth one-quarter to one-half of an American dollar during the Republican period. In 1934, Chinese farmers earned less than 3 silver dollars a month, and a school teacher, between 7 and 10 silver dollars (Chen Xingya 1936: 25). See also the estimated prices of daily goods in *tögrög* in Ulaanbaatar in 1927: Atwood 2002: 1065.

126  Sanjdorj 1980 [1963]: 90.

were not only spiritual but also material, economic, social and political. Pilgrimage was also an occasion to meet people, escape daily routine, sightsee and show oneself "in full pomp and state to as many observers as possible."[127] The tourist dimension of pilgrimages is not a recent phenomenon,[128] and the boundaries between 'religious' pilgrims and 'secular' tourists were blurred, especially in a pre-modern society that did not think of religion as a separate entity. In one of his autobiographies, the famous Buryat lama Dorjiev uses the Tibetan expression *gyelkham dönmé nyülba*, 'wandered aimlessly in the countries.' According to Norbu's commentary, this expression

> could be translated as [being a] 'tourist.' It is the sort of humble expression a pilgrim would use if asked what he or she was doing: "oh, just wandering aimlessly." ... To speak boastfully of an act of faith would mean to sacrifice any merit that might have resulted from it."[129]

While the great majority of Mongol travelers to Wutaishan were undoubtedly pilgrims, others journeyed for other motivations. On the pretext of making a pilgrimage, some were actually, or were also, traders, tourists, beggars or runaways fleeing justice, war or misery. On the other hand, on the pretext of accompanying a delegation, an emperor, a relative or a friend, some also worshipped at the monasteries and offered donations. Another major motivation which does not appear in the stone inscriptions is burial (see below).

In addition, some families took their son to Wutaishan to place him as a novice in a monastery, and delegations of monks from Inner Mongol monasteries journeyed to Wutaishan to obtain official recognition from the Changkya Khutugtu for a new reincarnation. Even if the boy was generally chosen beforehand from a local noble family, it was an official obligation for them to journey to Zhenhaisi: there, they asked the Changkya Khutugtu to read *sūtras* for seven days to help the soul of the former reincarnation find a new body. Once the reincarnation was approved by the Changkya Khutugtu, they went back to Mongolia, where they could announce the news officially.[130]

---

127   Haslund-Christensen (1935: 25), describing families of pilgrims who came in 1927 to join the Great Maitreya Festival of Batu Khaalga Süme in Inner Mongolia.

128   As pointed out by Turner and Turner (1978: 20), "A tourist is half a pilgrim, if a pilgrim is half a tourist."

129   Martin and Norbu 1991: 9, 51 n. 2.

130   Song Wenhui 2000: 34.

### Mongol Pilgrims' Spiritual and Mundane Expectations as Expressed in Steles

Few sources inform us about the material and spiritual motivations of Mongol pilgrims. Although the formal language of steles and certificates of donation only reflects 'official' and general expectations, it at least helps us define the vocabulary of prayers, merit-making and offering. The inscriptions will be supplemented with qualitative, subjective accounts written by pilgrims and travelers, with contemporary observations and with stories told to me personally by Mongols.

The texts of steles and certificates more or less follow the same general structure, with an upper section (called 'head') expressing the wish that the inscription will last forever, a prayer, the name of the monastery that receives the offering, the names of donors, and the amount and purpose of the donation (Appendix 2). They end with general wishes and more personal wishes in return for the 'pure and white merits' stemming from the offerings and the act of pilgrimage. The names of the living donors are followed by those of their deceased relatives. Sometimes only the father and mother of the main donor are mentioned, but some steles give the names of thirty to forty donors along with up to thirty deceased persons (TY51, 1924).[131]

General wishes focus on saving all the sentient beings, so that they forever enjoy peace and happiness, and on propagating Buddhism. Personal wishes are for the donor's deceased relatives and for him/herself and his/her family: most of the steles use formulas such as "pay back [the gift of birth given by one's] father and mother, who deserve gratitude." Throughout the Buddhist world, donors accomplish pious deeds to produce merit for their parents (Appendix 2).[132] Donors frequently offer money for a ritual to redirect (joriul)[133] merit accumulated in this way towards "the benefit of those who are deceased and (all) the sentient beings." The Pusading inscription (1936) expresses the wish to save the former generations of banner princes from saṃsāra. The donors also wish that, through the accumulated merit, the obstacles (kharshi) on their path

---

131   LH22 (1920) lists twenty-seven donors, plus five other living beneficiaries (perhaps older or ill devotees who stayed home) and four deceased relatives; LH29 (1929) lists eight donors and eleven deceased relatives.

132   Indian votive inscriptions dated from the second to the first centuries BCE studied by Gregory Schopen express wishes that one's deceased parents obtain nirvāna as the result of an act of pūjā undertaken by living descendants (more than ninety percent of the inscriptions from Ajanta declare that the intended beneficiaries are the donors' parents) (Schopen 1997, esp. "Filial Piety and the Monk in the Practice of Indian Buddhism: A Question of 'Sinicization' Viewed from the Other Side," 56-71).

133   Joriul: direct toward, cause to strive, turn one's merit over somebody else.

to liberation or to a better reincarnation are erased. The inscriptions and certificates all end with the ultimate wish to be reborn at the 'golden feet of
Mañjuśrī' and obtain the sanctity/holiness of Buddha (or of Vajradhara). Patrons extend these wishes to their descendants and future reincarnations, while
they pray for their deceased relatives to immediately reach the kingdom of
Shambhala or Sukhāvatī's Pure Land. Here again, Wutaishan is linked to both
Sukhāvatī's heaven and to Shambhala.

Accumulating merit and gaining a higher reincarnation for oneself or for living or dead relatives on a higher level of cyclic existence is the official, 'orthodox' motivation behind any Buddhist pilgrimage. [134] The Mongolian word for
the Buddhist notion of merit (or virtue), *buyan*, also means 'good luck,
fortune, prosperity' (*buyan, buyan kheshig*, 'merit-favor'), which is an indication
of the extent to which mundane and spiritual aims are intermingled. Pilgrims
were also—or were primarily—seeking happiness, fortune, health, longevity,
reputation and prosperity in this life and in their future lives through contact
with the sacred site. To beckon good fortune, the donors use verbs indicating
growth, such as 'rise,' 'increase,' 'expand,' 'strengthen,' and expressions like "as
long as their chance, fate and glory rise higher up like the new moon" (SF72,
1898; LH27, 1929; TY54, 1930). The vocabulary of wishes of the steles and certificates includes:[135]

- *nasun buyan*: 'age merit,' i.e., longevity. For example, "strengthen (ensure)
  ten thousand long lives under the feet of the holy master" (SF58, 1896);
- *khei mori*: lit. 'wind-horse' (depicted on flags printed with a wish-granting
  jewel), like in Tibetan, designates the 'ever living prospering spirit': *khei
  mori* was believed to be a vital component of the human body along with
  breath (*ami*), soul (*sülde*) and spirit (*sünesü*), bones and blood. Consequently, it also means 'good luck/fortune' (*khei moritai*, 'lucky, fortunate,
  endowed with success') and 'well-being.'[136] The wishes of increasing *khei*

---

134   Miller has emphasized the importance of accumulation and growth ("the underlying
      pressure towards expansion") in Tibetan Buddhism: a Buddhist community tends to
      accumulate merit, spread the religion, found new monasteries, recruit new monks to fill
      them, and accumulate property (1961: 431). The stone inscriptions all use expressions such
      as 'capital of merit' (*buyan-u khöröngge*) and verbs indicating growth, development and
      expansion (see Appendix 2).

135   On the notions and terminology of chance, good fortune, grace and destiny in the
      Mongolian world (*khei mori, sülde, kheshig, buyan kheshig, aja*): Bawden 1985b: 14 *sq.*;
      Bawden 1990; Hamayon 1990: 377, 627-630.

136   The meaning is the same in Tibet: "In fact, it is a symbol of the idea of well-being or good
      fortune. This idea is clear in such expressions as 'the increase of the *rlung-rta*' (*rlung-rta*

*mori* and longevity are central to the popular religious practices of the Mongols;

- *buyan kheshig*:[137] 'merit-favor,' fortune;
- *tsog jali, tsog jilde, tsog sülde*: grandeur, splendor, magnificence, glory (*tsog* also means 'energy, spirit');
- *aldar*: fame, renown, reputation;
- *uchiral*: fate, circumstances; *tsog uchiral*: good fortune;
- *sürüg nemegde-, sürüg mal arbid-*: increase of flocks and herds;
- *ger khotalaar amur mendü*: well-being, "peace and health for the entire family."

Pilgrimage clearly appears as an individual practice to accumulate merit for a better reincarnation, to be blessed with *kheshig*, to increase one's *khei mori* and *nasun buyan*, and to remove 'pollution' through meritorious acts, offerings and contact with the sacred. This vocabulary, which is common to Mongolian prayers, such as "Wind-horse incense-offerings,"[138] points to the fact that pilgrimage devotional practices also respond to the religious needs of herdsmen. The Buddhist notion of merit (which must be accumulated) here conflates with indigenous notions of vital energy (which must be increased) and fortune (which must be shared). Chapter 7 will show how contact with numinous traces and saints at particular sites allows a person to increase his/her *khei mori* and *buyan kheshig*.

To sum up the wishes expressed in the texts of the steles and certificates, the donors' efforts, penance, donations and prayers to Mañjuśrī result in the accumulation and multiplication of a 'capital of pure and white merits.' These merits will allow them to gain a better reincarnation, eventually in a paradise or in Shambhala, for their dead relatives and for their descendants, as well as to extend longevity, increase good luck and fortune, and strengthen reputation and

---

       *dar-ba*) when things go well with someone, and 'the decline of the *rlung-rta*' (*rlung-rta rgud-pa*) when the opposite happens" (Karmay 1993: 151).

137    Both *khei mori* and *kheshig/buyan kheshig* can increase or decrease, but *khei mori* is a kind of vital energy, a component of one's being, while *kheshig* is not. *Kheshig* is initially a part of offerings made to ancestors, then it is shared between the members of the clan; from ancestors' blessings, it came to designate good fortune, grace, prosperity (as the result of blessings) and also, after the eighteenth century, imperial favor (Atwood 2000). *Kheshig* circulates but can be harnessed and contained in certain forms; it must be shared, otherwise it can be lost. Someone who has a lot of *kheshig* must help others, practice charity and share his/her fortune. *Buyan kheshig* is not something that one receives: it is produced by one's good deeds or believed to be sent by the Buddha.

138    *Khei morin-u sang* (Bawden 1990).

glory for themselves. More generally, accumulated merit can also deliver all sentient beings from the ocean of sufferings and propagate the *dharma*. Finally, donors hope that their future reincarnation will be reborn at the golden feet of Holy Mañjuśrī and immediately obtain Buddhahood.

### General and Personal Expectations

The conventional, standard vocabulary of steles can still be heard in the speech of present-day Mongol pilgrims, who often mention *buyan*, *khei mori* and 'gaining a better reincarnation' as their main motivations. But more simply, a common answer to the question "Why do you go on pilgrimage to Wutaishan?" is "Any good Buddhist must go to Wutaishan at least once in a lifetime." Although it is not a mandatory duty comparable to the *hajj* for a Muslim, a great number of Mongol Buddhists made (and still make) the vow to go to Wutaishan once in their lives. They sometimes decide to embark on the journey following a prescient dream, in which a monk or Mañjuśrī himself has told them to undertake the pilgrimage. For instance, in the 1970s a pious Buddhist from Amdo dug up a small bronze statue of Mañjuśrī; he concluded that his eight-year-old son had a specific relation with Mañjuśrī. Later, the young boy dreamt that Mañjuśrī told him to restore Buddhist activities in Shifangtang. The boy therefore went to Shifangtang on Wutaishan to become a monk.[139]

Nineteenth-century sources confirm that going to Wutaishan was sometimes the most important vow a Mongol could make in his/her life. In 1883, Gilmour wrote that some Mongols used to journey to Wutaishan quite often, sometimes as often as once a year, hoping that each new visit would ensure happiness in a new life:

> One visit made by a pilgrim is said to ensure him happiness for the period of one of his future lives, two visits for two lives, three visits for three lives, and so on. In this way every devout Mongol endeavours to make at least one pilgrimage to this mountain during his lifetime, a number of them go frequently, and there are some who endeavour to visit it every year. In addition to this promise of happiness after death, a journey to Wu T'ai is frequently prescribed as a cure for disease, and the merit of making these journeys is supposed to be transferable, so that it is not uncommon thing to meet Mongols going to Wu T'ai, not on their own account, but for the benefit of others.[140]

---

139     See his biography in Li Xi 1994. For similar prescient dreams for Chinese pilgrims: Gimello
           1992: 103.
140     Gilmour 1970 [1883]: 143.

The stone inscriptions do not mention specific motivations or aspirations, but ancient and modern practices as well as biographical sources confirm that specific goals—such as finding a cure for an illness, seeking a vision, serving penance or countering a curse—are generally superimposed on more general motivations. Wutaishan was also a main destination for Mongols who wanted to have children. In Chapter 7, we will see in more detail the two main places on Wutaishan which were especially visited by those praying for a child: the Mother's Womb-Cave and Guanyindong Monastery.

One source of information about an individual Mongol's reasons for making the pilgrimage comes from Li Xiangzhi:

> Barbarians (*dazi* 韃子) give offerings. The Mongol barbarians have an honest nature; they especially value filial piety and submission [to their parents]. If a father or mother falls ill, and because where they live, medicine is underdeveloped, ... their medicine is made from herb roots and tree bark, there is nothing that can cure diseases. This is why after Mongols have contracted a disease and tried without success to be cured, [their son] has no other solution than [to go to] Wutaishan and make a vow (*xuyuan* 許願) [to be cured].[141]

Swiss reporter Walter Bosshard, who traveled in Mongolia in 1935-1936, gives another reason for making the pilgrimage. Bosshard met a certain Arach, a lama of Prince De's (Demchugdongrub, 1902-1966) entourage, who offered his services as a guide to Höhhot. From Höhhot, Arach planned to go to Wutaishan. Although he was poor, his larch-wood bowl was plated with silver, and his knife's sheath was inlaid with turquoise. Arach had been a lama in Urga but had fled the persecutions in Mongolia. When his flocks and herds died, he believed he was the victim of a curse. He decided to leave everything and, destitute and alone, to undertake a pilgrimage to Wutaishan. "I have to separate from my family. The evil spirits harass me relentlessly. My camels and sheep are dying. This is my punishment, for I would never have lusted after earthly goods."[142] He wanted to consecrate the rest of his life to Buddhism on Wutaishan, "in order to be delivered from all the sufferings of this earth and enter in the empire of delights, nicer than all the paradises."[143] But later, when his horse refused to walk, he went back home.

---

141    Li Xiangzhi 1932: 181.
142    Bosshard 1954 [1950]: 93-94.
143    Bosshard 1954 [1950]: 98.

Mongol pilgrims may go on pilgrimage to supplicate Mañjuśrī or to fulfill a promise to make the journey in return for some request already granted. Their privations, offerings, prostrations and circumambulations must be somehow equivalent to the blessings they have received. Requesting some favor from a deity and undertaking a pilgrimage in return is a symbolic transaction found in all pilgrimages: the vow of 'payment' establishes a relationship of dependency, of debt between deity and pilgrim which has been called the 'feudal paradigm'—the patron being the deity of the site, the client being the pilgrim.[144]

Alan Morinis' typology of the various individual motivations and aspirations can be applied to the Wutaishan pilgrimage:[145] the majority of pilgrims made a 'devotional' pilgrimage (aiming at an encounter with or worship of the shrine deity, in this case, Mañjuśrī, as well as the sacred 'traces' of buddhas, *bodhisattvas* and saints) and an 'instrumental pilgrimage' with finite, worldly goals (like obtaining a cure for an illness). Others make a 'normative' pilgrimage according to life cycles (especially for old or dying pilgrims), an 'initiatory' pilgrimage aimed at the transformation of self (for Buddhists meditants), or a 'wandering' pilgrimage (for some *badarchi lamas* and hermits).

The few biographies of Chinese pilgrims to Wutaishan show similar motivations: [146] to 'meet' Mañjuśrī, see one of the mysterious phenomena of the terraces, fulfill a pledge (after having been given an heir, a cure), accumulate merit in this world and secure benefits for themselves and their family in the next one, as well as receive blessings through contact with the sacred land.[147] However, while many motivations were similar, Mongol and Chinese performed different devotional practices and rites at the sites they visited. What's more,

---

144    Preston 1992: 42; also Eade and Sallnow 1991: 24.

145    Morinis 1992: 10-12.

146    For instance, Tian Chang'an and Liang Heng, eds. 2003. Interviews with present-day Han devotees show similar motivations. I did not carry out research on Tibetan accounts.

147    According to Birnbaum (1984: 11), in the first millennium CE, the primary aim of the Wutaishan pilgrimage, like Central Asian pilgrimages of the time, was not to gain merit but to have a spiritual experience—a vision quest seeking genuine teachings from the *bodhisattva*. Then a further element was added to the motivation for pilgrimage: the specific personal exchange with a deity consisting of making a vow (*xuyuan*) and the redemption of vows (*huanyuan* 還願). According to Karl L. Reichelt, motivations for undertaking a Buddhist pilgrimage in China are 'to seek help' (*qiuen* 求恩) in case of sickness, failed business deals, poor harvests, particular sins, calamities or real religious need; the pilgrims take a vow at the nearest temple, inform the deity that they will go on pilgrimage, and during the pilgrimage they 'give back' the vow (*huanyuan*) (Reichelt 1934 [1928]: 293). See also Naquin and Yü 1992: 12. For similar motivations in Tibetan pilgrimages: Buffetrille 1996a: 318 *sq*.

Wutaishan appears to be a major spot for Mongols to be buried in, and even to die in, which it is not for Chinese.

### Mongol Burial on Wutaishan

Mongol burial on Wutaishan, if better documented, would have deserved a whole chapter. There is no mention of Mongol burials in Duke Migwachir's travel account, in Mongolian guidebooks or songs (except the song recorded by Timkowski, cf. p. 200), or in the detailed Chinese records by Li Xiangzhi, Zhang Dungu or Gao Henian. However, a few Western travelers noticed the great number of Mongols journeying to Wutaishan carrying the bones or cremation ashes of their deceased parents, or ashes of monks, in order to bury them in the holy land of Mañjuśrī so that they would acquire religious merit and gain a better rebirth. According to the Lazarist fathers Huc and Gabet, who traveled in Mongolia and Tibet in 1844-1846 but did not actually visit Wutaishan:

> The most celebrated seat of Mongol burials is in the province of Chan-Si [Shanxi], at the famous Lamasery of Five Towers (Ou-Tay) [Wu-t'ai]. According to the Tartars, the Lamasery of the Five Towers is the best place you can be buried in. The ground in it is so holy, that those who are so fortunate as to be interred there are certain of a happy transmigration thence. The marvellous sanctity of this place is attributed to the presence of Buddha, who for some centuries past has taken up his abode there in the interior of the mountain. In 1842 the noble Tokoura ... , conveying the bones of his father and mother to the Five Towers, had the infinite happiness to behold there the venerable Buddha ... . it is certain that the Tartars and the Thibetians have given themselves to an inconceivable degree of fanaticism in reference to the Lamasery of the Five Towers. You frequently meet, in the deserts of Tartary, Mongols carrying on their shoulders the bones of their parents to the Five Towers, to purchase almost at its weight in gold, a few feet of earth, whereon they may raise a small mausoleum. Even the Mongols of Torgot perform journeys occupying a whole year, and attended with immense difficulty, to visit for this purpose the province of Chen-si.[148]

Alley and Lapwood wrote in 1935:

---

148    Huc 1928 [1924]: 93-94.

[It] is considered to be a fortunate thing to be buried in Wu T'ai, there being many accounts of pious elders being carried thither from far Mongolia so that it might become their last resting place.[149]

This practice was particularly common for Inner Mongol laypersons and lamas,[150] but it has also occasionally been observed with Khalkhas and Buryats. The Kanjurwa Khutugtu explains in his biography:

For religious and economic reasons, then, the great monastic center at Wu-t-ai-shan had important links both to Peking and to Mongolia and later many of our people desired to be buried there. Our people believed that a burial there would assure one of a good rebirth in the realm of Manjushri, the protector of scholars and the venerable deity of this monastic center. Some of our people traveled for a year at great expense and difficulty to visit Wu-t'ai-shan.[151]

Describing funerary customs among the Alashan Mongols, an article explains that after death, the body would remain at home for a period of three to seven days. Then,

if a body was to be buried, a lama would first be invited to come and choose a grave site ... Sometimes a lama might be invited to come afterwards and to carry the ashes to Wutai Mountain.[152]

Some Mongols also carried their dead relatives to be buried in Kumbum Monastery.[153]

There were important formalities required to bury one's parents' bones or ashes on Wutaishan "and for each particular case the authorization of the Bogdochān [i.e., the Manchu emperor] is necessary," wrote Pokotilov in 1893.[154] According to the 1728 "Regulations of the Court of colonial dependencies," Emperor Yongzheng gave orders about burial on Wutaishan:

---

149    Alley and Lapwood 1935: 119. Also Pokotilov 1935 [1893]: 77.
150    Taveirne 2004: 438 about Ordos Mongols.
151    According to his biography, written by Jagchid and Hyer 1983: 106-107.
152    State Nationalities Affairs Commission of China 1986: 136.
153    Narsu and Stuart 1994: 102.
154    Pokotilov 1935 [1893]: 77.

[In] general, it is forbidden to send the bones of lamas, [Chinese Buddhist] monks, Daoists, bannermen, Mongols and others to Wutaishan to be buried. If a Mongol *da lama* or other wishes his bones to be sent to Wutaishan to be buried, he should submit a request to the [Lifan]yuan, which will memorialize to the Throne to ask for an imperial edict [to approve it]. Resident lamas and [Chinese Buddhist] monks can be buried on Wutaishan but at a certain distance from the monasteries.[155]

Still in the 1880s, the Russian Mongolist A.M. Podneev added:

A khubilgan who wishes to be buried in these mountains must during his lifetime solicit the Bogdokhan [the Manchu emperor] for permission for such a burial and, without that official action and the Bogdokhan's consent, a burial in Wu-t'ai-shan is quite impossible according to the law. This rule applies not only for khutukhtus but is equally for princes and in general for all Mongols.[156]

Judging from the considerable size of the Mongol cemeteries on the mountain, we can conclude that these formalities were certainly simplified or omitted in the late Qing dynasty, when the state's interest in Wutaishan declined, and Mongols probably were free to bury their dead there in the Republican period. Pokotilov wrote:

Besides, it is required that if the corpse was brought within a coffin, it will be buried as it is, because according to the Chinese law this is considered the only possible and decent form of burial. But transportation of coffins to Wutai is rare because the cost of funerals is high. However, the burial of corpses that were previously incinerated is much more common, and [their transportation] is incomparably cheaper.[157]

Although in some parts of Inner Mongolia Qing-dynasty Mongols used to bury their dead in coffins, it is indeed difficult to imagine transportation of coffins to Wutaishan. Other sources inform us about the transportation of cremation ashes, placed in a small white bag or box, to Wutaishan.[158] The Mongols also

155   *Lifanyan zeli*, Qianlong reign, manuscript version quoted by Chen Bo 2010: 24; repeated in
      the *Qinding Lifanyuan zeli* 1817: *juan* 59, 22a.
156   Pozdneev 1978 [1887]: 365.
157   Pokotilov 1935 [1893]: 77.
158   Narsu and Stuart 1994: 102.

transported in a jar or in a small box the bones left after the corpse had decomposed, usually collected three years after death, for a second burial on Wutaishan.[159]

The urns containing the cremated remains of reincarnate lamas and abbots from Mongol monasteries were also carried to Wutaishan to be buried in *stūpas*.[160] Pozdneev noted that in Mongolia the corpses of high-ranking lamas were generally cremated or mummified; however,

> there are khubilgans who are not buried in Mongolia but taken to Tibet or to Wu-t'ai-shan. The ashes of such dead are gathered in a special box which is then put in a suburgan, and thus they are sent to their destination on a white camel. It is said that in Tibet such suburgans are placed in the idol-temples, and in Wu-t'ai-shan in special cemeteries for which the Mongols are said to have a certain plot solicited from the Bogdokhan [the Manchu emperor]. It is remarkable that burial in Wu-t'ai-shan is considered more sacred by the Mongols even than that in Tibet.[161]

Pokotilov recounts that those who performed these journeys had to carry gold to buy several square *chi* of land and then erected small funerary *stūpas* or brick *bungkhang* ('tomb, mausoleum,' here designating small brick structures for noblemen) on the plot.[162] The ashes were not buried underground but placed within these brick structures.[163] A simpler burial was small funerary mounds erected above the ashes and funerary 'memorials' (epitaphs?) on very small plots, which made the cemeteries densely crowded and compact.[164] Alley and Lapwood noticed "an extraordinary number of tombs, usually in the form of small *stūpas*."[165] At the end of the nineteenth century, according to Rev. Edkins:

> On the hillsides the graves are exceedingly numerous. Cemeteries in the plain, in the vicinity of the monasteries, are also not rare. The Gegens of the Yung-ho-kung monastery in Peking are brought here to find a final

159   Tibetans used to carry the skulls of their dead to Mount Kailash (Charles Ramble; personal communication, November 2011) and to other pilgrimage destinations (Jest 1975: 360).

160   Song Wenhui 2000: 34.

161   Pozdneev 1978 [1887]: 365.

162   1 *chi* 尺 = 0.32 m.

163   Mongols generally avoided digging the soil so as to not hurt the spirit-masters of the land.

164   Pokotilov 1935 [1893]: 77.

165   Alley and Lapwood 1935: 119.

resting-place. White tombs, enclosing an urn which contains the ashes of the departed, are everywhere seen.[166]

Probably because of the cramped conditions, large cemeteries were created at a certain distance from the main monasteries. Before 1949, elderly Mongol devotees, instead of making the entire journey to the five terraces, used to climb to Dailuoding, bury the ashes of their family members in the vicinity of the monastery and collect pine cones from the holy pines planted within Dailuoding to bring back home as a precious souvenir of their dead.[167] Tombs can still be seen on the slope south of Dailuoding Monastery. It even appears that very few monks (mostly, local monks) were buried within the monasteries. The five first *jasag lamas* of Wutaishan in fact each have a funerary *stūpas* in a compound at Fenglingu 楓林谷, the valley that extends from Shuxiangsi to Fenglinsi. Each *stūpa* has an imperial stone inscription recording the lama's biography; in front of the stele, offerings used to be given on an altar four times a year during the Qing dynasty.[168] However, the other *jasag lamas* had their funerary *stūpa* within Pusading.

The largest cemetery for lamas and for some high-ranking lay pilgrims was located behind Pusading,[169] on the right side of the path leading to Shouningsi.[170] Some Inner Mongol reincarnated lamas, such as the Chagan Diyanchi Khutugtus in eastern Inner Mongolia, had dedicated places for burial of their lineage (Fig. 25): a small temple run by three disciples of the Seventh Chagan Diyanchi, named Ruiyingsi (which is also the Chinese name of the Chagan Diyanchi's Monastery in Inner Mongolia), was built in Fenglingu Valley around the great funerary *stūpa* of Samdan Sangbu, the founder of the lineage.[171]

The custom of burying the ashes of dead relatives on Wutaishan has resumed since the end of the Cultural Revolution. Mongols coming mostly from Inner Mongolia, but also from the Republic of Mongolia, wish to be cremated after

---

166  Edkins 1893 [1878]: 240-241; also Pokotilov 1935 [1893]: 77.

167  Lian Kaowen 1993: 39.

168  Zhao Gaiping and Hou Huiming 2006.

169  Pokotilov 1935 [1893]: 77.

170  For a photograph taken in 1918 of the old 'lama cemetery' behind Pusading: Zhang Yuanji and Zhuang Yu 1925: pl. 12. For pictures of funerary Chinese-style and Tibetan-style *stūpas*: Ono Katsutoshi and Hibino Takao 1942: 26. On their map of Taihuai and the Numinous Vulture Peak, a large cemetery is indicated between the peak and the river, east of Yuanzhaosi and Luohousi, at the spot of the present-day village.

171  Cui Zhengsen 2002: 53. In 1907, a certain Ombo Sengge from this monastery offered a hundred taels to Tayuansi (TY28, 1907). Rebuilt between 2003 and 2006, it is now a branch temple of Luohousi.

death to "get a better life in the next reincarnation" and thus arrange for their
ashes to be brought to Wutaishan by a relative, generally a grandson. They buy
increasingly expensive plots of land on Wutaishan.[172] The large cemeteries on
the hillsides are extended every year. Nowadays, the three largest are located
south of Santasi around the funerary pagoda of the monk Miaofeng (the slope
provides an excellent vista over Pusading, the Great White Stūpa and the main
valley) (Fig. 26),[173] behind Pusading on both sides of the path leading to
Shouningsi,[174] as well as around the *stūpa* of Pakpa (Puensi). Other cemeteries
and scattered Mongol tombs are found in Fenglingu Valley, to the south of Upper Shancaidong,[175] to the north of Dailuoding, at the foot of the Western

---

172    Information from interviews I conducted in the Republic of Mongolia, Inner Mongolia
       and on Wutaishan.
173    See the general view in Ono Katsutoshi and Hibino Takao 1942: 42. In the same cemetery,
       the urns of the Chinese abbots of Xiantongsi are buried in brick tombs resembling yurts.
174    In 2012, the cemetery located on the right side of the path leading to Shouningsi was
       destroyed and partially relocated higher up, on the left side of the path.
175    The cemetery for Tibetan masters near Shancaidong, known as the Cooling Charnel
       Ground in Tibetan (Durtrö Chenpo Silji), is most revered by Tibetans (Duan Jinjin 2008:

FIGURE 26     *Mongol laypersons' tombs, cemetery on the way to Sanquansi.*
              © ISABELLE CHARLEUX, 2010.

Terrace,[176] at Huayangou 華嚴谷 around the *stūpa* of Pakpa,[177] and on the way
to Fomudong (Fig. 6).

The ashes of lamas (mostly Tibetan, Mongol and Han Gélukpa lamas of
Wutaishan, but also a few lamas from Amdo) are buried in Tibetan-style white
*stūpa*s. The burial sites of Inner Mongol laypersons tend to imitate these *stūpa*s:
the pyramidal brick structures with a stele written in Mongolian and/or in Chinese are sometimes even topped with a *stūpa* summit (Fig. 26). Other Mongol
tombs are small vaulted subterranean brick chambers with a surface opening in
the slope. According to the tombs' steles, the great majority house the remains
of laypeople from eastern Inner Mongolia (Khölön Buir, Jirim, Xing'an Leagues),
Höhhot and Ordos. I could not find dated tombs predating 1980, but most of the

---

78, quoting a Tibetan guidebook). Still in the twenty-first century according to Chou Wen-
shing, it is "considered equal in spiritual potency to the eight great charnel grounds in
India for practioners, and has been home to the remains of many masters" (2011b: 129).

176  Fischer 1923: 101.

177  See Online Appendix B: "Puensi." This is an old *stūpa*-cemetery for monks; the *stūpa* of a
National Preceptor (*guoshi*) is identified by a stele.

tombs' steles have no date and several cemeteries have been relocated. I have heard that these cemeteries were indeed much older but that in the 2000s new *stūpa*s were erected for the many bones found in the course of construction of new villages.

Interestingly, burial on Wutaishan goes against usual Mongol burial customs. While it not surprising that high-ranking Mongol lamas were buried on the mountain, burying laypersons on Wutaishan goes against archeological data and twentieth-century observations of herders' customs. Anthropologists generally insist on the importance for rural Mongols of being laid to rest in their homeland: a special site is chosen, with the help of an astrologer, on a slope or at the top of a mountain, in a 'higher, pure place' (*öndör tseber gajar*).[178] Pastoralists believe that the dead in the vicinity will protect their descendants; besides, the location of a burial site allows herders to claim the surrounding (winter) pastures.[179] In fact, the Mongols used to legitimate their use of the resources (i.e., the pastures) of a locality through the placement of their dead— a practice which is common to many societies. Among the Buryats, it was believed that dead ancestors, collectively localized on the mountains used by their descendants as summer camps, became the master-spirits of the land.[180] According to Pozdneev, princes who died abroad, except those who died in Tibet or Wutaishan, were always brought back to their own banner to be buried—meaning that only those who were 'fortunate' enough to die in Tibet or Wutaishan were buried there.[181] Making an exception for Wutaishan (and Tibet), the Mongols would not bury their relatives on mountains located far from home.

Moreover, in the modern period, except for some great masters who were mummified, and for nobles,[182] Mongols did not build tombs, burial mounds or monuments to remember the burial site of their dead. Commoners used to wrap their dead in a cloth and place them directly on the ground to be devoured by wild beasts and birds (if bones were left, they were later buried or

---

178    Delaplace 2009.

179    Delaplace 2009: Chapter 3, esp. p. 147-165. Winter pastures are called 'lineage encampments' and are said to be inherited from the ancestors.

180    Hamayon 1990: 623-633; also Humphrey 1995 about 'chiefly landscapes'; on the relation between the dead and the masters of the land: Delaplace 2009: 139-141.

181    Pozdneev 1978 [1887]: 612.

182    In the Qing period, aristocrats placed their dead in a sacred area on high mountains within their homeland, either in a coffin underground or in a wooden hut or a brick *bungkhang* (see Zhukovskaya 1990 for the sepulture of five princes of the Jasagtu Khan Aimag whose bodies were dried out in a sitting, praying posture). This could also be the case for lamas: Shirendev 1997: 34.

placed in a wooden box and cremated). Sometimes the corpse was cremated and the ashes put in a small box or bag, which was later taken to a place identified by a lama as the final resting place for the deceased. The idea behind choosing 'exposure' and cremation was that the body and its traces should quickly disintegrate: grass should cover the place as fast as possible so that it becomes indistinguishable from the open steppe. For commoners, the memory of the particular spot, although marked by a stone, was erased after two or three generations.[183]

Nonetheless, many Buddhist Mongols found burial on Wutaishan preferable to that in their homeland, despite the fact that placing their dead on Wutaishan would not secure any rights to pastures on the sacred mountain. The aim therefore was purely religious: Buddhist death rituals focus on the purification of bad karma in order to obtain a good rebirth. Death is the crucial moment when karmic potentialities are activated and determine a new existence in *saṃsāra*. Because Wutaishan is a 'Buddha land,' burial there was an assurance that one would attain a more favorable rebirth in a pure land,[184] as stressed by donors' wishes repeated in the stone inscriptions to be reborn in Sukhāvatī and Shambhala. Wutaishan was viewed somehow as a direct access to a paradise. Through the numinous sites, especially the presence of relics of Śākyamuni and great saints, the soil of Wutaishan confers blessings to those who touch and absorb it (see Chapter 7); it purifies and sanctifies the dead who were buried in it. Similarly, G. Schopen evidenced the importance of burial *ad sanctos* in ancient India (small funerary *stūpa*s surrounding the great *stūpa* of Sanchi) and in Mount Kōya 高野山 in Japan (around the tomb of Kōbō Daishi 弘法大師/Kūkai 空海, 774-835), because the relic and the actual Buddha are religiously one and the same.[185] Burial at Mount Kōya also ensures rebirth in Amitābha's paradise.

The great number of names of deceased relatives recorded on the votive stone inscriptions, not to mention on funerary steles, shows that commemorating the dead was a major preoccupation on Wutaishan. Mongols ordered special services in the monasteries for their dead parents' well-being and reincarnation (see Chapter 6). Nowadays, Inner Mongol families still often journey to Wutaishan to commemorate their dead; they visit the tombs and offer blue scarves, alcohol, fresh fruit, plastic flowers and incense (this may be a

---

183    Delaplace 2009.
184    A euphemism for 'die' is 'become a buddha/a deity/an icon' (*burkhan bol-*), which is not considered incompatible with the idea of rebirth.
185    Schopen 1997.: "Burial *ad sanctos*."

recent practice, since ethnographers have observed that in Mongolia today people do not visit cemeteries, which are believed to be haunted).[186]

In addition, some old or dying Mongols especially journeyed to Wutaishan to die there,[187] a practice occasionally observed in pilgrimages of other religions.[188] Gilmour mentions Mongols who were suffering from disease awaiting death in Wutaishan temples.[189] Many other pilgrims died on the road. As noted by Swallow in 1903:

> Generally when a Lama died on the road [to Wutaishan] his body was burnt, and his companions would bring his bones to be buried near some of the temples. Cases had occurred where men, in order to gain merit, had been burnt alive by their comrades, and their bones were buried in prominent places.[190]

Some monasteries took the responsibility for the burial of lama-pilgrims who had stayed in their precinct.[191] Lozang Menlam, the Monguor lama from Choné Monastery (in Amdo) who founded Shifangtang to provide shelter to itinerant lamas, had a brick *stūpa* of the *putongta* 普同塔 type ('*stūpa* of universal unity,' a term from Chan Buddhism to designate funerary *stūpa*s for deceased monks, Mo. *tügemel tegshi suburga*)[192] built at about one hundred meters from the monastery. He ordered that, if a monk-pilgrim died at Shifangtang, Luohousi

---

186   Delaplace 2009. This would deserve further study.

187   Some old Mongols hoped to die on Wutaishan, but there was no cliff for suicides like on Chinese pilgrimage mountains (Wudangshan, Taishan, Emeishan) and no specific connection with an underworld for dead persons (see Grapard 1982 about Japanese sacred mountains). The only Chinese story of suicide that I could find on Wutaishan is that of a woman who ran away to Wutaishan to escape her arranged marriage and jumped off from Saduoyai 薩埵崖 Escarpment or Mahāsattva Peak, but her body was never found and people believed she flew into the sky (she is depicted on the Cifusi map).

188   This is not the case in Tibetan pilgrimages (Katia Buffetrille, personal communication, 2009).

189   Gilmour 1970 [1883]: 151.

190   Swallow 1903: 179. Foreign accounts describing lamas' practices should be taken with a pinch of salt.

191   Li Xiangzhi (1932: 64) describes the funeral of a monk from Tayuansi, half the cost (five hundred silver dollars) being paid by his disciples, the other half by his monastery.

192   A modern *putongta*, with small cases for deceased Chinese monks arranged around a central statue of Kṣitigarbha, stands at the back of Puhuasi. Other monasteries, such as Mimoyan and Wenshusi, also had a *putongta*. Accordong to Prip-Møller (1967 [1937]: 172-175, ill. 211, 212), a *putongta* can have one or several inaccessible subterranean chambers beneath for the ashes, to which channels or openings lead from the base or sides of the

Monastery had to supply three hundred pounds of timber for his cremation. The ashes were then put in a box inside the *putongta*. Water flowed at the *stūpa*'s base; the boxes were put side by side and each time a box was added, the box at the front was carried away by the water.[193] This *putongta* is the Tibetan-style *stūpa* that now stands alone near the Qingshui River. The construction of such *stūpa*s shows the necessity of dealing with lama-pilgrims' burials: *putongta*s for lama-pilgrims were located outside monasteries (in conformity with the imperial edict) and were clearly distinct from resident lamas' funerary *stūpa*s. I do not know if other *shifangtang* monasteries also took the responsibility for burying laypersons who had died in their precinct, but, as seen before, their monks also used to escort back to Mongolia ill or tired pilgrims.

### The Pilgrims' Journey

The stone inscriptions show the Mongol pilgrims as they present themselves, but we need to rely on other sources to know how they actually traveled. Although it is not possible to give a precise description of their peregrinations to Wutaishan, some travelers' records offer a glimpse of how the pilgrims prepared for their journey and reached the sacred site—their means of transportation, their equipment, the route they took and the places they stopped at along the way. How Mongol pilgrims traveled to Wutaishan is linked to their material prospects and to their hopes and expectations: pilgrimages of commoners traveling on foot amid extreme adversity contrast with those of princes and officials bringing their family, guards and servants in caravans of twenty or thirty persons riding camels and horses. [194]

#### Preparation and Observances

Once the decision to undertake the pilgrimage was sealed by a vow, the pilgrim had to prepare himself for the journey. Present-day Mongol pilgrims take all kinds of precautions before going on pilgrimage. Like for any other travel, they ask a lama astrologist or check in an almanac whether the day of departure is auspicious for traveling and whether the journey will be safe.[195] They go to the

---

pagoda above. The number of rooms below varies: some are for monks, other for nuns, others for laypersons.

193    Wei Guozuo 2004: 42-43.
194    Li Xiangzhi 1932: 181-182.
195    For preparation of present-day Tibetans going on pilgrimage, and especially clothing and rituals of purification: Buffetrille 1996a: 390; Buffetrille 1997: 76.

nearest monastery or to their 'family lama' to ask for blessings and obtain names of monks or relatives living on Wutaishan. In Urga, the *badarchi lamas* used to pass under the 'Stūpa [That One] Crawls Under' (Shirgaadag suburga/Shurgadag suvraga, built over an archway) when they left on their pilgrimage.[196]

Lay and monk pilgrims often respected certain observances during pilgrimages such as vows of fasting or abstinence from meat.[197] Such vows were also taken by Mongol devotees on the 8th, 15th and 30th day of every lunar month and on major holy days.[198] Yet the vow of vegetarianism was certainly much less mandatory than it was for Chinese pilgrims.[199] During a pilgrimage, hunting was prohibited.

### Practical Matters

Mongol pilgrims had to obtain a travel permit or passport from the administration of their banner. Regardless of their status as nobles or as commoners, Mongols were confined within the defined territorial limits of their banner and could not travel, nomadize or go on pilgrimage outside their banner without authorization; otherwise they incurred fines. Officials, even princes and dukes, had to ask for a leave of absence (*chilüü guyu-*).[200] Groups of laypeople requested a group passport from the civil authorities: on these were written the individuals' names, the number of people, their banner and the time, destination and purpose of travel.[201] Monks had to obtain a passport from their monastery. Generally speaking, pilgrims' passports were easily obtained. The Shabi office (the office of the Jebtsündamba Khutugtu's estate) readily delivered free travel permits to go to Wutaishan and Tibet to the people belonging to the

---

196   Majer and Teleki 2006: 35, quoting Pürev 1994: 45.

197   Mo. *batsag, matsag, batsag-un sanwar*, Tib. *nyenné*, Skt. *upavāsatha*. Regarding vows such as vegetarianism in Tibetan pilgrimages: Ekvall and Downs 1987: 29; Buffetrille 1997: 88. But Buffetrille (2003) wrote that Tibetans drank alcohol during pilgrimage festivities: "pilgrimage retains the air of festival, expressed in song, dance, games, and the consumption of alcohol," and Kapstein (1998: 96) compared the carnival atmosphere to that of a pilgrimage to Woodstock. On Wutaishan, this carnival atmosphere is especially observed during the Sixth Month Festival.

198   Pozdneev 1978 [1887]: 574-578.

199   On observances of Chinese pilgrims, who respect silence and vegetarianism during their pilgrimage: Reichelt 1934 [1927]: 294-295; see also the guidebook for pilgrims *Chao si da mingshan luyin*, Republican period.

200   Altanzayaa (2000: 146), quoting a letter to the throne.

201   About passports to Wutaishan preserved in the archives of Alashan: this chapter, p. 15, 215.

Shabi estate.[202] According to Owen Lattimore, in 1941 "pilgrims and casual travelers move without hindrance across banner frontiers."[203]

Travelers' accounts show a major difference between journeys in the Mongolian-speaking world and those abroad. Buryat pilgrims still felt almost at home when they arrived in Urga. What made the difference was hospitality. In Mongolia, walking pilgrims could travel with no other means than their backpack: they enjoyed the hospitality of other Mongols and received extra food and offerings en route from alms-givers. Similarly, when traveling in Tibet, Mongol pilgrims received Mongol hospitality in Mongol-populated areas of the Tsaidam (in Eastern Tibet), but this trickled out when approaching Lhasa. Nevertheless, "Mongolian lamas do know how to get along with very little at times," as Pozdneev wrote, speaking about lamas from a college of doctrine. "I happened to see in Urga tsanid lamas who with 200 or even 170 silver *liang* [taels] managed not only to travel to Tibet, but even to live there for about two years."[204]

In the early twentieth century, the Mongol economy was still partially based on pastoral products, and the pilgrims needed cash money to undertake their pilgrimage abroad. Pilgrims sold horses and sheep in exchange for silver money before leaving for, or on the way to, Wutaishan.[205] As for princes or officials travelling in caravans,

> they go to Zhangjiakou, Datong or Suiyuan, where a *wenbu* [*ombo lama*, fund-raising monk] sent by a monastery of Wutaishan waits for them. After having welcomed them, the *wenbu* of the monastery leads them to the mountain. In every inn they stop for the night, in every place they stop to have a meal, the prince does not have to manage or care for anything; he only has to follow and pay the expenses. If there is any problem, the *wenbu* will speak and translate for the two parties.[206]

### The Walking Pilgrims' Equipment

While Mongol journeys in caravans (for moving to a new pasture or for trade) are documented,[207] travels on foot are not. In Mongolia, pedestrian travelers were essentially lay pilgrims and *badarchi lamas* who lived a peripatetic life (Fig. 27). They had to carry heavy baggage:

---

202  Andreyev 2001b: 171.
203  Lattimore 1942: 189).
204  Pozdneev 1978 [1887]: 276.
205  Li Xiangzhi 1932: 181-182.
206  Li Xiangzhi 1932: 181-182.
207  Lattimore 1928; Avery 2003.

FIGURE 27     *A lama student traveling from one monastery to another and a wandering lama.*
© FORBATH 1936: BETWEEN P. 103-104.

They prepare a backpack with a wooden frame (*beijiazi* 背架子) to carry
their luggage, put their silver dollars in a bag, and walk on foot to Wutaishan to
give everything up as offerings.[208]

The equipment carried by the *badarchi lamas* has been described by Gochoo
as "equivalent to a whole family in movement" [209] (Fig. 28). The average set of
gear included fifty-four objects:

- the 'backpack,' a tall bag with a two-part wooden frame made of curved
  willow sticks (83 × 79 cm.);
- a tent (2 × 2 m.) with ten stakes;
- a 'Tibetan cauldron,' the lid of which is used as plate and cup (23.5 cm. in
  diameter), and a leather bag for the cauldron, in which are stored tea, salt, a
  spoon, etc.;

---

208    Li Xiangzhi 1932: 181.
209    Gochoo 1970 [1963]. See also Heissig 1972, II: 743-744 for a detailed description of the
       *badarchi* and his appearance.

FIGURE 28    *Equipment of the badarchi lama.* © GOCHOO 1970 [1963]: 74. Painting "One day
in Mongolia," by B. Sharav (1869-1939), circa 1915, detail representing a
badarchi, Zanabazar Museum of Fine Arts, Ulaanbaatar.
© ISABELLE CHARLEUX.

- a felt mattress or carpet with cotton-lining (158x74 cm.) and its cover, and a
  goatskin to protect the mattress from dampness;
- a cotton strap with two brass rings—a rope to tighten the backpack and
  hold the tent in place;
- an aluminum flask for water;
- 5 kg. of food: (wheat?) flour (1 kg.), barley flour (1 kg.),[210] meat dried for five
  years (1 kg.),[211] dry cheese (1 kg.) in individual bags; salt (in a bamboo case
  or goat leather bag), one or two goat leather bags for tea (1 kg.),[212] designed
  to withstand heat and humidity, and 8 empty bags (1 kg.);
- small individual bags containing herbs from Lhasa (for fumigations), herbs
  from Erdeni Juu Monastery, juniper from Otkhon Tngri Mountain, incense
  sticks, *khadag*, herbs to burn against enraged dogs and three divination
  dice;
- a dark-colored *deel* (robe-coat), black Mongol boots, a *joshoo* hat, a belt,
  underwear, rosary beads, a wide red scarf on the left shoulder, an amulet

---

210    Up to the early twentieth century, the staple foods for Mongols, as well as for Tibetans,
       were roasted barley, milk products and tea.

211    *Bortsa*: dried beef, mutton or camel meat cut into strips or put into powder and dried. It
       was eaten raw, mixed with hot water, or cooked into noodle soup.

212    When short of tea, Mongols use substitutes such as thyme (*ganga*) and *terelji* (a kind of
       rhododendron), which also have medicinal properties.

box with representation of deities, a knife, two staffs—to shoo away dogs
when the *badarchi lama* approaches a yurt and to pitch his tent.

*Badarchi lama*s also carried a breviary and various ritual texts—such as *Ariun sang* (an incense offering prayer for purification) and *Gürim* (a variety of rites to avert, repel or exorcise misfortune)—and sometimes a small portable altar. Destitute travelers had a smaller backpack with no tent.

Judging from ancient pictures, it seems that Mongol pilgrims did not wear any special clothing for the pilgrimage,[213] but, when describing the pilgrimage to Erdeni Juu, Lham Pürevjav explains that pilgrims used special headgear, robe-coats (*deel*) and gloves.[214] What visually distinguished pilgrims from ordinary devotees were their backpacks and the multiple amulets they carried over their robe-coats. Some also carried a weapon for protection against the dangers of the journey,[215] but most Mongol pilgrims, like Tibetan pilgrims, relied on amulets and talismans (Mo. *buu*, < Ch. *fu* 符) to protect them against robbers and against the dangers of the mountain paths and the bad weather at the mountain passes. They prayed along the way with rosary beads and prayer wheels. Describing Mongol pilgrims, Chinese agent Ma Ho-t'ien wrote:

> [E]ach wore at his neck a bronze box about an inch square with a bronze Buddha inside. The face of the image was made of gold and the body was wrapped in red and yellow silk and satin. Along with this hung another box of glass and tin with a painting of Tsong-kha-pa inside. The little bronze Buddha had been presented to them by the Dalai Lama when they went through Tibet, and hence was of special value.[216]

Even the poorest pilgrims wore amulets.[217] Amulets need to be consecrated by a lama and be in contact with the body to be effective. They can be diagrams and drawings inscribed with spells on paper or cloth, wrapped in a cloth, wound with threads or sewn up in leather pouches: these were carried about the neck, tied round the arms or the body. Some were worn all the time, such as the one

---

213    Present-day elderly Khalkha pilgrims wear their best *deel* to undertake a pilgrimage.
214    Lham 2011: 51-53.
215    Edkins 1893 [1878]: 238.
216    Ma 1949: 14-15.
217    The following information comes from Mongol and Kalmyk friends, from observation on the field and from the literature on amulets and amulet boxes in the Tibeto-Mongol world: Skorupski 1983; Le Calloc'h 1989; Clarke 2001; D'ianakova 2001: 62; Vinkovicz 2003; Lang 2007: 33-36.

given by a lama on the day of birth,[218] or protection knots (*janggiya*, knotted cloth or string given by a lama, usually at a collective blessing ceremony) worn around the wrist.[219] Pilgrims also carried specific amulets for travel, kept in boxes. Amulet boxes (*guu* < Tib. *gau*) can be quite big (up to 12-13 centimeters) and heavy. Small ones were worn on a strap around the neck against the chest (for men and women), and larger ones were worn across the shoulder, on the right side under the arm (for men), fixed to the belt (for men) and sometimes at the back to prevent dangers coming from behind. A pilgrim could carry up to twelve boxes on his body. Those who traveled in a caravan fixed an amulet box around the neck of the leading animal. At the completion of the journey, the largest boxes were kept on the household altar.

The amulet box itself, when inlaid with precious or semi-precious stones having specific qualities, and decorated with the Eight Auspicious Symbols or the wish-granting jewel (*cintāmaṇi*), also had protective properties. Silver boxes were commissioned to a silversmith or a jeweler; worn on the outside of the coat, they were also visible symbols of wealth and status. They contained a miniature painted image, a molded clay image (*tsatsa*) or a small cast-copper figurine of a protective deity, as well as written charms to prevent the dangers of travel and all kinds of small protective objects: grains of sanctified wheat, a scrap of ritual scarf that had covered a famous icon, any object worn by a revered figure (a bit of clothing, of *khatag*),[220] leaves of sacred trees and so forth.

Lamas and lay devotees, at home as on pilgrimage, also carried a rosary (*erikhe*) around the wrist or, more frequently, hanging from their neck.[221] On pilgrimage, when walking they muttered the prayer *Oṃ maṇi padme huṃ!*, all the

---

218    These are miniature paintings representing particular deities that were "assigned to individuals through astrological chance, for each person's time of birth placed them in relationship to specific deities. Further, individuals in Mongolia who encountered particular problems in regard to finances or sexuality or health could, after consultation with astrologers and monks, purchase burhany zurags of deities whose influences were especially relevant to their problems" (Davis 2010; also Humphrey 1998: 427).

219    Buryat and Kalmyk laymen who have taken the vows of an *ubashi* had the distinctive custom of wearing a red ribbon over their right shoulder upon taking vows (Pozdneev 1978 [1887]: 180).

220    *Khadag* (Tib. *khatak*) are long scarves made of silk or cotton, usually yellow, black, white or blue; the longest have woven pictures of buddhas (generally Amitāyus, *bodhisattva* of long life).

221    Rosaries were personal objects, and one was not supposed to use someone else's. In Tuva, the rosary was buried along with the person: it was believed that after rebirth the deceased would once again use it to count prayers. See D'ianakova 2001: 62-63 about Tuvan rosaries; Pozdneev 1978 [1887]: 220.

while counting beads, in order to be protected against misfortune and difficulties on the road. They usually bought a large wooden rosary made on Wutaishan, which was (and still is) an important 'souvenir' for Mongol pilgrims.[222] They also prayed with hand prayer wheels, though these are not used anymore.

### Time for Traveling

Going on pilgrimage is generally a personal choice. According to information given by modern Mongols, there is no particular moment to undertake the pilgrimage, but, generally speaking, most sacred sites are especially visited on festival days because religious activities performed on major holy days yielded greater merit than those done at another time.

Did the pilgrimage season correspond to periods of inactivity for herders? How could they leave their flocks and herds for part of the year? In pilgrimage sites of Mongolia, summer (especially mid-July) and autumn were, and still are, the pilgrimage season, the time when great monastic festivals take place and *naadum* (Cyr. Mo. *naadam*), the three 'male' games—horse racing, wrestling and archery—are held throughout the country. The Finnish linguist Gustav J. Ramstedt explains the reason why Mongols did not store hay for their animals in summer: "that is when the great horse races are held and besides, people are generally on pilgrimages then."[223]

By contrast, Wutaishan seems to have been frequented by Mongol pilgrims almost all year round. According to the ritual calendar of Pusading in 1940 (Table 8), the busiest months were the first (New Year) and sixth months of the Chinese lunar calendar, yet every month also had a major event. Chinese travelers noticed that Mongols came continuously from the fourth to the tenth lunar month and were especially numerous during the fall, when horses were fat and healthy, ready to be sold before winter.[224] In summer, the population of the mountain doubled from one to two thousand, including the pilgrims.[225] The sixth lunar month was a period marked by the Great Sixth Month Festival as well as by ritual dances and the Great Mule and Horse Fair. Zhang Dungu wrote that Mongols left when snow began to fall, closing off the mountain.[226]

---

222    Nowadays on Wutaishan all pilgrims wear a rosary, a marker that distinguishes them from tourists.

223    Ramstedt 1978: 83

224    Tian Pixu *et al.* 1883: *juan* 3, 9b; Bai Meichu 2010 [1925]: *juan* 2, 154.

225    Lao Li 2004: 99, figures for the early twentieth century.

226    Zhang Dungu 1911: 24.

Conversely, Gilmour, and later Gao Henian, confirmed that Mongol and Tibetan monks came all year round, even "in the dead of winter."[227] Speaking of a road that was highly frequented in winter by large camel caravans of pilgrims, Fischer observed that "in winter the Mongols look on this pilgrimage like birds of passage going to a warmer climate."[228] Although mountain passes were sometimes closed by snow, cold winters on Wutaishan did not prevent Mongols, accustomed to low temperatures, from going on pilgrimage. Winter is a low season for nomadic herders, who, in summer, are busy shearing sheep, milking animals, making milk products, preparing stocks of food and fodder, and organizing *naadum*. Pokotilov (in 1889) even asserts that Mongol pilgrims were much more numerous in winter, from the tenth to the third month of the following year, and that "in summer the sacred mountain is relatively empty, and many lamas [from Wutaishan] journey to Mongolia to organize alms-rounds." This unabated flow of pilgrims in winter created the necessity of importing large quantities and varieties of food.[229] The herders who left their cattle and sheep in Mongolia probably preferred going on pilgrimage during the low season (winter), while the pilgrim-cum-traders certainly preferred going to Wutaishan in summer and fall in order to fatten their animals and sell them at the Great Mule and Horse Fair or in autumn. For those who traveled with herds and yurts, the journey to Wutaishan was not all that different from their nomadic lifestyle back home. It must be pointed out also that Mongols especially came to Wutaishan when high clerics resided there, such as the Thirteenth Dalai Lama in 1908.

### Different Ways of Reaching the Sacred Place: Traveling on Foot or in Great Prostrations

Whatever the means of transportation, pilgrimage is a physical adventure. There were four ways of traveling to Wutaishan: on foot, in great prostrations, mounted on horse or camel (or carried in a mule litter) and, in the twentieth century, by motorized transportation. Beginning in 1918, a bus company offered a regular service between Urga and Kalgan, organized by the Chinese government.[230] Some found it more convenient to go first to Beijing: in 1908

---

227  Gilmour 1970 [1883]: 141; Gao Henian 2000 [1949]: 109. Mongol caravans preferred traveling long distances in winter to escape heat. Those who traveled in summer moved only at night, when temperatures dropped.

228  Fischer 1923: 89, 100. According to Richthofen (1903: 131), Mongol pilgrims especially came during the coldest season.

229  Pokotilov 1935 [1893]: 67.

230  Roerich 1933: 81. Andrews (1921: 180) adds: "The motor service for passengers which the Chinese Government maintains between Kalgan and Urga is a branch of the

Mannerheim met Buryats on Wutaishan who had come by train via Beijing and the town of Baodingfu (250 kilometers from Wutaishan).[231]

Although traveling alone on foot over a long distance was generally seen by outsiders as a sign of poverty, in Buddhism it was first and foremost a form of penance and a way to obtain greater merit.[232] The pilgrim's merits were increased by the difficulties of the journey, a fortiori if he/she walked. Traveling on foot was seen as particularly praiseworthy for Mongols, horse-riding folk who generally hate walking for any great distances and who usually wear boots completely unsuitable for walking. In Mongolia, as in Tibet, monasteries had a stele or a sign requiring anyone to dismount one's horse, sometimes as far as one kilometer from their entrance.[233] As a sign of piety, modern Mongol devotees going to a temple fair generally walk for at least the last few hundred meters.

Ordinary lama-pilgrims always traveled on foot, while high lamas generally rode horses. Yet there were some high clerics who chose to walk. When the *jasag lama* of Wutaishan was preparing a pilgrimage to Tibet by sedan chair around 1878, the Buryat lama Jangchup Tsültrim Pelzangpo (Agwan Dorjiev's main tutor) told him, "To make pilgrimage to Tibet sitting in a sedan chair held up by men would be meaningless."[234] As a result, the *jasag lama* went on foot to Tibet, in spite of his old age.

The study of stone inscriptions and passports shows that many pilgrims traveled in groups. Others walked alone, but, when approaching their goal, they often joined other Mongol or Chinese groups. Blofeld thus met a group consisting of two Chinese pilgrims in sedan chairs, a Mongolian lama on a horse, two muleteers and some six or seven Mongol pilgrims proceeding on foot.[235]

Western travelers made note of the great exhaustion of the pitiable pilgrims they met on their way who had made a vow to walk or prostrate. John Blofeld noticed that pilgrims preferred to walk, and he told the story of an old Mongol who had walked all the way from northern Manchuria, spending over two years

---

　　　Peking-Suiyuan Railway and has proved successful after some initial difficulties due to careless and inexperienced chauffeurs.

231　Mannerheim 1969 [1940]: 691.

232　In Tibetan pilgrimages in general, walking or progressing in great prostrations is the norm, but in the pilgrimage to Amnye Machen, many Gologs make the pilgrimage on horseback (Buffetrille 1997).

233　Pozdneev insists that in Mongolia pilgrims must approach a monastery on foot (1978 [1887]: 58-59).

234　Martin and Norbu 1991: 12-13, quoting Agwan Dorjiev's 1923 autobiography.

235　Blofeld 1948: 87.

on the road.[236] Walter Bosshard met a pitiable monk-pilgrim in Dörben Kheükhed Banner (Ulaanchab League) on the way to Wutaishan and wanted to help him. He was lying on the road, his back leant against a bundle to protect him from wind and rain; his robe and shoes were in tatters and his monk's hat so worn that one could not distinguish its color. He had walked for five months from a monastery in Manchuria and was about to reach Shira Mören Süme, a main monastery of Dörben Kheükhed. Although Wutaishan was still several months ahead, he refused to ride in Bosshard's car:

> I want to do my pilgrimage on foot. How could I let myself be driven in such a car and give up all the virtues I have accumulated up to this day? ... Your devil's car cannot increase the number of my virtues![237]

Pilgrims on foot were often described as poor mendicants. Henning Haslund-Christensen speaks of "emaciated wanderers who spent years of their lives in penitential journeys from one Buddhist holy place to another":

> From all the corners of Central Asia [these pilgrims in prostrations] work their ways to the holy places of pilgrimage and the goal may be as remote as Wu-t'ai Shan of the many legends, or Dzarung Khashor [Bodnath Stūpa in Kathmandu], the domed pagoda in still more remote Nepal ... . Alone or in small groups they crawled along across steppes and deserts, over mountains and rivers, overcoming all obstacles that met them on their way. When the route lay through unpopulated and barren country its length was doubled, for food and water had to be carried with them, and every time the pilgrim had measured out a few hundred yards he had to return over the same stretch to fetch the indispensable provisions... . Such pilgrimages often take years and frequently the frail body does not reach its goal. The thought that Death may meet them on the way has no terror for the faithful, for the soul that is set free on such a journey rises to a higher plane than that on which he lived during his time on earth and the ultimate goal draws nearer ... . Many times in dismal and Godforsaken regions I have come upon such dying pilgrims. And I have tried to still the hungry conscience of the well fed by filling them up with my superfluity of material goods. They have accepted them with friendly but impersonal gratitude. They have sat by my fireside, covered in rags but which a soul made whole. I have listened to their words and understood that these

---

236    Blofeld 1959: 88.
237    Bosshard 1954 [1950]: 199-201.

expressed what was for them a deep and sincere truth. And I have sat there and watched them resume their agonizing course towards that enticing distant goal, followed their tardy disappearance.[238]

Some pilgrims walked in a state of stupor. Haslund-Christensen met a pilgrim going to Urga who could walk and sleep at the same time—"strictly speaking he slept all the time."[239]

Many lay and monk pilgrims chose to go to Wutaishan (or to Kumbum, Labrang or even to Lhasa) making full prostrations every third step (*unaju morgü-*, lit. 'to fall down and bow') without interruption until reaching their destination. This type of walking prostration involves dropping to the ground, with arms stretched out in front; the pilgrim then draws a line on the ground with the tips of the fingers, thus marking the place his/her body has reached (Fig. 29). After rising, the pilgrim takes three steps, with the third step reaching the previously drawn line; from here the pilgrim again makes a bow, stretching out on the ground, and so on. Even more so than walking, the journey performed in great prostrations takes on as much spiritual significance as the destination itself. Foreigners like Edkins, who traveled in 1872, were very impressed by these pilgrims:

[A]long the road [from Beijing to Wutaishan] may occasionally be seen more than usually devout pilgrims prostrating themselves on the ground all the way to the sacred mountain. Their idea is this: Woo-tai is the favoured region of the Buddhas and of Manjoosere, its great Bodhisattwa. To bow down and fall at full length before the images is meritorious. To do this all along the road must be far more meritorious. The pilgrim says to himself: - "I will make a vow. I will therefore prostrate myself at every third step. Though the distance is long, I shall arrive in a month, two months, or three, and I can walk back without prostrations on my return." It is only the Mongols that do this. We do not hear of the Chinese making this sort of painful pilgrimage. The Mongols are willing on account of their reverence for Woo-tai-shan and a wish to conform to a fashion that has grown up among them ... [240]

These pilgrims protected their hands with pieces of wood tied on with leather thongs, and their elbows and knees with pieces of cloth, and they wore a

238   Haslund-Christensen 1935: 28.
239   Haslund- Christensen 1954 [1932]: 172.
240   Edkins 1893 [1878]: 211.

FIGURE 29    *Pilgrim progressing in great prostrations from his home to*
*Wutaishan. Detail of the 1846 Cifusi map, print preserved in*
*Güden Süme, Jaya-yin Khüriye, Tsetserleg, Republic of Mongolia.*
© ISABELLE CHARLEUX, 2009.

kerchief round their heads in order to prevent injury to their foreheads.
Gilmour describes the technique of a Mongol lama:

> He had a piece of wood in his hand, and with it marked the ground as far
> forward he could reach, then got up and walked forward to the mark, tak-
> ing care, however, to keep a good way inside it. He was constantly mutter-
> ing something or other, both when upright and then prostrate.[241]

Rockhill observed in 1887:

> It is no uncommon sight, when travelling over one of the roads leading
> there, to see devout Mongols journeying thither on foot and making a full-
> length prostration every two steps [sic], measuring the whole distance
> with their bodies. Months are frequently taken in performing this highly

---

241    Gilmour 1893: 102.

meritorious deed, for three or four miles a day when gone over in this fashion are enough to exhaust the strongest man.[242]

According to Swallow in 1903:

> We heard many wonderful tales about the pilgrims; men had come on foot from three thousand miles away, knocking their heads on the ground—some one, and some even three times for every step they walked. Most of them came begging their way, and had been known to die from hunger and fatigue when within sight of their Mecca.[243]

Travelers were generally more impressed by the piety of the Mongols than by that of the Chinese pilgrims, but Chinese pilgrims too were known to occasionally make even more impressive prostrations, when they ascended mountains loaded with chains or with saddles and bridles, [244] spectacular demonstrations of piety that were commonly criticized by literati as being born of credulity and fanaticism.[245] There were also a few Chinese monks who chose to make the pilgrimage on foot performing prostrations all the way.[246] For instance, the Chan master Xuyun reached Wutaishan in great prostrations every third step in 1882-1883 to pay back his debt of gratitude to his parents. While he was almost dying of cold, Xuyun was saved by a beggar named Wenji (who was none other than Mañjuśrī), who accompanied him to his destination, carrying his belongings, and probed him with questions.[247] Stories of Mañjuśrī appearing on the road to help miserable pilgrims are common among the Chinese and Mongols. Modern Inner Mongols say that the 'Black Mañjuśrī' (the main dragon king) of Wanfoge sometimes appears on the road to accompany and protect the pilgrims on their journey back home. When on Wutaishan, they particularly worship this statue (Chapter 6).[248] The *bodhisattva* who saves exhausted and sick

---

242   Rockhill 1890: 10. Pozdneev (1978 [1887]: 392-393) wrote: "I know a lama among the Chahars who went performing bows from Doloon nuur to Wu-t'ai-shan, and on another occasion, when going to Tibet, measured his length from the Tibetan border to Lhasa."

243   Swallow 1903: 182.

244   Some Chinese also dressed "in the crimson garb of criminals with saddles on their backs and a bit in their mouths while they climbed the mountain on all fours ... to fulfil a vow made the year before to the goddess that they would return to their shrine in this manner if she would cure their ailing parent" (Goodrich 1998: fig. 4).

245   Yü 1992: 228.

246   Reichelt 1934 [1928]: 294.

247   Xuyun 1988: 13-17.

248   Information from U. Hurelbaatar and U. Ujeed, confirmed by other pilgrims.

pilgrims along the way recalls the many stories about apparitions of Kōbō Dai-shi on the Japanese Shikoku 四国 pilgrimage or visions of Santiago on Europe's Santiago de Compostela pilgrimage.[249]

Nowadays, a few Mongol pilgrims still travel this way; they are usually men accompanied by a young boy, who carries a begging bowl and cares for their belongings. Some also travel alone, with a backpack or a small cart to carry all their necessities. They first cover the distance they plan to walk for the day, leave their cart, then walk back to their starting point and make prostrations up to the cart. If they find a place to sleep overnight, the next day they return to the spot where they made their last prostration and start again from there. A few years ago, an old woman traveling this way to Wutaishan from Naiman Banner in eastern Inner Mongolia had her cart stolen on the way close to her destination; she then had to go back home. She made the pilgrimage again a year later, starting the prostrations afresh from home, and this time made it to the mountain.[250]

### Mounted Pilgrims

By contrast, many pilgrims traveled riding horses, mules, donkeys or camels (Fig. 30). Pokotilov pointed out in 1889 that the Mongol pilgrims generally traveled with their own yurts and herds.[251] Other carried *maikhan*s, travelers' cloth tents, which are easily transportable. Large enough for a family, these tents offer minimal protection from wind and cold.[252] Pilgrims riding horses or camels were nobles, officials and wealthy Mongols journeying in large caravans with their family members; high clerics and lay pilgrims traveling alone or in small parties; and pilgrims traveling with their flocks and herds so as to offer the animals to Wutaishan monasteries and/or sell on the mountain.

Writing in 1932, Li Xiangzhi contrasts the 'ordinary pilgrim' traveling on foot, with 'princes' caravans:

> [Mongol pilgrims] go on foot ... Others will hit their body and head [against the ground in great prostrations] every fifty or hundred steps, so that the vow of curing their father or mother can be fulfilled. They make vows related to their own life [too]; thus, although it is superstition, we can see they are sincere, and when it is time to give back their vow [they prepare to go on pilgrimage] ... . But if they are princes or officials and

---

249   Reader 2005: 10-11.
250   Information from U. Ujeed, 2010.
251   Pokotilov 1935 [1893]: 70.
252   It has a ridgepole, supported by two upright poles, and outer ropes to stabilize it.

FIGURE 30      *Traveling lama pilgrims.* © FRANCK 1923: BETWEEN P. 145-146.

have made an official vow, it is not as hard [as for commoners].... They
bring all their family with them—wife, sons, daughters—as well as guards
and servants, from eighteen to twenty or thirty persons. They ride on camels and horses, or are carried in a mule litter, and they carry tents, that is,
Mongol yurts.[253]

West of Dolonnor in 1844, Father Huc and his fellows met the long caravan of a
Khalkha princess from Mergen Wang Banner, with camels and a carriage upon
four wheels.[254] Fischer, who describes the amazing traffic on the roads to
Wutaishan in 1917, noticed that caravans of Mongol pilgrims with fifty camels
were a common sight on the mountain.[255] He also encountered in the vicinity
of Datong, a

> column of 111 camels and 13 ponies moving slowly from North to South,
> with its Mongol riders of both sexes. The Chieftain, in fine heavy silk and
> fur, rode at the head of this imposing column. In its rear followed a "Lo T'o
> Chiao" or closed sedan chair carried as a litter between two big mules.[256]
> The chair was occupied by a number of children of the Chieftain; they
> proceeding [sic] to Mount Wu-T'ai Shan on a pilgrimage.[257]

---

253    Li Xiangzhi 1932: 181-182.
254    Huc (1928 [1924]: 38-39) understood 'Five-Towers' (Wuta) instead of 'Five Terraces'
         (Wutai).
255    Fischer 1923: 93.
256    The mule litter (*jiaoche* 轎車) was a covered palanquin with shafts at each end, which
         were fitted to the harness of two mules, one before and one behind. This was also the
         means of transportation used by Chinese officials and Western travelers on the mountain
         roads.
257    Fischer 1923: 106.

Nobles and reincarnations traveled with large retinues of attendants and servants, and were followed by those in charge of driving carts or leading a train of several hundred sheep, to supply them with provisions on the road.[258] Mongol scholar Altanzayaa gives the example of the exceptionally reduced retinue of the Fourth Jebtsündamba, who journeyed to Wutaishan with the official tour of the four Khalkha *aimag*s in 1813: he was accompanied 'only' by the *tusalagchi jangjun beile* Namjildorji, a staff of thirty-one lamas in charge of organizing the journey,[259] plus monks and laymen leading the herds and driving the carts.[260] By comparison, in 1839 the Fifth Jebtsündamba traveled to Beijing and then to Wutaishan with a retinue of three thousand monks.

### *The Road to Wutaishan: Bringing the Nomadic Lifestyle to the Mountain*

To reach Wutaishan, Mongol pilgrims spent from a minimum of ten days away from home, crossing northern Shanxi, to a maximum of five years if starting from farther afield and advancing by doing full prostrations.[261] The main pilgrimage road to Wutaishan for Khalkhas and Mongols of central Inner Mongolia followed the great trade roads and generally stopped at Longshengzhuang 隆盛莊 (Fengzhen County 豐鎮縣, Inner Mongolia), a flourishing trading center of the Chakhar steppes between Kalgan and Höhhot, on the Longzhuang River 隆莊河 (Map 7). According to Pozdneev, every year between one and ten thousand pilgrims followed this road to Wutaishan, stopping at Longshengzhuang to purchase goods before entering Inner China. Longshengzhuang also had a cattle market, where Chakhar Mongols sold horses, oxen and sheep to Chinese coming from Beijing in exchange for tea, cloth and flour.[262] Then the pilgrims crossed the northern part of Shanxi: Datong, Yingxian 應縣, Fanzhixian and Hongmenyan 鴻門岩, eventually arriving at the village of Taihuai.[263] Hongmenyan, located between the Northern and Eastern Terraces, at the border between Fanzhi and Wutai Counties, was the 'northern gate'—one of the four 'gates' of Wutaishan according to the cardinal points. In winter, this route

---

258   Prjevalski 1876: 156.

259   Two *soibong*s (< Tib. *söpön*, 'healing master', here, head of the Jebtsündamba's staff), two *donir*s (< Tib. *drönnyer*, secretary of a monastery); two *takhilchi*s (lama in charge of sacrificial offerings), two *sula daakhu lama*s (lama without official post), eight *khiya lama*s (adjudants) and fifteen *khaalgachi*s (doorkeepers).

260   Altanzayaa (2000: 146-147) dates the journey to 1814, but in actual fact the pontiff visited Wutaishan in 1813 and died shortly after, in the same year.

261   Blofeld 1959: 128; Yan Tianling 2004: 42.

262   Pozdneev 1971 [1896]: 28.

263   Ono Katsutoshi and Hibino Takao 1942: 129-133.

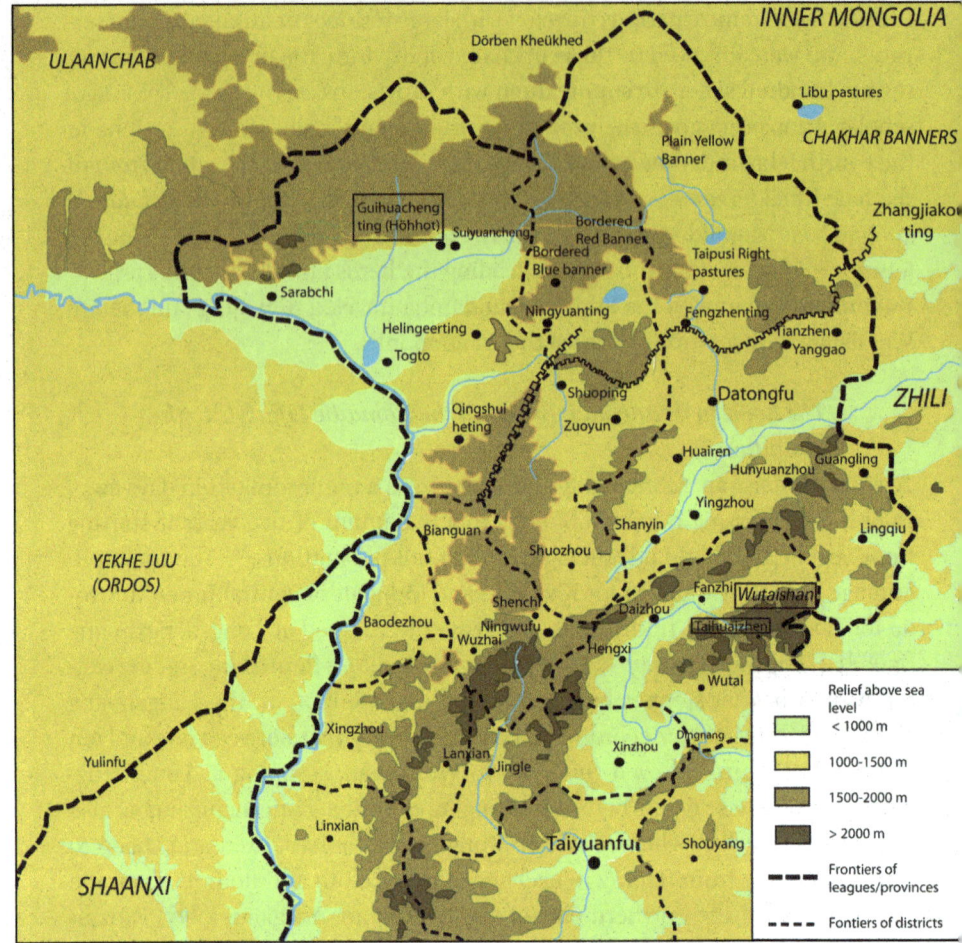

MAP 7        *Topographical map showing the northern part of Shanxi in 1820.* © ISABELLE
CHARLEUX (*based on the map by Tan Qixiang et al. 1982, nos. 20-21 and nos. 57-58*).

was heavily used by Mongol camel caravans. It was difficult because of its high
passes and rivers crossings (wheeled carts were practically not used).[264] From
Datong to Taihuai it took about five days: two easy days through the plain, and
three days with steep differences in height.[265]

---

264    Alley and Lapwood (1935: 116) wrote that "recent severe summer rains had washed away
       several of the poorly constructed bridges, so that streams had to be forded, making it
       necessary for passengers to alight and be carried across by vociferous countrymen at the
       expense of a few coppers."

265    Fischer 1923: 100 (who actually describes the return trip).

The western road through Daizhou and Ekouzhen 峨口鎮 was of easier access and seems to have been as heavily trodden as the northern one. Inner Mongols from the eastern Inner Mongol banners (Jirim, Juu Uda, Josotu Leagues, Bargu banners) as well as lamas from Beijing followed the old imperial road from Beijing through Baodingfu, Dingzhou 定州, Fuping County, the Great Wall's Changchengling 長城領 Pass (1,350 meters above sea level) and Shizui, a journey which took about ten days.[266] On average, caravans of thirty to forty pilgrims walked or rode up to 70 to 90 *li* (35-45 kilometers) a day. Camel caravans traveled in the winter season (November to the end of March) for ten to sixteen hours a day, at 3 to 5 kilometers an hour. A camel caravan usually made the journey from Urga to Kalgan in thirty to fifty days (horses were much faster).[267]

Along the main roads crossing Shanxi, several monasteries boasted specific relics in order to be integrated into the Wutaishan circuit. For instance, at a day's walk from the village of Taihuai was Wenshusi (Mañjuśrī Monastery), a Tibetan monastery near Daizhou that Mongol pilgrims visited and that was famous for enshrining the forty- to fifty-centimeter-long sandals of Śākyamuni (or of Mañjuśrī), which appeared to be made out of tree bark.[268] Coming from Beijing, just after Changchengling Pass before reaching Shizui, was the Arsan Bolog Monastery (Rashiyan Bulag, or "Holy Water Spring"), run by twelve lamas who all came from eastern Inner Mongolia when Edkins stopped there in 1872.[269] Mongol pilgrims also left a donation stele dated 1860 at the famous Yungang Caves in the vicinity of Datong.[270]

Traveling through Chinese territory entailed great hardship for Mongols. James Gilmour took the Mongols' defense:

> There is no more severe test of the earnestness of the religious devotion of the Mongols than their being willing thus to journey for days through the country of unsympathetic Chinamen, whose language they do not understand, and who lie in wait for their money, ready to fleece them at every turn.

---

266 Edkins 1893 [1878]: 211. It took three and a half days for Rockhill (1895: 768) to travel from Baodingfu to Beijing in 1887.

267 Andrews 1921: 180; Avery 2003: 77.

268 Rochechouart 1992 [1878]: 693-694; Chavannes 1912: 168.

269 Edkins 1893 [1878]: 223.

270 This stele dated 'Xianfeng 10' (1860) is almost illegible. I thank Olivér Kápolnas for having sent me a picture of it.

Although many pilgrims traveled into China with their own tent and herds, they could not live completely self-sufficiently: they had to buy fodder and fuel and even pay to water their animals, as well as pay taxes. Some pilgrims also brought their cattle, sheep and carts with them for other reasons and these large caravans organized for them to be looked after by other Mongols at the foot of the mountain (except for the animals destined to be offered or sold).[271] Travelers who rode camels did not stop along the way at Chinese inns, where camels were not admitted.[272]

However, the Chinese were accustomed to welcoming Mongol pilgrims, some of whom stopped at inns established every forty-five *li*, paying for room and board,[273] or in poor farmhouses, where they could find cheap beds.[274] The inns were heated by large *kang* beds, on which the guests could spread out their bedding.[275] Lama pilgrims left Tibetan inscriptions on the walls of such inns.[276] Many Shanxi traders and shopkeepers learned to speak Mongolian and opened shops and inns for the Mongols, with notices written in Mongolian at the entrance such as: "The men of this inn are honest and mild, everything is ready and cheap, therefore, O ye Mongols, our brothers, you could not do better than rest here."[277] Some Chinese shopkeepers even married Mongols.[278]

The return journey from Wutaishan was generally made in a hurry.[279] Wingate observed in 1900:

> [O]n the pass we met several Mongols with their ponies hurrying back to their native soil, their pilgrimage completed. One Mongol was prostrating himself full length on the ground nine times, making his last ke-t'ou to the P'u-sa-t'ing, the principal temple of this Mongol Mecca.[280]

---

271    Gilmour 1970 [1883]: 149.

272    Segalen 1967: 146.

273    Blofeld 1959: 122.

274    Blofeld 1948: 87.

275    Blofeld 1948: 87.

276    Edkins 1893 [1878]: 213.

277    Gilmour 1970 [1883]: 149. Jiang Weiqiao (1918: 16) details the prices and the menus of inns on the way to Wutaishan.

278    Gilmour 1970 [1883]: 149; Yan Tianling 2004.

279    Blofeld 1959: 132. I could not find much information on the return journey, except for the tradition of solemn addresses (*jorig*) declaimed to banner chiefs and high dignitaries once back home (Serruys 1977: 602-603).

280    Wingate 1907: 275.

### Conclusion: Typology of Pilgrims

The Mongol pilgrims to Wutaishan had a variety of expectations, interests and preoccupations, ranging from penance to tourism and trade. Many details will remain unknown; for instance, were the motivations to go on pilgrimage identical for men and women, for Khalkhas, Buryats and Inner Mongols? At least we can propose a simplified typology of Mongol pilgrims according to their status, mode of travel, aims and expectations:

1. The noblemen, officials and high lamas who visited Wutaishan with their suite, traveling in caravans, and recorded their donations on steles. Their motivations were as much religious as political;
2. The solitary pilgrims or small group of pilgrims—monks and laypersons, including wandering lamas—traveling on foot, some of them travelling performing full-length prostrations;
3. Small groups of mounted pilgrims traveling with tents and a few animals to offer to the monasteries, and yearly organized trade caravans of pilgrims-cum-traders, with their tents and herds;
4. Pilgrims who went to Wutaishan especially to bury a relative and/or pray for their dead parents.

Most pilgrims traveled in groups of persons of the same family, encampment or monastery, or in different groups who pooled their energies to help each other, often led by a lama. To pay for their pilgrimages, princes raised special taxes among their subjects. Traders instead brought animals to sell, hoping to make a profit that would cover their travel expenses and offerings. (The percentage of pilgrims-cum-traders may have been quite high, like in pilgrimages to Lhasa.) However, some pilgrims spent a half or a third of their entire belongings to get to Wutaishan, or even everything they owned. Others survived by begging.

The significance of the journey itself varied according to the mode of transportation. The pilgrimage was probably less important for mounted pilgrims than for penitents performing great prostrations and for pilgrims traveling on foot for days and weeks, enduring the hardships of the road and sometimes falling ill, getting robbed or even dying along the way.

We have seen how the last component of Preston's scale of spiritual magnetism was difficulty of access—due to either intrinsic (geography, various dangers) or extrinsic factors.[281] Whether Wutaishan was difficult to access actually depended on the period (peace or conflict), on the mode of transportation and

---

281   Preston 1992: 33-38.

on imposed rites of penance (fasting, great prostrations). For many pilgrims, the journey to this sacred mountain was the most adventurous experience of their lives.[282] The difficulties and sufferings of the journey were expected to increase the pilgrims' merit and purify the body of defilement.[283] By voluntarily enduring pain, pilgrims accumulated guarantees that their request would be granted by Mañjuśrī. Yet, on the whole, the Wutaishan pilgrimage was a well-organized affair: it was not actually a perilous adventure. Even if they were afraid of being cheated by Chinese traders, Mongols knew they would find relatives and help in specific monasteries, as well as groups of people to travel with, and would be able to put their yurts up in Wutaishan's tranquil pastures. The pilgrimage to Wutaishan was in fact far less risky, dangerous and expensive for ordinary Mongol families than the pilgrimage to Lhasa was.

For commoners bounded to their territory, traveling to Wutaishan once in a lifetime was certainly an 'exotic' journey that allowed them to cross boundaries, at least the physical ones, and get a glimpse of Chinese lifestyle, eat Chinese food, sleep in Chinese inns and purchase various Chinese commodities in market towns along the way. The walking pilgrims, especially those progressing in great prostrations and those who took vows such as abstention from meat and hunting during the whole journey, may have indeed had some kind of 'liminal experience' according to Turner's theory.[284] They certainly experienced, by the end of their journey, some degree of transformation through the direct contact with the divine and the exhausting practices of prostrating and circumambulating. By contrast, princes and Buddhist dignitaries who were used to traveling 'abroad' do not seem to have adopted habits when they journeyed to Wutaishan that were any different from when they crisscrossed Mongolia or visited Beijing. Likewise, the commoners who traveled with their herds, and especially those who went every year and sold their beasts at the market, simply appear to have adopted a particular kind of nomadization that varied little from the practices of their daily lives.[285]

---

282   Gilmour 1970 [1883]: 149

283   About the suffering body in the pilgrimage discourse: Eade and Sallnow, 1991: 16-23.

284   Turner proposed that pilgrims undergo a transformative and equalizing experience freed from the structure of ordinary society—they wear special clothing or other markers distinguishing them from ordinary worshippers, respect particular taboos and carry out distinctive actions; during a pilgrimage, rules of behavior are altered or suspended (Turner and Turner 1978: 7-9). For a discussion of Turner and Turner's arguments: Coleman and Eade, eds. 2004: Introduction.

285   Similarly, Buffetrille (1997: 99-100) observed that the Golog pilgrims' lifestyle on Amnye Machen does not truly differ from their everyday life.

# The Mongols on Wutaishan: Interactions and Encounters

Now that we have a more precise idea of who the Mongol pilgrims were in the late Qing and Republican periods, why they went especially to Wutaishan and how they reached their destination, let us examine what they actually did on the mountain—the sites they visited and the rituals they paid for. This chapter still focuses on Mongols but also deals with interactions and encounters between different ethnic and religious communities: the religious landscape of Wutaishan was shared between two traditions of Buddhism, plus Chinese popular religion, and between three main ethnicities. By studying the Mongols' specific practices and the sites they worshipped, I will question whether they made the same pilgrimage as the Tibetans and Chinese or a different one, and I will examine how lay and monk pilgrims and locals interacted with each other—in religious, daily and commercial activities. Was the Wutaishan pilgrimage one or many? A related question is this: Did pilgrims have a feeling of *communitas*, sharing common goals, expectations and experience, or did they behave as individuals with distinct faiths, social status and ethnicities? In other words, should we follow Elverskog's stimulating theory regarding the role of Wutaishan in the creation of a 'Mongol identity,' a 'Qing identity,' a 'Qing culture,' and a Qing 'cosmopolitanism' uniting Mongols, Chinese and Tibetans?

## Accommodation and Reception of Pilgrims

### Accommodating Mongol Pilgrims

The resident monks and shopkeepers, including Chinese, took initiatives to welcome and accommodate Mongol pilgrims on Wutaishan. The Mongols had four options for lodging: living in their own yurts, renting a room in inns or a house, staying in monasteries' hostelries or staying in private houses of (lama) relatives. Many Mongols carried their own yurt and stayed with their sheep and cattle in the pastures near Dailuoding and on the slopes of the Southern Terrace. For instance, when the Fourth Jebtsündamba journeyed from Höhhot to Wutaishan in 1802 "together with his lamas, officials and many servants," they "set up their tents on the land just below and to the east of Shuxiang Temple and stayed there."[1]

Some stayed in inns run by Chinese or rented a house at or near the village of Taihuai. Over half of the houses in Taihuai belonged to monasteries or to wealthy lamas, who rented them to pilgrims.[2] Edkins noticed near Pusading "a collection of buildings looking like a small town, where the animals belonging to travelers and to the monasteries are taken care of"[3]: the pilgrims staying in inns could leave their animals there—probably those that they were planning to donate to the monasteries.[4]

North of Pusading, "lodging-rooms for lamas formed quite a little town," and many pilgrims resided there.[5] Jiang Weiqiao counted about three hundred houses for lamas behind Pusading.[6] On their doors were pasted parallel auspicious sentences in Mongolian, in the Chinese fashion:

> May your age be the same as that of the pines in the southern mountains;
> May your happiness abound as the waters of the Eastern Sea.[7]

Lay pilgrims could probably also reside in this district, since Edkins added that:

> Many Mongol women were seen in this part, probably all belonging to pilgrim parties, who find quarters in rooms provided for them. Many ranges of buildings had upper and lower verandahs. Elsewhere are seen Tibetan houses with their small square windows in the upper part of a strong high wall.[8]

---

1  Dznyā na shrī man's Tibetan guidebook *Ri bo rtse lnga'i dkar chag rab gsal me long* 1994 [after 1827], passage transl. by Gray Tuttle, email, September 2011.

2  Edkins 1893 [1878]: 239-240.

3  Edkins 1893 [1878]: 234.

4  Before 2009, Taihuai extended southwest and west of Lingjiu Peak, on the two banks of the Qingshui River. Sadly, most of the village, along with its inns, was razed to the ground between 2007 and 2009 in order to accommodate the influx of tourists with Wutaishan's new status as a UNESCO World Heritage Site.

5  Edkins 1893 [1878]: 229; Pokotilov 1935 [1893]: 77.

6  Jiang Weiqiao 1961 [1918]: 22.

7  Edkins 1893 [1878]: 231.

8  Edkins 1893 [1878]: 229-230. Gilmour (1970 [1883]: 146) confirms that the houses south and north of Pusading were built in Tibetan style.

FIGURE 31    *Yurt in front of the Scripture Hall of Tayuansi.* © BOERSCHMANN
1937: ILL. BETWEEN P. 36-37.

Mongol yurts were many on the mountain. Within Gélukpa monasteries, yurts
served to receive important guests (Fig. 31).[9] Today, Tibetan-style buildings and
Mongol yurts have now totally disappeared from the Wutaishan landscape.

The *shifang* monasteries provided accommodation for pilgrims in a hostelry
with rooms ranging from dormitories for the poor to suites for those who could
afford them.[10] Generally speaking, Gélukpa *shifang* monasteries, such as Luohousi and Qifosi, had rooms for Tibetan and Mongol pilgrims, and Chinese
Buddhist *shifang* monasteries had rooms for Chinese pilgrims. That said, a few
Chinese monasteries (for example, Xiantongsi) also lodged Mongol pilgrims
who offered significant donations and who considered themselves to be specific donors of the monastery. *Shifang* monasteries served as hostels, restaurants and tourist information bureaus; men and women did not mix.[11] They
could lodge from thirty or fifty up to a hundred monk-pilgrims.[12] Small monasteries, such as Shancaidong, provided lodging for the poorest pilgrims,[13] while

9    Zhang Dungu was invited inside a yurt within Tayuansi. Cf. the picture of a yurt in
     Zhenhaisi (Li Xiangzhi 1932: ill. between p. 21).
10   The two-storied hostelry of Luohousi is located in the first courtyard.
11   Blofeld 1938: 35.
12   Li Xiangzhi 1932: 179.
13   Blofeld 1959: 125.

some quarters of Tayuansi were reserved for Mongol princes along with their retinue and mounts.[14] Tayuansi occasionally welcomed Chinese and Western travelers and treated them as 'official guests.'[15] High-ranking visitors and personal guests stayed in the abbot's quarters. Pusading had a 'lodging palace' for high-ranking monks, which served as a residence for emperors Kangxi and Qianlong and for the Thirteenth Dalai Lama.[16] It also had some luxury rooms for wealthy pilgrims, with a "*kang*, rich carpets, wall frescoes, chairs and tables."[17]

Because Mongols went on pilgrimage in ever greater numbers during the nineteenth century, two new accommodation centers for Tibetan and Mongol monk pilgrims were founded in 1822 and 1831 respectively: Cifusi and Shifangtang.[18] In nineteenth-century Mongolia, as in China, monk-pilgrims who could prove their status in a *shifang* monastery were immediately integrated into the monastic activities for the duration of their visit and participated in rituals and chanting.[19] The monasteries thus organized the lodging of Mongol pilgrims as soon as they arrived on Wutaishan according to their 'importance.'

### Reception in a Monastery

In Gélukpa monasteries, it was the duty of the *ombo lamas*—the same lamas who organized almsrounds in Mongolia—to receive the pilgrims: "these lamas are talkative and versatile; they ensure visitors' entertainment and a pleasant stay."[20] In Chinese Buddhist monasteries, this was the duty of the *zhikeshi* 支客師: their role was crucial in attracting donations, and particularly active, win-

---

14    Fischer 1923.

15    Mannerheim 1969 [1940]: 691; Irving 1919: 157; Swallow 1903: 179; Zhang Dungu 1911: 24; Chavannes 1912: 166; Fischer 1923: 89; Segalen 1967: 135.

16    The Thirteenth Dalai Lama later resided in Pushousi.

17    Blofeld 1948: 91.

18    Yang Yutan et al. [1985] assert that Shifangtang also welcomed male and female lay pilgrims. An Inner Mongol prince resided at Cifusi in 1935 (stele CF6). Nowadays the main lodging centers for Tibetan and Mongol pilgrims (laypersons and monks) are Luohousi and Shifangtang. Cifusi was revived in the 1990s as a Chinese Buddhist monastery and is no longer a *shifang* monastery.

19    Pozdneev 1978 [1887]: 275-276. About the credentials and elaborate rites governing a request for residence in Chinese monasteries (*guadan* 掛單): Welch 1973 [1967]: 10-16. About Chinese monks who request for residence in the Wutaishan monasteries: Li Xiangzhi 1932: 179. A Mongol pilgrim who visited Wutaishan in the 1990s wrote that lama pilgrims could enroll in Shifangtang and find a job after the very next day (Tian Chang'an and Liang Heng, eds. 2003: p. 45). Nowadays Mongol and Tibetan lamas behave as 'religious tourists' (as in Tibetan pilgrimage sites) and do not participate in monastic activities or daily offices.

20    Pokotilov 1935 [1893]: 65.

some and chatty monks were chosen for this office.[21] Li Xiangzhi provides insight as to how, in 1932, Mongol pilgrims were received according to their status and the amount they donated when arriving on the mountain. Apparently, if Mongol pilgrims had sold cattle, sheep and horses for three hundred to five hundred *yuan* before making their way to a Wutaishan monastery

> the monks of this monastery make an estimation of their offerings, divide them into three (categories), upper, middle and lower, and treat the donors (according to their offerings). The monks feed them for three to five days, giving them good meals such as mutton shoulder for the donors of the upper category. After having offered them [to the upper category of pilgrims] this excellent meal, the monks give them ordinary food. Those who stay up to one month or forty days (on the mountain) to fulfill their promise (*huanyuan*) and worship the Buddhas give their offerings, and when they have offered everything, they request some food to go back home. Some only keep a small amount of money for their travel expenses to return home on foot: this is how ordinary Mongol pilgrims give offerings.
>
> ... As for princes and officials ... After they arrive on Wutaishan, if [the prince] is a Xiantongsi donor, then he stops at Xiantong[si]; if [the prince] is a Pusading donor, then he stops at Pusading. When the monastery sees the donor arriving, [the monks] first serve him a meal (*xiamafan* 下馬飯), mutton shoulder plus various dishes. The donor to the monastery presides over the banquet. Also, a room is prepared for him. The following day [the donor] lightens lamps in the monastery, burns incense, worships the Buddhas, and then gives his offerings. For instance, if he brought 10,000 silver (dollars), he first offers at least 5,000 or 6,000 (silver dollars) to the monastery where he stays ... and later gives 3,000 or 4,000 (silver dollars) to the other monasteries. After he has worshipped at the Five Terraces and visited the monasteries, he buys a few wooden bowls of Wutaishan and bronze Buddha statues, and goes back home with his empty bags.[22]

Wealthy Mongol donors developed personal links and were 'attached' to a specific monastery for several reasons: first, those who had previously given offerings to *ombo lamas* from a certain Wutaishan monastery as he traveled the width of Mongolia were sure to be welcomed by this monastery as privileged

---

21    Pokotilov 1935 [1893]: 65.
22    Li Xiangzhi 1932: 182-183.

donors when they went on pilgrimage to Wutaishan.[23] As seen from Li Xiangzhi's account, this could also be a Chinese Buddhist monastery. This may also
explain why Mongols could bring their son to become a monk in a Chinese
monastery on Wutaishan.[24] Secondly, Mongols often had a relative or an acquaintance in a Gélukpa monastery on Wutaishan and would first donate to
that particular monastery.

### Great Moments of *Communitas*: The Festivals of Wutaishan

#### *The Great Sixth Month Festival*

The sixth lunar month (which generally falls in July) was the busiest period on
the mountain: the Great Sixth Month Festival attracted thousands of Mongol,
Tibetan and Chinese pilgrims. During the same period the Great Mule and
Horse Fair took place. Mongols were so numerous during the sixth month that
they had difficulty finding lodging.[25] The importance of the Great Sixth Month
Festival on Wutaishan is evidenced in the 1846 Cifusi map, which depicts the
great procession in its central part.

The festival opened with ten days of chanting and debating from the 6th to
the 13th day of the sixth month of the Chinese lunar calendar. It was attended
by all the lamas from Wutaishan's monasteries,[26] in addition to thousands of
Mongols and other pilgrims, who sat together cross-legged in the monasteries.[27]

> During the later part of the service several rich laymen walked down the
> rows of seated lamas and distributed alms. After this they performed the
> koutou before the Grand Lama's throne and presented him with 'hardas'
> [*khatag*] or ceremonial rolls of blue silk, which he accepted and then, as a
> sign of favour, placed upon the bent neck of the donors.[28]

In a later account, Blofeld described three Chinese who offered donations,
which were then redistributed among the pilgrims:

---

23    The pilgrims who offered a donation to a 'department' (*aimag*) of Urga were accommo-
      dated in that same department and would send their son there if the latter was ordained
      a lama (Pozdneev 1971 [1896]: 53).
24    Nan Yang 1998.
25    Rochechouart 1992 [1878]: 695.
26    Edkins 1893 [1878]: 235-236.
27    Blofeld 1959: 131.
28    Blofeld 1938: 30.

They proved to be well-to-do laymen who desired to gain merit by offering alms to the entire company. The High Lama introduced them with a few words, after which they bowed to the assembly and spoke in their turn. Lama officials then came forward and received great bags of money from them, which they proceeded to distribute, picking their way carefully between the rows of silent pilgrims who sat with their hands cupped above their crossed legs to receive the gifts.[29]

The climax of the Great Sixth Month Festival was the *cham* dance performed on the 14th day in front of the Mañjuśrī hall of Pusading.[30] The *cham* was introduced on Wutaishan in the seventeenth or eighteenth century.[31] In the late nineteenth century, sixty lamas at once performed the dance.[32] On the next day, a grand three-kilometer-long procession carrying a statue of Mañjuśrī (or perhaps of Maitreya)[33] in a palanquin was led by lama dancers and lama musicians, followed by "several high lama officials clad in splendid robes of yellow brocade and high layered hats"[34] and, last of all, by the *jasag lama* in a sedan chair.[35] The *da lama* of Tailusi and the 'lamas with a seal' were also carried in sedan chairs,[36] while others rode white horses with silver bridles and finely

---

29   Blofeld 1948: 99.

30   For the organization of the *cham*: Edkins (1893 [1878]: 235-236; Ono Katsutoshi and Hibino Takao 1942: 192-196, 205-212 (pictures taken during the festival: lamas playing music p. 14-16, masked dance p. 15-18, 20, spectators p. 16, 23, *jasag lama* p. 20, procession p. 21-23, *jasag lama* carried in a sedan chair p. 21); Wei Guozuo 1999 [1997]: 77-78. For a comparison with the ritual dances in Beijing Yonghegong: Ono Katsutoshi and Hibino Takao 1942: 212 (table).

31   Wei Guozuo (1999 [1997]: 78) gives the date 1721; Wang Bin and Guo Chengwen (1989) write that the *cham* ritual was introduced in the Kangxi period. Zhao Peicheng (2004) asserts that Qianlong decided to introduce the *cham* ritual to Wutaishan. None of them give their sources.

32   Edkins 1893 [1878]: 236.

33   The identity of the processional central statue is the object of debates, and I could not find out from which temple it came from. According to the *Wutaixian zhi* (1988: 584), Zhao Peicheng (2004) and Chou (2007: 120), it was Maitreya, but Blofeld (1948: 101; 1978: 143-144) asserts it was the '*bodhisattva* of Wisdom' (Mañjuśrī). In Mongolia, the Maitreya processions—one of the main festivals—are organized following the New Year and use a specific cart with a green horse head.

34   Blofeld 1938: 29.

35   Gao Henian 2000 [1949]: 65 (description of the procession in 1905); Li Xiangzhi 1932: 177-178; Blofeld 1938: 29..

36   Wei Guozuo 1999 [1997]: 78.

FIGURE 32     *Statue of Mañjuśrī or Maitreya carried in procession during the Great Sixth*
              *Month Festival. Detail of the 1846 Cifusi map, Rubin Museum of Art, New York.*
              © KARL DEBRECZENY.

woven saddle carpets.[37] Blofeld's vivid detailed description matches well with
the representation of the procession on the Cifusi map (Fig. 32). He wrote that
the procession was comparable to "a Roman Triumph in scale and probably
surpassed it in the lavishness of equipment and paraphernalia."[38]

> Then came the chair of the deity, supported on the shoulders of eight
> men, followed by the rest of the procession in the following order—a col-
> umn of banner bearers, the devil dancers, a great crowd of lamas and
> people, more musicians, the temple intoners, bearers of ritualistic objects
> and then the Grand Lama himself, preceded by several officials and car-
> ried in a huge sedan chair of red lacquer upon the backs of a number of
> perspiring men. His face was partly concealed by a long black silken fringe

---

37    Blofeld 1948: 101.
38    Blofeld 1938: 30-32; Blofeld 1948: 101; Blofeld 1959: 131-144.

suspended from this hat, in such a way that he could see but not be seen. Immediately behind him were the bearers of his enormous ceremonial umbrella and giant fan, both about twenty feet high. Last of all came an imposing looking gentleman in silk robes, who rode upon a horse with a scarlet saddle and silver bridles ....

The path was bordered by huge purple flowers and multitudes of buttercups and other wild flowers, but today these paled into insignificance beside the glory and colour of the procession. Little altars were set up at intervals along the way, bearing candles, incense burners and trays of offerings. At each one, as soon as the Grand Lama's chair reached it, the procession stopped and a high official from one or the other temple advanced towards him, bowing three times to the ground and offering a ceremonial strip of blue silk, after which the gongs sounded and the procession moved on. At the gates of the various temples along the route, the same ceremony was repeated, sometimes accompanied by the thundering of mighty Tibetan horns from within. At last, after passing through several densely crowded streets, the destination was reached.[39]

The observers were filled with wonder before the brightly colored garments and hats, the precious metals, silks and brocades gleaming in the sun, the thundering music, the shining golden statue and the shot of cannons.[40] The procession was followed by 180 great lama dignitaries in official robe,[41] plus their followers from each of the Wutaishan monasteries, on foot or riding horses, and four to five hundred monks and laypersons walking behind.[42] The *jasag* lama

was preceded by two resplendent figures bearing long poles to which was attached a horizontal silken banner or curtain, of which the lower edge was only some three feet above the ground, so that the whole formed a moving screen for His Holiness. As he approached, individuals would spring from the ranks of spectators lining both sides of the route, hurl themselves under his screen and then roll hurriedly out of the way of the oncoming lama.[43]

---

39   Blofeld 1938: 30-32.
40   A man shooting cannons is visible on the Cifusi map, at the foot of Pusading.
41   The yellow Gélukpa version of the official mandarin robe (Blofeld 1959: 143-144).
42   Wei Guozuo 1999 [1997]: 77-78; Blofeld 1959: 143-144.
43   Blofeld 1959: 143-144.

FIGURE 33     *Procession, Great Sixth Month Festival.* © ONO KATSUTOSHI AND
HIBINO TAKAO 1942: 21.

FIGURE 34

*Procession, Great Sixth Month
Festival.* © ONO KATSUTOSHI
AND HIBINO TAKAO 1942: 22.

Gao Henian describes the great procession followed by civil and military officers and by a crowd of monks coming from everywhere carrying alms bowls
and receiving great quantities of offerings on the way.[44] The procession gathered in front of the Mañjuśrī hall of Pusading, left the monastery by the back
(north) door, crossed the Cave of Four Gates (Simendong 四門洞, since destroyed) and the Officials' Bridge (Guanqiao 官橋, at the village of Dongzhuang
東莊, represented on the Cifusi map) and moved along Pushousi, Yingfang
Street 營坊街 (north of Taihuai), Shifangtang and Luohousi, where a second
*cham* was performed. Then the procession started again, advancing along Yanglin Street, the touring palace of the Qing emperors, and stopped in front of the
triumphal arch of Tayuansi. The *jasag lama* made full prostrations in front of
the Great White Stūpa, went through Xiantongsi and returned to Pusading.[45]
The procession therefore circled around Lingjiu Peak in the clockwise direction
of Buddhist circumambulation. Some authors describe slightly different routes
for the procession, whose route may have been organized differently from one
year to the next.[46]

Although the Great Sixth Month Festival was a Tibetan Buddhist festival,
Chinese popular deities were added to the list of Tibetan Buddhist deities,[47]
and all monks and pilgrims of Wutaishan attended it. In addition to the exorcist
function of the *cham*, this great ritual also aimed at taming the mountain deity
(the Dragon King)[48] and renewing the oath he made to protect Buddhism. As
explained by Chou Wen-shing, "*cham* parades a new pantheon of Wutaishan
deities that extends far into Tibetan and Mongol history and deep into Wutaishan's local and pre-Buddhist heritage."[49] It was certainly a main occasion for
building *communitas* between all pilgrims and resident monks.

---

44    Gao Henian 2000 [1949]: 65.
45    Wei Guozuo 1993 [1988]: 77-78; Zhao Peicheng 2004.
46    Li Xiangzhi 1932: 177-178) describes the procession going as far as Shuxiangsi and then
      back to Luohousi. Zhao Peicheng (2004) and *Wutaixian zhi* (1988: 584) give a different
      route.
47    Chou 2007: 120, quoting Hibino Jobū, *Godaishan*, Tokyo: Hebonsha, 1995: 251-257.
48    Gao Henian 2000 [1949]: 65.
49    Chou 2007: 120. The *cham* and the great procession have enjoyed a revival since 1987, and
      the organizers have striven hard to rediscover the very particular music of this ritual (text
      and pictures in Huang Yongsong and Dai Qing 1991: 28-33).

### The Ritual Calendar on Wutaishan

The Great Sixth Month Festival was the most important event on Wutaishan, but the ritual calendar counted dozens of other important dates.[50] Table 8 gives for the year 1940 the ritual calendar of the main Chinese Buddhist monastery and of the main Tibetan Buddhist monastery, Xiantongsi and Pusading.[51] In the year 1940 Xiantongsi organized twelve festivals; among them were common Chinese festivals, such as the Ghost Festival and the Mid-Autumn Festival, but there was also a Gélukpa festival: the Tsongkhapa Butter Lamps Festival. Pusading organized twenty-four festivals a year, including two *cham* rituals. Half of the festivals of both monasteries were organized in winter. The liveliest month in terms of number of rituals was, of course, the sixth month, but thirteen rituals were performed during the first lunar month to celebrate the New Year and expel evil influences. Mongol pilgrims coming to Wutaishan during the low season were certainly attracted by these dynamic events.

The Mañjuśrī Festival on the 1st day of the first month at Pusading corresponds to the Tibetan Great Prayer Festival (the Mönlam) celebrated in Tibet and in Mongolia. But whereas Mongol monasteries usually organized a grand Maitreya procession around monasteries or whole cities on that day, on Wutaishan Mañjuśrī presided over the entire first month. As in Mongolia, the anniversary of Tsongkhapa's death (or Tsongkhapa Butter Lamps Festival) was held on the 15th day of the tenth month (or from the 23rd to the 25th day of the tenth month),[52] and Śākyamuni's descent from Heaven (Lhalé bappé düchen, Ch. Tiangongfo 天公佛) was celebrated on the 22nd day of the ninth month.[53] The differences between the calendars of Pusading and Xiantongsi reflect the practice common in Mongolia to change the dates of rituals so that pilgrims and locals can attend as many festivals as possible. Except for the Great Sixth Month Festival, we have no description of the organization of these rituals. Small monasteries held only the main festivals, which often consisted of adding

---

50    Our sources here follow the Chinese calendar, but it was unclear whether the Gélukpa monasteries of Wutaishan followed the Tibetan or the Chinese lunar calendar. In early twentieth-century Ordos, the Mongol monasteries followed the Tibetan calendar, while the princes followed the Chinese one.

51    I have no data for the late Qing period, and this organization may have been quite different in the nineteenth century. My main source is Ono Katsutoshi and Hibino Takao 1942: 148-149; see also *Wutaixian zhi* 1988: 584-585.

52    This day is sometimes considered as being Tsongkhapa's birthday. On the importance of this festival in Mongolia: Majer 2008: 126-128. On festivals in Mongolia: Pozdneev 1978 [1887]: Chapter 5; Majer and Teleki 2005-2006.

53    Pozdneev 1978 [1887]: 384.

recitations and chanting to the everyday service.[54] In addition to celebrating the Gélukpa and Chinese Buddhist festivals, the many small Chinese temples (those to Guandi, the God of Wealth or the Jade Emperor) in Taihuai and in other villages organized processions and communal rituals.

## Mongol Pilgrims' Ritual Practices and Offerings at Monasteries

Many travelers and Chinese pilgrims have described the intense devotional life on Wutaishan, and especially the Mongols' practices. Besides prostrations and circumambulations, pilgrims performed specific rituals at certain places. I will question here whether these served as ethnic markers to distinguish Mongols and Tibetans from Chinese devotees or whether Tibetan, Mongol and Chinese Buddhists imitated each other and performed identical, borrowed or syncretic practices.[55]

---

54 The dates of only eleven of the twenty-eight contemporary revived festivals more or less correspond to that of the 1940 festivals (Avalokiteśvara's birthday, Mañjuśrī's birthday, Weituo's birthday, Kṣitigarbha's birthday, Śākyamuni's birthday, the Great *Cham* Festival, Ullambana, the Mid-Autumn Festival, Tsongkhapa Butter Lamp Festival, anniversary of Tsongkhapa's death, Śākyamuni's enlightenment). Besides, they now last only one day (or two days for the *cham* festival), versus up to four days in 1940. The other festivals performed in the 2000s are: New Year from the 20th day of the twelfth month to the 20th day of the first month, Maitreya's birthday on the 1st day of the first month, Śākyamuni becoming a monk on the 8th day of the second month, Śākyamuni's *nirvāṇa* on the 15th day of the second month, Samantabhadra's birthday on the 21st day of the second month, Buddha's mother's birthday on the 16th day of the third month, Five dragon kings' birthday and Qielan *bodhisattva*'s birthday on the 13th day of the fifth month, one-month opera in Wanfoge (sixth month), Avalokiteśvara's enlightenment on the 19th day of the sixth month, Mahāsthāmaprāpta *bodhisattva*'s birthday on the 13th day of the seventh month, Dīpankara's birthday on the 20th day of the eighth month, Avalokiteśvara's ordination on the 19th day of the ninth month, Bhaiṣajyaguru's birthday on the 30th day of the ninth month, Bodhidharma's birthday on the 5th day of the tenth month, Amitābha's birthday on the 17th day of the tenth month, Huayan pusa's birthday on the 29th day of the twelfth month (Xu Hong 2007: 49).

55 I here refer to the 'weak' meaning of the term 'syncretism' as defined by Albera 2009: 322: "pour dénoter la circulation et le mélange de pratiques et de croyances hétéroclites," versus the 'strong' meaning, i.e., the formation of a new, syncretic identity. About the controversial notion of syncretism in history of religions: Stewart and Shaw, eds. 1994.

TABLE 8    *Ritual calendar (lunar months) of Xiantongsi and Pusading in 1940*

| Lunar month | Day | Xiantongsi | Pusading |
|---|---|---|---|
| I | 1 | | Mañjuśrī |
| I | 2-3 | | God of Wealth |
| I | 1-8 | Wansheng fahui 萬聖法會 (for the peace of the country) | |
| I | 8 | Eight Immortals festival | |
| I | 8-9-10 | | Qingjing daochang 清靜道場 (清淨道場? Pariśuddhi ritual: ritual of complete purification) |
| I | 14 | | Amitāyus |
| I | 15 | | Mañjuśrī |
| I | 18 | | Five Mañjuśrī-s |
| I | 19 | | Thousand-hand thousand-eye Avalokiteśvara |
| I | 22 | | Śākyamuni's descent from Heaven |
| I | 24 | | Tsongkhapa |
| I | 25 | | Tsongkhapa's disciples |
| I | 27-29 | | 5 classes of Dagangsu 大剛素[a] |
| II | 19 | Avalokiteśvara festival | |
| IV | 2-5 | Mañjuśrī's birthday (in common with nine other Chinese monasteries) | |
| IV | 4 | | |
| IV | 6-9 | Śākyamuni's birthday | |
| IV | 8-10 | | Qijian daochang 啟建道場 (Ordination ritual) |
| IV | 8-18 | | Avalokiteśvara |
| V | 5-10 | | Śākyamuni |
| VI | 3 | Weituo's birthday | |
| VI | 6-15 | | Shenghui daochang 勝會道場 |
| VI | 14 | | *Cham* ritual |
| VI | 27 | | Tsongkhapa |
| VII | 11-16 | Ullambana (Ghost festival) | |
| VII | 14 | | Bhaiṣajyaguru |
| VII | 15 | | Śākyamuni |
| VII | 30 | Kṣitigarbha's birthday | |
| VIII | 10 | | Śākyamuni |

| Lunar month | Day | Xiantongsi | Pusading |
|---|---|---|---|
| VIII | 15 | Mid-autumn festival | |
| IX | 22 | | Śākyamuni's descent from Heaven |
| X | 1 | Kṣitigarbha's visit to hells | |
| X | 23-25 | | Anniversary of Tsongkhapa's death |
| X | 25 | Tsongkhapa lamp festival | |
| XI | | | Chuijiafo 吹迦佛* |
| XII | 8 | Buddha's enlightenment | |
| XII | 29 | | *Cham* ritual |

ª   I could not find these terms in dictionaries of Buddhism such as the *Foguang dacidian*.
SOURCE: ONO KATSUTOSHI AND HIBINO TAKAO 1942: 148-149.

### Basic Devotional Gestures

Mongol pilgrims seem to have performed the same gestures on Wutaishan as they did in Mongolia. The first basic devotional gestures, bowing with hands joined and kowtowing (*mörgö-*),[56] are common to Mongols, Tibetans and Chinese. On Wutaishan as in Mongolia, Mongols used to kowtow thrice in front of the main gate of a monastery before entering.[57] While making prostrations, kowtows, circumambulations or simply walking, they used to mutter simple prayers and turn their rosary beads.[58] Mongols and Tibetans recited the words "*Oṃ maṇi padme huṃ!*"[59] while Chinese recited the homage to Amitābha (*Namo Amituofo* 南無阿彌陀佛). Both prayers also worked as a greeting on Wutaishan.[60]

The first main devotional practice of Mongol pilgrims is that of making full-length prostrations. Both Mongols and Tibetans performed these within the monasteries, in the direction of the main icons and *stūpa*s, and on the roads—

---

56   *Alaga khabsur-*, or *alaga ben khamtud-*, 'join the palms,' means bowing with the upper part of the body, in a gesture of imploration, request, prayer and greeting; *namanchilaju jalbira-*: to pray; *jalbira-*: 'pray' while sitting or in prostration while muttering a prayer of solicitation (palms are closed but do not touch one another). *Namanchila-* has the same meaning, but here with a prayer of contrition, of repentance.

57   About entering a monastery in Mongolia, see Pozdneev 1978 [1887]: 58-59.

58   See Rochechouart 1992 [1878]: 696; Gilmour 1970 [1883]: 146; Fischer 1923: 91-92, 93-95; Edkins 1893 [1878]: 236; Alley and Lapwood 1935: 118; Blofeld 1938: 29; Blofeld 1959: 128.

59   Mongols also recite incantations (*mantra* or *dhāraṇī*) of various buddhas, *bodhisattva*s and other protective deities, which were taught to them by a lama.

60   Edkins 1893 [1878]: 102.

every third step, their hands protected by rags or pieces of wood. Within the monasteries, they prostrated on wooden planks that were about two meters long and three feet across, raised slightly from the ground at one end and pointing toward the icon or the *stūpa*.[61] The main places where prostrations are intensively practiced nowadays are in front of the Great White Stūpa and on the staircases leading to Pusading and Dailuoding. The 108-step stairway to Pusading represents the 108 passions the pilgrims crush with their feet, so that by the time they reach the gate they are cleansed from defilement and freed from sufferings.[62] The pilgrims silently counted each stair or prayed while turning their 108-bead rosary.[63]

The second main devotional practice is circumambulation, by walking or in great prostrations. Mongol pilgrims fixed in advance a number of prostrations and circumambulations to attain and came back day after day to achieve them.[64] To count the rounds, they made a mark on the ground with chalk. With their circumambulations they hoped to "destroy calamities and attract benedictions, become Buddha and immortal, or obtain a better reincarnation."[65] The number of circumambulations around the Great White Stūpa varied; even if 3 appears to be the strict minimum,[66] as in circumambulation of monasteries in Mongolia, some pilgrims tried to reach a total of 10,800 rounds, or else 84,000 rounds (the number of Śākyamuni's relics),[67] turning the prayer wheels all the while. According to Blofeld:

> These wheels were kept continuously revolving by a succession of Mongol pilgrims, who walked round and round at a steady pace, fingering their rosaries with their left hands and patting the wheels with their right ... it was the ambition of these pilgrims to make ten thousand eight hundred

---

61  Blofeld 1938: 29. See Pozdneev's (1978 [1887]: 389-390) precise description of how Mongols perform great prostrations in front of a Mongol temple.

62  Payne 1929: 509.

63  Rockhill (1895: 767) adds, "on every step were locks of human hair, offered to the god in the hope that the giver might be reborn in the paradise over which he rules." Nanshansi and Longquansi are also reputedly reached by a 108-step stairway (although neither of them has this exact number).

64  They used to do the same when they circumambulated monasteries of Mongolia: bows and circumambulations were multiplied in case of misfortune such as the loss of a sheep, illness, death, cattle plague, etc. (Pozdneev 1978 [1887]: 392).

65  Li Xiangzhi 1932: 62.

66  Li Xiangzhi 1932: 62.

67  Gao Henian 2000 [1949]: 111.

complete circles of the dagoba, this number corresponding exactly to one hundred times the number of beads on a Buddhist rosary.

... Another novelty... was the presence of several Mongols scattered about the courtyard who stood facing the tower from all sides and who threw themselves flat on their faces before it time and time again. They too were striving to make the number of their prostrations mount up to the giant figure of ten thousand eight hundred. Naturally they had to come back day after day to achieve this purpose.[68]

The 1721 Mongolian guidebook emphasizes the enormous benefits of prostrating and circumambulating 108 or 10,000 times around the Great White Stūpa, Mañjuśrī's Hair Stūpa and the *stūpa* of Luohousi.[69] The inscription LH46 (s.d.) mentions three circumambulations (*ergin toguri-*) of the 'marvelous blissful Five[-Peak] Mountain.' Duke Migwachir, who visited Wutaishan in 1938, wrote that he made the circumambulation (*ergil mörgül*)[70] of the following monasteries: Wanfoge, Shuxiangsi, and Fanxianshan (Lingyingsi).[71] It seems that this basic (Indo-)Tibeto-Mongol practice was much more common around monasteries than it is now. Perhaps circumambulation paths (Mo. *goroo*) have been abandoned or erased. Nowadays it is generally difficult to circumambulate the monastic compounds: no path marked by prayer wheels and *stūpa*s surrounds the walled monasteries like in Mongolia and Tibet, and, in many cases, when monasteries are erected on cliffs near ravines, circumambulation is impossible.[72] Circumambulation is not practiced by Chinese and can be viewed here as an ethnic marker for Tibetans and Mongols.[73]

Inside the halls, pilgrims bowed on a cushion or made a full prostration in front of each main statue before giving offerings. They placed their forehead against the pedestal or feet of the Buddha, if they could reach them, and

---

68    Blofeld 1948: 93-94. In 2010 I met a woman from Khölön Buir who made 108 circumambulations a day around the Great White Stūpa for fifteen days; she did not visit other places at Wutaishan.

69    *UTAOSC* 27a, 36a, 38a, 43a.

70    In Mongolia, before entering inside a monastery, devotees circumambulate it three times in a clockwise direction around the entire monastery wall. For descriptions of pilgrims making great prostrations while circumambulating the city of Urga: Ramstedt 1978: 44-45; around Baldan Bairawun Kheid: Geleta, in Forbath 1936: 244-246, 258-259.

71    Miγvacir 2008 [1942]: 404-405.

72    Nowadays, Mongols and Tibetans only circumambulate *stūpa*s and Lingjiu Peak, following the path taken by the Sixth Month procession.

73    However, present-day Chinese often follow this Tibeto-Mongol practice around the Great White Stūpa: pilgrims tend to borrow from others' ways.

touched the images with their right hand when possible. Chinese pilgrims always kowtowed with three sticks of incense and let them burn in the incense-burner placed in front of every hall. Mongols burned juniper (*artsa*), as in Mongolia.[74]

The individual or collective donation ritual seems to have been the same as nowadays. The monks opened the shrines and temples and received the pilgrims' offerings.[75] They rang a bell or a gong, and/or lit candles according to the amount donated.[76] In 1923 Fischer described at Pusading:

> A Mongol pilgrim stood there praying. We observed how fervently he prayed, and bowed, and kowtowed; he folded his hands; he brought the folded hands up to his face and forehead and down in prayer to his knees. He then took a string of small copper cash with square holes from his neck—took about 30 off and laid them on the offering table. Observing this, we two also put sixty cash (*i. e.* six cents in copper coins) on the offering altar; thereupon the priest lighted two small oil candles and struck the gong in reply to our charity.[77]

Pilgrims offering major donations were personally welcomed by the abbot and invited to take a meal in the Guest Department.[78] After the donation, they were given paper certificates with the stamp of the monastery's seal,[79] or their name was carved on steles. Blofeld describes a Chinese pilgrim taking with him a yellow banner on which he intended to have the vermilion seals of each of the temples of the Five Terraces stamped.[80]

Within monasteries, the main devotional practices distinguishing Tibetans and Mongols from the Chinese were circumambulation and the turning of

---

74    Miγvacir 2008 [1942]: 406.
75    Edkins 1893 [1878]: 226.
76    Rochechouart (1992 [1878]: 696-697) writes that the monks received the donation before opening the temples.
77    Fischer 1923: 96-97.
78    Li Xiangzhi 1932: 182-183.
79    Rochechouart (1992 [1878]: 698) describes the seal being imprinted on pilgrims' bodies; he himself preferred having it stamped on a piece of yellow silk.
80    Blofeld 1948: 102. Similarly, nowadays Pusading delivers pilgrimage certificates to Tibetan and Mongol pilgrims in the Mañjuśrī hall. Pilgrims also purchase a simple cloth map of Wutaishan and ask in every monastery they visit that its seal be printed on it. The practice of collecting temple stamps proving that the pilgrim has made the pilgrimage is common in Europe (like for the pilgrimage to Compostella) and in Japan (pilgrimage to Shikoku: Reader 2005: 22).

prayer wheels. The Mongols never adopted typical Chinese Buddhist practices such as mutilation (burning one's head with an incense stick, burning a finger or a whole arm), suicide as an offering to the Buddha,[81] releasing animals (*fang-sheng* 放生)[82] and burning firecrackers.[83] Although vegetarianism was also observed by some devout Mongols, it was and still is one of the main observable religious markers for Chinese monks and lay devotees. Some typical practices at Tibetan pilgrimage sites such as lifting and carrying heavy stones while circumambulating were not observed on Wutaishan.[84]

### Attending Offices

Mongol pilgrims generally attended the morning office in the monastery of which they considered themselves specific donors.[85] The assembly hall was a main place of interaction between the monastic community and the pilgrims: the monks gathered to recite liturgy and chanted while laypersons knelt, prayed and honored the Buddha images or listened to the chanting.[86] Fischer provides a detailed description of the Chinese service, followed by his observation of the Tibetan service at Tayuansi, both attended by Mongols:

> The procession of Ho-shang [*heshang*], headed by the Abbot who carries in his hands "the most precious," starts from the Pagoda, followed by the musician and choir of the temple, in the rear of whom the Mongol pilgrims living at the temple participate, and who close the religious march through the temple compound towards the main sanctuary. There, for an

---

81    For instance Yü 1992: 227, 233 about Putuoshan.

82    *Fangsheng* was an important Buddhist practice in China (and in Theravada countries of Southeast Asia). It was occasionally practiced in Inner Mongolia, probably under Chinese influence. On other Chinese pilgrimage practices: Goodrich 1998.

83    In his modern guide to Wutaishan, Khejok Rinpoché warns the pilgrims that "it is not a Buddhist practice to light firecrackers at a holy place" (Lim 1999).

84    On these practices: Buffetrille 1997: 81.

85    Pokotilov (1935 [1893]: 65) details for 1889 the timetable of Chinese monks, who woke up at 1:00 a.m. for the early morning office that ended at 3:00 a.m., attended the second office from 10:00 a.m. to noon, had their main meal, and attended a third office from 6:00 to 8:00 p.m. In some places, only two or three monks attended the third office because the others were sleeping. Present-day Tibetan Buddhist monasteries hold an early morning service (around 6:30 a.m.), and a second one later in the morning (between about 10:00 and noon); Chinese Buddhist monasteries have one (at 10:00 a.m.) or two morning services (one at 4:00, 5:00 or 6:00 am and one at 10:00 am) and an afternoon service (between 3:00 and 5:00 p.m. or later).

86    Some monasteries do not allow the laypersons to enter the hall when the monks are praying.

hour, chanting goes on at each service, which also means visits around to the various temple-images of gods and disciples of Buddha holding prominent positions. While services go on the pilgrims offer silken gauze and shawls called Ha-ta [*khatag*], also quantities of Mongolian butter, as well as other products, such as are seen day by day in the offering urns of the temple. And while this Chinese-Buddhist service takes place, called the "Ho-Shang nien-ching," a second service in a small sanctuary on the upper platform of the pagoda also takes place, the "Lama nien ching" or Tibetan-Mongol prayers which are participated in also by the visiting pilgrims. Of course as in Buddhistic services, flutes and other instruments are used, as well as the "Fish" and other drums, spanned with parchment, both of metal and wood. During the service the pilgrims inside the temple and the outside spectators prostrate themselves dozens of times, repeatedly kowtowing their entire length on the floor, bringing their foreheads in bowing right down to the ground. While offerings were made, hundreds of small oil lamps were lit. Following the inner procession around were also pilgrim women ... And those outside on the cold stone ground before the temple, prostrate in kowtow, or kowtowing on the five feet heavy wooden boards any number of times in communion, all these sights and features make Mount Wu-t'ai, during the pilgrim season, most interesting.[87]

Chinese pilgrims also attended offices in Gélukpa monasteries.[88]

In present-day morning services at Luohousi, Mongols, Tibetans and Chinese sit along the wall, on the ground or on a cushion, join their hands in praying gesture and listen to the monks chanting. A dozen pilgrims queue to receive blessings from the chanting lamas: one by one they bow in front of a lama who, without interrupting his chanting, touches or hits each pilgrim's head with his book or bell; the pilgrim then places a one-*yuan* banknote as an offering on the lama's table before moving on to the next lama to repeat the same gestures (Fig. 35). Others pour seeds onto a *maṇḍala* of offerings held out by a lama. As observed by Blofeld, at the end of each service,

a few drops of holy water were poured into the hands of all present from an ornamented silver jug, to which peacock feathers were attached. Each man then carried the water reverently to the top of his head and to his mouth.[89]

87    Fischer 1923: 91-92.
88    Gao Henian (2000 [1949]: 65) attended the office at Pusading.
89    Blofeld 1938: 33.

FIGURE 35     *Pilgrims attending a ritual and being blessed by lamas, Luohousi.*
              © ISABELLE CHARLEUX, 2007.

### Donations to Request Specific Rituals

The stone inscriptions mention a number of specific rituals requested by lay pilgrims in the temples. They also sponsored parts of a planned ritual (*möngkhe khural*, [eternal] assembly) in the assembly hall. This is the second most frequent item on which donations were spent, according to the stone inscriptions, after donations made to buy farmland (see below). These rituals aimed at gaining personal benefit by making use of the lamas' Tantric power. The most common ritual requested by Mongols was the recitation of the *Zangjidmulum*, for which 50 taels were paid, according to the few inscriptions that mention a price.[90] The *Zangjidmulum*,[91] usually translated as "Prayer of good actions—

---

90    SF5, 1873; SF55, 1896; also SF165, 1931. In the inscriptions, to pay for a ritual or an icon is *mönggöle-*, a term usually meaning 'to silver, cover with silver leaf.'

91    < Tib. *bZang spyod smon lam*; full Tibetan title: *bZang spyod smon lam gyi rgyal po*, Skt. *Ārya Bhadracaryapranidhānarāja*. It is sometimes written on prayer flags to gain spiritual merit.

the king of aspiration prayers"[92] is the final part (sixty-second section) of the *Gandavyūha sūtra*, which is the last section of the *Avataṃsaka sūtra*. Although it is well known in Mongolian as *Irüül-ün khaan*[93] (The king of prayers), the steles always cite the Tibetan name according to Mongolian phonetics. The prayer starts with "I bow to the blessed Mañjuśrī," and ends with "In order to enjoy good virtue in all, may I fulfill the holy wishes of Mañjuśrī ... may I also acquire all his rebirths."[94] In present-day Republic of Mongolia and Inner Mongolia, it is the first prayer people request to be recited either in a monastery or at home by a visiting lama, and it is the most important text to be recited at any occasion.[95] As mentioned in Chapter 3, these rituals may have been performed in Mongolian (which is not the case nowadays on Wutaishan).

The second ritual requested by Mongol donors was the *Altan tarabchimbu* (Mo. *altan*, 'gold' or 'golden' and < Tib. *Thar pa chen po*), Sūtra of the great liberation written with golden [ink].[96] A stone inscription at Shifangtang records a donation of 100 taels for the recitation of the *Altan tarabchimbu* on the 8th, 15th, and 25th day of the first month of every year and the recitation of a prayer to Avalokiteśvara on the 15th of the fourth month (SF17, 1881).[97] The *Altan tarabchimbu* deals with the path towards becoming a buddha, salvation from a lower rebirth and the removal of sins.[98] There is a Mongolian saying that goes: *Tal-i tuulakhu targun mori, tamu-yi tuulakhu Tarabchimbu*, meaning "A strong horse to cross the steppe, the *Tarabchimbu* to cross hell." People would

---

92 Aspiration prayers, such as "the King of Aspiration Prayers," the aspiration prayer to Maitreya, the meritorious wish prayer, the aspiration prayer for Sukhāvatī and aspiration prayers for Shambhala, are actually wishes for the future, usually to be born in a pure land, or to have a better reincarnation in a future life.

93 Short for *Qutuɣtu sayin yabudal-un irügel-ün qaγan*, "The King of Prayers of Holy and Good Deeds."

94 *Zangjidmulum*: Pozdneev 1978 [1887]: 417.

95 I thank Uranchimeg Ujeed for this information (email, January 2010). In present-day Mongol monasteries, it is also recited during the daily assemblies (Majer 2008: 131). It is one of the 'six prayers' (*jurgaan irüül*, see Majer 2008: 134) commonly read in Mongol monasteries, and is considered especially useful in removing the effects of 'white gossip' and cursing ('white gossip' are praises and compliments stemming from envy, jealousy or rumors, but with no intention to harm).

96 *Kanjur mdo sha* 328.

97 Other inscriptions mentioning the *Altan tarabchimbu* are SF113, 1918; SF26, 1885; SF48, 1894; LH45, 1935.

98 This explanation is given in the list of recitations proposed by Dashichoiling Monastery of Ulaanbaatar. In Dashichoiling, this text can be requested any day. If it is requested (and paid for), then it is read by one of the lamas participating in the daily chanting. I thank Zsuzsa Majer for these clarifications.

read the *Tarabchimbu* (or have it read) when alive and then have it read for them again after death in order to avoid going to hell.[99]

The third ritual mentioned in the steles was the *Dara ekhe mandalshiua*, the "four-*maṇḍala* offering to (Green) Tārā."[100] According to modern observation, four *maṇḍalas* representing the world are prepared as offerings to Green Tārā, the female *bodhisattva* of enlightened activity. The ritual can last a whole day, and the sponsor has to pay for all the material needed to prepare the altar.[101] It is performed for the purification of sins and to obtain well-being and success in one's worldly affairs and especially at work. A mother would request this ritual for the well-being of her children or to ensure healthy delivery if she is pregnant. In present-day monasteries of Mongolia, it is commonly performed on the 8th day of every month.[102] In the Wutaishan stone inscriptions, donors offered 50 taels (SF118, 1919) to 100 taels (SF8, 1880) for the performance of this ritual.[103]

Many stone inscriptions mention that the donors ordered a ritual of recitation of 'the *Kanjur*.'[104] The *Kanjur* is usually read to accumulate merit but also to gain prosperity, health and security. The *Kanjur*, or, more often, several texts selected from different volumes of the *Kanjur*, are read on specific dates in monasteries of Mongolia;[105] but when this reading is ordered by individuals, it always means reciting certain parts of it by selecting several texts from different volumes, never the whole *Kanjur*.

These rituals belong to the category of *jasal-un nom* ('texts to repair, correct'): "these are remedy prayers i.e. texts read to correct bad states or conditions (illnesses, sufferings, misfortune or bad luck) and to secure prosperity,

---

99    U. Ujeed (email, January 2010).

100   Also written *Dara ekhe-yin mangdasuua* or simply *Mandalshiua*; < Skt. *Tārā maṇḍala*, Tib. *zhiba*. The Tibetan title of this ritual dedicated to Tārā is *sGrol ma'i sgo nas mandal bzhi ba*. For the origin of this ritual composed in the eighteenth century from various texts: Stein 1988: 2, n. 1; Beyer 1973: 170-226 (with a translation of the ritual text).

101   Beyer 1973: 174.

102   U. Ujeed (email, January 2010); Majer and Teleki 2005-2006. The ideal moment for this ritual depends on the aim of the donor (Beyer 1973: 173).

103   See steles SF8, 1880; SF47, 1894; SF51, 1894; SF85, 1904; SF96, 1907; SF118, 1919; SF127, 1921; SF173, 1931; LH45, 1935.

104   *Γanjuur mönggülejü* (SF39, 1888; LH17, 1909), *γanjuur mani mönggülejü* (SF31, 1888).

105   In Mongolia, the *Kanjur* recitation was performed in monasteries that gathered several hundred monks; the sheets were distributed among the monks, who each read different texts at the same time. After the recitation, devotees carried a volume each and circumambulated the monastery three times.

happiness or success."[106] In fact, the *Zangjidmulum/Iruül-ün khaan* and the *Tarabchimbu*, together with the *Altan gerel (Suvarṇaprabhāsa sūtra)* were books kept in most Mongol families. People either read them by themselves or asked literate people to read them out loud; they also regularly invited monks to read them.[107] Asking lamas to recite prayers, and especially the *Zangjidmulum* and the *Mañjuśrīnāmasaṃgīti*, is still a popular request on Wutaishan.[108]

According to the Wutaishan steles, besides texts requested to be recited at the time of donation, Mongol donors also paid for rituals to be performed every month or at fixed dates of the year. A stele of Shancaidong records donations for a ritual at three in the afternoon on the 15th day of the first month, the 8th day of the fourth month and the 15th day of the seventh month of every year, plus a *mani-yin büteel* prayer on the 25th day of the tenth month (SCD1, 1907).[109] In a Shifangtang inscription, the donors offer 100 taels of silver for a ritual to Sarvavid Vairocana and Bhaiṣajyaguru every year on the 6th day of every month, to begin with the 6th day of the eleventh month of the Year of the Rooster (SF63, 1887).[110] In the main inscription of Cifusi, a total of 2,215 silver *yuan* are offered for daily recitations of a ritual to Tārā, to Chodba Nöngnei, of the *Tarabchimbu*, a reading of the *Kanjur* and a recitation of the *Mani migzum khorlo* (CF6, 1935).

Many inscriptions mention donations for *dungchud* (or *düngchüd*), which are often coupled with a recitation, such as *Ganjuur dungchud* or *Mandalshiua dungchud*, or with the name of a deity: *Manzushiri-yin dungchud*. This transcribes the Tibetan *tongchö*, 'a thousand offerings,' i.e., an offering ritual that might include a thousand butter lamps, a thousand cups of water, a thousand sacrificial cakes (*baling*, < Skt. *bali*), a thousand flowers, a thousand fumigations and so on. It can be related to any deity or any text. On Wutaishan, rituals of *Ganjuur dungchud* were paid for with sums between 50 taels (SF53, 1895; TY54,

---

106    Majer and Teleki 2005-2006; also Majer 2008: 42.

107    U. Ujeed (email, January 2010).

108    These Tibetan texts are popular in present-day monasteries of Inner Mongolia and the Republic of Mongolia. In Dashichoiling Monastery, these two rituals can be requested by individuals at the monastery's office (Zsuzsa Majer, personal communication, January 2011). These readings usually do not request the presence of the donors: see Majer and Teleki 2005-2006; Majer 2008: 41-46, 136-139, 154.

109    Evocation of a deity through contemplation and recitation of a *dhāraṇī*.

110    *Jilbüri-yin mön sarayin mön edür günreg otaci qurayulqu möngke-yin qural bayiyulqu tuqai-dur mönggü nigen jayun lang ergüged.* Günreg is the abbreviation of Günreg Nambarnanzad (< Tib. Künrik Nampar Nangdzé), Skr. Sarvavid Vairocana.

1930) and 100 taels (SF11, 1881).[111] As in Mongolia, a special financial unit, or trea-sury (*jisa*), could be set up to organize these rituals.[112]

Less wealthy donors could certainly purchase a recitation for less than 50 taels, according to their financial means.[113] Nowadays it is common on Wutai-shan to sponsor a ritual that is already part of the regular liturgical calendar or to share (*khubi oro-*) a recitation: a text, such as *Irüül-ün khaan*, is recited in the monastery's daily assembly and, at a specific moment during the ceremony, a lama (usually the disciplinary master) reads aloud the names of the dead and living relatives of each donor along with their date of birth.[114] After the ritual, following Chinese custom, a lama writes the names of the dead and living rela-tives on individual tablets or papers of, respectively, yellow and red,[115] which are put in the main hall or in a Chinese-style ancestral hall.[116]

---

111    Other inscriptions mentioning *Ganjuur dungchud*: SF9, 1880; SF27, 1885; SF32, 1888; SF33, 1888; SF36, 1888; SF39, 1888.

112    *Möngke yanjuur dungcud-un jisa bayiyulju* (SF25, 1885; SF39, 1888); *mandalsiu-a otaci-yin qural-un jisatu* (SF56, 1896); *möngke otaci jisa* (SF12, 1881).

113    In the Republic of Mongolia, up to the 1990s, donors who requested recitations usu-ally paid the amount they could afford, but now there are fixed prices for reading texts. Most requests for recitations for a specific situation are made following the advice of a lama. Prices range from 200 to 10,000 *tögrög* (around 20 cents to US$12 in 2008): Majer 2008: 155, 167-168, 177-178. However, speaking about Inner Mongolia, U. Ujeed adds that the text or ritual requested depended on the requester's financial capacity.

114    Observation by U. Ujeed when she visited Wutaishan in 1999, on the 15th day of the sixth lunar month when there was a major monastic service. This practice is also common in the Republic of Mongolia: Majer and Teleki 2005-2006.

115    As seen above, names of deceased and living relatives were written on stone inscriptions, but it is unclear to me whether the custom to write them on Chinese-style tablets or papers was already practiced by lamas in the early twentieth century. Nowadays, these are an important source of income, and some Gélukpa monasteries build Chinese-style ancestral halls to house them. Another Chinese ritual adopted by Gélukpa monasteries consists of petitioning a deity via a request on a yellow slip of paper, to be burned and thus transmitted to the afterworld.

116    I observed such a ritual in 2012. At Zhenhaisi, forty Mongols from Ulaanbaatar paid for an 'insurance ritual' (*daatkhalyn khural*) to obtain good fortune, money, success at work and good health, as well as insurance for the future (*daadkha-* means "to entrust one's hopes to a deity, say one's prayers, with an enumeration of requests for protection from all dangers, for well-being, prosperity"). A lama wrote on red and yellow papers the names of the donors' living and dead relatives, for 100 *yuan* each, to be placed into the main temple (see Online Appendix H).

### Donations to Buy Farmland

About two thirds of the inscriptions record donations to buy farmland for monasteries.[117] This was especially the case for donations of 30 to 50 taels to Shifangtang. Although it may seem strange that nomadic herders offered agricultural land to monasteries, in China farmland is a common endowment as a lasting way to feed the monks and therefore perpetuate the *sangha* (monastic community). We have seen in Chapter 3 that the first source of income for Wutaishan's monasteries was the rent and produce from their lands (forty-one monasteries owned 83.817 *mu* in 1935) located in Shanxi and Hebei Provinces. Mongol pilgrims thus offered to monasteries farmlands, which were then rented out to Chinese farmers.

The minimum and most common donation recorded on steles is the purchase of two *mu* (Mo. *muu*) of arable land, for 30 to 50 taels, in the nineteenth century and one to three *mu*, for 50 or 100 taels, in the 1920s-1930s (in the Qing and Republican periods, a *mu* was equivalent to 6.144 ares, i.e., 614.4 square meters). The largest recorded land donation is sixty *mu*, at a cost of 600 taels (XT2, 1923). Of course, the value of arable land depended on its location and quality and changed over time. The Mongols offered their donations to the monastery's treasury charged with buying farmland, and the figures given in the inscriptions may be mere approximations of acreage.[118]

### Construction and Restoration of Monasteries

A few steles mention financial contributions made to erect or repair buildings: restoration and construction at Tayuansi (see Chapter 5), construction of a *stūpa* in Shifangtang (SF133, 1922), of a small hexagonal pavilion for a statue (DLD1, 1691) and so on.[119] In 1658, the First Chakhar Diyanchi from Höhhot received from Emperor Shunzhi the authorization to spend 30,000 taels of white silver to repair the blooming lotus and the *stūpa* at Luohousi, as well as four monasteries and a number of roads and bridges on Wutaishan (LH1). A Mongol

---

117   (*Usun*) *gajar tariyalang*, arable land for agriculture (with water). Ex. *tariyalang-un yajar dörben muu abcu talbiyad nigen jayun lang ergükü* (SF26, 1885); *dörben muu yajar tariyalang abcu mönggü nigen jayun lang ergübe* (SF28, 1886).

118   Most of the inscriptions mention the purchase of farmland without specifying the acreage.

119   It seems that steles recording financial contributions to erect or repair temples made up a much higher proportion on other Chinese pilgrimage sites such as Wudangshan (Lagerwey 1992: 31). Most of the steles erected after 1990 on Wutaishan record Chinese, Mongol and Tibetan names of donors who contributed towards construction and restoration.

prince restored all of the temples on the Five Terraces before 1912.[120] Henry Payne relates in 1929 that a Mongol prince visited Wutaishan every year, bringing large sums of money for the upkeep of the monasteries, and that three large temples under construction were all being built using funds from votive offerings from Mongolia and Manchuria.[121] Mongol princes and reincarnated lamas also restored temples at Nārāyaṇa Cave and Lingyingsi.[122] To gain merit, some donors participated personally in building temples on Wutaishan;[123] others financed the reconstruction of ruined temples, such as Pushousi, an old Jin-dynasty monastery rebuilt in the Guangxu period by a Khalkha lama named Yönden.[124]

### Offerings of Icons, Prayer Wheels and Other Donations

Mongols commissioned paintings, appliqués and statues and paid for prayer wheels[125] to offer to the Wutaishan monasteries.[126] They donated statues of Bhaiṣajyaguru (Otachi) for 23 or 50 taels,[127] of Avalokiteśvara (Nöngnei),[128] Amitābha (Abida), Amitāyus (Ayushi),[129] Tārā (Dara ekhe), Sitātapatrā (Chagan Shikhürtei),[130] Guhyasamāja (Sangdui), or Saṃvara (Demchig, < Tib. Déchok).[131] Several of these deities are linked to longevity (Amitāyus, Sitātapatrā) and healing (Bhaiṣajyaguru).[132]

A common offering was small stone reliefs of Mañjuśrī. Around 2009, about a hundred such reliefs were dug up near the source of the Sanquansi Spring

---

120  Gao Henian 2000 [1949]: 115.

121  Payne 1929: 508.

122  Gao Henian 2000 [1949]: 115-117, 120; Wang Lu 1995: 28.

123  Blofeld 1959: 126.

124  Wei Guozuo 1993 [1988]: 167.

125  *Dungšuur [dungsiyur] mani-yin kürdün bütüke-*, "to complete a hundred million prayer wheels."

126  SF54, 1896; SF65, 1897 (120 taels); SF143, 1925.

127  It is not always clear if the texts speak of an icon or a text: *otaci mönggüleju* (SF4, 1873; SF7, 1874; SF37, 1888).

128  SF99, 1908; LH21, 1919; SF77, 1899; SF147, 1928.

129  SF47, 1892; SF97, 1908.

130  SF6, 1873. The cult of this deity is widespread in Mongolia.

131  SF56, 1896.

132  In 2007, donors from Shili-yin Khota had two *thangka*s depicting Amitāyus and Bhaiṣajyaguru made at Lhasa for 15,000 *yuan* and offered them to Luohousi, as explained in their long inscription, which includes a prayer similar to texts of stone inscriptions (to increase 'pure white' merit, fulfill wishes, get rid of sufferings for the donors and all living beings and obtain the sanctity of buddhas). The *thangka*s are hung in the great Buddha hall of Luohousi.

(Fig. 36). The name of the *bodhisattva* is carved in Tibetan on the back.[133] On
some of them is added (in ink on the back) the name and origin of the Mongol
donors, sometimes with the date: a Mongol lama patron from a Kharachin banner in the nineteenth century; a donor from a Khorchin banner; a certain Lub-
sanjurabu from Ordos Otog Banner, etc.[134]

According to the steles, another common practice was the distribution of
small amounts of money or food (*tsab*) and tea (*tsai*, or *manja*, < Tib. *mangja*,
honorific for tea for the lamas) to the lamas during ceremonies, as donations
(*zed pog*, Tib. *gyépok*, 'donation, alms'), or a gift of money to feed the monks for
a whole year.[135] Inscriptions also mention offerings of 'eternal lamps' (*möngkhe
jula*) and incense burners.[136]

Pilgrims offered numbers of ceremonial scarves that were put on altars
and on statues, in addition to great temple banners, silken embroidered altar

---

133    See also Chou 2011b: 138 and Fig. 4.16.
134    Nowadays, Mongol pilgrims offer small reliefs of Mañjuśrī to be placed along the walls of
       the Mañjuśrī hall of Luohousi.
135    SF14, 1881; SF57, 1896; LH31, 1930; TY36, 1911.
136    LH31, 1930; SF18, 1882; SF35, 1888 (70 taels).

decorations and Mongol rugs.[137] Blofeld describes a temple's sumptuous interior with painted ceiling, carpets, a lacquered altar with more than a hundred votive lamps, a porcelain incense burner, three large plates heaped with precious and semi-precious stones presented by pious pilgrims, and great banners inscribed in Chinese, Tibetan and Sanskrit hanging from the ceiling.[138] Temple decorations, mostly made of silk brocade, hung in front of the main statues. Bought by pilgrims, they were changed on holy days and in honor of special visitors. They include pillar coverings (made of silk or carpets), temple banners (*jaltsan*, < Tib. *gyeltsen*, long round cylinders sewn together and made of three materials of various colors, denoting the three sections of the Buddhist doctrine), round, umbrella-like canopies (*shikhür*, Tib. *duk*), brocades hanging at the top of pillars (*pen*), lanterns (*denlu*, < Ch. *denglong* 燈龍), *badan* (< Tib. *badang*, long, broad bands sewn together and made from material in five colors: blue, white, red, yellow and green) and so forth.[139] Most of this paraphernalia was sold in shops on Wutaishan.

Requests for recitations, plus offerings of statues, prayer wheels and farmland were often listed in the same stone inscriptions, worded as such: "Four-*maṇḍala* offering to Tārā" and the "Prayer of good actions"; the "Four-*maṇḍala* offering to Tārā" and the "Sūtra of complete deliverance of the soul."[140] There are numerous other examples. The stele of Shancaidong records an offering of 10,000 taels to complete a 'hundred million' prayer wheels and a thousand (statues of?) Tārā (SCD1, 1907). The inscription LH22 (1920) lists the following offerings: a 'hundred million' prayer wheels (150 taels), a *dungchud* ritual (50 taels), a *mani* (prayer) ritual (50 taels) and one *mu* of farmland (50 taels). The inscription XT2 (1923) lists sixty *mu* of farmland (600 taels), a reading of the *Kanjur*, a *dungchud* offering to Mañjuśrī (500 taels), a thousand statues of Amitāyus (*Ayushi burkhan*) (100 taels) and two *mu* of farmland (20 taels). Some donations were not limited to the monastery where the stele stands; for example, LH46 (s.d.) mentions gifts to many different monasteries—an offering of arable land, restoration of temples and of the Great White Stūpa, gifts to the clergy and an offering to have a statue covered in gold (leaf) (see also LH1, 1658).

---

137    Fischer (1923: 92) describes in Tayuansi: "before the entrance to the main service building, there was hung in front of the door a heavy 9'x12' rug of camel hair with large dragon designs and interwoven Manchu and lama characters."

138    Blofeld 1948: 92.

139    Pozdneev 1978 [1887]: 155-156.

140    SF15, 1881; SF89, 1905; LH45, 1935; SF59, 1896; SF60, 1896; SF140, 1925.

### The Circuits of the Mongol Pilgrims

As in other Mongol pilgrimages, the sites that that were considered most sacred by the Mongols on Wutaishan were of three kinds: the monasteries and the holy images they enshrined, the sacred relics and other numinous traces, and the living reincarnations. The natural numinous traces will be dealt with in the following chapter.

There was no fixed circuit linking sites in a definite order. All pilgrims first started at the Great White Stūpa and the monasteries of Lingjiu Peak, bowed to the sacred icon of Mañjuśrī in Pusading or to the one in Shuxiangsi to announce their arrival and inform Mañjuśrī that they came to fulfill a vow.[141] After that, they continued their pilgrimage according to their priorities, the length of their stay and the weather (for those who planned to walk to the terraces). The duration of their stay ranged from a week to one, two or three months, depending on one's financial means and the aims of the visit. [142] Those who came with cattle and sheep to trade either sold them at the sixth-month Great Mule and Horse Fair or stayed throughout the summer to sell them in the fall. The 'great pilgrimage' (*dachao* 大朝), which meant visiting the main monasteries, the most famous icons and the numinous traces of the Five Terraces took anywhere from one week to a whole month in the early twentieth century.

They used the main village as their base. The terraces were reachable from Taihuai via a long, winding road, for mounted visitors and mule-litters (now used by cars), and via abrupt paths and shortcuts, for walking pilgrims: to reach the North Terrace, there was

> a direct path of 25 *li* [12.5 kilometers] from Wu T'ai village, in preference to the longer 40 *li* [20 kilometers] mule-litter track which runs first up to the pass between the North and East Peaks.[143]

Present-day walking pilgrims generally climb the Eastern Terrace first in order to watch the sunrise, following a trail that starts from Bishansi; then they walk towards the Northern, Central, Western and Southern Terraces. Reaching the

---

141    According to Li Xiangzhi, Inner and Outer Mongols kowtowed in front of the Mañjuśrī statue of Pusading as soon as they arrive on Wutaishan (Li Xiangzhi 1932: 8); also Blofeld 1948: 91.

142    Li Xiangzhi (1932: 182-183) spoke of Mongol pilgrims who stayed one month or forty days. The Wutaishan pilgrimage is very different from other Chinese pilgrimages, such as Taishan, Huashan, Wudangshan or Emeishan, which usually require no more than one or two days (in addition, "such precipitation was a sign of reverence," Lagerwey 1992: 320).

143    Alley and Lapwood 1935: 119.

terraces was extremely difficult in winter; visiting all of them took three or four days on foot even in fine weather.[144] Once there, pilgrims found accommodation in one of the temples on the terraces, which were staffed by a few monks,[145] or in a monastery on the way to the Southern Terrace such as Qingliangqiao or Shiziwo.

The capricious weather and steep paths made the visit to the terraces dangerous, but it was (and is still) believed that great spiritual rewards resulted if one succeeded.[146] With the mountain's sudden snowstorms, thunderstorms and hailstorms that can blow even in mid-summer, its frequent rain and fog, not to mention misleading paths opened up by herds but going nowhere, pilgrims could (and still can) easily get lost. Stories abound of pilgrims getting lost in the dark or in the fog and being saved by an emanation of Mañjuśrī. This is why Mongols, Chinese and Tibetans often joined together and formed a group when walking from one terrace to the other.[147] The weather is sometimes so bad that it is not possible at all to walk to the terraces for several months in a row. A story attributed to the Qianlong emperor explains how climbing to Dailuoding to worship the Five Mañjuśrīs became an alternative to actually going to the terraces: it was called the 'small pilgrimage [replacing] the terraces' (xiao chaotai 小朝臺).[148] Nevertheless, the small pilgrimage is said to be for the sick or dying and for elderly pilgrims.[149] Before the eighteenth century, pilgrims who could not go to the terraces worshipped the five Ming-dynasty stūpas of Xiantongsi.[150]

---

144   Blofeld 1948: 96.

145   According to Gao Henian (2000 [1949]: 63, 115), no monks lived on the Western, Southern (in 1903), Central and Eastern Terraces (in 1912). Li Xiangzhi (1932: 127-149) counted a few monks on the five terraces in 1932. Blofeld (1938: 35-36) wrote that the Southern Terrace possesses two tiny guest rooms, where men and women were separated, and that at the Northern Terrace two tiny rooms "had the complete floor raised with heated pipes beneath."

146   Many pilgrims content themselves with visiting two or three terraces at a time, due to bad weather or physical tiredness. The Chinese authorities of Wutaishan try to discourage pilgrims from walking by building roads to the terraces and by keeping the small paths devoid of any markings. Tibetans and Mongols still generally prefer to walk (besides, they often cannot afford the high cost of motorized transportation).

147   Gao Henian 2000 [1949]: 117.

148   See Online Appendix B: "Dailuoding."

149   Lim 1999.

150   Jiang Weiqiao 1961 [1918]: 20; Gao Henian 2000 [1949]: 109.

### The Main Monasteries Worshipped by the Mongols

The pilgrimage of Duke Migwachir, who traveled there in 1938 but spent only five days on the mountain, is quite representative of the minimum tour for a Mongol. As soon as he arrived in the village of Taihuai (traveling from Beijing, which itself took four days), he worshipped the Mañjuśrī statue of Shuxiangsi. Although he acknowledged that the Great White Stūpa was the central place of worship, this statue in his eyes was the most important site of Wutaishan. Over the course of three days, he visited the Great White Stūpa, Xiantongsi, Pusading and Manibadara Monasteries (Shancaidong) and offered tea to the monks of Wanfoge. He climbed up Fanxianshan Hill and, after having circumambulated the monastery on the top, threw wind-horse papers from the terrace and burned incense. He spent his last night in Taihuai and, the day after, he worshipped Guanyindong, "comparable to Mount Potala," and crawled into the Mother's Womb-Cave (Fomudong). The following day, he visited Zhenhaisi and left for Beijing.[151] Migwachir conveniently started with the central places around Taihuai and ended with sites on the way back to Beijing. However, we could also interpret this order differently: he started with the most 'orthodox' sites praised in the guidebooks and enshrining the most ancient relics and ended with more recent, more Tibetan (Guanyindong, Zhenhaisi) and less orthodox (the Mother's Womb-Cave) sites.

Other sources point to the main monasteries frequented by Mongol pilgrims. Old lamas of the Kharachin Banner in Inner Mongolia remember some of their highlights from Wutaishan: they stayed in Shifangtang, climbed to Pusading, admired the stele of the Begging Mañjuśrī at Yuanzhaosi and saw the statue of Mañjuśrī with a Buckwheat Head at Shuxiangsi.[152] The Khorchin song "Utai-yin jam" lists more or less the same places and monasteries (fourteen monasteries, three cave temples and a *stūpa*) but in an order that certainly does not correspond to the pilgrims' circuit (Appendix 3). The prayer from Ordos mentions the terraces and their numinous traces, as well as twenty-five monasteries (of which I could identify sixteen: see Online Appendix E). The stone inscriptions also inform us about which monasteries Mongols sponsored. Besides Shifangtang, Tayuansi and Luohousi, between one and seven inscriptions stand in eleven Gélukpa monasteries of the Qing and Republican period, in five Chinese Buddhist monasteries, in the temples of the five terraces and at a few numinous sites such as Fomudong (Online Appendix A1: Table A). This list is not

---

151    Miүvacir 2008 [1942]: 403-407.
152    Song Wenhui 2000: 34. For the highlights of these monasteries, see Online Appendix B. The *TÜAG* (8b-11b, text in Kápolnas 2008) lists fourteen monasteries and seven numinous traces; the *UTAOSC* lists only nine identifiable monasteries and a great number of *stūpas*.

exhaustive since some steles have disappeared, but their concentration in a few monasteries certainly points to the places favored by Mongol donors. Other Gélukpa monasteries, such as the imperially sponsored Tailusi (located on the western road to Beijing), were not on the circuit followed by Mongol pilgrims.

Like the Chinese, the Mongol pilgrims also worshipped the 'ten scenic spots of Wutaishan'[153] and Chinese Buddhist monasteries, such as Xiantongsi, Shuxiangsi, Dailuoding, Bishansi, Nanshansi and Mimoyan 秘魔岩, along with relics of Chinese monks and heroes.[154] Li Xiangzhi expresses his surprise at the number of 'barbarian' donors who burn incense before the Great Mañjuśrī Hall of Xiantongsi.[155] As evidenced by Table 1, Mongol donors also erected stone inscriptions in Chinese Buddhist monasteries, while Chinese donors had very few steles erected in Gélukpa monasteries. The Mongols thus viewed Wutaishan as a pan-Buddhist site, not only as a Tibeto-Mongol Buddhist site, and considered the Chinese tradition as worthy of respect.

### *The* Stūpas *and Relics*

Relics (*śarīra*) and places of evocation of deceased saints and incarnated *bodhisattva*s forge a sacred geography of the mountain: "the power of the living person is sedimented and preserved after his death in the power of the place."[156] Wutaishan, as told for instance in the 1721 Mongolian guidebook, owes its sacredness to the presence of relics and 'traces' (such as footprints) of Śākyamuni and Mañjuśrī.

The Great White Stūpa was built to enshrine one of the nineteen relics of Śākyamuni that were found in China before the Tang dynasty (according to tradition, a relic of Śākyamuni was enshrined in Mongolia's Erdeni Juu).[157] In a lateral courtyard, a smaller *stūpa* is said to preserve a hair of Mañjuśrī. These relics are not visible, but the pilgrims could absorb some of their power by

---

153 Chapter 2, note 61.

154 Although they did not visit monasteries such as Zhenhaisi and Guanyindong Chinese pilgrims occasionally made donations to a Gélukpa monastery. For instance in 1702, Shanxi merchants asked Emperor Kangxi for permission to build a pavilion in Pusading (Yang Zengwu 2005: 107-108; another example in Tuttle 2011: 170).

155 Li Xiangzhi 1932: 69. On Mongols' donations to Xiantongsi: Pokotilov 1935 [1893]: 70.

156 Eade and Sallnow 1991: 8, Schopen 1997: 114-147, article "Burial *Ad Sanctos* and the Physical Presence of the Buddha in Early Indian Buddhism: A Study in the Archaeology of Religion."

157 Late biographies of Zanabazar mention a relic of Śākyamuni bestowed by the Third Dalai Lama to Abadai Khan in 1585, which was enshrined in Erdeni Juu (see Bawden, ed. 1961: 36-37). In 2012, Mongolia claimed to have rediscovered this same relic (http://www.infomongolia.com/ct/ci/3295, accessed on June 26th, 2013).

seeing, worshiping, touching and circumambulating the *stūpa*s. After having completed their full-length prostrations in front of the great Buddha hall in the direction of the Great White Stūpa, pilgrims circumambulate the *stūpa*.[158] Blofeld describes in 1938:

> Round this devout worshippers circle again and again, touching the doors with their foreheads at each complete turn to show their reverence. Many of them walk slowly round hundreds of times each day, their minds in deep meditation all the while.[159]

Edkins noticed "Mongol women pushing each wheel as they walked round in token of respect to Buddha. They were each followed by a Mongol attendant."[160] The sixty-one Mongolian stone inscriptions located around the circumambulation path (Online Appendix A1: Fig. B and C), confirm the central place occupied by the Great White Stūpa in the Mongol *imaginaire* of Wutaishan.

Other *stūpa*s enshrined various kinds of relics ranging from body relics of saints and contact relics (the begging bowl or the robe that had belonged to a saint, for instance) to numinous traces. The most important (contact) relic outside of the central complex for Mongols was the holy *stūpa* of Rölpe Dorjé in Zhenhaisi. Wang Chang, who traveled in Qianlong's suite in 1792 a few years after the Changkya's death, mentions Mongol 'princes and dukes' who came to worship his *stūpa*.[161] It has been seen to emanate rainbow light rays on a few occasions over the last few centuries.

Śāriputra's funerary *stūpa* in Yuanzhaosi, the *stūpa* that preserves the hat and robe of Pakpa Lama in Puensi, and the *stūpa* of Baohuasi, believed to enshrine a lock of Tsongkhapa's hair, were also meaningful places of worship for Mongols. The Pine Tree Holy Stūpa of Luohousi preserved a numinous trace: built above a miraculous tree, it commemorates a miracle. Other relics were visible and even touchable by pilgrims, such as the long tooth of Mañjuśrī and handprints of the *bodhisattva* in the rock at Jingangku, and the mummy of the warrior-monk Wulang at Wulangmiao. Although it enshrined the remains of a Chinese hero, this latter was run by lamas and subsisted thanks to the

---

158    Jiang Weiqiao 1918: 21; Ono Katsutoshi and Hibino Takao 1942: 13. Nowadays, Tibetan lamas advise pilgrims to go straight to worship the Great White Stūpa as soon as they arrive on Wutaishan "before having anything to eat or drink or looking after one's personal needs" (Lim 1999).

159    Blofeld 1938: 29. See other descriptions: Payne 1929: 509; Gao Henian 2000 [1949]: 109-110; Li Xiangzhi 1932: 62; Blofeld 1959: 128-29.

160    Edkins 1893 [1878]: 237.

161    Wang Chang 1999 [1792]: 22nd day.

generosity of Mongol pilgrims in the early twentieth century.[162] The Cifusi map shows a great number of Tibetan-style *stūpas* and Chinese pagodas: some were relic *stūpas*, but others guarded passes, served to guide pilgrims or were erected to mark a particular spot or to tame a site. Many have disappeared along with their history and legends.

### Worship of Specific Icons

Icons and relics were crucial objects to possess in the competition between monasteries, all the more so if they had some magical characteristic.

> At Wu T'ai, there is an image in a little temple over the gateway of the vil- lage. From this idol, we were told quite seriously, light streams far and near on certain days of the month. This of course raises the fame of the temple, and brings revenue .... it is on devices like this that the lamas rely, to keep up the reputation of themselves and their temples.[163]

The two statues most worshipped by Mongols on Wutaishan were the two 'true portraits' of Mañjuśrī, both being inspired by a version of the story of King Ud- dyana's Sandalwood Buddha—artists being incapable of drawing the Buddha's likeness, the Buddha/Mañjuśrī manifested himself in front of them. The oldest 'portrait' of Mañjuśrī—the eighth-century statue of Zhenrongyuan/Pusa- ding—served as a model for the Mañjuśrī statues of Wutaishan. Although the original no longer survives, the new golden statue that replaced it in 1482 in the Great Mañjuśrī Hall was commonly believed to be the same as the Tang-dynas- ty 'true image.'[164] After the drop in Qing patronage in the mid-nineteenth cen- tury, we know that Pusading became heavily dependent on Mongol donations.[165] Yet, except for the stele recording a donation of 8,800 taels of silver, offered in 1936 by a prince from the Juu Uda League (PSD1), no other Mongolian stele is found in this monastery.

The story of the Shuxiangsi's 'true portrait' of the *bodhisattva*, Mañjuśrī with a Buckwheat Head (Mo. Gulir terigütü Manzushiri), originates in a develop- ment of the same legend.[166] Measuring 9.87 meters high, it is the largest

---

162    Li Xiangzhi 1932: 98.

163    Gilmour 1970 [1883]: 231, other example p. 145.

164    When Li Xiangzhi (1932: 8) visited the monastery, he was told that the Mañjuśrī statue was 'the true image.'

165    Fischer 1923: 10.

166    Cf. Online Appendix B, "Shuxiangsi"; Mongolian version of the legend: Miyvacir 2008 [1942]: 404.

FIGURE 37     *Mongols worshipping the Shuxiangsi statue.* © ONO KATSUTOSHI AND HIBINO
              TAKAO 1942: 24.

Mañjuśrī statue on Wutaishan (Fig. 9, Fig. 37). The presence of a Mongolian
inscription and the fact that a whole guidebook was dedicated to this Chinese
monastery confirm its importance for Mongol pilgrims. Other famous icons of
Mañjuśrī that gave their name to their monasteries depicted on the map of
Wutaishan in the Badgar Choiling Süme, such as Mañjuśrī With a Cart (in Qixiansi) and Old Mañjuśrī (in Shouningsi), were particularly worshipped by
Mongols (these have not survived).[167]

---

167  Modern Chinese guidebooks list ten main statues with their corresponding lore: Mañjuśrī
     with the Arrow and Mañjuśrī-Yamāntaka at Pusading, White Mañjuśrī at Luohousi,
     Mañjuśrī with the Lantern at Qingliangqiao, Mañjuśrī with a Buckwheat Head and
     Bathing Mañjuśrī at Shuxiangsi, Mañjuśrī with a Thousand Bowls and Benevolent
     Mañjuśrī (Ganlu 甘露 Mañjuśrī) at Xiantongsi, Mañjuśrī Going Out of the Mountain (or
     Old Mañjuśrī) at Puhuasi, *dharmapāla* Mañjuśrī with Nine Heads and Eighteen Arms at
     Mingyuechi, and Black Dragon King Mañjuśrī (Xiexi 寫戲 Mañjuśrī) of Wanfoge (Zhou
     Rubi and Li Guangyi 2007: 402). Five of these statues are attributed a specific color: Black
     Mañjuśrī of Tayuansi (actually of Wanfoge), Yellow Mañjuśrī of Pusading, White Mañjuśrī
     of Luohousi, Green Mañjuśrī of Xiantongsi, and Blue Mañjuśrī of Shuxiangsi. Several of
     them are different buddhas and deities identified with Mañjuśrī (the Bathing Mañjuśrī of

FIGURE 38       *Sandalwood Buddha statue, Dailuoding.* © ISABELLE CHARLEUX, 2009.

While these sites and icons were must-sees for all pilgrims, another icon was especially meaningful for the Mongols: the Sandalwood Buddha of Dailuoding (Fig. 38). In 1691 on Wutaishan, a group of Mongols from Beijing offered to

Shuxiangsi adopts a posture that usually characterizes Śākyamuni) or with manifestations of Mañjuśrī (the Dragon King), or they originate from the Chinese Tantric local tradition.

Dailuoding a copy of the Sandalwood Buddha of Beijing (stele DLD1, 1691). Of the many replicas of the Sandalwood Buddha made in Mongolia and Buryatia, the Dailuoding version is the earliest documented copy made by Mongol donors. Present-day Inner Mongols do not know the story of the original Beijing statue and of its disappearance (during the Boxer Rebellion), and especially go to Wutaishan to worship this statue.[168]

Another must-see sculpture was the Blooming Lotus Revealing the Buddhas of Luohousi, which was said to attract Mongols like a magnet (Fig. 39).[169] Li Xiangzhi writes that the lama-keeper used to say to pilgrims,

> You are not devout enough, the offerings are not enough, the lotus will not open: add offerings, add offerings!' The pilgrims prostrate and add offerings and the lotus opens.[170]

Bai Meichu wrote that when the lotus opened,

> Mongols are filled with wonder; they respect and worship it. They prostrate to the ground and throw gold, silver and other things they brought altogether in the middle [of the lotus]. From this we learn that the monks of Wutaishan deceive the Mongols and [exploit] the degree of their devotion.[171]

Back home, the Mongols claimed to have seen the buddhas appear on Wutaishan. The pilgrims thought the lotus opened especially for them, though the monks revealed the subterranean mechanism to learned visitors such as Gao Henian.[172]

On Wutaishan, some deities and their icons were interpreted differently by Chinese and Mongols. Several temples (Fomudong, Yuhuangmiao/Puhuasi) had an icon called the 'Mother of Buddha(s)' (Fomu 佛母), an epithet of Prajñāpāramitā: this archetypal female deity was commonly identified as Tārā

---

168    Fieldwork in Wutaishan, 2007, and Ü. Hürelbaatar, personal communication, 2008. Two other representations of the Sandalwood Buddha are carved in low relief: one is embedded in the Great White Stūpa; the other one is in Yuanzhaosi.

169    Bai Meichu 2010 [1925]: *juan* 2, 153; Wei Guozuo, 1993 [1988]: 61-64. Luohousi is now the preferred monastery of Mongol pilgrims because it houses the largest Mongol community and has a distinct Mongol flavor (Mongol-speaking monks and information on rituals written in classical Mongolian). On its Mongol abbot: Nan Yang 1998.

170    Li Xiangzhi 1932: 20.

171    Bai Meichu 2010 [1925]: *juan* 2, 153.

172    Gao Henian 2000 [1949]: 119.

FIGURE 39     *The 'blooming lotus revealing the buddhas' of Luohousi.*

by the Mongols and the Tibetans and as Guanyin by the Chinese. Indra (Dishitian 帝釋天), like other Hindu gods, was represented as a minor deity in several Chinese Buddhist monasteries. In the late Ming, Daoists occupied the Indra Temple (Dishigong 帝釋宮) and renamed it Yuhuangmiao, thus identifying the Chinese Jade Emperor with Indra. However, the Mongol lamas who managed this temple (now known as Puhuasi) in the late nineteenth century worshipped the same deity under the name of Khormusta Tngri.[173]

The cult of Wanfoge's Dragon King developed in the early twentieth century. Mannerheim heard about this 'god of rain' and 'guardian angel' of Wutaishan and wrote that it "is generally asserted that he seldom refuses anything he is asked for. He is particularly gracious to the 36 villages of Yutai Shan [Wutaishan]."[174] Nowadays, this cult has almost superseded that of the *bodhisattva*;[175] yet, while in the 1900s-1930s it was customary for the locals to merely ask the deity for propitious weather, he now receives all kinds of prayers from all Wutaishan's pilgrims, and especially from Inner Mongols. The vows previously made before Pusading's and Shuxiangsi's 'true images' of Mañjuśrī are now made before the Black Dragon King of Wanfoge.[176]

### Worship of Reincarnations, Saints and Ascetics

The presence of a high reincarnation or saint on Wutaishan enhanced the attractive power of the place and could be a major motivation to undertake the pilgrimage. Rölpé Dorjé and the Thirteenth Dalai Lama attracted thousands of Mongol devotees to Wutaishan. D'Ollone described Mongol princes in caravans of thousands of camels visiting the Dalai Lama on Wutaishan in 1908,[177] and Mannerheim, who traveled along the road from Wutaishan to Höhhot, counted up to 2,500 Mongols who journeyed to Wutaishan in winter to worship him (Table 2): "We met a considerable number of Mongols on the road, travelling in small groups either on foot or on horseback with their savings, to the Dalai

---

173    See Online Appendix B: "Puhuasi." Khormusta Tngri is the Mongol form of Ahura Mazda, identified with Indra by the Uyghur Buddhists and transmitted to the Mongols during the fourteenth century.

174    Mannerheim 1969 [1940]: 693; also Blofeld 1938: 34.

175    Contrary to many other pilgrimage sites in the world where the cult of the personified saint replaced the cult of the chtonian deities when ecclesiastical control was enforced (Eade and Sallnow 1991: 6-7), the two cults with their different interpretations and practices coexisted on Wutaishan.

176    Vows made in the early morning are said to be more efficient, and pilgrims sometimes line up at two in the morning. Some even go back home without visiting any other monasteries.

177    Ollone 1911: 303.

Lama." These pilgrims were both men and women, "some with packs tied to their backs, other riding donkeys, mules, horses and camels."[178] The pilgrims attended mass teachings, empowerments and blessings, even asking these masters for specific initiations.[179] During collective blessings, they hoped to be touched by the lama's hand (*adis ab-*), and they received blessed amulets, protection knots and pills.

The high reincarnations redistributed part of the donations they received to the Wutaishan monasteries and their communities for the performance of rituals for the benefit of all living beings. In 1781, Rölpé Dorjé allocated to the ritual funds of the religious community one third of the ten thousand taels offered to him by Qianlong to extend his residence. In 1925, the Ninth Panchen Lama received many donations and offered three thousand silver dollars to Pusading.

Mongols showed great reverence not only towards renowned reincarnations but also to ascetics, including Chinese hermits, who practiced meditation within caves or monasteries.[180] Mongols from Beijing were deeply impressed by the Chinese ascetic known as Lichan Laoshi 立禪老師 ('Master Who Meditated Standing'), who practiced *samadhi* for thirteen years without sleeping: "Everybody knew of his reputation: he hides deep in the mountain to reduce his heart to ashes and annihilate his intellect" (stele DLD1, 1691). They built a hexagonal pavilion on the spot where he had planted a wooden pole, in which they enshrined a copy of the Sandalwood Buddha. In addition, Li Xiangzhi described the great reverence Mongols had shown in 1899 towards a sixty-year-old Chinese female ascetic from Zheli Province: this woman meditated for three years, days and nights on a platform at Xiantongsi, and the Mongols who visited the monastery believed she was a deity, made prostrations in front of her and gave her offerings. She used to bless them with water poured into their hands, and the Mongols washed their face with this blessed 'Buddha water' which could erase all calamities and make grace flow down on them.[181] Zhang Dungu also mentioned a Mongol woman sitting in meditation in a temple in 1911; even in the cold and snow, she mumbled invocations all day long. All the Mongols who saw her kneeled with respect and offered her food; it was said that she was certain to become a buddha.[182]

---

178   Mannerheim 1969 [1940]: 698.
179   On Mongol initiation rituals, see Pozdneev 1978 [1887]: 578-580. Mass teachings to commoners especially developed in the early twentieth century with the Panchen Lama's tours.
180   Many hermits lived in Wutaishan's caves. See for instance Chen Xingya 1936: 46.
181   Li Xiangzhi 1932: 76-77.
182   Zhang Dungu 1911: 25.

## When Pilgrims Go Shopping

Purchasing goods on Wutaishan was also an important component of the pilgrimage:

> The vacant spots between them [i. e., the temples] are taken up by shops where are sold all those things pilgrims delight in the world over, beads, books, amulets and images; also little wooden bowls and plates of poplar wood, for which the place is famous, and which are carried hence all over Mongolia and Tibet.[183]

The markets in the late Qing dynasty were on Yanglin Street, Yingfang Street 營坊街 and Taiping Street 太平街 (the main streets of Taihuai).[184] Yingfang and Taiping Streets had about twenty Chinese shops selling flour and daily products.[185] The Yanglin Street market, stretching out from Xiantongsi to either side of the 108 steps leading to Pusading, had narrow lanes that were densely crowded with thirty to forty Chinese family businesses.[186] "The bazaar close to Poo-sating is full of life. Mongols are constantly here buying from the Chinese shopkeepers."[187] The street was crowded with Mongol pilgrims and residing monks.[188] These small shops belonged to the monasteries and were rented out to the Chinese.[189]

The shops sold all sorts of Tibetan-style ritual objects—wooden bowls, rosaries (made of wood, glass, seeds or precious stones), incense and incense burners, metal lamps, lacquer dishes, books, bells, amulets, prayer wheels, prayer books in Mongolian and Tibetan printed in Beijing, vajras ('thunderbolt-diamond,' a ritual instrument), glass, precious stones, seeds, silver reliquaries, statues, paintings of Tibetan Buddhist deities and Chinese gods, banners, charms

---

183 Rockhill 1895: 766.
184 The village had a population of about two thousand in 1940 (Ono Katsutoshi and Hibino Takao 1942: 142). Chen Xingya (1936: 64) counts two thousand monks and one thousand shopkeepers. On the organization of Taihuai: Jiang Weiqiao 1918: 23. Ancient photos of Taihuai: Ono Katsutoshi and Hibino Takao 1942: 3 (Taihuai); 7 (view from Pusading), 11 (travelers riding a donkey; crowd at Yanglinjie). On present-day artisans: Huang Yongsong and Dai Qing, 1991: 11-20.
185 Jiang Weiqiao 1918: 22.
186 Bai Meichu 2010 [1925]: juan 2, 92.
187 Edkins 1893 [1878]: 228; Pokotilov 1935 [1893]: 70.
188 Pokotilov 1935 [1893]: 70.
189 Xin Butang and Zheng Fulin 1995: 30.

in one, two or three languages, and three dimensional *maṇḍalas*.[190] Most of these objects were manufactured in the Dai Prefecture (to which Wutaishan belonged during the Qing dynasty).[191] The shops also sold furniture and cooking utensils for the yurt, food and sweets, snuff, ceramics—everything that a Mongol family needed could be bought there. Herbal medicine from Wutaishan was renowned in North China and was sold in Hebei and Shanxi.[192] Other merchants sold antiques, leather objects,[193] "beautiful silks and satins figured with dragons and flowers worthy to be used as presents to the highest lamas.... . Considering the smallness of the village, it was amazing to see such a variety of goods, many of them extremely valuable."[194] In the 1890s, lamas could buy a high-quality robe for seventy taels and a more ordinary one for half that price; they were dyed on Wutaishan with a local burgundy color that was renowned as far as Beijing for its durability and magnificent brightness.[195]

During the late Qing and Republican periods, Chinese traders mostly came from Dai Prefecture (Fanzhi, Wutai and Guo 崞縣 Counties) as well as Xinding 忻定.[196] They were the same merchants who crisscrossed Mongolia, Xinjiang and Ningxia.[197] From September to June, goods were brought to Wutaishan on camelback, as seen on the Cifusi map, and large droves of camels were seen grazing throughout the valley.[198] For the summer months, from June to August, camel traffic was replaced by ox and pony carts.[199]

The Mongols were the main clients of the shops of Taiping and Yanglin Streets, and bargaining was done in Mongolian only.[200] Mongols rushed into the shops and loved buying and bargaining,[201] but they were said to pay exorbitant prices for the goods.[202] The Chinese took advantage of the Mongols'

---

190    Edkins 1893 [1878]: 237-238, Rockhill 1895: 767; Bai Meichu 2010 [1925]: *juan* 2, 74, 92; Ono Katsutoshi and Hibino Takao 1942: 142; Blofeld 1948: 92-93; Blofeld 1959: 123.

191    Bai Meichu 2010 [1925]: *juan* 2, 75.

192    Li Xiangzhi 1932: 154-155.

193    Bai Meichu 2010 [1925]: *juan* 2, 92.

194    Blofeld 1948: 92-93.

195    Pokotilov 1935 [1893]: 67.

196    Yan Tianling 2004: 42-43; Li Xiangzhi 1932: 177.

197    Bai Meichu 2010 [1925]: *juan* 2, 75; Yan Tianling 2004: 42-43.

198    Edkins 1893 [1878]: 228; Fischer 1923: 98.

199    Andrews 1921.

200    Bai Meichu 2010 [1925]: *juan* 2, 92.

201    Edkins 1893 [1878]: 237-238.

202    Swallow 1903: 179.

ignorance and "the money the Mongols brought to donate to Buddhist temples
and lamas usually wound up in the hands of Shanxi merchants."[203]

The most common souvenirs brought back by Mongol pilgrims were wooden
bowls, rosaries made of pine, cypress, elm or silver birch, and bronze statues of
Buddha.[204] The production of wooden bowls made from outgrowths of willow
roots, particularly prized by Mongols and Tibetans, has continued up to the
present day: they were reputed to be unbreakable, to stay cool even when holding hot food (and during the summer) and to be ideal for storing meat and oil
because of their natural preserving qualities.[205]

### Wutaishan as a Market of Buddhist Icons

Wutaishan was one of the main places where Mongols bought Tibetan Buddhist painted and sculpted icons, along with Dolonnor, Beijing and Höhhot.
Wutaishan's workshops were located within the shops on Yanglin Street, where
"hundreds of skilled craftsmen [were] painting or making images of the gods
from brass, silver and even gold."[206] Apparently, the craftsmen were all Chinese.[207] Wingate wrote that "the chief industry of the place is the making of
copper and bronze idols."[208] Though there was a booming trade in such idols,
their production is not documented, and at present very few pieces in museum
collections and Mongol monasteries are identified as coming from Wutaishan.[209]

Mongol nobles and Buddhist dignitaries commissioned works in silver or
bronze,[210] as well as *thangka*, to Wutaishan craftsmen to offer to monasteries
on the mountain or to bring back to Mongolia. The large appliqué of Tsongkhapa in the Newark Museum (Fig. 40) was probably commissioned on Wutaishan to a Chinese artist by a Mongol woman from the Ongniud Banner (Juu

---

203   Jagchid 1999: 31.
204   Li Xiangzhi 1932: 182-183.
205   Han Heping and Wang Miao 1999: 96. On present-day production of wooden bowls:
      Huang Yongsong and Dai Qing, 1991: 34-37.
206   Blofeld 1938: 34; Blofeld 1959: 123.
207   Blofeld 1959: 123; Halén 1987: 4.
208   Wingate 1907: 277. Pokotilov, who traveled there in 1889, is the only author who asserts
      that all the articles sold on the mountain were imported except for the wooden cups and
      wooden rosaries (1935 [1893]: 70). In 1930-1932, large statues for Wutaishan monasteries
      were also commissioned from Beijing workshops (Montell 1954 [1943]).
209   See for example Reynolds 1990; Halén 1987; Meinheit 2011; and the exhibit entitled "Wutai
      Shan: Pilgrimage to the Five-Peak Mountain" (May 10th – October 16th 2007) organized at
      the Rubin Museum of Art in New York (catalogue: Debreczeny 2011: 49-94).
210   Blofeld 1948: 93.

FIGURE 40      *Large appliqué of Tsongkhapa containing a letter in Mongolian sewn inside
dated 1805, made to be offered to Shancaidong.* © NEWARK MUSEUM, NEW
JERSEY (PHOTOGRAPH PROVIDED BY THE NEWARK MUSEUM).

Uda League), whose younger brother was a monk in Drépung Monastery. We know from the letter in Mongolian sewn inside, dated 1805, that it was destined to be hung in Norzang Cave, i.e., Shancaidong.[211] In the eighteenth century, Nanei [Nöngnei] Beile, ruler (*jasag*) of the Khalkha Darkhan Beile Banner (Ulaanchab League) went on pilgrimage to Wutaishan and brought back a statue of Mañjuśrī and some *sūtras*; back in Mongolia, full of faith, he decided to found a monastery, Batu Khaalga Süme, where he enshrined these objects. Also, the statues, texts and ritual objects of Moroi-yin Süme were especially commissioned to Wutaishan artisans. [212] Many statues and *thangka* that were preserved in Mongol monasteries were indeed brought from Wutaishan.[213]

However, the main production of the Wutaishan workshops seems to have been small-sized bronze statues and miniature paintings produced on a large scale. Pilgrims brought them in Wutaishan temples to have them consecrated by a lama or by famous icons. A few such small statues and paintings found in Mongolia have recently been attributed to Wutaishan (Fig. 41).[214] Much work still needs to be done in order to identify and characterize the Gélukpa Buddhist art on Wutaishan.[215]

There was a printing house in Pusading which certainly kept woodblocks for printing guidebooks.[216] Books printed on Wutaishan were said to be of a better quality than those from Beijing.[217] Other monasteries printed prayer books, as well as images, to be sold to pilgrims, such as the Cifusi map, the Buddha's footprints and Mongolian guidebooks.

---

211   Reynolds 1990: 32-38.

212   Ch. Molimiao 莫力廟, Khorcin Darkhan Wang Banner, Jirim League.

213   Altanzayaa 2000: 141-142.

214   From a number of stylistic elements, Carmen Meinert identified a 'Wutaishan style' of small-sized statues and miniature paintings, most of them dated to the nineteenth century, which she believes were brought back by pilgrims from Wutaishan to Mongolia (cat. 33, cat. 136, cat. 267, cat. 351). According to her, "Features characteristic of paintings and sculptures produced in the workshops of Mount Wutai are whorls of hair in the form of a net, narrow petals standing out in relief from broad lotus petals outlined on a smooth surface and a stylized design imitating lotus petals outlined on the smooth back of the lotus pedestal." She, however, identified other statues not fitting this description as artwork from Wutaishan (cat. 113) (Meinert, ed. 2011: 102, catalogue of a private collection of Mongol art).

215   Nowadays workshops producing bronze icons are still active on the mountain, but the Gélukpa monasteries generally import their icons from Amdo or Nepal.

216   Altanzayaa 2000: 142-143, 148.

217   Roerich 1933: 83. However Edkins (1893 [1878]: 238) wrote that the books sold on Wutaishan were brought from Beijing.

FIGURE 41

*Buddha Śākyamuni, statuette, cast bronze, gold leaf, 3.5 cm high, nineteenth century. This statuette may have been brought back by pilgrims from Wutaishan to Mongolia.*
© PUBLICATION BY COURTESY OF THE PRIVATE COLLECTOR, CORRESPONDENCE THROUGH CARMEN MEINERT.

### Śākyamuni's Footprints for Sale

The first Buddhist images represented Buddha's presence by his footprints only (Skt. *buddhapada*). Throughout the Buddhist world, footprints are said to be a spontaneous manifestation and are a common way to indicate the presence of a buddha, a deity or an accomplished master possessing spiritual power.[218] The footprints (*gishkigsen mör-ün orom*, 'pressed/trampled trace or footprint') not only recall their presence, but also the taming and empowerment of the mountain (*uula-yi adistidla-*) through the act of treading, pressing one's foot into the earth.[219] On Wutaishan, great masters, *bodhisattva*s and even Mañjuśrī's lion left their footprints in the rock (Fig. 44, Fig. 45).

Pilgrims to Wutaishan bought block prints of the Buddha's footprints as souvenirs. The woodblocks were carved after Śākyamuni's footprints engraved on the stele commonly referred to as "Foji lingxiang zhi bei 佛蹟靈像之碑," dated

---

218    Hummel (1971) and Selig Brown (2004) recount the history, decoration and symbolic significance of paintings and prints of handprints and footprints in Buddhist countries and especially in the Tibetan world.

219    *UTAOSC* 11a, 44b–45a.

FIGURE 42

*Relief of the Buddha's footprints on the base of the Great White Stūpa, Tayuansi.*

1582 and located in a southern niche of the Great White Stūpa (Fig. 42).[220] The footprints are very large, measuring 50 × 22 centimeters.[221] They are decorated with the usual *lakṣaṇa*s found on Chinese Buddha footprints (*svastika*, Moon King, Vajra Pestle, Double Fish, Treasure Vase, Thousand-Spoked Wheel, Brahma Peak/*uṣṇīṣa*, and Sword). Below them is a Chinese text of about thirty columns, which is preserved in a longer version in the *Qingliangshan zhi* (1596)[222] and is based on seventh-century Chinese pilgrim Xuanzang 玄奘's account of

---

220 The stele was roughly colored in blue, red and black up to the mid-2000s, when all traces of painting were removed. Similar steles were erected in Buddhist monasteries of China: Selig Brown ed. 2004: 70, n. 70; Debreczeny 2011: 64-66, cat. no. 14.

221 Most of the Buddha's footprints in South and Southeast Asia are gigantic (Selig Brown 2004: 15).

222 *Qingliangshan zhi* 1887 [1596]: *juan* 2, 9b-10a.

his nineteen-year peregrination in the West.[223] It explains that, according to Xuanzang's *Great Tang Records on the Western Regions*, before his death, in the city of Pātaliputra (India), Śākyamuni, while standing on a high stone, told his disciple Ānanda that he would leave his footprints on it for all living beings. Those who worshipped them would see the extinction of all sufferings and will be reborn in the presence of the Buddha. Xuanzang brought back to China from Pātaliputra a print of the footprints adorned with the *lakṣaṇas*, and Emperor Taizong had it carved for his ancestral temple. In 1582, the footprints were then re-carved for the Great White Stūpa of Tayuansi.

This stele was one of the most important places of veneration for Tibetans and Mongols;[224] the footprints' history is mentioned in Mongolian and Tibetan guidebooks of Wutaishan.[225] Two Qing-dynasty block prints and a painting of Wutaishan's Buddha footprints are preserved in museum collections:

– A woodblock print with pigment on cotton dated 1659-1658 is preserved in the Rubin Museum in New York (Fig. 43).[226] A Chinese text inserted between the feet condenses the *Qingliangshan zhi*'s version of the story and adds that the Wutaishan *da lama* A-wang-lao-zang (the first *jasag lama*) donated the money to have the image painted and published.[227] The Tibetan text written below the footprints informs us that the woodblock for this image was carved at Pusading. According to Karl Debreczeny, "This woodblock print would have been a relatively affordable image that a Mongol might have brought back as a souvenir from his pilgrimage to Five-Peak Mountain."[228]

– A woodblock print on cloth purchased by the Austrian collector Hans Leder (1848-1921) in Urga, now in the Linden Museum of Stuttgart,[229] was studied by S. Hummel. It resembles the above-mentioned print but with a nineteen-line Tibetan text below, which quotes Xuanzang's account. It ends with a prayer mentioning Mahākāla, Lhamo and Yama. Although the print has almost completely faded, the Tibetan text is still legible.

---

223   *Da Tang Xiyuji* 大唐西域記, "Records of the Western Regions of the Great Tang Dynasty" (Hummel 1971: 404, reproduction of the original between p. 396-397). See also Selig Brown 2004: 28.

224   According to a modern Tibetan guidebook, their worship helps purify defilement and be reborn in a pure pand (Duan Jinjin 2008: 78).

225   *TÜAG* 10a; *ZMRBDB*, Tibetan passage and German translation in Hummel 1971: 401.

226   It is preserved in the Rubin Museum of Art, New York (C2006.66.438 (HAR894)) and was published in Selig-Brown ed. 2004: 64; Debreczeny 2011: 64-66, cat. no. 13.

227   Debreczeny (2011: 64-66, cat. no. 13) transcribes and translates the text.

228   Debreczeny 2011: 64.

229   Nr. 23897, 87 × 53 cm. Hummel 1971, ill. and Tibetan text between p. 396-397, translation p. 397-398.

FIGURE 43    *Woodblock print of Buddha's footprints with pigment on cotton dated 1659-1658,*
*bearing Chinese and Tibetan texts.* © RUBIN MUSEUM OF ART, NEW YORK
(C2006.66.438) (HAR894, PHOTOGRAPH PROVIDED BY THE RUBIN MUSEUM
OF ART).

– A beautifully colored Tibetan-style *thangka* shows the golden footprints on a black background, surrounded by Śākyamuni, *bodhisattva*s and various Tibetan Buddhist deities (*yidam, dharmapāla*s) and symbols.[230] According to the Rubin Museum's caption, this *thangka* was acquired as a souvenir by a pilgrim who visited Wutaishan. It may have been painted by a Mongol artist over a woodblock print.[231]

Like the Cifusi map, the woodblock prints of Buddha's footprints were cheap mass products that were reproducible and could be colored in various ways or and even integrated into a painting; they range from simple black-and-white prints to elaborate *thangka*s painted with gold. In addition, being prints of a print, they do not differ from the original Śākyamuni footprints and possess "the same beneficient charisma as the original."[232] Prints of Buddha's footprints and prints of the Cifusi map belonged to the large category of Wutaishan 'pilgrimage souvenirs,' which also included icons, rosaries, wooden bowls, as well as soil, water, etc. from the mountain: not only were they material proof that a pilgrim had completed his/her journey but they also created a personal connection with the 'power' of the site and were worshipped back home.

### The Exportation of Wutaishan Buddhist Items

The artistic production of Wutaishan was also exported to Urga, Beijing,[233] and as far away as Buryatia. In 1860 a high dignitary came from the Wutai region to the Buryats of Barguzin with a large quantity of goods for trade.[234] Painters from Wutaishan frequently traveled to Urga at the end of the nineteenth century. Along with painters from 'Yinzhou' in Shanxi,[235] they had established seven workshops in Urga; they painted *thangka*s and made statues out of wood, clay and papier-mâché.[236] In 1909, Dr. G.J. Ramstedt's Finnish expedition purchased sixty-three brightly colored *thangka*s that were probably made on Wutaishan and a print of the 1846 map in a 'Beijing shop,' that is, 'an agency representing the Wutaishan monasteries' in Urga.[237] G. Roerich also mentions

---

230  Dimensions: 78.7 × 54.6 cm. It is dated to the nineteenth century and is preserved in the Rubin Museum of Art, New York (C2003.37.1). See Selig-Brown ed. 2004: 65; Debreczeny 2011: 66-67, cat. no. 14. Selig-Brown, ed. 2004: 70, n. 81) believes a pounce may have been used to reproduce the footprints.

231  Debreczeny 2011: 67.

232  Hummel 1971: 397.

233  Rockhill 1895: 766.

234  Humphrey 1998: 49.

235  An error in the text; the author possibly meant Xinzhou 忻州.

236  See Pozdneev 1971 [1896]: 69.

237  Halén 1987.

shops in early twentieth-century Urga called 'Ribo Tsénga *püüse*' (< Ch. *puzi* 鋪
子, 'shop') that imported small bronze statues and ritual paraphernalia (musical instruments, lamps, incense, monks' garments) from Wutaishan and Dolonnor, in addition to prayer books from Beijing and Wutaishan.[238]

Wutaishan was thus a trademark for religious objects, and the Mongols came
to identify a distinct 'Wutaishan artistic style' which inspired sculptors. C. Meinert suggested that small Mongol statues were influenced by this Wutaishan
style or even that "artists of Mount Wutai" may have worked in Mongolia.[239]
Several icons of Urga, such as the great statue of Lhamo in papier-mâché standing in the Juu Temple of the Choijin Lama-yin Süme (Temple of the Oracle
Lama), erected from 1904 to 1908, are attributed to "Mongol masters of the Utai
School."[240] In the same monastery, the faces of the sixteen *arhat*s are said to
have been modeled after Wutaishan's *arhat*s.

### Wutaishan: A Main Place of Contact Between Chinese, Mongol and Tibetan Cultures

A core of monasteries was visited by all pilgrims, but Mongols had their preferences as well as specific practices that they shared with Tibetans, such as circumambulation and throwing wind-horse papers.[241] The rituals they requested
show how much they were concerned with obtaining a favorable reincarnation,
health and longevity, clearing away defilement and sins and transferring merit
to their living and dead relatives. Their donations of money and farmland were
important contributions to the general economic and religious development of
Wutaishan in the late Qing period, and more specifically to the prosperity of
Gélukpa communities. Finally, Mongol pilgrims brought back souvenirs, and
many of them engaged in trade. The pilgrimage to Wutaishan was therefore an
opportunity for major economic exchange for Mongol herders, Wutaishan
monks and Chinese merchants.[242] Taihuai was a busy trade center that allowed

---

238   Roerich 1933: 83. There are now several Ribo Tsénga/Utaishan shops in Ulaanbaatar, right
      next to the Dashichoiling Monastery and south of Gandan Monastery. A monk from
      Dashichoiling journeys every year to Wutaishan to buy icons and ritual objects to sell
      them in the Dashichoiling shop.

239   Meinert, ed. 2011: cat. 41, cat. 89.

240   According to a local Mongol, 2009.

241   I do not have enough information about the Tibetans' pilgrimage to judge to what extent
      it differed from the Mongols'.

242   On the contribution of the Tibetan pilgrimage to the circulation of goods, particularly
      small items of value: see van Spengen 2000: 122-129.

for a population of traders, shopkeepers and even peasants and beggars to live off the success of the pilgrimage. In the words of the Kanjurwa Khutugtu (referring to the period 1920-1945):

> For many generations Wu-t'ai-shan was an economic center as well as a religious center because many pilgrims came there; great sums of money circulated from the many donations made to the monastic temples and because of the service activities that catered to the pilgrims.[243]

But were interactions limited to commercial matters, and how far might they have expanded into the fields of religion, intellectual exchange or personal friendship, for instance? Did these different peoples cohabitate without conflict? Could they share a feeling of *communitas*? Theories in pilgrimage studies can help us make sense of the very rich Wutaishan material. I will discuss two hypotheses made by Elverskog (2011) about Wutaishan as a key place of *communitas*, first among Mongols and second between Mongols, Mandchus, Tibetans and Chinese in the Qing empire.

### Communitas *between Pilgrims on Wutaishan?*
Although Victor Turner's well-known concepts of *'communitas'* and 'liminality'[244] have been seriously challenged by anthropologists,[245] often emphasizing the role of individual experience in pilgrimage,[246] some particular case studies show that the Turnerian model should not be abandoned altogether.[247] Turner's theories were based on the study of homogeneous, mono-confessional pilgrimage sites, yet they prove even more interesting when applied to shared pilgrimage sites.[248] Due to their long tradition of cohabitation between different schools and religions, most Chinese pilgrimage sites seem to be shared

---

243   Jagchid and Hyer 1983: 106-107.
244   Turner 1978, Turner and Turner 1978. His theory was inspired by the work of Arnold Van Gennep on rites of passage.
245   Notably Ekvall and Downs 1987: 47; Morinis 1992: 7-8; Eade and Sallnow 1991: 4-5; Albera 2009; Couroucli 2009: 178, n. 1.
246   In the conclusion of the book he edited with M. Couroucli, Albera (2009: 351) prefers to speak of pilgrims having common needs and goals but rarely interacting with each other.
247   See for instance Nancy Frey's study of the present-day Santiago pilgrimage; Holmes-Rodman's study of a healing shrine in New Mexico (in Badone and Roseman, eds. 2004).
248   See the different studies on places where Christian and Muslims cohabitate around the Mediterranean Sea: Albera and Couroucli, eds. 2009 (especially the articles of Couroucli and Valtchinova). For an example of a pilgrimage shared by Hindus and Buddhists in Nepal: Buffetrille 1994.

between Buddhist and Daoists, or between Chinese and Tibetan Buddhists, with more tolerance than, for instance, sacred sites frequented by both Christians and Muslims in the Middle East.[249]

Do the sources used here to study the Wutaishan pilgrimage allow us to speak of a *communitas* according to Turner's meaning, i.e., at the margins of or outside society, in a state of liminality or antistructure, characterized by the spontaneity of relationships and the abolition of social distinctions?[250] I argue that temporary forms of *communitas*, where "persons normally segregated in secular or profane society are, at least symbolically, integrated into a fluid, ecstatic community of common religious purpose,"[251] were certainly almost palpable on Wutaishan at some precise moments: collective rituals (especially the Great Sixth Month Festival procession), mass teachings and, above all, collective visions and miracles such as the 'Buddha lights' that were seen by large groups of people irrespective of ethnicity and rank. Rölpé Dorjé's biography indeed records that crowds of people witnessed light phenomena on the mountain, especially during and after Tibetan Buddhist empowerment rituals.[252] Moreover, in the eighteenth century, the throngs of Chinese, Tibetans and Mongols asking for blessings, teachings and initiations from Rölpé Dorjé, along with the communities of 'foreign' and Chinese monks performing rituals together under the leadership of the *jasag lama*, evoke forms of *communitas*. In the 1930s, Alley and Lapwood mention

> a huge procession of lamas, Chinese priests and pilgrims, who had been attending an initiation ceremony at a temple up the valley. These were estimated to be about 3,000 persons in all, and their coloured gowns and robes as they filed along the mountain path showed up well against a hillside already bright with flowers.[253]

Pilgrims following the great procession of the Great Sixth Month Festival or queuing to enter the Mother's Womb-Cave mixed with each other. Because of the dangers of the roads and the risk of getting lost, pilgrims of different

---

249   Naquin and Yü 1992, "Introduction."

250   According to Turner, pilgrimage is fundamentally antistructural: the rules and constraints of daily life being temporarily suspended, pilgrims experience egalitarian relationships and create a new community.

251   Gimello 1992: 136, n. 43, also 105, 132, n. 31.

252   Biography of Rölpé Dorjé, transl. Chen Qingying and Ma Lianlong 1988: 248-249.

253   Alley and Lapwood 1935: 119.

ethnicities occasionally traveled together on the roads leading to Wutaishan and formed groups when they climbed to the terraces.

*Communitas* is naturally present in the discourse as well. Since Mañjuśrī can appear on the mountain in many guises to test one's level of compassion, people say that one has to be kind to everybody because anybody could be Mañjuśrī in a guise;[254] thus, in general, pilgrims consciously adopt an attitude of generosity and friendly behavior. Khejok Rinpoché's modern Tibetan guide says, [255] for instance, that "in a pilgrimage, the pilgrims would cultivate a mind of faith and devotion on the way there."[256] Nonetheless, pilgrim discourse, like official propaganda of the site, tends to overemphasize harmony and brotherhood over disappointment and tensions, and we must be very cautious about such claims.[257] Susan Naquin observed on the Chinese pilgrimage to Miaofengshan that pilgrims did behave as if they formed one harmonious family, but that

> private feelings of discomfort, annoyance, or disappointment were to be suppressed; individuals were subtly pressured into such behaviour by their own and others' expectations.[258]

Therefore, it would be safer to speak of peaceful cohabitation, religious tolerance and curiosity for 'the other'[259] rather than a robust *communitas* in Turner's terms that truly levels the gap between ordinary pilgrims, monks, aristocrats

---

254   See for instance Tuttle 2006a: 19. Nowadays many beggars in rags hope that people will give them money in case he/she could be the *bodhisattva*.

255   Born in 1936, Khejok Rinpoché is the sixth reincarnation of the Ganden Datsang Lhündrup Ling (Dhétsang Monastery) in Eastern Tibet. Now teaching in Australia, he made a pilgrimage to Wutaishan in 1999.

256   This guide available on the Internet is based on information provided by Khejok Rinpoché during the pilgrimage he led to Wutaishan in 1999 (Lim 1999).

257   Many scholars working on pilgrimages have pointed out this ideal of harmony and solidarity, which is often far from the observed practices.

258   Naquin 1992: 364.

259   Comparing the sharing of religious sites in the Balkans and in India, Hayden (2002) argues that competitive sharing is compatible with the passive meaning of tolerance—i.e., non-interference—but incompatible with the active meaning of tolerance—acceptation of the Other, respect and recognition while disagreeing with others' beliefs and practices. Positive, active tolerance would be an illusion in the process of the complete appropriation of a holy site by a group. Albera (2009: 356) criticizes Hayden and prefers to highlight the plurality of situations and the difficulty of building theories. See also Hayden's reviews in *Current Anthropology* 43/2, and especially Bowman's comments.

and literati, or between different nationalities.[260] Temporary moments of *communitas* certainly happened on Wutaishan, but cohabitation and tolerance were probably more common than interactions and cultural exchange. As I will show below, my sources rather describe situations that are closer to Eade and Sallnow's theory, which views pilgrimage as a mosaic where actors are heterogeneous and viewpoints are diverse.[261] The Wutaishan pilgrimage is "capable of accommodating diverse meanings and practices," though it cannot be considered as being 'void' of beliefs and symbols.[262]

### A Communitas *between Mongols?*

The stone inscriptions offer us a glimpse of the Mongol donors as they wanted to appear on stone in perpetuity: they do not talk about impoverished herders and indebted nobles (which the donors actually were): on the contrary, they showcase the extreme generosity of all patrons towards the Wutaishan monasteries. These Mongols traveling in groups mixing men and women, nobles,

---

260    Similar observations for a mono-confessional pilgrimage site are made by Buffetrille (1997: 88 and 2003): in present-day Tibet, "pilgrimage groups as a rule do not mix with one another"; "there is not necessarily good fellowship, brotherhood and equality among all the pilgrims ... which does not exclude mutual aid in case of difficulty"; "the quality of *communitas* that Turner (1969, 1974, 1978) observes in all the pilgrimages he studied, is in general not present in the Tibetan world, except during very short periods ... contrary to what one might think, differences of social status persist during the pilgrimage." See also Huber 1999: 18. But Kapstein (1998: 112), who insists on the festive dimension of a pilgrimage, does not reject the Turnerian model.

261    Eade and Sallnow deconstructed both the first trend of pilgrimage studies, of Durkhemian inspiration, that considers pilgrimage as an element of social cohesion that participates in the construction and the maintenance of larger collective identities such as territorial, political or religious communities, and Turner's theory. Both are still valid in pilgrimage studies, though. See for instance in the Tibetan context Huber's study of a peripheral, popular pilgrimage where identities and cultural practices were forged anew (1999: 3-6; 174); see also Albera 2009.

262    In opposition to other theories that emphasize a pilgrimage site that is 'full' of beliefs and symbols, Eade and Sallnow insist on its property of 'void,' "capable of accommodating diverse meanings and practices," of offering to "a variety of clients what each of them desires" (1991: 15). They advocate analyzing each specific pilgrimage in terms of its particular social context and its "historically and culturally specific behaviors and meanings" (1991: 3-5). Pilgrimage resists analysis and theorization: "if one can no longer take for granted the meaning of a pilgrimage for its participants, one can no longer take for granted a uniform definition of the phenomenon of 'pilgrimage' either." Yet Eade's introduction to the second edition of *Contesting the Sacred* (2000) acknowledges that this argument may have been overstated.

lamas and commoners, and pooling their money to pay for rituals and offerings to monasteries would seem to embody the image of a brotherhood.

Elverskog, who argued that a distinct pan-Mongol identity emerged at the end of the Qing dynasty, cemented by Buddhism and by the heritage of Ching-gis Khan, alongside a local identity attached to one's banner,[263] proposed that the Wutaishan pilgrimage played a prominent role in the creation of a 'Mongol identity.'[264] The pilgrimage may have fostered "bonds between the stratified social hierarchies institutionalized by the Qing state," and thus

> it is possible to imagine that Mongols of all social ranks came to share a new 'Mongol' *communitas* .... at Wutai Shan the boundaries and nature of what it meant to be Mongol, must have been both challenged and recon-ceptualized.[265]

As Elverskog acknowledges, this is a deduction "based on an awareness of the larger historical context" but not on textual evidence. In fact, the sources I have studied do not confirm Elverskog's hypothesis, although Mongols' conscious-ness of a common identity may certainly have been enhanced during the pil-grimage by the simple fact of speaking the same language and travelling together in a foreign territory. The stone inscriptions, with their conventional formulas and semblance of brotherhood, do not tell us the whole story. Other sources, for example, reveal that commoners expressed their resentment and anger when they had to pay for their ruler's journey to Wutaishan. Therefore, following Eade and Sallnow's theory, I would rather say that what actually stood out on Wutaishan was not a specific group's ethnicity or religious affiliation but rather the great variety of pilgrims and reasons for making the pilgrimage: in fact, it is more accurate to speak of Wutaishan *pilgrimages*. Rather than forge a sense of ethnic or religious identity among Mongols (or among the Chinese or Tibetans), Wutaishan seems to underline the social differences between pil-grims: penitents walking in great prostrations, well-off pilgrims enjoying a com-fortable journey and giving ostentatious offerings, monk-pilgrims seeking spiritual encounters, traders looking for the best price, and curious tourists. There is no evidence allowing us to validate Turner's theory of the crossing of social frontiers, of *communitas* between rich and poor, high lamas and penitents.

---

263   Elverskog 2006.
264   Elverskog 2011.
265   Elverskog 2011: 254.

### Communitas *in a Cosmopolitan Qing Empire or Mutual Incomprehension?*

Elverskog's second hypothesis is that Wutaishan was the ideal place where all the Buddhist populations of the Qing empire met and intermingled, developed a sense of sharing a 'Qing identity'[266] and experienced a 'Qing *communitas*,' where "Chinese literati, Mongol herders, Tibetan lamas and Manchu bannermen all came together, jostling shoulders at temples and caves in the pursuit of blessings and merit":

> Coming into contact with the enormous cultural and religious diversity of the Qing empire, in many cases no doubt for the first time, must also have been an amazing experience... pilgrimage to Wutai Shan created the field where such ideas could grow... it was the main, possibly the only place, where all of these new ideas were not only in the air, but also accessible to the widest range of social actors found in the Qing empire... . Pilgrimage to Wutai Shan therefore played a fundamental role in familiarizing the Mongols with the new cosmopolitan culture of the Qing since they not only partook of it while at the mountain, but also brought it home... . Indeed, how many places in the empire could Mongol nomads, Tibetan lamas, Manchu officials, and Chinese peasants all come together in direct contact and shop for the same commodities, much less partake in the same religious ceremony?[267]

This Qing cosmopolitanism experienced on Wutaishan would have made cultural exchange possible,[268] and in this favorable context Mongols created Sino-Mongol syncretic works in fields as diverse as Buddhist art, literature, theatre and astrology. And it is true that some learned Mongols acted as intermediaries in the transmission of Chinese Buddhist history, literature and sciences and helped bridge Tibeto-Mongol and Chinese Buddhist traditions. Great figures such as Mergen Gegeen or Gombojab had an interest in the Chinese Buddhist

---

266    Elverskog argues in his book *Our Great Qing* (2006) that 'Qing dynasty Mongols' acquired a 'pan-Qing identity': they viewed themselves—thanks to the propaganda orchestrated by the Qing emperors—as members of a broader community including Chinese, Manchus and Tibetans, into a multicultural empire which entailed a certain 'porousness between Qing culture(s).'

267    Elverskog 2011: 260-262.

268    Elverskog (2011: 255) defines 'Qing cosmopolitanism' as "the ability of the various peoples within the Manchu state to see, think and act beyond the local, be they Mongol, Tibetan, Manchu, or Chinese"; but "notions such as being Mongol, Tibetan, or Chinese did not dissipate into a fog of Manchu cosmopolitanism." See also Nietupski 2011.

tradition and historiography; Chinese-speaking Mongols of eastern Inner Mongolia, Höhhot, Beijing and Chengde translated the great Chinese novels into Mongolian and translated, compiled or used as main sources Chinese works about religion, geomancy, astrology and medicine.[269]

Indeed, Mongol worship of Wutaishan must not be seen through the lens of Tibetan Buddhism alone but must be understood as the veneration of an ancient Buddhist holy site connected to India, as well as the veneration of an ancient Chinese Buddhist site.[270] Buddhism provided what was in effect a cultural lingua franca.[271] The stone inscriptions and pilgrims' records clearly show that, if the different ethnic groups can be said to have had their own preferences, Mongols sponsored monasteries of both traditions, while Chinese laypeople were looking for Tibetan initiations.[272] The Mongolian and Tibetan guidebooks and the 1846 map included old Chinese lore of the sacred mountain. Wutaishan was the only place in China where Mongols worshipped Chinese icons on a large scale. In his guidebook, in fact, Rölpé Dorjé speaks of 'the pilgrims' without any distinction. Sanctity and efficacy (of relics, of sacred icons, of great Buddhist masters) prevailed over sectarian and ethnic differences. The blurred visual frontier between a Gélukpa and a Chinese Buddhist monastery on Wutaishan perhaps enhanced the feeling that Buddhism was one, though its traditions were many.

On a similar note to Elverskog, Gray Tuttle has argued that the Tibetan (monastic and lay) elite and the Qing imperial elite (Manchu and Mongol) formed a "stable, mutually supportive community," of which, however, the Chinese were excluded.[273] Based on my own research, on Wutaishan these elites may well have interacted with each other, especially during the emperors' tours, but the sources I have used cannot confirm or invalidate Tuttle's hypothesis for late Qing-period Mongol commoners. Visiting Chinese Buddhist temples and

---

269    Atwood 1992-1993: 17; Elverskog 2011: 257-258.

270    According to Elverskog (2006), Mongols have been convinced that they belonged to a single Buddhist continuum extending from India to Mongolia. Being Mongol (within the Qing empire) had become synonymous with being a Gélukpa Buddhist and a subject of the Qing emperor. Historiographers rewrote the history of Buddhism in Mongolia, inserting it in the longer history of Buddhism: Chinggis Khan and his descendants were recognized as reincarnations of ancient Indian and Tibetan kings, making the history of Mongolia actually have its starting point in India.

271    Kapstein 2009: xvii.

272    As seen in Chapter 3, Chinese interest in Tibetan Buddhism before the 1930s may have been underestimated, at least for the early Qing period and in some places such as Beijing, Wutaishan and Gansu (see the volume edited by Kapstein, ed. 2009).

273    Tuttle 2005: Chapter 1.

worshipping ancient icons do not necessary entail inter-ethnic and inter-religious dialogue. I would say that before being a 'cosmopolitan Qing pilgrimage site,' for Mongol devotees Wutaishan was first of all the holy residence of a revered *bodhisattva* where one could increase one's vital force and fortune and ensure happiness in future lives. The pilgrimage was first and foremost *personal.*

Again following Eade and Sallnow, I propose that the Wutaishan pilgrimage has a plurality of meanings, viewpoints and practices, where egalitarianism and nepotism, fraternity and conflict, unity and divisiveness cohabited. The prejudices, xenophobia or, at best, indifference that are commonly seen nowadays, along with mutual respect, tolerance and some temporary forms of *communitas*, certainly already existed a century ago.[274] Elverskog may have overestimated the extent of cultural exchange and the cosmopolitan culture of the pilgrimage. Even though Mongol commoners may have known stories translated from Chinese that circulated in Mongolia, used objects made in China and worshipped icons housed in Chinese Buddhist temples, this does not mean that they were interested in interacting with Chinese pilgrims or resident monks. Except in moments of danger or of fear of getting lost and other above-mentioned temporary forms of *communitas*, I found no example of pilgrims of different nationalities mixing with each other. The cultural and linguistic gap has always existed between Tibetan, Mongol and Chinese pilgrims. Gray Tuttle has in fact shown that interactions between Chinese and Tibetan Buddhism at the level of monastic teaching and practice were, before the 1930s, dampened by language and geographical barriers.[275] Except for Chinese shopkeepers and traders who learned to speak some Mongolian,[276] Mongolian-speaking Chinese monks and some learned Mongols fluent in Tibetan or Chinese, the main cause of mutual incomprehension between the communities was, first of all, language.[277] In 1912 the Chinese lay Buddhist Gao Henian, who enquired about the history and stories about Wutaishan, complained that he could not converse with the lamas.

As further evidence of the divide that could exist between pilgrims, early twentieth-century Chinese sources give some insights into Chinese judgments of Mongol and Tibetan monks and pilgrims on Wutaishan. Chinese pilgrims

---

274   About a Bulgarian pilgrimage, Valtchinova (2009: 114) showed that relations between pilgrims of different religions or traditions are in perpetual renegotiation.

275   Tuttle 2005: Chapter 1.

276   Yan Tianling 2004, quoting Zhang Dungu 1911, and Bai Meichu 2010 [1925]: *juan* 2, 92.

277   This was also true in the case of medieval European pilgrimages, where language barriers and the absence of promotion of cultural exchange led to mutual incomprehension, contempt and swindling (Sumption 1975: 192).

and travelers completely ignored the Tibetan Buddhist tradition. In Chinese scholars' eyes, the Mongols appeared exotic because of their costumes and, above all, because of their ostentatious religious fervor, which has been labeled as superstition in modern China. Buddhist layman Zhang Dungu criticized Mongol lamas for whom monkhood was a lucrative job, while recognizing that some pious and ascetic Mongols had no fear of suffering in their search for *nirvāṇa*. Yet, on the next page, he described the repulsive filthiness of Mongols' faces and clothing and was shocked by men and women mingling in monks' quarters and sitting together around the *kang*.[278] Describing the image of a woman under a bull having sexual intercourse with it (probably an image of Yama), he explains that when the Xiongnu 'barbarians' were exterminated by the Han dynasty only one woman was left and had a son with a bull, who is the ancestor of all the Mongols. His depiction of the monks who all drank alcohol and ate meat, did not respect their precepts, did illegal things and possessed everything from land and shops to women is part of the general anticlerical discourse of the time, and especially that targeting lamas.[279] I have no comparable sources from a Mongol angle; thus, I can only extrapolate from contemporary observations.[280] But there is no doubt that the different ethnic communities observed each other with curiosity and interest, even if it was to pick out the other's faults and vices.

---

278 Zhang Dungu 1911: 24-25. On page 17 he quotes a local saying: "[At Wutaishan] houses built from piled rocks do not fall, monks at the gate are not bitten by dogs, lamas in the bed-chamber do not trouble people."

279 Charleux 2002a. According to my field observations, in the 2000s, in spite of the growing influence of Han Gélukpa lamas, the fact that Inner Mongols can communicate in Chinese, and the general interest of the Chinese in the Tibetan Buddhist tradition, on the whole Tibetan, Mongol and Chinese pilgrims do not mix with each other and do not share food. Veiled tensions and jealousy caused by religious and racial prejudices are observed behind the apparent *communitas* that stems from the pilgrims' discourse and behavior. Chinese Buddhist monks typically consider the Tibetan and Mongol monks as 'impure' because they eat meat and have a freer life than their own: "they are not true monks." Chinese pilgrims feel they are discriminated because Tibetans are exempted from the expensive entrance tickets, while they are not. They criticize Tibetans and Mongols for being ignorant, filthy and superstitious, but they show curiosity towards Tibetan customs and sometimes approach Tibetan groups to examine their hand-prayer wheels and clothes. When a Mongol or a Tibetan reads aloud a stele inscription, Han Chinese surround him/her, manifest some surprise and ask him questions about the text.

280 Nowadays, Mongol and Tibetan lamas complain that the Chinese are racist and do not try to understand their tradition. They believe that the Chinese circumambulate *stūpas* to obtain good luck in making money. For mutual criticisms of Tibetan Buddhists and Chinese Buddhists in the Republican period: Tuttle 2005: 70-72.

# CHAPTER 7

# Mongolized Wutaishan and Mongol Wutaishans: Appropriation and Substitution

Following McKay, we can observe on Wutaishan the two antithetical processes: a process of 'systematization'—the institutionalization of a pilgrimage site by religious and political authorities, which create material structures of worship to control the site and compose guidebooks to integrate it within a belief system—and a process of 'contestation'—pilgrims making their own pilgrimage, survival of earlier beliefs, and competition between various traditions over the control of a site. With these two forces at play, the Wutaishan pilgrimage site is not a static place but one in perpetual transformation.[1]

The pilgrims themselves appropriated the pilgrimage and brought in their own practices and interpretations. This appropriation is especially visible in their rituals at natural numinous sites: for Mongols, Wutaishan was not only a pilgrimage to Buddhist icons and relics but also a pilgrimage to the mountain's numinous rocks and springs. Some of their practices at these spiritually potent sites are common to pilgrimages all over the world, though their interpretations often differ. We have seen in Chapter 1 that Mongol pilgrims especially valued natural numinous rocks, caves and springs of their homeland, which could bring material benefits through the absorption of, or contact with, some of the mountain's 'power.' Even when these numinous sites were appropriated and resanctified by monasteries, as they often were, they still did not lose their spiritual power. Mongol pilgrims were able to bring back home with them some of Wutaishan's power by collecting 'portions' of the sacred mountain home (soil, water, flowers, ice, etc.) and by claiming that sites of the Mongol countryside were equivalent or identical to Shanxi's Wutaishan. As we will see, there was no replica in Mongolia of famous temples or icons of Wutaishan: these substitutes or 'surrogate Wutaishans' in Mongolia were said to be equivalent to the original thanks to local lore, miraculous manifestations and exceptional numinous sites, in particular, womb-caves. But could they fully replace the pilgrimage to Wutaishan?

---

1    McKay 1998: 2-3.

## Absorbing the Mountain's Power

The pilgrims' practices at natural numinous sites differed from their practices at built sites. Within a monastery, the pilgrims attended rituals, had contact with monks and were received in the Guest Department, when they made a significant donation. The resident monks served as intermediaries between pilgrims and the sacred site: they hosted and looked after the pilgrims, introduced them to the monastery's history, icons and special features, and explained the gestures and other devotional practices that were expected to be performed. They often served as guides to the terraces, on the pilgrims' demand or spontaneously. However, when a numinous site was not appropriated by a monastery but stood on its own or was protected by a hermitage kept by no more than one or two monks (such as Zaoyuchi or the Mother's Womb-Cave), the pilgrims visited it without the mediation of resident monks and, as observed on other pilgrimage sites, adopted informal behavior that contrasted with their formal and codified behavior within temples.[2] With less institutional control, devotional practices at numinous sites were turned towards worldly expectations, i.e., bringing good luck and material benefits in this life. (The clergy might later provide a Buddhist interpretation to legitimize these practices.) Furthermore, on numinous sites, the pilgrims tended to imitate what others did and could also adopt rituals that did not belong to their tradition. Borrowed practices are often observed in pilgrimage sites shared by different religions or religious schools.[3]

Everything that grew on Wutaishan was filled with the spiritual power of the holy site, and some of this power could be transferred to the individual pilgrim and to his/her animals grazing on the holy land.[4] This transfer, as explained by Toni Huber in reference to Tibetan pilgrimages,

is about a direct (and observable) physical, sensory relationship of person and place through *seeing* (in both the sense of direct encounter (*mjal*) and 'reading' and interpreting the landscape, etc.), *touching* (by contacting the place), *positioning* (body in relation to place), *consuming/tasting* (by

---

2  On pilgrimages ranging in structure from the highly formal (stressing social ritual), like the *hajj* to Mecca, to the highly informal ('open behavorial code,' oriented towards personal expression): Morinis 1992: 14-15.

3  See the different articles in Albera, ed. 2009, about holy sites located far from the central power, where inter-confessional frontiers become blurred. According to them, holy sites that stand outside the control of religious or political authorities are believed to have more efficacy.

4  Buffetrille 1996a: 296-307.

ingesting place substance), *collecting* (substances of the place), *exchanging* (place substance with personal substance/possessions), *vocalizing* (prayers addressed to the place or specific formulas), and even in some cases *listening* (for sounds produced by the place).[5]

For Tibetan and Mongol learned clerics, the five senses, and first of all vision, are the "key to understanding what is powerful about Five-Peaked Mountain."[6] For ordinary pilgrims, touching and tasting were perhaps just as important as seeing.

### Touching and Positioning

Full-length prostrations not only were performed to increase one's merit but also to connect the whole body with the sacred ground. On present-day Wutaishan, Mongols and Tibetans touch the *stūpa*s, the statues, the holy trees and sometimes the steles with their forehead and hands. Like the Chinese pilgrims, they vigorously massage with their hands or rub their body on Mañjuśrī's footprints at Zaoyuchi;[7] they lie on the two-meter-high stone called "Mañjuśrī's Bed at Qingliangsi" and practice meditation on special stones, in caves or on the pedestals of large steles (Fig. 44, Fig. 45). This later practice, usually called 'incubation' and known in many pilgrimage traditions,[8] was common in Mongolia. In the early twentieth century, Mongols used to lie on a large slab of stone at Choijin Lama-yin Süme in Urga to recover from a disease.[9] In Mergen Süme (Inner Mongolia), devotees rub their feet and joints on a 'disease-healing stone' to cure their fevers and aches.[10] In the Jokhang of Lhasa one can rub his or her back against a particular mural thought to relieve back pain.[11] As in pilgrimages

---

5      Huber 1994: 38.

6      Schaeffer 2011: 229.

7      The *White Beryl* mentions tens of thousands of footprints attributed to Mañjuśrī. (Dorje 2001: 48-49). Nowadays, most of the handprints and footprints of saints and deities are not touchable or accessible, or they have disappeared: footprints and handprints of Śākyamuni at Tayuansi, Mañjuśrī's handprint at Jingangku; footprints of Mañjuśrī's lion at the Western Terrace; Rāhula's footprint at Luohousi; Lichan Laoshi's footprints at Dailuoding and so on.

8      Morinis 1992: 11; Couroucli 2009: 192. See for instance the incubation on the 'stone of Celtic fevers' inside the cathedral Notre-Dame of Le Puy-en-Velay, France. On the cult of *menhir* linked with healing and fertility magic in France: Éveillard and Huchet 2006: 8-31.

9      Geleta/Forbath 1936: 257-258.

10     Humphrey 2006: 78.

11     Warner 2008: 202. Conversely, according to Katia Buffetrille, the practice of rubbing one's body on footprints is not attested in Tibetan pilgrimages (personal communication, 2009).

FIGURE 44    *Footprints of Mañjuśrī, Zaoyuchi.* © ISABELLE CHARLEUX, 2007.

FIGURE 45    *Footprints on the Northern Terrace. Detail of the 1846 Cifusi map, Rubin Museum of Art, New York.* © KARL DEBRECZENY.

all around the world, touching or rubbing one's body aims at transferring the power of the sacred site onto one's body. Mongols say it aims at increasing one's *khei mori* (ever-living prospering spirit) or *sülde* ('soul'). In her visit to the White Rock in the Khentii Mountains (Republic of Mongolia), Rebecca Empson writes that before entering the cave,

> we rubbed our bodies against a flat upright rock (*möngö šiddeg čuluu*, literally the money sticking stone) that stood at the base of the Rock and is said to gather a magnetic 'energy' from lightning (*cahilgaan cahildag soronzon inergi čuluu*, a stone energised by magnetic and electrical flashes).[12] This was meant to be good for our heart, liver and kidneys.[13]

Devotional practices at the White Rock consisted of touching various crevices with one's "ears, fingers, head, nose, face and eyes so they may be revitalized," rubbing oneself "against a smooth surface for one's left and right kidney," taking off one's clothes and covering one's body in fine sands that line the bank of the small stream and, finally, jumping into the stream: "This whole process constituted a kind of 'treatment,' whereby the Rock gave birth to us anew."[14]

The Mongols' practice of burying their dead on Wutaishan is, in a way, the apex of this physical contact, in that the deceased is 'absorbed' within the holy mountain: the numinous power of the mountain's earth purifies and ensures a good reincarnation.

### Consuming and Collecting

The pilgrims—Mongols, Tibetans and Chinese alike—all practiced 'collecting' just about every part of the mountain (water, earth, stone, plants, etc.) to be used on the spot or carried back home for later use. These substances are believed to contain the residual power (Tib. *jinchen*) which pervades the holy land.[15] Collecting substances is a universal pilgrimage practice; naturally, the Wutaishan practice has a Buddhist take: such substances could, for instance,

---

12   According to the modern emic interpretation, the aim is to be revitalized by the 'magnetic' (*sorunja*) energy of the rock/mountain.

13   Empson 2010: 138-139.

14   Empson 2010: 139.

15   Huber 1999: 15. As shown by Rebecca Empson (2011: Chap. 2), Mongols use to separate portions of valuable things and livestock they have to part with (umbilical cords, pieces of tail hair for herd animals that were sold) and hide them in the household chest in order to (re)generate growth.

purify the body and 'wash off defilement.'[16] Earth collected from distant holy pilgrimage sites was deposited inside *stūpas*. In Yuan-dynasty Beijing, soil from Wutaishan and Bodhgayā was deposited inside the White Stūpa during the consecration ritual.[17]

Wutaishan boasts more than twenty sacred springs and ponds. Nowadays, as in every pilgrimage site in Mongolia, pilgrims carry empty bottles and jerry cans to fill and bring back home. The most sacred spring for Mongols was the Prajñā Spring (Borequan). It is said that one receives Mañjuśrī's blessings by taking this 'Wutai sacred water,' or 'wisdom water' and that one will effortlessly gain wisdom after drinking it. The Manchu emperors and great lamas drank only water from the Prajñā Spring when they resided on Wutaishan. It also served to bathe the statues on the 8th day of the fourth month, the festival of Śākyamuni's birthday. Tibetans, Mongols but also Chinese monks and nuns choose this spot to perform their preliminary practices of the 'one hundred thousand water offering.'[18] Other renowned waters on the mountain include the sweet-tasting spring trickling from Avalokiteśvara Cave (Guanyindong), which was believed to be especially efficient for infertile devotees hoping to be blessed with children;[19] the sacred water (*foshui* 佛水, 'Buddha water') of Mingyuechi, collected especially during the Sixth Month Festival;[20] the water of Baisha Spring 白砂泉 in Zunshengsi, reputed to cure a hundred different illnesses; the milky water of Baishui Pond 白水池 near Jingangku (used to wash one's eyes)[21] (Fig. 46); the sacred spring of Chaoyang Cave in Yuhuachi (said to cured a hundred illnesses); the holy water of Qingliang inside the Arhat Cave near Qingliangsi; the wells of Sanquansi; the spring of Baohuasi; and the so-called 'Samantabhadra water' with healing powers found in a small cave of Shancaidong. According to Blofeld, pilgrims collected Samantabhadra water with small earthen bottles:

> Putting my hand within, I found it to form a shallow basin holding about two inches of water. The curious thing about this water is that it never

16    Huber 1999: 17. Mumford's informant, Lama Dorje (*Himalayan dialogue* 1988: 97, quoted by Buffetrille 1997: n. 99) explains why pilgrims bring back stones, earth or water: the earth and its nutritious value are deteriorating since the 'Good Age' but are preserved in 'power places': bringing back soil and stones and putting them in *stūpas* will delay the deterioration of the planet.

17    Franke 1994: 181.

18    Lim 1999.

19    Gao Henian 2000 [1949]: 63.

20    Wei Guozuo 1993 [1988]: 135-136.

21    Gao Henian 2000 [1949]: 114.

becomes deeper than two inches, yet if any is removed, it still reaches that level. There is no sign of a spring or a pipe, therefore the Mongols think it holy and use it as medicine.[22]

Furthermore, Mongols called Wannianbing 萬年冰 (Ice of Myriad Years) 'the ice that never melts' and collected it "to work cures on their sick friends at home."[23] Holy water could also flow from statues such as the fourth *arhat* in Guanyindong: this sweet water was said to cure diseases and annihilate adversity.[24] Pilgrims collected water dripping from the roof of Pusading's Water Dripping Hall for future use as a medicine, or they put small mounds of flour under the roof so that the dripping water was absorbed by the flour, with which they later made pills.[25]

Not only water but also soil, dust and the fruits and bark of trees were gathered to bring back home: pine cones from Dailuoding;[26] bark of the sacred tree at Wulangmiao (peeled to serve as medicine); and '*śarīra*-golden sand' (*jinsha shelizi* 金沙舍利子) collected in a torrent above Baiyunsi 白雲寺 (also used as medicine).[27] Pilgrims rubbed the stone of Niuxinshi 牛心石, the 'rock with a bull's heart,' and collected the dust to serve as a panacea. On the Eastern Terrace, they picked the petals of wild flowers and took them back to their sick relatives, "who then receive by this method the direct blessing of Wen Shu [Mañjuśrī]."[28] According to Edkins, these flowers were dried to make medicine, and pilgrims purchased them in little packets; they made tea by infusing them in hot water.[29] The grass and water of the excellent pastures of Dailuoding and the Southern Terrace attracted herders who came to fatten up or cure their animals before selling them (Fig. 47). Once back home, the Mongols kept the water, soil, stones and flowers on their altars to bring fortune and prosperity and to use as medicines. They often carried earth from Wutaishan in a reliquary for protection.

---

22    Blofeld 1959: 125-127; 1938: 34; also Blofeld 1948: 96.

23    Gilmour 1970 [1883]: 147.

24    Li Xiangzhi 1932: 124-126.

25    David-Neel 1940: 123.

26    On Tibetan pilgrims who collect stones and earth from Amnye Machen to be either kept at home as relics, deposited later inside a *stūpa*, or used later as medicine: Buffetrille 1997: 79, 81. Chinese pilgrims also collect soil and water from the Four Grand and Famous Mountains of China.

27    Gao Henian 2000 [1949]: 119.

28    Alley and Lapwood 1935: 118.

29    Edkins 1893 [1878]: 233-234.

FIGURE 46　*Pilgrim-monk from Labrang Monastery (Amdo) giving holy water to a pilgrim from Amdo, Puleyuan.* © ISABELLE CHARLEUX, 2007.

FIGURE 47　*Horses grazing of the slopes of the Northern Terrace.* © ISABELLE CHARLEUX, 2007.

When they arrived at the Qingshui River near Linyutang 淋浴堂, south of Taihuai, pilgrims used to bathe in it to purify themselves before entering the sacred area of Wutaishan. I do not know whether Mongols actually entered the water: in Mongolia today, although pilgrims do bathe in pools from mineral springs or in therapeutic muds,[30] bathing in rivers is generally prohibited. It is more likely that they sprinkled the water from this river, as well as from other rivers, springs and ponds, over their body. Two travelers on Wutaishan describe seeing Mongol pilgrims at 'Fanjiasi 梵家寺':[31]

> We met a small procession of Mongols from Outer Mongolia, several of the younger members of which wore foreign dress, while their elders wore the old-fashioned bright silks. They all stopped at a sacred spring below us, bared their heads and washed them in the spring waters. As we came up the younger ones noticed us, and quickly abandoned their reverential attitude, looking rather uncomfortable; the elders, however, went on with their little ceremony, oblivious of our intrusion.[32]

### Seeing

We have seen in the previous chapters the importance of collective visions and individual apparitions experienced by all kinds of pilgrims, as well as the identification of encountered humans and animals with Mañjuśrī. The interpretation of visions differed according to the ethnicity, religious background and social status of the witnesses. High Mongol clerics, such as the Chagan Diyanchi and Zanabazar, experienced visions and revelations, and their accounts proposed a representation of the sacred land populated with many deities and visionary experiences; however, we have no written sources telling us how ordinary pilgrims experienced and interpreted visions. For Tibetan and Mongol pilgrims, the Cifusi map, which depicts apparitions at every sacred place, may have served as a guide to the divine landscape of Wutaishan.

### Mantic Practices

On Wutaishan, pilgrims multiply mantic practices linked to the interpretation of omens, to the belief that future events can be foretold by specific prior events or acts. These practices may be linked to the association of Wutaishan

---

30   See an example of bathing in a pool of health-giving water in the Dayan Deerekhi pilgrimage in Khövsgöl Province: Galdanova, Zhukovskaya and Ochirova 1984.

31   According to them, this monastery is situated "on a small peak overlooking from the south the main group of buildings": it may be Fanxianshan.

32   Alley and Lapwood 1935: 119.

FIGURE 48     *Five-color 'prayer horse' papers thrown from Fanxianshan.*
© ISABELLE CHARLEUX, 2010.

with astrological texts: in a certain sense, the mountain's power guarantees the veracity of the resulting interpretation. Nowadays, using the wax of lamps, pilgrims paste coins onto stone inscriptions; if the coin sticks, the wish will be fulfilled (Fig. 56).[33] At Fanxianshan, Tibetans and Mongols used to (and still) throw five-colored Tibetan 'prayer horse' papers from the flat area outside Nantian 南天 Gate, said to be connected with the Sky (Fig. 48); if they fly, this pre-

---

33    On a similar practice observed in Istanbul: Couroucli 2009: 186. Other pilgrims pasted coins merely as offerings (which is a very common practice on holy rocks and cliffs in Mongolia) or because they were simply imitating what others did, thinking, "It must bring good luck."

dicts good fortune.[34] In Nanshansi and at the entrance of Pusading, the characters *foguo shandi* 佛國善地 (Buddhist Country Land of Bliss, Pure Land) are written on a wall: pilgrims stand at ten or twenty meters away, close their eyes and walk towards the wall; if they reach the inscription, this foretells they will be reborn in the Pure Land. As in other Mongols' divinatory/propitiatory practices, these acts are generally performed again and again till the result is positive.

### Votos and Ex-votos

The Mongols offered personal objects such as their jewels, silver ornaments, and robes to monasteries; they also left ex-votos like children's shoes, a common practice in Mongolia (as in China) to thank a deity for having granted a child. These offerings are believed to keep something of their owners, thus creating an unbreakable bond between the pilgrims to the sacred land.[35] A common voto is a red ribbon, red string or strip of red paper bearing auspicious inscriptions, fastened to trees. Near Wenshudong, devotees worshipped the Śala (Suoluo 娑羅樹) Tree (*Shorea robusta*).[36] At Zhenhaisi, they worshipped the two pine trees planted by Rölpé Dorjé: one was said to bless couples with children, the other to bestow longevity. Present-day Mongols and Tibetans hang hundreds of red ex-voto plaques around these pine trees. They buy five-colored wind-horse flags in the Taihuai shops and hang them on trees on the slopes of Wutaishan or around *stūpas*. Some write their vows and their name in Mongolian on prayer flags.[37]

The above-described practices that aim to absorb or transfer some of the numinous power of Wutaishan are also found in pilgrimage sites in Mongolia and do not differ from Tibetan practices. As for Chinese pilgrims, they similarly collect, touch, offer ex-votos and sometimes have visions, but they also have

---

34    Nowadays Tibetans pick up 'prayer-horse' papers that have fallen down in order to throw them again, thus ensuring good fortune for those who had thrown them before. This practice is also observed at Guanyindong.

35    The Mongols believe that personal objects, and especially their hats and garments, are 'charged' with their personal energy.

36    Gao Henian 2000 [1949]: 64. The tree is represented on the Cifusi map. In Indian literature, Śākyamuni's mother gave birth to him under a *śala* tree (wish-fulfilling tree). Pusading preserved the painting, with a poem by Qianlong written in his own hand, representing a *śala* tree; the painting was offered in 1780 to the Sixth Panchen Lama (Berger 2003a: 193-196 about an engraved version);

37    See Online Appendix H. The practice of putting padlocks (on guardrails and banisters, for instance) inscribed with wishes—symbolic of one's commitment to carrying something out—is now observed all around the world.

practices unique to them, such as offering incense to specific rocks and trees. The ritual practiced at the Mother's Womb-Cave of Wutaishan, however, seems to be particularly connected to Mongol indigenous practices.

## The Caves of Wutaishan

Mountain caves are an essential component of Tibetan and Mongol pilgrimages.[38] They were generally of difficult access before the construction of stairways in the late twentieth century.[39] They range from small meditation caves, where there is hardly enough room for one person to sit, to large caves turned into temples (Fig. 49). Retreatants and hermits such as Rölpé Dorjé searched for such spiritually potent sites to increase the efficacy of their meditations. Mongols and Tibetans especially worshipped Shancaidong, a small cave-shrine sheltered by a temple, where Rölpé Dorjé lived before the construction of Zhenhaisi,[40] and Avalokiteśvara Cave/Guanyindong, a hermitage located high up on a hill just north of Nanshansi where the Sixth Dalai Lama, the Thirteenth Dalai Lama, as well as Avalokiteśvara were believed to have meditated (Fig. 51).[41] Back home, the pilgrims would say, "I meditated at the place where the Sixth Dalai Lama meditated." Vajra Cave (Jingangku) attracted Mongols and Tibetans both for its ancient Chinese past and because it was another residence of Rölpé Dorjé, like nearby Puleyuan. It is still a must-see for all pilgrims. Since the Tang or maybe the Song dynasty, the entrance has never again been opened, but pilgrims visited a nearby artificial grotto with a subterranean corridor that leads to a half-buried Tibetan-style *stūpa*, as well as Boresi—the monastery built near Vajra Cave. In his guide Li Xiangzhi described many other caves that are no longer visible or accessible, with stalactites, subterranean lakes, optical phenomenon when light enters, miraculous statues and relics, and ascetics in meditation (Guanyindong, Yuhuachi, Mimoyan, Cifusi).[42] At Mimoyan, it is said that if one looks inside a hole in a rock he can see his/her previous life.[43]

---

38    Ekvall 1964: 241; Ekvall and Downs 1987: 105-106; Humphrey 1995: 135-162; Buffetrille 1996a; Buffetrille 1997. On caves in Buddhist scriptures and traditions: Stein 1988; Birnbaum 1989-1990: 118-120.

39    For a typology of the Wutaishan caves: Birnbaum 1989-1990.

40    Pokotilov 1935 [1893]: 83. See "Guanyindong" and "Shancaidong" in Online Appendix B.

41    Zhao Gaiping and Hou Huiming 2006. On this cave see also Birnbaum 1989-1990: 134.

42    Sixteen caves or complexes of caves are described in Online Appendix B.

43    According to a lama who had lived on Wutaishan, interviewed by Olivér Kápolnás (personal communication, September 2012).

FIGURE 49      *Shituolin, cave where a hermit is said to have meditated and died, located above*
               *Wenshusi.* © ISABELLE CHARLEUX, 2010.

### The Mother Womb-Cave

Among the many numinous sites of Wutaishan, Mongols' favorite place was, and still is, the Mother's Womb-Cave (Ekhe-yin Umai, Ch. Fomudong), located on a cliff northeast of the Southern Terrace. Present-day Mongols who stay only one or two days on Wutaishan first visit the Mother's Womb-Cave "to be reborn under the protection of Tārā," and travel agencies advertise trips to Wutaishan by showing a picture of the cave.[44] A Chinese monk, Beiyue 悲月, has been restoring and revitalizing the place since 1996 and has collected one million *yuan* in donations to build a kilometer-long stone stairway and path leading to the cave.[45]

The Mother's ritual involved touching and thus absorbing the mountain's power. Although the cave is said to have been discovered in the Ming period,

---

44    http://www.ikhayan.com/detail.html?detail=aghpa2gtΥΧlhbnιLCΧιEVG91chi5Rgw,
      accessed January 20, 2011.
45    See his biography: An Jianhua 2002.

FIGURE 50     *Avalokiteśvara Cave Monastery (Guanyindong)*. © ISABELLE CHARLEUX, 2012.

the earliest evidence of the ritual of crawling into this womb-cave that I could find is in the 1721 Mongolian pilgrimage guidebook: this cave "where a thousand Buddhas dwell" is called 'the Gate of the Buddhas' (*burkhan-u khaalga*). By crawling inside, those who follow the supreme *dharma* will rid themselves of the 'ten black sins' and bad destinies, remember their previous births and obtain enlightenment and the holiness of the Buddha. But those who live by ruse and lies, upon crawling inside the cave, will be tortured.[46] On the 1846 Cifusi map, a man is seen pushing the bottom of a pilgrim struggling to get inside the small hole (Fig. 51). This ritual, called in Mongolian "to cause/make [someone] to crawl through the mother's womb" (*ekhe-yin umai shirguulkhu*), was also popular among the Chinese, as evidenced by Gao Henian's visit to the cave, in 1899 and 1912, and Chen Xingya's visit in 1934.[47] In his account, Duke Migwachir relates his visit to 'Ekhe-yin Agui':

> [T]here is a hole measuring 8 *cun* [25.6 centimeters, which is only just enough for a naked man to pass through]. I, the Duke, took my clothes off except for the trousers. I entered inside with my head and a hand first while a *heshang* pushed my feet hard with his shoulders, and finally I just managed to get into it. The head is larger than the body; if the head enters, whatever the size of the body, the body can pass through thanks to the joints. If one does not believe this, he should pierce a 7-8-*cun* hole in his own yurt and go through it: then he will know. [But] this is a real hole. Looking inside with a lamp, I saw that it was as big as a room; there were many clay Buddhas. Soon it was cold and I wanted to get out, but when I said that, the monk closed the entrance [behind me] and, frightened by all kinds of things, I had to make promises [to get him to help me back out]. Then the monk pulled and, since I had no choice, I promised to pay again. I crawled, one hand in the back, the other one on the ear. My head with one hand went out, and then the monk pulled me out with both his arms. If nobody pulls, one cannot get out.[48]

Mongol lore and practices concerning this cave bring to light a lived religion.[49] In an article dated 1957, Ferdinand Lessing (who visited Wutaishan in 1930 or

---

46     *UTAOSC* 51b-52a.

47     Gao Henian 2000 [1949]: 119-120; Chen Xingya 1936: 34. See also Blofeld 1938: 34-35.

48     Miyvacir 2008 [1942]: 406-407.

49     See a description of the cave and its ritual in Birnbaum 1989-1990: 137-140. Stein (1988: 7-9) and Birnbaum compare the Mother's Womb-Cave ritual with the lore of Vajra Cave and Nārayāṇa Cave (Eastern Terrace).

1931) gave a full description of the cave according to his interviews with a Russian Adventist missionary and the Khalkha dignitary Dilowa Khutugtu (1884-1964). His description is more or less similar to that of Duke Migwachir: the hole, about three feet above the ground, with a diameter of 10-12 inches (25.4-30.5 centimeters), is shaped like a *yoni* (literally 'vagina' or 'womb,' symbol of the Goddess in Hinduism). The pilgrims were advised to remove all excess clothing or even to undress completely.[50] According to the Dilowa Khutugtu, a Chinese monk, nicknamed 'the midwife' by the Mongols, assisted the pilgrims and told them how to crawl in (Fig. 52):[51]

To enter the grotto the pilgrim would first insert his right arm and his head. The priest would stand below the hole, facing the entrance. The visitor would step on the priest's shoulder and try to enter the hole by extending his right arm and squeezing his right shoulder through. When he had proceeded so far, he would brace his feet against the shoulders of the priest in order to gain thrust enough to enter the grotto completely.

Then the pilgrim would find himself in a very narrow but widening passage, some three feet long and one foot high, which may be termed as the cervix. Bending and twisting to the left, the tube led into the inner chamber, the matrix, which allowed room for two people to stand.[52] In its center was an altar bearing a stone statue of a deity, possibly Tārā or Kuan-yin [Guanyin],[53] both goddesses of mercy and salvation.

A small lamp in front of the statue gave off a very faint light. The visitor was supposed to touch the altar with his forehead. The blessings expected from this religious rite were ridding oneself of sins and obtaining a favourable reincarnation. The way back was difficult because some visitors were liable to become frightened when they saw the small opening through which they had come and also when they saw the stones, projecting from the walls of the grotto, which they had hardly noticed on their way in because of the darkness.

Often the pilgrims had been impressed with stories of how some persons felt handicapped in gaining the exit because of their sins....

---

50    Although Birnbaum (1989-1990: 139, n. 71) finds this difficult to accept, this is told by Migwachir, by Lessing's Russian informant (Lessing 1957b: 95) and by Gao Henian (2000 [1949]: 119). On the Cifusi map, the pilgrim's trousers are visible.

51    Nowadays the hundreds of pilgrims queuing to enter the cave have plenty of time to study a board with diagrams and explanations on how to crawl through.

52    Actually five or six persons (a maximum of nine) can stand in the 'matrix.'

53    The statue worshipped nowadays is Guanyin.

FIGURE 51      *Pilgrim being pushed into the narrow passage at Ekhe-yin Umai; naked*
              *Vajrayoginī above Zhenhaisi. Detail of the 1846 Cifusi map, Rubin Museum of Art,*
              *New York.* © KARL DEBRECZENY.

FIGURE 52   *A Mongol pilgrim pushes her husband inside the Mother's Womb-Cave at Fomudong.* © ISABELLE CHARLEUX, 2012.

FIGURE 53   *Pilgrim walking in great prostrations to Ekhe-yin Umai. Stone relief on the screen-wall at the foot of the stairs leading to Longquansi, 1912.*
© ISABELLE CHARLEUX, 2010.

sometimes obese persons found their way out easily while thin people might got [sic] stuck in the "bottle-neck". The return was made headfirst with the left arm extended into the passage.[54]

Gao Henian experienced strange phenomena inside the cave, which contained deep water where thousands of small lights were dancing.[55] With the help of the 'midwife,' the pilgrim would come back and be informed that he/she had been within the womb of the Mother of Buddhas and that he/she had been re-born.[56]

The pilgrim had to pay a fee in order to enter the narrow passage and an additional 'ransom' fee to leave the grotto.[57] The 'midwife' was said sometimes to leave devotees stuck and free them only after they had made a vow to offer donations to the clergy: if a person was unable to crawl his/her way out again, he/she was declared by the lamas to be an exceptionally great sinner, and they would release him/her only after he/she had agreed to pay an exorbitant 'ransom.'[58] The Dilowa Khutugtu confirms that the pilgrims had to pay an entrance fee (this is a rare mention of the existence of a fixed entrance fee at a Wutaishan site before the late twentieth century):

> In front of the hole is a stone altar set with offering lamps. In former times the pilgrims deposited merely a few brass coins ("cash") on the altar. Later the admission fee was set at two coppers, and additional donations for the rite were to be made at the discretion of the pilgrims.[59]

The Mother's Womb-Cave is nowadays just as popular among Han tourists and pilgrims as it is among Tibetans and Mongols. According to written and oral accounts (including many blogs),[60] present-day pilgrims believe they can erase their sins, get rid of all the evils from their previous life,[61] obtain a second life and even be reborn as a buddha. They are told that the Mother's Womb-Cave is

---

54     According to the Dilowa Khutugtu, interviewed by Lessing 1957b: 97-98.

55     Gao Henian 2000 [1949]: 119-120.

56     Birnbaum 1988-1989: 139-40. Gao Henian (2000 [1949]: 119-120) does not mention any 'midwife' and had to ask for help to enter the cave; he climbed on someone's back and was pushed inside. Nowadays, pilgrims help each other under the supervision of a monk.

57     According to Lessing's interviews with the Russian missionary in 1931.

58     Lessing 1957b: 96-97.

59     Interviewed by Lessing 1957b: 97.

60     Zhang Minghui 2005: 36; An Jianhua 2003; Zhang Guixiang 1999; Zhang Minghui 2005.

61     *Tuotai huangu* 脫胎換骨: "get rid of the carnal envelope and change bones, become a new man."

the very womb of Śākyamuni's mother and, like Śākyamuni, they will be reborn out of her armpit. The stalactites inside the cave are said to be women's entrails.[62] Pilgrims often shout and cry, frightened by the experience (Raoul Birnbaum was told that "Mongolians, famous for their fervent piety, invariably cry when they enter the inner chamber").[63] When they come out, exhausted and covered with dust, they really do feel like children; they say they feel transformed and regret their past sins.

As stressed by Lessing and Rolf Stein, womb-cave rituals are generally not documented in the official and clerical records,[64] and they are often the object of contempt or indifference from the Buddhist clergy. Crawling inside a narrow cave belongs to beliefs and practices that were not considered worthy of attention by literati and clerics. The Chinese gazetteers mention the discovery of the cave in the Jiajing period of the Ming dynasty, when a monk named Daofang 道方, walking there late at night, followed ten thousand dots of lights into the cave; inside he saw rows of jade buddha images. When he became lost in the cave, he chanted the name of Guanyin, vowing to devote a sacred image to the deity; at that moment, the ten thousand lamps turned into a single light that guided him out.[65] In his pilgrimage guide, Rölpé Dorjé retells Daofang's discovery, simply replacing Guanyin's name with Mañjuśrī's but says nothing about the Mother's Womb-Cave ritual itself.[66] The 1721 Mongolian pilgrimage guidebook is the only guidebook I have read that mentions it.[67] Lessing, who bases his study of caves of initiatory rebirth on oral sources, qualifies this practice as "more or less secret," and his Tibetan teacher, the *dorampa lama* Lozang Zangpo "pretended never having heard about such an outrageous rite."[68]

---

62  Stein 1988: 10.

63  Birnbaum 1989-1990: 138, n. 70.

64  Lessing 1957b: 95; Stein 1988: 1, 5. In his extensive survey of womb-caves throughout the Asian world, Stein compares the cave rituals in Tibet, China, Nepal, India, Southeast Asia and Japan.

65  *Qingliangshan zhi, Qingliangshan xinzhi, Qinding Qingliang shan xin zhi*, CLŠASB (references in Online Appendix B). Recent accounts (An Jianhua 2002: 27; An Jianhua 2003: 33) tell half a dozen variants that embellish and develop the initial story. The Dilowa Khutugtu also mentioned a Thousand Buddhas Stūpa (Qianfota 千佛塔) where the thousand Buddhas of the present eon once descended upon that *stūpa* and then issued from the opening of the Mother's Womb-Cave (Lessing 1957b: 98). This story creates a link with the Chinese name (Qianfodong) and the legend of the cave.

66  *ZMRBDB*, Chinese translation, p. 10.

67  The *TÜAG* (11a) only mentions the name "Cave Where a Thousand Buddhas Dwell."

68  Lessing 1957b: 95, 97. On similar attitudes of priests toward popular practices at a Catholic pilgrimage: Eade and Sallnow 1991: 23.

However, some of the Mongol clerics who visited Wutaishan, such as the Dilowa Khutugtu and the Fourth Jebtsündamba Khutugtu, were well aware of this ritual.[69] The Fourth Jebtsündamba even wrote a Tibetan inscription on a stele erected at the entrance of the cave, which specifies that whoever enters the cave reduces his sins and secures for himself a better reincarnation.[70] In Mongolia, where this ritual is widely practiced, womb-caves were often integrated within monasteries and, in some places, lamas even adapted a 'short liturgy' that was recited by a monk:

> An old Mongolian lama who allegedly had officiated at such ceremonies produced a few Tibetan texts which he said were recited at this occasion. They turned out to be the *Saddharmapundarīka sutra* (Mongolian: *Cayan lingxu-a*), a *sādhana* (Mo. *bytygel*) evocation of Mahākāla (M. Gombo, Tibetan: Mgon-po) and an invocation to Tārā. "No specific texts were used for this rite, the lama said."[71]

Quoting another informant, Lessing wrote that at such sanctuaries in Inner Mongolia the lamas performed the (*Dara ekhe*) *mandalshiua*,[72] the four-*mandala* offering to Tārā that ensures a healthy delivery for pregnant women (see Chapter 6).

As for Wutaishan's Mother's Womb-Cave, Khejok Rinpoché's guide gives a Tibetan Buddhist interpretation of the ritual of what Tibetans call the Ḍākinī Cave:

> On the rock ceiling at the entrance of the cave one would see a naturally formed triangular hole called the dharma sphere. One enters the inner sanctum through a small opening to emerge again from the inner sanctum through the same hole again, to symbolically go through the birth process from Vajrayogini (Vajravarahi)'s womb. The inner cave is said to resemble a womb with rock formation that resemble the ribs and the organs and the shape of the opening bears resemblance of the vagina. The famous Jangya Rinpoche [Changkya Khutugtu Rölpé Dorjé], the lama of Emperor Chien-Lung [Qianlong], meditated on the Naropa lineage of Vajrayogini (Narokhadro) here and attained the inner dakini pureland

---

69    Lessing 1957; Stein 1988.
70    According to the Dilowa Khutugtu, interviewed by Lessing 1957b: 97. This inscription is not visible anymore.
71    Lessing 1957b: 96.
72    Lessing 1957b: 96.

state. He had a vision of Vajrayogini and when he emerged from the cave, every person he saw was a daka or a dakini to him and everywhere he went appeared to him as the mandala of the deity. It is possible to do dakini tsog or other practices outside the cave with offerings set up inside. Recently a group performed tsog here and there was a flower rain followed by a gentle hail storm. The event was talk-of-the-town for many days.[73]

I do not know whether Khejok Rinpoché's mention of Rölpé Dorjé having a vision of Vajrayoginī inside the Mother's Womb-Cave has a textual basis or not, but Rölpé Dorjé wrote several texts about the *Cakrasaṃvara tantra* (which is linked to Vajrayoginī), and it would be interesting to search for mentions of the Wutaishan cave in the colophons of these works.[74] In addition, the Cifusi map depicts an apparition of naked red Vajrayoginī drinking blood out of a human skull in a cloud above Zhenhaisi, just below the cave (Fig. 51). Vajrayoginī clearly makes the link between the Mother's Womb-Cave and the residence of the Changkya.

### The Womb-Cave Ritual in Tibetan and Mongol Pilgrimages
The womb-cave ritual is widely practiced in Mongolia, and some of these caves have become major pilgrimage destinations (see Chapter 1). Like in Tibet, some caves are linked to Nyingmapa teachings and lore about Padmasambhava.[75] Pilgrims who crawl into the womb-cave described as the "birth passage of the mother consort of Kālacakra, Lord of Shambala [Shambhala]"—near Khamar-un Kheid, a monastery founded in the nineteenth century by the great lama-poet Danjinrabjai in Dorngovi Province—are said to be reborn "as Kālacakra deities. They can now enter the Kālacakra *maṇḍala*."[76] Danjinrabjai also founded, or re-founded at a site allegedly 'opened' by Padmasambhava,[77] Lobonchin-bu Süme in Alashan (which is also connected with the lineage of the Dilowa Khutugtu).[78] At Lobonchinbu Süme, there is also a famous cave known as the Cave of the Ḍākinī; it is not technically a womb-cave but a narrow vertical tunnel cave that ensures a good rebirth. The pilgrims come out of the descending passage covered in a red dust, which is also collected and used to make medi-

---

73   Lim 1999.

74   I thank Françoise Wang-Toutain for this information. Many caves and shrines studied by Stein (1988) in the Tibetan and Hindu worlds are also linked to Vajrayoginī.

75   Stein 1988.

76   "Pilgrimage in the Gobi—Danzanravjaa's Shambala Dornogobi" 2008.

77   See Chapter 1, note 103.

78   The Eighth Dilowa revived religious activities there in the 2000s.

FIGURE 54

*A Mongol pilgrim crawling into the womb-cave of Tövkhön Kheid, Bat Ölzii Sum, Övörkhangai Province, Mongolia.* © DON CRONER.

cine.[79] At Alkanay (now a national park, where Buddhist meditants go on retreats), near Chita in Buryatia, the small cave, also known as Mother's Womb, is linked to Padmasambhava;[80] it is also known as a dwelling place of Cakrasaṃvara and his five *ḍākinī*s.[81] Moreover, Gélukpa monasteries of Inner Mongolia, such as Gilubar Juu (Left Baarin Banner)[82] and Labrang-yin Süme (Chakhar),[83] and of the Republic of Mongolia, such as Tövkhen Kheid (Övörkhangai Province) and Baldan Bairawun Kheid (Khentii Mountains),[84] were also built above or close to womb-caves (Fig. 54). Interestingly, great figures

---

79    Charleux 2002b.

80    Empson 2010: 138-139.

81    Surun Syrtypova, personal communication, August 2013.

82    Yesibaljuur 2010: 69-70, 123; Heissig 1972, II: 756.

83    About sixteen kilometers from the Khada-yin Süme, Goul Chagan Banner (Lessing 1957b: 95-96).

84    Croner 2008b.

connected to these monasteries, such as Danjinrabjai, Zanabazar, the Fourth Jebtsündamba and Jamyang Zhépa, all visited Wutaishan and may have established a link between Wutaishan's Mother's Womb-Cave and the womb-caves of the monasteries they founded.

Womb-caves are also found in regions where Buddhism is absent or marginal, such as among the Buryats of Cis- and Transbaikalia and among the Tuvans, or in places where Buddhism still coexists with shamanic beliefs:[85] the so-called Mother's Belly (Ekhe-yin Khebeli) at the White Rock in Khentii Province (Republic of Mongolia), in a territory inhabited by Buryats; and the Mother's Womb at Altan Shirguul (Chiyanjin County, Jarud Banner, Jirim League in Inner Mongolia). According to E. Chiodo,

> In the past, the shaman conducted rituals at the "mother's womb" in Altan Sirγuul in spring. On this occasion, a sheep was sacrificed to the spirit of the cave and domestic animals were consecrated. Later, the Layičing [a kind of 'white shaman,' a ritual specialist who worships Buddhist deities side by side with those of the popular religion] took charge of the performance of these rituals. Altan Sirγuul is a famous site of pilgrimage. People come to this place from near and far, make their offerings to the spirit of the caves, and crawl through the narrow crevice of the cave. When a person comes out of the cave it is as if he or she came out from his/her mother's womb. Nowadays, people perform the rebirth ritual in Altan Sirγuul without the participation of ritual specialists.[86]

E. Chiodo adds, quoting legends collected by the Jarud researcher Khong Miliyan, that this womb-cave was believed to be the birthplace of Buddha.[87] In Tsagan Üür County, Khövsgöl Province (Republic of Mongolia, near the border with Siberia), the shamanist deity Dayan Deerekhi is worshipped in a cave that works fertility magic. Dayan Deerekhi is said to bestow wealth, particularly for descendants, and to look after children. There, people climb through the vertical Mother's Womb—a narrow passage covered with permanent ice—believed to bring health, wealth and children. The cult of these caves, associated with praying for children, certainly existed a long time ago and was later added to Dayan Deerekhi's other functions.[88]

---

85    Chiodo (2000b: 86, n. 230) believes that Buddhists contributed to keeping the cult of the 'mother's womb' alive, but the following examples show that this ritual has remained alive in non-Buddhist regions too.

86    Chiodo 2000b: 85, n. 230, quoting Nima 2005.

87    Chiodo 2000b: 85, n. 230, quoting Qong Miliyan, *Altan sirγuul-un domuy*, unpublished.

88    Galdanova, Zhukovskaya and Ochirova 1984.

In the absence of womb-caves, narrow tunnel-caves (such as the one at Lobonchinbu Süme), as well as tight passages within the pedestal of statues or *stūpa*s, may convey the same womb symbolism.[89] An example is found in the pedestal of an eighteenth-century iron *stūpa* of Amurbayaskhulangtu Monastery: pregnant women crawl under the *stūpa* so that their child is purified of sins.[90] In Maitreya festivals of Inner Mongolia, when the statue of the *bodhisattva* is carried clockwise around the monastery, people gather and compete to crawl underneath the statue and inside the tunnel formed by the lamas upholding the palanquin to ensure that they will be reborn into the world when Maitreya appears in the future.[91]

Stein has shown in his extensive study on the cult of the Mother Earth that other esoteric Buddhist traditions have fully integrated this 'rebirth' ritual. In Japan, the womb-cave is identified with the Garbhadhatu *maṇḍala* ('Womb-world *maṇḍala*'), where the practitioner can reunite himself with Vairocana, attain Buddhahood in this life and be reborn, in the sense of being newly endowed with esoteric knowledge and powers.[92] In a popular Khmer initiatory rite centered on the Birth Cave of Phnom Sampau near Battambang described by François Bizot, the villagers 'die' while entering the cave and 'come back to life' when they reappear. The tellurian incubation is a symbolic death followed by the symbolic rebirth of the initiate in a higher mode of existence, thus breaking the chain of reincarnations.[93] Basing himself on other examples in the Tibetan and Hindu worlds, Stein argued that this ritual was, before anything else, a Buddhist ritual borrowed from Hinduism and clearly related to the cult of Tārā: he claimed that it certainly does not have non-Buddhist precedents.[94]

Conversely, considering the importance of the womb-cave in indigenous practices of Asia, especially in non-Buddhist regions, I argue that it is an ancient Inner Asia ritual linked to the cult of the Earth and later reinterpreted and reappropriated by Buddhism. We have already seen that womb-caves are also present in non-Buddhist or barely-Buddhist regions. Furthermore, in the case of the Dayan Deerekhi Cave in Khövsgöl, the womb-cave ritual appeared

---

89    Crawling under pedestals, statues or pillars with a hole is also documented in other parts
       of Asia (Stein 1988: 15). Lessing (1957) mentions a cult in India where polluted persons
       pass through an image symbolizing the *yoni*.

90    Corneille Jest, personal communication, 2008, and Stein 1988: 14.

91    See pictures of the Maitreya Festival at Mergen Süme, Inner Mongolia, in Ujeed 2006:
       45-47. I also observed in Mongol temples devotees crawling under the bookshelves
       stacked with the *Kanjur* in order to be blessed by the word of the Buddha.

92    Hardacre 1983.

93    Bizot 1980.

94    Stein 1988: 6.

abhorrent to the local lamas, who tried to contain and neutralize its power, indicating that the ritual could be perceived as non-Buddhist.[95] The Mongols may have borrowed it from the Turks, who especially worshipped Mother Umai (*umai* meaning 'womb'), protector of newborns and young children.[96] Besides, Stein, who lists a great number of 'testing' ritual caves and passages, could not find examples of womb-caves in Tibet and in the Himalayas. The many narrow caves and passages he cites, along with their practices and mythologies generally linked to the underground world and resurrection from death,[97] do not exactly have the characteristics of womb-caves either—i.e., narrow enough for a human body to pass through and leading to a dead end evoking a womb— except perhaps in literature. Unlike womb-caves, the numerous narrow caves and tunnels of Tibetan pilgrimage sites are used for the ritual testing of one's positive or negative karma.[98] If the pilgrim succeeds in going through the narrow passage, he/she is ensured of the purification of his/her sins and a better rebirth, and is released from the terror of the intermediate state between death and rebirth (*bardo*). Therefore, pilgrims with 'bad karma' may get stuck. "It is believed the clefts and passages change size automatically to allow any morally suitable candidate to pass through, regardless of his or her actual body shape and size."[99] Tibetans refer to these passages as 'narrow paths' (*tranglam*), or

---

95  Galdanova, Zhukovskaya and Ochirova 1984; Humphrey 1995: 149-150.

96  See this chapter, note 106. According to the ancient Turks' myhtogenesis, ten boys born of the union of a human and a she-wolf grew up in a cavern and took wives from the outside. Several generations later they came out from the cavern.

97  These are found all around the world: France, Morocco, Russia, Palestine (Bowman 2009: 35), India, etc. In the Western literature, see Michel Tournier's *Vendredi ou les limbes du Pacifique*: Robinson Crusoe entered, naked, with some difficulty, inside a cave which he identified as the womb of Speranza Island. There, he stayed prostrated in a foetal position, "suspended in a happy eternity," regressing in his souvenirs, haunted by his mother. When he crawled out, he felt as naked and white as a baby. He returned there several times, to find this "state of inexistence" where time has stopped, this 'lost innocence,' these 'white tenebras' comparable to milk, deep into the "female nature of Speranza." He remembered his mother and his childhood and eventually understood how life and death were close to each other (1996 [1972]: 121-133).

98  For instance in Western Tibet (two stones called the Bardo defile at Mount Kailash); Central Tibet (Ganden Monastery; Terdrom near Drigungtil); Amdo (Amnye Machen, Drakkar Treldzong in Peltang); Nepal (Tarap in Dolpo, the Halase-Māratika caves in Eastern Nepal—these caves are shared by Hindus and Buddhists: Buffetrille 1994: 8-9); Bhutan ... See Stein 1988: 11-23; Ekvall 1964: 241; Jest 1975: 356; Buffetrille 1996: 367-370; Buffetrille 1997: 98-100; Huber 1999: 19.

99  Huber 1999: 19.

'paths to hell' (*nyellam*) because they represent the Gates of Hell (those who pass will escape from hell) or the way leading to a pure land.[100]

By contrast, most of the narrow caves of Mongolia, Buryatia and Tuva are dead ends that closely evoke a womb, and the terminology focuses on the mother ('womb,' 'belly'): Ekhe-yin Agui (Mother's Cave), Ekhe-yin Umai (Mother's Womb), or Ekhe-yin Khebeli (Mother's Belly). The crawling into the grotto corresponds to the *regressus ad uterum* and to the act of conception.[101] In Mongol epics, dead heroes are placed into a cave, which brings them back to life.[102] When they crawl out of the cave, the Mongols believe they have been reborn (*ireejü törö-, dakhin törö-*) and are guaranteed purification of their sins and a more favorable rebirth: they are as pure and sinless as a child. Regarding Tövkhen Kheid Monastery, "legends say that at the time of Zanabazar people who entered this cave through its crevice would come out of it newly born and purified."[103] The entrance of the womb-cave of Labrang-yin Süme was ornamented with a lotus pattern symbolizing the *yoni*: "It was through the opening of this stone that the faithful seeking purification from their sins were supposed to crawl into the cave in order to become reborn, cleansed of all defilement (*nigyl ariγalxu-jin tula* [*nigül arilgalkhu-yin tula*])." But, according to another lama, the rite was first and foremost "a symbolic act aiming at obtaining an advantageous rebirth."[104] The pilgrim had to undress completely before entering and, when inside, had to make nine prostrations in front of a statue of the Green Tārā. In Mongolia, the womb-cave ritual is not a ritual to evaluate one's good or bad karma (in which one succeeds or fails) but rather a ritual requiring a physical effort to free oneself from sin. As shown by Lessing, sin is imagined as something material, to be scrapped off, physically removed by crawling through a narrow passage. And it is not only the Buddhist notion of 'sin' (*nigül*) or 'bad karma' that Mongols want to scrape off, but also pollution, defilement (*bujar*, from contact with a dead body, for instance), curses (*khariyal*) and misfortune. In addition, by penetrating into the core of a mountain's source of power, the

---

100    Buffetrille 1994: 9-12; Buffetrille 1998: 23. These testing rituals can be performed not only in caves (which can be artificial grottoes) but also in openings within a rock, in narrow passages between two rocks, or on a narrow natural stone bridge across a deep ravine. Stein (1988) opposes the motherly character of matrix caves to the male character of rocks under which a subdued demon is pressed. On a similar Chinese merit-testing ritual on Putuoshan: Yü 1992: 229.

101    Stein 1988: 1.

102    Meng Huiying 2000: 243; Chiodo 2000b: 85, n. 230.

103    Chiodo 2009: 85, n. 230, quoting Sükhbaatar 2001: 268.

104    Lessing 1957b: 96.

pilgrims absorb some of its spiritual energy and increase their personal life force.[105]

For Mongols, the womb-cave ritual is also—and perhaps, first and foremost—a fertility ritual. They revere Mother Earth (Etügen Ekhe) as an important deity,[106] and their word for 'mother' (*ekhe*) frequently appears in the names given to natural features of the landscape. In pilgrimage sites such as Alkanay, these caves are especially visited by childless couples or people wishing to help the childless have babies.[107] The Ekhe-yin Umai of Gilubar Juu was especially visited by people hoping to have a child and by those wishing to 'repair' misfortune;[108] the Ekhe-yin Khebeli of Tövkhen Kheid is said to ensure fertility and increase one's *khei mori* (Fig. 54).[109] The Buddhist aim of this ritual, to be reborn purified of one's sins, often obscures its more pragmatic goals—to obtain children, to benefit from the contact with the Mother Earth Goddess, to be revitalized and healed by the Earth's 'magnetic energy,' to increase one's fortune or *khei mori*, and to purify oneself from defilement and curses.[110] Conversely, there is apparently no association with Mother Earth or requests for children in the Tibetan and Himalayan 'testing' ritual performed in narrow passages and caves.[111]

---

105 See for instance Empson 2010: 138-139. Hardacre gives the same reason for mountain ascetics who meditate in caves in Japan: "absorb the maximum spiritual power of the mountain and the deities who dwell there" (1983: 150).

106 Etügen has ancient origins tracing back to the Turks (who called her 'Umai'). In the Mongol empire, while the Sky rose in importance and became more abstract, Etügen was relegated to the domestic cult; she ensured the fecundity of the herds and the fertility of the soil, she protected children, herds and the native country, and she was a source of treasures buried underground. On Umai/Etügen's history among the Turks, Mongols and Tungus: Lot-Falk 1956; Meng Huiying, 2000: 237-244. On the cult of the mother-deity Umai (Ome Niang Niang) and of female fertility spirits concerned with bringing children into the world and ensuring their health among the Daur, Manchus and Tungus peoples: Humphrey and Onon 1996: 286-293; Meng Huiying 2000: 237-244. An example of the cult of Mother Earth in present-day Republic of Mongolia is the Mother Rock Eji-yin Khada in Töv Province.

107 "A Gate to God, 9/18/05" 2005.

108 Meng Huiying 2000: 242-243.

109 According to personal observations, 2009.

110 For Humphrey (1995: 150), the cave ritual belongs to shamanic spirit cults; its power derives "from the untamed sexual drives of the female spirits within." This can also be the shamans' interpretation of an old popular ritual.

111 In Tibet, childless people who ask for children go to certain lakes or stones (Jest 1975: 360, 365; Katia Buffetrille, personal communication, 2009).

The Wutaishan Mother's Womb-Cave appears for Mongols as a particularly effective place in which to request children. Scholars working among the Ordos in the early twentieth century have mentioned Wutaishan as the first place to go for childless couples: "To obtain children, women who can afford it often resort to pilgrimages either to Ou t'ai chan (Chansi ) or to another renowned place of pilgrimage."[112] "Women make pilgrimages to Wutaishan as well as to local shrines such as a Chinese goddess of fertility near Yulin for Ordos Mongols."[113]

Oral sources clearly relate several Mongol womb-caves known for their fertilizing power to the famous Wutaishan cave. Lobonchinbu Süme's womb-cave is known as the 'daughter' of Wutaishan's Ekhe-yin Umai. A learned Tibetan historian, Nyima Dorjé, told Birnbaum that "it is inappropriate to enter the mother cave [at Wutaishan] if one previously has entered the daughter cave [at Lobonchinbu Süme?]."[114] It seems to be a matter of precedence: one must visit the mother at Wutaishan before visiting the Mongol daughter. Local people make a link between Dayan Deerekhi's ('shamanist') womb-cave and Wutaishan's Mother's Womb-Cave: "cases are known of people from Zakamen going for the 'gift of progeny' to U-tai, where there also was a cave, Utain Umai."[115]

We will never know whether it was the Tibetans, the Chinese or the Mongols who first squeezed into the Mother's Womb-Cave on Wutaishan. According to Stein, there are no true womb-caves in Tibet. Birnbaum thinks that this ritual may originate in "native Chinese traditions, lightly cloaked in Buddhist garb."[116] However, Stein could not find any evidence that the Chinese developed rebirth symbolism and ritual around their caves: Wutaishan's Mother's Womb-Cave would thus be the only known example of a cave of initiatory rebirth in Han China.[117] Han Chinese who crawled into the Mother's Womb-Cave at Wutaishan may have in fact been following a Mongol practice. The womb-cave ritual is an ancient Inner Asian fertility ritual of Earth-worship, which is likely to have been exported to Wutaishan: the Mongol pilgrims may have simply transplanted it to a Wutaishan cave that perfectly matched their requirements: a

---

112   Mostaert 1956: 292.

113   Taveirne 2004: 443. Another famous place to ask for children in Inner Mongolia was the shrine of Ishi/Eshi Khatun—the 'Lady-Mother,' i.e., Sorkhakhtani Begi (d. 1252), Khubilai Khan's mother—in Ordos Wang Banner (Okada 1990).

114   Birnbaum 1989-1990: 138, n. 70.

115   Galdanova, Zhukovskaya and Ochirova 1984: 7.

116   Birnbaum 1989-1990: 140.

117   Stein 1988: 5. This is not completely true, according to Vincent Durand-Dastès and Kristofer Schipper (personal communication, 2007). There exists, for instance, a Chinese womb-cave at Tianlongshan 天龍山, southwest of Taihuai, not far from Wutaishan.

womb-like grotto accessed through a narrow passage. Another possibility is that Tibetans first used it as a karma-testing cave or/and as a Buddhist initiation cave and that, later, Mongols interpreted the ritual as a fertility ritual.

### Legendary Tunnel Caves of Wutaishan

Another type of cave that seems to be an extension of womb-caves is the tunnel cave or 'gate' leading to a distant place in a very short amount of time. Tunnel caves formed a particular type of subterranean network that linked great 'power places,' essentially making Wutaishan, Lhasa, Kathmandu and Bodhgayā very close to one another. A cavity was said to connect Jingangku to Bodhgayā in India: according to Tibetan and Mongol lore, Padampa Sanggyé went from Wutaishan to India to retrieve the Uṣṇīṣa vijayā dhāranī sūtra in one day in order to put an end to epidemics (Chapter 4).[118] Another secret tunnel was said to connect Jingangku with the Northern Terrace. The Wutaishan Mother's Womb-Cave is also described as a tunnel cave in a local legend:

> A twelve-year-old boy crossed the mountain through the tunnel cave every day to reach the distant place where he studied. On a rainy night his mother went to wait for him with an umbrella, saw a strange light on the mountain, and her son suddenly appeared in front of her, with dry clothes on. He said that he had gone through the cave with an old woman leading travelers. The mother saw the cave and understood that the old woman was Buddha's mother saving people.[119]

A few examples of tunnel caves are known in Mongol holy sites. In Lobonchinbu Süme, a cave extends into a tunnel that allegedly allows one to reach Central Tibet in only one day's walk. It is said that once a monk sent a dog down the passage; since the dog never reappeared, the monk presumed the story to be true, but no human being has ever attempted the experiment.[120] Agui Bogdayin Süme, a small monastery near Rashi Choiling Süme (Dalad Banner, Ordos) was founded around a cave, at the back of which was a deep hole that, according to the monks, communicated with Kumbum and Lhasa.[121] In these cases, the underground passage served to connect the local shrine to the great

---

118  David-Neel (1940: 137-142) entered a tunnel (Jingangku?) supposedly connecting Wutaishan to Lhasa in a matter of days.

119  Zhang Guixiang 1999: 35.

120  Charleux 2002b.

121  Narasun and Temürbayatur 2000: 197-204.

pilgrimage centers.[122] According to a legend collected in Inner Mongolia in 1934 by Owen Lattimore, when the Yuan dynasty collapsed, the Mongol emperor Togon Temür is said to have fled through a tunnel cave, perhaps from the Yungang temple caves, up to Northern Mongolia.[123] Similar legends are found in Tibet; for instance, the caves of Drakkar Treldzong (White Rock, Castle of the Monkeys) in Amdo contain galleries that are believed to lead to the realm of the *nāgas* and legendary caverns beneath Lhasa.[124]

On Wutaishan there is a particular kind of tunnel cave that cannot be entered; called 'the eye of the sea' (*haiyan* 海眼), it connects with the sea and can cause flooding if not blocked by a *stūpa*. It reflects the complex subterranean water system under the mountain. The legendary story of the foundation of Zhenhaisi (i.e., Monastery that Subdues the Ocean) tells that Mañjuśrī blocked the *haiyan* with a cooking pot to avoid a terrible flood of water from the Northern Sea caused by the Dragon King. A cave of Yuhuachi was said to communicate with Zhenhaisi's *haiyan*, thus allowing water to flow into the cave. The waters of Sanquansi were said to connect with the Black Dragon Pool (Heilongchi) of the Northern Terrace;[125] the water from Nārayāṇa Cave supposedly flowed to Fuping to the south and Fanzhi to the west.[126] This lore that developed from unexplained phenomena, such as a level of water in ponds that never changes (Taihuaquan of the Central Terrace, spring of Shancaidong), confirms the exceptional configuration of the holy mountain. These legends echo the Tibetan and Nepalese lore about the origin of some famous lakes such as Kukunor in Amdo.[127]

---

122    On similar underground connections in the Indian world: Preston 1992: 44.

123    Lattimore 1979: 237-239.

124    Ekvall and Downs 1987: 105. These caves, which include a womb-cave, are located in Peltang (east of Kukunor Lake). See also Allen 1997: 435-451; Epstein and Peng 1994: 23-24; Huber 2008: 1.

125    Wei Guozuo 1993 [1988]: 196-197.

126    Gao Henian 2000 [1949]: 115, other example p. 117.

127    About Kukunor Lake: the Jokhang temple could not be erected owing to the presence of a lake under the chosen site. A subterranean passage then drained the water from Lhasa to Amdo, where it formed the Kukunor Lake. Padmasambhava prevented the Kukunor Valley from being entirely flooded by blocking the hole with the top of the mountain Mahādeva (Buffetrille 1999). Another example is the Tibeto-Nepalese legend explaining how Mañjuśrī drained the lake that covered the Kathmandu Valley: Mañjushrī used a tunnel running from Lhasa to an opening in a cliff in the Kathmandu Valley, now called Lhasa's Cave (Lhasa Pāku). Pilgrims believe that the money they throw into the cave reaches Lhasa (Corneille Jest, personal communication, 2006). A similar story is found in Beijing: on Qionghua Island 瓊華島 (Beihai Park 北海), where Emperor Shunzhi had a

## Mongol Pilgrimages Related to the Wutaishan Pilgrimage

The connection between the womb-cave of Wutaishan and that of Lobonchinbu Süme, between Jingangku and India, are part of a greater discourse on local pilgrimage shrines that are related to, or function as substitutes for, great pilgrimage centers located abroad. Visiting the surrogate pilgrimage was generally said to be equivalent to journeying to the 'original' site. Through the creation of replicas, a sacred site moves closer to the pilgrims' home: it is not the pilgrim who travels abroad but the pilgrimage center that travels to the pilgrims, transferring the numinous power of the original. Wutaishan's Lingjiu Peak itself was compared and named after the Vulture Peak in India. Surrogate pilgrimages exist throughout the Buddhist world: it is like worshipping the same deity in different temples.[128]

In ancient history, Wutaishan was 'replicated' in many places—in Japan,[129] Korea,[130] North China,[131] Tibet[132]—generally to compensate for the impossibility or the difficulty of accessing the original site,[133] or as part as imperial

---

white *stūpa* built in 1651, a well called a *haiyan* was said to link up to the sea (Arlington and Lewisohn 1987 [1935]: 83).

128　In Tibet, local pilgrimages to mountains were numerous, and the merit gained there was seen as equivalent to those obtained on international pilgrimages to places such as Lhasa, Kailash or Bodhgayā (Large Blondeau 1960: 226). On Christian replicas of the Holy House of Nazareth, of Lourdes and other shrines: Coleman and Elsner, eds. 1995: 104-106.

129　A Japanese replica of Qingliangsi was erected on Atago Mountain 愛宕山 (northwestern part of Ukyō-ku) in the early eleventh century: Chikurin-ji 竹林寺. One of the eighty-eight monasteries of the Shikoku Island pilgrimage circuit was founded in the eighth century on Mount Godaisan (i.e., Wutaishan), Kōchi Prefecture.

130　Five temples were built on five terraces called Wutaishan in Korea during the Late Silla dynasty (668-935) on Mount Odae 五臺 (Cui Wenkui 2004: 19-20; Wang-Toutain 2007).

131　A southern Wutaishan,' on the southern side of Zhongnanshan, twenty-five kilometers south of Xi'an, place of devotion to Guanyin (Yü 1992: 194); a 'small Wutaishan' at Panshan 盘山 (mountain range in Hebei); another 'small Wutaishan' in the Taihang Range west of Beijing, with a monastery founded in the Northern Wei and visited by two Liao emperors, as well as a copy of Shuxiansi.

132　See Chou 2007: 127, n. 41.

133　Because it was impossible for Liao and Tangut (Xixia dynasty, 1032-1227) emperors to personally visit Wutaishan, they built replicas of Wutaishan within their own kingdom. The "History of the Liao dynasty" (*Liaoshi* 遼史) mentions two Khitan emperors who visited Wutaishan; however, Wang-Toutain (2007) believes that the fraught relationships between the Liao and the Song certainly prevented them from undertaking the pilgrimage. Instead, they probably visited the replica called 'Eastern Wutaishan' which included ten monasteries in a five-peak mountainous configuration near Yuzhou 蔚州 in Hebei Province. The Xixia built a 'Northern Wutaishan' in the eleventh century to the west of

programs of replication of holy sites.[134] Some of these Wutaishans were substitute pilgrimages ranging from the replica of one or several monasteries and icons in a site reminiscent of the five-terrace configuration of the original to mere literary comparisons or references to Shanxi's Wutaishan.[135] Others may have been viewed as the 'original,' the true residence of Mañjuśrī, their promoters thus considering Shanxi's Wutaishan a surrogate. For example, in the Korean replica, each terrace had a temple with its own deity, color and particular *sūtra*, so the replica was a true *maṇḍala*; according to the Korean origin myth, a thousand Mañjuśrīs manifested there instead of at Shanxi's Wutaishan.[136]

Did Mongols replicate Wutaishan in the steppe, for practical reasons of distance, affordability and hardship of travel, and/or as a discourse on the equal status of Mongolia and China as Buddhist holy lands? I found only one site that claims to replicate Wutaishan temples in Mongolia: Prince 'To' (Togtokhtör Wang), who visited Wutaishan in 1840, built Utai Uula-yin Kheid, a monastery that was explicitly modeled on Wutaishan temples near present-day Tamsagbulag (Khalkh Gol County, Dornod Province, Republic of Mongolia) (Fig. 55).[137]

Inner Mongols certainly seem to have viewed Wutaishan as a unique, original, non-replicable pure land, in particular for burial; on the other hand, it was almost a Mongol place, in terms of geography, ecology and cultural appropriation. But several popular pilgrimages are said to be related, compared or affiliated to Wutaishan. Shine Usun Juu in Ordos (Otog Banner), founded in the late eighteenth century, was compared in local songs with Wutaishan.[138] Ugtum Monastery, a very large institution in a Buryat region of the Republic of Mongolia, was known as 'the Wutaishan of Mongolia.' And, as we have already seen, Lobonchinbu Süme's womb-cave, considered to be the daughter of the Wutaishan cave, was meant to be visited only after one had already crawled into the Wutaishan 'mother' cave, giving it its due respect. Yet, on the contrary, Buryats say that one should visit Alkanay before going to worship Wutaishan:

---

their capital (in the foothills of the Helan Mountains 賀蘭山, Ningxia Province, west of Yinchuan), which included the replication of several Wutaishan monasteries (Cui Wenkui 2004: 18-19; Gimello 1994:506-508; Dunnell 1996: 35-36, 192-193 n. 53 and 56).

134   Qianlong's two replicas of Shuxiangsi (in the Western Hills and in Chengde) and his replica of Pusading (in the Western Hills) were not pilgrimage sites: they were erected for the personal use of the imperial clan and for political reasons.

135   Surrogate pilgrimages of Wutaishan from the seventh to the twelfth century were studied by Cui Wenkui 2004; Wang-Toutain 2007.

136   I thank Chou Wen-shing for this information.

137   Altanzayaa 2000: 141; Tsedendamba 2009: 418-419.

138   Mostaert, ed. 1937: 141.

FIGURE 55    *Luvsansharav, "Monastery in Utai" (Utai Uula-yin Kheid in Dornod Province),*
*late twentieth century, 95 × 120 cm, oil on canvas. Uranchimeg (ed.) 2000: 84.*

The Buryats believe that Alkanay has a sacred connection with Wutai.
Before one goes to worship at Mount Wutai, he must first visit Alkhana
[Alkanay], because in Wutai he would be asked by the gods if he had
bowed to Alkhana. If not, then it is not worth going so far [to Wutai].[139]

Gilubar Juu was called 'Little Wutaishan'[140] or 'White Wutaishan' during the
Qing dynasty; and modern Khalkha pilgrims call Tövkhen Kheid 'the Wutai-
shan of Mongolia.' According to oral sources from Shili-yin Gool and Juu Uda
Leagues, there were no fewer than five Wutai(shan)s, which were distinguished

---

139    Surun Syrtypova, personal communication, August 2013.
140    Dashbalbar County, north of Dornod Province.

by color (Map 2).[141] Yellow Wutai is Shanxi's Wutaishan.[142] White Wutai is Gilu-bar Juu in the Left Baarin Banner (Fig. 5), while Red Wutai Monastery (Ulaan Utai-yin Süme) is a monastery affiliated to the Prince Monastery (Wang-un Süme) of the Left Khuuchid Banner (Shili-yin Gool League; now in the village of Khögjiltü, ten kilometers southwest of Jir-ün Gool Balgasu, Right Üjümüchin). Green Wutai Monastery (Nogoon Utai-yin Süme) is Abural Nüüleskhüitü Süme of the Left Khuuchid Banner (now in the village of Erdenidalai, Ejinnuur Balg-asu, Left Üjümüchin Banner). This Green Wutai is certainly the mountain that Pozdneev calls 'Wutaishan' in the Left Khuuchid Banner (at the frontier with Üjümüchin), so called because several miracles happened there.[143] The fifth Wutaishan is Blue Wutai, the 'Old' Khorgo Mountain, a sacred place at Altan-shilggatsagan (Biligütei Balgasu, Abaga Banner, formerly called Khorgo Aimag or Badag Aimag, in Argalchin Sumu, Right Abaganar Banner) (Map 2).[144] Pil-grims came from afar to worship Tsongkhapa at Old Khorgo, which had a sa-cred cave with a *stūpa* at the entrance, two small temples, an *oboo*, inscriptions on a cliff, and parietal paintings.[145]

Discourse on the equivalence of the 'Five Wutais' are based on local lore about light manifestations and on the natural characteristics of the sites. Mon-gols from Shili-yin Gool say that the Five Wutais of Five Colors were created by the emission of five-colored lights coming from Śākyamuni's hair. The place where the yellow light fell is Yellow Wutai; the place where the blue light fell is Blue Wutai, and so on: the five places became blissful (*adistidtu*) pure lands (*dagshin oron*). The lights of each of the five colors turned into a *bodhisattva*.[146] In this popular Mongol version of the five Mañjuśrīs emanating on the five ter-races of Shanxi's Wutaishan, thanks to golden rays from Buddha's *uṣṇīṣa*,[147] the five terraces have become five different Wutais. Another legend asserts that

141    Belgünütei and Bükeqada 2010: 1-26, first chapter on "Mongγulcuud-un mörgül-ün orun—tabun Utai-yin tuqai angqan-u sinjilge": 1-3. I thank Olivér Kápolnás for having sent me a copy of this chapter.

142    Shanxi's Wutaishan would be called 'Yellow Wutai' because the mountain blooms with yellow flowers (Belgünütei and Bükeqada 2010: 6). See the praise prayer "Utai sang-un mani" translated in Online Appendix E.

143    Pozdneev 1977 [1896-1898]: 277.

144    Others say that Blue Wutai is located in the ancient Right Khuuchid Banner (between the modern village of Khairakhan, Jirgalangtu Sumu, in Abaga Banner, and the nearby village of Badarakhu, Ejinuur Sumu, Left Üjümüchin Banner) (Belgünütei et al. 2004: 321.)

145    For a general presentation of Blue Utai: Belgünütei and Bükeqada 2010: 2-3.

146    Belgünütei et al. 2004: 321.

147    This motif originates from the *Pad ma bka' thang*: see Chapter 4.

Gilubar Juu/White Wutai has precedence over the others because it concentrates all five miraculous lights into one, white light.[148]

In a legend about Red Utai inspired from the *Journey to the West*,[149] when Tangsug Lama (or Xuanzang), the famous Tang-dynasty monk who traveled to India to bring back Buddhist scriptures, was about to leave for India, Buddha told him to release the monkey 'of' (born from a) stone (Sun Wukong 孫悟空), whom he had imprisoned under a rocky mountain with five *stūpa*s for having committed a crime in heaven. Tangsug Lama released the monkey from the mountain, which then exploded into five pieces. The places touched by the pieces became the Five Wutais.[150] Tangsug Lama is also said to have traveled to the site of Gilubar Juu: he saw in a vision a protector who advised him to establish a monastery; he then excavated and built a temple.[151]

Although Shanxi's Wutaishan is much bigger in terms of the number of temples and *stūpa*s (for instance, Red, Blue, White and Green Wutai only have one assembly hall),[152] the Five Wutais have a comparable numinous natural environment, with healing springs and extraordinary rocks, and are said to emit marvelous lights of the color corresponding to their name—especially Shanxi's Wutaishan and Gilubar Juu (White Wutai). On Wutaishan in 1769, Tagtanwangchug (r. 1727-1786), the *jasag beile* of Aru Khorchin, met the Second Jamyang from Labrang and later invited him to Mongolia. The Jamyang did travel to Mongolia and, around 1770 on the site of Gilubar Juu, he saw a miraculous white light illuminating all the surroundings. Following his directions, a cave was discovered containing the (Liao-dynasty) stone Buddha in *parinirvāṇa*, and he had the monastery (re)built. The appellation *gilubar* comes from this radiant white light (*gilbaga*).[153]

---

148   Belgünütei and Bükeqada 2010: 4.

149   The *Xiyouji* was translated into Mongolian in the eighteenth century and was extremely popular: Atwood 1992-1993.

150   Belgünütei and Bükeqada 2010: 6, quoting Lubsangjamsu 2002. In the *Xiyouji*, it is said that Sun Wukong was first trapped inside five pillars forming a cage, which were the five fingers of Buddha's hand, and then imprisoned under the mountain for five centuries. Other legends about the Five Wutais are developed by Belgünütei and Bükeqada 2010: Chapter 1.

151   Galsang et al. 1994: 279.

152   Belgünütei and Bükeqada 2010: 7-10.

153   In another source it is the prince of Baarin who invited the Jamyang Zhépa to establish Gilubar Juu (Galsang et al. 1994: 280-281). A legend says that while Śākyamuni was preaching he suddenly laughed. His disciples asked him once why he was laughing, and he told them, "While I am sitting here explaining the Dharma, people from a place in the East believe I am dead and are making my portrait in *nirvāṇa*." The disciples asked where

The five sites also boast of numinous traces of Buddhas and protectors, such as footprints, magic statues, miraculous stones in the shape of Buddhas, as well as legends about them. In Red Wutai, there are icons of Börte (Grey) Lhamo and Damjin (Dorlig, i.e., Damchen Dorjé Lekpa) and hoofprints of Lhamo's mule;[154] in Green Wutai are an icon of Lhamo, many hoofprints of her mule and so on.[155] At Gilubar Juu, the mountain south of the monastery has the shape of Paldan Lhamo; a gigantic *dharmapāla* is carved on a red cliff, below the four syllables *Oṃ maṇi padme huṃ!*[156] Some of these numinous traces have been left by past kings and emperors such as Gesar/Geser (at Gilubar Juu) and Chinggis Khan—devotees in Green and Red Utai revere his seat, his footprints, the hoofprints of his horse and the trace of his yurt (carved into the rock)—in the same way that Chinese emperors and heroes of the past left traces on Shanxi's Wutaishan.

Lastly, the Five Wutais also have natural caves, especially womb-caves. In Green Wutai, pilgrims crawl in a hole of Shirguul Cliff to be cleansed from diseases, obstacles and sufferings.[157] The Red, Green and White Wutais each have a natural Golden Toad Narrow Passage (Altan Melekhei-yin Shirguul). There are also hell paths with 108 steps (Tamu-yin Jam, in Green and White Wutais). Pilgrims generally visit these numinous sites following a specific order. At Gilubar Juu, pilgrims first worship the Liao-dynasty Buddha in *parinirvāṇa* in the central cave, known as Khebtege Juu (the 'Reclining Jowo'), and then test their luck, or their karma, at the 'Five Extraordinary Sites' and the 'Three Paths': they climb the Hell Path—if somebody manages to climb this vertical cliff three times, he/ she will not fall into hell[158]—before crawling through the Altan Melekhei Narrow Path, circumambulate the difficult path around Cindamani (Cintā-maṇi) Stone, crawl into the Ekhe-yin Umai Cave, and drink water from the (now dried-up) Onggod Khuddug Spring.[159]

---

this place was, and Śākyamuni's five fingers emitted five miraculous lights that glanced off to form a rainbow, and the white light combining all the colors appeared above what will become Gilubar Juu (Belgünütei and Bükeqada 2010: 4).

154  Bükeqada 1999: 140; 140-142.

155  Bükeqada 1999: 140; 144-146.

156  Galsang et al. 1994: 275-289; Yesibaljuur 2010.

157  Bükeqada 1999: 144-146.

158  Another ritual linked to hell was observed at Jaya-yin Khüriye: under the floor of the Galdan Juu Temple there was a tunnel-like passage: devotees entered a dark hole, crawled along the narrow passage and had 'a glimpse of hell while they were alive,' which was meant to dissuade them from committing sins and encourage them to do meritorious deeds. They went out through an opening on the left.

159  Galsang et al. 1994: 282-287; Yesibaljuur 2010: 62-63, 71.

To sum up, although Mongol pilgrimage places were occasionally compared to Tibetan sites,[160] Wutaishan seems to be the main point of reference for Mongols. The presence of a womb-cave (and its association with child-giving and fertility), other numinous traces on the landscape and light manifestations seem to be the most distinctive features explaining why a Mongol sacred place was called Wutai, or compared to or related to Shanxi's Wutaishan. At Lobon-chinbu Süme and Gilubar Juu, the characteristics that recall Wutaishan are the womb-caves, the number five (five caves, five *ḍākinīs*, five extraordinary sites), the holy springs, and their popularity as local pilgrimages. Sometimes the connection was tenuous; despite Tövkhen Kheid being 'the Wutaishan of Mongolia,' its womb-cave is the only element linking it to Wutaishan. Also, there is no particular reference to specific monasteries or statues of Wutaishan or to the five terraces and five manifestations of Mañjuśrī in the Mongol Wutais. Gilubar Juu, said to be the 'incomparable palace of Mañjuśrī,'[161] might have been called 'Little Wutaishan' because the affluence of pilgrims at its festival was comparable to that of Wutaishan. Only three years after Pozdneev's visit to the (Green) Wutai of Keft Khuuchid, local people

> tell how for many years some kind of unusual noise was heard coming out of the midst of the mountains till finally the local lamas began to take an interest in it. The latter consulted people familiar with the locality who first of all found a connection between these mountains and the well-known Mount Wu-t'ai-shan, and then concluded that the area was generally holy and must show signs of harbouring a deity. When they looked over this mountain more closely, the lamas did find on a rock there an image of the burkhan of Ayusha [Ayushi] that had not been made by the hand of a man and several Tibetan letters, likewise not man-made, that formed an inscription of a dharani formula.[162]

In fact, when lamas wanted to promote a local pilgrimage and attract devout Mongols, it was in their interest to compare their monastery to Wutaishan, the pilgrimage place par excellence in modern Mongol history. This may also have been the case of the Tibetan site called Ribo Tsénga (the Tibetan name for

---

160    Chagan Diyanchi-yin Kheid, a major pilgrimage shrine in eastern Inner Mongolia, is known as 'the Tibet of the East.'

161    According to the guidebook to Gilubar Juu written by the Tenth Panchen Lama (1938-1989) (*Manzusiri ülisi ügei ordun Gilubar ayula-yin orun-u yarcay*, in Yesibaljuur 2010: 196-204).

162    Pozdneev 1977 [1896-1898]: 277.

Wutaishan), located southwest of Lhasa.[163] This discourse naturally claims identity between the original and the surrogates. Mongol guidebooks to monasteries naturally emphasize the holiness of a site by saying that worshipping this particular monastery is equivalent to worshipping all the other places.[164] Scholars Belgünütei and Bükeqada go as far as asserting that, according to "Mongolian and Chinese historical sources,"[165] the above-mentioned Five Wutais were sacred 'Mongol' places already since the fourth century BCE, since they were located in the territory of the Xiongnu/Khünnü empire.[166] They propose that the term 'Utai/Wutai,' sometimes written as 'Uta' in Mongolian, is an indigenous Mongol word that is identical to *uda*, the willow, a tree that has an important symbolism in shamanism.[167] The Wutais located in the heart of Mongol territory would therefore be more 'original' than the one in China's Shanxi Province.

While these local pilgrimages may be older than Mongols' worship of Shanxi's Wutaishan, they never replaced the great pilgrimage to Wutaishan for Mongols: they remained 'Little Wutaishans' or 'daughters.' Besides, there is no general consensus about the validity of there being one or several surrogates, for several regions in Mongolia claim to have a Wutai. Undoubtedly, these surrogates developed completely independently up to the moment when a learned

---

163    Hugh Richardson, commented in 'Jam dbyangs Mkhyen brtse'i dban po et al. 1958: 166, n. 683: "Ri bo rtse lnga, the Mountain of the 5 peaks, is the Tibetan counterpart of the famous Wu t'ai shan in China (it is a ridge of rocky pinnacles to the south of 'U śaṅ. HR)."

164    Such as the guidebook of Yekhe Juu of Ordos, 1802, translated from Tibetan into Mongolian in 1849 (ed. Narasun and Temürbaγatur 2000: 371-391). On similar discourses about Tibetan pilgrimage sites: Epstein and Peng 1994: 24: "the centrifocality of a given place appears to be the abiding strategy in virtually all pilgrimage guides in any case. However, this tendency is simultaneously undercut by the second and stronger tendency to connect it with various frontiers," that is, with more important pilgrimage places in Tibet.

165    The authors subscribe to the thesis developed by Gombojab (*rGya nag chos byung* "History of Buddhism in China," 1736), who, drawing on the *History of the Han Dynasty*, asserts that Buddhism penetrated the Xiongnu as early as the first century BCE, when the statue of a 'gold man' which he identified as a buddha, was offered to a Chinese general by a Xiongnu chief (see Elverskog 2006: 112-113). It is known that Chinese monks converted some of the nomad populations of northern China to Buddhism as early as the fourth century CE, but no connection can be established between these populations and the thirteenth-century Mongols.

166    Belgünütei and Bükeqada 2010: 20-19. The Xiongnu, a people of still unknown ethnolinguistic affiliations centered in Mongolia, founded a confederation in the fourth or third century BCE, bringing under their rule many of the neighboring Turkic, Mongolic and Iranian peoples. Modern Mongols view them as their ancestors, thus asserting the great ancientness of the Mongol nation.

167    It is used in sacrifices to obtain benefits (Belgünütei and Bükeqada 2010: 21-22).

cleric saw correspondences and announced a connection with Shanxi's Wutai-shan.

## Conclusion: The Mongols' Appropriation of Wutaishan

On Wutaishan, the worship of natural numinous sites was as important, if not more important, for pilgrims than worship at temples, *stūpa*s and saints. Men and women practiced the same rituals and had access to the same sites.[168] Many of these practices, such as drinking holy water, fastening ribbons to trees, crawling into a narrow hole, etc., are universally shared practices that can have different meanings and interpretations.[169] The importance of the numinous sites, as well as the ritual practices and narratives associated with them, sug-gests a popular appropriation of the mountain, in the same way that burial of one's dead relatives staked a claim to the land. The spiritual significance of these sites informs us, in a different way from the Tibetan and Mongol guide-books, about how the Tibetans and Mongols reshaped the mountain, disrupted and subverted the clerical Buddhist project by reasserting old beliefs and prac-tices: it is ultimately the pilgrims who create the pilgrimage. Sacrality is built through practices, and just by visiting the site the pilgrims help make the site more numinous.

We do not know how, when and by whom these practices were brought to Wutaishan: they are not documented by official records because they do not belong to any learned tradition and because the eminent monks never consid-ered them important compared, for instance, to manifestations of Mañjuśrī. However, we can assume that both the lamas, overcoming their disdain for such popular practices to please and attract Mongol and Tibetan devotees, and the pilgrims themselves who already practiced them in their local pilgrimage sites, imported them to Wutaishan. The high-ranking lamas who traveled between Tibet, Wutaishan and Inner Mongolia certainly played a role in this transmis-sion and in building links between the Wutaishan Mother's Womb-Cave and Mongol womb-caves.

The process of systematization and institutionalization is a slow one, but pragmatic practices are enduring. Although interpretation of these rituals may have changed, their contemporary revival at numinous sites and the custom of

---

168   In some Tibetan pilgrimages, such as the Kawa Karpo or Tsari, women are excluded from certain rituals (Buffetrille 1997: 108; Huber 1999: 120).

169   See for instance Bowman 2009: 33-35.

burying one's relative on Wutaishan seem to be the driving force behind the revival of the pilgrimage since 1980.

Wutaishan therefore has various meanings for Mongols: it is the residence of Mañjuśrī mentioned in Indian *sūtra*s and sanctified by the relics of Śākyamuni Buddha; it is one of the four Buddhist mountains of China with a prestigious past and miraculous icons, as well as a Tibeto-Mongol *néri* mountain with hidden treasures and footprints of saints, *stūpa*s and temples to circumambulate; lastly, it is a place to be buried to ensure rebirth in a pure land. In a single pilgrimage, the Mongols were thus able to carry out at once a 'pragmatic' cult of the mountain, a Chinese Buddhist pilgrimage and a Tibeto-Mongol Buddhist pilgrimage.

The terraces of Wutaishan do look like some Mongol sacred mountains, with an abundance of sacred rocks, springs and numinous sites. The mountain irradiates a power that can be transferred and absorbed to heal, bring good luck and ensure to those buried there rebirth in a paradise. But unlike Tibetan *néri* summits and most Mongol mountains—which remained virgin, devoid of ritual architecture due to their remoteness, great altitudes and extremely harsh environment—Wutaishan was also a human-built site with hundreds of monasteries, *stūpa*s, hermitages and shrines. Following Chinese custom for pilgrimage sites, temples and *stūpa*s were built on top of each terrace so that monks could live and meditate there and so that pilgrims too could stay there and have a chance to personally experience the mysterious phenomena of the holy mountain. However, while the temples and *stūpa*s are periodically ruined due to meteorological conditions, the numinous sites cannot disappear.

# Conclusion

Wutaishan possesses all the components that make a 'spiritual magnetic site' according to Preston's criteria. It boasts numinous traces such as springs associated with healing and good fortune. It is a site of apparitions of supernatural beings —Mañjuśrī, Tsongkhapa, Avalokiteśvara, Padmasambhava transmitting revelations, sacred texts and icons that were hidden when people were not ready to understand them or in times of troubles, to be revealed in their time. Wutaishan also had a geography sacralized by prestigious monasteries, relics and miraculous icons, and by the presence of Indian, Tibetan and Mongol saints and reincarnations. It was an awe-inspiring site combined with accessibility to a deity.[1] Like Chinese mountains and some Japanese pilgrimage sites, Wutaishan includes more than a hundred built and natural sites. With their high altitude and harsh climate, plus various dangers ranging from tigers to storms, the terraces were difficult to access, requiring great effort and courage to reach. The pilgrimage was enhanced by acts of contrition (like progressing in full-length prostrations) and fasting. Yet dangers and hardships were less compared to journeys to Tibet, and the excellent pastures and vivid markets of Wutaishan appeared especially attractive to Mongol herders, who could bring their flocks with them. Women equally participated in the pilgrimage, and there were no specific prohibitions or places forbidden to them. In addition, the prestigious past of Wutaishan, which was remembered in local legends, connected the holy mountain to religious and political figures of ancient Tibet, China and India. The abode of Mañjuśrī never ceased to be an international pilgrimage site since the first millennium and, in the modern period, became increasingly associated with supernatural efficacy for Mongols.

For Mongols, Wutaishan could compete with the great Tibetan pilgrimage sites, which, comparatively speaking, attracted more monks and a smaller variety of social groups. As for the 'national' and local Mongol pilgrimages, and especially Urga, while their importance must not be underestimated, they could not completely replace the journey to Wutaishan. In the sacred geography of Mongolia, Wutaishan was located geographically abroad (yet not far) but spiritually at the heart of Mongol territory; it was shared by all Mongol groups, because it was not the particular mountain of a local Mongol community.

Since the Tang dynasty, Wutaishan was also an important site for the ritual protection of the dynasties that ruled China and served as ideal ground for the Yuan and the Qing empire-building projects. We have seen that the role of the

---

1   Preston 1992: 33-38.

Qing emperors in the promotion of the pilgrimage among Mongols was weak compared to its promotion by the local clergy (especially the *ombo lamas*) and by the Mongols themselves, from lamas who wrote prayers and prescribed the pilgrimage as a cure to oral accounts of returning pilgrims. The number of pilgrims, the amounts of their donations, and their literary and visual production about Wutaishan show that the Mongols' craze for the holy mountain surpassed the initial encouragement. They not only recycled and distorted Buddhist lore and Sino-Manchu stories but also developed a unique popular folklore, Wutaishan being even included in shamanistic invocations. These productions are both causes and consequences of the pilgrimage: they stemmed from the experience of pilgrims and, when diffused, prompted future pilgrimages.

How can we explain that Mongols' pilgrimages to Wutaishan culminated during a period of economic depression and troubles, when Mongols' identity and social status were being redefined and when anticlerical discourses rose among the population, targeting a poorly educated clergy condemned for its corruption, lust and parasitism?[2] Explanations are as many as the types of pilgrims: princes financed their pilgrimages by levying special taxes on their subjects; pilgrim-traders made profits by selling horses, oxen and sheep at a high price; penitents and poor pilgrims begged for food, while others spent all their savings in donations. The significant Mongol contribution to the Wutaishan economy, which allowed some circulation of resources, may have been partially counterbalanced by the profits made by the pilgrim-traders. The importance of donations to the Wutaishan monasteries also allows us to re-evaluate the prevalent picture of economic stagnation and to nuance it according to the period and places.

The variety of pilgrims, of aims and types of pilgrimages allows us to draw a picture with much sharper contrasts compared to the simple picture of *communitas* and of Qing dynasty cosmopolitanism. Some monasteries and sites were worshipped by all pilgrims, while others were especially visited by Mongols and Tibetans. The Mongols particularly liked caves and monasteries that had a venerable Chinese or Indian past (the Great White Stūpa and Buddha's footprints, Shuxiangsi, Xiantongsi) but neglected other sites which were praised in the Chinese gazetteers. Their patronage of Chinese institutions in the late nineteenth and early twentieth centuries contributed to the survival of some temples and monasteries such as Wulangmiao and Yuhuangmiao/Puhuasi. Except for learned lamas from Tibet and Mongolia who came to Wutaishan to meet each other, interactions between common pilgrims seem to have been limited.

---

2  Bawden 1989 [1968]: 160-172.

Because of differing pilgrimages and expectations, the Mongols' common faith in Wutaishan's sacredness did not act as a cement uniting Buddhist Mongols.

Whatever the role of the Manchu emperors and the Buddhist institutions in creating, promoting and canalizing the pilgrimage to Wutaishan, the Mongols undertook the pilgrimage for several reasons that have nothing to do with promotion by the court or by the Wutaishan monasteries, such as burying their dead, shopping, or crawling into the Mother's Womb-Cave (the fertility and re-birth ritual of which was, and still is, one of the major moments of the Mongols' journey). The practices and rituals that Mongols performed on Wutaishan did not greatly differ from those they performed in Mongolia, and some, like crawling into the womb-cave, were even adopted by the Chinese pilgrims. By creating new sites, legends and rituals, the Mongols, like the Tibetans, thus transplanted and superimposed their own pilgrimage traditions and narratives (revelations, apparitions, stories) onto the ancient Chinese traditions, deeply leaving their mark on Wutaishan's religious culture. Not only, but by their pres-ence, their yurts, flocks and herds, their tombs and steles, their specific rituals, they brought a distinct Mongol flavor to the holy mountain.

Burial on Wutaishan appears to be a major element that distinguished the Wutaishan pilgrimage from other pilgrimages in Tibet or in Mongolia. As in other Buddhist sites of Asia, such as Mount Kōya in Japan, burial on a sacred mountain that was empowered by relics ensured rebirth in a pure land. On Wutaishan, the Mongols were preoccupied with death and after-death destiny, and they requested salvation rituals to avoid going to hell. The fact that often the Mongol pilgrimage to this holy land was made to bury the dead, purify one-self of sins and avoid the sufferings of hell made it not just a pilgrimage but a journey between death and (a better) rebirth.

Wutaishan's Mother's Womb-Cave was seen as superior to all the other womb-caves found in Mongol pilgrimages, and the mountain itself was consid-ered a cut above the other secondary substitutes found back home. This was even more the case with burial on Wutaishan. No other pilgrimage site of Mon-golia or Tibet was chosen for burying the dead. For laypersons, the two options for burial were one's ancestral pastures or, for that fortunate minority of Bud-dhist devotees, Wutaishan. In present-day Inner Mongolia, Buddhists still want to be buried on the sacred Chinese mountain, but is this because they have lost their pastures or can no longer legitimate their pasture rights through burial?

## Wutaishan's Legacy in Mongolia

International pilgrimages are often responsible for the diffusion of new ideas and material culture. By crossing a part of Shanxi, many ordinary Mongol families had the opportunity to observe Chinese Buddhist and lay culture, to prostrate in front of Chinese Buddhist icons, and to buy books and Buddhist souvenirs.

Through the many pilgrims who visited Wutaishan, and the Wutaishan monks who crisscrossed Mongolia, Wutaishan's culture exerted a deep influence on Mongol art and literature, and became part and parcel of the Mongol identity. References to Wutaishan were commonly included in Mongol lore, prayers, blessings, eulogies, stories of saintly lives, as well as in sayings and anticlerical mockery of *badarchi lamas*. According to Mongol scholar Altanzayaa, *ombo lama* would be a term of foreign origin that came to designate the monks responsible for welcoming pilgrims in Khalkha monasteries, and the monks who keep the treasuries of reincarnated lamas.[3]

In a certain way, the Mongol craze for Wutaishan can be paralleled to the contemporaneous success of Shambhala, which was the most praised holy land in the nineteenth and early twentieth centuries—but an extra-earthly kingdom, though identified by some as being a real, reachable place. Shambhala is described as a Pure Land, and its core (its capital city) is surrounded by a ring of mountains. Wutaishan and Shambhala are listed among the five 'Especially Excellent Sites of Empowerment' of Jambudvīpa in the Mongol cosmology. Several holy men were expected to be reborn in Shambhala and participate in the ultimate war against the enemies of Buddhism: the Panchen Lama would be the last king of Shambhala, the Jebtsündamba Khutugtu would be General Hanumanda, and Mañjuśrīkirti, one of the three main kings of Shambhala, would be an incarnation of Mañjuśrī.

Recently, the Khamar-un Kheid founded by Danjinrabjai in the Gobi, has become the main pilgrimage center of the Republic of Mongolia.[4] It is believed to be the main 'portal' to Shambhala in Mongolia, "seen as the epicenter of spiritual energy" and a constant flow of pilgrims from different regions of Mongolia and from western countries rush to make the pilgrimage every year.[5] In its two temples—the Red (Nyingmapa) temple, that enshrines the famous

---

3   Altanzayaa 2000: 141.

4   Wallace 2008: 50.

5   Sharavdorj, who served as Mongolia's Minister of Defense until 2007 converted to the Nyingmapa School and used his political connections and own funds to restore the monastery (Wallace 2008: 50).

thousand-knive statue of Padmasambhava, and the Yellow (Gélukpa) temple—, rituals are performed to "protect pilgrims of Shambhala from harm." Women circumambulate the breast-like *oboo*s first, and men afterwards. The pilgrims visit the thirteen caves where disciples of Danjinrabjai meditated during 108 days, as well as his personal cave. They crawl inside the womb cave, and "stretch on the open ground to absorb the Shambhala healing energy."[6] Khamar-un Kheid and its Shambhala mythology has now replaced Wutaishan for many pilgrims of the Republic of Mongolia.

### Rupture and Revival

In pilgrimage literature, some authors have noted the extraordinary persistence of pilgrimages through periods of internal and external change: the history of pilgrimage centers moves at a slow pace and tends to be conservative.[7] But pilgrimage is also "an on-going and dynamic process" open to outside influences and change; it intensifies at certain periods, dies of over-institutionalization or persecution, and sometimes revives after a period of decline.[8] The early twentieth century is generally seen as a period of political and religious rupture;[9] Mongols were by then no longer part of "Our Great Qing."[10] Yet the continuous erection of steles and records of donations after the fall of the Qing allows us to challenge the previously temporally bounded units of the Qing and the Republic. The Wutaishan case is a good example showing that a pilgrimage has a temporality that is different from political, religious and social history. However, the contemporary Mongol pilgrimage deeply differs from the early twentieth-century pilgrimage. The developments and destruction of the twentieth and twenty-first centuries on Wutaishan help us understand why we must be extremely cautious in using present-day Mongol journeys to Wutaishan to illustrate Qing-dynasty and Republican-period pilgrimages.

---

6    "Pilgrimage in the Gobi—Danzanravjaa's Shambala Dornogobi" 2008, video posted on Youtube about the Dalai Lama's birthday on July 6th.

7    Morinis 1992: 23-24.

8    Preston 1992; Coleman and Eade 2004: 10.

9    For Chinese religion, Goossaert and Palmer (2011) date this rupture to 1898.

10   For Sino-Tibetan relations, Gray Tuttle (2005) highlights the period of the 1930s and 1940s as a major turning point, with the creation of nation-states, the redefinition of the place of religion in the public space and the role of Buddhist culture as a cement linking Chinese, Tibetans and Mongols.

### Wutaishan in the Communist Era

The last Mongolian stone inscription is dated 1940, and although some individual pilgrims journeyed to Wutaishan after that date, they left no trace of their pilgrimage. After the 'liberation' of Wutai County in 1946 and Mao Zedong's journey to Taihuai in 1948, monks returned to the Wutaishan monasteries. Impressed by Wutaishan's temples, Mao expressed the wish to protect the Wutaishan Buddhist heritage. Inventorying and protecting Buddhist cultural institutions and relics was the task of the Buddhist Association. As a result, several monasteries were spared, and Buddhist activities flourished again,[11] that is, up to the summer of 1966, when the Cultural Revolution reached the mountain. Then all the monasteries were closed, and thousands of monks were sent for re-education in labor camps. Because of the isolation of the Wutaishan mountain range, its monasteries were not hit as hard as those in other Chinese provinces. Despite being plundered, most monasteries escaped destruction, and some of the central ones came out relatively unscathed, managing even to preserve their statuaries and paintings. However, the venerable Jingangku and nearby Puleyuan were destroyed with canons around 1970 to build a summer residence for Lin Biao.

### The Revival of the Buddhist Communities on Wutaishan

Monastic life on the mountain was revived in the 1980s, when a certain degree of religious freedom was again allowed in China. Old and young monks and nuns gradually returned to Wutaishan and reopened the monasteries. Because most of them now come from other areas of China, the specific local ritual practices, and especially the musical traditions, could only be preserved in a few monasteries.[12] There came a great wave of reconstruction and restoration of more than sixty monasteries, along with roads, stairs and bridges, spurred by the rapid economic growth of the 1990s and 2000s. In the 2010s, monasteries were extended to accommodate the growing number of monks and lay pilgrims. Several former Tibetan monasteries were turned into Chinese Buddhist monasteries (Sanquansi, Shouningsi, Baohuasi, Puansi, Cifusi) and nunneries or school for nuns (Qifosi, Pushousi, Jifusi). Qinghai Lama of the Han Gélukpa School, following the flourishing tradition of masters Fazun and Nenghai, took

---

11     Szczepanski 2008: 60. A 1956 census counted seventy Mongol, seven Tibetan and three Manchu monks (Wei Guozuo 2004: 50).

12     Szczepanski 2008: 70.

over Chinese and Tibetan Gélukpa monasteries (Yuanzhaosi, Shancaidong, Guangzongsi, Santasi, Tayuansi, Jixiangsi, Yanjiaosi, and Jifusi).[13]

Overall, the number of Tibetan lamas residing on Wutaishan has increased since the 1990s,[14] and the 2000s saw a renewal of Tibetan Buddhist practice, with a significant multi-ethnic following.[15] The monasteries are now more or less divided according to ethnic communities. But thanks to the dialogue between Gélukpa and Chinese Buddhism initiated by Fazun and Nenghai, the Chinese Gélukpa community, which initially was ethnically Han, now accepts Mongols from Inner Mongolia and Tibetans from Amdo in their ranks (the language spoken in these monasteries being Mandarin). Inner Mongol and Tibetan nuns also enroll in Chinese Buddhist nunneries to receive nun ordination, which does not exist in Tibetan Buddhism.

Through the Han Gélukpa School, but also through visiting Tibetan masters, Tibetan Buddhism played a major part in the Buddhist revival. In 1987, the great Nyingmapa master Jikmé Püntsok (Khenpo Jigpün, 1933-2004), who had established the Larung Buddhist Institute near Serthar in 1980 in Sichuan Province, led a group of several thousand disciples to Wutaishan, most of them Han. There, he performed rituals of the Great Perfection tradition, gave mass teachings and empowerments, as well as revealing Buddhist texts and statues and in turn concealing texts within the mountain. He offered statues to Wutaishan monasteries and reconsecrated icons.[16] Jikmé Püntsok helped revitalize the Tibetan Buddhist tradition on Wutaishan and laid a common ground for Chinese and Tibetans, though his Nyingmapa followers encountered some opposition from the local Gélukpa clergy. Other Tibetan masters of Gélukpa, Nyingmapa or Rimé traditions, such as Dilgo Khyentsé, Akya (Ajia) Rinpoché, Khejok Rinpoché, Dzongsar Khyentsé Rinpoché and Sakyong Mipham Rinpoché, have contributed to re-empowering Wutaishan through initiations and treasure-discovery, and to reviving the pilgrimage. New miracles were spotted by crowds, especially during rituals and initiations. The rituals Jikmé Püntsok performed at the Great White Stūpa, at Qingliangsi and at Nārāyaṇa Cave were accompanied by apparitions of Mañjuśrī in the sky, along with colored haloes,

---

13 Tuttle 2006a; Bianchi and Rinaldo 2010. The reason is that Chinese monks and nuns were the first to re-occupy these monasteries. On contemporary Wutaishan, see also Szczepanski 2008; Chou 2011: Chapter 4.

14 Tuttle 2006a.

15 In 2010, local monks said to me there were a thousand lamas and five thousand *heshang*s living on Wutaishan; other surveys give a number of three thousand resident monks and up to five thousand monks in summer, including pilgrim-monks (Zhou Rubi and Li Guangyi 2007: 408).

16 Chou 2011: Chapter 3.

rainbow lights and so on.[17] In 1999, just after Khejok Rinpoché said his prayers in front of Rölpe Dorjé's *stūpa*, twenty or so monks witnessed rainbow light rays emanating from the *stūpa*.[18] A fabulous, golden-winged bird was seen in auspicious clouds above Qifosi on December 12, 1998.[19] New numinous traces continue to be discovered. For instance, in the 1990s, Miaosheng 妙生, the Chinese abbot of Puhuasi, noticed that the mountains seen from Lingfengsi 靈峰寺 took on the shape of the profile of the Buddha's face; from then on people have gone there to worship the 'Big Buddha Looking Upwards' (Yangtian dafo 仰天 大佛), especially at sunrise or when it rains.[20] Shituolin 屍陀林 (the Cemetery Forest), a cave were a hermit meditated and died, located above Wenshusi, is especially visited by Tibetans (Fig. 49).[21]

Because Buddhist institutions in Inner Mongolia are struggling to survive (owing to many factors, including state control, absence of reincarnations and leading figures, reputation of monks, cutting off with Tibet, lack of monastic vocations, sinicization and rural exodus), Mongols monks presently do not play an important role in the global revival of Tibeto-Mongol Buddhism in China. On Wutaishan, Mongol monks are now much less numerous than Tibetan monks from Amdo. Those who report miracles and discover new numinous sites, write new guidebooks and propagate new stories are Chinese Buddhist monks and Tibetan and Han Chinese lamas writing in Chinese or Tibetan, and the Mongols are no longer authors of pilgrimage lore.

### The Return of the Pilgrims

Pilgrims started returning to Wutaishan in the 1980s, but the large-scale pilgrimage and the festivals were revived only in the 1990s. The political, religious and economic dimensions of the pilgrimage—including lifestyles, means of transportation, access to the sites, organization and staff of the monasteries— have been deeply transformed since 1949. Because of the redefinition of the role of monks and monasteries in society as a whole, the practice of collecting alms outside of Wutaishan has disappeared.

---

17    Germano 1998: 84-87; Chou 2011b: Chapter 4, quoting his biography.

18    Lim 1999.

19    See the pictures in Zhou Rubi and Li Guangyi 2007: 194, 195, 199.

20    See the picture and other examples of mountain crests looking like Buddha's face in Wen Fuliang et al. 2004: 187-190.

21    This name, which was provided to me by Chinese nuns, obviously refers to Śītavana, the charnel ground near Bodhgayā. Another Shituolin on Wutaishan is the Cooling Charnel Ground near Shancaidong.

The institutionalization and control of the site by the political authorities, along with the development of mass tourism and of Chinese settlements, have transformed the landscape. In 2007-2009, a large part of Taihuai bordering the central complex of monasteries was razed to the ground (and a thousand residents forcibly resettled) to mark the inclusion of the site in the UNESCO list of heritage. Rock blasting in the search of precious metals has also altered the landscape and recently caused damage to murals and statues at Jingesi.

Wutaishan now attracts a great number of tourists. New roads (and soon, a highway) and frequent buses bring tourists and pilgrims from all of China, Taiwan, Mongolia, Japan, etc.: Wutaishan is now only six or seven hours away from Beijing, three or four hours from the big cities of Taiyuan and Datong, and about twenty-four hours from Lhasa by train and buses. Visitors come from April to October, when the mountain and its shopping center bustle with activity; winter is no longer a pilgrimage season. The profane activities of Chinese urban life (tourism, construction work, markets, private companies, village life, karaoke and so on) are now more visible than the religious activities, and speakers blast Chinese profane music in the central area.

As recent scholarship has shown (Preston; Eade and Sallnow; Hiroshi Tanaka Shimazaki; Reader), in a modernized and secularized world, the general erosion of the penitential dimension of pilgrimages, the increasing number of tourist-pilgrims, and the shortening of stays have all had negative effects on the 'spiritual magnetism' of mountains such as Wutaishan. With the new means of transportation, the journey itself now takes on much less importance than worship at the shrines. It is not only the dangers and physical hardships that have disappeared but also all the 'holistic vision of the world.' On Wutaishan, the sacred is more and more separated from the profane in time and space, and nature is increasingly tamed by buildings and roads that reach the terraces.

Pilgrims (who also engage in some tourism and shopping) adopt strategies to differentiate themselves from tourists (who also worship statues and burn incense) by taking up specific dress and attributes (pilgrim's incense bags, rosaries) and by walking only (except for some who take a van to visit the terraces).[22] They also avoid taking pictures, except for pictures of their group with monks to whom they made a donation or who served as guides.

Most of the Mongol pilgrims I interviewed and followed stayed two or three days and contented themselves with the 'small pilgrimage';[23] a minority

---

22    On pilgrimage and tourism, see the volume edited by Badone and Roseman 2004.
23    I interviewed Mongols in Inner Mongolia during my many fieldworks there between 1993 and 2012; Mongols in the Republic of Mongolia (Ulaanbaatar, Arkhangai and Övörkhangai

stayed a week and climbed to the terraces,[24] and some lay devotees from Inner Mongolia stayed about one month in a monastery, attending daily teachings and practicing meditation. Individual pilgrims are few and tend to aggregate with other pilgrims. Pilgrims are faced with a dilemma: either they chose walking only and cannot do the whole pilgrimage (on foot they can visit only one or two terraces, weather permitting)[25] or they collectively rent a van.

As noted by Ian Reader about the Shikoku pilgrimage in Japan, pilgrim groups can perform a more complete and intense pilgrimage than a lone walking pilgrim, by using modern means of transport and enjoying collective prayers and the explanations of a guide.[26] Yet Online Appendix H shows how contemporary pilgrims visit from five or six sites and up to nineteen sites within three days. The list of must-see sites has slightly changed compared to the early twentieth-century list, and many minor places have been forgotten or destroyed. Since the majority of pilgrims directly arrive at Taihuai by car or bus, the temples along the route, such as Guangjisi 廣濟寺 or Zunshengsi 尊勝寺 (Wutai County, south of Taihuai), are much less visited than before, not to mention the monasteries located off the beaten track. Not only has the time spent been reduced but also the movements that were central to the pilgrimage; for instance, circumambulation around monasteries is not performed anymore. The circuits have been simplified, and the narratives and representations have lost most of their profusion and richness; for example, the only modern Mongolian guidebook (written in Uyghur-Mongolian script) is a translation from the Chinese, and the Cifusi map has been forgotten (although those who read Tibetan have access to different narratives).

The reasons for visitors' shorter stays on the mountain are not only the pace of modern life and transportation but also the cost of traveling to and staying on Wutaishan. Except for Tibetan pilgrims, all visitors have to pay a high fee to enter the mountain (168 *yuan* plus 50 *yuan* for transportation, in 2010) plus

---

Provinces) in 2009 and 2013, and Mongol pilgrims and monks on Wutaishan between 2007 and 2012.

24    Tibetan lay pilgrims stay no more than three or four days on the mountain and come from various parts of Amdo and from Lhasa (by train). One of their motivations is to meet, receive blessings and travel with lamas, which they cannot do freely in Tibet. Chinese pilgrims typically travel with the lay association attached to the monastery of south or southeast China to which they belong, and they generally cannot afford to stay more than three or four days.

25    For similar questions about the validity of half a pilgrimage, which also entails the disappearance of the 'communal and festive aspect of the pilgrimage': Buffetrille 2003.

26    Reader 2005: 36.

entrance fees to the main monasteries (5 to 10 *yuan* each).[27] Most pilgrims stay within the monasteries and in cheap inns (10 to 15 *yuan* a bed in a dormitory of two to four beds) but bring their own food because they cannot afford the high price in the restaurants. Only special taxis and minibuses are allowed to go to the terraces and ask more than 100 *yuan* per pilgrim, although tour group negotiate cheaper prices.

In addition, Inner Mongols and Mongols of the Republic of Mongolia now belong to two different countries. Inner Mongols are Chinese citizens and many of them have become sinicized. Inter-ethnic communication between Inner Mongols, Chinese and Tibetans is facilitated by the fact that many Tibetans and Inner Mongols can speak Chinese, and the monks' communities are not completely segregated. However, between Inner Mongols and Mongols from the Republic of Mongolia the gap is actually widening.

Buddhist Inner Mongols I interviewed all say that Wutaishan is an important pilgrimage site for them. They travel in small groups, often accompanied by a lama, and reside in the Mongolian-speaking Luohousi (where they often have acquaintances) or in cheap inns. On Wutaishan in 2007, I met a family of five Mongols from Ordos who come every year in July for the Great Sixth Month Festival. In 2009, I interviewed a group of six Mongols from Tongliao (eastern Inner Mongolia), composed of laypersons from two different families and a lama, who were coming to Wutaishan for the second time. Among them, one woman was thinking of becoming a nun in a Wutaishan nunnery. They say that people from rural areas, especially the elderly, wish to visit Wutaishan at least once in their life to gain merit for a better reincarnation and also, after death, to have their ashes buried there, because Wutaishan is a place 'for the cult of the dead.' Some Mongols carry their parents' funerary urns to be buried on the sacred land. Others journey to Wutaishan to accompany their aged parents so that they may be able to pray and find peace before they pass away, or when someone has recently died in their family. For instance, a Khorchin pilgrim living in Beijing, who wrote a few pages describing her pilgrimage in the 1990s accompanying her elderly mother to Wutaishan, recounts that their pilgrimage could not be complete if they did not climb to the Northern Terrace. They walked slowly to the terrace while praying *Oṃ maṇi padme huṃ!* "Each step allows one to remove a little bit of sin, suppress a bad thought, and avoid doing a bad thing, thus one can increase his share of happiness." They succeeded in getting to the Northern Terrace, but due to bad weather conditions, they had great difficulty getting down. Having fulfilled her wish to visit Wutaishan, the mother

---

27   Even those who have a lay Buddhist registration (*jushiji* 居士記) must pay. This card allows them to enter for free in the monasteries of their province only.

informed her daughter that she could now die. Once back in Beijing, the daughter herself felt transformed by the adventure.[28]

A few Inner Mongols still journey in great prostrations from their home to Wutaishan, spending months on the road. Some even undertake the pilgrimage once or twice a year, because "it is auspicious, good for the present." In any case, they take back with them some earth from the mountain to keep on their altar at home, showing it the same respect as they do towards Buddha images. These pilgrims' motivations and expectations are likely to be, to a major extent, the same as those of their predecessors. But is it still conservatism and only conservatism when practices persist in the face of so much change? When it takes more courage and defiance to carry on?

Conversely, for Mongols from the Republic of Mongolia, the pilgrimage is an expensive journey in a foreign country. The expenses and difficulties of traveling abroad, added to strong anti-Chinese feelings, have greatly reduced the power of attraction of the Chinese mountain. In the decades since 1990, Buddhism has had to find a new place in the Republic of Mongolia, a country attempting to forge a new national identity in the context of post-communist secular modernity, and new national pilgrimage sites have been promoted as substitutes for pilgrimages abroad. Devotees are commonly advised by the Buddhist authorities to pay their devotions at the main shrines of their country rather than traveling abroad. For instance, a female Buddhist from Ulaanbaatar (around forty years of age) whom I interviewed in 2009 in Arkhangai asked a lama if it was 'compulsory' to go on pilgrimage to 'Utai-Gümbüm' i.e., Kumbum Monastery and Wutaishan. "Going to Utai-Gümbüm (or Gümbüm-Utai)" is one of the modern expressions used to designate a pilgrimage (abroad), and some Mongols believe Wutaishan and Kumbum are one and the same, or at least very close to each other. The lama answered that it was equivalent for her to worship the holy sites of the Republic of Mongolia: "Going to Utai-Gümbüm is either for very pious people, or for those who want to travel around." She believes that the most sacred place in her country is Khamar-un Kheid (known as the 'gate of Shambhala,' in the Gobi Desert) because "it is the center of Mongolia's magnetic energy," and she goes there every year on pilgrimage. Another Mongol I interviewed in 2009, an eighty-year-old from Arkhangai, was told by a lama of Wutaishan that it was not necessary anymore to go on pilgrimage to Wutaishan because "we have Erdeni Juu and Tövkhen Kheid in Mongolia." Similar to what has been observed for Christian pilgrimages in late medieval England, the decline of Mongols' international pilgrimages correspond to nationalism, the

---

28    Tian Chang'an and Liang Heng, eds. 2003: 62-71.

indigenization of Buddhism and the creation of Buddhist sites in Mongolia, plus the difficulty of traveling abroad.

Yet some Buddhist Khalkhas still list Wutaishan as a main pilgrimage site. Small groups journey to the mountain by bus and train; they generally take the opportunity to visit Höhhot, Kumbum and Beijing along the way, only staying one to three days on Wutaishan because of the high cost of transportation, food and lodging (Online Appendix H). They are made visible thanks to their distinctive dress and behavior. Most of them travel in small tours organized by monks from Gandan and Dashichoiling, in Ulaanbaatar,[29] or by a travel agency. In 2009, radio ads for tour operator Tenger Travel, which were broadcast in Ulaanbaatar, encouraged filial Mongols to give a pilgrimage to Wutaishan to their parents as a birthday gift,[30] and, in a street near the Ulaanbaatar Hotel, large posters by the same company advertised, "Offer a trip to the holy land of Utai [Wutaishan][31] and Gümbüm [Kumbum] to your gray-haired father and mother!" Tenger proposed four trips via train and bus:

- a seventeen-day trip to visit Erenhot [Erlian, at the Sino-Mongol border], Kumbum, Höhhot, Wutaishan and Beijing for a total of 6,220 kilometers and a cost of about US$500, but only one day and a half are spent on Wutaishan;[32]
- a thirteen-day trip to Wutaishan and Kumbum via Erenhot and Höhhot (5,480 kilometers), for about US$370, with two days on Wutaishan, and, for the same price, a ten-day trip to Wutaishan and Beijing via Erenhot and Höhhot;
- an eight-day trip to Lhasa by train, through Beijing, for US$1,390.

A female Buddhist devotee from Ulaanbaatar (aged around fifty) whom I met in 2010 had made five pilgrimages to Wutaishan and Kumbum, one of which was to accompany her elderly mother. Each time, she spent only two nights on Wutaishan out of a total of ten to seventeen days in China. She always took an organized tour because "it is almost impossible to reach Wutaishan alone." Her

---

29  A lama of Dashichoiling Monastery in Ulaanbaatar gathers pilgrims every year, and the shops selling Buddhist objects near monasteries advertise the trip.
30  I thank Pierre Palussière for the pictures of the ad in the streets of Ulaanbaatar and for introducing me to the website, which offers a variety of "Buddha tour excursions abroad" (*Buddha tour gadaad ayalaluud*) ("Tenger Travel internet website").
31  *Ariun dagsin: ariun* < Cyr. Mo. 'pure, holy,' and Tib. *dakzhing*, 'pure land.'
32  "Tenger Travel internet website" and "Ikh ayan internet website".

most salient memories were the Mother's Womb-Cave and the blessings given by a renowned lama from Inner Mongolia who had also traveled to Wutaishan.

All in all, Mongols now constitute only a small minority of the pilgrims; they are diluted among the masses of Chinese pilgrims (not even counting the tourists). The trade dimension has disappeared and their offerings are insignificant compared to donations from the Chinese (from China, Taiwan, Singapore) and Japanese. Instead, we can observe a de-mongolization of the mountain compared to the early twentieth century, when Mongolian script appeared on steles, banners, name plaques, prayer wheels and tombs inscriptions (most of this heritage was destroyed during the Cultural Revolution). The practice of carving donation steles in Mongolian ceased after 1940. All the steles are now carved in Chinese, and one cannot distinguish those written by Chinese donors from those written by Inner Mongols who have taken a Chinese name. Mongols arriving with their flocks and camel caravans and pitching their yurts in the pastures have disappeared from Wutaishan's landscape. They do not have personal ties with specific Wutaishan monasteries anymore. Mongol pilgrim-monks are no longer integrated into the life of *shifang* monasteries for the time of their visit; the vast majority of resident and pilgrim lamas now come from Amdo.[33] The guidebooks, maps, prayers and songs composed by Mongols are forgotten. Although Inner Mongols try to reappropriate Wutaishan through their presence (as pilgrims, as monks, as tourists), their donations and their ever-growing cemeteries, the distinct Mongolian flavor of Wutaishan has practically vanished, and even their tombs are generally inscribed with Chinese characters.

---

33    About two thousand lamas come every year from Labrang and its region and stay one month in July. They do not reside in a monastery or participate in rituals but rather rent a room in the 'Tibetan District' north of Taihuai (in 2007, a five-bed room in a courtyard was rented for 300 *yuan* a month) and visit monasteries using modern Tibetan guidebooks.

# Appendices

Three appendices are presented below: a synthetic table of the monasteries of Wutaishan, a study of the Mongolian stone inscriptions, and a Khorchin song.

More materials are presented in Online Appendices on the "open archive HAL-SHS" website at the following URL: https://halshs.archives-ouvertes.fr/. The online appendices include:

- a list of steles presented by monastery in chronological order, with for each of them the name and origin of the main donor, the date and the amount of the donation, and a summary of the text for the most important ones (Appendix A2). Synthetic tables give an overview of this corpus of stone inscriptions (Appendix A1), and six examples of paper certificates recording donations are presented (Appendix A3);
- a catalogue of the main monasteries and numinous sites visited by Mongol pilgrims with their different names, localization, legends, notes on their history (focusing on the Qing and Republican periods), main features, present state, sources (including stone inscriptions) and photographs (Appendix B) ;
- a list of the main travelers to Wutaishan who left records in the Qing and Republican periods, along with a summary of seven Mongolian, Chinese and Japanese accounts (Appendix C);
- a list of Mongolian gazetteers and guidebooks on Wutaishan, with a summary of two of them  (Appendix D);
- two praise prayers to Wutaishan (Appendix E);
- the transcription of the text of a booklet in accordion form entitled "Great Enterprise of Restoration of the Main Assembly Hall of Ganjuur Süme on Wutaishan" written by the abbot of this monastery to request from Mongols the exorbitant sum of fifty thousand taels to repair the monastery, dated 1919 (summarized in this book, p. 142-143). The forty-nine pages following the introductory text, destined to receive the names of donors, were left blank.
- a transcription and a translation of the Mongolian texts of the 1846 Cifusi Map (Appendix G);
- some notes and photographs on contemporary Mongol pilgrimages (Appendix H);
- a list of the twenty-three *jasag lama*s of Wutaishan (Appendix I);
- and a list of references cited in the appendices.

© KONINKLIJKE BRILL NV, LEIDEN, 2015 | DOI 10.1163/9789004297784_011

# Main Monasteries of Wutaishan, Early Twentieth Century

*   The date under brackets in column 3 gives the period when the monastery was turned into a Gélukpa monastery. The names of the largest monasteries are written in bold. See the Online Appendix B for details on the main 'numinous sites' and the temples and monasteries visited by Mongols. P. Preserved; D. Destroyed; R. Rebuilt; D* Monastery destroyed except for a *stūpa.*

| Monastery's name in Chinese and Mongolian | English name | Date of foundation/refoundation | Affiliation in the late Qing period (date) | Main sights and 'numinous traces' | Present state |
|---|---|---|---|---|---|
| **Lingjiu Peak** | | | | | |
| (Dabao) **Tayuansi** (大寶塔院寺) - Burqan gegegen-ü šaril-tin gereltü yeke cayan suburga | (Great Precious) Stūpa Cloister Monastery Big White Illuminated Stūpa of the *Śarīra* of the Enlightened Buddha | Tang/Ming | Ch. Buddhist | Great White Stūpa enshrining Śākyamuni's relic; Mañjuśrī's Hair Stūpa; stele of Śākyamuni's footprints; revolving library | P. |
| **Xiantongsi** 顯通寺 (Dafu Lingjiusi 大孚靈鷲寺) - Γayiqamsiγtu tegüs süme; Ubadistu süme; Altan kürel süme | Clear Understanding Monastery (Great Faith Numinous Vulture [Peak] monastery) Monastery Having Magic Powers; Golden Bronze Monastery | Northern Wei | Ch. Buddhist | Beamless Hall; Thousand Bowl Mañjuśrī; Bronze Hall; Five Pagodas... | P. |
| **Luohousi** 羅睺寺 - Raqu-yin süme | Rāhu(la) Monastery | Northern Wei/ Tang | Tib. Buddhist (17th century) | 'Blooming lotus revealing the Buddhas'; statue of Mañjuśrī as White as Milk; Pine Tree Stūpa | P. |
| **Yuanzhaosi** 圓照寺 - Tegüs geyigülügci süme; Altan yanjuur süme | Perfect Radiance Monastery Golden *Kanjur* Monastery | 1309 | Tib. Buddhist (15th century) | Śāriputra's funerary *stūpa*; stele of the begging Mañjuśrī | P. |
| **Pusading** 菩薩頂 (Zhenrongyuan 真容院; Da Wenshusi 大文殊寺) - Bodisadua-yin orgil; Busading keyid | Bodhisattva Peak/ Bodhisattva's *Uṣṇīṣa* (Cloister of the True Countenance; Great Mañjuśrī Monastery) | 5th century/ Tang | Tib. Buddhist (15th century) | Residence of the *jasaġ lama*, Mañjuśrī with the Arrow, Water Dripping Hall | P. |

| Name | Date | Tradition | Notes | |
|---|---|---|---|---|
| Shuangyang 丁刀至 (Guangrensi 廣仁寺) - Arban jüg-ün duyang; Örüsiyel badarayuluyci süme / Ten Direction Hall (Vast Benevolence Monastery) | Shunzhi/1831 | Tib. Buddhist (branch of Luohousi) | Lodging center for Tibetan and Mongol lamas | P. |
| Wanfoge 萬佛閣 (Wuyemiao 五爺廟) - Tümen burqan-u asar, Qara luus-un qayan-u süme / Ten Thousand Buddha Pavilion (Fifth/Five Lord(s) Temple) | 1616 | Ch. Buddhist | Black Dragon King/Black Mañjuśrī and his four associates | P. |
| Guangzongsi 廣宗寺 - Itügen delgeregülügci süme, Otaci-yin süme / Ancestor Honor Monastery, Bhaiṣajyaguru Monastery | 1507 | Ch. Buddhist | Bronze Tile Hall | P. |

**Around Lingjiu Peak**

| Name | Date | Tradition | Notes | |
|---|---|---|---|---|
| Shuxiangsi 殊像寺 or 殊祥像 - Tuli terigütü Manzusiri / Mañjuśrī Image Monastery, Mañjuśrī with a Flour's Head | Tang/Yuan | Ch. Buddhist | Mañjuśrī with a Buckwheat Head; 'Bathing Mañjuśrī' | P. |
| Fanxianshan 梵仙山 (Lingyingsi 靈應寺) - Siditu süme; Dangsurung Peak / Brahman Immortal Mountain (Numinous Answer Monastery) | Ming or before | Ch. Buddhist | Chinese temple dedicated to a Fox spirit; terrace to throw 'wind-horse' papers | P. |
| Lingfengsi 靈峰寺 - Ling feng se süme / Numinous Peak Monastery | Tang | Ch. Buddhist | Ming dynasty relic pagoda | D.* |
| Wenshusi 文殊寺 (Guang'ansi 廣安寺) - Manzusiri-yin süme / Mañjuśrī Monastery | 18th century | Tib. Buddhist (Qianlong) | | P. |
| Puhuasi 普化寺 (Yuhuangmiao 玉皇廟) - Bükün-i gegeregülügci süme / Universal Transformation/Conversion Monastery (Jade Emperor Temple) | Ming | Tib. Buddhist (ca 1872) | | P. |

| Monastery's name in Chinese and Mongolian | English name | Date of foundation/refoundation | Affiliation in the late Qing period (date) | Main sights and 'numinous traces' | Present state |
|---|---|---|---|---|---|
| Shancaidong 善財洞 - Šuddana-yin ayui; Manibadara-yin süme | Sudhana Cave | Ming | Tib. Buddhist (Qianlong) | Rölpé Dorjé's meditation cave; sacred spring | P. |
| Dailuoding 黛螺頂 (Daluoding 大螺頂) - Qara labai-yin orgil | Black Conch Peak (Great Conch Peak) | Tang or Ming | Ch. Buddhist | Sandalwood Buddha; Five Mañjuśrīs; sacred pine trees | P. |
| Santasi 三塔寺 - Turban suburγan-u süme Noγuγan dhar-a eke-yin süme | Three Stūpa Monastery Green Tārā Monastery | Ming Wanli period | Tib. Buddhist (Qing) | Three stūpas | D./R. |
| Sanquansi 三泉寺 - Turban bulaγ-un süme | Three Spring Monastery | Yuan | Tib. Buddhist (18th century) | Three springs | P. |
| Shouningsi 壽寧寺 - Nasun öljei batudqaqu süme; Ebügen Manzusiri | Everlasting Tranquility Monastery Everlasting Tranquility Monastery Old Mañjuśrī | 6th century/1007 | Tib. Buddhist (13th century) | Relics of the Third Prince, statue of Old Mañjuśrī | P. |
| Cifusi 慈福寺 - Buyan ibegegci süme; Asaraltu buyantu süme | Merciful Blessings Monastery | 1814 | Tib. Buddhist | Lodging center for Tibetan and Mongol lamas | P. |

### South and southwest of Taihuai

| Qixiansi 棲賢寺 - Merged orusiγci süme; | Respite the Worthy Monastery | Yuan | Ch. Buddhist | Statue of Mañjuśrī on a cart pulled by an ox | D. |

| | | | | | |
|---|---|---|---|---|---|
| **Nanshansi** 南山寺 - Emünetü aγula-yin süme | Southern Mountain Monastery | 1295-1297 | Ch. Buddhist | 108 stairs, relic *stūpa* of Monk Puji | P. |
| Guanyindong 觀音洞 - Qomsim bodisadua-yin aγui; Aryabalu-yin aγui-yin süme | Avalokiteśvara Cave | 18th century | Tib. Buddhist | Sixth Dalai Lama's cave; sacred spring | P. |
| Wenshudong 文殊洞 | Mañjuśrī Cave | | Ch. Buddhist | Giant tree in the shape of a pipal | P. |
| Tiewasi 鐵瓦寺 - Temür degebürtü süme | Iron Tile Monastery | Yuan | Tib. Buddhist (18th century) | | D. |
| Wanfodong 萬佛洞 - Tümen burqantu aγui | Ten thousand Buddha Cave | Tang/Yuan | Ch. Buddhist | Cave; relic *stūpa* | P. |
| Zhenhaisi 鎮海寺 - Luus-i daruγsan süme; Jangya gegeen-ü suburγa | Subduing the Ocean Monastery / Monastery that Subdues the Water Spirit(s) / *Stūpa* of the Changkya Khutugtu | Late Ming | Tib. Buddhist (1710) | Relic *stūpa* of Rölpé Dorjé, two sacred trees | P. |
| Mingyuechi 明月池(Guanhaisi 觀海寺) - Tungγalaγ saran naγur (Dalai barilaγci süme) | Bright Moon Pool, (Contemplating the Ocean Monastery) | Northern Wei/ Ming | Ch. Buddhist | Fierce black statue of Mañjuśrī with nine heads and eighteen arms; sacred spring | P. |
| Puansi 普安寺/普庵寺 | Universal Peace/Hermitage Monastery | Northern Wei | Tib. Buddhist (Qing) | | D. |
| Baiyunsi 白雲寺 - Caγan egülen süme | White Cloud Monastery | (Tang?) Kangxi | Ch. Buddhist | Imperial traveling lodge | D./R. |

| Monastery's name in Chinese and Mongolian | English name | Date of foundation/refoundation | Affiliation in the late Qing period (date) | Main sights and 'numinous traces' | Present state |
|---|---|---|---|---|---|
| Fomudong 佛母洞 (Qianfodong 千佛洞) | Mother of Buddha Cave (Thousand Buddha Cave) | 16th century? | Ch. Buddhist | Womb-cave | D./R. |
| Eke-yin umai | Mother's Womb | | | | |
| Linyutang 淋浴堂 | Wash Monastery | Qing | Destroyed | Pilgrims took a bath in the river | D. |
| Rizhaosi 日照寺 | | Northern Qin | Ch. Buddhist | Belonged to Nanshansi | D. |
| Jingesi 金閣寺 - Altan qarsitu süme | Golden Pavilion Monastery | 766–767/1555 | Ch. Buddhist | Statue of thousand-armed Avalokiteśvara | P. |
| Qingliangsi/shi 清涼寺/石 - Ariyun serigün süme | Clear and Cool Monastery/Stone | 472–473 | Ch. Buddhist | Giant stone called Mañjuśrī's bed, 10 caves | D./R. |

**North and Northwest of Taihuai**

| Monastery's name in Chinese and Mongolian | English name | Date of foundation/refoundation | Affiliation in the late Qing period (date) | Main sights and 'numinous traces' | Present state |
|---|---|---|---|---|---|
| Guanghuasi 廣化寺 - Yeke nigülesküi süme | Vast Compassion Monastery | (Northern Wei)1822 | Tib. Buddhist (1822) | Sixteen stone statues of *arhat*; *dhāraṇī* pillars, *stūpas*, pine tree planted by the First Changkya | P. |
| Pushousi 普壽寺 - Tügemel öljei süme | Universal Longevity Monastery | 1202 | Tib. Buddhist (Guangxu) | Offered to the Thirteenth Dalai Lama in 1908 | D./R. |
| Qifosi 七佛寺 - Doluyan burqan-u süme | Seven Buddha [of the Past] Monastery | 1180 | Tib. Buddhist (1734?) | Icon of Vajrapāṇi; *dhāraṇī* pillars, pagoda | P. |

| Name | Translation | Date | Affiliation | Relics / Notes | Status |
|------|-------------|------|-------------|----------------|--------|
| Jifusi 集福寺 (Hongquansi 洪泉寺) - Buyan quriyayci süme (Rasiyan bulaγ-un süme) | Accumulated Blessings Monastery (Vast Spring Monastery) | Guangxu reign | Tib. Buddhist | | P. |
| Bishansi 碧山寺 (Puji(chan)si 普濟禪寺) - Kökimdüg aγula-yin süme (Bükün-i tedkügci süme); Bilig baramid-un süme | Azured Mountain Monastery (Universal Salvation Monastery) Prajñāpāramitā Monastery | Northern Wei | Ch. Buddhist | Ordination center for Chinese monks | P. |
| Puensi 普恩寺 (Xitiansi 西天寺) - Si tiyan se | Universal Benefaction Monastery (Western Heaven [India] Monastery) | Yuan | Tib. Buddhist (Yuan or 15th century) | Relic stūpa of Pakpa Lama | D.* |
| Baohuasi 寶華寺 (Zahuasi 雜花寺) - Erdeni-yin süme | Precious Flower Monastery | 849 | Tib. Buddhist (1711) | 'Stūpa that came flying' enshrining a lock of hair of Tsongkhapa; sacred spring; Avalokiteśvara statue that pours water | D.* – R. |
| Jingangku 金剛窟 (Boresi 般若寺) - Vcir-un aγui | Vajra Cave (Prajña Monastery) | 767 | Tib. Buddhist (early 18th century?) | Cave where Buddhapāli disappeared in 683; Mañjuśrī's tooth and handprint | D./R. |
| Puleyuan 普樂院 - Olan-i bayasqayci süme | Universal Joy Cloister | Tang/1765 or 1766-1769 | Tib. Buddhist | Sacred spring, residence of Rölpé Dorjé | D. |
| Wulangmiao 五郎廟, Taiping Xingguosi 太平興國寺 - U lang-un süme | Wulang Temple Great Peace and Prosperity of the State Monastery | 982 | Tib. Buddhist (18th century?) | Mummy and iron stick of Wulang; sacred tree | D./R. |

| Monastery's name in Chinese and Mongolian | English name | Date of foundation/refoundation | Affiliation in the late Qing period (date) | Main sights and 'numinous traces' | Present state |
|---|---|---|---|---|---|
| **Towards the terraces** | | | | | |
| Eastern Terrace – Wanghaisi 望海寺 | Viewing the Ocean Monastery | Northern Wei | - | Nārāyaṇa Cave (Ch. Naluoyanku 那羅延窟; Douli 斗笠 Stupa; Guanlaishi 觀來石; Zaolinpo 棗林坡 (Slope of the Jujube Tree Forest) | D./R. |
| Northern Terrace – Lingyingsi 靈應寺 | Numinous Answer Monastery | Northern Wei | - | Heilonggong 黑龍宮 (Palace of the Black Dragon) with Heilongchi 黑龍池 (Black Dragon Pool); relic *stupa* of Tang dynasty Master Yinfeng 隱峰; Baishuichi 白水池 (White Water Pond) | D./R. |
| Central Terrace – Yanjiaosi 演教寺 | Teaching Monastery | Northern Wei | - | *Stupa* of an Indian monk; Taihuaquan 太花泉 (Great Floriate Spring); Taihuachi 太花池 (Great Floriate Pond); Wenshu fatai 文殊法臺 (Terrace where Mañjuśrī Preached the Dharma); Wannianbing 萬年冰 (Ice of Myriad Years [that] never melts); Qixiandong 七仙洞 (Seven Immortals Cave) | D./R. |
| Western Terrace – Faleisi 法雷寺 | Thunder of Dharma Monastery | Northern Wei | - | Print of Mañjuśrī's lion claws, Niuxinshi 牛心石 (Oxen's Heart Stone); Bagongdeshui 八功德水 (Eight [Extraordinary] Merits Water); Wenshu xibochi 文殊洗鉢池 (Pond where Mañjuśrī Washed his Bowl); Ersheng duitanshi 二聖對談石 (Stone where Two Saints Discussed) | D./R. |

| Southern Terrace – Pujisi 普濟寺 | Universal Salvation Monastery | Northern Wei | - | Samantabhadra *stūpa*; Bailongchi 白龍池 (White Dragon Pool); Chajianling 插箭嶺 (Escarpment with the Sticked Arrow) | D./R. |
|---|---|---|---|---|---|
| **Yuhuachi** 玉花池 (Wanshoushan 萬壽山) - Qas cecegtü keyid (Tümen öljeitü süme), Tabun jaγun bandida | Jade Flower Pool (Ten Thousand Longevity Mountain) / Five Hundred Pandits | 7th century/770 | Tib. Buddhist (17th century?) | Stone pond of 500 foreign monks, 350 iron statues of *arhats*, Chaoyangdong 朝楊洞 Cave | D./R. |
| Zaoyuchi 澡浴池 | Bathing Pool | 1729 | Ch. Buddhist | Pond; footprints of Mañjuśrī | D./R. |
| Qingliangqiao 清涼橋 (Jixiangsi 吉祥寺) - Öljei orusiγci süme | Clear and Cool Bridge (Auspicious Monastery) | Northern Wei | Ch. Buddhist | Mañjuśrī holding a red lantern | D. |
| Fenglinsi 楓林寺 - Batucaγan süme | Maple Tree Grove Monastery / Strong White Monastery | Ming | Ch. Buddhist | Relic *stūpa* of Chetian 徹天 Heshang | D./R. |
| **Longquansi** 龍泉寺 (Jiulonggang 九龍崗) - Luus-un süme | Dragon Spring Monastery / Monastery of the Dragons | Northern Song | Ch. Buddhist | Funerary *stūpas* of Monks Puji and Xiujing Wengong; spring, 108 stairs | P. |
| Zhulinsi 竹林寺 - Qulusutu-yin süme | Bamboo Grove Monastery | 771-805/Ming | Ch. Buddhist | Ancient 'manifestation monastery'; octagonal pagoda | D.* – R. |
| Shiziwo 獅子窩 - Arslangtu-yin orun | Lions' Lair | 1586 | Ch. Buddhist | 35 m. tall octagonal pagoda (1599-1604) | P.* |
| Jindengsi 金燈寺 - Altan jula-tu süme | Golden Lantern Monastery | Yuan | Ch. Buddhist | | D. |

| Monastery's name in Chinese and Mongolian | English name | Date of foundation/refoundation | Affiliation in the late Qing period (date) | Main sights and 'numinous traces' | Present state |
|---|---|---|---|---|---|
| **Outside the terraces** | | | | | |
| Tailusi 台麓寺 - Tai lu se süme | Terrace Foothill Monastery | 17th century | Tib. Buddhist | Residence of the *da lama*; cliff carved of characters said to be 'natural' (Tailuziyai 台麓字崖 or Xieziyan 寫字岩), cave, imperial stele | D. |
| Yongquansi 湧泉寺 (Folinsi 佛林寺, Zaoyuchi 澡浴池) | Monastery of the Spring that Gushes Out (Buddha Grove Monastery) | 1683 | Tib. Buddhist | Sacred spring where pilgrims used to bath; residence of the third *da lama*, imperial steles | D. |
| Gufosi 古佛寺 - Erten-ü burqan-u süme | Old Buddha Monastery | Ming | Ch. Buddhist | Clay Buddha statue | P. |
| Mimoyan 秘魔岩 (in Fanzhi County) | Secret Magic Monastery/ Escarpment | Tang | Ch. Buddhist | Dragon Cave and 9 other caves; sacred spring, relic *stūpa*; inscriptions on a cliff | P. |

# A Study of the Mongolian Stone Inscriptions of Wutaishan

### Comparison of the Chinese and Mongolian Stone Inscriptions

The most ancient and venerable Chinese steles, and first of all the imperial ones, stand in front of the main halls, while Mongolian steles are usually relegated to back court-yards (Xiantongsi, Tayuansi). However, some imposing Mongolian steles stand in a po-sition symmetric to Chinese inscriptions in front of the Buddha hall: for instance, in the first courtyard of Dailuoding, the bilingual Mongolian-Chinese stele (Chinese at the back) recording an important Mongol donation in 1691 stands parallel to a Chinese stele dated Wanli 20 (1592). The same can be said of inscriptions at Yuanzhaosi (YZ4, 1898), Shouningsi (SN1, ca. 1664) and Pusading (PSD1, 1936).

The corpus of Chinese steles includes imperial inscriptions and non-imperial in-scriptions written by the monasteries' abbots or by groups of donors. The majority of the Qing imperial inscriptions were carved in the Kangxi period to record ostentatious religious patronage on the occasion of an emperor's visit. Kangxi wrote twenty inscrip-tions, and Qianlong, eleven. While steles are usually written to be read and inform the visitor of the generosity of the patrons, large imperial Chinese steles are often too big to be legible, for instance, the 1786 four-language imperial stele of Pusading is 4.8 me-ters high. Chinese steles were continuously erected from the Yuan to the Republican period, [1] with peaks during the Wanli and Kangxi periods and the Republican period. The two Chinese monasteries with the largest number of Chinese steles are Tayuansi and Nanshansi (Table 1). The twenty Chinese steles of Nanshansi recording donations from 1885 to 1935 reflect the great popularity of Puji's school among the Chinese.

### Stone Inscriptions: A Chinese Tradition?

The Wutaishan Mongolian steles are referred to in their own texts as *khöshiye chuluu*, 'funerary monument, commemorative inscription,' a term that also designates 'a tomb-stone, a border stone':[2] the etymology points to a possible funerary origin and to the

---

1   See the Yuan-dynasty steles of Shouningsi, Jilesi/Nanshansi and Tayuansi.

2   *Chuluu* means 'stone'; *khöshiye* is a monument, a stele, a tombstone; but also a tumulus, a burial place, a tomb. The following terms are also found in the Wutaishan inscriptions to designate a stele: *pailuur* (from Chinese *pailou* 牌樓, 'ceremonial archway'), *pailuur chuluu* or *khöshiye chuluun-u pailuur*: (stone) 'stele, ceremonial archway, and portal'; *temdeg pailuur*,

act of recording something by marking the soil with a lasting monument.[3] The steles' 'head' (*manglai*, 'forehead') often expresses in Mongolian or in Chinese the wish that it may last forever.[4]

In many locations throughout the Mongol and Yuan empires, the Mongol emperors erected steles placed on the back of a stone tortoise commemorating historical events, a tradition which was continued by rulers and monastic communities on a much smaller scale in the following centuries.[5] In addition, steles erected by former dynasties, such as the Turkic inscriptions of the Orkhon Valley, are still standing today in the Mongol steppe. Qing-dynasty Mongol donors occasionally carved their name, if not on steles,[6] then on the *stūpas* they paid for, such as those bordering the Gandantegchilen Monastery of Urga to the north and west and upon Erdeni Juu's fortified wall. The Mongols were not unfamiliar with stone inscriptions; however (contrarily to Chinese, who systematically erect a stele when founding or restoring a temple), they never used this medium on a large scale in Mongolia, and scholars usually do not count stone as a major medium for writing in Mongol culture.

On Wutaishan, Mongols adopted the Chinese religious custom of erecting stone inscriptions to make the donors' activities known to all visitors; however, no Mongolian inscription has been found on bells or on incense burners, while this is common practice in the monasteries of Mongolia.[7] The largest Mongolian donation steles of Wutaishan, topped with dragons and standing on a tortoise, use the same codes as the Chinese imperial steles and sometimes stand parallel to a Chinese inscription.

---

*batu temdeg pailuur*: 'monument, stone inscription' (lit. 'stele-certificate, stele as a firm mark'); *tsamkhag*: 'tower, turret, bastion, stronghold.'

3   Other modern Mongolian terms for steles include *bichig-tu khöshiye* ('monument having an inscription'), *temdeg chuluu* ('mark-stone'), and *chuluun nom* ('stone book'). Present-day Mongols place unwritten stones, also called *temdeg chuluu*, to remember the location where their dead are set down in the open steppe to be eaten by animals and birds (Delaplace 2009: 100, Fig. 16; 134).

4   *Möngke kösiy-e cilayu*, or *möngke pailuur cilayu*, 'eternal stone inscription'; *mingyan yalb[yalab]-un kösiy-e*, 'stone inscription of [which will last] a thousand *kalpas*' (SF156, 1930); and occasionally in Chinese, *qianwan gu liu fang* 千萬古流芳, 'which would endure forever' (SF144, 1927), or *wan gu* 萬古, 'ten thousand old.'

5   See, for instance, the so-called stele of Chinggis Khan (1225), the stele of Möngkhe Khan (1257, with Chinese inscriptions, Khövsgöl Province), the stele of Tsogtu Taiji (1624, Töv Province) (*History and Culture of the Mongols* 2006: 260-263), the Mongolian and Chinese stele of Huayansi, forty kilometers east of Höhhot (1581), the stele of Olan Süme (Inner Mongolia) dated 1594, etc.

6   See the 1929 stele commemorating the transportation to Urga of a complete set of the *Tanjur* (*History and Culture of the Mongols* 2006: 260-262; Wallace 2009: 90-91).

7   Incense burners of Erdeni Juu, Choijin Lama-yin Süme and Gandan in Khalkha Mongolia, of Yekhe Juu and Shireetü Juu (Höhhot) in Inner Mongolia.

### *Typology of Mongolian Stone Inscriptions*

The Mongolian steles can be placed into three categories according to their physical characteristics (Fig. 57):

- Category A includes seventeen more refined and/or larger steles with a head, lateral decorations and sometimes a prayer in Tibetan or in Lantsa script.[8] Some stand on a tortoise and the head is decorated with dragons, imitating imperial inscriptions. Recording the largest donations, they are located in front courtyards and along the circuit of circumambulation around the Great White Stūpa. The stele of Yuanzhaosi (YZ4, 1898) in front of the great Buddha hall, is embedded in a roofed brick structure standing on a tortoise (Fig. 57); it measures 126 × 61 centimeters plus a head with dragons (20 × 14 centimeters), inscribed with the Chinese words *gongde bei* 功德碑, "stele of merit." Different stones were used for these steles; sometimes the script is too small and the carving is not deep enough, making the text difficult to read.

- Category B includes nineteen small or medium-sized steles without decoration, not even a head for most of them. Many were carved on a poor-quality white stone, so, although they sometimes record important donations, they are often completely or partially illegible.

- The great majority of steles (Category C) are embedded in a low wall, a balustrade or in a special place inside three monasteries: Shifangtang, Luohousi and Tayuansi. The steles of Shifangtang are all of the same size: 60 × 36 centimeters (except for a larger one, SF124, east of the Mani Hall, which measures 90 × 42); they are embedded in balustrades surrounding the Mani Hall and the Buddha hall, as well as in the lower part of the Buddha hall. In Luohousi, twenty-eight steles (also measuring 60 × 36) are embedded in a screen-wall in the Stūpa Courtyard. In Tayuansi, forty-eight steles are embedded in the low wall bordering the Great White Stūpa to the north.[9] Other thin steles of various sizes sit against walls in Luohousi, Xiantongsi and Yuanzhaosi: they seem to have been removed from a screen-wall or a wall; many of them are broken. These steles of Category C are easy to decipher, firstly because their location preserved them from degradation, and secondly because in most cases the white stone is covered with a black revetment: it is not the stone itself but the coating that is carved, and the white script therefore stands out against the black background. Unfortunately, the coating often disintegrates in the lower part of the stele, and the script disappears with it.

---

8 There are three in Tayuansi, two in Luohousi, one in Pusading, two in Xiantongsi, one in Lower Shancaidong, one in Dailuoding, four in Cifusi, one in Yuanzhaosi and two in Shouningsi. See the abstracts of some of their texts in Online Appendix A2.

9 The fact that all the steles are of the same size indicates that they were carved to fit in the screen-wall; however, one is cut into two pieces to fill the space.

FIGURE 56        *Three examples of steles showing marks of veneration: 1) in Guanyindong; 2)*
                 *same stele in Guanyindong, three years later; 3) in Shifangtang.*
                 © ISABELLE CHARLEUX, 2009.

FIGURE 57        *Examples of Type A (YZ4, 1898 and stele in Lantsa, Tibetan and Mongolian in*
                 *front of the stūpa of Luohousi).* © ISABELLE CHARLEUX, 2010.

Great variations are observed in height and width; for instance, steles of Category A range from 60 × 36 to 170 × 73 centimeters (without the head and tortoise); steles of Category B have different sizes, between 130 × 59 and 160 × 75. As a comparison, the largest stele of Wutaishan is the four-language square inscription written by Emperor Qianlong in 1786 and located in the east wing of Pusading: it measures 4.80 meters in height.

### The Polyglot Stone Inscriptions[10]

Except for a few multilingual imperial inscriptions (three in Pusading, one in Xiantongsi), the multilingual inscriptions of Wutaishan were carved to record Mongols' donations. Of the twenty-three multilingual inscriptions I found, twelve belong to Category A and record particularly remarkable donations (Table 9).[11] The various languages are written on the same face or on the two faces of the stele. Three steles are written in Mongolian, Tibetan and Chinese on the same face; these are located in Tayuansi (TY7 and TY9, on the north side of the Great White Stūpa's pedestal, Fig. 1) and in Shifangtang. Two have the *mantras* of Avalokiteśvara and Mañjuśrī (*Oṃ maṇi padme huṃ!* and *Arapacana*) written in Lantsa, Tibetan and Mongolian on the head (LH1, LH2).

In bilingual Mongolian-Chinese inscriptions, the Chinese text is not a translation of the Mongolian one; in fact, it is often shorter. The vocabulary and formulas of the Chinese texts are modeled on the Chinese donations stele and thus give precise details on the context and the amount of the donation and the rituals that followed it. In contrast, the largest section of the Mongolian texts contains prayers and wishes. One of the reasons for these differences is that the Chinese texts were often written and signed by the Chinese abbot of the monastery, who wanted to record the material aspect of the donation, while the Mongolian texts were written following Mongol patterns. For instance, in stele TY1, dated 1853, the Mongolian text starts with a prayer to Holy Khutugtu Mañjuśrī, followed by the full title, name and origin of the donor offering 300 taels to buy land for the monastery. On the other hand, the 'corresponding' Chinese text is modeled on Chinese donation steles: it begins with a series of questions ("What makes the spirit/the gods powerful? They are powerful thanks to sincerity. How can sincerity be communicated? It can be communicated thanks to material offerings."),[12] followed by an explanation of how the *bodhisattva* Mañjuśrī stored relics

---

10  Among the 'Mongolian steles,' I counted polyglot steles recording Mongols' donations, but I did not count the imperial steles.

11  In Table 9 only the steles where all scripts are more or less of an equal length are listed, but many other steles are written in Mongolian with a Chinese head (such as *gongde bei*, 'stele of merit') and/or a Chinese date at the end of the text or on the back side, or with a head in Lantsa (used for *dhāranīs*) and/or Tibetan (*Oṃ maṇi padme huṃ!*).

12  *Shen he you er ling hu? Yi cheng ling er. Cheng he you er shu hu? Yi zi shu er* 神何由而靈乎。以誠靈耳。誠何由而輸乎。以資輸耳.

TABLE 9 *The twenty-three polyglot steles of Mongol donors (into brackets, script only on the 'head'; in bold, trilingual steles)*[a]

| | Monastery | Date | Languages | Category | Faces | Donation |
|---|---|---|---|---|---|---|
| LH1 | Luohousi | 1658 | **Lantsa, Tib., Mo.** | A | 2 faces | 30,000 taels |
| LH2 | Luohousi | 1659 | (Lantsa, Tib.) Mo. | A | 1 face | |
| DLD1 | Dailuoding | 1691 | Mo., Ch. | A | 2 faces | Construction of a pavilion |
| SX1 | Shuxiangsi | 1665 | (Lantsa, Tib) Mo., Ch. | B | 1 face | |
| SN1 | Shouningsi | Kangxi period | (Lantsa), Mo., Ch. | A | 2 faces | Restoration of Shouningsi |
| SN2 | Shouningsi | 1774 | Mo., Ch. | A | 1 face | 1,452 taels |
| LH3 | Luohousi | 1775 | Mo., Ch. | B | 1 face | |
| LH4 | Luohousi | 1829 | Mo., Ch. | - | | |
| LH5 | Luohousi | 1830 | Mo., Ch. | - | | |
| LH6 | Luohousi | 1831 | Mo., Ch. | - | | |
| TY1 | Tayuansi | 1853 | Mo., Ch. (1/3$^{rd}$ of the text) | B | 1 face | 300 taels |
| SF1 | Shifangtang | 1835 | **Mo., Tib., Ch.** | B | 1 face | |
| TY3 | Tayuansi | 1869-97 | (Tib.) Mo., Ch. | A | 1 face | 12,000 taels |
| BH2 | Baohuasi | 1873 | Tib. Mo. | B? | 2 faces | |
| TY7 | Tayuansi | 1887 | **Mo., Tib., Ch.** | A | 1 face | 500 taels etc. |
| TY9 | Tayuansi | 1894 | **Tib. (58 lines), Mo. (10 lines), Ch. (2 lines)** | B | 1 face | 1,800 taels etc. |
| SCD1 | Shancaidong | 1907 | Mo., Ch. (2 lines) | A | 2 faces | 10,000 taels |
| TY40 | Tayuansi | 1915 | Mo., Tib., Ch. (1 line) | A | 1 side (Ch. at the back) | 5,200 taels |
| XT1 | Xiantongsi | 1918 | Mo., Ch. | B | 1 face | 1,000 taels |
| SF149 | Shifangtang | 1928 | Tib., Mo. | C | 1 face | 200 yuan |
| CF6 | Cifusi | 1935 | Mo., Ch. | A | 2 faces | 1,315 yuan |
| PSD1 | Pusading | 1936 | Mo., Ch. | A | 2 faces | 8,800 taels |
| BH3 | Baohuasi | Republican period | Tib., Mo. | A | 2 faces | |

[a] LH4, LH5, and LH6 are listed in the *Catalogue of Ancient Mongolian Books and Documents of China* (1999) as being located around the *stūpa*. They were removed because they had become illegible.

in (the *stūpa* of) Tayuansi Monastery which emitted magical lights and that 'a prince' (*junwang*, without even mentioning his name or origin)—with an 'awakening mind' (*bodhicitta*) offered 300 taels as an 'eternal offering' to buy incense and lamps. So different was the Mongol style that the Mongolian text of stele TY3 even omits to mention the large sum of 10,000 taels, reported instead in the Chinese text.

In 1774, the monks of Shouningsi became concerned about the poor state of their monastery and organized a fundraiser: the Mongolian text of the stele records twenty-three donors, or groups of donors, mostly from Höhhot, Chakhar, eastern Inner Mongolia and Beijing. It is unclear whether they journeyed to Wutaishan or subscribed to an almsround organized by *ombo lama*s from Shouningsi traveling across Mongolia. The adjacent Chinese text mentions that "Mongol donors from the ten directions all gave offerings, precious things," and lists donations from twenty-one abbots and monks from Wutaishan Gélukpa monasteries.[13] The donations collected during the almsround range from 8 to 600 taels (total: 1,275 taels; average donation: 67 taels), while local abbots and monks offered smaller amounts, from 1 to 275 taels (total: 550 taels; average donation: 26 taels).

### *Mongolian Script, Language and Carving of the Stone Inscriptions*

The Mongolian script of the steles uses Inner Mongolian particularities:[14] contractions of words,[15] as well as of particles of grammatical functions such as particles of declension attached to base-words,[16] dialectal forms and phonetic renderings.[17] These particularities reflect Inner Mongolian writing habits, or the actual (Ordos or Chakhar) pronunciation, or both.[18] The cases often do not follow the usual forms.[19] The letters *y* and *j* are often non-differentiated. Occasionally we find *g* in words with velar vowels and *γ* in words with front vowels, and vowel harmony is not always respected. These orthographic irregularities are not 'mistakes,' given that, in the nineteenth century, spelling was not fully standardized and non-official documents were influenced by oral pronunciation and dialectal forms. The steles of Wutaishan thus represent a particular corpus for the study of the evolution of (Inner) Mongolian language in the Qing and Republican periods.

We know nothing about the carvers, but they may have been Chinese who reproduced in stone a text written by a Mongol without themselves knowing or hardly knowing the Mongolian alphabet, which (only occasionally) resulted in mistakes, omissions, aberrations and non-respect of vowel harmony. Similarly, the carvers of the

---

13    See Online Appendix A2: Shouningsi, SN2, 1774.

14    The mark of palatalization of *s* preceding *i* is marked with two dots: *ši. I* is not always carefully traced and often looks no different from *a* or *e* (like in *šijin* for *šajin/šasin*).

15    *Tabilang* for *tabin lang*, *jayulang* for *jayun lang*.

16    *Jisdu* for *jisa-du*, *jilun* for *jil-un*, *sarayin* for *sara-yin*, *γarun* for *γar-un*, *narun* for *nar-un*.

17    *Juryan* for *jiryuyan*, *cecin* for *cecen/secen*, *dungšuur* for *dungsiyur*, *ejin* for *ejen*, *qatan* for *qatun*...

18    On attempts to reconcile the written language with the spoken one: Kara 2005: 126-127.

19    *Burqan-yin* instead of *burqan-u*, for instance.

wooden printing blocks of the great number of eighteenth- and nineteenth-century Mongolian books published by the Beijing printing houses were Chinese.[20]

In most inscriptions, there are several lines which start above the rest of the text (*mör degdeekhü yosu*, 'line elevation'), marking respect towards *bodhisattva* Mañjuśrī, towards prayers directed to him, towards Wutaishan as well as towards the Qing emperor's reign title when giving the date. Several steles are difficult to read because their text is not written in homogeneous vertical lines (for instance, TY39, 1911): names and words are added between the lines; vertical lines are divided into two other lines and then join and merge into one line.

The frames present decoration of lotuses, floral and geometrical patterns, depictions of books (SF66, 1897), bamboo (SF54, 1896), parasols (SF59, 1896), Chinese-style men and women (SF95, 1907), the Eight Precious Things, i.e., the symbols of Chinese scholars (TY7, 1887; TY40, 1915), or flowers and other auspicious patterns (TY56, 1934).

### General Structure of the Inscriptions

The main donor listed in the stone inscriptions is referred to as 'supreme (or distinguished/respectable) alms-master' (*öglige-yin ejin* [*ejen*]). The 'alms-master,' translating Tib. *yöndak*, designates the layperson who supports the community of monks, which is referred to as 'offering site' (Tib. *chöné*, Mo. *takhil-un oron*)—but in the Wutaishan inscriptions the 'alms-masters' were often themselves members of the clergy. This relationship, whereby the patron provides material support and protection to the *sangha* (monk community), while the clergy is in charge of guiding living beings along the path to enlightenment through blessings, prayers, rituals and initiations, is a fundamental principle of Buddhist society usually known in Tibetan as *yönchö* or *chöyön* (contraction of *yöndak chöné*). In the *yönchö* relationship, the two are not on equal footing, for the donor is subordinated to the lama in the religious realm.[21] It is based on the 'economy of karmic merit,' by which deeds create merit that are accumulated and transferred to others. By supporting the monastic community, the lay patron also earns merit, securing a better rebirth for himself/herself. In turn, the monks, by purifying themselves in observing ethical precepts, achieving personal enlightenment and taking the *bodhisattva* as an ideal for the benefit of all, accumulate vast quantities of merit that can be transferred towards living or dead laypersons.[22]

As expected, the Mongol word for the Buddhist notion of 'merit,' *buyan* (< Skt. *punya*), is central in the texts of steles: the stone inscriptions use expressions such as

---

20    Kara 2005: 107.
21    Ruegg 1991 & Ruegg 1995. For the application of this relation to Mongol sovereignty: Sagaster 1976: 9-49; Elverskog 2006: 42 sq. For the economic aspects of this relationship: Miller 1961.
22    Miller 1961; Illich 2006: 182.

'capital of merit' (*buyan-u khöröngge*)[23] and verbs indicating growth, development and expansion: *delgere-*: 'to increase, expand, spread, develop, blossom'; *badara-*: 'to spread, expand, develop, blossom, become clear, manifest, public' (e.g., *shashin-i/nom-un üiles badaran delgere-*); *mandu-*: 'to rise, become higher, propagate, spread, prosper, develop'; *arbiji-, arbid-*: 'to grow in number, increase, accumulate'; *nemegde-*: 'to be added, to increase.' Merit is also 'harvested,' or 'collected,' i.e., accumulated (*buyan khuriya-*). As seen in Chapter 5, *buyan* also refers to mundane expectations, and formulas to beckon good fortune (*khei mori* and *buyan kheshig*), health, longevity (*nasun buyan*), reputation (*aldar*) and prosperity could be multiplied, such as: "as long as their chance, fate and glory rise higher up like the new moon,"[24] and "strengthen (ensure) ten thousand longevities under the feet of the holy master."[25]

Below I dissect the rhetorical structure of inscriptions in order to understand the pilgrims' expectations. Similar formulas and vocabularies are found in most of the stone inscriptions, especially those of Category C; a few texts are almost identical.[26] They generally follow the model below:

1. The head often reads "eternal stone inscription,"[27] "stone inscription of a thousand *kalpas*," in Mongolian or Chinese,[28] *gongde bei*, "stele of merit" in Chinese,[29] the name of the monastery in Tibetan,[30] formulas like "expand the rule of Buddhism,"[31] formulas of salutation (*om sain amugulang boltugai*), prayers (*namo Amituofo* 南無阿彌陀佛, "Homage to Amitābha," *Oṃ maṇi padme huṃ!*) or the date in Mongolian.

2. Some inscriptions start with a salutation, like in the colophons of scriptures and prayers: "Homage to the guru!"; "I pray to the saint savior Holy Mañjuśrī/powerful

---

23    *Khöröngge* means 'seeds, grain, yeast, ferment, origin; capital, property, estate, means, resources, funds.' It also has the connotation of 'sharing;' for instance, when one inherits of his/her father's property: this meaning comes from the ferments kept by Mongol families to produce fermented drinks. Ferments were transmitted generation after generation and therefore symbolized family continuity.

24    *Kii [kei] mori coy uciral anu sin-e sarayin metü degegside manduju delgeregser* (SF72, 1898). Similar expressions are: *coy jali kii mori aldar sineyin saran-u gerel metü ulam degegside mandun delgeregseger* (LH27, 1929); *nasun buyan ki mori coy uciral sin-e sarayin gerel metü manduju badaraysayar* (TY54, 1930).

25    *Tümen nasutu boydan ejen-ü ölmei dour-a batudqaju* (SF58, 1896).

26    SF77, 1899; SF78, 1899; SF78, 1899.

27    *Möngke kösiy-e cilayu; möngke cilayun pailuur; möngke kösiy-e bosqabai; möngke camqay bayiyulbai; möngke pailuur cilayu; möngke buyan-u pailuur.*

28    *Mingyan galab-un kösiy-e, qianshi bei* 千世碑 (SF156, 1930).

29    SF62, 1897; YZ4, 1898; SF102, 1910; SF103, 1910.

30    *Nub-phyogs kun-'dus gling*, i.e., Shifangtang (SF6, 1873; SF14, 1881).

31    *Sijin [šasin]-u törü badaraqu* (SF55, 1896).

victorious Mañjuśrī!";[32] "I pray to the Three Jewels";[33] or *manggalam* (< Skt. *mangalam*, 'blessing, good fortune, happiness').

3. Then comes the destination of the offerings—the monastery itself—which is praised as the center of Buddhist faith on Wutaishan: "in the eternal treasury[34] of the [name of the monastery] of Cold and Pure Wutai where the Dharma is propagated" (SCD1, 1907).[35] Wutaishan is named an "extremely marvelous central place of the pure doctrine."[36] Gélukpa Buddhism is referred to as the "religion of the second victorious Tsongkhapa,"[37] since Tsongkhapa is viewed as a second Buddha (SF55, 1894; also SF50, 1894). SF131 (1922) starts with: "Shifangtang (in) Wutai Cold and Pure, the pure land, where dwells the one [Mañjuśrī] who forgives with love, with a mind of immense compassion, all living beings as if each were his only son, surrounded by all the buddhas and *bodhisattvas*."[38] The thirteen monasteries of Amdo or the thirteen monasteries of Lhasa (Baruun Juu) are often cited in reference to Shifangtang, which was built by an Amdo monk and which maintained close relations with Amdo monasteries: "In the eternal assembly treasury of Shifangtang Monastery, which is the Eastern summary (of)[39] the thirteen monasteries of Amdo, established on the cold and pure mountain of Wutai, abode of Holy Mañjuśrī."[40] Thirteen (the center plus the twelve points of the

---

32    *Namu guru manzuširi* (SN2, 1774); *namu manzuširi-dur mörgümü* (SF148, 1928); *namu gürü qutuytu getülgegci boyda manzuširi-dur mörgümü* (LH25, 1922); *abural getülgegci boyda manzuširi-dur mörgümü* (SCD1, 1907); *erketü ilayuysan manzuširi* (SF183, Republican period).

33    *Degedü yurban erdeni-dür mörgümüi.*

34    In Mongol monasteries, the building housing the treasury is often called *möngkhe jisa.*

35    For instance: "In the treasury of eternal fields of Shifangtang that vastly expands the prospering Yellow Faith in the territory of Pure Wutai" (SF138, 1925: *Ariluysan u-tai-yin orun-a amuyulangtu sir-a-yin šašin* [*šasin*] *asuru delgeregülün bayiyuluysan ši vang tang keyid-ün möngke tariyalang-un sang-du* [...]). Another example: *abural getülgegci boyda manzuširi-yin orun-a serigün tungyalay utai šan ayula šašin nom-yin* [*-un*] *üiles-ün badaran delgereysen* [*delgeregsen*] *yeke yayiqamsiqtu* [name of the monastery] *möngke yajar tariyalang-un jisdu* [*jisa-du*] (YZ4, 1898).

36    *Ariluysan nom-un töb yajar asuru yayiqamsigtu u-tai oron.*

37    *Qoyaduyar ilayuysan boyda zongqab-a-yin šašin.*

38    *Ayuu yeke nigülesküi sedkil-iyar qamuy amitan-i yayca köbegün metü enerin örüšiyegci burqan bodisadu nar bükün-ece küriyelün orusiysan ariyun orun serigün tungyalay-a u-tai ši vang tang*; similar formula in SF132, 1922 and SF133, 1922.

39    *Quriyangyui* means "collection, abridgment, summary, sum, total, inclusive"; it probably means here that Shifangtang is seen as the Eastern counterpart of a group of thirteen monasteries of Amdo and of Lhasa.

40    *Boyda manzuširi orun u-tai-yin serigün tungyalay ayulan-a bayiyuluysan amdu-a arban yurban keyid-üd örün-e jüg-yin quriyangyui ši vang tang keyid-yin möngke qural-un jisadu* [*jisa-du*] (SF31, 1888); *öründü* [*örün-e-dü*] *jüg-ün barayun juu andu-a* [*amdu-a*] *arban*

compass) is probably here a symbolic figure (see the groups of thirteen *oboos* in Mongolia); thirteen is a number commonly found in Mongol practices and rituals.[41]

According to the stone inscriptions, the donations are made to the *jisa* (< Tib. *chisa*, "community property, corporate property, communal good"), the monastic treasury or finance office that managed agricultural land, buildings, livestock and storehouses for keeping food, cloth and so on, and that engaged in trade and money-lending. The *jisa* system permitted allocation of funds for specific purposes that were not immediately vital to the *sangha*, such as a ritual, maintenance of a temple, or participation in economic activities.[42] The *jisa* constituted a reserve allowing the *sangha* to become economically independent from the patrons.[43]

4. The text provides the name of the main donor, called *erkhim yekhe öglige-yin ejin* [*ejen*], and a list of other donors—monks or laypersons, with their names, kinship position and/or official rank within the clergy, nobility or administration—and region of origin. The donors are said to act 'out of sincere faith and reverence.'[44]

5. The names of the main donor's deceased relatives (*nasun-aca nögchigsen*) are included, sometimes simply replaced by 'father and mother' (*echige ekhe*).

6. The text records that the donors make a donation, in taels of silver in cash or the equivalent in head of cattle and sheep, to the treasury in order to buy arable land. They can also pay for a ritual to be held annually on a certain date.

7. Next, it is said that the donors 'erect' or 'carve a votive stone inscription' (*batu temdeg pailuur* or *khöshiye chuluu*) as a "firm symbol of eternal merit";[45] or "as an offering for future successors."[46]

8. The donors make general wishes to save all living beings and propagate Buddhism thanks to the "strength of pure and white merit" (*ariun chagan buyan-u khüchün-iyer*) stemming from these offerings and other meritorious actions (*sain üiles*). They wish to "deliver all mother-sentient beings from the ocean of *saṃsāra*"[47]; "for the sake

---

   *yurban keyid bükün-i tobcilin quriyaysan ši vang tang* (SF142, 1925). Similar formulas SF38, 1888; SF65, 1897; SF91, 1905; SF95, 1907.

41    Bawden 1985a.

42    Robert J. Miller (1959, 1961) has given a detailed study of the economy of Inner Mongol monasteries and especially of the '*jisa* mechanism.' See also Lkham Purevjav 2012.

43    Large Mongol monasteries had ten to twenty, fifty or up to a hundred *jisas*, because every monastic department had its own treasury: the main one was that of the main assembly hall, then came treasuries of faculties, of reincarnated lamas, of temples, and of particular rituals.

44    *Cing ünen süsüg bisirel-ün egüdece; cing ünekü süsüg bisirel-ün egüdece* [*egüden-ece*] *joriju.* On the use of *egüde*(*n*), lit. 'door,' to indicate the source of faith: Serruys 1977: 602, n. 159.

45    *Möngke buyan-u batu temdeg kösiy-e cilayun bayiyulba* ( SCD1, 1907).

46    *Qoyisi jalyamjilaju ergüy-e kemen batu pailuur bayiyulba* (SF8, 1880).

47    *Eke boluysan qamuy amitan-i orcilang-un dalai-aca getülgekü* (LH35, 1931).

of all mother-sentient beings of the six kinds,"[48] so that "the totality of the mother-sentient beings forever enjoy peace and happiness."[49] The 'mother-sentient beings' (lit. "all the sentient beings who have been mothers") translates the Tibetan *margyur sem-chen*: any sentient being may have been our mother in a previous life. Donors generate a feeling of gratitude for each sentient being, and then express the wish that all of them achieve happiness and avoid suffering. The 'six kinds' refer to the six realms of reincarnations in the realm of desire (*kāma-dhātu*): as a human, a god, an *asura* (jealous god), a *preta* (a hungry ghost), an animal or a suffering being in hell. Other formulas include "Thanks to the strength of the very white and pure merit, all the sins accumulated from immemorial times [lit. the time without beginning] [in] the *saṃsāra* of all the sentient beings are cleansed away. May all the births enjoy happiness and tranquility and avoid the sufferings of unfavorable destinies!"; "the supreme Yellow doctrine of liberation [will] emit light like ten thousand sunrays."[50]

9. The donors then wish to "especially pay back/return the favor of [the gift of birth given by their] father and mother, who deserve gratitude"[51]; pay back the 'beneficient holy lama' (*achitu bogda lama*, i.e., Mañjuśrī) or 'root-master lama' (*ündüsün bagshi lama*),[52] and re-direct merit thus accumulated towards "the benefit of those who are deceased and (all) sentient beings."[53] They wish that, through the accumulated merit, the obstacles on their way to liberation or to a better reincarnation are erased, that "the obstacles inside and outside the supreme donors who support and propagate the doctrine are pacified."[54] The following sentence expresses the wish that their vows be fulfilled: "This being done, thanks to the strength of the white and pure merit [thus accumulated], (may) all those wishes be accomplished according to my will."[55]

---

48   *Eke boluysan jiryuyan jüil qamuy amitan-u tusadur [tusa-dur] joriju* (LH22, 1920).

49   *Eke qamuy amitan bükün-e amuyulang jiryalang egüride edleged* (SCD1, 1907).

50   *Ariyun cayan buyan-u kücün-iyer aliba amitan bükün-ü orcilang terigülsi ügei cay-aca quriyaysan nigül kilince-yi cöm arilyayad törül büküi mayu jayayan-u joblang-yi ulu abun amuyulang jiryalang-i edlegsügei* (SF138, 1923); *abural degedü šir-a-yin šašin bum naran-u gerel metü sacurayad* (LH25, 1922).

51   *Ilangyuy-a acitu ecige eke-yin aci qariyulqu* (SF72, 1898).

52   SF39, 1888; SF71, 1898; SF96, 1907; SF174, 1931.

53   *Nasun-aca nögsigsen-ün tuqai kiged amitan-u tusa-dur joriyulun* [...] (SF64, 1897).

54   *Šasin-i delgeregülün tedkci erkim öglige-yin ejed-tei-ü yadayadu dotuyadu-yin qarsi nögcil ciqula amurliyad* (SF51, 1894; SF93, 1906). Also: *buyan-u kücün-iyer erkim öglige-yin ejen tan-u aliba qarsi nögcil büküd ciqula amurliyad jokilduqu-yin nögcil nasun buyan ki mori coy uciral sin-e sarayin gerel metü manduju badaraysayar* (LH22, 1920); *ene metü üiled-degsen [üileddügsen] buyan kücün-iyer qarsi nögcil ciqula amurliyad jokilduqui-yin nögcil bolju aliba sanaysan üiles sedkilcilen bütüged* (SF66, 1897).

55   *Ene metü egüdesen ariyun cayan buyan-u kücün-iyer sanaysan aliba üiles bükün sedkicilen bütüjü* (SF72, 1898). While at first only the main donor was called *öglige-yin ejen*, the donors now appear as a collective (*öglige-yin ejed*) in the last part of the inscriptions.

10. The last wish found in most inscriptions is to be reborn at the golden feet of the *bodhisattva* Mañjuśrī, whose name starts on a new line and is elevated as a mark of respect: "May [we] be reborn inseparably under the lotus of the enlightened feet of the holy lama Mañjuśrī and obtain the sanctity of Buddha,"[56] or "the sanctity of Vajradhara."[57] *Ölmei* is the honorific for 'feet'; *lingkhua* (or *liangkhua, liankhua*, < Ch. *lianhua* 蓮花) designates the lotus where the buddhas stand.[58] This expression translates the Tibetan honorific expression *zhappé*, "a lotus below the foot."[59] Donors also wish to be reborn at the feet of Tsongkhapa.[60] These wishes can be extended to descendants and future reincarnations.

We also find the following expression: "We worship the Holy Savior Mañjuśrī. May we obtain the path to enlightenment following the brilliant religion of Holy Tsongkhapa."[61] *Bodi mör* translates Tibetan *lamrim*, "stages of the path to enlightenment," here referring to Tsongkhapa's teachings and major work, the *Lamrim chenmo*. Mañjuśrī is generally invoked as 'savior'—by the late sixth century, the *bodhisattva* of Wutaishan was already prayed to as a savior whose aid was particularly to be invoked in times of 'decline of the Law.' But he is also called 'holy lama' or 'supreme lama,' which is quite unusual for a *bodhisattva*.[62]

---

56    *Boyda blam-a manzuširi-yin gegegen-e ölmei lingqu-a dour-a qayacal ügei dayan töröjü burqan-u qutuy-i olqu boltuyai* (YZ4, 1898); *boyda manzuširi-yin altan ölmei-e dour-a darui türgen-e burqan-u qutuy-i olqu boltuyai* (SF89, 1905); *boyda manzuširi-yin gegegen-lüg-e qayacal ügei töröged ecüs-dür burqan-u qutuy olqu boltuyai*); "may we pray continuously to the golden holiness of Saint Mañjuśrī [etc.]" (*boyda manzuširi-yin altan gegen-e ürgüljide mörgügseger burqan-u qutuy türgen-e olqu boltuyai*, SF72, 1898).

57    *Vacir dar-a-yin qutuy-i darui törgen-e olqu minu boltuyai* (SF70, 1898; SF71, 1898; SF106, 1916; SF108, 1916; SF109, 1916; LH45, 1935). On Vajradhara in relation to Mañjuśrī: Davidson 1981: 18: n. 52. In the *Mañjuśrīnāmasaṃgīti*, Vajradhara/ Vajrapāṇi asks Śākyamuni to learn the litany of names of Mañjuśrī.

58    For instance *degedü manjuširi-yin ölmei-yin linqu-a* [*sic*]-*yin toyusun-dur sitüjü*: "relying on the dust of the lotus of the feet of the supreme Manjushri" (Rintchen 1964: 15, no.1213).

59    Serruys 1977: 585, n. 40.

60    *Boyda blam-a zongyab-a-yin gegegen ba abural getülgegci boyda manzuširi-yin gegegen-u altan ölmei liangqu-a-u* [-*yin*] *dour-a örgülji mörgügseger dayan töröku boltuyai* (SF38, 1888).

61    *Getülgegci boyda manzuširi-du mörgüged boyda zongkaba-yin gegen šasin-i dayan bodi mör-yi olqu boltuyai* (SF65, 1897; also SF13, 1881; SF50, 1894; SF130, 1922).

62    *Boyda blam-a manzusiri* (SF31, 1888; SF46, 1890; SF52, 1894; SF59, 1896 etc.); *degedü blam-a manzusiri* (SF2, 1862). In the inscription of the Cifusi map, Mañjuśrī is also called 'supreme lama.' In Tibetan Buddhism, a meditant for whom the master has the nature of a buddha, and thus can be indistinguishable from a buddha or a great *bodhisattva*, could call Mañjuśrī a 'lama'; on the other hand, a *bodhisattva* can be called 'lama' when he gives

The patrons may also express the wish that their deceased relatives immediately reach the kingdom of Shambhala[63] or the Pure Land Sukhāvatī:[64] "By the strength or the highest, pure-white merit stemming from these deeds, may all the mother-sentient beings of the six realms enjoy peace and happiness, be freed from sin and suffering and, besides being reborn in paradise, find holiness."[65]

11. The last sentence in the steles gives the date of the inscription, referring to the Manchu era or to the Mongol calendar, such as "Made on a holy day, the 15th of the seventh month of the 33rd year of Guangxu"[66]; "On a good auspicious day of the middle month of spring, in the year of the White Male Monkey."[67] The Mongol denomination of years follows cycles of sixty years: the year of the White Male Monkey, for instance, can be 1800, 1860 or 1920; but there is generally no ambiguity because the date of the stele or of the preceding or following steles is often added in Chinese.

teachings. But the expression 'supreme lama Mañjuśrī' has no equivalent in Tibetan (I thank Françoise Wang-Toutain for these remarks).

63   *Šambala-yin orun kürcü* (TY59, s.d.; TY32 and TY33, 1910).

64   Suhvati (PSD1, 1936); Divaajang (written Davajin, Devejing: YZ4, 1898; TY33, 1910), < Tib. Dewachen.

65   *Ene metü üileddegsen [üileddügsen] degedü ariyun cayan buyan-u kücün-iyer eke boluysan jiryuyan jüil qamuy amitan amuyulang jiryalang-i edlejü. jobalang nigül arilaju. devejing-du törükü-ece yadan-a qutuy-yi olqu [boltuyai]* (YZ4, 1898).

66   *Badarayultu törü-yin yucin yurbaduyar on doluyan sarayin [sar-a-yin] arban tabun-a sayin edür bayiyulba* (SCD1, 1907). *Sayin edür* is Tib. *düzang.*

67   *Cayan becin jilun [jil-un] qaburun [qabur-un] dumdadu sarayin öljeitü sayin edür-e* (LH22, 1920). On calendars and time-reckoning in Qing-dynasty Mongolia: Baumann 2008: Chapter 4; Atwood 2002: Appendix E.

# Khorchin Song "Utai-yin jam"[1]

Sung by Shilj, recorded by Nachin (Nacinšongqur and Türgenbayar, eds. 1990: 778-784)

*degegesi-ban macuqu degter jam*
*debajan-dur orusiqu utai-yin jam :*

*doγuγsi-ban γulγuqu dosuγur jam*
*tunuju degdekü toγuruutu-yin jam :*

*uruγu baγubal aγulan jam*
*usutu-yin dabaγ-a ceng siye ling :*

*ögede qarabal egülen jam*
*önggeyim-e qadatu γuvan yün düng :*

*oriγaju muskiralduqu oγtarγui jam*
*olan yenderetü pu sa ding :*

*ebügen burqan mansir-un jam*
*eke-yin umai sirγuqu aγui :*

*cinaγsi orubal cuvan yün düng*
*caγan suburγatu bait a se :*

*anusi-ban ergibel ü lang miγou*
*öndör taγitu dai lü ding :*

*jang he se-dur jalbariqu jam*
*jebei ögsükü cang lou se :*

*γoul-un köbege temderikü jam*
*γulir terigütü-dür kürkü musgiγ-a :*

---

1   I thank Elisabetta Chiodo for having sent me a copy of this song, and Uranchimeg Ujeed for her corrections.

*γaγca süjügcid-ün cuburaqu jam*
*ger-e [kar-a?] mansir-dur mörgügülkü cubay-a :*

*dereng keyid-ün dabayan jam*
*dingša duyulduqu manitu-yin ayui*

*cindamani cayan cakiyurtu jam*
*ceceg-iyer quralaqu γoul-tai yolumta :*

*bars sümetü bardayatu jam*
*bandi tabun jayu šoyumal qada :*

*köndei kögügergelekü keyimöri keyid-ün jam*
*kölberim-e orgil daki noyuyan suburya :*

*mayidar cayan šorung jam*
*mil boyda-dur baralaqu [barayalqaqu] asq-a :*

*manan küdeng tunuraqu jam*
*möngke rasiyan sürcikü bulay :*

*uyalja tuyaljitu ulayan jam*
*uran mancir dalalqu qayirqan :*

*ayusyi jirüke uyaraqu jam*
*eke dar-a mösiyekü orgil :*

*altan gereltü ariyabalu-yin jam*
*amidu burqan moturalaqu ordu :*

*cilayun qayalyatu cabcimal jam*
*cakilyan suyunaylaqu odun arsi [qarsi?].*

*quva ya ling-un qas jam*
*quvar miraljaqu feng šüi ling :*

*qomsim bodisadu-a jalaraqu jam*
*qur-a-yin solungγ-a mataraysan qarsi :*

*Su cayan sümbürtü duyang*
*Sünesü mör dalalaqu qorlutu :*

*Arca ʒandan arqayiljaysan jam*
*Ariyun küjis borgiysan egüde :*

*Narasu mayilasu nangkiljaysan jam*
*Nara sara tuvalaysan congqu :*

*yarudi yalbingy-a dongyuduysan jam*
*yanjuur danjuur duyulduysan bušuy :*

*bilig-ün görügesü toylaysan jam*
*bidiriyan otyaryui-du siryuysan yandir [yanjir ?] :*

*eregül engke-ber ebsiyelgekü jam*
*erdeni-yin luu ebkereldügsen jisa :*

*labari cimeg-iyer siryuyulqu jam*
*lama bandi-dur uytuydaqu tangkim*

*juu-yin orun-du jorciqu jam*
*jamšambali-yin jobalang-ece jayiluyulqu orun :*

*zanbutib-un toyusun-ece angyijirayulqu yajar :*

*ünen mör-dür kötülkü jam*
*ügegüü bayan-i tegsilekü eki :*

*möngke siditü utai-yin jam*
*mingyan yalba sunuljan bui!*

The stepped road to climb upwards
The road of Utai located in Sukhāvatī

The [?] road to glide downwards
The road of the cranes that sink and float

When [one] goes down, it is the mountain road
And the Usutu Pass [Pass with Water] Ceng Siye Ling

If [one] looks upwards, it is the road of clouds
Towering rocky Guwan Yün Dung [Guanyindong]

The sky road that rolls and winds
Pu Sa Ding [Pusading] with many terraces

The road of Old Buddha Mañjuśrī [Shouningsi]
The cave in which one crawls through Mother's womb [Fomudong]

If [one] goes further, there is the Tsuwan Yün Düng
Baitasi with the white *stūpa* [Tayuansi]

If [one] turns back, there is U Lang Miyou [Wulangmiao]
The high-terraced Dai Lü Ding [Dailuoding]

The road where one prays at the Jang he se
The Cang Lou Se that is ascended through a defile

The road that runs alongside the river's shore
The twist that leads to the Flour-Headed One [Shuxiangsi]

The road along which those with only [devout] faith file past one after the other
The path to worship Luminous [or 'Black'] Mañjuśrī

The road of the pass of Dereng Kheid
The Manitu-yin Agui where is heard [the sound] *dingša*

The road with *cintāmaṇi* white flint
The homeland with a river that rains with flowers

The dangerous pass with the Tiger Monastery [Tailusi]
The cliff [in the shape of] statues of the five hundred *bandi* [*arhat*]

The road of Kheimori [Wind-horse] Monastery, that bridged over a gorge [?]
The green *stūpa* at the sloping peak

The road of the towering white peak of Maitreya
The cliff to have an audience with '*mil* holy' [Milarépa]

The road with the fog that settles to the bottom
The spring that sprays the ambrosia of eternity

The red road that makes *uulja tuulji* patterns
The mountain where the wise Mañjuśrī beckons [pilgrims?]

The road that moves the heart and lungs
The summit where Tārā smiles

The road of Avalokiteśvara with the golden ray
The palace where Amitābha blesses with his hands

The road opened by cutting rocks, with stone gates
Star Palace [?] where lightening rises in a column

The jade road of Quva Ya Ling
Feng Shui Ling where flowers dazzle

The road where Avalokiteśvara proceeds
The palace where a rainbow of rain bends

The temple with Sumeru white as milk [Luohousi?]
With a wheel that beckons
The route for souls [to follow]

The road where juniper and sandalwood grow randomly
The door from which pure incense rises in clouds

The road where conifers and cypress move in the wind
The window lit by the sun and by the moon

The road where *garuḍa* and phoenixes sing
The threshold where one can listen to the *Kanjur* and *Tanjur*

The road where antelopes of wisdom play [perhaps a reference to the two deers/
   antelope surrounding the *dharma* wheel at the entrance of a Buddhist
   temple]
The *Ganjir* roof finial that penetrates the beryl sky

The road makes one yawn in peace and health
The treasure where dragons of jewels are curled up.

The road that makes one crawl through canopy ornaments
The great hall where one is received by lamas and novices

The road to travel to the land of *jobo* [Lhasa]
The place that allows one to escape the sufferings of Shambala

The place that frees from the dust of Jambudvīpa

The road which leads one on the path of truth
The beginning [or source] that equalizes rich and poor

The eternal magical road of Utai
Stretches for a thousand *kalpa*s!

# Bibliography

*T*: *Taishō shinshū Daizōkyō* 大正新修大藏經 [The Buddhist Canon, comp. Taishō era, 1912-1926]. Edited by Takakusu Junjiro 高楠順次郎 and Watanabe Kaigyoku 渡邊海旭, Tokyo: Taisho issaikyo kankokai, 1924-1932), 100 vols.

Aerdingdu 阿爾丁夫. 1997. "Luobusang Danjin "Wutai shan lüxing zhinan" chengshu, kanxing niandai kao" 羅卜桑丹津《五臺山旅行指南》成書、刊行年代考 [Research on the date of completion and publication of Lubzangdanjin's "Guide to Wutaishan"]. *Nei Menggu shehui kexue* 內蒙古社會科學 1997-3: 35-37.

Ahmad, Zahiruddin. 1970. *Sino-Tibetan Relations in the Seventeenth Century*. Roma: Istituto Italiano per il Medio ed Estremo Oriente (Serie Orientale Roma, 40).

Albera, Dionigi. 2009. "Conclusion. Pour une anthropologie de la traversée des frontières entre les religions monothéistes." In Albera and Couroucli, eds. 2009: 321-359.

——— and Maria Couroucli, eds. 2009. *Religions traversées. Lieux saints partagés entre chrétiens, musulmans et juifs en Méditerranée*. Arles: Actes Sud/MMSH (Études méditerranéennes).

Albera, Dionigi and Benoît Fliche, 2009. "Les pratiques dévotionnelles des musulmans dans les sanctuaires chrétiens: le cas d'Istanbul." In Albera and Couroucli, eds. 2009: 141-174.

Allen, N.J. 1997. "'And the Lake Drained Away': An Essay in Himalayan Comparative Mythology." In Alexander Macdonald, ed., *Mandala and Landscape*, 435-451. New Delhi: D.K. Printworld.

Alley, Rewi and Ralph Lapwood. 1935. "The Sacred Mountains of China: A Trip to Wu T'ai Shan." *The China Journal* 22(3) (March): 114-121.

Altanzayaa, L. 2000. "Mongolyn burkhany shashny tüükhend kholbogdokh Utain tukhai zarim medee" [Some informations about Utai in relation to the history of Mongol Buddhism]. *Studia Historica Instituti Historiae Academiae Scientiarum Mongoli* 32: 138-148.

An Jianhua 安建華. 2002. "Beixin Guyue du zhongsheng" 悲心孤月度眾生 [Life of Beixin Guyue]. *Wutaishan yanjiu* 五臺山研究 2002-2: 26-28.

———. 2003. "Chaobai Fomudong" 朝拜佛母洞 [Worshipping Buddha Mother Cave]. *Wutaishan yanjiu* 2003-2: 33-35.

Andrews, Roy C. 1921. *Across Mongolian Plains: A Naturalist's Account of China's "Great Northwest."* New York and London: D. Appleton.

Andrews, Susie, 2011. "Tales of Conjured Temples (*huasi*) in Qing Period Mountain Gazetteers." *Journal of the International Association of Tibetan Studies* 6 (December): 134-162: http://www.thlib.org/collections/texts/jiats/

Andreyev, Alexander. 2001a. "An Unknown Russian Memoir by Aagvan Dorjiev." *Inner Asia* 3(1-2): 27-40.

———. 2001b. "Indian Pundits and the Russian Exploration of Tibet: An Unknown Story of the Great Game Era." *Central Asiatic Journal* 45(1): 163-180.

———. 2001c. "Russian Buddhists in Tibet, from the End of the Nineteenth Century – 1930," *Journal of the Royal Asiatic Society*, Series 3, 11(3): 349-362.

Aris, Michael. 1989. *Hidden Treasures and Secret Lives: A Study of Pemalingpa (1450-1521) and the Sixth Dalai Lama (1683-1706)*. London and New York: Kegan Paul International.

Arlington, L. C. and William Lewisohn. 1987 [1935]. *In Search of Old Peking*. Hong Kong, Oxford and New York: Oxford University Press [Peking: Vetch].

Atwood, Christopher P. 1992-1993. "The Marvellous Lama in Mongolia: The Phenomenology of a Cultural Borrowing." *Acta Orientalia Academiae Scientiarum Hung.* 46(1): 3-30.

———. 1996. "Buddhism and Popular Ritual in Mongolian Religion: A Reexamination of the Fire Cult." *History of Religions* 36(2): 112-139.

———. 2000. "Worshipping Grace: The Language of Loyalty in Qing China." *Late Imperial China* 21(2) (December): 86-139.

———. 2002. *Young Mongols and Vigilantes in Inner Mongolia's Interregnum Decades, 1911-1931*. Leiden, Boston, Köln: Brill, 2 vol.

———. 2004. *Encyclopedia of Mongolia and the Mongol Empire*. New York: Facts On File.

Avery, Martha. 2003. *The Tea Road: China and Russia Meet Across the Steppe*. Beijing: China Intercontinental Press.

Bai Meichu 白眉初, 2010 [1925]. *Lu Yu Jin sansheng zhi* 魯豫晉三省志 [Annals of three provinces: Shandong, Henan, and Shanxi]. Beijing: Beiping shifan daxue shidixi (Zhonghua Minguo shengqu quan zhi 中華民國省區全志, vol. 3), 1925, esp. *juan* 2: "Shanxisheng zhi" 山西省志. – Reed. Beijing: Zhongyang dixueshe, 2010, vol. 4.

Badone, Ellen and Sharon R. Roseman, eds. 2004. *Intersecting Journeys: The Anthropology of Pilgrimage and Tourism*. Urbana: University of Illinois Press.

Baumann, Brian. 2008. *Divine Knowledge: Buddhist Mathematics According to the Anonymous Manual of Mongolian Astrology and Divination*. Leiden and Boston: Brill.

Baumer, Christoph. 2011. *China's Holy Mountain: An Illustrated Journey into the Heart of Buddhism*. London: I.B.Tauris & Co Ltd.

Bawden, Charles, ed. 1961. *The Jebtsundamba Khutukhtus of Urga*. Text, transl. and annotations of a Mongolian biography of the Jebtsündamba Khutugtu dated 1859. Wiesbaden: Otto Harrassowitz (Asiatische Forschungen, 9).

———. 1976. "The Offering of the Fox Again." *Zentralasiastische Studien* 10: 439-473.

———. 1985a. "Arban γurban sang. A Buddhist Element in the Mongolian Epic?" In Walther Heissig, ed., *Fragen der mongolischen Heldendichtung* II, 37-48. Wiesbaden: Otto Harrassowitz

———. 1985b. "Vitality and Death in Mongolian Epic." In Walther Heissig, ed., *Fragen der mongolischen Heldendichtung* III, 9-24. Wiesbaden: Otto Harrassowitz.

———. 1989 [1968]. *The Modern History of Mongolia*. London and New York: Kegan Paul International.

———. 1990. "Mongol 'Wind-horse Offerings'." In Tadeusz Skorupski, ed., *Indo-Tibetan Studies*, papers in honour and appreciation of Professor David L. Snellgrove's contribution to Indo-Tibetan studies, 29-36. Tring (U.K.): Institute of Buddhist Studies.

———. 1994. *Confronting the Supernatural: Mongolian Traditional Ways and Means*. Wiesbaden: Otto Harrassowitz.

Bazarov, Andrey. 2010. "Buddhist Canon and Social Reality: Some Results of Field Research in Buryatia (2006-2009)." Paper read at the Twelfth Seminar of the International Association for Tibetan Studies, Toronto.

Beckwith, Christopher I. 1987. "The Tibetans in the Ordos and North China: Considerations on the Role of the Tibetan Empire in World History." In Christopher I. Beckwith, ed., *Silver on Lapis: Tibetan Literary Culture and History*, 3-12. Bloomington: The Tibet Society.

Beixin 悲心. 1996. "Tayuansi beiwen" 塔院寺碑文 [Stone inscriptions of Tayuansi]. *Wutaishan yanjiu* 1996-4: 32-44.

Belgünütei and N. Bükeqada. 2010. *Mongγul teüke-yin sudulγan-u ügülel-üd* [Research articles on Mongol history]. Hailar: Öbür Mongγul-un soyul-un keblel-ün qoriya.

———, N. Bükeqada and Uriyangqan Gangγanceceg. 2004. *Sili-yin γoul-un γajar-un nere-yin domuγ* [Legends on the place names of Shili-yin Gool]. Hailar: Öbür Mongγul-un soyul-un keblel-ün qoriya.

Bell, Sir Charles Arthur. 1987 [1946]. *Portrait of a Dalai Lama: The Life and Time of the Great Thirteenth*. London: Wisdom.

Berger, Patricia. 2001. "Miracles in Nanjing: An Imperial Record of the Fifth Karmapa's Visit to the Chinese Capital." In Marsha Weidner, ed., *Cultural Intersections in Later Chinese Buddhism*, 145-169. Honolulu: University of Hawai'i Press.

———. 2003a. *Empire of Emptiness: Buddhist Art and Political Authority in Qing China*. Honolulu: University of Hawai'i Press.

———. 2003b. "Lineages of Form: Buddhist Portraiture in the Manchu Court." *The Tibet Journal* 28: 109-116.

———. 2011. "The Jiaqing Emperor's Magnificent Record of the Western Tour." *Journal of the International Association of Tibetan Studies* 6 (December): 349-371: http://www.thlib.org/collections/texts/jiats/

Beyer, Stephan V. 1973. *The Cult of Tārā: Magic and Ritual in Tibet*. Berkeley: University of California Press.

Bhardwaj, Surinder Mohan. 1973. *Hindu Places of Pilgrimage in India. A Study in Cultural Geography*. Berkeley: University of California Press.

Bianchi, Ester. 2008. "Protecting Beijing: The Tibetan Image of Yamāntaka-Vajrabhairava in Late Imperial and Republican China." In Monica Esposito, ed., *Images du Tibet au 19ᵉ et 20ᵉ siècles*, 329-356. Paris: École Française d'Extrême-Orient (Études thématiques 22-1).

———. 2009. "The Chinese lama Nenghai." In Kapstein, ed. 2009: 295-346.

——— and Arianna Rinaldo. 2010. "Cina e Tibet: Wutaishan come luogo di incontro." In *La Cina e il mondo. Atti dell'XI Convegno dell'Associazione Italiana Studi Cinesi, Roma, 22-24 Febbraio 2007*, 359-382. Roma: Edizione Nuova Cultura.

Biography of Rölpé Dorjé: Thu'u-bkwan blo-bzang chos-kyi nyi-ma (1737-1802), *Khyab bdag rdo rje sems dpa'i ngo bo dpal ldan bla ma dam pa ye shes bstan pa'i sgron me dpal bzang po'i rnam par thar pa mdo tsam brjod pa dge ldan bstan pa'i mdzes rgyan* [A beautiful ornament of the virtuous (Gélukpa) teachings: A brief exposition of the complete liberation story of the embodiement of the master Vajrasattva, the glorious holy lama, Yéshé Tenpé Tonme Palzanpo (The glorious and pure lamp of the wisdom teachings)], 1792-1794, in Collected Works of Thu'u-bkwan blo-bzang chos-kyi nyi-ma, vol. 1. – Ed. *lCang-skya rol-pa'i rdo rje'i rnam-thar*, Lanzhou: Kan su'u mi rigs dpe skrun khang, 1989.

Birnbaum, Raoul. 1983. *Studies on the Mysteries of Mañjuśrī: A Group of East Asian Maṇḍalas and their Traditional Symbolism.* Boulder (Col.): Society for the Study of Chinese Religions (Monograph; 2).

———. 1984. "Thoughts on T'ang Buddhist Mountain Traditions and Their Context." *T'ang Studies* 2: 5-23.

———. 1986. "The Manifestation of a Monastery: Shen-Ying's Experiences on Mount Wu-t'ai in T'ang Context." *Journal of the American Oriental Society* 106(1) (Jan. - Mar.): 119-137.

———. 1989-1990. "Secret Halls of the Mountain Lords: The Caves of Wu-t'ai shan." *Cahiers d'Extrême-Asie* 5 (Kyôto): 115-140.

———. 2004. "Light in the Wutai Mountains." In Matthew T. Kapstein, ed., *The Presence of Light: Divine Radiance and Religious Experience*, 195-226. Chicago and London: University of Chicago Press.

Bizot, Francois. 1980. "La grotte de la naissance: Recherches sur le Bouddhisme Khmer II." *Bulletin de l'École Française d'Extrême-Orient* 67: 221-269.

Blofeld, John. 1938. "The Festival of the Sacred Mountain." *China Journal* 28: 25-37.

———. 1948. *The Jewel in the Lotus: An Outline of Present Day Buddhism in China.* London. Sidgwick & Jackson, published for the Buddhist Society.

———. 1959. *The Wheel of Life. The Autobiography of a Western Buddhist.* London: Rider & co.

Blondeau, Anne-Marie. 1996. "Foreword." In Anne-Marie Blondeau and Ernst Steinkellner, eds., *Reflections of the Mountain. Essays on the History and Social Meaning of the*

*Mountain Cult in Tibet and the Himalaya*, vii-xi. Vienna: Verlag der Österreichischen Akademie der Wissenschaften.

Boerschmann, Ernst. 1923. *Picturesque China - Architecture and Landscape. A Journey through Twelve Provinces*. New York, Brentano's.

————. 1937. "Die grosse Gebetmühle im Kloster Ta Yüan Sï auf dem Wu Tai Schan." *Sinica-Sonderausgabe* (Frankfurt): 35-43.

Bormanshinov, Arash. 1998. "Kalmyk Pilgrims to Tibet and Mongolia." *Central Asiatic Journal* 42: 1-23.

Bosshard, Walter. 1954 [1950]. *Sous la yourte mongole: À travers les steppes de l'Asie Centrale*, transl. from German by Marie-Laure Rouveyre (*Kühles Grasland Mongolei. Zauber und Schönheit der Steppe*, 1950). Paris: Amiot-Dumont (Bibliothèque des voyages).

Bowman, Glenn. 2009. "Processus identitaires autour de quelques sanctuaires partagés en Palestine et en Macédoine." In Albera and Couroucli, eds. 2009: 27-52.

Bredon, Juliette. 1922. *Peking. An Historical and Intimate Description of its chief Places of Interest*. Shanghai, Hong Kong, Singapour, Hankow and Yokohama: Kelly & Walsh.

Brook, Timothy. 2002. *Geographical Sources of Ming-Qing History*. Ann Arbor: Center for Chinese Studies, University of Michigan (Michigan monographs in Chinese Studies, 58).

Brunnert H.S. and V.V. Hagelstrom. 2007 [1912]. *Present Day Political Organization of China*, revised by N. Th. Kolessoff, transl. from the Russian by A. Beltchenko and E.E. Moran. London: RoutledgeCurzon [Shanghai: Kelly and Walsh, Ltd].

Buffetrille, Katia. 1994. "The Halase-Maratika Caves (Eastern Nepal): A Sacred Place Claimed by Both Hindus and Buddhists." *Pondy Papers in Social Sciences* 16. Pondichéry: Institut Français de Pondichéry, 70 p.

————. 1996a. "Montagnes sacrées, lacs et grottes. Lieux de pèlerinage dans le monde tibétain. Traditions écrites, réalités vivantes." Unpublished doctoral thesis. Nanterre: Université Paris X, Laboratoire d'Ethnologie et de Sociologie Comparative, vol. 2.

————. 1996b. "One Day, the Mountain Will Go Away... Preliminary Remarks on the Flying Mountains of Tibet." In Anne-Marie Blondeau and Ernst Steinkellner, eds., *Reflections of the Mountain. Essays on the History and Social Meaning of the Mountain Cult in Tibet and the Himalaya*, 77-90. Vienna: Verlag der Österreichischen Akademie der Wissenschaften.

————. 1997. "The Great Pilgrimage of A-myes rma-chen: Written Traditions, Living Realities" In Alexander W. Macdonald ed. *Mandala and Landscape*, 75-132. New Delhi: D.K. Printworld.

————. 1998. "Reflections on Pilgrimages to Sacred Mountains, Lakes and Caves." In McKay 1998: 18-34.

————. 1999. "The Blue Lake of A-mdo and its Island: Legends and Pilgrimage Guide." In Toni Huber, ed. 1999: 105-124.

————. 2003. "The Evolution of a Tibetan Pilgrimage: The Pilgrimage to A myes rMa chen Mountain in the 21st Century." In *21st Century Tibet Issue. Symposium on Contemporary Tibetan Studies*e, 325-363. Taipei: The Mongolian and Tibetan Affairs Commission.

Bükeqada, N. 1999. *Sili-yin youl-un süme keyid* [Monasteries of Shili-yin Gool]. Hailar: Öbür Mongγul-un soyul-un keblel-ün qoriya (Mongγul ündüsüten-ü süme keyid-ün bürin ciγulγa, 4).

Bulaγ. 2003. *Šasin surtaγun* [Doctrine of Buddhism]. Höhhot: Öbür Mongγul-un surγan kümüjil-ün keblel-ün qoriya, 2 vol.

Bulag, Uradyn E. 2007. "From Empire to Nation: The Demise of Buddhism in Inner Mongolia." In Uradyn E. Bulag and Hildegard G.M. Diemberger, eds. *The Mongolia-Tibet Interface: Opening New Research Terrains in Inner Asia. Proceedings of the Tenth Seminar of the IATS, 2003*, 19-58. Leiden and Boston: Brill.

Cai Hong 彩虹. 1999. "Shifangtang" 十方堂. *Wutaishan yanjiu* 1999-1: 23-25.

Campbell, C. W. 1903. "Journeys in Mongolia," *The Geographic Journal* 22(5) (Nov.): 485-518.

Cartelli, Mary Anne. 2012. *The Five-Colored Clouds of Mount Wutai: Poems from Dunhuang*. Leiden: Brill.

*Catalogue of Ancient Mongolian Books and Documents of China* 1999. Ürinkiyaγa, ed., 1999. *Zhongguo Menggu wen guji zongmu* 中国蒙古文古籍总目—*Dumdadu ulus-un erten-ü mongγul nom bicig-ün yerüngkei γarcaγ*. Beijing: Beijing tushuguan chubanshe, 3 vol.

Cerensodnom, Dalantai and Manfred Taube. 1993. *Die Mongolica der Berliner Turfansammlung*. Berlin: Akademie Verlag.

Chai Zejun 柴澤俊. 1999. "Wutaishan jilüe" 五臺山紀略 [Chronicles of Wutaishan]. In *Chai Zejun gu jianzhu wenji* 柴澤俊古建築文集 — *Collected works of Chai Zejun on ancient architecture*, 65-77. Beijing: Wenwu chubanshe.

Chandra Das, Sarat. 1991 [1902]. *A Tibetan-English Dictionary*. New Delhi: Gaurav Publishing House.

Chang, Michael. 2001. "A Court on Horseback: Constructing Manchu Ethno-Dynastic Rule in China, 1751-1784." Unpublished doctoral thesis, University of California.

*Chao si da mingshan luyin* 朝四大名山路引 [Road index for the pilgrimage to the Four Grand and Famous Mountains]. s.n., Republican period.

Charleux, Isabelle. 2002a. "Les 'lamas' vus de Chine: fascination et répulsion." *Extrême-Orient Extrême-Occident* 24 (October): 133-151.

————. 2002b. "Padmasambhava's Travel to the North: The Pilgrimage to the Monastery of the Caves and the Old Schools of Tibetan Buddhism in Mongolia." *Central Asiatic Journal* 46(2): 168-232.

———. 2006. *Temples et monastères de Mongolie-Intérieure*. Paris: Comité des Travaux Historiques et Scientifiques and Institut National d'Histoire de l'Art.

———. 2011a. "Cong Bei Yindu dao Buliyate: Mengguren sheyezhong de zhantan foxiang" 从北印度到布里亚特：蒙古人视野中的旃檀佛像 [From North India to Buryatia: The 'Sandalwood Buddha' from the Mongols' perspective]. *Palace Museum Journal* 故宮博物院院刊 154 (2011-2): 81-99.

———. 2011b. "Kangxi/Engke Amuγulang, un empereur mongol? Sur quelques légendes mongoles et chinoises." *Études mongoles et sibériennes, centrasiatiques et tibétaines* 42 (2011), online (http://emscat.revues.org/index1782.html).

———. forthcoming. "The Mongols' Devotion to the Jowo Buddhas: The *True Icons* of Lhasa and Beijing and their Mongol Replicas."

Chavannes, Édouard. 1910. *Le T'ai Chan. Essai de monographie d'un culte chinois*. Paris: E. Leroux.

———. 1912. Articles "Tai-yuan-fou au Wou-t'ai-chan," and "Wou-t'ai-chan." In Claudius Madrolle, ed., *Northern China, the Valley of the Blue River, Korea*, 163-166, 166-168. Paris, London: Hachette & Company.

Chayet, Anne. 1985. *Les Temples de Jehol et leurs modèles tibétains*. Paris: Recherche sur les civilisations (Synthèse, 19).

Chen Bo 陳波. 2010. "Qingdai Wutaishan: yige lishi renleixue de guancha" 清代五台山—一个历史人类学的观察 [Wutaishan in Qing dynasty China: A historical anthropology observation]. *Sichuan daxue xuebao* 四川大學學報 169 (2010-4): 21-26, 56.

Chen Qingying 陳慶英 and Ma Lianlong 馬連龍 (transl.). 1988. *Zhangjia guoshi Ruobi-duo-ji zhuan* 章嘉國師若必多吉傳 [The biography of the national preceptor Changkya Rölpé Dorjé]. Beijing: Minzu chubanshe, 1988 (Chinese translation of Thu'u-bkwan Blo-bzang Chos-kyi nyi-ma's biography of Rölpé Dorjé).

Chen Xingya 陳興亞. 1936. *Jin Cha Sui youji* 晉察綏遊記 [Travel record in Shanxi, Cha(khar), and Sui(yuan)]. Beijing: Beiping jingcheng yinshuju, 71 p.

Chia, Ning. 1993. "The Lifanyuan and the Inner Asian Rituals in the Early Qing (1644-1795)." *Late Imperial China* 14(1) (June): 61-63.

Chiodo, Elisabetta. 1989-1991 and 1992-1993. "'The Book of Offerings to the Holy Cinggis Qagan.' A Mongolian ritual text." *Zentral-Asiastische Studien*, 1st part: 22 (1989-1991): 190-220; 2nd part: 23 (1992-1993): 84-144.

———. 2000a. *The Mongolian Manuscripts on Birch Bark from Xarbuxyn Balgas in the Collection of the Mongolian Academy of Sciences. Part 1*. Wiesbaden: Harrassowitz (Asiatische Forschungen 137).

———. 2000b. *Songs of Khorchin Shamans to Jayagachi, the Protector of Livestock and Property*. Paderborn, München, Wien and Zürich: Verlag Ferdinand Schöningh.

————. 2009. *The Mongolian Manuscripts on Birch Bark from Xarbuxyn Balgas in the Collection of the Mongolian Academy of Sciences. Part 2*. Wiesbaden: Harrassowitz (Asiatische Forschungen 137-2).

Chou, Wen-shing. 2007. "Ineffable Paths: Mapping Wutaishan in Qing Dynasty China." *The Art Bulletin* 89(1) (March 2007): 108-129.

————. 2011a. "Maps of Wutai Shan: Individuating the Sacred Landscape Through Color." *Journal of the International Association of Tibetan Studies* 6 (December): 372-388: http://www.thlib.org/collections/texts/jiats/

————. 2011b. "Where Our Journeys End: Visions, Exchanges, and Encounters in Early Modern Representation of Wutaishan." Ph.D. dissertation in History of Art from the University of California, Berkeley.

————. 2014. "Visions in Translation: Place-Making in Zhangkya Rölpé Dorjé's Guidebook to Wutai Shan." Paper presented at the International Association of Buddhist Studies 17, University of Vienna, Austria.

Clarke, John. 2001. "Ga'u: The Tibetan Amulet Box". *Arts of Asia* 31(3): 45-67.

Cleary, Thomas (transl.). 1985-1986. *The Flower Ornament Scripture: A Translation of the Avatamsaka Sutra* (translation of Śikṣānanda's Chinese version). Boston and London: Shambala.

CLŠASB. *Cing liyang šan aγulan-u sine ji bicig* [New gazetteer of Qingliangshan]. Mongolian translation of Lao-zang-dan-ba's *Qingliangshan xinzhi*, 1701, prefaced by Kangxi, 10 chapters. – Modern ed. *Utai serigün tungγalaγ aγula-yin jokiyangγui*, by Lubsangdamba (Lao-zang-dan-ba), Na. Batujiryal and R. Soyultu, eds., Höhhot: Ündüsüten-ü keblel-u qoriy-a, 2000.

Coleman, Simon and John Elsner, eds. 1995. *Pilgrimage: Past and Present in the World Religions*. Cambridge (Mass.): Harvard University Press.

———— and John Eade, eds. 2004. *Reframing Pilgrimage: Cultures in Motion*. London and New York: Routledge.

Couroucli, Maria. 2009. "Saint Georges l'Anatolien, maître des frontières." In Albera and Couroucli, eds. 2009: 175-208.

Croner, Don. 2006. 2008a. *Mongolia Adventure*. Ulaanbaatar: Polar Star Books.

————. 2008b. "Mongolia. Khentii Aimag. Baldan Bereeven Khiid." Don Croner's World Wide Wanders, October 21, 2008, internet website: http://www.doncroner.net/Archives/2008_10_19_archive.html (accessed April 10th, 2009).

Crossley, Pamela K. 1999. *A Translucent Mirror: History and Identity in Qing Imperial Ideology*. Berkeley: University of California Press.

Cui Wenkui 崔文魁. 2004. "Wutaishan yu Wutaishan tu" 五臺與五臺山圖 [Wutaishan and its maps]. *Wutaishan yanjiu* 2004(3): 17–23.

Cui Zhengsen 崔正森. 1999. "Qingliang laoren Awang Laozang" 清凉老人阿王老藏. *Wutaishan yanjiu* 1999-3: 27-30.

———. 2002. *Wutaishan liushiba si* 五臺山六十八寺 [Eighty-six monasteries of Wutaishan]. Taiyuan. Shanxi kexue jishu chubanshe.

———. 2003. "Zhenhaisi fojiao jianshi" 鎮海寺佛教簡史 [Short history of Buddhism at Zhenhaisi]. *Wutaishan yanjiu* 2003-4: 5-14.

——— and Wang Zhichao 王志超. 1995. *Wutaishan beiwen xuanzhu* 五臺山碑文選注 [Annotated selection of Wutaishan stelae]. Taiyuan: Beiyue yishu chubanshe (Wutaishan yanjiu congshu zhi si).

Damdinsüren, C. 1977. "Ülger domgiin jargalant oron Jambal" [Jambhala, blissful place in legends]. *Zentralasiastische Studien* 11: 351-388.

Danjiong Rannabanza 丹迥冉納班雜 and Li Decheng 李德成. 1997. *Mingsha shuang Huang si: Qingdai Dalai he Banchan zai jing zhu xidi* 名剎雙黃寺－清代達賴和班禪在京駐錫地 [Famous monasteries the two Huangsi － Qing dynasty residence of the Dalai and the Panchen in the capital]. Beijing: Zongjiao wenhua chubanshe.

David, Armand (abbot). 1867-1868. *Journal d'un voyage en Mongolie fait en 1866*. Paris: musée d'Histoire naturelle, 1867-1868, 2 vol. (Bulletin des Nouvelles Archives).

David-Neel, Alexandra. 1940. *Sous les nuées d'orage*. Paris: Plon.

Davidson, Ronald M. 1981. "*The Litany of Names of Manjusri*––Text and Translation of the *Manjusrinamasamgiti*." In Michel Strickmann, ed., *Tantric and Taoist Studies in Honour of R.A. Stein, Mélanges Chinois et Bouddhiques*, 1-69. Brussels: Institute Belge des Hautes Études Chinoises.

Davis, Stevan. 2010. "The Miniature Paintings of Mongolian Buddhism: Tsaklis, Thangkas and Burhany Zurags." http://asianart.com/articles/burhanyz/index.html, published: April 8.

Dawson, María Teresa. 2001. "The Concept of Popular Religion: A Literature Review." *Journal of Iberian and Latin American Research* 7(1): 105-132.

DeFrancis, John. 1993. *In the Footsteps of Gengis Khan*. Honolulu: University of Hawai'i Press.

Debreczeny, Karl. 2011. "Wutaishan: Pilgrimage to Five Peak Mountain." *Journal of the International Association of Tibetan Studies* 6 (December): 1-133: http://www.thlib.org/collections/texts/jiats/

Delaplace, Grégory. 2009. *L'Invention des morts. Sépultures, fantômes et photographies en Mongolie contemporaine*. Paris: Centre d'Études Mongoles et Sibériennes and École Pratique des Hautes Études (Nord-Asie, 1).

Demiéville, Paul. 1952. *Le Concile de Lhasa: Une controverse sur le quiétisme entre bouddhistes de l'Inde et de la Chine au VIIIe siècle de l'ère chrétienne*. Paris: Imprimerie Nationale de France.

Dharmatāla, Damchø Gyatsho (Dam-chos rgya-mtsho Dharmatāla). 1987 [1889]. *Rosary of White Lotuses, Being the Clear Account of How the Precious Teaching of Buddha Appeared and Spread in the Great Hor Country*, transl. from Tibetan and annotated by Piotr Klafkowski, Wiesbaden: Otto Harrassowitz [*Padma dkar-po'i phreng-ba*].

Di Cosmo, Nicola. 1998. "Qing Colonial Administration in Inner Asia." *The International History Review* 20(2): 287-309.

D'ianakova, V.P. 2001. "Lamaism and its Influence on the Worldview and Religious Cults of the Tuvans." *Anthropology & Archeology of Eurasia* 39(4) (Spring), special issue on "Buddhism (Lamaism) in Russia": 52-75.

Dorje, Gyurme. 2001. *Tibetan Elemental Divination Paintings, Illuminated Manuscripts from the White Beryl with the Moonbeams Treatise of Lo-chen Dharmashri*, commentary and translation by Gyurme Dorje. London: John Eskenazi and Sam Fogg.

Duan Jinjin 段晶晶. 2008. "Wutaishan yu zangchuan fojiao shengji" [Wutaishan and sacred historical sites of Tibetan Buddhism] 五臺山與藏傳佛教聖蹟. *Xizang daxue xuebao* 西藏大學學報, 2008-1: 75-78.

Dunnell, Ruth W. 1996. *The Great State of White and High: Buddhism and State Formation in Eleventh-Century Xia*. Honolulu: University of Hawai'i Press.

Dupront, Alphonse. 1987. *Du Sacré. Croisades et pèlerinages. Images et langages*. Paris: Gallimard.

Dznyā na shrī man (Yé[shé] Pen[den]). 1994 [after 1827]. *Ri bo rtse lnga'i dkar chag rab gsal me long* [The clear mirror: A guide to Five-peaked Mountain]. – Ed. Zi ling: mTsho sngon mi rigs dpe skrun khang, 1994.

Eade, John. 2000. "Introduction." In Eade and Sallnow, *Contesting the Sacred. The Anthropology of Christian Pilgrimages*, ix-xxvii. Urbana: University of Illinois Press.

——— and Michael J. Sallnow. 1991. *Contesting the Sacred. The Anthropology of Christian Pilgrimage*. New York and London: Routledge.

Edkins, Joseph, Rev. 1893 [1878]. *Religion in China; Containing a Brief Account of the Three Religions of the Chinese: With Observations on the Prospects of Christian Conversion Amongst that People*. London: Trübner & Co.

Ekvall, Robert B. 1964. *Religious Observances in Tibet: Patterns and Functions*. Chicago and London: The University of Chicago Press.

——— and James F. Downs. 1987. *Tibetan Pilgrimage*. Tokyo: Institute for the Study of Languages and Cultures of Asia and Africa.

Elverskog, Johan. 2003. *The* Jewel Translucent Sūtra. *Altan Khan and the Mongols in the Sixteenth Century*. Leiden and Boston: E. J. Brill (Brill's Inner Asian Library, 8).

———. 2006. *Our Great Qing: The Mongols, Buddhism, and the State in Late Imperial China*. Honolulu: University of Hawai'i Press.

———. 2007. "Wutai Shan in the Mongol Literary *Imaginaire*." Paper presented at the "Conference Wutaishan and Qing Culture," New York, May 12-13, 2007.

———. 2011. "Wutai Shan, Qing Cosmopolitanism and the Mongols." *Journal of the International Association of Tibetan Studies* 6 (December): 243-274: http://www.thlib. org/collections/texts/jiats/

Empson, Rebecca M. 2010. "'Enclosing' for Growth: Including or Excluding People from Land in Northeast Mongolia." In Isabelle Charleux, Roberte Hamayon, Grégory

Delaplace, and Scott Pearce, eds., *Representing Power in Modern Inner Asia: Conventions, Alternatives and Oppositions*, 123-148. Bellingham: Western Washington University.

———. 2011. *Harnessing Fortune. Personhood, Memory, and Place in Mongolia*. Oxford: British Academy and Oxford University Press.

Epstein, Lawrence and Peng Wenbin, 1994. "Ganja and Murdo: The Social Construction of Space at Two Pilgrimage Sites in Eastern Tibet." *Tibet Journal*, special edition: *Powerful Places and Spaces in Tibetan Religious Culture* 19(2): 21-45.

Éveillard, James and Patrick Huchet. 2006. *Croyances et rites populaires*. Rennes: Éditions Ouest-France.

Everding, Karl-Heinz. 1988. *Die Präexistenzen der lCaṅ skya Qutuqtus: Untersuchungen zur Konstruktion und historischen Entwicklung einer lamaistischen Existenzenlinie.* Wiesbaden: Harrassowitz.

Fang Qingqi 方慶奇 and Wang Xuebin王學斌. 1994. "Wutaishan Wenshu pusa" 五臺山文殊菩薩 [*Bodhisattva* Mañjuśrī of Wutaishan]. *Wutaishan yanjiu* 1994-1, Part 1: 9-17; 1994-2, Part 2: 20-24.

Farquhar, David M. 1955. "Mongolian Manuscripts in Washington." *Central Asiatic Journal* 1: 161-218.

———. 1978. "Emperor as Bodhisattva in the Governance of the Ch'ing Empire." *Harvard Journal of Asiatic Studies* 38(1) (June): 5-34.

Fischer, Emil S. 1923. *The Sacred Wu Tai Shan in Connection with Modern Travel from Tai yuan fu via Mount Wu Tai to the Mongolian Border*. Shanghai: Kelly and Walsh.

Forbath, Ladislaus. 1936. *The New Mongolia*, as related by Joseph Geleta; translated from the Hungarian by Lawrence Wolfe. London and Toronto: W. Heinemann.

*Fozu lidai tongzai* 佛祖歷代通載 [A comprehensive registry of the successive ages of the Buddhas and the patriarchs], by Monk Nianchang 念常, before 1340. – Ed. Beijing: Shumu wenxian chubanshe, [s.d.].

Franck, Harry A. 1923. *Wandering in Northern China*, illustrated with 171 unusual photographs by the author, with a map showing his route. New York; London: The Century Co.

Franke, Herbert. 1987. "Tibetans in Yüan China." In John D. Langlois, ed., *China under Mongol Rule*, 296-328. Princeton: Princeton University Press.

———. 1994 [1984]. "Tan-pa, a Tibetan lama at the court of the Great Khans." in *China under Mongol Rule*. Herbert Franke, Hampshire (GB) and Vermont (USA): Variorum, 157-180 [*Orientalia Venetiana 1, Volume in onore di Lionello Lanciotti, Mario Sabattini ed.*, Firenze: Leo S. Olschki Editore, 1984].

———. 1994. "Consecration of the 'White Stûpa' in 1279." *Asia Major* 7(1): 155-183.

Galdan (tusalaγci). *Erdeni-yin erike* [Jewel Rosary], 1859. – Ed. Ardajab, Höhhot: Öbür Mongγul-un arad-un keblel-un qoriya, 1999.

Galdanova, G.P, L.N. Zhukovskaya, and G.N. Ochirova. 1984. "The Cult of Dayan Derkhe in Mongolia and Buryatia," transl. by Caroline Humphrey. *Journal of the Anglo-Mongolian Society* 9(1-2): 1-11.

Galsang, Kügjiltü and Batubayar. 1994. *Juu uda-yin süme keyid* [Monasteries of Juu Uda]. Hailar: Öbür Mongγul-un soyul-un keblel-ün qoriya (Mongγul ündüsüten-ü süme keyid-ün bürin ciγulγa, 2).

Gao Henian 高鶴年. 2000 [1949]. *Ming shan youfang ji* 名山游訪記 [Record of visits to famous mountains]. Beijing: Zongjiao wenhua chubanshe [1st ed. 1949].

Gao Lintao 郜林濤. 2000. "Basiba yu Wutaishan" 八思巴與五臺山 [Pakpa and Wutaishan]. *Wutaishan yanjiu* 2000-4: 27-28, 48.

———. 2004. "Huangjiao zai Wutaishan de chuanbo" 黃教在五臺山的傳播 [The expansion of the Gélukpas at Wutaishan]. *Cang sang* 滄桑 2004-1: 96-97.

Gao Minghe 高明和. 1996. "Tayuansi jianzhu yu suxiang gaishu" 塔院寺建筑與塑像概述 [Architecture and painted sculptures of Tayuansi]. *Wutaishan yanjiu* 1996-4: 10-16.

Gao Shiqi 高士奇 (1644-1703). 1989 [ca. 1700]. "Hucong xixun rilu" 扈從西巡日錄 [Daily record of following in the retinue of Kangxi's Western Tour], 27 fol., in *Qingyin tangji* 清吟堂集, ca. 1700– Ed. *Siku quanshu* 235, 271-287, ed. Taibei: Xin wenfeng chuban gongsi, 1989 (Congshu jicheng xubian 叢書集成續編, 235).

"A Gate to God, 9/18/05", 2005. http://www.northcountrypublicradio.org/news/naj/naj7.html (accessed September 25th, 2007).

Germano, David. 1998. "Re-membering the Dismembered Body of Tibet: Contemporary Tibetan Visionary Movements in the People's Republic of China." In Melvyn C. Goldstein and Matthew T. Kapstein, eds. *Buddhism in Contemporary Tibet*, 53-94. Berkeley, Los Angeles and London: University of California Press.

Gilmour, James. 1893. *More About the Mongols*, selected and arranged from the diaries and papers of James Gilmour by Richard Lovett. London: The Religious Tract Society.

———. 1970 [1883]. *Among the Mongols*. New York: Praeger.

Gimello, Robert. 1992. "Chang Shang-ying on Wu-t'ai Shan." In Naquin and Yü 1992: 89-149.

———. 1994. "Wutaishan during the Early Chin Dynasty: The Testimony of Chu Pien. *Chung-Hwa Buddhist Journal* 中華佛學學報 7: 501-611.

Gochoo, C. 1970 [1963]. "Le Badarci mongol," transl. from Mongolian by Sarah Dars. *Études Mongoles* 1 (Nanterre), 70-77 ["Mongol badarchny tukhai." *Studia Archaeologica* 2 (Ulaanbaatar, 1963): 36-42].

Goodrich, Anne S. 1998. "Miao Feng Shan." *Asian Folklore Studies* 57(1): 87-97 (personal account of a pilgrimage made in 1931).

Goossaert, Vincent and David A. Palmer. 2011. *The Religious Question in Modern China*. Chicago: University of Chicago Press.

Grapard, Allan G. 1982. "Flying Mountains and Walkers of Emptiness. Toward a Definition of Sacred Space in Japanese Religions." *History of Religions* 21(3): 195-221.

Grupper, Samuel H. 1984. "Manchu Patronage and Tibetan Buddhism during the First Half of the Ch'ing Dynasty. A Review Article." *Journal of the Tibet Society* 4: 47-75.

*Gu Yanwu* 顧炎武 (*1613-1682*) 1956 [*seventeenth century*]. *"Wutaishan ji"* 五臺山記 [Notes on Wutaishan], seventeenth century – In *Gu tinglin wenji* 顧亭林文集, Taipei: Xinxing shuju, 1956, *juan 5: 2b-4a* (transl. in *Inscribed Landscapes: Travel Writing from Imperial China* with annotations and an introduction by Richard E. Strassberg, Berkeley: University of California Press, 1994, 353-660).

*Guang Qingliang zhuan* 廣清涼傳 [Expanded record of Clear and Cold] 1060. By Yanyi 延一. T. 2099, vol. 51: 1101a-1127a.

Hackman, Heinrich. 1914 [1912]. *A German Scholar in the East: Travel Scenes and Reflections*, transl. from German by Daisie Rommel. London: Kegan Paul, Trench, Trübner & Co., Ltd. (*Welt des Ostens*, Berlin: Karl Curtius, 1912).

Halén, Harry. 1987. *Mirrors of the Void, Buddhist Art in the National Museum of Finland, 63 Sino-Mongolian Thangkas from the Wutaishan Workshops, a Panoramic Map of the Wutai Mountains and Objects of Diverse Origins*. Helsinki: National Board of Antiquities.

Hardacre, Helen. 1983. "The Cave and the Womb World." *Japanese Journal of Religious Studies* 10(2-3): 149-176.

Hargett, James M. 2006. *Stairway to Heaven: A Journey to the Summit of Mount Emei*. Albany: Statue University of New York Press.

Hamayon, Roberte. 1990. *La Chasse à l'âme. Esquisse du chamanisme sibérien*. Nanterre: Société d'ethnologie.

Han Heping 韓和平 and Wang Miao王苗. 1999. *Wutaishan*五臺山. Hong Kong: Xianggang Zhongguo lüyou chubanshe.

Haslund-Christensen. 1935. *Men and Gods in Mongolia* (*Zayagan*), translated from Swedish by Elizabeth Sprigge and Claude Napier. London: Trench, Trubner & Co

———. 1954 [1932]. *Tents in Mongolia: Adventures and Experiences among the Nomads of Central Asia*; translated from the Swedish by Elizabeth Sprigge and Claude Napier. London: Kegan Paul, Trench, Trubner.

Hayden, Robert M. 2002. "Antagonistic Tolerance: Competitive Sharing of Religious Sites in South Asia and the Balkans." *Current Anthropology* 42(2): 205-231; "Commentary" by Glenn Bowman. *Current Anthropology* 43(2) (April): 219-220.

He Zhang Lianjue 何張蓮覺. 1934. *Ming shan youji* 名山遊記 [Record of travels to famous mountains]. Hong Kong: Donglian jueyuan (preface dated 1933), 67-73.

Hedin, Sven A. 1933. *Jehol: City of Emperors*. New York: E.P. Dutton & Co.

———. 1943. *History of the Expedition in Asia: 1927-1935*, in collaboration with Folke Bergman. Part II: *1928-1933*. Stockholm: Göterborg Elanders bocktrykeri aktiebolag,

1943-1945, 3 vol. (Reports from the Scientific Expedition to the North-Western Provinces of China under the Leadership of Dr. Sven Hedin).

Heissig, Walther. 1950. "A Contribution to the Knowledge of Eastmongolian Folkpoetry." *Folklore Studies* 9: 153-178.

———. 1953. "Some Glosses on Recent Mongol Studies." *Studia Orientalia* 19(4) (Helsinki 1954): 1-14.

———. 1954. *Die Pekinger Lamaistischen Blockdrucke in mongolischer Sprache. Materialien zur mongolischen Literaturgeschichte.* Wiesbaden: Otto Harrassowitz, 1954 (Göttinger Asiatische Forschungen, 2).

———. 1959. *Die Familien- und Kirchengeschichtsschreibung der Mongolen, Materialien zur mongolischen Literaturgeschichte,* vol. I: 16.-18. Jahrhundert. Wiesbaden: Otto Harrassowitz, 1959 (Asiatische Forschungen, 5).

———. 1972. *Geschichte der mongolischen Literatur,* Band I: 19. Jahrhundert bis zum Beginn des 20. Jahrhunderts; Band II: 20. Jahrhundert bis zum Einfluss moderner Ideen. Wiesbaden: Otto Harrassowitz.

———. 1973 [1970]. "Les religions de la Mongolie." In Giuseppe Tucci and Walther Heissig, *Les Religions du Tibet et de la Mongolie,* transl. from German by R. Sailley, 337-488. Paris: Payot, 1973 [Stuttgart, 1970] (Les Religions de l'humanité).

———. 1976a. "Eine Anrufung des 'Weissen Alten' in der Staatsbibliothek Preussischer Kulturbesitz Berlin." *Folia Rara* (Verzeichnis der Orientalischen Handschrifter in Deutschland, Suppl. 19): 51-60.

———. 1976b. *Die mongolischen Handschriften-Reste aus Olon süme Innere Mongolei (16.-17. Jhdt.).* Wiesbaden: Otto Harrassowitz.

———. and Klaus Sagaster. 1961. *Mongolische Handschriften, Blockdrucke, Landkarten.* Wiesbaden: Franz Steiner Verlag (Verzeichnis der orientalischen Handschriften in Deutschland, 1).

Heller, Amy. 1996. "Mongolian Mountain Deities and Local Gods: Examples of Ritual for their Worship in Tibetan Language." In Anne-Marie Blondeau and Ernst Steinkellner, eds., *Reflections of the Mountain. Essays on the History and Social Meaning of the Mountain Cult in Tibet and the Himalaya,* 133-140. Vienna: Verlag der Österreichischen Akademie der Wissenschaften.

Heller, Natasha. 2008. "Visualizing Pilgrimage and Mapping Experience: Mount Wutai on the Silk Road." In Philippe Forêt and Andreas Kaplony, eds. *The Journey of Maps and Images on the Silk Road,* 29-50. Leiden and Boston: E. J. Brill.

Henrion-Dourcy, Isabelle. 2007. "Un rite en l'honneur de Khawa Karpo. Quelques notes sur le double culte à un dieu-montagne au Tibet." In Joël Noret and Pierre Petit, eds., *Corps, performance, religion. Études anthropologiques offertes à Philippe Jespers,* 263-281. Paris: Éditions Publibook Université.

Henss, Michael. 2001. "The Bodhisattva-Emperor: Tibeto-Chinese Portraits of Sacred and Secular Rule in the Qing Dynasty." *Oriental Art* 3: 1-16.

*History and Culture of the Mongols*. 2006. Ulaanbaatar: International Institute for the Study of Nomadic Civilizations.

Hsu, Sung-peng. 1979. *A Buddhist Leader in Ming China: The Life and Thought of Han-shan Te-Ch'ing*. University Park: The Pennsylvania State University Press, translation of Hanshan's autobiography: *Hanshan laoren zuxu nianpu*, 1622.

Huang Hao 黃顥. 1993. *Zai Beijing de zangzu wenwu* 在北京的藏族文物 [Tibetan cultural heritage in Beijing]. Beijing: Minzu chubanshe.

Huang Yongsong 黃永松 and Dai Qing 戴晴. 1991. *Wutaishan luoma dahui* 五台山騾馬大會 [Great Mule and Horse Fair of Wutaishan]. Taibei: Hansheng zazhishe.

Huber, Toni. 1994. "Putting the *Gnas* Back into *Gnas-skor*: Rethinking Tibetan Buddhist Pilgrimage Practice." *The Tibet Journal* 19(2) (Dharamsala): 23-60.

———. 1999. *The Cult of Pure Crystal Mountain. Popular Pilgrimage and Visionary Landscape in Southeast Tibet*. New York and Oxford: Oxford University Press.

———. ed. 1999. *Sacred Spaces and Powerful Places in Tibetan Culture: A Collection of Essays*. Dharamsala, H.P.: Library of Tibetan Works and Archives.

———. ed. 2008. *A Holy Land Reborn: Pilgrimage and the Tibetan Reinvention of Buddhist India*. Chicago: University of Chicago Press.

———. 2000. *The Guide to India: A Tibetan Account by Amdo Gendun Chöphel*. Dharamsala: Library of Tibetan Works and Archives.

Huc, Régis Evariste (1813-1860). 1928 [1924]. *Travels in Tartary, Thibet and China, 1844-1846*, translated by William Hazlitt; edited with an introduction by Professor Paul Pelliot. London: Routledge, 2 vol. [1st ed.1924].

Hummel, Siegbert. 1971. "Die Fusspur des Gautama-Buddha auf dem Wu-t'ai-shan". *Asiatische Studien* 25: 389-406.

Humphrey, Caroline. 1974. "Inside a Mongolian Tent." *New Society* (October 31): 273-275.

———. 1993. "Avgai Khad. Theft and Social Trust in Post-Communist Mongolia." *Anthropology Today* 9(6): 13-16.

———. 1995. "Chiefly and Shamanist Landscapes in Mongolia." In Eric Hirsch and Michael O'Hanlon, eds., *The Anthropology of Landscape: Perspectives on Place and Space*, 135-162. Oxford: Clarendon Press.

———. 1998. *Marx Went Away – But Karl Stayed Behind*. Ann Arbor: University of Michigan Press (updated ed. of *Karl Marx Collective*, 1983).

———. 2006. "Prophecy and Sequential Orders in Mongolian Political History." In Rebecca Empson, ed., *Time, Causality and Prophecy in the Mongolian Cultural Region*, 61-97. Cambridge: Globe Oriental.

——— and Hurelbaatar Ujeed. 2013. *A Monastery in Time. The Making of Mongolian Buddhism*. Chicago: University of Chicago Press.

——— and Urgunge Onon. 1996. *Shamans and Elders: Experience, Knowledge and Power among the Daur Mongols*. Oxford and New York: Clarendon Press.

Hurcha, N. (=Qurca). 1999. "Attempts to Buddhicize the Cult of Chinggis Khan." *Inner Asia* 1(1): 45-57.

"Ikh ayan internet website": http://www.ikhayan.com/detail.html?detail=aghpa2gtᴙxl hbnıʟcxıᴇᴠɢ91chjoʀgw (accessed on January 20, 2011).

Illich, Marina. 2006. "Selections from the Life of a Tibetan Buddhist Polymath: Chankya Rolpe Dorje (Lcang skya rol pa'i rdo rje), 1717-1786." Unpublished doctoral thesis. Columbia University.

Irving, Christopher (=Sir Reginald Fleming Johnston). 1919. "Wu-Ta'i-Shan and the Dalai Lama." *The New China review* (May): 151-163.

Ishihama, Yumiko. 2005. "The Image of Ch'ien-lung's Kingship as Seen from the World of Tibetan Buddhism." *Acta Asiatica* 88: 49-64.

―――石濱裕美子. 2011. *Sinchō to Chibetto bukkyō: bosatsuō to natta Kenryūtei* 清朝とチベット仏教: 菩薩王となった乾隆帝 [The Qing dynasty and the Tibetan Buddhist world: The Qianlong emperor who became a Buddhist king]. Tokyo: Waseda Daigaku Shuppanbu, 2011.

Ishtavkhai, N. 1998. *Mörgölchidöd zoriulsan tailbar* [Explanations to pilgrims]. Erdenet.

Jagchid, Sechin. 1999. *The Last Mongol Prince. The Life and Times of Demchugdongrob, 1902-1966.* Bellingham: Western Washington University.

―――and Charles R. Bawden. 1970. "Notes on the Ranks and Titles of the Mongol Nobility During Manchu Times." In *Proceedings of the 9th Meeting of the PIAC (Ravello, 26-30 September 1966)*, 139-153. Napoli: Istituto Universitario Orientale, Seminarion di Turcologica.

―――and Paul Hyer. 1983. *A Mongolian Living Buddha: Biography of the Kanjurwa Khutughtu.* New York: State University of New York Press.

Jagou, Fabienne. 2004. *Le 9e Panchen Lama (1883-1937). Enjeu des relations sino-tibétaines.* Paris: École Française d'Extrême-Orient.

Jalsan. 2002. "The Reincarnations of Desi Sangye Gyatso in Alasha and the *Secret History* of the Sixth Dalai Lama." *Inner Asia* 4(2): 347-359.

'Jam dbyangs Mkhyen brtse'i dbang po, et al., 1958. *Guide to the Holy Places of Central Tibet.* Roma: Istituto Italiano per il Medio ed Estremo Oriente.

Jambal. 1997 [1959]. *Tales of an Old Lama,* transl. by Charles Bawden. Tring (U. K.): The Institute of Buddhist Studies, 1997 (Buddhica Britannica, Series Continua VIII)— from a Mongolian text recorded and edited by Ts. Damdinsüren: *Övgön Jambalin yaria,* 1959, reed. in *Tüüver zokhiol,* 1969.

Jest, Corneille. 1975. *Dolpo. Communautés de langue tibétaine du Népal.* Paris: Éditions du Centre national de la recherche scientifique.

Jiang Weiqiao 蔣維橋 (1872-1958). 1961 [1918]. *Wutaishan jiyou* 五臺山記遊 [Travel record to Wutaishan], *juan* 10, 1918. – In Lao Yi'an 勞亦安, ed., *Gujin youji congchao* 古今遊記叢鈔, 3. Taibei: Taiwan Zhonghua shu ju, Minguo 50 [1961], 48 *juan,* 15-26.

Jing, Anning. 1994. "The Portraits of Khubilai Khan and Chabi by Anige (1245-1306), a Nepali Artist at the Yuan Court." *Artibus Asiae* 54(1-2): 40-86.

Junast. 1991. *Basiba zi he Menggu yuwen xian – II: Wenxian wenji* 八思巴字和蒙古语文献·II 文献文集– *The Mongolian Monuments in 'Phags-pa Script* II: *Collection of Monuments.* Tokyo: Tokyo University of Foreign Studies.

Kápolnas, Olivér. 2008. "Az Öt-ormú hegy leírása." Unpublished manuscript.

Kapstein, Matthew T. 1998. "A Pilgrimage of Rebirth Reborn. The 1992 Celebration of the Drigung Powa Chenmo." In Melvyn C. Goldstein and Matthew T. Kapstein, eds., *Buddhism in Contemporary Tibet: Religious Revival and Cultural Identity*, 95-119. Berkeley (Ca.): University of California Press.

———. 2004. "The Strange Death of Pema the Demon Tamer." In Matthew T. Kapstein, ed., *The Presence of Light: Divine Radiance and Religious Experience*, 119-156. Chicago and London: University of Chicago Press.

———. 2009. "Preface" and "Introduction: Mediations and Margins." In Kapstein 2009: xv-xviii, 1-18.

———, ed. 2009. *Buddhism Between Tibet and China.* Boston: Wisdom publications.

Kara, György. 2000. *The Mongol and Manchu Manuscripts and Blockprints in the Library of the Hungarian Academy of Sciences.* Budapest: Akademiai Kiadó.

———. 2005. *Books of the Mongolian Nomads. More than Eight Centuries of Writing Mongolian.* Bloomington: Indiana University, Research Institute for Inner Asian Studies (Uralic and Altaic Series).

Karmay, Samten G. 1993. "The Wind-horse and the Well-Being of Man." In Charles Ramble and Martin Brauen, eds., *Anthropology of Tibet and the Himalaya*, Proceedings of the International Seminar, September 21-28 1990 at the Ethnographic Museum of the University of Zurich, 150-157. Zurich: Ethnological Museum of the University of Zurich.

———. 2005 [1998]. "Concepts of Territorial Organization and their Transformation into Buddhist Sacred Sites", paper presented at the eighth seminar of the IATS, Indiana University, July 25-31, 1998. In Samten G. Karmay, *The Arrow and the Spindle. Studies in History, Myths, Rituals and Beliefs in Tibet*, 31-52. Kathmandu: Mandala Book Point.

Kelényi, Béla, ed. 2003. *Demons and Protectors. Folk Religion in Tibetan and Mongolian Buddhism.* Budapest: Ferenc Hopp Museum of Eastern Asiatic Art.

Khan, Almaz. 1995. "Chinggis Khan, From Imperial Ancestor to Ethnic Hero." In Stevan Harrel, ed., *Cultural Encounters on China's Ethnic Frontiers*, 248-277. Seattle and London: University of Washington.

Kler, Josef (CICM). 1957. "Die Windpferdfahne oder K'ï-mori bei den Ordos-Mongolen." *Oriens* 10: 90-106.

Köhle, Natalie. 2008. "Why Did the Kangxi Emperor Go to Wutai Shan?: Patronage, Pilgrimage, and the Place of Tibetan Buddhism at the Early Qing Court." *Late Imperial China* 29(1): 73-119.

Klafkowski, Piotr, ed. 1979. *The Secret Delivrance of the Sixth Dalai-Lama as narrated by Dharmatāla.* Wien: Viener Studien zur Tibetologie und Buddhismuskunde, Universität Wien.

Krueger, John R. 1966. "Catalogue of the Laufer Mongolian Collections in Chicago." *Journal of the American Oriental Society* 86(2) (April): 156-183.

Kürelbaγatur (=Hurelbaatar), ed. Forthcoming. *Utai-yin Mongγul ögligecid-ün kösiye* [Steles of Mongol donors of Wutaishan]. Höhhot.

Lagerway, John. 1992. "The Pilgrimage to Wu-tang Shan." In Naquin and Yü, eds., 1992: 293-332.

Lamotte, Étienne. 1960. "Mañjuśrī." *T'oung Pao* 48(1): 1-96.

Lao Li 老李. 2004. "Dao Wutaishan qu baifo" 到五臺山去拜佛 [Going to Wutaishan to worship Buddha]. *Baolin* 報林 2004-1: 97-102.

Lalou, Marcelle. 1930. *Iconographie des étoffes peintes (paṭa) dans le Mañjuśrīmūlakalpa.* Paris: Librairie orientaliste Paul Geuthner, 1930.

Lang, Maria-Katharina. 2007. "Die Sammlung Hans Leder. Mongolische Ethnographica im Museum für Völkerkunde Wien." Research report of the project "Bearbeitung der Mongolei-Sammlung des Forschers Hans Leder im Museum für Völkerkunde Wien." Wien.

Large-Blondeau, Anne-Marie. 1960. "Les Pèlerinages tibétains." *Sources orientales* 3: Les Pèlerinages (Paris: Le Seuil): 203-245.

Lattimore, Owen. 1928. "Caravan Routes of Inner Asia: The Third 'Asian Lecture.'" *The Geographical Journal* 72(6) (December): 497-528.

———. 1942. *Mongol Journeys.* London: The Travel Book Club.

———. 1979 "A Mongol Legend of the Founding of Peking." *Central Asiatic Journal* 23(1-2): 237-239.

——— and Isono Fujiko, eds. 1982. *The Diluv Khutagt. Memoirs and Autobiography of a Mongol Buddhist Reincarnation in Religion and Revolution.* Wiesbaden: Otto Harrassowitz.

Le Calloc'h, Bernard. 1989. "Amulettes himalayennes décrites par Csoma de Körös." *Revue de l'Histoire des Religions* 206(3): 271-282.

Lee, Don Y. 1981. *The History of Early Relations between China and Tibet: From Chiu T'ang-shu, a Documentary Survey.* Bloomington: Eastern Press.

Lessing, Ferdinand D. 1957a. "Bodhisattva Confucius." *Oriens* 10(1) (July 31): 110-113.

———. 1957b. "The Question of Nicodemus." *Studia Altaica. Festschrift für Nikolaus Poppe zum 60. Geburtstag am 8. August 1957*, 95-99. Wiesbaden: Otto Harrassowitz.

Lham, Pürevjav. 2011. "Erdene-Zuu Monastery as a Major Pilgrimage Center of Khalkh Mongol." In Matsukawa Takashi and Ayudai Ochir, eds., *The International Conference* on *"Erdene-Zuu: Past, Present and Future,"* 51-72. Ulaanbaatar: The "Erdene-Zuu Project" and the International Institute for the Study of Nomadic Civilizations.

Li Jicheng 李冀诚. 1988. "Zangchuan fojiao yu Wutaishan 藏传佛教与五臺山 [Tibetan Buddhism and Wutaishan]." *Wutaishan yanjiu* 1988-4: 18-21.

Li Kecheng 李克城. 1995. "Cong Bukong zhi Zhangjia: mizong zai Wutaishan de fazhan" 從不空至章嘉——密宗在五臺山的發展 [From Bukong to Changkya: The development of esoteric Buddhism at Wutaishan]. *Wutaishan yanjiu* 1995-3: 21-27.

Li Xi 黎曦. 1994. "Lama Ge-sang" 喇嘛格桑. *Minzu tuanjie* 民族團結 1994-10: 38-39.

Li Xiangzhi 李相之. 1932. *Wutaishan youji* 五臺山游記 [Travel record of Wutaishan]. [Taiyuan]: Shanxi Bingzhou xinbaoshe, Minguo 21, 188 p., ill.

Lian Kaowen 廉考文. 1993. "Dailuoding" 黛螺頂. *Wutaishan yanjiu* 1993-4: 38-30.

Liddle, T. Hodgson. 1909. *China: Its Marvel and Mystery.* London: George Allen and Sons.

Lim, Thomas. 1999. "Pilgrimage to Wutaisan, the Sacred Mountain of Manjushri." Based mainly on information given by Khejok Rinpoché during a pilgrimage to Wutaisan led by Rinpoché in 1999; website of the Buddhist International Alliance: http://www.b-i-a.net/Wutaisan.htm, accessed December 24th, 2010.

Lin, Shen-yu. 2007. "The Tibetan Image of Confucius." *Revue d'Études Tibétaines* 12 (March): 105-129.

Lin, Wei-Cheng. 2014. *Building a Sacred Mountain. The Buddhist Architecture of China's Mount Wutai.* Seattle (Wa.): University of Washington Press.

Lindahl, Jared R. 2010. "The Ritual Veneration of Mongolia's Mountains." In Jose Ignacio Cabezon, ed., *Tibetan Ritual*, 225-248. Oxford: Oxford Unity Press.

Liu Shufen 劉淑芬. 1996. "'Foding zunsheng tuoluonijing' yu Tangdai zunsheng jingchuang de jianli: jingchuang yanjiu zhi yi" 《佛頂尊聖陀羅尼經》與唐代尊勝經幢的建 立——經幢研究之一 [The *Ushnīsha vijayā dhāranī sūtra* and the building of *dhāranī* pillars in Tang China: A study of *dhāranī* pillars], *Zhongyang yanjiu yuan lishi yuyan yanjiu suo jikan* 中央研究院歷史語言研究所集刊 67(1): 145-193.

Lkham Purevjav. 2012. "Patterns of monastic and Sangha developments in Khalkha Mongolia." In Bruce M. Knauft and Richard Taupier, eds. *Mongolians after Socialism: Politics, Economy, Religions*, 249-268. Ulaanbaatar: Admon.

Lokesh Chandra. 1961. *Eminent Tibetan Polymaths of Mongolia, Based on the Work of Ye-śes-thabs-mkhas.* New Delhi: International Academy of Indian Culture (Śatapitaka Series 16)

Lomakina, Inessa. 2006. *Mongol'skaya stolitsa, staraya i novaya* [Mongolian capital: New and old]. Moscow.

Lopez, Donald. 1998. *Prisoners of Shangri-la. Tibetan Buddhism and the West.* Chicago and London: University of Chicago Press.

Lot-Falk, Evelyne. 1956. "À propos d'Ätügän, déesse mongole de la terre." *Revue de l'histoire des religions* 149: 157-196.

Lowdermilk, W.C. and Dean R. Wickes. 1938. *History of Soil Use in the Wu T'ai Shan Area* (Monograph issued under auspices of the NCBRAS). Shanghai.

Lu Minghui 盧明輝 and Liu Yankun 劉衍坤. 1995. *Lü Meng shang. 17 shiji zhi 20 shiji Zhongyuan yu Menggu diqu de maoyi guanxi* 旅蒙商——17世紀至20世紀中原與蒙古地區的貿易關係 [Itinerant merchants in Mongolia: Trade relations between the Central Plain and Mongol territories from the seventeenth to the twentieth centuries]. Beijing: Zhongguo shangye chubanshe.

Lu Zhongwei 陆仲伟. 2002. *Zhongguo mimi shehui* 中國秘密社會 [Secret societies of China]. Vol. 5: *Minjian huidaomen* 民間會道門. Fuzhou: Fujian renmin chubanshe.

Lubsangdorji, J. 2002. "Buddhist Lamas and Mongolian." *Mongolica Pragensia '02*: 101-128.

Lubsangjamsu, G. 2002. "Mongγul-un orun ulaγan Utai" [Red Wutai in Mongolia]. *Üjümücin* (2002), 34 p.

Ma, Ho-t'ien (= Ma Hetian). 1949. *Chinese Agent in Mongolia*, translated by John De Francis. Baltimore: Johns Hopkins Press.

Macdonald, Alexander W. 1998. "Foreword." In McKay, ed. 1998: ix-xi.

Maiskii, Ivan M. 2001 [1921]. *Orchin üyeiin Mongol* [Mongolia in the modern period], transl. from Russian by C. Otkhon. Ulaanbaatar: Khevleliin sogoo nuur kompani [*Sovremennaya Mongoliia*, Irkutsk].

Majer, Zsuzsa. 2008. "A Comparative Study of the Ceremonial Practice in Present-day Mongolian Monasteries." PhD. Dissertation, Eötvös Loránd University, Department of Inner Asian Studies, Budapest.

———— and Krisztina Teleki. 2005-2006 with some annotations in 2007: "Survey of Active Buddhist Temples in Ulaanbaatar." Oulan-Bator, http://www.mongoliantemples.net/static/ulaanbaatar-active-monasteries.php, accessed January 25, 2011.

———— and Krisztina Teleki. 2006. "Monasteries and Temples of Bogdiin Khüree, Ikh Khüree or Urga, the Old Capital City of Mongolia in the First Part of the Twentieth Century". Oulan-Bator, www.mongoliantemples.net (183 printed pages), accessed January 25, 2011.

Mallman, Marie-Thérèse de. 1964. *Étude iconographique sur Mañjuśrī*. Paris: École française d'Extrême Orient.

Mannerheim, Carl G.E. 1969 [1940]. *Across Asia from West to East in 1906-1908*. Oosterhout: Anthropological publications, 2 vol.

Marchand, Ernesta. 1976. "The Panorama of Wu-t'ai Shan as an Example of Tenth Century Cartography." *Oriental Art* 22(2): 158-173.

Martin, Dan. 1990. Bonpo Canons and Jesuit Cannons: On Sectarian Factors Involved in the Ch'ien-lung Emperor's Second Goldstream Expedition of 1771-1776 Based Primarily on Some Tibetan Sources." *The Tibet Journal* 15(2): 3-28.

————. 1994. "Pearls from Bones: Relics, Chortens, Tertons, and the Signs of Saintly Death in Tibet." *Numen* 41: 273-324.

———— and Thupten J. Norbu. 1991. "Dorjiev: Memoirs of a Tibetan Diplomat." *Hokke bunka kenkyū* 法華文化研究 17: 1-105.

McKay, Alex. 1998. "Introduction." In McKay, ed. 1998: 1-17.

————. ed. 1998. *Pilgrimage in Tibet*. Richmond (Surrey) and Leiden: Curzon Press, International Institute for Asian Studies.

McKeown, Arthur. 2010. "From Bodhgayā to Lhasa to Beijing: The Life and Times of Śāriputra (c.1335-1426), Last Abbot of Bodhgayā." Unpublished doctoral thesis, Harvard University.

Meinert, Carmen, ed. 2011. *Buddha in the Yurt. Buddhist Art from Mongolia*. Munich: Hirmer Verlag, 2 vol.

Meinheit, Susan. 2011. "Gifts at Wutai Shan: Rockhill and the 13rd Dalai lama." *Journal of the International Association of Tibetan Studies* 6 (December): 411-428: http://www. thlib.org/collections/texts/jiats/

Meng Huiying 孟慧英. 2000. *Chenfeng de ouxiang——Samanjiao guannian yanjiu* 塵塵封的偶像: 薩滿教觀念研究 [Idols of the 'dusty world': Study of the concept of shamanism]. Beijing: Beijing chubanshe.

Merleau-Ponty, Maurice. 1945. *Phénoménologie de la perception*. Paris: Gallimard "Tel."

Miaozhou 妙舟. 1993 [1935]. *Meng Zang fojiao shi* 蒙藏佛教史 [History of Tibeto-Mongol Buddhism], 1935, 7 *juan*. – Ed. Yangzhou: Jiangsu Guangling guji keyinshe, 1994.

Miγvacir 2008 [1942]. *Mergen-i bayasqaγci caγan teüke: Alaša qosiγun-u baraγun güng-ün iledkel šastir* [White history that rejoices the sages: Report of the Western Duke of Alashan Banner]. Höhhot: Öbür Mongγul-un arad-un keblel-ün qoriya.

Miller, Robert James. 1959. *Monasteries and Culture Change in Inner Mongolia*. Wiesbaden: Otto Harrassowitz (Asiatische Forschungen, 2).

————. 1961. "Buddhist Monastic Economy: The Jisa Mechanism." *Comparative Studies in Society and History* 3(4) (July): 427-438.

(Shi) Minghe (釋)明河. 1996 [Ming period]. *Buxu gaoseng zhuan* 補續高僧傳 [Complement to the "Continuation of the biographies of eminent monks"], 26 *juan*. – Ed. Shanghai: Shanghai guji chubanshe, 1996.

Montell, Gösta. 1954 [1943]. "The Idol Factory of Peking." *Ethnos* 1(4): 143-156.

Morinis, Alan. 1992. "Introduction: The Territory of the Anthropology of Pilgrimage." In Alan Morinis, ed. *Sacred Journeys: The Anthropology of Pilgrimage*, 1-27. Westport (Conn.): Greenwood.

Mostaert, Antoine (CICM). 1941-1944. *Dictionnaire ordos*. Beijing: The Catholic University, 3 vol. [Monumenta Serica, 5].

————. 1956. "Matériaux ethnographiques relatifs aux Mongols Ordos." *Central Asiatic Journal* 2: 241-294.

————. 1969. *Manual of Mongolian Astrology and Divination*, with a critical introduction by the Rev. Antoine Mostaert. Cambridge (Mass.): Harvard University Press.

Munkh-Erdene, Lhamsuren. 2006. "The Mongolian Nationality Lexicon: From the Chinggisid Lineage to Mongolian Nationality (from the Seventeenth to the Early Twentieth Century)." *Inner Asia* 8: 51-98.

Murata, Jiro 村田治郎. 1957. *Chü-yung-kuan I. The Buddhist Arch of the Fourteenth Century at the Pass of the Great Wall Northwest of Peking*. Kyoto: Kyoto University, Faculty of Engineering.

———— and Fujieda Akira 藤枝晃. 1955. *Chü-yung-kuan II. The Buddhist Arch of the Fourteenth Century at the Pass of the Great Wall Northwest of Peking*. Kyoto: Kyoto University, Faculty of Engineering.

Nacinšongqur and Türgenbayar, eds. 1990. *Küriye arad-un dayuu-yin tegübüri* [Collection of folk songs from Khüriye]. Höhhot: Öbür Mongγul-un arad-un keblel-ün qoriya.

Nakata Nie 中田美繪. 2009. "Godaishan Monju shinkō to ōken—tōchō Daisō ki nawakeru Kinkakuji shūchiku no bunseki o tsūjite" 五臺山文殊信仰と王権——唐朝代宗期における金閣寺修築の分析を通じて [The Mañjuśrī's cult on Wu-t'ai-shan and kingship: Through an analysis of the reconstruction of Chin-ko-ssu during the reign of Tai-tsung in the T'ang]. *Tōhōgaku* 東放學 117 (January): 40-58.

Nan Yang 南陽. 1998. "Luohousi guanjia Suonadaerji" 羅睺寺管家素那達爾吉 [Suo-na-da-er-ji, intendant of Luohousi]. *Wutaishan yanjiu* 1998-1: 21-22.

Naquin, Susan. 1998. "Sites, Saints, and Sights at the Tanzhe Monastery. *Cahiers d'Extrême-Asie* 10: 183-211.

————. 2000. *Peking. Temples and City Life, 1400-1900*. Berkeley, Los Angeles, London: University of California Press.

———— and Yü Chün-fang, ed. 1992. *Pilgrims and Sacred Sites in China*. Berkeley: University of California Press (rpt. Taipei: SMC Publishing).

———— and Yü Chün-fang. 1992. "Introduction." In Naquin and Yü, ed. 1992: 1-38.

Narantuya, C. 2005. *Mongol urlagiin ünet büteelüüd. Ayuurzanin Altangereliin tsugluulgaats—Treasures of Mongolian Art. Collection of Altangerel Ayurzana*. Ulaanbaatar: The Asian Art antique gallery.

Narasun, S. and Temürbaγatur. 2000. *Ordus-un süme keyid* [Monasteries of Ordos]. Hailar: Öbür Mongγul-un soyul-un keblel-ün qoriya (Mongγul ündüsüten-ü süme keyid-ün bürin ciγulγa, 5).

Narsu and Stuart, Kevin. 1994. "Funerals in Alxa Right Banner, Inner Mongolia." *Mongolian Studies* 17: 98-103 (material collected by Narsu in 1988).

Natsagdorj, Sh. 1963. *Khalkhyn tüükh – Manjiin erkhsheeld baisan üyeiin khalkhyn khuraangui tüükh (1691-1911)* [History of the Khalkhas. Concise history of the Khalkhas in the period of the Manchu domination (1691-1911)]. Ulaanbaatar: Ulsyn khevleliin khereg erkhlekh khoroo.

Nekorpa. "Pilgrimage Guide to Otgontenger." http://nekorpa.org/projects/otgontenger-mongolia/ accessed October 17, 2014.

Ngag dbang bstan dar. 2007. *Dwangs bsil ri bo rtse lnga'i gnas bshad* [Pilgrimage Guide to the Clear and Cool Five Peak Mountain]. Beijing: Krung-go'i bod rig dpe skrun khang.

Ngawang Lhundrup Dargyé. 2011. *The Hidden Life of the Sixth Dalai Lama*, transl. Simon Wickham-Smith. Lanham, MD: Lexington Books.

Nietupski, Paul K. 2009. "The 'Reverend Chinese' (*Gyanakpa tsang*) at Labrang Monastery." In Kapstein, ed. 2009: 181-213.

———. 2011. "Bla brang Monastery and Wutaishan." *Journal of the International Association of Tibetan Studies* 6 (December): 327-348: http://www.thlib.org/collec tions/texts/jiats/

Nima. 2005. "Eke-yin umai kiged mongɣul soyul sedkiküi" [Reflection about Mother's womb and Mongol culture]. *Öbür Mongɣul-un ündüsüten-ü yeke surɣaɣuli* 2005-2: 25-46.

Okada, Hidehiro. 1990. "The Chakhar Shrine of Eshi Khatun." In Denis Sinor, ed., *Aspects of Altaic Civilizations*, III, 176-186. Bloomington: Indiana University.

Ollone, Vicomte Henri d', Commandant. 1911. *Les Derniers barbares. Chine, Tibet, Mongolie*. Paris: Pierre Lafitte & co.

*OMSA. Orud-un manglai serigün aɣula-yin orun-u nomlal süsüg-ün lingqu-a-yi delgeregül-ügci ɣayiqamsiɣ-tu naran-u tuɣ-a kemekü orusiba* [Teaching on the Clear and Cool Mountain, the Very Best of the Places: Marvelous Sun Rays That Causes Lotuses of Devotion to Blossom], written by lCang skya Rol pa'irdo rje and completed by his disciples (original title: *ZMRBDB*), transl. *biligtü güüsri* Dgeleng damcuvas' (Tib. dGe legs dam chos), appendix by the Second Changlung Arya Bandida Agwang Lubsang Danbi Jalsang. Peking xylograph, 1831, 156 fol.

Ono Katsutoshi 小野勝年 and Hibino Takao 日比野丈夫. 1942. *Godaisan* 五臺山 [Wutaishan]. Tōkyō: Zayuhō Kankōkai.

*Pad ma bka' thang*. Biography of Padmasambhava revealed by the fourteenth-century treasure discoverer O rgyan gling pa (1323-ca. 1360), transl. into English by Kenneth Douglas and Gwendolyn Bays, *The Life and Liberation of Padmasambhava*. Berkeley: Dharma Publishing, 1978, 2 vols.

Pander, Eugen. 1994 [1889]. *Lalitavajra's Manual of Buddhist Iconography*, Sushama Lohia ed. and transl. New Delhi: International Academy of Indian Culture, Aditya Prakashan Śata-pitaka Series, 379) [*Das lamaische Pantheon*, Berlin].

Payne, Henry. 1929. "Lamaism on Wutaishan." *Chinese Recorder* 60(8): 506-510.

Pegg, Carole. 2001. *Mongolian Music, Dance and Oral Narrative. Performing Diverse Identities*. Seattle and London: University of Washington Press.

"Pilgrimage in the Gobi—Danzanravjaa's Shambala Dornogobi." http://www.mongo lianmatters.com/mongolia/2008/09/pilgrimage-in-the-gobi-desert/, video posted on October 20th, 2008.

Pokotilov, D. 1935 [1893]. "Der Wu T'ai Schan und seine Klöster." *Sinica-Sonderausgabe*, 1935: 38-89 [transl. by W. A. Unkrig of two chapters (p. 47-116) of *U-taj. Ego prošloe i nastojaščee, U-taj* (Zapiski Imp. Russk. Geogr. Obshchestva po obshchej geografii, 22. 2). Saint Petersbourg, 1893, 152 p].

Poppe, Nicholas, Leon Hurvitz and Okada Hidehiro. 1964. *Catalogue of the Manchu-Mongol Section of the Toyo Bunko*. Seattle: The Toyo Bunko and the University of Washington Press.

Pozdneev, Aleksei M. 1971 [1896]. *Mongolia and the Mongols*, vol. I, transl. from Russian by J.R. Shaw and D. Plankrad. Bloomington: Mouton & Co., 1971 [Saint Petersburg].

———. 1977 [1896-1898]. *Mongolia and the Mongols*, vol. II, transl. from Russian by W. Dougherty. Bloomington: Mouton & Co. [Saint Petersbourg].

———. 1978 [1887]. *Religion and Ritual in Society: Lamaist Buddhism in Late 19th-century Mongolia*, transl. from Russian by Alo Raun and Linda Raun, ed. John R. Krueger. Bloomington: The Mongolia Society [Saint Petersburg] (The Mongolia Society Occasional Papers, 10).

Preston, James J. 1992. "Spiritual Magnetism: An Organizing Principle for the Study of Pilgrimage." In Morinis, ed. 1992: 31-46.

Prip-Møller, Johannes. 1967 [1937]. *Chinese Buddhist Monasteries: Their Plan and its Function as a Setting for Buddhist Monastic Life*. Hongkong: Hongkong University Press, 1967 [Kopenhagen, London].

Prjevalsky, Lieut.-Colonel N. 1876. *Mongolia: the Tangut Country, and the Solitudes of Northern Tibet, Being a Narrative of Three Years' Travel in Eastern High Asia*, transl. by E. Delmar Morgan; with introduction and notes by Colonel Henry Yule. London: S. Low, 2 vol.

Pürev. 1994. *Mongolyn uls töriin töv* [The center of the Mongolian state]. Ulaanbaatar.

Pürevjav, S. 1961. *Khuv'sgalyn ömnökh Ikh Khüree* [Urga/Yekhe Khüriye before the Revolution]. Ulaanbaatar: Ulsyn khevleliin khereg erkhlekh khoroo.

*Qinding Lifanyuan zeli* 欽定理藩院則例 [The Imperially Commissioned Regulations of the Court of Colonial Dependencies], compiled in 1817, revised in 1826, 64 *juan*. – Ed. Guangxu 16 (1890), s. l.

*Qinding Qingliangshan zhi* 欽定清涼山志 [Imperially sponsored gazetteer of Qingliangshan], compiled in 1785, printed by the Palace Publishing House in 1811, 22 *juan* (Library of the Institut des Hautes Études Chinoises, Paris).

*Qingliangshan xinzhi* 清涼山新志 [New gazetteer of Qingliangshan] edited by the Chinese lama Lao-zang-dan-ba, third *jasag da lama* of Wutaishan, 1694, 10 *juan*, with a preface by Lao-zang-dan-ba. – 1st emended reprint by the Palace Publishing House in 1701 with an imperial preface. – Emended editions in 1785, published in 1811; 1887.

– Reprint Danqing tushu gongsi 丹青圖書公司, 1985 (Zhongguo fosi shizhi huikan, 30).

*Qingliangshan zhi* 清涼山志 [Gazetteer of Qingliangshan], compiled by (Shi) Zhencheng (釋)鎮澄 (1546-1617), a monk from Shiziwo, Wutaishan, preface dated 1596, 10 *juan* (compiled on the basis of a 20 *juan* draft written by Abbot Qiuya 秋厓 during the Zhengde period). – First reprint and revision in 1661, by A-wang-lao-zang (preface by A-wang-lao-zang and imperial preface). – Reprint in 1707. – Reprint in 1755 with a new preface (new blocks were carved). – 1887 reprint of the 1755 edition with Qianlong's preface. – Ed. 1887, Library of the Institut des Hautes Études Chinoises, Paris.

Qiao Ji. 2007. *Menggu fojiao shi. Bei Yuan shiqi (1368-1634)* 蒙古佛教史——北元時期 (1368-1634) [History or Mongol Buddhism: Northern Yuan period (1368-1634)]. Höhhot: Nei Menggu renmin chubanshe.

Ramble, Charles. 1995. "Gaining Ground: Representations of Territory in Bon and Popular Tradition." *The Tibet Journal* 20(1) (Spring): 83-124.

———. 1997. "The Creation of the Bon Mountain of Kongpo." In Alexander W. Macdonald, ed. *Mandala and Landscape*, 133-232. Delhi: D.K. Printworld.

Ramstedt, Gustav John. 1978. *Seven Journeys Eastward, 1892-1912: Among the Cheremis, Kalmyks, Mongols, and in Turkestan, and to Afghanistan*, transl. from the Swedish and ed. by John R. Krueger. Bloomington: Mongolia Society.

Rasidondug, Sh., in collaboration with Veronika Veit (transl.). 1975. *Petitions of Grievances Submitted by the People (18th-beginning of 20th Century)*. Wiesbaden: Otto Harrassowitz.

Rawski, Evelyn S. 1998. *The Last Emperors. A Social History of Qing Imperial Institutions*. Berkeley, Los Angeles and London: University of California Press.

Ray, Himanshu Prabha. 1994. "Kanheri: The Archaeology of an Early Buddhist Pilgrimage Centre in Eastern India." *World Archaeology* 1994-1: *Archaeology of Pilgrimage*: 35-46.

Reader, Ian. 2005. *Making Pilgrimages: Meaning and Practice in Shikoku*. Honolulu: University of Hawai'i Press.

Reichelt, Karl Ludvig. 1934 [1928]. *Truth and Tradition in Chinese Buddhism: A Study of Chinese Mahayana Buddhism*, transl. from the Norwegian by Kathrina Van Wagenen Bugge. Shanghai: Commercial Press.

Reischauer, Edwin O. (transl.). 1955. *Ennin's Diary: The Record of a Pilgrimage to China in Search of the Law*. New York: Ronald Press Company.

Reynolds, Valrae. 1990. "A Sino-Mongolian-Tibetan Buddhist Appliqué in the Newark Museum." *Orientations* 21(4) (April): 32-38.

Rhie, Marilyn. 1977. *The Fo-kuang ssu, Literary Evidences and Buddhist Images*. New York: Garland Publishing.

Rinchen Sangpo. 2009. *"Unveiling the Truth"* (Dngos myong bden pa ra sprod). Documentary film ("Tibet TV"): http://www.tibetonline.tv/videos/77/unveiling-the-truth. Accessed on May 15th, 2010.

Richthofen, Ferdinand Freiherr von, 1903. *Baron Richthofen's Letters, 1870-1872*. Shanghai: Printed at the North-China herald office.

Rintchen, B. (Academicien Prof. Dr.). 1964. *Catalogue du Tanjur imprimé*. New Delhi (Śata-pitaka Series, 33).

*Rixia jiuwen kao* 日下舊聞考 [Legends of old about the capital], ed. Yu Minzhong 于敏中, *ca* 1785, 160 *juan*. – Ed. Beijing: Beijing guji chubanshe, 2000, 4 vol.

Robinson, David M. 2008. "The Ming Court and the Legacy of the Yuan Mongols." In David M. Robinson, ed., *Culture, Courtiers and Competitive. The Ming Court (1368-1644)*, 365-421. Harvard: Harvard University Asia Center.

Rochechouart, comte Julien de. 1992 [1878]. *Excursions autour du monde. Pékin et l'intérieur de la Chine*. Paris: Plon. Extract reproduced in Ninette Boothroyd and Muriel Détrie, eds., *Le Voyage en Chine. Anthologie des voyageurs occidentaux du Moyen Age à la chute de l'empire chinois*, 693-699. Paris: Robert Laffont, 1992 (Bouquins).

Rockhill, William W. 1890. "An American in Tibet: An Account of a Journey through an Unknown Land." *The Century Magazine* (November) 41: 4-17.

———. 1894. *Diary of a Journey through Mongolia and Tibet in 1891 and 1892*. Washington: Smithsonian Institution.

———. 1895. "A Pilgrimage to the Great Buddhist Sanctuary of North China." *The Atlantic Monthly* 75(452) (June): 758-769.

———. 1910. "The Dalai Lamas of Lhasa and Their Relations with the Manchu Emperors of China, 1644-1908." *T'oung p'ao* 11: 1-104.

Roerich, George. 1933. *Sur les pistes de l'Asie centrale*, transl. by M. de Vaux Philippau. Paris: Librairie orientaliste Paul Geuthner.

——— and Gedun Choepel, transl. 1979 [1976]. *The Blue Annals* by Gö Lotsawa, Delhi: Motilal Banarsidass.

Ruegg, David S. 1991. "Mchod-yon, Yon-mchod and Mchod-gnas/Yon-gnas: On the Historiography and Semantics of a Tibetan Religio-Social and Religio-Political Concept." In Ernst Steinkellner, ed., *Tibetan History and Language, Studies Dedicated to Uray Géza on His Seventieth Birthday, Wiener Studies zur Tibetologie und Buddhismuskunde*, heft 26, 441-453. Vienna: Universität Wien.

———. 1995. *Ordre spirituel et ordre temporel dans la pensée bouddhique de l'Inde et du Tibet. Quatre conférences au Collège de France*. Paris: Collège de France (Publication de l'Institut de civilisation indienne, 64).

Sagaster, Klaus. 1967. *Subud Erike: Ein Rosenkranz aus Perlen. Die Biographie des 1. Pekinger lCang skya Khutukhtu Ngag dbang blo bzang c'os ldan, verfasst von Ngag dbang c'os ldan alias Shes rab das rgyas*. Wiesbaden: Otto Harrassowitz.

————. 1976. *Die Weisse Geschichte (Cayan teüke). Eine mongolische Quelle zur Lehre von den Beiden Ordnungen: Religionen und Staat in Tibet und der Mongolei.* Wiesbaden: Otto Harrassowitz (Asiatische Korschungen, 41).

Saiget, Robert J. 2009. "Buddhism thrives as China relaxes religious policy." *AFP*, July 7. http://www.buddhistchannel.tv/index.php/calendar_central/index.php?id=46,8342, 0,0,1,0, accessed on April 14, 2011.

Samuel, Geoffrey. 1993. *Civilized Shamans: Buddhism in Tibetan Societies.* Washington DC: Smithsonian Institution Press.

Sanjdorj, M. 1980 [1963]. *Manchu Chinese Colonial Rule in Northern Mongolia,* transl. and ann. by Urgunge Onon. London; C. Hurst and Company.

Sárközi, Alice. 1982. "A 17th Century Mongol *Mañjuśrīnāmasamgīti* with Commentary." *Acta Orientalia Academiae Scientiarum Hung.* 36(1-3): 449-468.

————. 1983. "Incense-Offering to the White Old Man." In Klaus Sagaster and Michael Weiers, eds., *Documenta Barbarorum: Festschrift für Walther Heissig zum 70. Geburtstag,* 357-369. Wiesbaden: Harrassowitz.

————. 1992. *Political Prophecies in Mongolia in the 17-20th Centuries.* Wiesbaden: Harrassowitz.

Sazykin, Aleksei G. 1988. *Katalog mongol'skikh rukopisei i ksilografov Instituta Vostokovedeniia Akademii Nauk SSSR* [Catalogue of Mongolian manuscripts and xylographs of the Institute of Oriental Studies of the Academy of Sciences of the USSR]. Moscow: Nauka.

Schaeffer, Kurtis R. 2011. "Tibetan Poetry on Wutai Shan." *Journal of the International Association of Tibetan Studies* 6 (December): 215-242: http://www.thlib.org/collections/texts/jiats/

Schneider, Richard. 1987. " Un moine indien au Wou-t'ai chan." *Cahiers d'Extrême-Asie* 3: 27-39.

Schopen, Gregory. 1997. *Bones, Stones, and Buddhist Monks. Collected Papers on the Archaeology, Epigraphy, and Texts of Monastic Buddhism in India.* Honolulu: University of Hawai'i Press.

Segalen, Victor. 1967. *Lettres de Chine.* Paris: Plon.

Selig Brown, Kathryn H., ed. 2004. *Eternal Presence. Handprints and Footprints in Buddhist Art.* New York: Katonah Art Museum.

————. 2004. "Handprints and Footprints in Buddhist Art." In Selig Brown 2004: 13-32.

Sen, Tansen. 2003. *Buddhism, Diplomacy and Trade: The Realignment of Sino-Indian Relations, 600-1400.* Honolulu: Association for Asian Studies and University of Hawai'i Press.

Serruys, Henry (CICM). 1974a. "Four Manuals for Marriage Ceremonies among the Mongols, Part I." *Zentralasiatische Studien* 8: 247-331.

————. 1974b. *Kumiss Ceremonies and Horse Races.* Wiesbaden: Harrassowitz.

————. 1977. "A Genre of Oral Literature in Mongolia: The Addresses." *Monumenta Serica* 31: 555-613.

Service, Robert G. 2007. "Notes on *The Beautiful Flower Chaplet*: A Nineteenth Century Mongolian Guide to the Shu-hsiang Szu of Wu-t'ai shan." *Mongolian Studies* 29: 180-201.

*Shanxi tongzhi* 山西通志 [Gazetteer of Shanxi] 1990 [1892]. By Wang Xuan 王軒 et al., comp. 1892, 184 *juan*+1 *juan*. – Ed. Beijing: Zhonghua shuju, 1990, 22 vol.

Shaw, Rosalind and Charles Stewart. 1994. "Introduction: Problematizing Syncretism." In Charles Stewart and Rosalind Shaw, eds., *Syncretism/Anti-Syncretism. The Politics of Religious Synthesis*, 1-26. London: Routledge.

Shirendev, Bazaryn. 1997. *Through the Ocean Waves. The Autobiography of Bazaryn Shirendev*, transl. by Temujin Onon. Bellingham: Washington University Press, Center for East Asian Studies.

Shu Ren 樹仁. 1997. "Xiantongsi jianzhu yu suxiang" 顯通寺建筑與塑像 [Architecture and painted sculptures of Xiantongsi]. *Wutaishan yanjiu* 1997-2: 6-13.

Shüreg, C. 1976. *Mongolchuudyn nom khevledeg arga* [Book-printing of the Mongols]. Ulaanbaatar.

————. 1991. *Mongol modon baryn nom* [Mongol xylograph books]. Ulaanbaatar.

Siklós, Bulcsu. 1996. *The Vajrabhairava Tantras: Tibetan and Mongolian Versions. English Translation and Annotation*. Tring (U.K.): The Institute of Buddhist Studies.

Silk, Jonathan. 1996. "Notes on the History of the Yongle Kanjur." In Michael Hahn, ed., *Suhrllekhāh: Festgabe für Helmut Eimer*, 153-200. Swisttal-Odendorf: Indica et Tibetica Verlag, 1996 (Indica et Tibetica 28).

Skorupski, Tadeusz. 1983. *Tibetan Amulets*. Bangkok: White Orchid Press.

Sneath, David. 2000. *Changing Inner Mongolia. Pastoral Mongolian Society and the Chinese State*. Oxford: Oxford University Press (Oxford Studies in Social and Cultural Anthropology).

Sperling, Elliot. 1983. "Early Ming Policy Toward Tibet: An Examination of the Proposition that the Early Ming Emperors Adopted a "Divide and Rule" Policy Toward Tibet." Unpublished doctoral thesis. Bloomington: Indiana University.

————. 2011. "13th Dalai Lama at Wutai Shan: Exile and Diplomacy." *Journal of the International Association of Tibetan Studies* 6 (December): 389-410: http://www.thlib.org/collections/texts/jiats/

Song Wenhui 宋文輝. 2000. "Mengzu renmin de Wutaishan qing" 蒙族人民的五臺山情 [The Mongol people's passion for Wutaishan]. *Wutaishan yanjiu* 2000-3: 33-34.

Song Yu 宋宇. 2010. "Qing zhengfu dui Wutaishan zangchuan fojiao de guanli" 清政府对五臺山藏傳佛教的管理 [The Qing government's administration of Tibetan Buddhism at Wutaishan]. In Li Shangquan 李尚全, ed., *Hanshansi foxue* 寒山寺佛學, 280-296. Beijing: Renmin chubanshe.

State Nationalities Affairs Commission of China. 1986. "Religion and Customs in Alashan, Inner Mongolia," transl. by Du Yanjun and Kevin Stuart. *Journal of the Anglo-Mongolian society* 12(1-2): 105-145.

Stein, Rolf A. 1987 [1962]. *La Civilisation tibétaine*. Paris: L'Asiathèque.

———. 1988. *Grottes-matrices et lieux saints de la déesse en Asie Orientale*. Paris: École Française d'Extrême-Orient.

Stevenson, Daniel. 1996. "Visions of Mañjuśrī on Mount Wutai (Visionary Experiences of the Tang-dynasty Monk Fazhao)." In Donald S. Lopez, ed., *Religions of China in Practice*, 203-222. Princeton: Princeton University Press.

Stewart, Charles and Rosalind Shaw, eds. 1994. *Syncretism/Anti-Syncretism: The Politics of Religious Synthesis*. New York and London: Routledge; and their "Introduction: Problematizing Syncretism."

Stoddard, Heather. 1999. "Dynamic Structures in Buddhist *Maṇḍalas*: *Apradakṣina* and Mystic Heat in the Mother *Tantra* Section of the *Anuttarayoga tantras*." *Artibus Asiae* 58 (3/4): 169-213.

Stuart, Kevin, ed. 1995. *Mongol Oral Narratives. Gods, Tricksters, Heroes, & Horses*, transl. by Nassenbayar et al. Bloomington: The Mongolia Society, Indiana University.

Sumption, Jonathan. 1975. *Pilgrimage: An Image of Medieval Religion*. London: Faber and Faber.

Sükhbaatar, Khatgin Osornamjimyn. 2001. *Mongolyn gazar usny neriin domog. Mongolian legends of the land*. Ulaanbaatar.

Svenbro, Jesper and John Scheid. 1985. "Byrsa. La ruse d'Élissa et la fondation de Carthage." *Annales. Économies, Sociétés, Civilisations* 40e année, no. 2: 328-342.

Swallow, R.W. 1903. "A journey to Wu Tai Shan, one of the Meccas of Buddhism." *Journal of the Manchester Geographical Society*: 173-182.

Szczepanski, Beth M. 2008. "*Sheng guan* in the Past and Present: Tradition, Adaptation and Innovation in Wutai Shan's Buddhist Music." Unpublished doctoral thesis. The Ohio State University.

Szerb, János. 1990. *Bustön's History of Buddhism in Tibet*. Wien: Verlag der Österreichischen Akademie der Wissenschaften (Österreichische Akademie der Wissenschaften, phil.-hist. Kl. 569).

Tan Qixiang 譚其驤 et al. 1982. *Zhongguo lishi dituji* 中國歷史地圖集 [Historical atlas of China]. Shanghai: Ditu chubanshe, vol. 8, "Qing shiqi" 清時期.

Tatár, Magdalena. 1976. "Two Mongol Texts Concerning the Cult of the Mountains." *Acta Orientalia Academiae Scientiarium Hung.* 30(1): 1-58.

Taveirne, Patrick. 2004. *Han-Mongol Encounters and Missionary Endeavours: A History of Scheut in Ordos (Hetao) 1874-1911*. Leuven University Press: Ferdinand Verbiest Foundation / impr. 2004

Teiser, Stephen F. 1996: "Introduction. The Spirits of Chinese Religion." In Donald S. Lopez, ed., *Religions of China in Practice*, 3-37. Princeton: Princeton University Press.

"Tenger Travel internet website": http://www.tengertravel.com (accessed on November 15, 2009).

Terentyev, Andrey. 2009. "Udayana Buddha Statue: Its Fate in Russia." In K.L. Dhammajoti and Y. Karunadasa, eds., *Buddhist and Pali Studies in Honour of the Venerable Professor Kakkapalliye Anuruddha*, 473-500. Hong Kong: The University of Hong Kong.

Thurman, Robert, ed. 1982. *Life and Teachings of Tsongkhapa*. Dharamsala: Library of Tibetan Works and Archives.

Tian Chang'an 田昌安 and Liang Heng 梁衡, eds. 2003. *Nanwang Wutaishan* 難忘五臺山 [Memorable Wutaishan]. Taiyuan: Zuojia chubanshe.

Tian Pixu 田丕緒 et al. 1883. *Wutai xinzhi* 五臺新志 [New Wutai Gazetteer], 1+4 *juan*. [China]: Chongshi shuyuan.

Timkowski, Georges. 1827. *Travels of the Russian Mission Through Mongolia to China and Residence in Peking in the Years 1820-1821*, transl. from Russian, with corrections and notes by Julius von Klaproth. London: Longmans, 2 vol.

Toh, Hoong Teik. 2004. "Tibetan Buddhism in Ming China." Unpublished doctoral thesis. Harvard University.

Tokiwa Daijō 常盤大定 and Sekino Tadashi 関野貞. 1928. *Shina bukkyo shiseki hyokai* 支那佛教史蹟評解 [Discussion of Buddhist historical sites of China]. Tokyo. Bukkyō shiseki kenkyūkai, vol. 5.

Tournier, Michel. 1996 [1972]. *Vendredi ou les limbes du Pacifique*. Paris: Gallimard.

Tribe, Anthony. 1994a. "Manjusri: Origins, Role and Significance (Parts I & II)." *Western Buddhist Review* 2: 23-49.

———. 1994b. "The Names of Wisdom. A Critical Edition and Annotated Translation of Chapters 1-5 of Vilāsavajra's Commentary on the Nāmasaṃgīti, with Introduction and Textual Notes." Unpublished doctoral thesis. University of Oxford.

Tsagaan, D. 1992. *Yaruu nairgiin tsomorlig* [Collection of poems]. Ulaanbaatar.

Tsedendamba, S. 2009. *Mongolyn süm khiidiin tüükhen tovchon* [Brief history of Mongolian monasteries]. Ulaanbaatar: Admon.

Tsevel, Ya. 1966. *Mongol khelnii tovch tailbar tol'* [Explanatory and concise dictionary of Mongolian language]. Ulaanbaatar: Ulsyn khevleliin khereg erkhlekh khoroo.

Tsyrempilov, Nikolai and Tsymzhit Vanchikova, comp. 2004. *Annotated Catalogue of the Collection of Mongolian Manuscripts and Xylographs MI of the Institute of Mongolian, Tibetan and Buddhist Studies of Siberian Branch of Russian Academy of Sciences*. Sendai-shi: Tōhoku Daigaku Tōhoku Ajia Kenkyū Sentā.

———. 2006. *Annotated Catalogue of the Collection of Mongolian Manuscripts and Xylographs MII of the Institute of Mongolian, Tibetan and Buddhist Studies of Siberian Branch of Russian Academy of Sciences*. Sendai-shi: Tōhoku Daigaku Tōhoku Ajia Kenkyū Sentā.

Tsybikov, Gonbochjab T. 1904. *Lhasa and Central Tibet* (Annual report of the Board of Regents of the Smithsonian Institution). Washington: Government Printing Office.

———. 1992 [1919]. *Un Pèlerin bouddhiste au Tibet* (transl. from Russian by Bernard Kreise. Paris: Peuples du Monde [Petrograd, 1919].

*TÜAG. Tabun üjügür-tü ayula-yin yarcay* [Guidebook of the Five-Peak Mountain], by the Qing monk Badmin tatr-a zay-a, eighteenth century, manuscript written with kalam, 16 fol. Collection of Prince Yunli, Archives of Inner Mongolia, Höhhot.

Turner, Victor. 1978. "Pilgrimages as Social Processes." *Dramas, Fields, and Metaphors: Symbolic Action in Human Society*. Ithaca: Cornell University Press.

——— and Edith Turner. 1978. *Image and Pilgrimage in Christian Culture: Anthropological Perspectives*. New York: Columbia University Press.

Tuttle, Gray. 2005. *Tibetan Buddhists in the Making of Modern China*. New York: Columbia University Press.

———. 2006a. "Tibetan Buddhism at Ri bo rtse lnga/Wutai shan in Modern Times." *Journal of the International Association of Tibetan Studies* 2: 1-35: http://www.thlib. org/collections/texts/jiats/#jiats=/02/tuttle/, accessed January 25th, 2011.

———. 2006b. "A Tibetan Buddhist Mission to the East: The Fifth Dalai Lama's Journey to Beijing, 1652-1653." In Bryan J. Cuevas and Kurtis R. Schaeffer, eds., *Power, Politics, and the Reinvention of Tradition. Tibet in the seventeenth and eighteenth centuries*, 65-90, Leiden and Boston: Brill.

———. 2011. "Tibetan Buddhism at Wutai Shan in the Qing: The Chinese-language Register." *Journal of the International Association of Tibetan Studies* 6 (December), 163-214: http://www.thlib.org/collections/texts/jiats/

Ujeed, Uranchimeg Borjigin. 2006. "Circulating Prophetic Texts. Ethical and Moral Aspects." In Rebecca Empson, ed., *Time, Causality and Prophecy in the Mongolian Cultural Region*, 21-60. Cambridge: Globe Oriental (Inner Asia Series).

———. 2009. "Indigenous Efforts and Dimensions of Mongolian Buddhism— Exemplified by the Mergen Tradition." Unpublished doctoral thesis, SOAS, Department of the Study of Religions, London.

Unesco. 2009. China's sacred Buddhist Mount Wutai inscribed on UNESCO's World Heritage List, Friday June 29, 2009, http://whc.unesco.org/en/news/523 (accessed November 18, 2011).

Uranchimeg, Ts. 2000. *Union of Mongolian Artists 2000*. Ulaanbaatar: Dino Publishing and Union of Mongolian Artists.

Uspensky, Vladimir L. 2006. *"Explanation of the Knowable" by 'Phags-pa bla-ma Blo-gros rgyal-mtshan (1235-1280)*, facsimile of the Mongolian translation with transliteration and notes, with special assistance from Inoue Osamu. Tokyo: Research Institute for Languages and Cultures of Asia and Africa.

———. 2007. "The Legislation Relating to the Tibetan Buddhist Establishments on Wutaishan Under the Qing Dynasty." Paper presented at the "Conference Wutaishan and Qing Culture." New York, May 12-13, 2007.

———. 2011. *Tibetskiy Buddizm v Pekine* [Tibetan Buddhism in Beijing]. Saint Petersburg, Saint Petersburg State University.

———, comp., Nakami Tatsuo, ed. 1999. *Catalogue of the Mongolian Manuscripts and Xylographs in the St. Petersburg State University Library*. Tokyo: Institute for the Study of Languages and Cultures of Asia and Africa.

UTAOSC. *Uta-yin tabun aɣulan-u orusil süsüg-ten-ü cikin cimeg orusiba* [A Guide to the Five Mountains of Wutai. Ornament for the Ears of the Devotees], written by Lubzangdanjin at A-wang-lao-zang's behest, printed in 1667 or more probably in 1721, 74+[1] fol. Peking xylograph preserved in the Library of the Hungarian Academy of Sciences, Budapest.

Valtchinova, Galia. 2009. "Le mont de la Croix: partage et construction de frontières dans un lieu de pèlerinage bulgare." In Albera and Couroucli, eds. 2009: 113-140.

Van Spengen, Wim. 2000. *Tibetan Border Worlds. A Geohistorical Analysis of Trade in Tibet*. London and New York: Kegan Paul International.

Vei Güo Cüo (=Wei Guozuo). 1988. *Utai-bar juyacaysad-tu* [Guide to Wutaishan], transl. Jaɣunasutu and Tümen. Ulaɣanqada (Chifeng): Dumdadu ulus-un juɣacal-un keblel-ün qoriya.

Verellen, Franciscus. 1995. "The Beyond Within: Grotto-Heavens (*dongtian* 洞天) in Taoist Ritual and Cosmology." *Cahiers d'Extrême-Asie* 8: 265-290.

Vinkovicz, Judit. 2003. "Charm Boxes and Their Secrets." In Kelényi, ed. 2003: 93-98.

Vreeland, Herbert H. 1962 [1957]. *Mongol Community and Kinship Structure*. Westport (Connecticut): Greenwood press (Behaviour science monographs).

Waddell, Austine. 1985 [1895]. *Buddhism and Lamaism of Tibet, with its Mystic Cults, Symbolism and Mythology, and in its Relation to Indian Buddhism*, rept. of *The Buddhism of Tibet and Lamaism* (London, 1895). Kathmandu: Educational Enterprise.

Wallace, Vesna A. 2008. "Mediating the Power of Dharma: The Mongols' Approaches to Reviving Buddhism in Mongolia." *The Silk Road* 6(1): 55-53.

———. 2009. "Diverse Aspects of the Mongolian Buddhist Manuscript Culture and Realms of Its Influence." In Stephen C. Berkwitz, Juliane Schober and Claudia Brown, eds., *Buddhist Manuscript Cultures: Knowledge, Ritual, and Art*, 76-94. Abingdon and New York: Routledge.

Wang Bin 王濱 and Guo Chengwen 郭成文. 1989. "Wutaishan jin'gangwu ji lamamiao daochang" 五臺山金剛舞及喇嘛廟道場 [Vajra dance and the ritual area of Tibetan Buddhist monasteries of Wutaishan]. *Wutaishan yanjiu* 1989-2: 33-34

Wang Chang 王昶 (1725-1806). 1999 [1792]. *Taihuai suibi* 臺懷隨筆 [Notes from Taihuai], 1 *juan*, 1792 – In Wang Xiqi 王錫祺, ed., *Xiao fang hu qi yu di cong chao* 小方壺齊輿地叢抄, vol. 2, *juan* 4. Lanzhou: Gansu wenhua chubanshe, 1999.

Wang Chien-ch'uan 王見川. 2008 [2004]. "Qingmo Minchu Wutaishan de Puji ji qi jiaotuan" 清末民初五臺山的普濟及其教團 [Master Pu Ji and His Religious Order in Wu Tai Mountain in the Late Nineteenth and Early Twentieth Century]. In *Hanren zongjiao, minjian xinyang yu yuyanshu de tansuo* 漢人宗教、民間信仰與預言書的探索. Taipei: Boyang wenhua, 128-169 (rpt., 1st ed. *Yuanguang foxue xuebao* 圓光佛學學報 9 (2004): 85-119).

Wang Jinping 王金平. 2005. *Shan you jiangzuo jilu – Shanxi chuantong jianzhu wenhua sanlun* 山右匠作輯錄――山西傳統建築文化散論 [Compilation on carpenters from Shanyou: Essays on the culture of Shanxi traditional architecture]. Beijing: Zhongguo jianzhu gongye chubanshe.

Wang Leiyi 王磊義, Yao Guixuan 姚桂軒 and Guo Jianzhong 郭建中. 2009. *Zangchuan fojiao siyuan Meidaizhao Wudangzhao diaocha yu yanjiu* 藏傳佛教寺院美岱召五當召調查與研究 [Survey and study of the Maitreya Temple and Udan Juu, Tibetan Buddhist monasteries]. Beijing: Zhongguo Zangxue chubanshe, 2009, 2 vol.

Wang Lu 王璐. 1995. "Wutaishan yu Xizang" 五臺山与西藏 [Wutaishan and Tibet]. *Wutaishan yanjiu* 1995-4: 22-29.

Wang-Toutain, Françoise. 2000. "Quand les maîtres chinois s'éveillent au bouddhisme tibétain. Fazun 法尊: le Xuanzang 玄奘 des temps modernes." *Bulletin de l'École Française d'Extrême-Orient* 87(2): 707-727.

———. 2007. "Les pèlerins aux Monts aux Cinq Terrasses. Dévotion populaire, dévotion impériale." Oral paper given at the international meeting "The Pilgrim's Satchel: Evoking Through Memories. The substitute pilgrimage to holy places in the ancient world and in the important living religions," Piedmont Region, Turin, October 2nd-6th.

Wang Xiangyun 王湘云. 1995. "Tibetan Buddhism at the Court of Qing: The Life and Work of Lcang-skya Rol-pa'i-rdo-rje (1717-1786)." Unpublished doctoral thesis. Cambridge (Mass.): Harvard University Press, Inner Asian and Altaic Studies.

———. 2004. "Wutaishan yu Zangchuan fojiao" 五臺山与藏传佛教 [Wutaishan and Tibetan Buddhism], paper read at the conference "Duoyuan shiye zhong de Zhongguo lishi – Di erjie Zhongguo shixue guoji huiyi" 多元視野中的中國歷史 — 第二屆中國史學國際會議, Qinghua University, Beijing, August 21-24, 2004 (website: http://166.111.106.5/xi-suo/lsx/Learning/meeting2004/Complete/wangxiangyun.pdf, March 15, 2007, 19 pages).

Wang Xuebin 王學斌 et al. 1994. "Jin xiandai mingseng" 近現代名僧 [Modern and contemporary famous monks], *Shanxi wenshi ziliao* 山西文史資料 1994-4: 137-184.

Wang Zhichao 王志超. 1994. "Wutaishan beiwen xuanzhu" 五臺山碑文選注 [Selection of annotated Wutaishan epigraphy]. *Wutaishan yanjiu* 1994-4: 35-41.

Wang Zhiyong 王志勇 and Cui Zhengsen 崔正森. 2000. *Wutaishan fojiao shi* 五臺山佛教史 [Buddhist history of Wutaishan]. Taiyuan: Shanxi renmin chubanshe, 2 vols.

Wang Zilin 王子林. 2006. "Qianlong yu Wenshu pusa – Fanzonglou gongfeng chenshi tanxi" 乾隆與文殊菩薩―― 梵宗樓供奉陳設探析 [Qianlong and *bodhisattva*

Mañjuśrī: A study of the arrangement of the pantheon in Fanzonglou]. *Gugong bowuyuan yuankan* 故宫博物院院刊 126-4: 122-131.

Warner, Cameron D. 2008. "The Precious Lord: The History and Practice of the Cult of the Jowo Shakyamuni Statue in Lhasa, Tibet." Unpublished doctoral thesis, Harvard University, Cambridge (MA).

Wayman, Alex. 1999 [1985]. *Chanting the Names of Mañjuśrī. The Mañjuśrī-Nāma-Samgīti Sanskrit and Tibetan Texts*, transl. with annotations and introduction. Delhi: Motilal Barnarsidas Publishers.

Wei Guozuo 魏国祚. 1993 [1988]. *Wutaishan daoyou* 五臺山导游 [Guide to Wutaishan]. Beijing: Zhongguo lüyou chubanshe, 2ᵉ ed.

———. 1999 [1997]. *Wutaishan daoyou* 五臺山导游. Taiyuan: Shanxi guji chubanshe, reed.

———. 2004. *Wutaishan daoyou* 五臺山导游. Taiyuan: Shanxi guji chubanshe, reed.

Weidner, Marsha. 2001. "Imperial Engagements with Buddhist Art and Architecture: Ming Variations of an Old Theme." In Marsha Weidner, ed., *Cultural Intersections in Later Chinese Buddhism*, 117-144. Honolulu: University of Hawai'i Press.

Weiers, M. 1967. "Zum Textfragment TM 40 aus der Berliner Turfansammlung." *Zeitschrift der Deutschen Morgenländischen Gesellschaft* 117: 329-352.

Welch, Holmes. 1968. *The Buddhist Revival in China*. Cambridge (Mass.): Harvard University Press.

———. 1973 [1967]. *The Practice of Chinese Buddhism, 1900-1950*. Cambridge (Mass.): The Harvard University Press.

Wen Fuliang 溫福亮, Zhou Rubi 周如璧 and Li Guangyi 李廣義. 2004. *Dudong Wutaishan* 讀懂五臺山 [Read and understand Wutaishan]. Taiyuan: Shanxi renmin chubanshe.

Wen Ming 文明. 2006. "Qianlong yu Sanshi Zhangjia huofo de shiyou qing" 乾隆與三世章嘉活佛的師友情 [Qianlong and the Third Changkya Khutugtu]. *Zijincheng* 紫禁城 2006-4: 72-80.

Wimmel, Kenneth. 2003. *William Woodville Rockhill, Scholar-Diplomat of the Tibetan Highlands*. Bangkok: Orchid Press.

Wickham-Smith, Simon. 2006. *Perfect Qualities: The Collected Poems of the 5th Noyon Khutagtu Danzanravjaa (1803-1856)*. Ulaanbaatar: Ongot khevlel.

Wingate, A.W.S. 1907. "Nine Years' Survey and Exploration in Northern and Central China (Continued)." *The Geographical Journal* 29(3) (March): 273-302.

Wong, Dorothy C. 1993. "A Reassessment of the *Representation of Mt. Wutai* from Dunhuang Cave 61." *Archives of Asian Art* 46: 27-52.

———. 2004. *Chinese Steles: Pre-Buddhist and Buddhist Use of a Symbolic Form*. Honolulu: University of Hawai'i Press.

*Wutaishan quantu* 五臺山全圖 [Complete map of Wutaishan]. s.n., s.l. (Library of the Institut des Hautes Études Chinoises, Paris, SB 2608).

Wutaixian zhi bianzuan weiyuanhui 五台縣志編纂委員會, ed. 1988. *Wutai xianzhi* 五台縣志 [Gazetteer of Wutai County]. Taiyuan: Shanxi renmin chubanshe.

Wuyungaowa 烏雲高娃 (Oyunguua). 1997. "Jiushi Banchan Nei Menggu zhi xing" 九世班禪內蒙古之行 [The travel in Inner Mongolia of the Ninth Panchen]. In Yang Jizeng, ed. 1997: 199-208.

Wylie, Turrell. 1965. "The Tibetan Tradition of Geography." *Bulletin of Tibetology* 2(1) ): 17-25.

Xiao Guang 曉光 et al., eds. 2003. *Ganzhuer miao* 甘珠爾廟 [Ganjuur Süme]. Höhhot: Nei Menggu wenhua chubanshe (Youmou wenhua ziliao yu yanjiu congshu).

Xiao Yu 肖雨. 1990. "Zhangjia guoshi yu Wutaishan" 章嘉國師與五臺山 [The Zhangjia National Preceptor and Wutaishan]. *Wutaishan yanjiu* 1990-2: 3-7.

———. 1996. "Pusading de fojiao lishi" 菩薩頂的佛教歷史 [Buddhist history of Pusading]. *Wutaishan yanjiu* 1996-1: 3-17.

———. 1998. "Luohousi fojiao shilüe" 羅睺寺佛教史略 [Brief history of Luohousi]. *Wutaishan yanjiu* 1998-1: 6-13.

———. 1999. Laozang danba ji qi 'Qingliangshan xinzhi'" 老藏丹巴及其「清涼山新志」 [Lao-zang-dan-ba and his 'New gazetteer of Qingliangshan"]. *Wutaishan yanjiu* 1999-3: 25-26.

———. 2003. "Wutaishan zhuming gaoseng Ruobi duoji" 五臺山著名高僧章嘉若必多吉 [Famous monk of Wutaishan Rölpé Dorjé]. *Wutaishan yanjiu* 2003-4: 28-32.

Xiao Yu 蕭宇. 1990. "Zhangjia hutuketu yu Wutaishan fojiao" 章嘉呼圖克圖與五臺佛教 [Changkya Khutugtu and Buddhism at Wutaishan]. *Wutaishan yanjiu* 1990-4: 11-15.

———. 1996. "Tayuansi fojiao jianshi" 塔院寺佛教簡史 [Short history of Buddhism at Tayuansi]. *Wutaishan yanjiu* 1996-4: 3-6.

Xiong Wenbin 熊文彬. 2003. *Yuandai Zang Han yishu jiaoliu* 元代藏汉艺术交流 [Sino-Tibetan artistic exchange during the Yuan period]. Shijiazhuang: Hebei jiaoyu chubanshe.

Xin Butang 辛補堂 and Zheng Fulin 鄭福林. 1995. "Wutaishan simiao jingji de tansuo" 五臺山寺廟經濟的探索 [Research on the economy of the monasteries of Wutaishan]. *Wutaishan yanjiu* 1995-3: 28-31.

Xu Hong 旭宏. 2007. *Wuyemiao: lifo qiyuan yibentong* 五爺廟禮佛祈愿一本通 [Wulangmiao: Guide to the Buddhist praying]. Höhhot: Nei Menggu renmin chubanshe.

Xuyun (1840?-1959). 1988. *Empty Cloud: The Autobiography of the Chinese Zen Master Xu Yun*, revised and edited by Charles Luk and Richard Hunn. Longmead: Element Books.

Yan Tianling 閻天靈. 2004. "Menggu ren 'chaotai' yu Meng Han goutong" 蒙古人"朝臺"與蒙漢溝通 [Mongols' pilgrimages and Sino-Mongol encounters]. *Wutaishan yanjiu* 2004-1: 41-44.

Yang Fuxue 楊富學. 2003. "Juyongguan huiwuwen gongdeji suo jian 'uday' kao" 居庸關回鶻文功德記所見uday考 [Examination of the term 'uday' in the Uyghur inscription (to record) merit at Juyongguan]. *Xibei minzu xueyuan xuebao* 40-42 (2003-1): 126.

Yang, Haiying. 2000. *Manuscripts from Private Collection in Ordus, Mongolia (1)*. Köln: International Society for the Study of the Culture and Economy of the Ordos Mongols (OMS e.V.).

Yang Jizeng 楊繼曾, ed. 1997. *Nei Menggu lamajiao jili* 內蒙古喇嘛教紀例 [Chronicles of 'Lamaism' in Inner Mongolia]. Höhhot: Nei Menggu wenshi shudian (Nei Menggu wenshi ziliao, 45).

Yang Yutan 楊玉潭 et al. 1985. *Wutaishan simiao daguan* 五臺山寺廟大觀 [Splendor of the monasteries of Wutaishan]. Taiyuan: Shanxi renmin chubanshe.

Yang Zengwu 楊增武. 2005. *Huangjia yu Wutaishan* 皇家與五臺山 [The imperial house and Wutaishan]. Taiyuan: Shanxi guji chubanshe.

Yesibaljuur. 2010. *Gereltü cayan Utai Gilubar juu-yin orun* [The place of Bright White Wutai Gilubar Juu]. Chifeng: Öbür Mongɣul-un sinjilekü uqaɣan teknik mergejil-ün keblel-ün qoriya.

Yoshida Hiroki 吉田宏哲. 1995. "Bukong sanzang yu wenshu xinyang" 不空三藏與文殊信仰 [Bukong and the Mañjuśrī belief]. *Wutaishan yanjiu* 1995-1: 26-28.

Yu Meian 喻昧庵. 1977 [1923]. *Xin xu Gaoseng zhuan* 新續高僧傳 [New "Continuation of the biographies of eminent monks"], 65+1 *juan*. – Ed. Taipei: Guangwen shuju, 1977, 4 vol.

Yü, Chün-fang. 1992. "P'u-t'o Shan: Pilgrimage and the Creation of the Chinese Potalaka." In Naquin and Yü, ed. 1992: 190-245.

*Yuanshi* 元史 [The Yuan History], [1370] 1976. By Song Lian 宋濂 et al., 1370. – Ed. Beijing: Zhonghua shuju.

Zha Luo 扎洛. 1998. "Tufan qiu 'Wutaishan tu' shishi zakao" 吐蕃求《五臺山圖》史事雜考 [Miscellaneous research on the historical event of Tubo (Tibetan empire) searching for a 'Map of Wutaishan']. *Minzu yanjiu* 民族研究 1998-1: 95-101.

Zhang Dungu 張沌谷. 1911. *Wutaishan can fo riji* 五臺山參佛日記 [Pilgrimage diary to Wutaishan]. *Dixue zazhi* 地學雜誌 3(1): 17-28; 3(2): 1a-5b.

Zhang Guixiang 張桂香 1999. "Fomudong tanqi" 佛母洞探奇 [Extraordinary visit to Fomudong]. *Wutaishan yanjiu* 1999-1: 35-36.

Zhang Minghui 張明暉. 2005. "Fomudong" 佛母洞. *Haiyan* 海燕, *Petrel* 2005-3: 36-37.

Zhang Yu 張玉. 1996. "Sanshi Zhangjia hutuketu yuanji qianhou shiliao xuanyi," 2nd part 三世章嘉呼圖克圖圓寂前后史料選譯(下) [Selected translations of historical materials about before and after the death of Third Changkya Khutugtu, 2nd part]. *Zhongguo diyi lishi dang'anguan* 中國第一歷史檔案館 1996-1: 38-43.

Zhang Yuanji 張元濟 and Zhuang Yu 莊俞. 1925. *Wutaishan* 五臺山. Shanghai: Shangwu yinshuguan, introduction and illustrations of Jiang Weiqiao's visit to Wutaishan in 1918.

Zhang Yuxin 張羽新. 1988. *Qing zhengfu yu lamajiao* 清政府與喇嘛教 [The Qing government and Lamaism]. Lhasa: Xizang renmin chubanshe.

Zhao Gaiping 趙改萍 and Hou Huiming 侯會明. 2006. "Jianlun Qingdai qianqi de Wutaishan zangchuan fojiao" 簡論清代前期的五臺山藏傳佛教 [Brief discussion on Tibetan Buddhism at Wutaishan in the eary Qing period]. *Xizang minzu xueyuan xuebao* 西藏民族學院學報 2006-1: 28-32.

Zhao Linen 趙林恩. 2001. "Cong Hongli de xun Tai shi kan qi dui fojiao de taidu" 從弘歷的巡臺詩看其對佛教的態度 [Hongli's attitude towards Buddhism as seen from the perspective of his poem on his tours to Wutaishan]. *Xinzhou shifan xueyuan xuebao* 忻州師范學院學報 17(4): 61-65.

Zhao Peicheng 趙培成. 2004. "Shitan Wutaishan zangchuan fojiao yu jin'gang shenwu" 試談五臺山藏傳佛教與金剛神舞 [On Wutaishan Tibetan Buddhism and Vajra dance]. *Xinzhou shifan xueyuan xuebao* 忻州師范學院學報 20(4) (August): 38-40.

Zheng Lin 鄭林. 1997. "Yuanzhaosi fojiao jianshi" 圓照寺佛教簡史 [Short history of Buddhism at Yuanzhaosi]. *Wutaishan yanjiu* 1997-1: 16-23.

Zhou Rubi 周如璧 and Li Guangyi 李廣義. 2007. *Wutaishan de gushi* 五臺山的故事 [Tales of Wutaishan]. Beijing: Zuojia chubanshe.

Zheng Sen 正森. 1987. "Wutaishan Tayuansi Dabaita" 五臺山塔院寺大白塔 [Great White Stūpa of Tayuansi of Wutaishan]. *Wutaishan yanjiu* 1987-1: 27-29.

Zhou Zhenhua 周振华 et al. 1998. *Wutaishan beiwen biane yinglian shifu xuan* 五臺山碑文匾额楹聯诗赋選 [Selection of stele inscriptions, placard inscriptions, couplets and poems from Wutaishan]. Taiyuan: Shanxi jiaoyu chubanshe.

Zhukovskaya. N.L. 1990. "The Main Directions of Soviet Ethnographic Research in Mongolia in the 1970's and 1980's." *Journal of the Anglo Mongolian Society* 13(1): 93-104.

*ZMRBDB. Zhing mchog ri bo dwangs bsil gyi gnas bshad dad pa'i padmo rgyas byed ngo mtshar myi ma'i snang ba*, by Rol pa'i rdo rje, revised and completed by two of his disciples, 5 chapters, printed at Songzhusi in Beijing in 1831 (two chapters written by Rol pa'i rdo rje between 1767 and 1786, published as *Ri bo dwangs bsil dkar chag mjugs ma tshang pa* in his early nineteenth century *gSung 'bum* [Collected Writings], vol. 5). – Republished as *Zhing mchog ri bo rtse lnga'i gnas bshad*. Xining, 1993. – Translated into Chinese by Wang Lu 王璐: "Sheng di Qingliangshan zhi" 聖地清涼山志. *Wutaishan yanjiu* 1990-2: 7-48.

# Index

## Index of Places and Peoples

**Religious Beings and Famous
Icons**

### Religious Texts and rituals

### Subjects